10.45

SOCIOLOGY

SOCIOLOGY SERIES

John F. Cuber, Editor
Alfred C. Clarke, Associate Editor

SIXTH EDITION

SOCIOLOGY

A
SYNOPSIS
OF
PRINCIPLES

JOHN F. CUBER

The Ohio State University

New York

APPLETON-CENTURY-CROFTS
Educational Division
MEREDITH CORPORATION

to
PEGGY BUCKWALTER CUBER

for her dedicated and creative
contributions to this edition

PREFACE

In the twenty years which have elapsed between the first and this sixth edition of *Sociology* the map of sociology has changed as radically as has the map of the world. Some of our innovations have come from theoretical work and empirical research of modest scope and import but have, nonetheless, added to the building blocks which we have so sorely needed. But mostly matters of larger compass have altered the image. During these twenty years social systems thinking, in one form or another, has approached a consensus, the parameters of which rather generally define the sociological enterprise. The study of power, once an almost esoteric — if not a downright suspect — subject, has now become accepted in the professional literature and has extended to the popular marketplace of ideas. And perhaps most important of all, the self-assurance about the monolithically scientific structure of the discipline which characterized our thinking in the early postwar years has been reconsidered. The excesses of the "fads and foibles," though played down in the official pronouncements of the establishment, have left their corrections nonetheless. Books like *The Sociological Imagination* and *Sociology on Trial* are widely read, and an uneasiness about some of our earlier assumptions haunts the thinking of many, especially among the younger generation of sociologists.

Benchmarks for the preparation of this sixth edition are, of course, implicit in the above paragraph. While the general structure of the book remains the same, the 20 percent of new materials attempts to incorporate the above perceptions. Specifically they include the following changes:

1. While earlier editions utilized social systems and structure-function frames of reference, these were not made explicit on the supposition that these were tools of the professional sociologist. Thus, they were not necessarily functional for the elementary student who is interested primarily in the *findings* of social science as they interpret his social world and who is only in rare instances occupationally oriented to becoming a sociologist. But even those for whom Sociology I is a terminal course are a little more sophisticated these days, and it can perhaps be more safely assumed that they can handle more rigorous conceptualizations. In this edition, then, social systems and structure-function concepts are more explicit.

2. The discussions of sociological method are much less dogmatic in this edition than in previous ones because, as I read the signs, the

characteristic sociologist is less inclined to intone a dogmatic doxology on the subject and more inclined to see that the tools of sociological research are fashioned by the professional inquirer to meet the needs of his problem and perhaps also his temperament. This edition "levels" with the student somewhat more forthrightly in terms of our own growing sophistication. Macro-sociology, for example, has not been laid to rest according to the schedule which some of the more articulate extremists of a decade or two ago had set forth. The sociological enterprise is still, as Alan Bates and other recent chroniclers have aptly shown, a highly pluralistic set of perceptions, types of intellectual craftsmanship, and even value positions. This edition tells the students all this a little more candidly.

3. Now that it appears respectable to talk about power in more accurate and more forthright terms than previously, a completely new chapter on social power and power structure is included in this edition. The subject is approached historically with particular attention to early work like the Lynds' X-Family in Middletown, gives some attention to the work of political scientists, but focuses attention primarily on contemporary implications of nonlegitimate power structures in a democratic ethos.

4. The treatment of race relations has been cast in a broader cross-cultural and historical perspective in order to meliorate the American's tendency to regard the concepts, traditions, and problems of race with which he is familiar as inherent in the scheme of things, rather than as a particular time-bound phenomenon.

5. The sociological outpouring has been prodigious and ubiquitous. The bibliographies contain a larger proportion of very recent meritorious works than do previous editions. Actually, the annotated bibliographies are bifurcated lists consisting of classical materials on the one hand and very recent ones on the other, not because nothing of import has been done in between, but because the more thoughtful student can better see the emergence of sociology by juxtaposing the classics with the ultra modern. Footnotes and documentation throughout the text have been deliberately kept to a minimum, since these extensive bibliographies are themselves the documentation for the materials found in this edition.

6. Not only does a discipline change in twenty years — so does a man. Almost with each edition, I have become less sure of the ethical legitimacy of the value-free stance. While still deeply respectful of the need for objectivity, I think this edition will show a greater willingness to take at least a few more value positions where the evidence legitimates them.

7. The remaining changes are in the miscellaneous and conventional categories: updating population statistics, introduction of illustrative materials which make current prima facie sense to students, and the refinement of passages which experience has shown to have been murky.

The original motivation for the first edition of *Sociology*, published over twenty years ago, was essentially pedagogical — to prepare a book if possible in such a way that a minimum of sociological content got lost in the mechanism of communication between the producer and the consumer of the intellectual product. Whether the durability of the book is any measure of the achievement of that goal, the original intention still holds. This sixth edition has again been prepared on a level of content and analysis which will best educate students, not one which would enlighten professional colleagues.

J.F.C.

CONTENTS

Part IV

Part V

Part VI

ILLUSTRATIONS AND TABLES

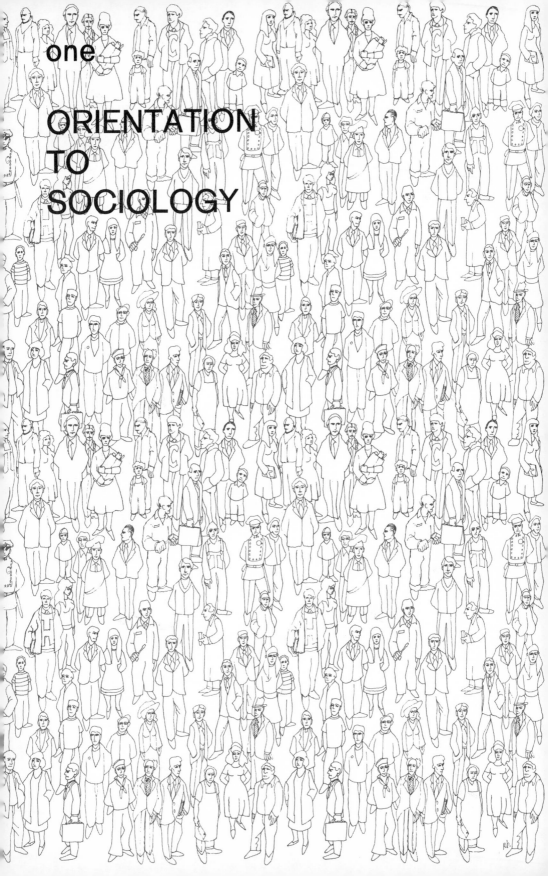

one

ORIENTATION
TO
SOCIOLOGY

1
SOCIOLOGY: A FIELD OF KNOWLEDGE AND A VOCATION

One of man's most glaring anachronisms is that he started to study himself *scientifically* several centuries *after* he had built up fairly impressive science about many other things but had only confident but erroneous assumptions about himself. And even today we may know more scientifically about space than we do about the astronaut!

There are, of course, numerous reasons why man was so tardy in studying himself scientifically. First, there have always been persons who have opposed the application of scientific modes of study to man, either because to study one's self seemed unbecoming or because it seemed impossible. Eventually, however, after concentrating for centuries on virtually every phenomenon in the universe *except* himself, man is coming at last to try to understand himself by the use of an analytical method of study called "science." The result is a group of knowledge systems called "the social sciences," one of them being sociology.

The specialized body of knowledge which we call sociology is vast and ever growing. It numbers hundreds of books and thousands of other writings. Some of these books are quite old, but despite their age they still contain the essential truths which later sociologists' researches have found to be fundamentally correct. On other books the printer's ink is hardly dry, but their significance is already evident. In view of the vastness of the sociological library which we now have, it is impossible to present within the pages of any one book all that we know about this field. Much less can an *introductory* book cover the field completely. In this book we shall, so to speak, cover only the ABC's of sociology. Thus the student should not expect that a mastery of this book will make him a sociologist, any more than the mastery of a college textbook in physics will make him a physicist. That objective would constitute a career.

3

Another way of describing the content and purpose of this book would be to call it a *résumé or synopsis of sociology;* it aims to introduce and discuss *briefly* the major contents of sociology. It does not contain *all* of the findings and most assuredly does not give *all of the evidence* underlying even the findings which are discussed. It will be reasonably complete, however, and the more interested student will secure from it a sufficiently well-rounded preparation in the subject, permitting him later to go on to more specialized courses in sociology and encounter no serious difficulty with his basic understanding, his technical vocabulary, or his point of view.

DEFINITION OF SOCIOLOGY

Some introductory textbooks contain brief, one-sentence definitions of sociology. Other writers prefer not to attempt a formal definition because they believe that such synoptical definitions are not only too brief to be meaningful to the beginner, but also may lead to serious misunderstandings. These writers simply offer "the whole book" as the student's best working notion of the scope of sociology. While there may be merit in this approach, there seems greater merit in at least attempting an approximate, terse definition, even though both writer and student realize that it has serious limitations. At least it is a beginning.

Sociology may be defined as a *body of scientific knowledge about human relationships.* The word *relationships* is a key word. Sociology is not concerned, for example, primarily with man as a biological being, nor with his history, nor with his accomplishments. Sociology is concerned with *man's behavior in relation to other men, with human interaction.* When we point out that sociology is not concerned primarily with man's biology, his history, or his accomplishments, we do not intend to imply that sociology is not at all concerned with these phenomena. Sociology is concerned with these phenomena, but *only as they are a part of, affect, or result from, human interrelationships.*

THE POINT OF VIEW OF MODERN SOCIOLOGY

Probably the most fundamental idea with which the beginning student of sociology must familiarize himself is what we call the "point of view." Many beginning students encounter unnecessary difficulty in this field because they are launched too soon into the study of the materials without first knowing *why* the materials are to be studied.

1. Sociology is knowledge, not direct treatment

Broadly speaking, there are two distinct kinds of competence which man has built up. One is *knowledge about things* and the other is *knowledge of how to do things*. Serious confusion arises from the failure to distinguish between these two.

The sociologist's chief duty is to build up the most accurate body of knowledge *about* human relationships that is possible. The *use* of this knowledge, like the use of the biologist's knowledge, remains largely for others to carry out. Thus, social workers, juvenile court judges, teachers, psychiatrists, parents, and many other people may put sociological information into practical use either in a professional way or in their own "personal" lives, very much in the same way that the physician puts into practical use the knowledges ascertained by biologists, chemists, and other discoverers. *Persons who use sociological knowledge, however, do not thereby become sociologists*, any more than the physician becomes a chemist or a biologist merely by using some chemical or biological knowledge.

One should *not* expect to find in sociology a set of knowledge ready to be used in the alleviation of human problems or in the treatment of social ills. These belong largely in the province of related applied fields such as "social work" and "public administration" for which, as a rule, training in sociology is considered prerequisite. Sociology, then, is a body of knowledge about the behavior of human beings; it has "practical value" often, but is usually put into practical operation by others than sociologists.

2. Sociological knowledge is based on evidence

A sociological statement is not true because some sociologist *says* it is, or for that matter because five hundred sociologists say it is. It is true only if and when sufficient numbers of observations or experiments have been made and critically examined to formulate a factual (or "empiric") basis for the statement. Thus, sociology is a field of knowledge *based on evidence*. This evidence consists of *observations of phenomena* —*repeated* observations of the same and related phenomena, which observations then constitute the established basis, or authority, for the statement.

When we use the term *observation* we do not mean merely "looking at" something. Scientific observation is a technical process involving much training in ways and means of *accurate* observation. The astronomer uses a telescope, the biologist a microscope, the physician a stethoscope—what all three have in common in the use of these precision tools is the purpose, namely, to *improve the accuracy of observations*. Each field of knowledge develops its own technical tools to improve the reliability and accuracy of its observation of the materials within its scope of study. The telescope is, of course, of no greater use to the physician than the stethoscope would be to the astronomer, and neither would be of much use to an economist. But the economist has developed certain other observational procedures, not necessarily mechanical instruments, which help him to improve the accuracy and precision of his observations. And so with the sociologist. He, too, has devised various technical procedures which enable him to observe his data more accurately than the person who merely uncritically "looks at" the people and things about him.

3. Sociology is mainly the study of what "is," not of what "ought to be"

The prime concern of sociology, as we have already seen, is to discover what is *true* about human beings and their relations to one another. Sociologists with few, even if conspicuous, exceptions are not advocates, are not reformers, are not preachers, and have no "axe to grind" other than this interest in building up the most nearly perfect body of knowledge about human beings that they can. Of course, every sociologist is a citizen, too, and *as a citizen* he usually has preferences for one political party over another, for one religion over another, or for one philosophy over another. But this part of him is his citizen-self, not his sociologist-self. Other specialists, of course, have the same compartments in their thinking. An architect may be a Democrat, a Catholic, and a conservative. He is these three things not, however, because he is an *architect*, but because he is a *person*. A second architect may be a Republican, a Protestant, and a radical. But in their *professional capacities*, their citizen roles, even their differences, are of no professional significance. And so it is with the sociologists; the personal predilections of sociologist *A* or of sociologist *B* are not a part of sociology.

An opposing position. It should be pointed out that there is a group of sociologists who believe that it is within the professional province of the sociologists to make recommendations as to what "*ought* to be," and what changes are desirable in human affairs.

C. C. Bowman [1] may be taken as representative of this point of view:

It is maintained that the scientific interest in society cannot be marked off sharply from an interest in societal welfare, since the two are inter-related. Stimulated by training along religious and humanitarian lines, a number of persons have entered the field of sociology in order to partici-pate in the "solution" of social problems. As their study progressed, at least some have come to realize that humanitarian sentiment per se is not enough. Consequently they have turned to science in order to implement their ideals with a substantial fund of knowledge.

On the other hand, and more relevant to our present purpose, a student of society may start out to be strictly scientific and develop a social-welfare interest as his knowledge grows. In any scientific pursuit, particularly in its applied aspects, it is an easy and natural step from objective knowledge to interest in improvement. . . .

This normal connection between scientific and welfare interests may be blocked by various factors. In this country conflicts between strictly scientific and welfare sociologists are apparent from time to time. A polarity of relationship tends to exist wherein the scientists are too detached and the welfare group too impatient. Such misunderstanding represents an early stage in the evolution of a new field of knowledge that is trying to free itself from moralistic preconceptions and the unsubstantiated opinions of common sense. It probably has no permanency. Certain sociologists be-come excited when the term *welfare* is mentioned, for in their minds it connotes the limited approach of traditional social work or "up-lift" activi-ties based upon great passion but little understanding. In the present dis-cussion the term is free from these connotations. The whole purpose is to oppose the view that interest in social betterment is imposed upon the scientific quest arbitrarily, if at all. It is maintained that, although the wel-fare interest is to be classified as ethical, it emerges readily from the profes-sional interest and activities of the social scientist and from the needs of the public.

Probably most sociologists, however, regard their primary pur-pose as that of *studying the existing scheme of things* with the view to learning what is true about it. At least it seems more fundamental to learn, first, what is true, before attempting to pass judgment on it or to

[1] C. C. Bowman, "Must the Social Sciences Foster Moral Skepticism?" *American Sociological Review*, Vol. 10 (December, 1945), p. 714. See also a later statement by the same author, "Is Sociology Too Detached?" *American Sociological Review*, Vol. 21 (October, 1956), pp. 563–568. This is a time-honored viewpoint and any number of similar opinions can be found scattered throughout both professional and popular writing.

advocate something else. The problem is complicated, however, and we shall devote a chapter to it later (Chapter 3).

4. Sociology is one of several social sciences

Sociology is not the only modern science which studies man. Biology, anthropology, psychology, social psychology, economics, political science, and others study some aspects of the behavior of human beings. These various fields study different aspects of man's behavior for the most part, although sometimes several may study the same aspect. During recent years, for example, there has arisen an attempt to integrate sociology, psychology, and anthropology into one science of human behavior. While we cannot at present be certain that this movement to merge the three fields will stand, there are many reasons to applaud the movement as a step in the right direction. It is not to be assumed, however, that progress in human knowledge could not continue if the various fields of knowledge remained separate. Up to the present time great strides in knowledge have been made, even though these closely related fields have remained somewhat distinct. Borderline studies like social psychology, with one foot in sociology and the other in psychology, have served as integrating points. Also numerous individual scholars have done their research on problems in which two or more social sciences converge and have made some important discoveries thereby.

As the matter now stands, we have several fields of knowledge all studying man's behavior, each presenting an impressive accumulation of tested knowledge, each staffed by a sizable group of professionally competent people. The truly educated person has no practicable alternative but to acquaint himself as fully and as precisely as he can with the main knowledges of *all* of these fields and then put them together as best he can. To do anything less is to leave gaps of ignorance in his understanding of himself and of other people.

5. There are professional disagreements within the field of sociology as in other fields

When one has studied any field of knowledge carefully, he will find that it has within it some rather marked differences in point of view and some downright conflicts. Not all psychologists agree, for example, on the correctness or value of psychoanalysis, and not all political scientists and historians agree on the utility of the United Nations. At the present time a sharp disagreement exists among physical scientists regarding the extent of the harmful effects of "fallout" resulting from the use and testing of nuclear devices.

Several factors are involved in these intraprofessional differences of opinion. (*a*) Not all persons are equally familiar with the facts involved because there are intraprofessional specializations. (*b*) Not all are equally unprejudiced or, for that matter, (*c*) equally capable of interpreting certain data. (*d*) Sometimes two or more points of view may both be correct, or at least both *tenable* for the time being or for different purposes.

But it is easy to exaggerate the extent and seriousness of these professional disagreements. If one could make a complete catalogue of the many items of information within the fields of, say, medicine, or psychology, or history, and then have each physician, psychologist, or historian check those on which he agreed with others in his field, one would find an overwhelming agreement on an overwhelming proportion of items. A 2 percent disagreement may cause a riot of controversy; the 98 percent agreement goes unnoticed!

Most modern fields of knowledge, however, welcome the somewhat varied viewpoints among their scholars. It is from differences that progress arises. If all sociologists agreed precisely on everything, one could conclude only that all possible knowledge was already known. Knowledge, quite to the contrary, is dynamic and ever changing. Today's truth may be tomorrow's error. The "knowledge" taught in a dozen departments of a modern college of thirty years ago would have to be repudiated today. In each instance someone discovered that his predecessors, and perhaps also he himself, were wrong about something.

Throughout this book there will occur frank admissions that on this or that problem, two or more points of view are currently tenable in the light of existing knowledge. In the vast majority of instances, however, that will not be necessary because substantial agreement has already been reached. This does not mean, however, that at some future time new discoveries may not revolutionize sociology as biology and physics have been revolutionized during the last century by the theories of evolution and relativity.

TECHNICAL LANGUAGE: TERMS AND CONCEPTS

One of the fundamental problems which one faces when he begins work in a new field is the necessity of learning the concepts which are employed and the words or terms which stand for the concepts. Until one learns what the biologist means by "vertebrates" or the economist by "marginal utility" or the political scientist by "sovereignty," he cannot penetrate very deeply into any of these fields. The student's problem here is more than just learning words; it is learning the *ideas* for which the words stand.

Fortunately, in all three of the cases just mentioned the terms have no popular meaning. If one hears the term *vertebrate, marginal utility,* or *sovereignty,* it is probable that the user of it has at least an approximate idea of what it means in the technical usage of the field of knowledge from which it comes. Unfortunately, not all technical language consists of words which have no popular usage. Words like *sympathy, emotion, race,* or *accommodation,* while technically employed in one or more of the social sciences, also have other meanings in the everyday language of literate laymen. Thus, one must not assume that he knows what the psychologist means by "intelligence" merely because he already has a notion that intelligence has something to do with "smart people." He must first learn exactly what the psychologist means *by* intelligence before he can ever understand what the psychologist can tell him *about* intelligence. Similarly for many of the words used in sociology, the student must be cautioned to learn the technical meanings and not rely on his commonsense vocabulary. It is unfortunate and confusing to have several usages of the same word in existence at the same time. But one has no recourse; he must use the language as it is. He must learn the correct usages of words and terms in the several contexts to which they customarily apply, if he is to be educated.

In summary, while ideas are represented by words, the word (or term) and the idea (or concept) are distinct. Usually it is more difficult to learn the concept or idea than it is merely to learn the label or term. A given term may have somewhat different meanings to different people, but despite these differences there may still be a general agreement or consensus. Finally, two or more quite distinct meanings or concepts may coexist for a given word and be basically and uncompromisingly different, such as the professional and the popular use of many of the words found in this or any other technical book.

SOCIOLOGY AS A VOCATION

Up to this point we have discussed sociology as an academic discipline. There is, however, another side, a more concrete one. Sociology is also an *occupation.* (The formalist may object that the occupation is really sociolog*ist*, but there is ample evidence in our language that a body of knowledge and a profession may both have the same name, for example, medicine, law, or theology.)

What do sociologists "do"? They perform chiefly four kinds of professional service: teaching, research, consultation, and administration. These services are performed for practically every type of organization found in America—government bureaus, including the armed forces, business, religious organizations, and, of course, educational organizations.

1. Teaching

The greatest proportion of sociologists spend the greatest proportion of their time in teaching. In 1959, 70 percent of the members of the American Sociological Association were teachers, 59 percent employed in liberal arts colleges.[2] The preponderance of teaching, however, is not as great at present as it was in the past, when practically all sociologists were exclusively or primarily teachers in universities or colleges. Teaching done by sociologists has two principal purposes—vocational and cultural. The vocational emphasis is relatively new, but a growing one. The catalogue of practically any major university will reflect the growing demand for sociology in the training programs of many vocations. Often these take the form of required work in sociology in order to qualify for the practice of some profession or occupation. A prominent example is social work, although to a less extent, but increasingly, sociology is a required course or curriculum for teaching, nursing, city planning, and other fields as well. When not required, it is frequently strongly recommended for virtually all fields.

The reasons for introducing sociology into the training curricula of so many professions and occupations are not always made explicit. A strong case, however, can be made for the inclusion of sociology for several reasons. It should help persons who work closely with people (who doesn't?) better to understand their associates, which, in turn, should result in more efficient work relations with them. The findings of sociology, rooted as they are in science, can and do provide better answers to many practical questions than can be derived from common sense, folklore, or tradition. Sociology may also be helpful to the individual in understanding himself, an indispensable skill which anyone can use.

But all instruction in sociology is not vocational. Some of it, like general education, is simply intended to develop the human intellect by providing new insights, new challenges, new information, which, added to that acquired from other disciplines, should somehow result in what

2 See M. W. Riley, "Membership of the A. S. A., 1950–1959," *American Sociological Review,* Vol. 25 (December, 1960), p. 921.

we call "an educated man." In this respect sociology is in no sense unique. It occupies a place in the community of scholarship in much the same way, and for much the same reason, as does history, philosophy, or English literature.

2. Research

An increasing number of sociologists, however, are employed either partially or fully at *research*.[3] Their task is to add something to human knowledge through the technical procedures which have slowly evolved in their profession. As we shall see in subsequent chapters, research does not mean simply reading what others have written or simply collecting facts, but is rather a complicated and technical set of procedures for securing reliable answers to important questions.

These research efforts are of two principal kinds, although sometimes they merge together. Perhaps the easier to understand is what we call *applied* or *practical* research. This is research designed to give answers to problems or questions already formulated and which have presumably some importance to someone. Sometimes this research is done by sociologists employed by the organization which wants the answers, in much the same way as a chemist or a physicist or an engineer may work solely as a research worker for a company like Du Pont. Other practical research is done under contract, a sociologist working either full or part time for the contracting party. The last fifteen years have seen a phenomenal increase in the extent of contract research performed by sociologists, either alone or as part of a research team including specialists from several disciplines. A list of such research projects would fill a large book. Suffice it to say that at one university during the last ten years contract research has been done by sociologists for many agencies, among them the following:

National Institute of Mental Health
National Science Foundation
The Office of Naval Research
The School of Aviation Medicine, U.S.A.F.
The Department of State
Three different hospitals—psychiatric, tuberculosis, and general
A chamber of commerce
A state nursing association
A state Council of Churches
Two separate Community Planning associations

[3] *Ibid.*

A metropolitan City Slum Clearance Authority
A subdivision of a State Department of Mental Hygiene and Corrections
  (for a study of alcoholism)
Several national research foundations, such as Carnegie Foundation, Ford
  Foundation, Kellogg Foundation, and others
Several private business concerns

These contract researches represented expenditures to the contracting parties of hundreds of thousands of dollars. The university in question, although a state supported one, derives 10.7 percent of its total income from research contracts, $16 million per year.[4] Only a small fraction of this total is for contract work in sociology, but the sociological research amounts to several hundred thousand dollars per year. Moreover, it should be pointed out that the department and the university in question are by no means the most outstanding or most noted for emphasis on contract research. For the country as a whole the number of man-hours and the number of dollars going into contract research of this sort is indeed impressive.

What kinds of research problems have sociologists been employed to solve? Again the range is wide and we shall have to content ourselves with a few examples. These will be put in nontechnical language, in terms of what the contracting parties wanted to know. In a number of cases much effort and time had already gone into attempts to solve the problem by people from other disciplines, but the attempts had not been successful.

The United States Air Force, through the School of Aviation Medicine, wanted an answer to the question: Why do so many pilots who have the necessary skills and abilities to fly planes either "wash out" late in the training period or resign when they get their wings? This is a tremendously practical problem, since it now costs in the vicinity of $100,000 fully to train an Air Force pilot. Everyone who cannot or will not fly at the end of this period constitutes a financial loss of $100,000, plus other immeasurable losses both material and psychological.

The nursing association would like to know the answer to this question: Why, after pursuing long periods of arduous education, do so many nurses exhibit low morale and, by implication, what can be done about it, since there is a nationwide shortage of nurses?

It has been known for a long time that juvenile delinquency is concentrated in neighborhoods of the city where it is practically *normal* to be

[4] Ohio State University Consolidated Summary Financial Report for fiscal year ending June 30, 1966.

a "bad boy" by more general community standards. But everybody is not a bad boy, even in these areas. How and why do the good boys manage to stay good, when it is normal to be bad? (This may also help us to explain why the occasional boy goes bad in groups where it is normal to be good.)

A few researches which have brought considerable attention to sociological methods of inquiry have been on a national scale, and very few people at the time the study was carried out knew that they were a part of it. One case in point occurred during World War II and had to do with the important practical problem of getting people to buy war bonds, not only to finance the war but also to keep money out of the marketplace so that inflation would not get out of hand. What kind of an appeal would work best, the Treasury Department wanted to know. Should the appeal be made to people's patriotism, to their self-interest (to curb inflation; that the bond is a good investment for the person holding it, or his children; that the bond is a safe form in which to keep one's savings), or what? Who should make the appeals—representatives of government, professional entertainers, or anonymous people reading commercials? To secure practical answers to these questions a large study was set up, the results of which are to be found in Robert K. Merton's *Mass Persuasion*.[5]

Discussion of this sort could be extended indefinitely, but perhaps enough has been said to indicate the wide range of questions which sociologists have been called upon to answer through their research efforts. The list and fields are ever growing.

In addition to applied research, sociologists also make another kind of inquiry, often called *pure research*. Pure research is also sometimes, but less often, done under contract from some sponsoring agency. The essential difference between pure and applied research is that the former is often concerned with finding answers to questions which have no immediate practical value. Sometimes, in fact, research is necessary in order to determine even what questions to ask. Hence, this kind of activity is also often called *basic research*. All fields of scientific inquiry have this same division between practical and basic research. Research in atomic energy thirty years ago, for example, was mostly in the category of basic research. Obviously not so today!

3. Consultation

Sociologists, in common with persons in almost all of the academic professions which have practical application, frequently serve in a capacity known as "the consultant." A person becomes a consultant be-

[5] Robert K. Merton, *Mass Persuasion* (New York, Harper & Row, 1946).

cause he has some special knowledge which is needed and for which the needing agency or person pays a fee. Thus, sociologists serve as consultants to city planning commissions, to business and other organizations with organizational problems, to courts in various capacities, to committees of state and federal legislatures, and to a wide variety of other ongoing enterprises. In their capacity as consultants, sociologists sometimes advise on research projects, determining whether or not they are feasible and if so, how they should be set up. Or they may advise on practical courses of action. Increasingly those persons in charge of important enterprises in our society are recognizing that decisions which were once made informally can now be made much better, and have a much greater probability of being correct, if persons with expertise can bring their knowledge to bear on the decisions. A number of consulting firms now employ sociologists full time in such capacities, but most of the consulting is probably still done by teaching or research sociologists who devote part of their time to this professional practice.

4. Administration

A fourth professional activity in which sociologists are employed we have loosely called "administrative." Their training as sociologists is required, or deemed better to qualify them, for any of a wide variety of professions and positions in the world of action, including such seemingly different tasks as public relations, personnel work in industry, government planning, the long-run development of private corporations, cities, and educational institutions. The list is extensive.

TRAINING

How much training is required for employment in these various fields? Generally speaking the qualifying degree is the Doctor of Philosophy, requiring a minimum of seven years of college training, three years beyond the ordinary A.B. or B.S. degree. There are a few limited and exceedingly minor vocational opportunities for persons with less training than this, but persons entering the job market today, whether in college teaching or research or administrative fields, will find that competition from "the Ph.D.'s" sets the tone of the job market. Moreover, for persons who may have vocational aspirations in this direction, it should be pointed out that there is a rigorous selection process that takes place in the last three years of this training, that is, in graduate school. Statistics indicate that, whereas 10 percent of Americans complete college, less than 1 percent receive the Doctor of Philosophy degree. There are, of course, factors other than skill and ability involved, but it is certainly safe to assume that persons who do not complete college in the top 10 to 20 percent nationally, so far as scholarship is concerned, are poor risks for successful graduate school achievement—at least in the better graduate schools. Finally it must be remembered that the Ph.D., exacting as it is, is yet not a "union card." There are numerous people who possess the doctor's degree in sociology, as in any other field, who for one reason or another do not secure satisfactory employment, advance to positions of responsibility and prestige, or otherwise become "successful" in their chosen vocation.

REWARDS: INTRINSIC AND EXTRINSIC

What are the rewards in this occupation? Rewards, here as elsewhere, are of several kinds. The extrinsic ones resolve themselves into income, miscellaneous working conditions, fringe benefits, and prestige. The financial rewards of academic sociologists compare very closely with those of other academic specialists, as shown by data compiled in a study conducted by The National Science Foundation in March of 1966.[6] A perusal of this data will give the interested student an idea of salaries among the several fields of science and also comparisons by age, type of employer, highest degrees granted, experience, and other breakdowns. Incomes of sociologists vary considerably from the average of slightly over $10,000. For example, a sociologist who is in the top 10 percent of professionals in his field receives an income ($17,000 per year) two and one half times as great as one in the lowest 10 percent.

Increasingly the fringe benefits of an academic or other scientific career are important considerations in computing total income. Substantial numbers of American colleges now provide free or greatly reduced tuitions to faculty members' children and furnish life and health insurance free or at greatly reduced rates. Retirement incomes are increasingly adequate, even in an inflationary economy. Thus, in these and in many other ways, hidden income must be added to the mere dollar income paid to persons in this profession.

Moreover, salaries and total income should not be confused. Increasingly, sociologists are finding it possible, if they so desire, to "moonlight," by which term is meant that various kinds of part-time employment are available and increasingly assumed. In this category should be listed writing, editing, consultant work, lecturing, and, of course, research under contract. At the present time enterprising

[6] *The American Sociologist*, Vol. I, No. 2 (February, 1966), p. 76.

experienced sociologists in major universities, who wish to do so and have the talents, can earn a total income of around $25,000 to $30,000 per year.

What about other kinds of rewards? These are difficult to discuss,

1. Types of Employment of Sociologists

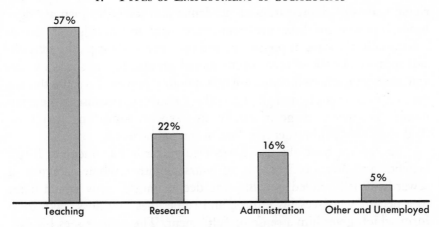

From "Sociologists in the 1964 National Register of Scientific and Technical Personnel," *The American Sociologist*, Vol. 1, No. 2 (February, 1966), p. 77.

2. Principal Employers of Sociologists

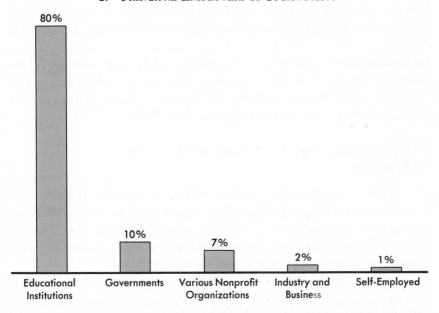

From "Sociologists in the 1964 National Register of Scientific and Technical Personnel," *The American Sociologist*, Vol. 1, No. 2 (February, 1966), p. 76.

because, unlike salaries and income, they have no common denominator. It may be important to one person that the college teacher works, on the average, about nine months a year and has three months for travel, study, other self-improvement, or whatever he wishes to do with it. To another person, "that is too much time on my hands with nothing to do." And so, also, with "prestige." Studies [7] show that, despite periodic waves of depreciation of academic and scientific men as "eggheads," people in these professions are held in the highest esteem —essentially the same as physicians and the very highest public officials, and appreciably above other occupational groups, like business owners and managers, whose incomes are considerably higher. To some this is a reward, even though intangible; to others a burden, because if the community bestows prestige it usually also expects something in return. And so some would rather live "less in the public eye."

So far we have discussed extrinsic rewards like income, fringe benefits, and prestige. There is, of course, another whole category of rewards, usually called *intrinsic*—the deeper satisfactions which come to a person who sees his efforts, and sometimes sacrifices, take some form which gives him a sense of fulfillment. The painter sees his canvas, the composer hears his music, and what of the scientist, specifically the sociologist? The teaching sociologist's rewards are essentially the same as those of any teacher: to teach human minds to substitute understanding for ignorance, to acquire skills, to correct misconceptions; slowly to see the integration of knowledge and character. This kind of "making of men" is for many people almost reward enough for the greatest efforts. To the research sociologist the reward pattern is a little different, less personal, less dramatic, resting more perhaps on the ultimate faith that what he is doing will somehow add to human knowledge or assist someone to solve a practical problem.

THE PURPOSES FOR STUDYING INTRODUCTORY SOCIOLOGY

It has been pointed out previously that one cannot hope to learn the whole body of knowledge called sociology from the study of any one book or from any one course. Obviously, then, the writer should indicate just what parts or aspects of the whole field of sociology he is striving to present. Four objectives are sought in this book:

1. To acquaint the student with the basic *point of view of sociol-*

[7] See, for example, Robert W. Hodge, Paul M. Siegal, and Peter H. Rossi, "Occupational Prestige in the U.S. 1925–1963," *The American Journal of Sociology*, Vol. 70 (November 5, 1964), pp. 286–302.

ogy. This has already been outlined in broad terms in the current chapter, but will need to be made more specific from time to time as we proceed.

2. To teach the student the *basic and more important information* which sociologists have discovered.

3. To give the student something of an idea of the *research procedures which sociologists use* in the discovery and testing of their research, that is, how sociological evidence is gathered and interpreted.

4. To acquaint the student with the *basic technical vocabulary* of sociology. Each field of knowledge develops a specialized vocabulary, with a precise and often technical meaning attached to words. In order that a person be competent, even in an elementary way, to do work in a field, he must familiarize himself with some of the specialized terminology.

These, then, are the results which may be expected from a first adventure in sociology.

SUMMARY

In this chapter we discussed, first, the "point of view" of modern sociology. It has been noted that among people not too well acquainted with sociology, or acquainted with an obsolete model of it, there is confusion concerning what sociology is. Among professional sociologists, however, there now exists a rather clear consensus concerning the field. These agreements are the following: (1) that modern sociology is a field of knowledge, not a reform movement, and not a therapy; (2) that the subject matter of sociology should consist only of the knowledges which are based on careful and repeated observations by well-trained persons employing tested methods of observation and analysis; (3) that sociology should be concerned primarily but not exclusively with the study of what *is*, not with speculation about what *ought to be;* (4) that sociology is only one of a group of social sciences which study human behavior, each of which has its own subject matter, point of view, and personnel, none having a corner on the whole truth; and (5) that sociology, like all fields of knowledge, contains differences in professional viewpoint, but we cherish these differences because out of them usually comes growth in human knowledge.

We then approached sociology from the point of view of the kind of work sociologists do—teaching, research, consultation, and administration—and considered briefly each of these lines of effort. Finally, the question of rewards, both extrinsic and intrinsic, was discussed.

SUGGESTED READINGS

Aubert, Wilhelm, *Elements of Sociology*. New York, Scribner, 1967.
It may be interesting to more serious students to compare the way "elementary sociology" is developed by Aubert, a European, to the way in which it is typically presented by American sociologists.

Bates, Alan P., *The Sociological Enterprise*. Boston, Houghton Mifflin, 1967.
This is a paperback which roughly parallels the point of view and coverage of the present chapter. Bates treats sociology both as an intellectual enterprise and as a vocation. His data and his insights "ring true" as a portrayal of the discipline.

Gouldner, Alvin W., and Miller, S. M., eds., *Applied Sociology*. New York, Free Press, 1965.
This is a collection of various materials, all of which are addressed to the practical use of sociology in various parts of American society.

Hinkle, Roscoe C., and Hinkle, Gisela J., *The Development of Modern Sociology*. New York, Random House, 1954.
An excellent short treatment of the emergence of sociology as a discipline and its major assumptions and divisions.

Mizruchi, Ephraim H., ed., *The Substance of Sociology: Codes, Conduct and Consequences*. New York, Appleton-Century-Crofts, 1967.
This is one of the best books of readings among the sizable crop which recent authorship has put forth. The editor shows a fine feeling both for the classics and for the gleanings of contemporary effort. Whether he reads from cover to cover or selectively on the basis of interest, the reader will secure from this book an uncommonly representative view of the sociological enterprise.

Parsons, Talcott, "Sociology as a Profession." *American Sociological Review*, Vol. 24 (August, 1959), pp. 547–599.
One of America's leading social theorists, writing principally to a professional audience, assays the nature of the profession and discipline of sociology.

Simpson, George, *Man in Society*. New York, Doubleday, 1954.
A short (85 pages) preface to sociology and the social sciences written in a mature, lucid way.

Smelser, Neil J., ed., *Sociology: An Introduction*. New York, Wiley, 1967.
Smelser's *Sociology* is an uncommonly good, advanced presentation of the field of sociology today. The more mature and serious student will find in it true intellectual excitement.

Timasheff, Nicholas. *Sociological Theory: Its Nature and Growth,* rev. ed.
    New York, Random House, 1967.
This is a useful book for those who would like to see contemporary sociology
in the light of its historical, theoretical antecedents. A field of knowledge can
never be really understood until seen against the backdrop of thinkers of the
past.

Valdes, Donald M., and Dean, Dwight G., *Sociology in Use.* New York,
    Macmillan, 1965.
There is currently a plethora of books of readings purporting to provide an
introduction to the field of sociology, all of which more or less accomplish this
purpose. Valdes and Dean differ from the genre in that their collection of readings intends primarily to present illustrations of how sociological work has been
put to *practical* use. This may or may not be important, depending upon
whether one holds to an intellectual conception or to a pragmatic conception of
what a field consists of. However, in terms of its stated purposes this book is
worth reading.

STUDY QUESTIONS

1. Why has man been so slow in studying himself scientifically?
2. Why is it difficult to give a one-sentence definition of sociology?
3. In what ways is the term *sociologist* often improperly applied?
4. Why is sociology not "therapy"? Illustrate.
5. What is the "field of knowledge" of sociology?
6. Why are most modern professional sociologists not advocates of any
    particular "ought to be"?
7. How may an interest in welfare grow out of a professional interest in
    sociology?
8. Why are most sociologists primarily interested in studying the existing
    scheme of things?
9. Why is it difficult to "integrate" the various present-day subject-matter
    divisions in the social sciences?
10. How do different points of view arise in any one field of knowledge?
    Why is this often overemphasized?

2
METHODS OF SOCIOLOGICAL STUDY

Some people assume that "knowledge" is something waiting in the universe to be discovered and, after discovery, thereafter forever "known" to man. Many times knowledge in this sense is "found," but only temporarily, like the idea current among educated people in Europe about 1500 that the earth was flat, or the "fact" held generally by chemists around 1800 that a substance called "phlogiston," [1] determined what materials would burn. Any school child *now* "knows" the falsity of these once-held "truths." The thoughtful man of today wonders, "How many of the things we now know *for sure*, aren't really true?" Existing knowledge is *made by men*, and by men using certain kinds of *ideas* and *physical tools*; as either the ideas or the tools change, the "findings" or "knowledge" or "truths" or "facts" also change. This is an endless process of creating and discarding knowledge. It applies to *all* scientific knowledge and in major degree to all knowledge.

In the first chapter we pointed out that differences of judgment among competent scholars is a common (and quite desirable) characteristic of *all* fields of knowledge, and especially so among the *sciences*. Some issues are relatively minor and refer to some minute point of the method used, or to some "slant" or "wrinkle" of the interpretation. Other issues are fundamental; they are rooted in the more profound personal makeup and educational experience of the scholars involved and often cannot be reconciled, because they are irreconcilable. They remain among us as vivid reminders that scientists and other scholars are not robots, but rather are self-conscious and self-directed human beings who come at life and at experience differently. Endless arguments about which one—or which "school"—is right and which wrong are enlightening and sometimes also amusing, but rarely do they resolve or settle the issues; more likely they sharpen the issues and in the

[1] For a classic discussion of this point see George Lundberg, *The Foundations of Sociology* (New York, Macmillan, 1939), pp. 10–12.

sharpening process the participants, and the bystanders, too, can better come to appreciate what is at stake.

With this background we shall discuss some of the basic differences among present-day sociologists regarding the proper methods of sociological inquiry. Some of the time we shall allow the proponents to "speak for themselves" in an effort better to secure the more subtle overtones of what they have to say.

But there also are substantial *agreements* among sociologists. These should not be neglected while we give attention to the more dramatic differences. Accordingly, then, we shall begin with a statement of some of the more generally agreed upon matters in sociological method. (It is to be noted that we are in this chapter *not* concerned with *all* agreements and disagreements among sociologists, but *only* with those agreements and disagreements *regarding methods of research* and study.)

SOME BASICS IN SOCIOLOGICAL METHODS

1. The imperative need for objectivity

a. Objectivity defined

The basic attitude or point of view which is essential for successful work in any science is objectivity. Objectivity means the *ability and the willingness to study the facts of a given field without prejudice*. It is essential to see things as they "really" are, even if this seeing is uncomfortable or not to one's liking or not to one's best interest. For example, the author's students frequently object vigorously to being informed that they have grown up in a state which ranks high in wealth and low in educational expenditures as compared to other states in the Union. Rather than seeing this as a social fact, actually a condition of their own lives, many seem to prefer to ignore it or to explain it away; a few even seem to denigrate those persons who point the fact out. To recognize that a fact exists and to consider its implications, causes, and consequences is the inescapable task of the scientific mind. Sentimentality, personal discomfort, and misguided conceptions of loyalty have no place in the scientific enterprise. Since much of the subject matter of sociology consists of understandings as close, if not closer, to the existing prejudices of people as this one, the student must be especially conscious both of the need for being objective and of the hindrances to objectivity which are constantly being encountered.

b. Lack of training in objectivity

We have not been trained to be objective. As a matter of fact, most persons are trained *not* to be objective. Everyone is more or less indoctrinated with prejudices about many things. It is always easy to recognize that the other person's views constitute prejudices, but it requires a considerable measure of objectivity to be able to recognize equally clearly that one is prejudiced himself. A man once complained to the writer that a friend of his who belonged to the opposite political party was "very prejudiced on political matters." He said that he had argued almost all night with the prejudiced man and could not change his political views. This complainant seemed quite innocent of the fact that *both* he and his political opponent were prejudiced, and that it was quite as significant that his own mind was not changed during the discussion as it was that the other man's was not. What he really said could be paraphrased this way: "I have intelligent ideas; he who agrees with me also has, but he who disagrees is either unintelligent, stupid, or prejudiced." This is more or less true of everyone, although, of course, all persons are not equally prejudiced or necessarily prejudiced in the same direction or about the same things.

c. "Loyalties" may curb objectivity

Everyone is indoctrinated not only with prejudices but also often with the idea that not to be prejudiced constitutes "disloyalty" to some person or to some principle. A student recently reported, for example, that in the study of history she had learned certain facts about the private lives of some of our nation's heroes which were not wholly complimentary to their characters. She protested the teaching of such information on the ground that it was "disloyal" not to be able to continue to believe that these men were above reproach. One is forced to conclude, then, that she would prefer to remain ignorant and keep her "loyalties" rather than know the truth and lose them. This is by no means an exceptional case. Illustrations of the same point could be found in the thinking of almost anyone. It is a quite natural outcome of our teaching children to be loyal to groups and to ideals. Every group with which we are affiliated indoctrinates us with prejudicial views of many things. This is true of our church, our political party, our race, our social class, even our age-groups.

d. Lack of objectivity may result from attempts to justify social position

One frequently finds it necessary, or at least more comfortable, to justify the things he does or the privileges he possesses. It is also useful to alibi failures and mistakes.

We learn popular clichés to justify the actions or ideas of our groups. Thus, numerous whites are quick to "explain" the superior advantages of whites in terms of the "lower capability of Negroes," omitting the remainder of the truth, namely, that Negroes are less well trained than whites, on the average, because whites, being in control, have not allowed Negroes to utilize their skills along many lines by denying them job and educational opportunities. It is easier to say that the Negro "does not have the necessary experience to do a white man's work" than to say that one has denied the Negro the opportunity to acquire the experience.

Sometimes unobjective information regarding one's community appears. For example, in one town located adjacent to a large city, the "Boosters' Club" boasts of the low death rate as compared to that of the larger adjacent city. The facts are correct as stated, but the reason is less complimentary. The city with the low death rate has no hospital, and its ill go to the adjacent city's hospitals for treatment, and, when they die, the deaths are recorded in the city which has the hospitals within its borders! But yet, somehow, it is comforting to many to be able to live in the city with the low death rate, even if it is only a statistical trick! The trick, however, is at the expense of those who really believe that they live in "a more healthful city."

e. Summary on objectivity

Perhaps enough has been said to indicate that coming to correct conclusions in social science is not made easy by the mere fact that one has been exposed to some of its raw materials in the course of growing up. As a matter of fact, it is largely because one has been exposed to many of the prejudicial interpretations that it is difficult for him to be objective and thus come to correct conclusions. One can see the "superstitions" in the other person's religion better than those in his own. He can see the "logical errors" in someone else's philosophy better than he can the equally logical errors in his own. He is taught to do this and is indoctrinated with numerous socially acceptable ways of thinking which make prejudice easy and objectivity difficult. Yet despite the difficulties, some measure of objectivity is attainable for almost everyone, and if they will work at it diligently, a great deal of objectivity about social phenomena is attainable by most. One of the by-products of studying this book should be a sharpened sense of objectivity about the matters with which it deals. The chief point to our discussion of objectivity was to show its importance, in fact indispensability, to successful work in sociology, and to point out some of the handicaps to attaining objectivity "overnight." Progress in mastering objectivity is usually slow.

The precise ways for achieving objectivity differ somewhat among sociologists. Here we are only making the point that it is agreed that objectivity *by some route* is a basic scholarly ideal of the utmost importance.

2. The importance of qualification

In studying sociology the student should be careful to note the qualifying words such as *sometimes, rarely, usually, on the average, as far as we know, presumably,* and so on. There is an important difference between the statements that "all men are born equal" and that "all men are born equal *in legal rights.*" The first is unqualified (and, incidentally, incorrect); the second is more nearly correct, although the word *all*, not further qualified as to place and time, would certainly raise grave doubts, because in numerous times and places great inequalities in legal rights have existed and still exist. In the United States at the present time, to be more exact, all people are born equal in legal rights *except* Negroes in some states, women, children born out of wedlock, orphans, and others. And, also, since abstract legal rights are often of no particular significance to the person unable to afford competent legal counsel, we need to add income or wealth or prestige as an additional inequality. Our original statement would be much more nearly in accord with the facts, and hence more nearly correct or true, if we restated it this way: "In America, around 1968, all legitimate, white males have the same theoretical, but not actual, legal equality."

Too much qualification can, of course, impede one unduly. Important as precision in scientific work is, it can be overdone and render the resultant generalization ridiculous. It is recorded that a scientist and a layman were riding through the country and passed a flock of sheep that had recently been shorn. The layman remarked, "Those sheep have just been shorn." The scientist is reported to have replied, after careful scrutiny of the sheep, "Well, it appears from where I am, that those which I can see have been shorn, on the side which I am observing, if my eyesight is correct." It is hardly necessary to qualify generalizations as guardedly as that; in fact, to do so may be unwise.

It is doubtful that the beginning student will overdo the qualifications of his statements and thoughts. Experience shows that he is much more likely to err on the side of omitting much needed qualification. This is especially important when reading sociological material or understanding correctly the instructor's statements. Laymen are usually not trained to see or to hear the finer distinctions, and it is the fine distinctions, often, which mark the difference between correctness and error.

In studying this book the student will do well to watch carefully for qualifying words and phrases of the following sorts:

1. Regarding the *degree of generality*—words like *all, always, sometimes, rarely, usually*.
2. Regarding the *time referred to*—all time, since the beginning, during our generation, before the Civil War.
3. Regarding the *place referred to*—the world, this continent, Ohio, the South Pacific peoples, north of the Mason-Dixon line, in cities, in large cities.
4. Regarding the *group referred to*—everyone, males, persons 30–34, white-collar workers, students in state universities.
5. Regarding the *conclusiveness of the evidence*—on the basis of this one experiment, in all cases studied, on the basis of research conducted in the United States.
6. Regarding the *extent of professional agreement* on points under discussion—a majority of scholars, a few scholars, almost without exception, a growing agreement, an increasing skepticism.

The difference between interpreting correctly, understanding passably, or being entirely wrong may, and often does, lie in the qualifying phrase. Frequently the difference between the scientifically correct generalization and the popular one is the qualification of the scientific one. "Like begets like," says the layman to genetics. "Yes and no," says the geneticist, as he goes on to qualify the statement in the light of the whole truth, as the truth is known to scholars in that field.

CAUSALITY, CORRELATION, AND SCIENTIFIC INTERPRETATION

A common error in much amateur (and some professional) interpretation of sociological facts relates to the matter of "correlation." The term *correlation* refers, simply, to the observed fact that two measured conditions are so related that as one increases the other also does and in the same degree. Thus, for example, there is a correlation between the size of cities and crime rates for certain kinds of crime. The bigger the city, the higher the number of offenses per 1000 people. (Correlation may also be negative; for example, as one condition gets larger, the related one gets smaller. An example of this would be the relation between the amount of education women have and the number of children they produce. The most educated women have the fewest children and the least educated have the most, on the average.) Correlations, both positive and negative, do not, however, prove anything whatsoever about the *causal* connections between the items correlated. This can be shown by an illustration from a recent research.

A researcher found that there was a positive correlation between the number of dates which college girls had and their grades. In other words, the girls who dated most received the highest grades and those who dated least got the lowest grades. When the facts of this correlation were revealed, some persons jumped quickly to the conclusion that *because* some girls dated a great deal they received higher grades in their school work. While such a causal relationship *might* exist, there is nothing in the statistical fact of a correlation which proves it. Why not?

When a correlation between two items exists, there may be any of four possible inferences regarding causes.

1. Item *A* (dating in our illustration above) *might* cause item *B* (good grades).
2. Item *B* (high grades) *might* cause item *A* (many dates).
3. The connection between *A* and *B* might be due to sheer chance. For example, one could show a correlation between the horsepower of automobiles in the United States from 1920 to 1950 and the number of persons adjudged insane in the United States. No one would seriously contend that there is any causal connection between these two items—just happenstance.
4. Item *A* (dating) and item *B* (grades) might both be caused by some other item, *C*, possibly a combination of good health, personality, and intelligence which could easily relate both to popularity as a date and to scholastic achievement. (Incidentally, this fourth possibility would seem the most probable one by which to interpret the correlation of grades and dates as found in the study reported.)

Great care should be observed when attempting to interpret the meaning or significance of a correlation. There is often the desire on the part of the interpreter to seize upon the one of the four possibilities which best suits his prejudices or his fears or his comprehension at the moment. Actually, the real test of the causality of two items cannot be made by the correlation. All that a correlation gives one is a clue as to the *possibility* of a causal connection—and even then one cannot determine whether *A* causes *B* or *B* causes *A* or *A* and *B* are both caused by *C* or by *CD!*

(The student should note that this discussion of correlation has been elementary and that we have completely avoided such technical questions as how to interpret coefficients of correlation of varying size. These questions may best await a course in statistics.)

SOME ISSUES IN SOCIOLOGICAL THEORY AND METHOD

1. The nature of science

Perhaps the most basic disagreements among sociologists, as well as among its interpreters and critics, grows out of differing conceptions of science itself. Discussions as to whether sociology is or is not a science often result in a confused and confusing dialogue in part because differing conceptions of science are being used by the various participants. At least three prevailing conceptions of science, all applicable to other sciences as well as to the social sciences, are extant. Unfortunately, meanings are not always spelled out, and sometimes one has to search a writer's or a speaker's communication for implicit, "between the lines," meanings in order to understand what *he* means by science.

One well-established meaning of the word *science* is simply that it consists of *empirical verification* of events and relationships. Thus, the knowledge that the earth is round; that water consists of H_2O, boils at $212°F$, and freezes at $32°F$; that the moon reflects light rays from the sun; or that women and men are equally intelligent are "scientific" propositions. All that is required is that observation and, if possible, measurement take place and that subsequent verification bear out earlier observations to form a verified and thus reliable understanding or comprehension of "how things really are." This is the earliest and most unsophisticated, yet in a way basic, meaning of science. All scientific fields contain numerous such items of information and descriptions of reality and continue to devote effort to furthering such knowledge.

A second meaning of science holds that science consists of *explanation* of relationships among observed occurrences. It is not enough to know that water "is" H_2O; we need also to know the various properties of hydrogen and oxygen and why one combination results in water and another in hydrogen peroxide. This is, of course, the function of hypotheses and theories in science building. The scientist seeks explanations as to *why*. Thus, there is the eternal search for the conditions under which certain events take place. Theories and hypotheses as explanations constantly undergo change as scientific minds reexamine their assumptions, collect new information, rethink their inferences, and in various other ways subject their explanations to more critical judgments and to new information. Thus, many of our understandings of the structure of atoms, the chemistry of chromosomes, and the nature of matter have been importantly transformed within the lifetime of many living scientists.

A third prevailing conception of science, which some scientists insist is the ultimate in scientific accomplishment, while others vehemently deny it, is that science exists only when the scientist's knowledge enables him accurately to *predict* occurrences. In this sense, thus, astronomy is manifestly scientific because the astronomer can predict eclipses or estimate distances between planets so that, among other things, space travel is possible. The biologist, too, is a scientist because he can predict the behavior of living organisms under various conditions, controlled or natural. One does not have to be a scientist, of course, to make accurate predictions; any farmer knows the gestation period for various kinds of livestock and so is able to predict the parturition dates of his animals. He can also predict the seasonal changes in temperature well enough to maximize his production of plants and to make the most effective use of seed, fertilizer, and his own efforts. Most teenage boys know enough about automotive mechanics to be able to predict the behavior of their hot rods under various conditions, such as fuel use, ignition adjustment, and the like.

It is amazing to observe how much accurate prediction may be done in various sciences without explanatory understanding. For example, long before man had a sufficiently scientific explanation of the nature of electricity, he was sophisticated enough to predict the behavior of electricity and to make it work for him—to produce heat and cold, supply power and light, and harness it in myriads of ways to facilitate communication. Similarly, biologists do not always know why various chemicals cure disease, and yet they are able to predict with dramatic accuracy that certain outcomes will occur.

Discussions about "the nature" of science unfortunately often degenerate into semantically ridiculous harangues because of the failure to recognize such basic distinctions as these. There are several common misapplications which perennially arise when considering the scientific standing of the social sciences. One of these is the assumption that since social scientists do not as a rule carry on their observations in laboratories and conduct experiments under controlled conditions, they therefore cannot claim scientific knowledge or explanation. This argument curiously equates science with a particular procedure, namely the use of the laboratory. If the laboratory were essential to the building of science, then the astronomer would have no science and such basic biological concepts as evolution would have no scientific standing, since they did not derive from the laboratory experiment! A second vulgarism maintains that nothing is scientific unless it is "exact," that is, that it *always* happens in a certain way. Yet modern physics, generally regarded as probably the most advanced of scientific fields, expresses practically all its propositions in terms of the mathematics of probability. It is minimally sufficient to establish a scientific proposition simply to demonstrate that the occurrence takes place *in fact* more often than it would by *chance*. For example, in order to have scientific standing, a drug need not cure every known case of a specified disease. It is sufficient that in a high percentage of instances it so performs as compared to cases in which the drug was not administered. It is even to be expected that there may be a small percentage of cases where the drug may be actually harmful, as in the cases of penicillin "poisoning." Obviously, the more nearly universal our knowledge is, the better we like it and the more useful it is for practical purposes. And certainly it is completely reasonable to assess the worth of a science in terms of how many of its important propositions have a high level of accuracy for predictive purposes. But to make precision the determining consideration is, in the present state of scientific endeavor, simply a naïveté.

2. "Hard" and "soft" science

In the professional jargon of science a distinction between "hard" and "soft" science is increasingly being used. *Hard sciences* are those sciences in which there is a large and impressive body of definitive findings. Moreover, these findings are based on experiment or other evidence which is conclusive and amply verified. Where used for practical application, they have become operational. Physics, astronomy, many aspects of chemistry, and some aspects of the biological sciences probably exhaust the category. *Soft sciences* are so designated for either of two related reasons. First, the data themselves may not quite live up to the standards of rigorous scientific requirements. Possibly the findings

have not been replicated sufficiently as yet, or there is a lurking doubt
as to whether the inferences drawn from the data are correct inferences. Or the samples may be in some ways dubious. In other words,
while the canons of scientific inquiry have been observed, there have
been too many compromises to warrant confidence. In another sense, soft
sciences refer to the subject matter. For example, in psychology and
sociology a great deal of research is done on attitudes. Assuming for the
moment that we have impeccable measures of attitudes, doubt still remains as to whether or not one can really predict overt behavior even
with a thorough knowledge of attitudes. Thus, for example, a man may
say he "believes in monogamy" and may do so quite sincerely, but this
may or may not determine his actual conduct in sexual matters. On the
other hand, there is reason to believe that we are further ahead with a
knowledge of attitudes than with no knowledge at all or with a merely
speculative or intuitive judgment as to what people will do. It comes
down, then, to how closely the conventional requirements for scientific
procedure have been approximated: not only are some sciences and
some findings soft, but some are softer than others.

3. Methods in science

a. Formal procedure

Another issue among sociologists, which they share with scientists
in other fields, is that of scientific method, or preferably, scientific
methods. One school of thought approaches the question in a formalistic manner. A classic sociological work,[2] acknowledgedly based on
its author's conception of physics, enumerates "canons" of scientific
procedure. These postulates, he says, should constitute the "frame of
reference" of sociology. In substance, the explanation is as follows.

1. *Uniformities in the universe.* We assume, first, that items in the
universe, whether we are talking about the planets, the composition of
blood, or the operation of the human mind, show uniformities and regularities which man can discover if he searches ably enough. The so-
called "unpredictability of things" is not really inherent unpredictability
at all, but rather current human ignorance concerning how the things
"work." Much that was unpredictable yesterday is readily predictable
today, and many things unpredictable to the layman are readily predictable to the expert. Accurate prediction is possible, however, only
for the person who knows enough about the uniformities to be able to
anticipate the future workings of them.

[2] *Ibid.*

2. *Uniformities revealed by observation.* A further assumption of science is that we learn the uniformities in the universe through *observation, rechecking our observations many, many times* in order that we may learn more precisely and certainly what the uniformities are.

3. *Verification.* It is the method of *verification* through which we *establish* our scientific finding. The precise ways in which we observe and verify vary for each field of knowledge, but fundamentally there is no substitute for the verification process. We must observe over and over again.

4. *Codification.* After verified observation has demonstrated that something is true, it becomes necessary to *codify* the finding in some definite way. The well-known chemical formula H_2O is such a statement. What it really means is that after repeated observations water has been found to consist of two "parts" hydrogen and one "part" oxygen. The finding could just as well be stated in a sentence as in a formula, but usage seems to have favored the formula H_2O rather than a sentence. Other findings of science cannot be stated so tersely. For example, the theory of evolution as discovered by biologists cannot be stated as a formula and can, in fact, hardly be stated accurately in a sentence. It is too involved for either, but is no less certain and surely no less important than some other finding which can be stated more tersely.

Scientific findings when stated in words are usually classified into *laws, theories,* and *hypotheses.* If the evidence indicates that the finding is clearly established and can be stated definitely without too many "ifs, ands, and provides," then it is called a "law." Examples are the "Law of Falling Bodies," "Boyle's Law," and the "Law of Diminishing Returns." Discoveries which are probably true, but for which the evidence is not quite so conclusive, are usually called "theories." It is necessary to emphasize, however, that a theory is not a guess, is not "a notion spun out of thin air," but is a truth for which there exists considerable but not final and conclusive evidence. Finally, there are "hypotheses." A hypothesis is an idea about which we are not yet sufficiently certain to permit us to call it a law or a theory, but there is, nevertheless, some evidence to support it. An idea usually does not remain a hypothesis very long. It is usually soon tested and if found true becomes a theory or a law, if found to be false is discarded. This may, of course, take a long time and require much effort.

Most fields of knowledge have some laws, some theories, and some hypotheses, although they do not always call their findings by these labels. Very often the term *principles* is used to cover all three. The point, however, to our discussion is simply that the findings of each field of knowledge vary in degree of definiteness depending on how much research underlies them, that the findings can be expressed in various ways, but that fundamentally they constitute a statement of what has been found to be true.

5. *Systematization.* The final step in science is to organize the laws, theories, and hypotheses into *systems* or *patterns of knowledge.* Some principles are large, overall truths which are fundamental to the rest of the science, such as evolution in biology or relativity in physics. Other truths are very specific, almost minute in nature, such as the law that water will solidify at 0° centigrade and vaporize at 100° centigrade at sea level and under other specified conditions. Obviously the broad principles, the subordinate principles, and the minute principles have to be arranged and woven together into the overall pattern of knowledge which makes up what we call summarily the "field."

b. Critiques of formal procedure

Outlining the matter in this way may lead to serious misconceptions. The first of such errors is the implication that research always and necessarily proceeds from step one through step five. In practice it seldom works this neatly. Often, for example, hypotheses are formulated late in the inquiry rather than being present at the beginning, particularly when original hypotheses are found during the experiment to have been faulty. Second, it is not an ironclad rule that research begin with a hypothesis. Most important of all, formal statements about scientific method fail to allow sufficient room for the *principle of serendipity.* Serendipitous findings in research are findings which the scientist stumbles upon, so to speak, in the course of working on something else. The classic example of this is the discovery of penicillin by Sir Alexander Fleming. Another well-known case is the vulcanization of rubber. Serendipity also works, of course, in social science; in fact it is likely that it plays an even more important role in the less developed sciences than in the more advanced ones. W. I. B. Beveridge[3] stresses that serendipitous findings are not really accidental, that they require unusual alertness, creativity, and probably breadth of knowledge to make the serendipitous discovery when the unanticipated conditions are present. Finally, there is the unfortunate implication in the above postulates that all scientists work more or less alike and that their productivity results from some overt performance of a physical regimen. Actually the scientific enterprise, regardless of the field, is essentially

[3] See Beveridge's excellent treatment in *The Art of Scientific Investigation,* rev. ed. (New York, Norton, 1957). Also available in paperback.

a mental enterprise, a creative act. The moment of truth is quite as likely to arrive when one is sitting with his feet on his desk smoking a cigarette as it is when he is pouring over his experimental paraphernalia. Many distinguished scientists in their autobiographical writings have attested to this. Moreover, there is a sort of specialization which grows up informally among scientists. In their professional shoptalk they frequently distinguish between "idea men" and "technicians." The idea men, like Darwin or Einstein, pursue problems of a very abstract and basic sort, while the technicians devote themselves to problems of more modest proportions which they rigorously check out with repeated experiments. When research is done in teams, administrators usually deliberately seek to combine the talents of idea men and technicians in order to maximize the probability of coming up with something worthwhile.

INFORMAL SOCIOLOGICAL METHODS

In sharp contrast to the foregoing kind of approach to sociological study is that implied in the following quotations, the first from a contemporary sociologist and the other from a revered sociological pioneer.

Sometimes one feels that sociology would prosper more, especially in America, if its practitioners forgot to think of it as a science. . . .[4]
We hear it questioned whether sociology is a science or a philosophy. It is both, and an art also.[5]

"Verstehen"

The word *Verstehen*, obviously German, is sometimes used to characterize this viewpoint, although it is not wholly satisfactory. It is difficult to translate adequately because it has no exact English equivalent. Loosely translated, *Verstehen* means "understanding" or "insight," but it also means more than these. In sociological literature it refers to a unique *kind* or *degree* of understanding and insight, like the understanding of a painting by the artist or the understanding of a personality by the psychiatrist. The difficulty with *Verstehen* is that no one can give a precise recipe for it, although some have tried.

Cooley puts it this way: It "is developed from contact with the minds of other men, through communication, which sets going a pro-

[4] R. M. MacIver, *Society: Its Structure and Changes* (New York, Ray Long and Richard R. Smith, 1931), p. ix.
[5] C. H. Cooley, *Life and the Student* (New York, Knopf, 1927), p. 160.

cess of thought and sentiment similar to theirs and enables us to understand them by sharing their states of mind. This I call personal or social knowledge." [6]

The difficulty of enumerating specific steps in the pursuit of informal methods in sociology is presented interestingly by Redfield.[7]

Let us here try to find out something about the nature of this non-formal aspect of social science through a consideration of three books about society that have long been recognized as important, influential, and meritorious: De Tocqueville's *Democracy in America*, Sumner's *Folkways*, and Veblen's *The Theory of the Leisure Class*. For from almost fifty to a hundred years these books have interested and have influenced many kinds of social scientists. . . . None of these books tells very much about research method, in the sense of teaching special procedures of operation with certain kinds of data. . . . There is nowhere in them any procedure, any kind of operation upon facts to reach conclusions which might not occur to any intelligent and generally educated person. . . .

. . . This requirement in the social scientist calls for gifts and for a kind of education different from that required of any physicist and very similar to what is called for in a creative artist. . . . So I say that social science, as practiced, is something of an art and that, as its best works are communicated, it has something of the personal and social values of all the arts.

Mills [8] is another proponent of informal method, which he characterizes as work "in the classic tradition" and which results in "the sociological imagination." Some of his own widely known and respected work is of this type.

It is easy to make a case for informal method. No one needs to labor the point that isolated facts mean little, that interpretation of facts and the integration of factual knowledge into larger and more meaningful wholes is the essential task. Nor is there anything automatically scientific about statistical study, the most widespread technique of formal sociological method. As Cooley [9] puts it, "Nothing is more illuminating or more fallacious than statistics. If the underlying material is trustworthy they may reveal its meaning; but numerical exactitude is often the only thing scientific about them."

[6] C. H. Cooley, *Sociological Theory and Social Research* (New York, Holt, Rinehart and Winston, 1939), p. 290.

[7] Robert Redfield, "The Art of Social Science," *American Journal of Sociology*, Vol. 54 (November, 1948), pp. 182, 190.

[8] C. Wright Mills, *The Sociological Imagination* (New York, Oxford University Press, 1959).

[9] Cooley, *Life and the Student*, p. 156.

Respected and lasting insights into human relationships have been achieved by sociologists and other observers of the human scene who have not followed strict scientific procedures. For example, in his famous study of *The Lonely Crowd*, in which Riesman and his close associates talked with a relatively few people about a wide variety of subjects in a highly creative way, Riesman was able to make penetrating discoveries about the American character (Chapter 4). Despite efforts to teach techniques of interviewing, skillful interviewing and interpretation of interview materials remains more an art than a technology.

Criticism of the informal approaches

Needless to say, informal sociology has its critics. Lundberg's criticism may be taken as representative.[10]

Eloquent defenses of insight and understanding, therefore, merely draw a red herring across the trail of the real question, namely: What are the methods of attaining understanding and insight? We want an objective description of the *technic*. The answer to this demand in some quarters is to wear one's collar backwards, to gaze into crystals or tea cups, or to go into a trance. While being duly impressed with the remarkable results of these technics, the hardier minds in every field have always demanded a more detailed description of the steps in the procedure. . . . Since verification by other qualified minds is the essence of scientific knowledge, the progress of science has been characterized by increasingly searching demands that the author of a generalization specify the steps by which he reached it.

The difficulty with informal methods as an operation is that the alleged "operation" is not defined. There is no neat recipe, no precise record of how step *A* leads to step *B* so that some skeptical person can rework the problem to determine whether he gets the same answer.

The interdependence of formal and informal method

In practice the sharp distinction some make between informal operations and strict empiric (scientific) ones seldom holds. Actually the two methods are interdependent—only the extremists of either view deny this, and even they do so more in theory than in practice.[11] Cer-

[10] G. A. Lundberg, *Foundations of Sociology* (New York, Macmillan, 1939), pp. 51–52.

[11] This point is well made by Robert Bierstedt, "A Critique of Empiricism in Sociology," *American Sociological Review*, Vol. 14 (October, 1949), pp. 584–591. See also Jessie Bernard, "Reply to Lundberg's Comments," *American Sociological Review*, Vol. 14 (December, 1949), pp. 799–800.

tainly when one examines the undisputed classics of social science, as Redfield suggests, he finds numerous important works, the significance of which does not come from devotion to strict scientific procedure. Numerous others fall into a middle category. Conclusions are not rigidly supportable by precise scientific steps, and yet hard, factual data are used in the research process. We shall not mention any of such here, but throughout the footnotes and bibliographies of this or any other sociological textbook, one will find the dependence of all sociologists on studies and writings which fall into this middle-of-the-road category, being neither rigidly empiric nor clearly informal, but an admixture of both.

The student who goes on with the study of sociology will learn a wide variety of methods and how to choose the most appropriate one for the problem at hand. Questionnaire construction, interview procedure, sampling techniques, as well as the formation of scales and statistical analysis of the data, when it is appropriate, are the a.b.c.'s of sociological method. These and others are the basic techniques which sociologists use and are constantly refining in their application of the tenets of science to the inquiry into the condition of man.

SUMMARY AND CONCLUSION

In this chapter we have compressed a great deal of work pertaining to the methods of sociological inquiry. First we pointed out that there are many routes to knowledge and that persons of equal competence are not necessarily oriented to the search in the same way. Two schools stand out and each makes a strong case for its position: formal scientific method and the informal approach. We have examined the viewpoints of both of these.

Some sociologists try to "solve" the above problem by making believe it does not exist. They say, and write, that there "really is no issue," that it is the function of informal method to suggest hypotheses, of statistics and other formal procedures to test them, and of informal procedures, again, to interpret the findings. This sounds good, and it sometimes really happens that way, but any student can see for himself that such does not often occur simply by comparing the methods used by the authors of articles appearing in the professional journals of sociologists and other social scientists.

The same conclusion will be reached by a mature examination of this or any other textbook in sociology: the "content" of the field comprises a mixture of strictly scientific material and a liberal amount of

Verstehen material as well. This condition is not pointed out to justify the current practices of sociologists or to attack them—but, rather simply, to get the facts of the matter before us as they *are*.

SUGGESTED READINGS

Berger, Peter L., *Invitation to Sociology: A Humanistic Perspective*. New York, Doubleday (Anchor Books), 1963.
This is an influential, widely known, and respected small paperback critique of the present state of sociology as a discipline. The author leans toward the humanistic rather than the formal scientific conception of the field.

Beveridge, W. I. B., *The Art of Scientific Investigation*, rev. ed. New York, Norton, 1957.
One of a very few broad-gauge considerations of what is really involved in the scientific enterprise, whether related to sociology or to some other scientific field. Several of Beveridge's formulations are treated in this chapter, but a reading of the entire book will be helpful in shaping a young scientist's sophistication.

Bruyn, Severyn T., *The Human Perspective in Sociology: The Methodology of Participant Observation*. Englewood Cliffs, N.J., Prentice-Hall, 1967.
A scholarly development of the thesis that sociological endeavor should be concerned more than it is with informal, but by no means pedestrian, participation by the sociologist in the society he studies.

Cooley, C. H., "The Roots of Social Knowledge," *Sociological Theory and Social Research*. New York, Holt, Rinehart and Winston, 1930. The article also appears in the *American Journal of Sociology*, Vol. 32 (July, 1926), pp. 59–79.
This is a classic statement of the dichotomy of knowledge—measurative and "human." Cooley stressed the large role of insight in what he considered to be the essence of sociology.

Cuber, John F., and Harroff, Peggy B., eds., *Readings in Sociology: Sources and Comment*. New York, Appleton-Century-Crofts, 1962.
This is a collection of fifty relatively short readings from a wide variety of sources intended to be used as supplementary readings with standard texts. The following selections are relevant to this chapter: Karl Pearson, "The Grammar of Science," pp. 15–20; Herbert Spencer, "The Study of Sociology," pp. 1–7; Robert Oppenheimer, "A Scientist Reflects on Science," pp. 20–27; Robert Bierstedt, "Sociology and Humane Learning," pp. 32–37.

Doby, John T., ed., *An Introduction to Social Research*. New York, Appleton-Century-Crofts, 1967.
This book is an excellent introduction for the student interested in research methods utilized by social scientists today. Parts may be somewhat technical, but taken as a whole it provides a realistic, and for the most part readable, account of how sociological expertise is carried out.

Lundberg, G. A., "Some Convergences in Sociological Theory." *American Journal of Sociology*, Vol. 62 (July, 1956), pp. 21–27.
Advances the hypothesis that despite long-standing divergencies among sociologists regarding theory and research methods, agreements are emerging. Technical.

McKinney, John C., *Constructive Typology and Social Theory*. New York, Appleton-Century-Crofts, 1966.
This is a recent reformulation of some long-standing concepts as to what the social scientist ought to be doing. If there is a true separation between theory and empirical endeavor in social science, this work would have to be classified as the former. Probably only of interest to the serious student.

Mills, C. Wright, *Images of Man: The Classic Tradition in Sociological Thinking*. New York, George Braziller, 1960.
In this book Mills attempts to reacquaint sociologists with what he considers to be neglected aspects of their professional origins. The introduction to this book, "The Classical Tradition," is an interesting interpretation of the present condition of sociology as seen by an off-beat analyst. The bulk of the book consists of excerpts from the classical writings out of which contemporary sociology has emerged. The introductory chapter, however, can profitably be read alone.

Mills, C. Wright, *The Sociological Imagination*. New York, Oxford University Press, 1959.
This is a book of uncommon importance in the development of the discipline of sociology. The author clearly adheres to the humanistic or informal sociological approach. His characterization of the errors which derive from the excesses of raw empiricism and grand theory will not soon be forgotten.

Redfield, Robert, "The Art of Social Science." *American Journal of Sociology*, Vol. 54 (November, 1948), pp. 181–191.
In this now classic statement Redfield takes the position that *in addition* to the scientific aspects of sociology and the other social sciences, there is an artistic aspect, a *Verstehen* function, which is important. He suggests three phases of which this "art" consists.

Stein, Maurice, and Vidich, Arthur, eds., *Sociology on Trial*. Englewood Cliffs, N.J., Prentice-Hall, 1963.
This well-known little book is probably destined to go down in history as a representative collection of essays, mostly critical of some of the thought-ways of contemporary sociology.

STUDY QUESTIONS

1. What different conceptions of "science" are there? Illustrate each.
2. Is sociology a science? Why and why not?
3. What are some of the issues in scientific method? Illustrate each.
4. What is meant by saying "The essence of science is method, not fact"? Explain and illustrate.
5. "Verification is the final test of a scientific generalization." Explain. Do you agree?
6. What is *Verstehen?* Illustrate.
7. "*Verstehen* procedures are inevitable not only in sociology but in all science." Illustrate this.
8. What are the arguments for and against *Verstehen* as a scholarly procedure?
9. In so-called "*Verstehen Sociology*," how does the qualified sociologist differ from the nonsociologist? Explain.
10. What is meant by "serendipity" in scientific work? Illustrate.
11. Distinguish "hard" and "soft" science. Illustrate.
12. Distinguish cause and correlation. Provide some illustrations other than those appearing in the text.

3
SOCIOLOGISTS AND THE PROBLEM OF VALUES

People cherish certain ideas or beliefs which are often called their "values." These ideas contain or express the judgments which people have of the relative worth or importance of things. In America, for example, we characteristically value highly such things as success, beauty, a high standard of living, education.

There are also value *disagreements* among people—even among close friends or members of a family. Current value disagreements which everyone has observed upon countless occasions refer to such important areas of life as religion, morals, politics, and philosophies of life. Sometimes these disagreements are so basic and irreconcilable that they even affect what persons regard as the "facts."

How do values relate to sociological work? This is a most troublesome and important professional problem. Unless the student becomes familiar with this problem, his sociological study will be both confusing and myopic.

SOME ELEMENTS OF THE PROBLEM

Science is itself a value

Science of all kinds seeks truth, irrespective of what or whose values may be jeopardized thereby. By seeking to avoid bias, science might seem, then, to have nothing to do with values whatsoever. Although this *is true for the method* of science, it is *not true for the goal* of science. *Why* does the scientist seek knowledge? Why, *ultimately*, does the scientist wish to discover accurate scientific knowledge?

The scientist seeks scientific truth because he accepts, *on faith and faith alone*, that out of the quest for more accurate knowledge will eventually come some good for mankind. He cannot be sure that that will be the result because demonstrable harm as well as good has resulted from scientific knowledge up to the present. Currently, among thinking men's greatest fears is the nuclear bomb which scientific man has created and which may destroy him. Even though less dramatic, many other scientific inventions have *so far* been of doubtful good. Yet science goes on apace, spurred by the hope and the faith that eventually, when there is "enough" knowledge, man may be the better for it.

Values are part of the subject matter of sociology

Having pointed out that science is itself one of our currently held values, we have only begun. So far, what we have said would apply to any science from physics to sociology. Sociology and the other social sciences, however, have another problem. It arises from the fact that part of the subject matter of sociology consists of values. An illustration at this point may be helpful.

A famous study which sociologists (and others) regard as one of the most outstanding sociological works of all time is Myrdal's *An American Dilemma.*[1] It is a study of Negro-white relations in the United States and was intended to be of practical as well as of theoretical use. The key idea in Myrdal's study is that of democracy. Under the American ideal of democracy, prejudice is often regarded as undesirable. Here we see at once that the heart of a sociological condition is the conflict between one value called "democracy" and another value which some people hold, namely, that Negroes are inferior and ought to be treated as such. The result is another set of values (anti-white prejudices among Negroes). The final evidence is the decision by a prominent research foundation to sponsor a research (another value) on race because of its "importance" (another value). Thus we see that often the very phenomena which we study are values, their causes, and their effects.

Values which people hold may be impediments to scientific work

Once a person accepts a value, he becomes somewhat biased or prejudiced thereby. This does not mean, for example, that all people who accept the value of democracy are necessarily *equally* biased or prejudiced, but merely that they are all likely to be somewhat blinded

[1] (New York, Harper & Row, 1944.)

to the real conditions and advantages to be found in a nondemocratic social system. Similarly, one may prefer rural life to city life, the Republican party to the Democratic party. One cannot escape having some values, and once he has them, they operate as prejudices or biases in his thinking. The difficulty which arises, then, is that a person's values (sometimes called "prejudices" or "biases") affect what he *sees* in a situation. A more disinterested party would "see" the situation quite differently. For example, for centuries we have recognized that the decisions of a court cannot be trusted to persons who have had some previous contact with the case because it affects their "judgment." So it is with scientific work—especially social. Prejudices are so numerous, so subtle, and so emotionally held that they may, and do, interfere with objectivity.

How can the values of the individual scientist be prevented from prejudicing his findings?

At present there is no entirely satisfactory way. Insulating the social scientist from the blinding and deceptive influences of his own prejudices is a perplexing and continuing problem. But great strides have been made. A considerable portion of the training of a professional sociologist goes into mastering the known techniques for reducing the ill effects of his own prejudices. A few of the accepted techniques follow. The student should recognize that only a few of the techniques will be mentioned here, and those only briefly. Our purpose is not to attempt to train professional sociologists but rather to assist beginning students in the comprehension of how values are "handled" by the sociologist.

1. *Rigorous training in the scientific ideal of objectivity* (freedom from value-prejudice) *and the importance of attaining it.* From this indoctrination the professional, and also to some extent the beginning student of sociology, comes to appreciate the great need for objectivity and the pitfalls in not being objective. By this self-discipline the apt student can minimize the operation of bias, but probably not eliminate it.

2. *Use of measuring devices to reduce error.* The history of measurement is a fascinating record of man's gradual triumph over inaccuracy of observation. The nonscientist can speak eloquently about "bigness," "smallness," "rapid growth," and the like, but the man who is informed by training in measurement can often abandon such vague and sometimes prejudice-laden usages and speak, instead, of "percent-

ages," *rates* of growth, or "ratios" of *A* and *B*. Present measurement skills in social and human behavior sciences enable us to measure such abstract and heretofore elusive phenomena as intelligence, attitude, and temperament. Truly these devices are not yet perfected, but great strides have been made. It has taken prejudiced men a long time to realize that women are as intelligent as they, but with the aid of an objective measuring device, such as an intelligence test, even a relatively prejudiced man cannot fail to see the mote in his eye.

3. *Verification by other scientists.* When values are suspected of coloring one's research, their influence can be discovered by the technique of comparing findings with another student whose values are different. Verification by having operations rechecked by another observer is similar to repeating one's observations or experiments. But it is even better than simple repetition. If one is blinded by prejudice, it does little good to repeat the prejudice-laden experiment over again, because the same factors which misled one once will likely mislead him again. But if another person verifies the facts and the operations involved in interpreting them, then we may be one step nearer to the ideal of circumventing the operation of the prejudice. For this reason most really worthwhile social science research being conducted today is the joint effort of several persons.

4. *Making values explicit.* Numerous sociologists believe that values impede research less when they are openly stated, so that the reader or listener or critic may be aware of them. The theory underlying this approach is that values are so powerful that he who holds them seldom can really eliminate them from his work, even though he may try. Hence, it is felt, it is better to lay one's values more or less bare so that critics may better know where to look for their influence in appraising the scientific worth of a study. Thus, to illustrate with an oversimplified example, would it not be easier to appraise a news commentator's evaluation of the news if the listener knew whether the commentator were a Republican or a Democrat, a Catholic or a Protestant, since each of these group memberships carries loyalties to different values?

If a person's biases are *unconscious*, of course, this device is useless. Suppose a man has an unconscious prejudice against Negroes or women or rural people; he cannot make these negative values explicit because he is not aware that he has them. In such cases other devices to detect and expose values would need to be employed.

So far as the beginning student of sociology is concerned, we may have made too severe a case for prejudicial influence in sociological work. Many problems in social sciences are not deeply overlaid with values, and it often suffices for most practical purposes merely to be *aware* of the value problem.

HOW SOCIOLOGISTS "STAND" ON THE PROBLEM OF VALUES

As we have said repeatedly, sociologists take varied positions on the relation of values to sociological work. Simpson [2] believes there are "three leading points of view on this general subject."

Type I: "The extreme behaviorist position" [3]

One long-standing view is that science is in its very nature non-ethical, that is, it should not be concerned with the scientists' values or with the direct application of scientific finding to practical matters; and the scientist (whether sociologist or physicist) should so work as to keep his own values strictly out of the endeavor. By inference, this applies to the sociologist working as a teacher quite as much as to the sociologist working as a researcher. In general, persons with this point of view seem to feel that to the extent that the sociologist can use statistics and verification by others he is "scientific" and his own values have minimum effect, if they are not avoided entirely.

There is a good bit of optimism in this position. No one can be *sure* that there are completely reliable ways by which the scientist can escape the contaminating influence of his own values upon his professional work, even if he tries very hard to do so and even if he uses statistical and other objective procedures. Values affect thinking in very subtle ways, and one may be led by them without knowing it. Moreover, there may be an inconsistency in this position stemming from (1) the fact that science itself is, as we have seen, one among many alternative values, and (2) the claim that the scientist *can* be value-free (regardless of how easy or difficult the latter may be). This problem is not strictly separable from what we said in the preceding chapter about sociological (and other scholarly) *method*. Maybe the "artistic" aspects of sociology are important, too, and worth cultivating. If we always must wait for verification *by formal means* before we can

[2] George Simpson, *Man in Society* (New York, Doubleday, 1954), pp. 78–81.
[3] George Lundberg, *Foundations of Sociology* (New York, Macmillan, 1939), pp. 29–31.

regard any and every discovery as "true," we may perhaps needlessly delay the whole process of gaining new knowledge. For these and other reasons, this view is sharply challenged in many quarters.

Type II: The value neutralization view

Many sociologists hold this view. They say, in effect, that the sociologist probably cannot be value-free; yet he can and should study values as objectively as he can, but that he should abstain from recommending values to the society or identifying himself as a sociologist with movements for value change. (These persons often set up a dichotomy of the citizen-self as distinct from the sociologist-self. For example, as a citizen the sociologist may have preference for a certain religious faith, but he should not allow his religious prejudices to dominate his "objective" study of facts which might run counter to his religious values.) While the writer knows of no way to prove it statistically, it is his judgment that the majority of present-day sociologists hold—in varying degree—to this view.

Probably persons who hold this middle view do so for either (or both) of two main reasons. Some really believe that personal values tend to impair the best sociological results. Others seem more concerned with the "public relations" angle, that is, with fears about their own and their colleagues' jobs and reputations, if their values show too clearly to powerful critics with opposing values. The recurrent attacks upon scholars, and especially upon social scientists, by governmental, church, and patriotic groups with apparently different values, certainly constitute a vivid reminder that the "safer" course of action may be to say as little as possible which might be interpreted (or misinterpreted) as "unsafe," "subversive," or "immoral." The history of science is strewn with the records of scholars and their works, highly regarded now, but castigated in their own time because their values showed. To the degree that the scholar has a sense of "mission," of course, he perhaps ought not to be concerned with himself, but rather solely with advancing truth. This is a nice ideal, but sociologists, as other scholars, are people, like to have favorable reputations, and wish to rear their children in psychological and physical comfort. Many sociologists feel that the net result of the constant surveillance of scholars by the "watchdogs" of the community is one factor working in the direction of holding back science—especially social science. There is, some think, a too strong tendency among sociologists to study and to teach such matters as are not likely to cause them and their employers "trouble."

Type III: The legitimacy of value espousal

Robert Lynd, in his *Knowledge for What?* [4] expresses this view probably most articulately, although many other sociologists say privately and sometimes also publicly that they agree with Lynd. (The long quotation from C. C. Bowman in Chapter 1, for example, would seem to be at least in partial agreement.) Lynd reviews a number of considerations such as those which we have already discussed, namely, that sociologists are people and have other connections with the society which gives them values, prejudices, bias, point of view, and so on, and that it is probably impossible completely to keep these contaminating factors from influencing sociological work. But he goes on to say that this is not to be regarded as bad; that sociologists, precisely because they are better informed about sociological matters than laymen, ought to indicate which values are better than others and recommend to the society what it should and should not do about this or that condition. It is argued that abdication by those who by professional training and experience know the most about society leaves important social decisions to those knowing less, which hardly seems rational.

In criticizing this view, Simpson points out that "Lynd's position must face the fact that different sociologists have different, varying, and sometimes mutually contradictory values," and that, therefore, "we might have as many sociologies as we have sociologists. . . . Such a condition would rob sociology of any claim to scientific status." The other side of the argument, as we have seen in the preceding chapter, is that scientific status may be only *one* of *various* conceptions of sociology and all might be worth retaining.

There is reason to believe that the once prevailing ideal of non-ethical work in sociology is being modified, if not replaced, by a candid acknowledgment that the social scientist can and should consider the ethical dimensions of sociological matters. In his foreword to *Transforming America*, appearing in 1967, Robin M. Williams, Jr., says, "The author has not tried to write a 'value free' book—as if he does not care whether a particular social pattern or its opposite prevails. . . . One can agree or disagree, but there will generally be no difficulty in discovering where he stands. This is as it should be." [5] Nor is this reappraisal limited to sociology. Scientists in many fields are more con-

---

[4] Robert Lynd, *Knowledge for What?* (Princeton, N.J., Princeton University Press, 1939).

[5] Raymond W. Mack, *Transforming America: Patterns of Social Change* (New York, Random House, 1967), p. ix.

cerned now than they have been for many years with the ethical considerations and dimensions and possible future implications of their work.

CONCLUSION

The student should appreciate that varying viewpoints on the proper handling of the problem of values exist at present among sociologists, and that sociological work is done by men and women of these various positions. There is probably little need for a complete agreement, as long as the people involved know the varying orientations which one another have and can make allowances in their own judgments for differing value positions. Finally, at the risk of being repetitious, it should be pointed out that the problem of values is by no means unique to sociology; it pervades all fields, especially in the social sciences. But probably sociologists are a little more explicit about it.

The student is entitled to know where the author of this book stands on the value question. Which of the three positions discussed above most nearly corresponds to the point of view from which this book has been written? The middle position best seems to fit, namely the view that (1) the values of the sociologist as teacher, researcher, or writer may stand in the way of the most objective discovery and portrayal of the "true" materials; (2) therefore, the sociologist should try to keep his personal values as much out of the enterprise as he can; (3) but this is an ideal and no one can achieve it all of the time, even though he strives to do so.

SUGGESTED READINGS

Etzioni, Amitai, "Social Analysis as a Sociological Vocation," in Arthur B. Shostak, ed., *Sociology in Action.* Homewood, Ill., Dorsey Press, Inc., 1966, pp. 317–323.
A middle-of-the-road position which neither goes so far as Lynd or Mills nor abdicates the involvement of sociologists in practical programs. The author's position seems to be that *within the limits of established knowledge* the sociologist may and should get involved in practical matters.

Gouldner, Alvin W., and Sprehe, J. Timothy, "Sociologists Look at Themselves." *Transaction,* Vol. 2, No. 4 (May/June, 1965), pp. 42–44.
This is a condensation of a questionnaire study of 3,440 sociologists out of the nearly 7,000 members of the American Sociological Association in 1964. This is an excellent compilation of what sociologists' agreements, disagreements, and

uncertainties are regarding the problem of values in sociology, as well as other matters.

Lundberg, G. A., *Can Science Save Us?* New York, Longmans, 1947.
This little book is a fine statement of the promise and the limitations of science as a tool for social control. Something of a classic.

Lynd, R. S., *Knowledge for What?* Princeton, N.J., Princeton University Press, 1939.
This is a widely known and important book. Lynd's thesis is that scientific objectivity among sociologists and other social scientists results in the loss of much of the scientists' contribution. He seems to advocate that sociologists espouse values and make their efforts "practical" in the sense that they orient their research and writing to public affairs and participate actively in championing the application of their findings to the direct improvements of social life.

Mack, Raymond W., *Transforming America: Patterns of Social Change.* New York, Random House, 1967.
While this is a somewhat general book analyzing the current condition of America, the book differs from most sociological writing in that the author does not hesitate to take a stand concerning what he approves and disapproves about the transformations—even though he does not advocate any specific courses of action. An uncommonly well-written, straightforward book.

Shostak, Arthur B., "A Sociologist in the War on Poverty," in Arthur B. Shostak, ed., *Sociology in Action.* Homewood, Ill., Dorsey Press, Inc., 1966, pp. 226–231.
A discussion of the ways in which sociologists have been involved in the practical federal programs known popularly as the "War on Poverty." Useful for securing insight into the problems which necessarily arise as a result of the involvement of the sociologist in practical programs.

Sussman, Marvin B., "The Sociologist as a Tool of Social Action," in Arthur B. Shostak, ed., *Sociology in Action.* Homewood, Ill., Dorsey Press, Inc., 1966, pp. 3–12.
Discusses very realistically and forthrightly the various ways in which sociologists are in fact oriented to practical action programs.

STUDY QUESTIONS

1. How do sociologists try to reduce the dominance of their personal values? Illustrate.
2. Give an example to illustrate that values are "the subject matter" of sociology.
3. What is meant by saying that "science is itself a value"?

4. How do values enter into the *selection* of research problems in fields other than sociology? Illustrate.
5. What is meant by "sociological behaviorism"? Illustrate.
6. What are the advantages in separating the person into two selves, "the citizen-self and the sociologist-self"? What problems arise when one attempts to do this?
7. What do you think of Lynd's position with respect to the legitimacy of value espousal by the sociologist?
8. What problems might arise if sociologists as a whole began to follow Lynd's suggestion?
9. What values do you recognize in your own thinking which you suspect might present difficulties for *you* in the study of sociology? What values might help you?

two

BACKGROUND UNDERSTANDINGS FROM CULTURAL ANTHROPOLOGY

4
THE MASS SOCIETY: A PRELIMINARY SKETCH

The dramatic event in twentieth-century America, overshadowing all else, even two world wars and a major depression, is the emergence of the United States as a mass society. There are few students of American society who do not agree with this. . . . Nor is there reason to doubt the hypothesis that the mass society is carrying out a vast liquidation of traditional values.[1]

One of the persistent images of anthropology is that it is the study of so-called "primitive peoples" and so-called "simple societies." While, to be sure, anthropologists have done a great deal of such research and to some extent still take field excursions to faraway peoples and strange places, they are increasingly giving attention to and reporting upon research on modern, complex societies, including the American.

Anthropologists are, however, not the only students of the contemporary scene. They share the responsibility for interpreting the American and other present-day civilizations with sociologists, economists, political scientists, social psychologists, and contemporary historians. None of these approaches exactly substitutes for any other, and sometimes there are sharp differences in findings and interpretations among them. Nevertheless, taken together and integrated around a sociological-anthropological point of view, they present an arresting picture of the current scene. This is the kind of effort which is presented in this chapter. We shall assemble a number of materials and ideas *to fashion a broad interdisciplinary interpretation of how American society seems to various professional social scientists.*

As seen in such broad perspectives, contemporary American society is a "new" society, a "mass" society, and an "urbanized" society. What do such terms designate, and what evidence and interpretations support such conceptions?

[1] From the preface to Don Martindale, *American Society* (Princeton, N.J., Van Nostrand, 1960), p. vii. Chapters 1–4 of this excellent book contain a lucid treatment of the mass society.

ANTECEDENTS

One of the important understandings concerning which practically all social scientists agree is the necessity for seeing current reality against the backdrop of history. One cannot adequately understand any present civilization or any present system of relationships among people without understanding that which came before, no matter how much contemporary knowledge he may amass. "We do not so much outgrow the past as we grow out of the past."

1. Pluralistic origins

One of the central historical facts about the origins of American society is diversity. America was peopled by relatively small groups from a wide variety of nation-states in Europe. There was little in common among such groups as the Puritan settlers at Plymouth Rock, the Catholics in Maryland, the Quakers in Pennsylvania, or the French in New Orleans. There was diversity of religion—and in those times religion was taken pretty seriously. There was diversity in language and in the class positions from which the settlers came—there were indentured servants, craftsmen, and aristocrats. Geography further influenced diversity. In the colonial era it was necessary to live close to the soil; the conditions of the natural environment placed inexorable limits upon what could and could not be done in food customs, styles of life, and architecture, and upon many other areas of life as well.

This diversity in ways of coming at life is richly documented in the historical period of the American Revolution and the founding of the Constitution. The great problem then, so great in fact that it was almost a miracle that a single nation emerged from the chaos, was the urgent necessity felt by many for each of the colonies to maintain its own identity. The idea of a strong central government, as we now have it, was as abhorrent as the idea of serving under a king, although there were a few extremists at that time who wanted each of these. What finally emerged was a very loose federation of "sovereign states," each jealous of its own autonomy and very reluctant to surrender any of it. It was only by very ingenious political maneuvering that the Constitution was ratified by the necessary numbers.

Out of this kind of historical context grew some of the ideas and ideals which historians and political philosophers identify as distinctly American—safeguards for the rights of diverse minorities, honoring of widely variant concepts of personal freedom, fear of powerful government, and a long continuing reluctance to surrender individual liberties to orderly legal regulation.

Pluralism by no means ended with the founding of the United States. It continued manifestly for at least another century. Slowly there emerged two distinct kinds of economic and social systems, the North and the South, which culminated for a variety of reasons in the Civil War over one hundred years ago. And, as everyone knows, even that war did not really settle many of the important differences in the economic, political, and social realms north and south of the Mason-Dixon Line.

Migration, chiefly from Europe, was a cardinal social reality until, and to some extent since, World War I. During the peak period, over one million immigrants came to the United States within a calendar year. In the twentieth century the migration has been chiefly from southern and eastern Europe and thus there has been brought—to an already diverse America—additional variations in religion, economic outlook, languages, and just about everything else. Eventually most of these diversities yield to the inexorable workings of the so-called "melting pot," but not immediately and not without considerable resistance.

Many astute observers from Europe during the nineteenth and early twentieth century have expressed surprise, if not bewilderment, at the successful cohesion of such diverse elements in an orderly and unified nation-state. It is commonplace for Americans to interpret their good fortune as due to the genius of the founding fathers of the Constitution, although it appears likely that this is an oversimplification of a much more complex process.

2. Rural origins

Originally, of course, American civilization was rural. The early settlers, like the Indians before them, were bound to the land, not in the sense of feudal property rights but in the sense that their survival depended on getting their food supplies and other essentials from a not always cooperative natural environment. The early settlements were in no sense urban—they were simply patterns of living together for protection and mutual aid. Even the so-called cities of the early American period would strike a modern American as quaint, if not repelling. They were small. There was little efficient communication between them and very little travel. The population of horses and cattle and other livestock was at least as great as the number of human inhabitants. A nation which originated with over 90 percent of the population deriving its sustenance from agriculture has now experienced a reversal; almost 90 percent are now engaged in nonagricultural pursuits. This reversal is all the more dramatic when one realizes that in the early decades of this nation very little change took place in this respect. The great revolution from rural to urban is chiefly the product of the present century.

THE MASS SOCIETY

People with sufficient maturity and education to read this book already know a good deal about contemporary human relations and society. College students know, or ought to, that the modern world is one of massive organization and that the coercive power of large organization over the individual is definitive. Even if we had to rely upon television and movie interpretations, we must by now realize, despite the oversimplifications, that we are living in a kind of world in which a remarkable sameness pervades the people and the situations in which they participate. To be sure, there are still some regional variations and sometimes some telltale reminders that one's classmates have come from different national groups or have distinctive religious convictions. But chiefly these are seen as impedimenta to be lived down or to be kept under wraps in the modern world—not adhered to in the prideful way in which these differences were worn in the past.

Everyone knows, or says he does, that things were not always this way, that the kind of human relationships which we now have evolved in a complicated historical process which is at least vaguely understood. But vague understanding is not enough for a sociologist—a trip to the zoo does not make one a zoologist. We need to look more closely, to analyze more precisely and with greater objectivity than is ordinarily achieved, in order to understand what the present human mélange really is.

It has been observed that the last thing which a creature in the ocean would identify would be water. Carrying this notion to our own sphere, it is equally true that some of the last characteristics which contemporary Americans—or for that matter, contemporary Russians—would recognize in their own society would at the same time constitute that society's most salient characteristics as seen by someone from the outside.

Probably the most fundamental features which have transformed the historical Western society, which is now often called a "mass society" by many professionals, are growing homogeneity and overt conformity. One of the reasons why the layman is likely to under-estimate the extent to which his potential individualism is atrophied is due to the many and subtle ways in which society influences his desires and rewards his conformity, thus tending to obliterate his individualism. For example, one says he earnestly desires to own a recording by a new television star, but he is likely not to recognize that he desires this par-ticular recording because, usually through no effort or choice of his own, he was exposed to it and not to something else as a result of his own curiosity or exploration. He desires to conform to the latest fad; he is not, as he sees it, coerced or unduly influenced. He maintains the illusion that this is his own choice. Curiously enough, Americans are typically very sensitive about being what they call "brainwashed," yet all are living in a society in which more and more of us are being brain-washed everyday in innumerable ways of which we are largely una-ware.

What are the sources of this "great sameness" which has settled increasingly upon the American society and also upon much of the Western world?

1. Mass communication

The external influences which play upon people are becoming in-creasingly standardized. For example, in the United States four national television networks and four national radio networks supply virtually all of the important television and radio programs and commercials, in-cluding the so-called public information and public affairs services. Anyone even remotely familiar with the radio and television industry is aware that there are few, if any, significant differences among the services of these four so-called competitors. The major reason for this sameness is, of course, that these networks are all trying to reach the maximal audience, and thus they scrupulously avoid offending any re-ligious, occupational, regional, or social group, since this would reduce the number of viewers and reduce the value of the program to the sponsor, to whom, of course, it represents a costly investment. The effect is to play down difference of all kinds as far as possible and to accent the common denominators of opinion, taste, and values.

Newspapers represent a similar influence in the direction of ac-centing uniformity and playing down differences. Between 1925 and 1955, for example, the number of English language newspapers in the United States decreased by 248, while the circulation of newspapers increased from 34 to 56 millions. In 1900, 42 percent of the cities of the

United States had daily newspapers with noncompetitive ownership; by 1954, 94 percent had noncompetitive ownership. In other words, at the present time not over 6 percent of American cities have local daily newspapers with competing ownership.[2]

There are many reasons, chiefly economic, which explain the concentration of our sources of information, entertainment, and education. We are not here concerned with these reasons—simply with the facts which together support the inescapable conclusion that uniformity in taste and information is exceedingly hard to escape, unless one turns to sources other than radio, television, and the newspapers for his intellectual stimulation. Not many do.

A number of students of contemporary society have been exceedingly critical of some of the personal manipulation which this kind of concentration of influence makes possible. One best selling popular book [3] has richly documented the effectiveness of the standardization of taste and intelligence which presumably results from such concentration of influence. Probably no one book, however, could succeed in giving a sufficiently complete picture of the great extent to which one or another kind of thought-control shapes the minds, the aspirations, the tastes, and the world view of the great mass of the American people.

2. Mass production and distribution

As every schoolboy knows, we live in a "mass-production economy." With the modern production and distribution systems which we have, we make vast numbers of identical units, and so it is possible to sell them at prices low enough that the items are available to great numbers of people of even modest financial circumstances. At the same time it is possible to pay wages to the great mass of partially skilled laborers which enable them to buy commodities which in previous times would have been reserved for the rich.

But the cycle of increasing production, it was found, needed further stimulation and so there was invented, and firmly established in American society, a practice known as installment buying. Very few durable items of consumer goods now need to be purchased outright by persons with steady incomes. In fact, it has become customary to advertise only the down payment and the monthly installment when trying to attract customers. This has had the effect, as intended, of greatly

[2] Wilbur Schramm, *Responsibility in Mass Communication* (New York, Harper & Row, 1957), p. 4.
[3] Vance Packard, *The Hidden Persuaders* (New York, Pocket Books, 1958).

increasing, at least in the short run, the amount of goods which the public is able to absorb. Whether or not in the long run installment buying greatly increases the volume of goods which a society can absorb is a question about which economists are not in complete agreement. There is, however, no disagreement that installment buying of identical mass-produced goods is an entrenched part of the American way.

It is easier to describe the practice of installment purchasing of goods and services than it is to appraise its subjective influences upon the people who live such budgeteered lives. It is not our purpose here to attempt such an evaluation. We are simply making the point that not only does almost everyone own the same collection of gadgets, but everyone has the same anxieties about down payments and monthly payments and is aware that everyone else is in the same boat with him. Thus, not only the external materials are mass-produced, so are the anxieties and the concerns and the skills at making one's way in the world.

3. Stronger government

In the modern mass society the citizens have come to rely more and more on the government to provide services which formerly were supplied either by persons for themselves or by some kind of private contract with a supplier. The "welfare state," which to some traditionalists has become a form of polite profanity, is not the whole issue. Many of the numerous and increasing rules, regulations, and controls no one seriously expects even a "conservative" government to abolish. Traffic tickets to jaywalkers, licenses for dogs which never leave the owner's premises, compulsory liability insurance for auto drivers are merely token illustrations of the increasing number and the increasingly restrictive nature of collective controls over the conduct of people. And the end is by no means in sight.

Part of the continued pressure to pass more and more laws requiring more and more people to do more and more things more and more alike goes on apace. One of the obvious reasons is that it is more convenient that way. If everyone is required to act in a certain way, then it becomes easier to "get along"; one always knows what the other person will do, because he has to do it. The real awkwardness, the real nuisance is that occasional person who insists on being different; the way to take care of him is to make a rule which will require him to do as others bid.

There are undoubtedly many other factors which would help to explain why the homogeneous-conformist accents, which are the essence of the mass society, have come to be what they are. Simply focusing on mass communication, mass production and distribution, and increasing government regulation, nevertheless, goes a long way to reveal the underpinnings of the contemporary order.

CONSEQUENCES

The mass society, whether one likes it or not, has had a number of consequences. The daily lives of people, their hopes and fears, and their ways of coming at life are strongly influenced by the configuration of circumstances which we have just described. A few of the consequences of these mass influences deserve brief preliminary consideration.

1. A sense of affluence

Ever since J. K. Galbraith wrote *The Affluent Society*,[4] this apt phrase has been a part of the daily discourse of informed people. The gist of the point is that following a decade or more of depression and slow recovery in which unemployment, financial reverses, modest incomes, and considerable austerity occurred, America, and to some extent much of the rest of the Western world, has experienced what appears in contrast to be bountiful times. Very probably World War II was the greatest single factor in bringing about the remarkable reversal. Nevertheless, the reversal occurred and in comparison to the thirties and forties, life in the fifties and sixties has seemed affluent indeed. This does not mean, to be sure, that everyone is rich and certainly not that financial problems for many people are not still the cardinal problems of living. The essence of the affluent society lies in the abundance of goods and services which the great mass of Americans and other people in Western civilization are enjoying and the rather remarkable freedom from serious ups and downs in business cycles which the past decades have brought.

Some critics have complained that Americans have thereby become a more materialistic people, that we revel not in our good deeds or our pure hearts, but rather in our inventories of installment-ridden goods. Whether or not there has been an appreciable increase in materialism as a result of current affluence is an exceedingly complicated question, one difficult in an objective evaluation to pass quick judgment upon. It is, of course, quite possible that these critics are right. Never-

---

[4] John K. Galbraith, *The Affluent Society* (Boston, Houghton Mifflin, 1958).

theless, the modern citizen lives his life inured in a prima facie luxury which the older person finds strange by comparison to the conditions of life which he can recall from his own past, just twenty or thirty years ago.

2. Fragmentation

The mass society appears to require a fragmented life for the participant in it. Work is increasingly specialized so that when one explains "what he does," he finds very few people who can really understand him. Often the best answer to the question is at the same time the vaguest one, "I work for Coca-Cola." Life at work and the rest of life are typically very, very different from each other, and there is little feedback from one to the other. There is a very general view to the effect that except for the professions, and not always then, work is no longer supposed to yield much satisfaction; the rest of life is to provide a kind of therapy, or at least diversion, to make the work world bearable.

3. High mobility

Within the mass society there is a great deal of personal movement. Part of this is coerced. Practically every male youth is required to spend some time in the armed forces, and it is not at all unusual to be "shipped" around the world. Many corporations have a policy of moving important as well as secondary personnel from one part of the country to another for a variety of efficiency reasons. But a great deal of mobility is also voluntary, either for financial betterment or because the climate may be better or just because it may be fun to move. Many people move from one part of the country to another with little fear of feeling strange in the new place, because people and circumstances have become so standardized that it takes but a short time, if any, to feel at home again. Every census shows a smaller and smaller percentage of population living in the states of birth.

4. Decline of provincialism

Accompanying our pluralistic and rural origins was a pervasive provincialism which is now demonstrably on the decline. Narrow attitudes are constantly being challenged by the mass media, increasing travel opportunities, more sophisticated education, and wider social experiences for people in all walks of life. Provincialism is no longer a necessary product even of small town life. "A man can be provincial in the biggest city or cosmopolitan in the smallest. . . . It is hard to be narrow . . . when one out of five Americans moves each year, when the small towner can often afford the same cars for his garage, or the same clothes for his wife as the old-rich east, when Ohioans or Kansans or Oklahomans routinely take a winter vacation in the Bahamas or cruise the Greek islands in summer . . ." [5] The same *Time* essay goes on to point out that in the mass society commerce and industry have taken on a nationwide and even international character. Atlanta, Georgia, for example, has branch offices for 410 of the 500 largest American corporations. The "local manager" as likely as not comes from a city other than the one he serves. The same holds true for other echelons of the corporation and for the personnel of colleges, ecclesiastical hierarchies, the armed services—even the recreational meccas like Miami Beach or the Bahamas, where one's next-door tourist may be a financial tycoon from Wall Street or a vacationing wheat farmer from Kansas.

5. The organization man

A decade ago William Whyte, Jr., wrote an extremely influential and provocative book called *The Organization Man*.[6] This phrase has become a byword. Whyte's inimitable portrait of the man who "takes the vows of corporation life" and the wife who must come to accept the fact that "her husband belongs first to the corporation" is to many millions of people nothing more than a blunt description of what they have already come to realize. For the Organization Man the central facts of life are belongingness and togetherness, and his success may well depend quite as much on his facility in adopting this way of life as upon any other skills he may have developed or talent he may possess. Putting the matter as we have may lead to the inference that there is a general resentment against the Organization-Man psychology. Except for occasional instances, this seems not to be the case. The overwhelming mass of people seemingly accept this mode of life as altogether natural and acceptable under the circumstances, and many of them are quite grateful for the protecting arm of the corporation with its abundant fringe benefits such as health insurance, life insurance, recreational programs, pensions, educational programs, and a whole host of protections against individual adversity. The consequence, again, seems a reinforcement of what we have pointed out several times before: a

[5] *Time*, Vol. 88, No. 17 (October 21, 1966), pp. 36–37.
[6] William Whyte, Jr., *The Organization Man* (New York, Simon and Schuster, 1956).

blurring of individual difference and an accenting of common problems, common orientations, and common satisfactions.

Individual identity is increasingly submerged in the larger mass of organization. Not only is this true at work, but also in religious organizations and community associations. Thus, at work and at play the typical American is submerged in categories of organization and, insofar as he thinks much about it, seems rather grateful for the large amount of security which this kind of life has brought him.

6. "Other direction"

David Riesman's *The Lonely Crowd*,[7] is another contemporary classic. One of the main threads in this original and highly respected interpretation of American life is the condition which he calls "other-direction." Putting it tersely, other-direction means that a person looks to his immediate associates for his standards of correct and incorrect behavior. In contrast, the inner-directed and/or tradition-directed person looks to longer standing "principles" and "authorities" for answers to questions of morality, propriety, etiquette, and other proscriptions for the good life. Riesman's research convinced him that other-direction has become the prevailing morality, if it can be so-called, in American society and thus has added a further and telling evidence of encrustation of conformity. The other-directed person, the prevailing person-type according to Riesman, is not a conformist simply in the things he owns, or in the recreation he follows, or in his artistic tastes. He is a conformist to the immediate group in a far deeper sense—his concepts of right and wrong, the important and the unimportant, the permissible and the disapproved derive from the group. Since the other-directed person is not geared in his moral precepts to any kind of eternal verities, he typically possesses an elastic conscience. But the elasticity is not of his own contrivance; rather it is that of the group with which he "runs around." The immediate group of his peers is the final arbiter of what is right or wrong, approved or disapproved. As the group changes, he changes. The greatest breach of morality is to break with the group; the act in question is secondary.

Riesman is careful to emphasize that not everyone is other-directed and that some people are a mixture of other- and inner-direction. But he seems to insist that other-direction is the prevailing psychology of man in the modern mass society and that more and more we are producing other-directed men.

[7] David Riesman, Reuel Denny, and Nathan Glazer, *The Lonely Crowd* (New Haven, Yale University Press, 1950).

7. Amorality

Another aspect of the mass society which has attracted the attention of many observers is a seemingly growing casualness about traditional moral precepts where the collective enterprise is concerned. A dramatic incident that comes to mind is the election of an ex-convict to the mayorship of Boston in recent years. The man's crime was no impulsive crime of passion but a rather deliberate and continued violation of law. The concept "white-collar crime" has come into wide usage to describe the activities of persons engaged in seemingly legitimate businesses and professions, but who in the course of their work systematically and more or less openly violate not only the modern laws but the time honored religious and moral precepts concerning proper conduct. The line between "smart business" and gross immorality has come to be so badly blurred that for millions there is no line at all.

Nor is this pervasive amorality limited to the business world. The following description from *Time* is by no means exaggerated. "It was just an ordinary day. Mom was at the store taking back a party dress she swore she had never once put on (it was only slightly stained with lipstick). . . . Sonny was in school, doing pretty well on a math test by dint of some judicious copying. . . . And Dad was busy at the office, adding a few fictitious lunches to his expense account." [8]

In the *Power Elite*, C. Wright Mills [9] coins the phrase "the higher immorality" to characterize the rather cynical disregard for moral precepts which he says typically characterizes elite persons in the high military, governmental, and business echelons. Perhaps more telltale, however, is the far more general characteristic in American society of "the public relations front"—the deliberate use of falsehood and misrepresentation, even by institutions supposedly dedicated to high purposes, when making bids for public acceptance or covering up a scandal.

These are probably simply extensions of a more diffuse amorality, such as legitimate falsification of the rate of speed at which a friend's auto was traveling when it struck a pedestrian. The essential point seems to be that in the large, impersonal society, many people, who are scrupulously moral toward persons they know and care about, are notably calloused and unmoral where the victims of their behavior are removed by time and space and less intimate relationships. For whatever reasons, the historical precepts fostered by the church and in-

[8] *Time*, Vol. 88, No. 11 (September 9, 1966), p. 26.
[9] C. Wright Mills, *The Power Elite* (New York, Oxford University Press, 1956).

corporated in our basic law seem not very convincing to large numbers of people, particularly when the consequences of their acts are not immediately visible to them.

8. Racketeering

Closely tied with the foregoing several points and in some degree simply a special case of some of them is a widespread occupation known as "racketeering." Racketeering practices are so normal in American society that for the most part they are no longer reported in the press, except now and then when a homicide or particularly sensational scandal comes to light. In the more genteel modern practice of racketeering, the crude methods reminiscent of the 1920's are in ill repute. There are better and more effective ways to today's racketeering which do not stir up much opposition and get the job done as effectively.

Business and industrial rackets in American cities have developed principally in the distribution of services and commodities. The racketeer has found that the soft spot in the American competitive system is the point of distribution of services and goods in the urban community, for it is in this area that competition is keenest and demand is greatest. Milk must get out. Bread must be distributed. Newspapers must go on the streets. Fish and poultry must be disposed of quickly. In other words, the racketeer found the vulnerable place in the American system of free enterprise and took advantage of it in the absence of effective laws and law enforcement.

Very few fields of distribution of services and goods in the large American cities have been able to stay out of the clutches of racketeers. Taking the outstanding rackets in New York City as an example, Thompson found that there were rackets in the clothing business, in the running of taxicabs, in the distribution of fish, in the poultry business, in the building and construction business, in the milk dealers' business, in the distribution of artichokes, and in the operation of movie houses.

The racketeer, therefore, became a new type of middleman dictator who was able to control and enforce the conditions of doing business. He set up a monopoly. He also became a stabilizer of business through his enforced regulations and prices. He became the illegal policeman of the distribution of services and goods. He is the invisible government of urban distribution who cannot be touched by legal government.[10]

The important aspects of the situation, which are insufficiently noted, seem to be these: (a) There is very little attention paid to the large amount of racketeering which has infiltrated into at least fifty

[10] Walter C. Reckless, *The Crime Problem*, 3rd ed. (New York, Appleton-Century-Crofts, 1961), pp. 191–192.

fields of business, as the Kefauver Committee [11] investigations of fifteen years ago pointed out. (*b*) Present methods of law enforcement are notoriously ineffective in curbing racketeering practices. (*c*) Most important of all, there is little sense of public outrage when the vast extent of racketeering activities is made public.

Conclusion

It should not be inferred from the foregoing that a blanket indictment of American society is intended. Quite the contrary. No indictment whatsoever is implied—we intend simply a candid camera description of a number of aspects of American society which are well known among professional social scientists but which are not widely recognized by many people who consider themselves well informed. There prevails today a kind of schoolboy conception of life which prefers to pretend that old platitudinous descriptions are true and offers reassurances, largely detached from reality, that the real world is something other than what it is. One certainly has the moral right to such views, but abdication of intelligence is not conducive either to informed citizenship or objective scholarship.

MASS SOCIETY AS A WORLDWIDE CONCEPT

Up to this point we have discussed the mass society as if it is distinctly American. It is, of course, not so. Most of the European nations, increasingly even including Russia, show many of the same characteristics. If it were not for the barriers of language and a few remnants of pluralistic origins, people from the United States would find, and some of them already have found, that the conditions of their lives and their attitudes and tastes are quite congruent with those of persons of similar class position in other nations of Europe, South America, and even here and there in Asia. This is what some observers have meant by the emergence of "one world."

But there are really still two worlds: (1) the modern, urbanized, mass society, as exemplified by the United States and increasingly approached by Russia, and (2) the so-called underdeveloped areas. The latter are essentially rural and derive their sustenance from the soil, chiefly by what seem to us to be archaic, almost superstitious modes of

[11] *Third Interim Report of the Special Committee to Investigate Organized Crime in Interstate Commerce* (Washington, Government Printing Office, United States Senate, Report No. 307, 1951).

cultivation and fabrication of raw materials for human use. Despite nominal nation-states, the great mass of people in the underdeveloped areas have been relatively untouched by the more cosmic political considerations which are of so great importance to the nations in the mass society. Numerous observers have pointed out that most of the rank and file people in the East and in Africa, for example, are often oblivious to the changes in political fortunes of the nations of which they are presumably citizens. They typically have no part in formulating political decisions, are illiterate or nearly so, and by and large couldn't care less whether their nominal leaders are allied with the East or the West or hold a capitalistic or communistic economic philosophy. The urgencies of existence are so stark and the life risks are so apolitical that only a very few ever find their way intellectually beyond the immediate exigencies of existence.

It hardly needs mentioning that the so-called "underdeveloped areas" are rapidly being developed. Both the United States and Russia, the two principal world powers, are spreading technical "know-how," first in agriculture and simple medicine, and later in industrial techniques, as a means to aligning the various underdeveloped areas to their respective sides. Each side sees this as a necessary condition to winning what is called the "cold war."

One should not lose sight of the fact, however, that underdeveloped areas have been served by various agencies in this country and others for a long time. Much of the activity of early missionaries was, in practice, as much educational and economic as it was theological. Thousands of hospitals and agricultural demonstration stations dot the world as evidence that for various reasons, chiefly humanitarian, efforts have been made to change the modes of life of simpler people to accord with Western ideas. Success in these respects has been very limited for reasons which will be made much clearer in the remaining chapters of this section. Nevertheless, whether motivated by political expediency or humanitarian zeal, the long arm of the mass society is increasingly encircling the globe, and it is no pipe dream to envision the passing of the "simpler" societies in the underdeveloped areas.

In the current popular simplitudes of our time, it is fashionable to think of the "two worlds" as the Anglo-American and the Russian. Actually these two have far more in common—and this may be what sharpens some political issues—than they have differences, as far as the prevailing life modes are concerned. The real contrasts in the present world are between the mass societies and the underdeveloped ones, and, as we have seen, the mass society is rapidly expanding.

Conclusion

In describing the mass society as we have, a certain degree of unreality may have been suggested and so needs to be corrected.

1. The mass society is *not yet a completed thing;* it is in the process of emergence, and the traditions with which it has broken are by no means completely extirpated.

2. Furthermore, the mass society *affects people in different circumstances differently.* To take an extreme illustration: to an Amish farmer in Lancaster County, Pennsylvania, or Holmes County, Ohio, life is still essentially rural, human relations are comparatively simple, and the mid-twentieth century has not yet quite dawned. Yet a close look at these and other dramatic remnants of the pluralistic past indicates that even they are having great difficulty maintaining their traditions despite vigorous efforts to do so. More to the point, however, are the run-of-the-mill farmers and small-town dwellers for whom there is considerable illusion that the old order is still with them. But the illusion is increasingly hard to maintain as the inroads of uniformity, centralized government, and technological organization press more and more heavily upon provincial custom, strong religious conviction, and independence of thought and action.

3. In short, what we have been saying in the above paragraphs, as earlier, is that *the mass society is a generalized interpretive and descriptive idea,* like the phrase "the American way of life" or "the industrial revolution," and that it is not a completely literal description of reality for every last person with complete consistency. It is, nonetheless, increasingly true as a relentless impersonal force whittling away at the older pillars of pluralism.

4. Nor is there any intention to deny the *strong sentimental appeal,* again particularly for older people, *of the older ways and the supporting ideas and ideals which better fit our national origins than our current realities.* One of the interesting social realities of this period of history is the continuing inconsistency between what people *say* about interpersonal relationships and society and what they, in fact, *do.* Thus, people who say "Honesty is the best policy" are nevertheless forced to use the "public relations front." Persons who believe in individualism, if they wish to find employment, must submerge their separate identities and become organization men. And persons with genuine moral conviction feel that they are faced with no real alternative but to hold to policies of personal living which are at best badly compromised versions of the principles they feel to be right.

5. All of this, then, by way of saying that *the mass society is a growing and engulfing system of human relationships for which few, aside from the present generation of youth, have much compatible precedent.*

6. The foregoing certainly should not be taken to mean that there is necessarily anything eternal or inherently good about the mass society. *Very probably the mass society, like all of its historical precedents, will one day become something else. But for our time and for the immediately foreseeable future, it appears here to stay.* All realistic considerations for individuals and groups must be worked out within the confines imposed by the mass society. There is, of course, especially among some older people, much sentimental nostalgia for the pluralistic society or some parts of it, and occasionally some individuals by one device or another can escape at least some of the impact of the mass society. But fewer and fewer want to and fewer and fewer are able to. The mass society is the inescapable backdrop against which life during the twentieth century must be lived by people in the Western world.

CONCLUSION

In this chapter we have taken an inclusive look at man in American society and to some extent in the world society. In order to understand more fully what we have glimpsed, it is necessary to get down to brass tacks, that is, to understand some of the concepts and information which sociologists and other social scientists have discovered and used, such as culture, ethnocentrism, personality structure, and the like. Moreover, there is need to examine more closely the process which we glibly call "social change." It is one thing to observe superficially, as we mostly have in this chapter, how the mass society seemed to emerge from a pluralistic configuration, but it is quite another thing to spell out the details and to understand the role of human relationships in the emerging process and in the final product. The remaining chapters in this section, and to some extent the entire book, will consist of analytical tools which should facilitate the understanding of the larger complexities.

SUGGESTED READINGS

Bell, Daniel, *The End of Ideology*. New York, Free Press, 1960.
This entire book is replete with analyses and interpretations pertaining to the mass society. Pages 21 to 36 are particularly provocative and relevant to the treatment in this chapter.

Cuber and Harroff (see Bibliographic note, p. 40): Don Martindale, "Formalization of Personal Identity," pp. 146–150; "Self Development Literature," pp. 154–159; David Riesman, *et al.*, "Three Types of Character Structure," pp. 150–154; William H. Whyte, Jr., "The Ideology of Organization Man," pp. 229–234; C. Wright Mills, "The Power Elite: The Higher Circles," pp. 248–253; Everett M. Rogers, "Government Agricultural Agencies: Growing Dependence on Uncle Sam," pp. 288–300.

Harp, John, and Taietz, Philip, "Academic Integrity and Social Structure: A Study of Cheating Among College Students." *Social Problems*, Vol. 13, No. 4 (Spring, 1966), pp. 365–373.
A careful study of cheating on the college campus, comparing students at different academic levels and in different fields of study. Shows in all categories a higher level of cheating by fraternity members and by students who plan to enter graduate school.

Larrabee, Eric, and Meyersohn, Rolf, *Mass Leisure*. New York, Macmillan, 1958.
This is a symposium dealing with various aspects of leisure in the mass society by a wide variety of observers and interpreters. It is to be read chiefly as descriptive material. Occasionally there are arresting and original hypotheses. It is not, strictly speaking, a sociological book.

Rosenberg, Bernard, and White, David M., *Mass Culture*. New York, Macmillan, 1957.
A symposium on many aspects of mass culture—advertising, motion pictures, magazines, television. Also some provocative theoretical chapters.

Schramm, Wilbur, ed., *Mass Communications*. Urbana, Ill., University of Illinois Press, 1960.
This is a collection of materials edited by a man who has done extensive and important research on communication in the mass society for a number of years. The student will find here a number of fresh interpretations and will be confronted by some challenging ideas about things which he has tended to take for granted.

Stein, Maurice, Vidich, Arthur J., and White, David M., *Identity and Anxiety: Survival of the Person in the Mass Society*. New York, Free Press, 1960.
An excellent collection of readings focusing on the psychological problems heightened by the complexities and frustrations of mass society. A wide range of subjects with competent authoritative authorship.

Van den Haag, Ernest, "Reflections on Mass Culture." *American Scholar*, Vol. 29 (Spring, 1960), pp. 227–234.
This is a critical interpretation of the mass culture which raises questions con-

cerning its *desirability* rather than simply its reality. The author feels that in American society efforts should be made to create a more autonomous culture rather than simply to succumb to the influence of the mass culture.

Vidich, Arthur J., and Bensman, Joseph, *Small Town in Mass Society*. Princeton, N.J., Princeton University Press, 1958.
This little book has become a classic. While there has been much speculation about the fate of the small town under the imprint of mass society, this is a study of what actually happened in a small town studied by the authors. This is no mere description, however; there are penetrating theoretical and interpretive themes.

STUDY QUESTIONS

1. What is meant by the mass society?
2. Why does the mass society differently affect people in different circumstances? In different sections of the country?
3. It was suggested in this chapter that the mass society poses more problems for the older than for the younger person. Do you think this is so? Why or why not?
4. What evidences of "other-direction" have you seen among your high school and college friends? Comment.
5. In what sense is present day American society an "affluent society"? In what sense is the phrase "affluent society" misleading?
6. Compare and contrast the mass society and the so-called underdeveloped societies.
7. Someone has said that trying to operate the mass society with attitudes and habits derived from the pre-existing society is like trying to drive a sports car with a buggy whip. What do you think is meant by the remark and to what extent do you agree *and* disagree with it?
8. What is meant by the Organization Man? What is the difference between being an Organization Man and simply working for an organization?
9. It has been said that aside from the older professions, and possibly even there, the most important skills in modern society are those which enable one to manipulate people. Why is this skill so important in the present world and what evidences do you see that people really act on such a premise?
10. It has been said that it is difficult to draw a line between a racket and many legitimate businesses. Why do you think this might be so and what do you think about it?
11. Why do social scientists tend to use the word *a*morality for disapproved acts of other-directed persons and *im*morality for the inner- or tradition-directed persons? What are some of the implications of this distinction?

5
CULTURE AND SOCIETY

Two basic concepts of social science, not merely of sociology, are culture and society. Somewhat arbitrarily we shall begin with culture. Understanding culture is fundamental to the understanding of the human being and of groups.

For the present it is sufficient to define a culture as the way of life of any society. This way of life includes innumerable details of behavior. . . . They all represent the normal, anticipated (expected) response (acts) of any of the society's members to a particular situation. Thus, in spite of the infinite number of minor variations which can be found in the responses of various individuals, or even in those of the same individual at different times, it will be found that most of the people in a society will respond to a given situation in much the same way. In our society, for example, nearly everybody eats three times a day and takes one of these meals approximately at noon. Moreover, individuals who do not follow this routine are regarded as queer. Such a consensus (uniformity) of behavior and opinion constitutes a culture pattern; the culture as a whole is a more or less organized aggregate of such patterns.[1]

POPULAR MEANINGS OF THE WORD *CULTURE*

One frequently hears reference to some person as "cultured" or some act as "cultural." The implication is often clear in such usage that some other person is not cultured or some other act is not cultural. In other words, culture is popularly conceived in an evaluative way. Certain things are good or highly desirable or supposedly possessed of virtue, and are, therefore, called "cultural" to set them aside from the less good, the less valuable, and the less highly regarded things. *Social scientists do not use the term that way. All people have culture, although different persons and different groups have different cultures.*

[1] Ralph Linton, *The Cultural Background of Personality* (New York, Appleton-Century-Crofts, 1945), p. 19.

THE TECHNICAL MEANING OF CULTURE

How then, precisely, is culture defined in social science? What is the concept for which the word *culture* stands? Although there are several ways in which the idea can be worded, this way of stating it seems to be essentially accurate and yet reasonably simple: *Culture is the continually changing patterns of learned behavior and the products of learned behavior (including attitudes, values, knowledge, and material objects) which are shared by and transmitted among the members of society.* Like most definitions this one needs to be explained phrase by phrase and illustrated.

1. ". . . Learned behavior . . ."

This technical meaning of the word *behavior* should not be confused with the popular one implied in such sentences as, "Now, son, behave," because technically the son is behaving whether he is doing the approved thing or the disapproved thing. Putting a tack on the teacher's chair, playing truant from school, or telling a lie are all "behavior," even though one could hardly regard any of them as praiseworthy. Not all behavior is learned, but most of it is. Combing one's hair, standing in line, telling jokes, criticizing the President, going to the movie, and kissing one's aunt all constitute behaviors which had to be learned. So, also, is feeling angry or hurt because someone laughed at you, solving a problem in mathematics, or worrying about your health. Each of these had to be learned. One readily recognizes that he had to learn how to solve the mathematics problem, but he is apt to overlook the fact that he also had to learn to worry, to love his mother, or to use the latest slang word.

Conscious and unconscious learning. Sometimes the terms *conscious* learning and *unconscious* learning are used to distinguish the learnings which one accomplishes deliberately from the learnings which "just seem to happen" in the course of living. Recent advances in psychology and other social sciences are more and more dramatically showing how important and basic are the influences which play upon us *unconsciously*. These operate in many subtle ways and usually escape detection altogether, except, perhaps, by the most insightful and psychologically trained persons. For example, the ways in which a small child learns to handle such problems as a tyrannical father or a rejecting mother or a bullying brother often profoundly affect the ways in which that child, ten or fifty years later, handles his relationships with other people. In much the same way the more normal learnings, the kind which are typical of whole populations which have a common culture, may be unconscious.

Overt and covert behavior. Some behavior is obvious. People can be seen going to football games, eating with forks, or driving automobiles. Such behavior is called "overt" behavior. Other behavior is less visible, but no less real to the actor. Such activities as planning tomorrow's work, feeling hatred for an enemy, or wondering about the existence of the Devil are behaviors, too. Behavior of this sort—that is, which is not openly visible to other people—is called "covert" behavior in contrast to "overt" behavior. Both, of course, may be learned.

Thus, we have seen that conscious and unconscious, overt and covert, behavior may be learned. We shall proceed now with further elements in our definition of culture.

2. ". . . Patterns of learned behavior . . ."

Our definition of culture indicated that the learned behavior of people is *patterned*. One's behavior is not just a list of items. There is a *relationship among these items*. Why are you reading this book at this moment? Whatever your reason, you will find that it is related to some other item of your total behavior. Perhaps you are curious to know what culture is. Perhaps you are just fulfilling a requirement in a course. If you think a bit you will observe that you either like or dislike this book, and perhaps, if you think long enough and accurately enough, you may be able to discover *why* you like it or dislike it. Thus the act of reading, the reason for reading, your attitudes and feelings toward the reading, as well as many, many other behaviors are interrelated. And so, of course, with everyone else. It would be difficult, indeed, for almost any normal person to find a wholly isolated or unrelated unit of learned behavior.

Another way in which behavior is patterned or fitted together is in the relationship between the behaviors of people when they are in contact. In order that one person may give, another must receive. Many of the learned behaviors making up each person's life have complementary behaviors in the life of someone else. If one will reflect for a moment upon the many behaviors involved in the following reciprocal and complementary relationships, this phrase of patterning will be more clear: husband-wife behavior, parent-child interaction, teacher-pupil relationship, employer-employee interdependence, and so on. Each person's behavior often depends upon some particular behavior of someone else. The point is not that the behaviors fit perfectly, or that they fit every time, or that one is necessarily conscious of the fitting. It is rather that, as a general rule, behaviors are somewhat integrated or organized with related behaviors of other persons.

We have now shown that much human behavior is learned and is patterned for both the person and the group.

3. ". . . And the products of behavior . . ."

The ideas which come to one are ready-made by *man*, that is, had to be fashioned by someone, somewhere, somehow. It is not necessary at this point to consider the specific questions of where and how some one notion or practice came into being; for example, why women powder their faces and cut their hair now, whereas well-dressed men in George Washington's day cut their hair quite similarly and then powdered it. The point is that the upper-class man of Washington's era who wished to be well groomed powdered his hair because this behavior was correct. It was "correct" simply because it resulted from the experience of the men who had preceded Washington. One learns behavior from others, and they in turn from others, until we get back eventually to the point of origin of the particular behavior in question. The act originally came into use as a result of someone's initiating behavior.

Another sense in which cultural learnings are the "products" of behavior may be seen in this way. As the person behaves, performs the acts making up his life, there occur changes *in him*. He acquires the ability to swim, to feel hatred toward someone, to think objectively, or to sympathize with someone. These attributes of his being are real and can be demonstrated by him quite readily. They have grown out of his previous behaviors.

In both ways, then, human behavior is the result of behavior. The experiences of other people are impressed on one as he grows up, and many of his traits and abilities have grown out of his own past behaviors. Of what, now, do these results consist? The next paragraphs will amplify somewhat more fully what is included among the "products" of behavior.

a. ". . . Including attitudes, values, knowledges . . . "

There is a widespread error in the thinking of many people who tend to regard the ideas, attitudes, and notions which they have as "their own," that is, that they are unique to one because they result from his "own experience." It is easy to overestimate the uniqueness of one's own attitudes and ideas. When there is agreement with other people it is largely unnoticed, but when there is disagreement or difference one is usually conscious of it. Let us take a simple instance. Select some friend of approximately your own age and sex and think of all the ways in which you are alike, of the things which you both do, the ideas on which you agree, and the likes and dislikes which you both have. The list of these close similarities in behavior would be impressive. Yet how could it be otherwise? You have both grown up, very roughly speaking, in the same or similar cultures. Therefore, obviously, you both speak the English language, and you both want to have more money. Your differences, however, may also be cultural. Suppose you are a Catholic and the other person a Protestant. You came in contact with one cultural religious stream of ideas, prejudices, and practices called "Catholic"; the other person came in contact with a somewhat different pattern of ideas, prejudices, and practices called "Protestant." (We shall not define attitudes and values at this point, except to say that they constitute chiefly "mind-sets" derived from culture.)

And so it is, also, with knowledge. How does one really *know*, for example, that the major ideas and truths which he accepts as correct are correct in fact? How can he determine that they are correct? He thinks about them, no doubt, but with what does he think? He thinks with his other knowledges, with the prevailing prejudices, and with the things which he "takes for granted" because others do, too. How does one *know* that 150 million divided by three is 50 million? He certainly has not carefully counted out 150 million items of something into three equal piles and then found that there are 50 million in each pile! Rather he learned a thinking method called "arithmetic," one of the mental processes of which is division. And so with other kinds of logic and other thought systems.

b. ". . . And material objects . . ."

Frequently as people behave, their behavior results in creating objects. Man's behavior has created an impressive array of material objects, from the crude flint choppers of the stone age to the skyscrapers, guided missiles, and electron microscopes of today. Men were behaving when they made these things. To make these objects required numerous and various skills which human beings have gradually built up through the ages. Man has invented the "know-how," he has preserved his knowledge, and he has organized and integrated it with other knowledge he had. And, behaving again, he has invented something else and so on and on.

Occasionally one encounters the view that man does not really "make" baseball bats, steel, or a battleship. All these things, it is sometimes argued, first existed in a "state of nature"; man merely modified their form, changed them from a state in which they were to the state in which he now uses them. The chair was first a tree, which man surely did not make. The glue which holds the pieces together probably came from the hoofs of a horse, which man certainly did not make. But the chair is more than trees and horse hoofs, and the jet airplane is more than iron ore, sap from a rubber tree, and so forth. Undeniably man *uses* nature, but the significant question is, *how* does he use nature? Nature contained wood, but not chairs. Nature contained dogs, but not Great Danes. Nature contained sand, but not the lens of a telescope. It seems a very unreal and indefensible point of view to deny that man has created these things which were fashioned not by nature, but by the ingeniousness of man's mind.

4. ". . . Shared by . . . the members of society . . ."

The patterns of learned behavior and the results of behavior are possessed not by one or a few persons, but usually by a large proportion. Thus, many millions of persons share such behavior patterns as Christianity, the use of automobiles, or the English language.

As has been pointed out previously, the numerous persons whose mode of life contains some one pattern of behavior need not be otherwise identical. Persons may share some part of a culture unequally as, for example, the majority of Americans do the Christian religion. To some of these Christianity is the all-important, predominating idea in life. To others it is less preoccupying, and to still others it is of marginal significance only. Not only do the various people share unequally in Christianity, but they share different aspects of it—Catholic and Protestant, liberal or conservative, as clergymen or as laymen. But Christianity is nevertheless shared, even though unequally and somewhat variously. The point to our discussion is not that culture or any part of it is shared identically, but that it is shared by the members of society to a sufficient extent that, given a person's culture, one can have a reasonably accurate idea of what that person does, how he looks, what he believes, and numerous other facts about him, even though not everything about him.

5. ". . . Transmitted among . . ."

These cultural ways which we have been discussing are learned *by* persons *from* persons. Many of them are handed down by one's elders, by parents, teachers, and others of a somewhat older generation. Other cultural behaviors are "handed up" to elders. Most children have taught their parents more about the child culture than either the parents or the child are likely to recognize. Home economists, for example, have frequently pointed out that one of the ways of improving home-making standards is for adults to teach better standards to their children. Many a parent likewise comes gradually to be educated in the precisely correct and latest adolescent slang. Finally, some of the transmission of culture is among contemporaries, neither down from the elders nor up from the juniors. Styles of dress, recreational fads, political views, and the use of recent labor saving devices all tend to illustrate the point.

It is necessary to point out that the phrase "transmitted by" may not indicate too clearly exactly what is involved in the handing along of patterns of learned behavior. Transmission is really a shorthand word for the process of *teaching and learning*, which must go on whenever a behavior is passed along. One does not acquire a behavior pattern spontaneously. He learns it. That means that someone teaches him and he learns what is being taught. The parent who learns a slang phrase from his child probably does not recognize that he is learning something, any more than the child realizes that he has momentarily served as teacher. We see here again an example of the basic principle involved in cultural learning, namely, that much of the learning process both for the teacher and the learner is quite unconscious, unintentional, or accidental, but it is learning and teaching nevertheless.

6. ". . . Continually changing . . ."

There is one fundamental and inescapable attribute of culture: the *fact of unending change*. Few if any persons who live to maturity leave the identical culture which existed at the time of their birth. Phrases like "stagnant cultures" and "unchanging cultures" are misleading. All that squares with the facts is that some societies at some times change slowly, and hence in comparison to other societies seem not to be changing at all. But they are changing, even though not radically or obviously so.

People frequently (but not always) have a deep-seated distrust and fear of change. It is usually easier not to change—to drift along in the accustomed ruts, doing as one always did. That requires less thinking, and there appears to be less chance for making a mistake. But the behavior patterns of culture really constitute the techniques through which the people of the society meet and solve the many problems which periodically confront them. From moment to moment as one lives, he encounters problems and obstacles. When he is confronted with a problem he turns to the solutions for situations like that, which he has learned in the course of participating in culture. Man does not meet each recurring situation in *exactly* the same way each time, however. He makes modifications, large and small. He tries new ways, or he accidentally stumbles onto new ways of handling the situation. These new ways are transmitted to others, and already the culture is changed. The person who sets for himself the task of preserving the culture of the society permanently as it is at any one time has cut out for himself a hopeless and impossible task. At best all he can do is to slow down the unending and uncontrollable process of change, and even that is not as easy as it appears.

Summary: the meaning of culture

We have tried in this section to clarify the meaning of the fundamental concept, *culture*. To recapitulate: culture is a continually changing pattern of learned behavior and the products of learned behavior (including attitudes, values, knowledge, and material objects) which are shared by and transmitted among the members of society. Attention has been called to the facts:

1. That the behaviors of people are largely learned;
2. That they are organized into patterns;
3. That these patterns result from the teaching (conscious or unconscious) of other people;
4. That they exist both in the form of material objects and intangible thought-habits like attitudes and knowledges;
5. That they tend to be somewhat uniformly shared by the members of society, learned from and taught to each other largely unconsciously;
6. That these ways of doing and ways of thinking make up the pattern of human lives;
7. That these ways are constantly changing.

THE CONCEPT OF SUBCULTURE

Particularly in the mass society, the concept of culture which we have just outlined is less than fully apropos. What is missing is the more modern concept of the *subculture*, which means simply that *within the confines of some larger culture, there exist pockets of cultural differences which have most of the earmarks of the more encompassing idea, except that they apply less generally.* A few examples may help to focus the idea. Within many of the American Protestant denominations there exists a phenomenon known as *fundamentalism* which claims the allegiance of both laymen and clergymen and has a formal structure of ideas codified in books, common resolutions, and informal manners and morals. Similarly, there is a youth subculture in American society which is perhaps most conspicuously delimited by a somewhat different language (which even the aggressive adult has difficulty keeping up with); a distinctively different set of tastes regarding dress, music, and the arts in general; and a discernably different set of values, moral standards, and orientations to the future. The most interesting and significant implication of the subculture, however, is that it contains essentially the same structure, and the same principles relating culture and behavior apply. That is, behavior is not random or arbitrary; it is related, largely through other-direction, to a rationale, a set of principles which are regarded as self-evident by the young people in the system. There are also material culture objects, the current hair style, dress, and hit records, as well as the well-known linguistic forms which people in the supraculture like to call "slang." They are not slang, however, to the participants in the teenage culture; they are simply the approved, accepted modes of communication. Other subcultures are somewhat more enduring in the cultural forms which they strive to perpetuate. The familiar trichotomy of Catholic-Protestant-Jew, each, of course, subcultures in the larger American mass culture, are among the most enduring encrustations in the cultural landscape. Similarly, with such smaller entities as the Quakers and the Amish. As the student will see in a later chapter on stratification, even the socioeconomic status of a family carries with it a demonstrably distinct set of beliefs, values, and overt behaviors, as well as material culture objects which set persons of a given status clearly apart from those above and below them in the hierarchy of privilege and prestige.

In the mass society, then, the concept of culture as the social heritage must always be understood to be a complex, not a single logical entity. For practically everyone, *his* cultural heritage is something of a mixture of mass cultural elements and one or more subcultures which may or may not be consistent with one another.

SOCIETY AND SOCIAL SYSTEMS

Culture, however, is not the people. Although no analogy is useful without being at the same time inaccurate, we shall risk one which has served for some time to help clarify the distinction between society and culture. In some ways culture may be considered to be like a play, and the people of the society where the culture prevails may be considered as actors enacting the play. The play is, of course, visible only through the enactments of the actors. The actors get their lines from the play; although they are given some freedom of choice in interpreting the play, not very much "leeway" is usually permitted. The only tangible existence which the play has is in the portrayal of the players; the only knowledge one has of the players is the play which they enact.

Society, thus, may be thought of as the organized group of people who enact a culture. There are, of course, many weaknesses to this analogy. The people of the society do not "play" their culture. It is the only existence which, for the most part, they know; the very essence of their lives is that one culture. Moreover, the members of the society do not merely "enact" the culture; they *create* culture as they go along, carrying on, like the bride, with "something old and something new." But the illustration is useful in showing both the close relationship of culture and society, and yet also the basic distinction.

A society may be defined as a *group of people who have lived together long enough to become organized and to consider themselves and be considered as a unit* more or less distinct from other human units. The key phrase in the definition is a *group of people*. A culture, on the other hand, is a *group of behavior patterns*. The behavior patterns of the culture determine both the behavior and the organization of the persons of the society, but the behaving *people constitute the society*.

In recent years sociologists have largely replaced the concept *society* with the concept *social system*, which means the *network of relationships among people which grows out of their adherence to a given culture and/or subculture, from which they derive the proscriptions for their behavior and, of course, their interrelationships*. Thus, a nation is a social system, a religious denomination is a social system, a fraternity is a social system, the army is a social system, and a family is a social system. Obviously, the appropriate behavior for participation in each of these systems is somewhat different, but what all participations have in common is that the behavior of each individual is inter-related in some specified way or ways with the behavior of others; certain behaviors are tabooed; and all fit together into a more or less integrated and working system which makes up the collective enter-prise. Human behavior, to be understood realistically, must be compre-hended in this systemic sense. Most of what one must learn in order to function in collective enterprises consists of learning the rules and regulations (later to be discussed as "roles") which successful participa-tion requires. Failure to accomplish this is in one way or another pe-nalized: a person finds his participation in the system handicapped or, in extreme instances, he might be ostracized.[2]

REGULARITIES IN LEARNED HUMAN BEHAVIOR

So-called "pressure" to conform to the ways of other people is evident to almost everyone, particularly to the young, who in onerous ways experience one or another kind of "control" recurrently. Pressure to conform is no less strong for more mature people, but they, because of their maturity, usually are so thoroughly habituated to the patterns that the pressure is largely unnoticed except under unusual circum-stances. Society contains numerous devices to facilitate and assure con-formity. Basically there exists a reward and punishment system—one is rewarded for doing the appropriate things and punished for doing the inappropriate things.

The individual is virtually powerless to resist indoctrination as he participates in his culture. He has few real choices as to the fundamen-tals in the pattern. He speaks the language which prevails, engages as a rule in the activities in which he is supposed to, and acquires the knowl-edges, the prejudices, and the fears that are current. He seems bribed into conformity, coerced into being and doing what is expected.

Conformity to the patterns of one's culture is, however, not com-plete; the person still has choices, even if only the choices among the several alternatives contained in the culture.

All behavior not equally uniform

The persons of a society do not behave identically, even though similarities are often marked. People in a given culture attach different degrees of importance to the various patterns of behavior. The situation

[2] Most professional discussions of social systems are too technical for the beginning student, but a good elementary treatment is to be found in Alvin L. Bertrand, *Basic Sociology: An Introduction to Theory and Method* (New York, Appleton-Century-Crofts, 1967).

may be graphically portrayed in the following way. Suppose one thinks of the following continuum, graduated into degrees like a thermometer or a speedometer, as representing the various degrees of uniformity in behavior among the persons in a society.

3.

No Uniformity   Complete Uniformity

One could, then, distribute the various behaviors of people along this continuum. Thus, the following items for contemporary urban Americans may be approximately located.

4.

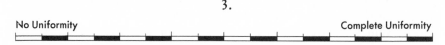

No Uniformity   Complete Uniformity

WHICH SHOE   KEEPING ONE'S   SHOWING   WEARING   DISAPPROVAL
ONE PUTS   YARD CLEAN   "RESPECT"   CLOTHES   OF BIGAMY
ON FIRST   TO OLD
                                        PEOPLE

The location of the various items along the continuum is, of course, very approximate. One cannot prove, for example, that showing "respect for one's elders" is 50 percent less uniformly observed than is "wearing clothes." The basis for locating "respect for elders" on the continuum is *in relation to other items*, that is, "respect for elders" is less uniform than "wearing clothes," but presumably more frequently found than is "keeping one's yard clean." Thus, each of the many acts making up the mode of life can be placed *somewhere* along this continuum. The point to our discussion is not that it is possible or necessary to place every act in its precisely correct position, but that each act *could* be placed as soon as sufficient research were done. Many acts can be approximately placed without formal research, as in the above examples.

"Mores," "folkways," and "undefined acts"

Sociologists have traditionally attached the words *mores, folkways*, and *undefined acts* to certain ranges along this continuum.

1. *Mores* [3] are usually defined as the must-behaviors, the basic and important patterns of ideas and acts of a people. Monogamy, wearing

[3] The classic treatment of the concept *mores* appears in W. G. Sumner, *Folkways* (Boston, Ginn, 1906). Sumner coined the phrase "mores have the authority of facts."

clothes, and loyalty to the government, especially in time of war, are illustrations of the mores. There may be some variations granted under a few "exceptional circumstances" which might arise, but on the whole these behaviors are said to be required if one is to live in present-day American society without suffering disprivilege. Some of the mores are written down in the law and carry stipulated penalties to be imposed upon violators. Many of the mores are not so formally set forth, but observance of them is no less compulsive. Informal methods of enforcement consist of such patterns as ridicule, gossip, and ostracism by one's associates. Many persons' behavior is said to be "held in line" not by fear of legal action but by fear of social ostracism, which can be more seriously and permanently harmful than formal legal action. For example, the loss of "reputation" of a physician is a far more serious penalty to him professionally than the fine which might be imposed for some malpractice. In one way or another, then, the society rigidly enforces some of its most important patterns of behavior—its mores.

2. *Folkways* are construed as somewhat less compulsive than the mores of the same society. Many of the folkways are not even really enforced, but rather are the expected or taken-for-granted things which most persons within the society perform similarly, even though under no rigid requirement so to do. Other folkways may be somewhat more compulsive. For example, the appropriate clothing for students to wear to class, while somewhat varied from campus to campus and region to region, is more or less agreed upon. Should a woman appear in a long gown or a man in overalls, neither would probably be disprivileged in any official way for so doing, but both would constitute "bad taste," and the wearers would probably be regarded as somewhat eccentric or "queer." Perhaps some mild pressure would be imposed, like ridicule or laughing at them. But few would consider this to be a serious breach of the moral code, or consider taking formal action to punish the students involved. The point is best illustrated perhaps by the fact that cases like the above are very few. Persons rarely *want* to wear other than the appropriate clothes, do not consider very seriously wearing anything other than the regularly accepted clothing for the occasion. Such is the nature of the folkways.

3. Finally, some acts are regarded as outside the province of social dictation, and it is of no real concern to anyone else what one does. No one cares which arm goes into the coat sleeve first or whether one prefers his coffee with or without sugar. Such acts are regarded as in the realm of one's own preference; any way is socially acceptable. These are the culturally *undefined acts*.

Range along the continuum

In terms of the already familiar continuum, folkways, mores, and undefined acts may be represented thus:

5.

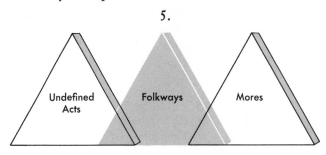

Again, the range covered by each of these three terms is only approximate. It might be difficult to determine, for example, whether taking frequent baths constitutes a folkway or a mos (singular of mores). Is daily bathing required for social acceptability or is it "just the expected, natural thing to do"? The answer would vary from social class to social class; it would then be a "borderline case," somewhere between folkway and mos for the general community. But it is still regarded as convenient to have the terms *mores, folkways*, and *undefined acts* for quick and approximate designation, even though the distinctions are not always clear-cut.

Position along the continuum varies with time as well as with place

There is nothing final or permanent about the position of any specific act along the continuum we have just discussed. Behavior considered essential at one time may gradually lose its compulsion until eventually it becomes largely undefined. The history of women's dress contains numerous illustrations. What would have been considered as "immoral, indecent exposure" in beach costume in 1900 is undefined and largely unnoticed conventional dress today. The reverse may also be true. Undefined acts and folkways may with the passing of time become regarded as increasingly important and hence "in the mores" of the group. At one time a person with a disease such as measles or whooping cough could come and go as he wished, whereas now he is required by both law and public opinion to remain isolated so that he will not infect others. The history of morals contains numerous examples of radical shifts in the societal definition of various acts.

Emphasis on cultural compulsion is misleading

Although it has been traditional for some sociologists and anthropologists to stress the compulsion feature underlying societal behavior patterns, this point of view leads to basic misunderstanding. At its worst, the view sets the person and the culture apart *as if* the culture were an active thing ordering people around and forcing them to do what they do not wish to do. Actually, of course, the culture is inseparable from the people of a society; the people are participants in the culture. To say that culture "forces" people to abide by social standards would be like saying that the game of football forces quarterbacks to call signals or centers to lean over the ball. The point is not that the game of football forces these men to behave in these ways, but rather that these men are participants in the culture of football, and the pattern simply consists of these behaviors.

Groups and individuals, not cultures, force persons to behave in stipulated ways

There is no denying the fact that persons are often required to act in ways which they do not prefer. The existence of laws tabooing some acts and requiring others illustrates the fact of social compulsion. But it is well always to note that the acts tabooed may reflect culturally patterned behavior quite as much as the acts approved. The member of a boys' gang which steals automobile tires is manifesting the boys' gang culture in which he is participating. The fact that this behavior is illegal, according to the standards of behavior set up by the people who made the laws, reflects merely a difference in judgments between the two groups. The controlling group of citizens, lawmakers, and law-enforcing officials are the ones trying to force the boys' gang to do what it does not wish to do, namely, refrain from the behavior pattern of automobile pilfering. *We may, then, speak of "social" compulsion, but not of "cultural" compulsion.*

Compulsion is not entirely arbitrary: values

Compulsion is not entirely a hit-or-miss thing which societies "just happen upon" or devise merely for the sake of making living onerous. Instead, compulsion may arise from the *ideas of importance* which the culture contains with respect to certain behaviors. These are called the cultural *values*. Compulsion is logical *if* it is important that an act be performed, or that it be performed in some precise way. If, for example, the Puritans of New England considered that man's chief responsibility was to God and that church-going was the minimum, inescapable evidence of devotion to God, then it was logical for them to pass strict laws requiring men and women to attend church services regularly. Moreover, if it is considered a serious moral wrong to murder a fellow-man, then severe penalties for murder are in order, assuming, of course, that such penalties deter murderers. And so on. In a later chapter attention will be drawn to the interesting and significant problem of what determines "logic" and "right," but here we are only concerned with making the point that the prevailing notions of the importance of certain behavior are the bases for requiring adherence to the societal standards of conduct.

Mores formulated in terms of taboo or of required action

Sometimes it is easier to describe a mos in terms of the requirement that the individual abstain from some act—*taboo*. The Ten Commandments constitute an excellent case in point. The "Thou shalt nots" of the Mosaic code are, moreover, the same kinds of prohibitions which are recorded in the laws of the United States. In other instances it is conventional to express the mores positively, that is, in terms of what one is under *obligation* to do. Thus, according to both law and custom, a man must support his wife and children, and adults are responsible for the maintenance of aged and indigent parents. Likewise, during time of war a person is more or less under obligation to serve his nation in some capacity suited to his talents, age, and marital status, and he is supposed to show more concern for his country's welfare and less for his own than under more normal circumstances.

Law and informal mores may not be consistent

There are numerous examples of discrepancies between what the law prescribes pertaining to human conduct and what the more informal mores of the people condone. Thus, despite clear and overwhelming evidence of murder, few juries will convict a man if the murder can be shown to have been in "self-defense" or if the victim had been involved in adulterous behavior with the murderer's wife, even though the law states nothing whatsoever about the legality of such exceptions. "You cannot legislate morality" is an adage containing much that is sociologically sound. When the mores conflict with law, in the long run the mores seem usually to "win out." Prohibition during the 1920's illustrates the difficulty of setting up laws which a substantial minority of the population do not consider to be in the true realm of moral taboos. Under conditions such as these, "lawlessness becomes normal."

The sovereignty of the mores over law occurs also in societies which are not democratic. It would be difficult, for example, to conceive of more severe or more certain punishment of nonconformers to law than that meted out by the Nazis in the occupied countries during the Second World War. Yet throughout the period of Nazi occupation in almost every country involved, fairly large and effective underground organizations flourished for the express purpose of circumventing the operation of the conqueror's law. In the United States prior to the Civil War, despite Supreme Court decisions and laws to the contrary, prominent and highly respected people in the North supported another type of widespread underground movement called the "Underground Railway" which made it possible for escaped Negro slaves to secure safe passage into the North. Every conceivable device was used and many of the devices employed were in themselves clearly illegal; but because the moral conscience of the people justified the objective of freeing Negroes, the illegality of their behavior seemed to be regarded as of little consequence. Many of the early extreme reforms of the Russian Revolution had to be modified or abandoned because the mores of the peasants of the vast country ran so completely counter to the laws passed by the new government that it was found necessary to make changes in the law providing for greater consistency with the prevailing, traditional mores.

The phrase *the mores* is frequently an oversimplification

Particularly under the conditions of modern mass society, the mores may be changing so rapidly or there may be so many different sets of mores in existence that it is difficult for a person who is completely objective to determine what the mores of his community are. For example, do the mores of America condone or condemn birth control? Studies have shown that the majority of married pairs, in numerous samples that have been investigated, either have practiced contraception or at least are not opposed to its practice. Yet large and prominent church bodies with millions of members have endorsed resolutions specifically condemning the practice. What, then, are "the mores" regarding contraception? Perhaps one can become more realistic with respect to behavior patterns if attention is drawn to the basic distinction between real and ideal patterns.

"REAL" AND "IDEAL" PATTERNS

When one closely observes the people participating in a social system he will find that they actually show two kinds of uniformities.[4] The first of these may be called *ideal* patterns. These are the models of exemplary conduct which are held up as standards of perfection. They represent what one "should do" or "ought to do" if he were to behave ideally. Ideal patterns are usually formulated in such a way that they are more or less unreal. If a person carried them out exactly, he would not only be regarded as naïve and queer, but probably would get into numerous practical difficulties in "reward" for his very virtuous conduct. Suppose one were at a party at which inferior food was served and where the guests were dull, and altogether it was a bad evening. At the end of the evening, when paying the hostess the customary compliment, should one lie and be "diplomatic," or should he tell the truth and offend her? Whichever he chooses to do, he thereby violates one or another of the social codes. It is probable that in most cases diplomacy takes precedence over the truth. Yet one does believe in telling the truth, even though he lies to his hostess. And he will no doubt punish his child for the serious offense of telling a lie!

There is a second set of behavior patterns. These are called *real*. They are "real" in the sense that they are what the people actually do, irrespective of what they are ideally supposed to do, or what they themselves believe they should do. In the previously mentioned dilemma regarding one's "honors" to the hostess, the real pattern is probably one of lying to the hostess if necessary in order to compliment her. In a similar vein one notes that most people agree with the ideal that it is wrong to steal, but many compute their income tax in such a way as to pay the government less than they know they ought to, without regarding such behavior as theft.

In a strictly logical sense, real and ideal patterns constitute inconsistencies. But if one is realistic in his observation of human beings, the conclusion cannot be escaped that ideal patterns and real patterns pertaining to the same acts are not so much inconsistent as "only different." That is not to say, however, that the ideal patterns are of no

[4] The original development of this idea is found in Ralph Linton, *The Study of Man* (New York, Appleton-Century-Crofts, 1936).

significance. Quite to the contrary. So long as ideal patterns exist, they tend to serve as checks upon real patterns, even though at some times the checks seem not to be very effective. There always seem to be some morally sensitive people in a society who take ideal standards somewhat seriously. Such persons perform the function of periodically reminding the members of the society of the inconsistencies between the real and ideal behavior patterns, and frequently they have originated significant changes making for a greater agreement between real and ideal patterns.

THE ORGANIZATION OF CULTURE

It has become customary to use technical language to characterize the various parts of culture. It is necessary for the student, therefore, to acquaint himself with this nomenclature.

The smallest unit of culture is called a *culture trait*. A group of related traits is called a *culture complex*. In contemporary America, for example, the automobile complex consists of a great many culture objects and behavior patterns having to do with the automobile and its usage; automobiles, filling stations, roadside parks, traffic laws, and automobile clubs are merely a few of the ramifications of the automobile complex.

The difference between a culture trait and a culture complex is not always as simple a distinction as the above paragraph seems to imply. What appears to one observer to be a culture trait might appear to another observer, who is able to analyze it further, to be a culture complex. Both usages are correct; it is a matter of the observer's ability to distinguish the different degrees or minutiae. Thus, an automobile would be called a "trait" if one were describing American culture to an Arab, yet to an automobile engineer an automobile is a culture "complex" consisting of such traits as the wheel, the internal combustion engine, four-wheel brakes, and the incredible number of technical features which taken together constitute an automobile. At the outset the student may have some difficulty in determining when to use the word *trait* and when to use *complex*. Generally speaking, if one is aware that the segment of culture being described is readily divisible into parts, then the word *complex* would probably be employed.

Complexes, like traits, are related to each other. The term *the culture pattern* is sometimes used to designate the overall organization of the culture, but sometimes is used in a more limited way, also. Thus one finds both in sociological and anthropological writing such phrases as "the culture pattern of the Eskimo" when it is quite clear from the context that the writer means the entire culture of the Eskimo. More commonly, major segments of the culture are referred to as patterns, for example, "the family pattern of the Trobrianders" or "the religious pattern of the Todas."

Trait-complex-pattern unity

It should be emphasized that the various traits of a culture derive their meaning and significance from the way in which they fit into the large complex to which they are related. *Objects or units of behavior have no meaning outside of their contexts.* This can readily be illustrated by observing a material culture object from another culture. Frequently the observer does not even know for what the object is used or how valuable it is in relation to other objects, unless and until he knows something else about the rest of the culture. A breastplate from the New Georgia Island natives is as meaningless to an American as a "number 2 iron" would be to a New Georgian.

At many points in this book attention will be devoted to the problems which center around the interrelation of the parts of culture. One of the greatest problems of living for the individual, and one of the greatest problems of controlling societies, is that of changing one aspect of behavior without upsetting a great many others which are related to it. The problems of war and the problems of reconversion to peace have both been greatly increased because of the lack of knowledge concerning how the parts of modern culture really fit together, or a refusal to follow the course of action which our knowledge would seem to indicate. This important principle shall be treated in considerable detail in several of its ramifications from time to time in subsequent chapters.

SUMMARY

In this chapter we have defined and explained the fundamental concepts of sociology—culture and society. This has been only a beginning, of course, because the whole book is about culture and society. Culture is the constantly changing patterns of learned behavior and the products of learned behavior (including attitudes, values, knowledges, and material objects) which are shared by and transmitted among the members of society. Society is the group of people who have lived together long enough to become organized and to consider themselves and be considered as a unit. When attention is focused upon some delimited set of interrelationships, the concept *social system* is now used. It has the utility of stressing the interrelatedness of human action.

A further purpose of this chapter has been to introduce the technical nomenclature customarily used in describing and analyzing culture and culture objects; patterns or uniformities in culture; folkways and mores; real and ideal culture patterns; and traits and complexes. Although sociological and anthropological writers are not entirely consistent in the use of these terms, each concept has a somewhat standardized core of meaning which has been defined and illustrated.

Cultures are organized and/or integrated. This does not mean that every single item of each culture is neatly and precisely integrated with everything else. It means rather that it is normal for the parts to be somewhat integrated and organized, and that culture traits receive their significance and meaning out of their relation to the rest of the culture.

SUGGESTED READINGS

Bain, Read, "Our Schizoid Culture." *Sociology and Social Research*, Vol. 19 (January–February, 1935), pp. 266–276.
A clever description of the "irrational contradictory" behavior characterizing our culture. Very tersely written in terms of a series of antitheses. An idea which should become familiar to everyone. The more serious student will profit from Bain's "Cultural Integration and Social Conflict." *American Journal of Sociology*, Vol. 44 (January, 1939), pp. 499–509. The treatment here is more profound.

Bredemeier, Harry C., and Stephenson, Richard M., "The Analysis of Culture," in Peter I. Rose, ed., *The Study of Society*. New York, Random House, 1967, pp. 119–133.
A very insightful treatment, though technical, distinguishing two kinds of cultural definition, the one telling people what to *perceive* and the other telling how they should *respond*.

Cuber and Harroff (See Bibliographic note, p. 40): William Graham Sumner, "The Mores," pp. 47–54; Robert S. Lynd, "The Pattern of American Culture," pp. 78–82; Ralph Linton, "Society," pp. 226–229; John Gillin, "Culture is Learned," pp. 59–61.

Hall, Edward T., *The Silent Language*. Garden City, N.Y., Doubleday, 1959.
A sophisticated and original book which interprets cultural behavior as a "silent" language of the people.

Jaeger, Gertrude, and Selznick, Philip, "A Normative Theory of Culture." *American Sociological Review*, Vol. 29 (October, 1964), pp. 653–669.
This paper takes a novel but perhaps important position regarding culture. The

authors attempt to bring together the popular and the technical meanings of culture as developed in this chapter. Will be interesting to the serious, humanistically-oriented student.

Linton, Ralph, *The Study of Man.* New York, Appleton-Century-Crofts, 1936.
This is a classic work on culture and society, written by a distinguished anthropologist.

Myrdal, Gunnar, and others. *An American Dilemma.* New York, Harper & Row, 1944, pp. 1031–1034.
An excellent critique of Sumner's concept of mores. In line with the view presented in this book.

Sumner, W. G., *Folkways.* Boston, Ginn, 1906.
A classic sociological-anthropological book. All sociologists and anthropologists are greatly indebted to Sumner for these early formulations, many of which, of course, are now somewhat modified.

STUDY QUESTIONS

1. Why will most people in a society respond to a given situation in much the same way?
2. What differences do you observe between the technical meaning and the popular meanings of the word *culture?*
3. How do we acquire our behavior patterns? How are they "patterned"?
4. If we are acquainted with a person's culture, why can we predict to a certain extent that person's behavior? Illustrate.
5. How is cultural learning a mutual interaction between contemporary people rather than a "handing-down" process?
6. What is the relationship between society and culture? Illustrate.
7. Why are there no static societies or unchanging cultures?
8. How are both material objects and "intangible" behavior part of culture?
9. How are culture objects and nonmaterial behavior related? Illustrate.
10. How does the reward-punishment system produce conformity to a culture?
11. Why is it impossible for the individual to be wholly "indoctrinated" by his culture?
12. Why do not all people show the same degree of conformity to all expected types of behavior?
13. How is conformity to culture "a relative matter"?
14. Why are some forms of behavior mores, others folkways, while others are just "undefined acts"?

15. Criticize: "For every mos there is a law, and for every law there is a mos."
16. What is the relation of the "real" to the "ideal" culture patterns? Illustrate.
17. How is the presence of "inconsistent" culture patterns a source of problems for a society? How does one know that they are "inconsistent" patterns? Illustrate.
18. What is the relation of the culture trait and culture complex to the culture pattern? Illustrate.
19. Give some examples of folkways becoming mores, and vice versa.
20. What is a "social system"? Illustrate.

6
VARIABILITY AND UNIFORMITY AMONG CULTURES AND SOCIAL SYSTEMS

SCIENTIFIC INTEREST IN COMPARING CULTURES

Everyone, it seems, is interested in the "quaint, queer folk" of other societies. Souvenir hunting among strange peoples is a common hobby. Travelers' tales *are* amusing. But *scientific* study of cultural variability has advanced considerably beyond the curio-hunting and naïveté of the layman. Modern behavior scientists' interest in cultural variability centers around certain *theoretical problems* pertaining to the different cultures in which man lives and has lived.

1. *How wide is the variation among cultures?* Is it literally true that "the ideas of one society make anything right, and of the next society make the same thing wrong"? Or are there some limits beyond which the variability does not go?

2. *Why do these variabilities exist?* Since man as a species is biologically constituted the same, why does he not behave everywhere the same, as the members of other species do?

3. *Are there uniformities common to all cultures?*

This chapter contains an introductory treatment of these three basic problems.

VARIABILITY AMONG CULTURES

It would be impossible to summarize even a very small fraction of the available material on cultural variability which ethnologists have discovered. There are hundreds of cultures in the world, and thousands of patterns in each culture. It must suffice to give a few examples, so that the student may get some understanding of the general situation. We shall therefore treat very briefly the extent of cultural variability in certain characteristic parts of culture.

1. Variability in sex-marriage-family behavior

Everywhere the human race is divided into two sexes, and everywhere human beings reproduce by the same biological process. There is, however, seemingly no end to culturally formed variations in how, when, and where the basic biological processes are to be carried out.

a. The makeup of the family illustrates variability convincingly. Some societies, like ours, are *monogamous;* that is, each adult person is permitted to have only one legal mate at a time. He is permitted remarriage only after the death of the previous mate or after a court decision (divorce) sets the marriage aside. Some societies have stricter monogamy than we do, because they prohibit divorce, and in some cases do not permit remarriage, even after the death of the mate. In many parts of the world *polygyny* is and has been permitted or required. Under the polygynous system, a man has multiple wives. If the man has great prestige, wealth, or power, the number of wives may run into the hundreds, as in the well-known case of King Solomon. Usually, of course, the number of wives is much lower, and often even in a polygynous society a man might not take advantage of the privilege of having multiple wives. Then, also, there is *polyandry*, the practice of one woman having multiple husbands. Polyandry is and has been much less common than polygyny. Finally, *group marriage* exists. Under this system a group of men are married to a group of women, not necessarily of equal number, each person having sexual access and economic legal rights to all or a number of the others. Group marriage is not widespread, but does exist in a few societies. It is important to note that there are innumerable details which make up a polygynous or polyandrous society, just as there are innumerable details which have to be observed in a society like ours in order to carry out our specific kind of monogamous system. For example, the colonial American mating system was monogamous, many native American Indian cultures were monogamous, and we are monogamous, but the details of each of these three systems varied greatly. Likewise in some polyandrous societies it is required that the multiple husbands be brothers, while in other societies it makes no difference. Thus, we see that in the mating arrangement every possible combination between the sexes has somewhere come to be accepted—one man to one woman; one man to several women; one woman to several men; and several men to several women.

b. Mate choice. In some societies a woman is not eligible for marriage until after she has borne one or more children. It is said that the logic of this practice is that childbearing is such an important function that no respectable man would want to risk marrying a woman who might prove to be infertile. Obviously, under such conditions, premarital sex behavior is not only permitted but necessary. In other societies unmarried men and women must not only remain chaste but are prevented from speaking to each other from the time of puberty until marriage. Frequently girls are not eligible for marriage until all older sisters are already married. Sometimes wives are purchased either in exchange for money, for property, or for the young man's labor. Sometimes the marrying persons choose each other, and sometimes their marriage is arranged by parents or some other persons. In some cases marriages are arranged between older men and infant girls, the marriage to be physically consummated when the girl attains maturity. Sometimes mates are "selected" by "falling in love."

A very prevalent aspect of mate selection arises from cultural patterns relative to the group from which the mate must be chosen, regardless of who does the choosing. Under *endogamy* the mate must be chosen from within some designated group to which the chooser also belongs. Thus in some cultures one must marry within his social class, his village, or his circle of blood relatives. The latter may operate so as to permit or even require first-cousin, brother-sister, or father-daughter marriage, although such cultures are not common. The opposite of endogamy is *exogamy*, the obligation to choose the mate from outside the group to which one belongs. Again, as in endogamy, "the group" may refer to blood relationship, class, or territorial group, although most generally it refers to blood relationship. It is to be noted, of course, that a culture may require *both* endogamy and exogamy. Thus, for example, our culture requires exogamous marriage so far as close blood relationship is concerned, but favors endogamy regarding race and, to some extent, social class and religion.

c. Family rule. Under the *patriarchal* family form—the most prevalent—authority is vested in the male head of the family. Sometimes that authority is so absolute as to include the right of life or death over the women and children. Usually, there are some limitations imposed by law or by informal custom. Less common than the patriarchate is the *matriarchal* family—authority vested in the woman head of the family with the male being subordinate. Contemporary American families are said to be "democratic," that is, not clearly patriarchal or matriarchal. But legally and by custom, male dominance is still quite in evidence, although it is increasingly being abridged.

d. Other variability in the sex-marriage-family sphere. Conspicuous in the encyclopedia of curios are such practices as sexual hospitality (lending of wives to overnight guests), Sutteeism (burning the wife on the funeral pyre of her deceased husband), and many others. Little more needs to be said in order to demonstrate the broad principle of wide variability. So vast are the variations among cultures that most persons find it impossible to "think up" a practice which does not already exist or has not already existed. Man has shown himself to be truly inventive in his social practices centering around sex, marriage, and the family.

2. Variability among religions

Man has, likewise, endowed almost everything at some time or other with supernatural power or existence: animals of various kinds, plants, planets, mountains, rivers, people (insane people, old people, dead people, children), storms, ancestors, dreams. In fact, it is very difficult to conceive of anything which is not or has not somewhere been regarded by man as "sacred." Moreover, in the name of religion, man performs the most varied and antithetical acts; meditation and dancing, feasting and fasting, silence and shouting, sex abstinence and sacred prostitution, acts of kindness and acts of cruelty, child care and infanticide (killing babies), love and hate. Again, there seems to be no end to man's ingenuity at inventing and building religions—no end, either, to the range of "explanations" as to *why* he does what he does, thinks what he thinks, or has "authority" to act in the way he does.

3. Variability in governmental systems

Every college student has studied, at least cursorily, enough history to permit him to illustrate governmental variability without much aid. Somewhere, men have lived and loved—even fought and died for —governmental systems as varied as democracy and dictatorship. Dictatorial or *absolutistic governments are of various sorts*—hereditary monarchies, elected persons given or taking permanent and complete authority, small cliques with power and indefinite tenure, autocratic powers by exclusive groups of the wealthy, and so on. *Democracy is likewise of very different varieties*—the British is not like the American, neither is it like the Swiss, and the democracy of primitive peoples is not like any of them. Nor is the American democracy of the 1960's like the American democracy of the 1860's, when neither Negroes nor women voted.

4. Variability in economic pursuits and ideas

Americans, living as they do in a highly competitive and wealth-conscious society, tend to "take for granted" that it is inherent in the "nature" of good human beings to "keep up with the Joneses," work hard, and be thrifty. Such a view is, of course, quite incorrect. There are numerous cultures in which pecuniary matters have no prominence, in fact are subordinated to other matters. Likewise, there are societies in which there is no concept of saving or notions of the virtue of hard work as we know them. Instead, one lives in these societies on the assumption that he works each day for the purpose of meeting that day's needs—tomorrow is another day. Regular work is not a sign of commendable character, but rather of stupidity, because a clever person should see that there are other values in life and that there are ways of avoiding regularity of work. "Savings" in some cultures are nonexistent.

Another widespread American notion which does not square with the facts is that people *always* work harder and more efficiently when there is "incentive of profit" or at least incentive of "personal reward for work." Such a notion is understandable as a rationalization to support our economic system, but as a scientific statement is, simply, incorrect. People are activated to exert effort by *many* different motives, only one of which is pecuniary self-interest. Much of the world's work, even in this culture, is done for reasons quite aside from financial gain.

The careful study of many cultures gives one perspective on many of his own cultural ideas. From such study he learns that our notions of what is valuable and important are by no means shared generally by people of other societies, that not all peoples *want* what we call "high standards" of living, that wealth does not necessarily bring power and prestige to its possessors, that people are motivated by many considerations other than money or wealth, that people work very effectively in cooperation as well as in competition, that people take pride and interest in and will sacrifice for communally-owned property, and that what is customarily regarded as private property in one society may be owned collectively in the next, or at another time in the same society. All economic systems seem "natural" to their practitioners and work fairly well, although not equally well, to provide man with the satisfactions of his basic needs.

Are each society's ways the best for it?

Frequently one encounters a point of view to the effect that each society's ways constitute "the best adjustment" which that people can make "to the existing situation." In one sense such a view is correct, provided one recognizes that the idea "best" is itself a cultural definition and varies, therefore, from culture to culture. Thus the "best adjustment" which a people "can" make depends on the ideas, knowledges, and values of the rest of their culture.

A tribe which tries to stop a typhoid epidemic by organizing large-scale witch hunts operates logically in terms of the culturally established fact that witches are responsible for disease. When we try to achieve the same end by inoculation and boiling drinking water we also are acting logically on the basis of our culturally established knowledge that disease is caused by bacteria. Most members of our society have never seen a germ, but they have been taught that germs exist and accept their existence without further proof. Our own not very remote ancestors would have found the witch hunt more logical than the inoculations.[1]

Frequently it is noted that the practices of some peoples involve consequences which jeopardize the health of members of the society. On the surface it would appear that it would be better if the practice were to be discontinued. The difficulty, however, is that the practice cannot be discontinued without doing violence to the basic values of the society. For example, it is well known that there are many ways of "making love," one of which is known as kissing. It is well known in our society that osculation spreads disease germs of many kinds, and, therefore, is clearly a menace to sound health. Knowledge of this fact, however, seems not to have resulted in the discontinuance of osculatory behavior. The conclusion is inescapable that even though kissing entails risk of infection with disease, the other values implicit in the behavior are regarded as important enough to justify the risk of infection. Is it, then, logical to say that kissing is the best adjustment to the existing conditions in American life?

Many other practices involve the principle that has just been illustrated. It seems better to say merely that practices are customary or habitual than that they can be objectively interpreted as the best adjustments. As will be discussed later, the origins of many practices are lost in antiquity. All that one knows is simply the observed fact that the practice exists, that it is not too poor an adjustment, because the group still exists, and that the practice usually seems more or less logical to the people in the social system in which it is found.

[1] Ralph Linton, *Cultural Background of Personality* (New York, Appleton-Century-Crofts, 1945), p. 102.

Summary: variability among cultures

The culturally approved and entrenched practices of the various societies are replete with variety, contrast, and antithesis. One is forced to the conclusion that man is so constituted biologically as to permit of highly varied modes of living, so varied that opposite practices can each meet his "needs" as an organism. It is also to be noted that each of these variant practices claims the loyalty of its practitioners, and thus may be regarded as satisfactory to them. Many persons are quick to observe, when commenting on alien customs, that "these people really don't know about other systems, because they are habituated to their own and do not get a chance to see others." What such superficial observation misses is that this identical logic could with equal justification be directed toward the practices of the observer's society! The view is sound enough, but not until one includes also his own cultural ways does he "get the point."

UNIFORMITIES AMONG CULTURES AND SOCIAL SYSTEMS

Variability, of course, is not the whole truth. While there are no universal cultural beliefs and practices in the strict sense of the word *universal*, there are numerous very widespread or near-universal practices and ideas. Thus, in order to complete our treatment of cultures, we must consider also those practices and ideas which stand out because they are so much more common. To illustrate this point, earlier it was noted that in some societies father-daughter marriages have been known to exist. While it is well to recognize this fact, one should not lose sight of the overwhelming fact that *as a rule* societies prohibit such marriages. The *incest taboo* (the prohibition of marriage to and/or sexual relations with persons of close blood relationship) is nearly universal, although there is considerable variation as to how close "close" is. Thus, for example, in some American states first-cousin marriage is prohibited because it is regarded as incestuous, while in other states it is permitted. Another near-universal, although apparently not nearly as universal as the incest taboo, is monogamy. Even though there are and have been numerous societies which have permitted or required polygyny, polyandry, and group marriage, closer observation reveals that among the rank and file of the people one spouse rather than multiple spouses has been the rule.

It would be impossible to catalogue here the many specific practices which show a high frequency among cultures. Such a list would be imposing. We shall, however, confine ourselves to a consideration of the more general similarities among the cultures of the world.

The main uniformities

Although, as we have seen, there is wide variability in the specific practices centering around sex, marriage, and the family, it is well also to note that every society has had *some* kind of a sex-marriage-family pattern. It is significant, then, first, that in no society is the individual free to do as he pleases, but instead must observe numerous taboos and other behavior requirements. Furthermore, every society which has survived has had some kind of formalized arrangements pertaining to the care of children by adults. (It is worth noting at this point, however, that there *may* have been societies in which adults did not protect children and, very possibly because they did not protect children, they failed to survive.)

On the basis of existing data it is possible to catalogue at least the following group of behavior *patterns* found in every known human society.

1. Language—not necessarily written language.
2. A sex-marriage-family system—widely variable as to details of content, but always present.
3. Age and sex differentiation, that is, a somewhat different, and often strikingly different, set of behaviors required of males and females and of persons of different ages.
4. Government functions—a generally recognized set of ideas and practices designed to handle disputes between persons or between groups and to make for cooperation to preserve the society from aggression.
5. Religion—a set of ideas and practices relating to the society's conceptions of the sacred.
6. Knowledges—a system of propositions regarded as true or correct, sometimes built up as a mythology, and sometimes by more or less scientific derivation.
7. Economic system—a set of beliefs and practices pertaining to making a living, property rights, and the relative importance of economic matters in the whole scheme of life.
8. Recreational or play activities—participation in certain activities for amusement.
9. Art—some kind of attempt to portray situations and create objects in nonutilitarian form.

It is to be noted carefully that the above list of *universal patterns* in culture is to be kept entirely distinct from the variabilities in the *content of culture*. For example, Germany, the United States of America, the natives of the New Hebrides, and the Roman Empire all have or had government, but in the rights of citizens, in the authority of rulers, and in the standards of justice, a long list of differences among these four societies could be made. Similarly, the family is universal, but one should always bear in mind that there are many specific content differences from society to society and from time to time.

REASONS FOR VARIABILITY

From days of antiquity, thinking men have speculated concerning the causes or reasons for the wide variety of cultural practices. Before social science developed it was fashionable to regard alien peoples as "bedeviled people" upon whom the wrath of God had been visited for some assumed sin. Their ways were frequently regarded as "perverted ways." They were "uncivilized," "savage," "barbarian," and certainly "backward." The naïveté implied in this mode of thinking is obvious, perhaps, to the person reading this book, but to many less-schooled (or differently schooled) contemporaries it still seems quite plausible.

Somewhat later in the development of interest in societies, a number of explanations of variability were advanced. These ideas still enjoy considerable respectability among some laymen. They will be discussed here and their fallacies pointed out, because the student will almost inevitably encounter them at some time or another.

Geographical environment is not a sufficient explanation

It is an obvious fact that geographical conditions vary throughout the world. It is not surprising, therefore, that uncritical people tried to explain variations in culture *solely* on the basis of variations in geography. It seemed an obvious explanation.

1. But one must be careful not to carry this explanation too far. In many societies people will be observed to be doing things which the conditions of their immediate environment would seem to prohibit. A Kentucky Colonel sipping his ice-cold lemonade on the Fourth of July is a case in point. Lemons do not grow naturally within hundreds of miles of the Colonel's veranda, and the ice would have to be made artificially at that time of year or preserved artificially from the preceding

winter. Thus, even though the environment would seem to preclude the ice-cold lemonade on the Fourth of July, the Colonel still goes on with his sipping. Throughout the world, man has for centuries been turning deserts into oases, forests into cornfields, swamps into truck gardens through the application of his scientific knowledge. Less and less is man dependent upon the *immediate* benefits of his natural environment. Tersely, but accurately, man modifies his geographical environment radically. Or, if one prefers to state the matter otherwise, man may use his geographical environment in such a way as radically to change its effects on him.

2. The chief difficulty, however, with regarding the geographical environment as a sole or sufficient explanation for cultural variability lies in another direction. The geographical environment always presents man with *alternatives*. As an example, let us consider the presence of snakes in some environment. If snakes are abundant in a given area, what does that fact *determine* so far as man's behavior is concerned? In one place or another man has been observed to make the following use of snakes: (*a*) man may eat the snakes; (*b*) man may make pets out of snakes as we do out of dogs, and therefore because of sentiment refuse to eat them; (*c*) man may worship the snakes; (*d*) man may largely ignore the snakes, as he often does. What, then, about a culture is determined because of this condition in the natural geographical environment? There are numerous cases in which vast natural resources, as they appear to us, remain largely or entirely ignored by the peoples of the area where the resources abound. To these people they are not resources at all. It is difficult, if not impossible, to find an inhabitable area in the world in which the environment does not present to man alternative usages of the elements which it contains. The geographical environment can never tell men what to *do* with them; that is always up to man.

3. Finally, it is to be noted that there are innumerable and important cultural practices which have no connection whatsoever with the natural environment. Questions of etiquette and morals are cases in point. History records a series of evolutions and revolutions in the cultures of Europe during the last few hundred years, during which period the seasons, temperature, rainfall, climate, topography, and native plants and animals of that part of the world have not changed. Obviously something else must constitute the explanation.

One should not assume from the foregoing paragraphs that the geographical environment has absolutely nothing to do with the specific content of culture. *The geographical environment, as we have pointed out, presents certain limitations and prohibitions to man as a culture builder. Although sometimes, to be sure, man circumvents these limitations by the application of his knowledge, some of them do persist.* Even when man modifies the existing geography of his area, he still must work within the limitations imposed by the natural order. But all of this is indeed a long way from explaining the vast variability among cultures which we have already observed.

Race is not an accurate explanation

"Race" is sometimes offered as an explanation of cultural variability. It is suggested that some races are "slower," or "less intelligent," or "temperamentally different," or possess "special skill," or have "different needs and interests." The evidence is entirely to the contrary. Three factual tests of this explanation can be made.

1. *The contemporary test.* Each of the three major races—White, Negro, Mongoloid—at the present time is found in a number of cultures showing wide variation. There are Negroes in Harlem slums and in the top-ranking professions in America, and there are several primitive Negro groups in Africa. Likewise with whites. Within the United States there are the "hillbilly whites" and "the poor white trash" of some areas in the South and the slum dwellers of "Blackboard Jungle" in the large Northern cities. They are all quite as "white" as are the members of the President's Cabinet. And so, also, there are wide cultural variations among the Mongoloids. *If* any one race were inherently different, then we should find the people of that race with a culture and society having distinct features. But, *in fact*, we do not find such.

2. *The historical test.* Furthermore, since "race traits" are inherited, race differences, if they are valid as an explanation of culture differences, would have to be consistent over long periods of time. If one race is different from others in 1955, it should also be in 1855 or in 1155 B.C. The evidence, again, shows that at one period of history some culture possessed by some one race is in the ascendancy, and at another period the culture of a different race is. Compare, for example, the white and the yellow races at about 4000 B.C. The yellow race in China had the world's most highly developed culture at that time. The white race at that time, and for a long time thereafter, was exceedingly primitive. We observe, also, that cultures rise and fall in their prestige and power positions in the world. Sometimes the cultures of one race are in the seemingly "higher" position, but other cultures of the same race at the same time are "lower." At a later time still another culture becomes

the "leader." If the theory of racial determination of culture were true, such oscillation would not be possible.

3. *The clinical-psychological test.* Finally, it is now possible to test representative samples of persons of various races in psychological laboratories to determine their relative intelligence, temperament, and special aptitudes. Such tests show conclusively that the commonly alleged wide differences among the races do not exist in fact. The several races are essentially the same, although not identical, in the mental endowments needed to make cultures. (Chapter 18 will treat the evidence in some detail.) Thus we see that the racial explanation of cultural variability is incorrect and must, *because of the evidence,* be discarded.

Why, then, do cultures vary?

At the present stage of our knowledge this question is not satisfactorily answerable, although certain data permit some tentative generalizations. Reviewing, we already have seen that:

1. Man's biological "needs" for food, sex activity, and protection *can* be "satisfied" in quite different ways.
2. The geographical environments differ.
3. Man invents new ways of doing and of thinking from time to time, that is, he is a problem-solving animal.

Here are the *raw materials of culture making and social action*—biological needs, the natural environment, and man's ingenuity. Thus, due to his constant inventiveness and reflective thinking, man strives always to have his interests and needs fulfilled. He has, here and there, somewhat different materials to work on, as provided by the natural environment. In one instance man comes out with behavior *A*—let us say, premarital chastity—as a "good policy." But in another instance man comes out with behavior *B*—which is premarital promiscuity—which for him in this situation also "works." Thus, we have two different—in fact opposite—cultural practices. Both fulfill needs; they *must* fulfill some needs or they could not exist.

Similarly with food. One man perhaps finds a fish accidentally thrown out of the water. He is hungry and eats it. His hunger is satisfied, and there are no bad after-effects. Fish eating is "in the culture" as soon as others take on his invention. Meanwhile in culture *B* no one "happens" on to a fish, but someone does experiment with snake eggs.

They meet the hunger needs, and snake-egg eating comes into culture *B*.

This trial-and-error process has sometimes been called "historical accident," and so it appears to be. Obviously, a large element of chance enters into the "choice" of practice *A* over practice *B*. Some students of behavior science have objected to the phrase "historical accident" because it is vague, and is really only a cover for our ignorance relative to *why* culture *A* invented fish eating and culture *B* invented egg eating when, theoretically, each had access to both fish and eggs. Eventually, we have reason to hope for a more precise explanation than the historical accident theory, but for the time being it is not possible to offer a much more accurate explanation. At least it cannot be attempted without going considerably beyond the evidence.

The history of science is replete with examples of scientific problems which were regarded as mere "chance outcomes" at one time, but which, after study, have been found to be causally determined and later predictable. It may be that, eventually, when more study has gone into analysis of the "historical accident" in culture building, we shall have a better answer to the question. But for the time being one must be content with some such statement as the following regarding culture variability: Within the limitations imposed by the geographical environment, man's problem-solving activities result in the selection of some behavior which meets his biological and psychological needs. This behavior may then become prevalent among the group and thus culturally established. Both the invention of the behavior and its acceptance depend on many interacting factors, most of which are themselves cultural. At the present stage of our knowledge of the factors involved, the outcome can rarely be predicted successfully. Negatively, we may say that neither race nor geography constitutes an acceptable explanation of most cultural variability because of the empiric (factual) tests which have been made and reported in the preceding paragraphs.

SUMMARY

This chapter has been devoted to an examination of the variations and uniformities among the cultures of the world. While there is great, in fact almost infinite, variation in the specific *content* of the various cultures, the overall *patterns* of culture possess notable uniformities. A number of these have been listed and briefly discussed.

Although it is difficult to establish the fact empirically, it appears probable that the uniformities stem from the inherent biological-psychological uniformities and/or needs of man as a species. Variations are somewhat more difficult to account for. The theological and other theories which in the past purported to explain cultural variability have now been superseded by two popular explanations that are completely untenable in the light of present knowledge but still hold many adherents. Neither the fact of race difference nor the fact of difference in the geographical environment can be accepted as a sufficient explanation for cultural variability. Both arise from false historical inference and inadequate factual evidence regarding man's cultural experience. Whereas it can be shown that the racial and the geographical explanations are both erroneous, it is not possible to substitute a wholly acceptable hypothesis in their place. Many social scientists use the "historical accident" explanation, but it is not entirely accurate because it implies that man is a more passive agent in culture formation than he in fact is.

SUGGESTED READINGS

Benedict, Ruth, *Patterns of Culture*. Boston, Houghton Mifflin, 1934.
This book is a classic. It contains abundant materials on the variations among cultures. Readable and accurate.

Casagrande, Joseph B., *In the Company of Man: Twenty Portraits by Anthropologists*. New York, Harper & Row, 1960.
"*In the Company of Man* is a collection of twenty nontechnical accounts of native informants, most of which are somewhat personal, thereby giving the reader not only a glimpse into the primitive culture, but also into the researcher-informant relationship." (Book review, *American Sociological Review*, Vol. 26 [August, 1961], p. 664.)

Folsom, J. K., *The Family and Democratic Society*. New York, Wiley, 1943, Chapters I, II.
This is a combination textbook and treatise on the family. Chapter I contains an interesting comparison of the American and the Trobriand Island family cultures. The comparison is made in parallel columns under a series of headings so that the reader can observe both the similarities and the differences under each subject, such as family rule, kinship arrangements, and so forth. Chapter II deals with similarities and differences among all family systems. The treatment of "limits to cultural variation" seems especially good.

Herskovitz, Melville, *Man and His Works*. New York, Knopf, 1948.
A good study of similarities among cultures. Done by a leading anthropologist.

Hollander, Paul, "Leisure as an American and Soviet Value." *Social Problems*, Vol. 14, No. 2 (Fall, 1966), pp. 179–188.

A discussion comparing leisure, the use of leisure, and concepts of leisure in Soviet and American societies. Has theoretical as well as descriptive relevance.

Kluckhohn, Clyde, and Leighton, Dorothea, *The Navaho*. Cambridge, Harvard University Press, 1946.
A classic study of the Navaho. This book is especially useful in showing the cultural variability of values and ethics. For example, "personal excellence is, then, a value, but personal 'success' in the white American sense is not." A good book for assisting the student to gain perspective on his culture.

Lewis, Oscàr, *The Children of Sanchez*. New York, Random House, 1961.
This book, consisting largely of autobiographical accounts of members of a Mexican family, gives a vivid, dramatic account of the deep implications of living in a particular culture and social system.

Murdock, G. P., "The Cross Cultural Survey." *American Sociological Review*, Vol. 5 (June, 1940), pp. 361–370.
A clear statement of the purposes and organization of the cross cultural survey —a monumental collection of data on cultures.

Nimkoff, M. F., ed., *Comparative Family Systems*. Boston, Houghton Mifflin, 1965.
A well-known sociologist of the family presents in this book an interesting and readable account of family systems in different parts of the world.

Parsons, Talcott, *Societies: Evolutionary and Comparative Perspectives*. Englewood Cliffs, N.J., Prentice-Hall, 1966.
This is a relatively high-level intellectual effort to look at society for the purpose of making comparisons—a challenging intellectual endeavor for the serious and more able student.

STUDY QUESTIONS

1. What are the similarities and differences among the three types of family rule?
2. Why is there no universally accepted "superior" governmental or religious or economic system? Illustrate.
3. What determines "the best adjustment" people make "to the existing situation"? Illustrate.
4. What general behavior patterns are found in every human society?
5. Why are these patterns *general* rather than specific?
6. How does the geographic environment limit, but not determine, cultural practices? Illustrate.
7. How does the biological nature of man limit, but not determine, culture? Illustrate.

8. How does the culture of a group limit, but not determine, cultural additions? Illustrate.
9. Why is race not a sound explanation for cultural variability? Explain with illustrations.
10. Why must a cultural practice fulfill a need in order to exist? What determines the "need"?
11. How do the three raw materials of culture-making permit cultural variability? Illustrate.
12. Criticize: "Cultural variability is inevitable for human kind."

7
ETHNOCENTRISM AND ITS IMPLICATIONS

Attention has already been drawn to the fact that the people of each society usually find it difficult, if not impossible, to think or act in ways other than those to which they have become habituated. Thus everyone tends to be "culture bound," although not all persons are bound in exactly the same way or to the same extent. The purpose of this chapter is to consider how the culture of a people limits its ability to think *objectively* and to act *realistically*.

ETHNOCENTRISM: A PROMINENT SOCIAL REALITY

Ethnocentrism defined

Ethnocentrism may be defined as *the tendency of persons to judge other cultures and actors in other social systems by the standards of judgment prevailing in their own*. When, for example, one has been reared in a society, such as ours, in which women are accorded social privileges comparable to those enjoyed by men, and in which great pride is taken in having "freed" women, it is difficult to observe another society in which women are accorded a different role without coming to the conclusion that the second society is not a "good" one. A person from the second society would probably come to the same negative conclusion about ours. A simpler but perhaps more terse illustration was suggested once by a school boy in whose community a foreign language-speaking family lived. Like most of his neighbors the boy was inclined to speak disparagingly of "these queer funny-talking people." When it was pointed out to him that, after all, language is only a medium for communicating ideas and that any language is about as good as any other after one has learned it, he listened politely as if he understood the explanation. He then dismissed the subject with the confident conclusion that "the trouble with foreign languages is that you can't say anything in them that makes any sense."

It is virtually inevitable that a person will use his familiar judgments and thoughtways when thinking about others. It is practically unavoidable, therefore, that persons tend to conclude that their cultural ways are the "best ways" of thinking and of doing. As a result, most persons come to regard other cultures with contempt and distrust. If one lives in a society in which people wear clothing, it is only natural to regard the people in a society which does not as "crude people" lacking somehow the "refinements" of "good taste." In America many people apparently feel that it is altogether proper for us to send missionaries all over the world to acquaint the people there with the religious, as well as many other, aspects of our culture. In fact many persons feel quite virtuous about such an undertaking, but would themselves oppose the efforts of other nations to instill their cultures here. Again, it is not uncommon to find somewhat sophisticated Americans amused if not disgusted by some of the unhygienic food habits of other peoples, it not somehow occurring to them that many of our own food habits are as dangerous, if not more dangerous, to sound health.

Conformity does not necessarily denote ethnocentrism

The fact that a person adheres to the modes of thought and action prevailing in his society does not in itself prove that he is ethnocentric. The underlying *reason* for his conformity is the important criterion. One may conform to the laws and customs of his society merely because it is more expedient to do so. A white may refuse to marry a Negro not because he necessarily regards Negroes as inferior, but simply because he realizes that a Negro-white marriage creates numerous and severe problems for the married pair and for their children. On the basis of *rational or realistic choice* he abstains from the Negro-white marriage.

"Loyalty," likewise, may or may not reflect ethnocentrism, depending upon its source. One may be loyal to some particular religion, school, or nation because after a careful objective examination of pertinent facts, he comes to the conclusion that that religion, school, or nation is the best for him. It should not be assumed, however, that such "rational loyalty" as we have just described is either common or easily attainable. It requires a high and uncommon degree of objectivity and a considerable amount of effort to attain even a measure of perspective on one's own culture. In a complete sense probably the goal is impossible to attain, but in a relative degree it can be approximated. It should at least be clear that not all loyalty is equally "blind." The member of the local "booster" club is not necessarily ignorant of the advantages of living in another town, but since he makes his living here, he can quite rationally concentrate upon the virtues of the local community for the sake of the benefits he might derive therefrom.

Ethnocentrism is largely inescapable

One should not dismiss lightly the patterns of thinking called ethnocentric. There is often the tendency among people unfamiliar with the ramifications of ethnocentrism in their own thinking to conclude that "broad-minded persons" like themselves, who strive to "free their minds of prejudice," are able to rise above such "narrow-minded attitudes" as these. The breadth or narrowness of one's "mind" is not, however, the point. Rather it is the knowledge and thinking *content of the mind* which determines the degree of ethnocentrism of a given person. The point is *not so much that a person is unwilling to think in terms of another cultural context, but that he is unable to.*

One says to a man, for example, "Put yourself in this woman's place." But can he? Can he know how this woman, as a woman, views many things? He may consider what she says about it, but there is so much at the same time which she cannot verbalize—in fact, the really basic values, the values ingrained in a person's existence by decades of living, are the hardest to verbalize. And even if these values and sentiments were accurately put into words, can the man interpret the words the way the woman means them? But this has been a relatively simple example.

Suppose we had said to a white man, "Put yourself in a Negro's position." Can he? Or, again, suppose you put yourself in the position of a cannibal. Can you imagine yourself in a cultural context of habits, sentiments, religion, joking, and so on, which might conceivably fit a cannibalistic pattern? In a very superficial way perhaps one could, but it would be indeed superficial. In the first place one of the most deep-seated ideas of our culture is a "respect for human life." So great is that respect that the practice of putting people to death is a very repulsive thought—except perhaps under the necessity of war or police action. Then, when eating the body of the victim is considered, innumerable other sentiments arise which one would be obliged, somehow, to neutralize before he could really understand the cannibalistic pattern. Cannibalism is, of course, of no great significance numerically or otherwise. We have used it as an illustration only. One would encounter the same difficulties in trying to understand any cultural pattern the values and practices of which are foreign to those of his own culture. Many have heard discussions between Catholics and Protestants regarding their religious thinking. So often each has occasion to say to the other, "But it isn't like that." Each recognizes that the other, however "open-minded" he may try to be, is not really able to participate even vicariously in the other's culture, because as he participates he does so as an outsider, using unconsciously the judgments, prejudices, and assumptions of his own cultural patterns, because he cannot escape them.

Ethnocentrism is taught

Almost everywhere there is evidence of this fact. Often, as one is taught "loyalty" to his community, his school, his social class, his country, or his religion, he is being taught to be ethnocentric about it. One is admonished in a half-hearted, conventional way to be "tolerant," but at the same time in innumerable ways he is being taught that tolerance toward certain other cultures constitutes "disloyalty" to his own. As one is taught the sufficiency of his own religion, his own country, his own social class, he is taught it in such a way that the others seem stupid, or inferior, or even dangerous. Frequently these teachings are couched in the most unctuous language and thinking. For example, "The Zulus are not necessarily bad; they are simply ignorant." After they have been educated—educated, that is, to accept *our prejudices* on matters—they can be as "good" as we are. One, therefore, would presumably have no prejudice against the Zulus—after they stop being Zulus, and think and act as we do.

Unconscious learning and teaching of ethnocentrism. Not only is ethnocentrism taught formally, much of it comes to the person through informal learnings. Note, for example, the ethnocentrism implied in the innumerable jokes which are supposed to demonstrate the penury of the Scotch, the business acumen of the Jew, and the ignorance of the "hillbilly." Seldom are these jokes told in a context which could be considered deliberately defamatory to these people or to their way of life. Instead they are told as jokes, *as if* for amusement only. They have the effect, however, of fixing certain ideas in the minds of people hearing and telling the stories. For example, the Scotch stories convey at least three notions: (1) that the Scotch are "tight" in money matters; (2) that being a Scotsman is per se evidence that a person is penurious; and (3) that it is not good to be penurious—one ought to be "like us." Not one of the above three has been proved factually. The first two could be empirically proved to be true or to be false, if someone took the trouble. The third is virtually indeterminable. There is no way in which one can determine, without prejudice due to the basic assumptions with which he approaches the problem, whether it is better to be penurious or somewhat more free with money. It is a matter of values. It all depends on what one has as his goal or objective, whether it is better to be thrifty or not. It is much like the age-old value issue, whether it is better to have loved and lost or never to have loved at all!

Movies, radio, and stage in modern society also reinforce our ethnocentrism and help to create it. Until very recently stage characterizations of Negroes, primitive peoples, and foreign peoples portrayed these minorities in such ways as to lead to the uncontestable conclusion that their ways were wrong, ridiculous, if not dangerous. Recently, more sympathetic presentations have become common, but most adults in American society developed their early, and often lasting, impressions from the earlier ethnocentric presentations. Again, as in the case of jokes, the intention to be ethnocentric was probably seldom deliberately planned, but the effect is the same as if it had been planned.

Deliberate teaching of ethnocentrism. In other instances ethnocentrism is deliberately taught through our strongest conformity-producing social institutions and agencies. Often such teaching is called "indoctrination." Many institutions in society have indoctrination as either their primary or incidental function. In the case of organizations for Americanization or for teaching religious doctrine, indoctrination is obvious enough. But in many other ways it occurs often in spite of our intentions. For example, it has become fashionable for American schools to disavow all indoctrination. Such a point of view may or may not be commendable, depending in part upon how ethnocentric one may be, but it is hardly attainable. If the schools did not indoctrinate with the thoughtways and the folkways, what, then, would they teach? Indoctrination is virtually inescapable in the course of teaching the child about his country, its literature, its history, its achievements, even its language per se which is replete with ethnocentric words and ideas. Although much has been achieved in recent years in the direction of less extremely and narrowly ethnocentric teaching of history in the public schools, it is easy to overemphasize the change. In studying about the Civil War a child in the North and a child in the South do not, somehow, get the same version. Nor does the English child read the same account of the American Revolution as the American child does. The tendency invariably is to interpret the facts so that they fit into the basic prejudice patterns of the society.

It is not to be assumed throughout this discussion that ethnocentrism is necessarily undesirable—or that it is desirable. It is our purpose to describe, not to evaluate. One is entitled as a citizen of a democracy quite as much to the view that it is right to be ethnocentric as he is to the view that ethnocentrism is a distorted view of the truth. Rather it is our purpose to find out as much as possible about the phenomenon of ethnocentrism, how and why it operates, and what its advantages and disadvantages to a society are.

Ignorance of a culture's sources aids ethnocentrism

The people of each society tend to regard their culture as their "own," as if all of the existing objects and ideas were invented by persons in that culture stream. Even among somewhat better informed persons, there is a tendency to minimize the culture's debt to other cultures. As a matter of historical *fact*, each culture contains a minimum of traits and patterns unique to it or actually invented by it. Instead, it is the rule for cultures to draw very heavily upon other cultures for their culture objects and ideas. If the whole truth were known to them, it would be difficult for intelligent people to be as ethnocentric as they tend to be. Somehow the unique contributions or inventions in a culture are played up, and the items borrowed or "stolen" from other cultures tend to be played down. As an illustration let us consider the following classic account of the cultural content of a "one hundred percent" American citizen. It is written as satire, but the point it makes is irrefutable. The author was a distinguished anthropologist and well acquainted with the facts which it contains.[1]

There can be no question about the average American's Americanism or his desire to preserve this precious heritage at all costs. Nevertheless, some insidious foreign ideas have already wormed their way into his civilization without his realizing what was going on. Thus dawn finds the unsuspecting patriot garbed in pajamas, a garment of East Indian origin; and lying in a bed built on a pattern which originated in either Persia or Asia Minor. He is muffled to the ears in un-American materials; cotton, first domesticated in India; linen, domesticated in the Near East; wool from an animal native to Asia Minor; or silk whose uses were first discovered by the Chinese. All these substances have been transformed into cloth by a method invented in Southwestern Asia. If the weather is cold enough he may even be sleeping under an eiderdown quilt invented in Scandinavia.

On awakening he glances at the clock, a medieval European invention, uses one potent Latin word in abbreviated form, rises in haste, and goes to

[1] Ralph Linton, "One Hundred Per Cent American," *The American Mercury*, Vol. 40 (April, 1937), pp. 427–429.

the bathroom. Here, if he stops to think about it, he must feel himself in the presence of a great American institution; he will have heard stories of both the quality and frequency of foreign plumbing and will know that in no other country does the average man perform his ablutions in the midst of such splendor. But the insidious foreign influence pursues him even here. Glass was invented by the ancient Egyptians, the use of glazed tiles for floors and walls in the Near East, porcelain in China, and the art of enameling on metal by Mediterranean artisans of the Bronze Age. Even his bathtub and toilet are but slightly modified copies of Roman originals. The only purely American contribution to the ensemble is the steam radiator.

In this bathroom the American washes with soap invented by the ancient Gauls. Next he cleans his teeth, a subversive European practice which did not invade America until the latter part of the eighteenth century. He then shaves, a masochistic rite first developed by the heathen priests of ancient Egypt and Sumer. The process is made less of a penance by the fact that his razor is of steel, an iron-carbon alloy discovered in either India or Turkestan. Lastly, he dries himself on a Turkish towel.

Returning to the bedroom, the unconscious victim of un-American practices removes his clothes from a chair, invented in the Near East, and proceeds to dress. He puts on close-fitting tailored garments whose form derives from the skin clothing of the ancient nomads of the Asiatic steppes and fastens them with buttons whose prototypes appeared in Europe at the close of the Stone Age. This costume is appropriate enough for outdoor exercise in a cold climate, but is quite unsuited to American summers, steam-heated houses, and Pullmans. Nevertheless, foreign ideas and habits hold the unfortunate man in thrall even when common sense tells him that the authentically American costume of gee string and moccasins would be far more comfortable. He puts on his feet stiff coverings made from hide prepared by a process invented in ancient Egypt and cut to a pattern which can be traced back to ancient Greece, and makes sure they are properly polished, also a Greek idea. Lastly, he ties about his neck a strip of bright-colored cloth which is a vestigial survival of the shoulder shawls worn by seventeenth-century Croats. He gives himself a final appraisal in the mirror, an old Mediterranean invention, and goes downstairs to breakfast.

Here a whole new series of foreign things confront him. His food and drink are placed before him in pottery vessels, the popular name of which —china—is sufficient evidence of their origin. His fork is a medieval Italian invention and his spoon a copy of a Roman original. He will usually begin the meal with coffee, an Abyssinian plant first discovered by the Arabs. The American is quite likely to need it to dispel the morning-after effects of over-indulgence in fermented drinks, invented in the Near East; or distilled ones, invented by the alchemists of medieval Europe. Whereas the Arabs took their coffee straight, he will probably sweeten it with sugar, discovered in India; and dilute it with cream, both the domestication of cattle and the technique of milking having originated in Asia Minor.

If our patriot is old-fashioned enough to adhere to the so-called American breakfast, his coffee will be accompanied by an orange, domesticated in the Mediterranean region, a cantaloupe domesticated in Persia, or grapes, domesticated in Asia Minor. He will follow this with a bowl of cereal made from grain domesticated in the Near East and prepared by methods also invented there. From this he will go on to waffles, a Scandinavian invention, with plenty of butter, originally a Near-Eastern cosmetic. As a side dish he may have the egg of a bird domesticated in Southeastern Asia or strips of the flesh of an animal domesticated in the same region, which have been salted and smoked by a process invented in Northern Europe.

Breakfast over, he places upon his head a molded piece of felt, invented by the nomads of Eastern Asia, and, if it looks like rain, puts on outer shoes of rubber, discovered by the ancient Mexicans, and takes an umbrella, invented in India. He then sprints for his train—the train, not the sprinting, being an English invention. At the station he pauses for a moment to buy a newspaper, paying for it with coins invented in ancient Lydia. Once on board he settles back to inhale the fumes of a cigarette invented in Mexico, or a cigar invented in Brazil. Meanwhile, he reads the news of the day, imprinted in characters invented by the ancient Semites by a process invented in Germany upon a material invented in China. As he scans the latest editorial pointing out the dire results to our institutions of accepting foreign ideas, he will not fail to thank a Hebrew God in an Indo-European language that he is a one hunderd per cent (decimal system invented by the Greeks) American (from Americus Vespucci, Italian geographer).

The last paragraph of the above quotation is very significant. It points out how the very *basic components* of the "American" way of life—language, religion, the number system, and so on—are really not American at all, except by importation and subsequent usage. It is true that each culture adds, subtracts, modifies these importations, but its basic debt to the other civilizations should not be overlooked, although it usually is.

Some reinforcements of ethnocentrism

At this point in our discussion the thoughtful student may quite properly wonder, if ethnocentrism is based so demonstrably on myth and illogic, why it persists, particularly among many educated people. The answer probably lies in some such generalization as the following: It is the nature of culture not only to provide meanings but also to provide reinforcements for these meanings through a depreciation of alternatives. Thus, for example, monogamy is not only "right" but polygamy is "immoral, unnatural, and even illogical." This amounts to a kind of double reinforcement. It has the effect of isolating the thought process from rational and objective consideration of alternatives.

Perhaps the student will grasp the virtual inescapability of ethnocentrism by a consideration of ways in which the ethnocentric stance operates in his own life and among his associates. We suggest that this can be done through the examination of a number of clichés which people habitually employ when the sufficiency of their particular thoughtways and folkways is challenged.

"But it's natural . . ."

One common belief is that one's own particular *modus operandi* or one's particular "way of looking at it" is more "natural" than some other. This implies that there is one basically correct way of doing or thinking which is inherent to man as man. All of the evidence points to the fallacy of this point of view. Virtually anything seems natural to one whose culture habituates him to it. It is "natural" for a cannibal to eat human flesh—but not for an American. It is "natural" for an Eskimo to get hungry for whale blubber—but not for you. It is "natural" for men in several different cultures to lend their wives to overnight guests as a demonstration of genuine hospitality—but not in the United States. What, then, does "natural" mean? It may refer to the acts and thoughts to which one becomes so thoroughly habituated that it is difficult, if not impossible, to conceive of any other proper or fitting way of acting or thinking. When the conditioning is complete enough, the person acquires the *illusion of inherency* of the act, that is, the notion that the act results not from mere habit, but from "the nature of things." Here lies the error, but it is a persistent error.

Perhaps the best test to apply in a specific case where "naturalness" is in question is the *test of universality*. Do all peoples, regardless of the culture in which they live, do or think or feel in the manner in question? If the answer is found—*found, not assumed*—to be "yes," then it seems scientifically justifiable to consider the behavior inherent and not culturally habituated. If, on the other hand, one people behaves in one way and another in another way, then if we call either's mode of behavior "natural" we must recognize that we mean natural *by habituation*—not inherently.

"But it's logical . . ."

Here again, as with the notion of naturalness, one may easily be ethnocentric without knowing it. The error again lies in the assumption that there is only one correct logical conclusion which can be drawn from given conditions. On the contrary there are several, perhaps innumerable, conclusions which can be reached logically from given conditions. Logicalness always depends upon the amount and kind of other knowledge which one possesses at the time he draws his conclusions. It also depends on what might be called "basic assumptions." For example, if one starts with the idea that the universe was the work of some purposive Being, then it seems logical to ascribe its normal workings and its irregularities to that Being's wishes or intents. The storm struck here instead of there because this Being wanted for some reason or other to have it so. On the other hand, if one begins with the assumption that the universe is not the creation of a purposive Being, then the above storm's explanation is not only not logical but ridiculous. Again, if one assumes that the earth is flat, then it follows logically that he should not go out near the edge so that he will not fall off, an explanation common in Columbus' time.

The point to note is that *logic is itself a cultural creation or invention.* Logic is a mode of thinking about certain items in the universe in an orderly fashion. The logic invented, or modified, by one culture is, therefore, not necessarily, or likely, to be exactly like that of the second culture. Science is one logic. Religion is another logic. Mathematics is a logic with a formal language of its own. Each is quite logical—but each is different.

It is also noteworthy that logic is used often as a mode of buttressing or "proving" some way of thinking after one has by nonlogical methods come to accept it. In this way logic may come to be used as a kind of formalized "sales talk" for some point of view. One cannot fail to have noted that opposite ideas or programs are both more or less logically supported by their proponents and more or less logically attacked by their opponents. Logic supports the Catholic faith and the Protestant faith and the non-Christian faiths; logic supports the Republican party platform and the Democratic platform. But *which* logic?

"But it's abnormal . . ."

What makes an act or an idea normal? Would it be regarded as normal if one of your classmates were to claim that he had had another life on earth before this one, that he had been a cat, or a goldfish in Mr. Vanderbilt's aquarium the first time? Surely, the student's mental faculties would be questioned. "A normal person would not believe that." A normal person *in this culture* and *at this time* would *usually* not accept such an interpretation of himself. But, again, there are cultures in which such an explanation would seem altogether plausible, if not obvious, to the people. There the "abnormal" person would be one who did not accept the idea. Thus, we see "normality" is essentially of the same cultural origin as the logical or the natural, and "abnormal" labels the act or idea or person which is out of the ordinary, too different to be acceptable. Obviously, what is regarded as normal or abnormal varies from culture to culture and from time to time in the same culture. It is certainly not abnormal for a woman to smoke, wear cosmetics, and dress in slacks at the present time, but not long ago any one of these behaviors would have rendered her not only abnormal but criminally so.

"But it's immoral . . ."

Morality, again, is a cultural definition as we have already seen in the chapter on cultural variability. History is replete with examples of acts and their opposites, ideas and their antitheses, which are both regarded as moral by the standards of valuation of two contemporary or successive cultures. It would be immoral to hold a Negro in slavery today in the United States, but one hundred years ago it was not so. Some people regard birth control as immoral, but others regard it as immoral to refrain from limitation of offspring.

Summary

In summary, we see that logicalness, like naturalness, is a mode of thinking which one derives from the cultural stream in which he functions. It is common to find persons resorting to the "it's natural" or "it's logical" mode of thought as a means of justifying their particular prejudice-system. These words are often used because in our culture "logic" and "nature" have become "virtue words." If something can be made to appear "natural," that is, inherent in the assumed scheme of things and not alterable by man, it takes on a certain authority and finality. Likewise, if some act or idea can be made to appear reasonable or logical, its authority and respectability are accordingly enhanced. Both of the ideas, logical and natural, are useful, but the problem arises out of their misuse, or at least their vulgarization, by persons who understand their implications incompletely, or have an insufficient knowledge of the facts and other data in the fields to which the terms are properly applied.

AN IMPORTANT RESEARCH

So far we have treated ethnocentrism in purely descriptive terms. We now turn our attention to the question of whether ethnocentrism can be measured and also to what more can be learned about it from attempts to measure it.

Adorno and his associates [2] constructed a scale to measure ethnocentrism which has received a great deal of attention. The techniques involved in making a scale to measure attitudes are much more complicated than they appear to be. Those students who go on to advanced work in statistics will eventually become familiar with the rather complicated mathematics and other logic involved in scale construction. All that we can say here is that Adorno's scale to measure ethnocentrism represents a sophisticated effort and that it is highly regarded by many students of psychology, sociology, and anthropology. This does not mean that it would not be possible to find critics of Adorno's methods. We shall present the findings, then, as those of a widely known and respected research, but not with the implication either that they are infallible or that someone else may not later come up with a better method for measuring ethnocentrism.

The first Ethnocentrism Scale consisted of 34 items,[3] on each of which an individual was to register an attitude. The 34 items fell into three subgroups or subscales: (1) attitudes regarding Negro-white relations; (2) attitudes toward minority groups, such as foreigners, political parties, religious and other minority groups; and (3) attitudes about patriotism, including the view that other nations are inferior and ought to be held subordinate to the United States, particularly when they hold values different from ours. A few of the items from the questionnaire follow: [4]

6. Any group or social movement which contains many foreigners should be watched with suspicion and, whenever possible, be investigated by the F.B.I.

12. The main threat to basic American institutions during this century has come from the infiltration of foreign ideas, doctrines, and agitators.

13. Present treatment of conscientious objectors, draft-evaders, and enemy aliens is too lenient and mollycoddling. If a person won't fight for his country, he deserves a lot worse than just prison or a work camp.

25. An occasional lynching in the South is a good thing because there is a large percentage of Negroes in many communities and they need a scare once in a while to prevent them from starting riots and disturbances.

[2] See the classic study by T. W. Adorno and others, *The Authoritarian Personality* (New York, Harper & Row, 1950), Part I, esp. Chaps. IV-VIII.

[3] Subsequent scales reduced this number to a final scale of only 20 items. *Ibid.*, p. 142.

[4] *Ibid.*, pp. 110–111.

Each informant was requested to mark each item in one of six ways in accordance with his views:

> strong agreement
> moderate agreement
> slight agreement
>   or
> strong opposition
> moderate opposition
> slight opposition

What did Adorno and his associates discover, then, when they thus measured ethnocentrism among Americans? Perhaps the first and most important finding is that ethnocentrism in one area of life tends to be accompanied by ethnocentrism in others, that is, if a person is ethnocentric about the white race, for example, he is also likely to be ethnocentric about his country and to be hostile toward minority groups within his country.

A second finding from this study is that even within a society which presumably exposes individuals to a more or less general pattern of culture, persons vary radically in the degree to which they are ethnocentric. One might assume a priori that all of the people growing up in a society would be equally ethnocentric about that society, since all have been exposed to the same kind of teachings. Apparently, however, such is not the case, since there is a *wide difference* in the degree to which various people are ethnocentric as measured by this scale.

A third finding is more technical, but may be the most important part of the whole study, namely, that high degrees of ethnocentrism seem to be found chiefly among persons of certain "personality types." More specifically, the most ethnocentric people are the ones who (1) are also "projective," that is, blame other people for their own difficulties, rather than more rationally trying to figure out their own responsibilities in the matter, and (2) are also against analyzing their own beliefs and feelings very deeply. At the risk of oversimplification, the study comes very close to concluding that the kinds of people who think that psychology (and sociology and anthropology) is "a waste of time" or "dangerous" are the kinds of people likely to be most ethnocentric. (3) Finally, the study concludes that persons whose approach to life is "authoritarian" (in contrast to "democratic") are the most ethnocentric.[5]

[5] There are many more findings in this study. We have discussed only those which have relevance to ethnocentrism.

The student is cautioned here, as elsewhere, against taking one study as completely conclusive. Even though the study is done very carefully by a technically competent group of people, there is still much that we do not know about ethnocentrism. An equally important caution, however, should be pointed in the other direction, namely, not to discount such findings as these, simply because they may prove to be personally unpalatable.

ADVANTAGES OF ETHNOCENTRISM
TO CULTURAL STABILITY

The word *advantage* in the above heading requires comment. "Advantage" is meaningless unless it is specified "for whom" or "for what" it is advantageous. In this section we shall consider the effect of ethnocentrism on the *preservation of* the existing culture of a society. Whether such preservation be desirable or not is quite another matter, but outside the scope of this discussion.

Ethnocentric thinking reduces or even
prevents criticism of the status quo

Insofar, however, as ethnocentric thinking occurs, it has the effect of strengthening the *status quo*. If, for example, one's religion is the "only true religion revealed to man by God," then there is not only no good reason to consider another religion, but every reason to shun and ridicule the others. If capitalism is the only really good and workable economic system, then one need have no concern about its being replaced by another, because no other system will be found to be good enough. On the other hand, other religions and other economic systems do "creep in" in places where ethnocentrism is insufficiently strong to prevent a consideration of the possible merits of other systems.

The term *subversion* has in recent times in the United States come to mean, to many people, any nonprejudicial learning about culture other than one's own. Derogation of other cultures is permitted; open-minded and objective consideration is per se suspect. The opportunity to learn new modes is thus sharply curtailed.

One is not to assume, of course, that the only factor resisting change is ethnocentrism; obviously there are many others, but ethnocentrism is certainly one of them. The observer's ethnocentric thinking must in some way be weakened or reduced or destroyed, before the existing scheme of things can be successfully evaluated.

Loyalty to one's society

Groups are often "strong" in proportion to the "loyalty" which their members give them. Insofar, therefore, as a society is able to maintain the ethnocentrism of its members, that is, can keep the members believing that the purposes and functions of that society are right, good, and desirable, that group is more secure. There is less danger of its going out of existence due to its members' apathy. A nation at war is a case in point. To the extent that the people of a nation agree that their cause is a just one, they will cooperate in fighting the war, even at great personal danger or loss of property. Their nation may, of course, actually lose the war, but the point is that their chances of winning are greatly enhanced by loyalty and that their loyalty is greater if their ethnocentrism is more deeply entrenched. On both sides in World War II, millions of men died, each believing that he was fighting for the perpetuation of a culture which was "right." Both sides believed that they were obliged to fight the opposing society, that they were involved in a righteous attempt to "protect" themselves.

Ethnocentrism may increase uniformity within the society

To the extent that one does not question the logic of the prevailing thoughtways, he is in harmony with them. And to the extent that a society can indoctrinate sufficient numbers of persons in the same way, its conflicts within itself tend to be reduced. There are thoughtful people today who believe that the chief problem of America as a nation is the diversity which one finds in the values of different classes, races, creeds, and religions. The multiplicity of value systems, it is argued, makes for no real meeting of minds, even when persons actually meet to talk things over, because there is no common basis of agreement which all can take as a point of departure for discussion. Whether this is a correct diagnosis of the problems of American culture or not, we shall discuss at a later point in this book. The proponents of this point of view, however, are probably correct when they point out that to the extent that we have common prejudices, that is, are ethnocentric with respect to the same social system, the resulting uniformity makes for a smoother functioning of the society.

On the other hand, when ethnocentric ideas and practices are directed toward subgroups in the society, such as radical or religious minorities, the effect is to weaken the larger society by fragmentizing loyalties, dissipating energies, and magnifying differences.

Summary

Ethnocentrism, measuring the worth of all things in terms of the standards of value of the existing culture, is, of course, circular thinking. The person gets indoctrinated with a set of values, Catholic or Protestant, Republican or Democratic, Christian or non-Christian, capitalist or communist, and thereafter judges other cultural streams in terms of the already indoctrinated ideas. It is not surprising, then, that he usually concludes that his ways are the best ways.

In this section we have seen how ethnocentrism helps to keep a culture from changing, by reducing or eliminating some of the criticism and discouraging really objective thinking about the culture. The more thoroughly ethnocentric person is likely to be more loyal when the society needs loyalty from him, Ethnocentric thinking, because it works against the indoctrination of new ideas and ways, makes for uniformity and temporary stability of the culture. Meanwhile the ethnocentric person receives certain measures of contentment and satisfaction from his confident acceptance of the all-sufficiency of his scheme of things, either because he is actually convinced that his culture benefits him or because he identifies himself with it in ways which he cannot or does not wish to measure selfishly. The net result of the operation of these and other influences is to make for a more closely-knit and integrated society. In the sense that such conditions make for a permanent and strong group organization, ethnocentrism may be said to be an advantage to the perpetuation of the group and of its culture. But there are also disadvantages of ethnocentrism to the group, and we now turn to a consideration of some of them.

DISADVANTAGES OF ETHNOCENTRISM

Ethnocentrism also has its negative aspects from the point of view of cultural preservation. No society lives in a vacuum; instead it lives among other societies, and the conditions of its existence are determined in no small part by what goes on in the other societies. A more ethnocentric society, while it has advantages through the blind loyalty of its members and through its refusal to accept disorganizing changes in its culture, faces certain disadvantages, especially in relation to other societies. For example, Nazi Germany and prewar Japan constituted two of the most ethnocentric large modern nations. In neither case did their ethnocentrism save them. At best we might say that their ethnocentrism put off the day of their defeat. In other respects it can be shown that their ethnocentrism may have been largely responsible for getting them into the conflicts as a result of which they were defeated. Although it is not altogether clear in the case of these two nations that their ethnocentrism was the determining factor or even the major factor in this chapter of their history, certainly it was a contributing factor.

Ethnocentrism hinders intersystem cooperation

Frequently societies, like persons, get along better with others, whether in competition or not, when they understand each other, respect each other, and in general can work together. Frequently societies may find it to their greater advantage to work together in order to attain mutually advantageous objectives. The overly ethnocentric society or group often finds that its ethnocentrism stands in the way and prevents or reduces the understanding necessary to work in harmony. Loyalty or patriotism may be so intense that essential cooperation between societies becomes difficult.

Future relations between America and Russia are an important case in point. About fifty years ago, when Russia overthrew capitalism by revolution, capitalistic peoples like ourselves became uneasy lest the communistic experiment in Russia should work. Many influential persons in America, however, not only hoped communism would fail, but were confident that it would. During the 1920's it was fashionable to debate the number of years it would take for the communistic experiment to fail, as if the *fact* of failure were a foregone conclusion. The experiment did not fail. Anti-Russian feelings ran high again just prior to World War II when Russia seemed to be casting her lot with the Nazis in Germany. This further intensified the suspicion and hatred of the Russian "scheme." When Russia finally entered the war on the side of the Allies, many were actually only half-hearted about her assistance. They regarded her as a somewhat impotent nation, large to be sure, but not a very decisive force, because her economic system was so backward as compared with ours. When Russia began giving a rather convincing account of herself in both an economic and military way, the ethnocentrism of millions of Americans concerning this "impossible Russian experiment" received a jolt. Here this "impotent, backward, ignorant people," without the spur of private property and profit, had become a powerful nation. Instead of ridiculing Russia, many came to fear her. International tension is frequently great between Russia and the Anglo-American bloc in the United Nations.

Relations between that nation and ours will probably continue to be strained as a result of the fears, ill-feelings, and misunderstanding which have been built up on both sides for so many years. It is not to be assumed that cooperation between Russia and the United States will be impossible in the future, but rather that it will be made more difficult than it needs to be by the strong ethnocentric beliefs common among both peoples.

Ethnocentrism hinders assimilation

The process of absorption of persons or groups of one culture into a larger group of different culture is called *assimilation*. One of the chief characteristics of the United States of the nineteenth and early twentieth centuries was the assimilation of millions of Europeans of various cultures into the American society. In the long run, assimilation is virtually inevitable, but the length of the run may be appreciably shortened if the members of each group are not too ethnocentric in their appraisals of the other group's culture. Two conditions made the Americanization of the European immigrant difficult. First, and proba-bly chiefly, the native American usually had no real appreciation of the culture which the immigrant brought with him. The immigrant was treated by most "Americanization" organizations as if he had "no real culture" at all before coming here. Insofar as there was superficial recognition of the culture with which he came, the incoming culture was regarded as an unpleasant and unfortunate perversion which had to be destroyed at the earliest possible moment. Partly as a result of the prevailing native attitude, but also as a result of ethnocentrism of the Europeans themselves, the immigrants frequently resisted assimilation by America as long as they could. They organized clubs, lodges, and even political groups; they sponsored foreign-language newspapers and sent their children to foreign-language schools. They tried to impose the foreign ways and ideas upon their children, who thus were torn between the American ways and the ways they were taught at home. The result was a great deal of conflict between parents and children of the second generation and a disproportionate amount of delinquency and crime in the second generation. This latter fact was seized upon by the "one-hundred-percenters" as evidence that immigration was a mis-take, that these foreigners were really inferior people anyway and should be kept in an inferior social position. Thus the ethnocentrism of both sides aggravated a difficult situation, caused a great deal of unhap-piness in both groups, and prolonged the solution of the problem for many years unnecessarily.

It is also thought by many persons that cooperative action between religious groups in America could be facilitated greatly if there were less ethnocentrism in this phase of modern culture. The situation frequently arises that two (or more) organizations really wish to accomplish an objective upon which their leaders agree, but the folk in the rank and file of both groups find it so completely impossible to acknowledge that any good thing could possibly come out of the other camp with its altogether mistaken ideas that the official agreements are not translated into action as was originally planned. Eventually, probably, some degree of assimilation will take place, but ethnocentrism will prolong the process and present many obstacles along the way.

SUMMARY

In this chapter attention has been drawn to the phenomenon called *ethnocentrism*. It has been shown that ethnocentrism is virtually universal among humans, and that it varies in degree and form among different cultures and among the different persons in a given society as well. The essence of ethnocentrism is evaluation—judging the worth of other ways of doing and other ways of thinking in terms of the values with which one has become indoctrinated by his own cultural experience. It results in prejudicial language and overt behaviors taking such organizational forms as the missionary movement, wars, and educational and religious indoctrination. Ethnocentrism has both advantages and disadvantages to the society as a result of its tendency to insulate the thoughts and ways of the people from the thoughts and ways of other peoples. The ability to recognize and analyze ethnocentrism is a basic professional prerequisite of the sociologist and also of the successful student of sociology.

SUGGESTED READINGS

Adorno, T. W., and others, *The Authoritarian Personality*. New York, Harper & Row, 1951, Part I, esp. Chapters IV–VIII.
A highly respected research in which ethnocentrism is measured and its relationship to personality factors demonstrated statistically.

Catton, William R. Jr., "The Functions and Disfunctions of Ethnocentrism: A Theory." *Social Problems*, Vol. 8 (Winter, 1960–61), pp. 201–211.
This is a sophisticated treatment of ethnocentrism which pursues a number of

the functions and dysfunctions which are discussed in this chapter. It also relates the theory to a number of happenings in recent history.

Fulbright, J. William, "The First Fifteen Years of the Fulbright Program." *Annals of the American Academy of Political and Social Science*, Vol. 335 (May, 1961), pp. 21–27.
This is an appraisal of the Fulbright Program for cultural interchange among nations written by Senator Fulbright, who fathered the idea. Discusses a number of problems involved in the interchange of educated personnel.

Hoffer, Eric, *The True Believer*. New York, New American Library, 1958.
This is an exceedingly well-known book in which the author, not a sociologist, presents an essentially macro-sociological analysis of extreme ethnocentrism and its consequences. Highly readable.

Kassof, Allen, "The Prejudiced Personality: A Cross-Cultural Test." *Social Problems*, Vol. 6 (Summer, 1958), pp. 59–67.
This is one of a very few studies of prejudice outside of samples taken from American society. The subjects were former citizens of the Soviet Ukraine.

Palmore, Erdman B., "Ethnophaulisms and Ethnocentrism." *American Journal of Sociology*, Vol. 67 (January, 1962), pp. 442–445.
This is a discussion of derogatory racial and ethnic nicknames as they appear in the *Dictionary of American Slang*. It shows how these ethnophaulisms support ethnocentrism, chauvinism, and discriminatory practices.

Rokeach, Milton, *The Open and Closed Mind: Investigations into the Nature of Belief Systems and Personality Systems*. New York, Basic Books, 1960.
This book is in the tradition of Adorno and others who have attempted better to understand how belief systems and other aspects of personality are interrelated. The book is not only on an important topic, but as one reviewer said, "is rich in theory, ideas, . . . and data. In sum, it is a book of rare excellence."

STUDY QUESTIONS

1. Why do people tend to judge other cultures by the standards of their own?
2. Why do Americans send missionaries to foreign countries?
3. Why is a person unable to think in terms of another cultural context? Illustrate.
4. How does society "teach" people to be ethnocentric? Illustrate with examples of unconscious fostering of ethnocentrism.
5. What is the relation between prejudice and enlightenment? Is either any more "cultural" than the other?

6. Why is the term *pure American culture* a myth?
7. Why is ethnocentrism a relative term? In what ways is it relative?
8. How does ethnocentrism tend to produce cultural stability?
9. What is the relation between ethnocentrism and "nationalism"?
10. Are local "boosters' clubs" ethnocentric? Or only "rationally loyal"?
11. How has ethnocentrism created majority-minority problems in the United States?
12. Why does the sociologist need to be able to "objectify" ethnocentrism? Illustrate.
13. How is ethnocentrism "a system of evaluation"? Illustrate.
14. Do you think that Adorno's attempt to measure ethnocentrism adds materially to one's understanding of this phenomenon? Why and/or why not?

8
CULTURAL
AND SOCIAL
CHANGE

A TIME PERSPECTIVE ON MODERN CULTURE AND SOCIETY

Culture origins largely an enigma

There is no scientific knowledge as to *precisely* when, where, or how man first began to create culture. The quest for knowledge about culture origins, however, has preoccupied many scholars' time and energies for centuries. Not all of the scholars were scientists; many were theologians or philosophers, and some of them have created "explanations," "theories," or sheer guesses. None of these explanations can, however, stand the test of empiric examination, because the prehistoric past is veiled in such obscurity. The problem persists largely because of the almost inconceivable antiquity of man's original activities in culture creation.

Science is not, however, entirely devoid of reliable information on some aspects of the genesis of human culture. While many facts about man's remote past have been lost, not all of the evidence from the earliest cultures has. Certain items of early material culture which did not decompose, such as stone tools, pottery, some paintings on the interior of caves, and other artifacts are present even today and can be observed and handled. The early nonmaterial culture, on the other hand, cannot be reconstructed, because prior to the appearance of writing and art, there is no tangible evidence of how the people lived, what they thought about, or why they happened on one invention instead of another.

The dangers of faulty inference from accurate factual data

We can, however, derive certain *inferences* concerning the folkways of some prehistoric peoples. If, for example, a people's skeletal remains are found in proximity with one another, accompanied by apparently valuable items like jewelry and placed in a characteristic position, it would seem reasonable to assume that these people buried their dead instead of simply abandoning the corpses. Again, if the people left paintings showing campfire scenes and men riding astride horses, one might infer that horse riding and campfire fraternization were among their folkways. Caution must be observed, however, not to assume too much from such inferential "evidence." From the above illustrations regarding primitive drawings of men riding horses, one still does not know whether to conclude that these people rode horses for pleasure or economic reasons or both; whether horseback riding gave a man higher or lower status than did some other form of locomotion; whether the horses were used solely for riding or only incidentally for riding, their chief function possibly being to provide meat or milk. For that matter we do not even know whether the horses were kept for utilitarian reasons or were regarded as sacred beasts like the sacred cattle of India. Thus, great caution must be observed in drawing inferences concerning a people's *habits* from the mere fact that a given artifact (material culture object) was possessed by or known to them. The even more significant question, namely, what did it *mean* to them, is almost impossible to determine from material remains alone. Prior to the preservation of writings, and to some extent even after that, this vital information has not been available.

Some inferences from known human history and archaeology

Anthropologists have, nevertheless, secured some sufficiently reliable information regarding human cultural beginnings and early development to permit one to piece together an approximate—but *very* approximate—chronology of some of man's early cultural evolution.

The earliest traces of culture are regarded by archaeological authorities to have appeared about a million years B.C. Translating such a time span into units which are more familiar, a million years is five hundred times as long as the period which has elapsed since the birth of Christ, or more than six thousand times as long as the period since the American Constitution was written.

The artifacts from these early cultures are, of course, quite crude. They consist of chipped stone tools, probably used by the people of that time for chopping or hewing. There is little evidence that for the next half million years, almost half the way up to the present time, much change in man's production of artifacts occurred. It seems probable, however, that nonmaterial culture could and did change during this tremendous era, but we have no artifacts or other definitive evidence to prove it.

By around 100,000 B.C. stone tools were supplemented by tools made of bone, and some tools showed technical work which was becoming increasingly precise. Noteworthy, perhaps, is the fact that tools which were made apparently around 100,000 B.C. were decorated with carvings and other evidences of nonutilitarian workmanship and interest.

From about 75,000 to 14,000 B.C. culture seems to have developed more rapidly. Specifically, for example, there is evidence that by around 14,000 B.C. men began to bury their dead, live in cave communities, use wood for tools in addition to bone and stone, and draw and paint recognizable images. By 10,000 B.C. human culture contained numerous material and nonmaterial elements familiar to us, such as agriculture, domestic animals, and pottery.

Several cautions should be observed by the student in thinking about the above data. (1) The dates are *very* approximate. It is not difficult to find two or more archaeologists of comparable ability and training whose judgment differs by several thousand years concerning the age of some item. While the sequence is roughly as we have indicated, the transition dates, that is, the dates chosen to mark the end of one period and the beginning of the next, are very arbitrarily chosen and can be justified only by convenience. (2) Many of the data are inferential, that is, our "facts" are often deductions from other facts and may be faulty, particularly when artifacts are used as the basis for determining the behavior of the people, as mentioned in preceding paragraphs. When one speculates concerning what this or that practice "meant" to this or that people, and "why" they behaved as they did, he is treading on very thin academic ice. (3) Development was *very* slow. A period like the span of years between the discovery of America and the present would be a mere moment in the history of civilization. The rapid change which characterizes modern life is something exceedingly new in human experience. Throughout most of man's existence the amount of culture change from generation to generation was almost imperceptible. (4) European civilization (and modern America, also, since it is an offshoot of the European) was one of the last major cultures to develop. The Near Eastern, the Oriental, and the Mediterranean cultures were well advanced while the Europeans were still primitive. The Chinese, for example, were living in palaces and the Egyptians had bronze plumbing at the time our European ancestors were wearing bearskins, eating raw meat, and living in crude huts.

SOME PRINCIPLES REGARDING CULTURAL CHANGE

Selective addition and loss of traits, not simple "accumulation"

One of the persistent errors in much thinking about culture change is the notion that man's culture "just accumulated," as if it were like the proverbial snowball rolling downhill, gaining size with each revolution, picking up virtually everything with which it came in contact, gathering momentum as it rolled, and guided by no purpose except the laws of the physical universe. Although culture does tend to accumulate new traits and patterns from time to time, it also loses such elements. Culture loses traits in several ways. Sometimes a people discards a culture trait because it has found something "better" to take the place of the outmoded trait. We are not concerned here with the important question of whether the new trait is "really better" than the old one or *why* it is better, but simply with the fact that under existing conditions the people whose prerogative it is to make the choice, either consciously or unconsciously choose to employ folkway *A* instead of folkway *B*, or artifact *A* instead of artifact *B*. The result is that down through time there are numerous instances of culture losing elements.

The additions to culture are not random, but are what is usually called "selective." As a rule there are numerous alternatives or choices. In the area of religion, for example, a people have an almost infinite range of phenomena which they may worship. To one culture it seems "fitting and logical" that people worship the moon, to another group it seems equally fitting and logical that they venerate ancestors, and to a third it seems fitting and logical to worship nothing at all. Adding or discarding a culture trait stems not so much from the mere *availability* of the trait as from the *relationship between the trait and the rest of the culture* into which it may or may not ultimately be absorbed.

Culture is, then, a unity: its various parts, while they need not fit perfectly together, need in some measure to be consistent, or at least need to *seem* to be consistent with one another. On the basis of this "strain for consistency," the selective adding and discarding of culture traits takes place down through time.

Great men and cultural change: a stubborn myth

One of the persistent errors in thinking about culture development is the overemphasis upon the influence of a few great men as inventors or innovators in culture. This is a gross oversimplification and leads to a recurring and serious error when one attributes some invention solely to "the work of this great man." It is well to consider the *other factors* which account for both the inventor himself and the incorporation of the invention into the culture.

1. *Few, if any, inventors ever created anything wholly new.* The inventor of the automobile, for example, only combined the four-wheel carriage and the internal combustion engine, both of which had been in existence for some time. The inventor of the carriage simply combined two of the two-wheel carts which were in existence before the four-wheel carriage. In other words, each inventor draws on the accumulated cultural storehouse of objects and ideas which are given to him by the persons and groups which came before him.

The same principle is operative in nonmaterial invention, that is, innovations in the folkways and thoughtways, the mores and laws of a society. The writers of the American Constitution, for example, did not start from scratch. Practically all of the ideas embodied in the American Constitution are to be found in the writings of the political philosophers in Europe for many years prior to the American Revolution. These ideas were known to many among the intelligentsia of America. The American Constitution was new, to be sure, but new only in the sense that it consisted of a selection and integration of these radical political ideas from Europe and of the governmental experiments and experiences of America itself. In short, the Constitutional Convention of 1787 chose *from among the available ideas* about government, integrated their choices, and the result was the American Constitution.

The atomic bomb looked like a miracle to the man on the street, but the principles of atomic energy were common classroom discussions in courses in physics in American universities for years. The atomic bomb inventors did create something new, but in the making of it were privileged to draw upon the accumulated knowledge and experimentation of generations of scientists and engineers, without whose knowledge no atomic bomb could possibly have been achieved in our time.

2. The inventor's *invention must be accepted by the society* before it can become a vital part of any people's existence. It is customary to refer to "men ahead of their times." This expression embodies an important principle pertaining to invention, namely, that the final determination of whether an invention will have acceptance lies not so much in the nature of the invention as in the conditions affecting its acceptance or rejection. The "greatness," as well as the mere appropriateness,

of an invention usually stems from the extent of its subsequent adoption and is frequently determined not so much by the intrinsic qualities of the invention itself as from how the invention is accepted and used.

3. Since inventions must draw upon preceding knowledges and techniques and must depend upon popularity for their eventual appraisal, they *can often be anticipated before they actually occur*. Moreover, there have been numerous instances in which the same invention has been invented several different times by different persons working independently.

The purpose in pointing out these facts regarding invention is obviously not to detract from the prestige of the inventor, who is usually a person of somewhat superior ability, but rather to correct the false belief that a few great men have largely directed the course of human development. It would be more accurate to say that these innovators in material and nonmaterial culture were *as much the product of their cultures as they were the creators of it*, even in the areas of culture to which their inventions pertained.

Is it becoming more difficult to invent?

One frequently hears that "so many things have been invented that it must be very difficult to make an invention now." The reverse is the truth. The more elements a culture has, the more a prospective inventor has with which to work. Since, as we have seen, all invention is really a combination of pre-existing elements, then the greater number of elements in a culture (the *culture base*) the greater is the number of possible new combinations which can be created.

Invention and diffusion

It is probably obvious that a culture can secure new elements from only two sources: either some person in the society in which the culture prevails creates a new artifact or a new idea (invention) or the new culture element comes to the culture from some other society (diffusion).

The role of invention often exaggerated

There is a tendency for the people of each society to exaggerate the inventiveness of their own group and to minimize their debt to the people of other societies. This is natural enough in view of people's propensity for being ethnocentric, but scientifically such a view constitutes a fundamental error. By way of illustration, suppose we make a list of ten important elements of our material culture and ten from our nonmaterial culture. Such a list might include:

Material Culture Elements	*Nonmaterial Culture Elements*
houses	Christianity
railroads	democracy
radio	English language
fire, i.e., artificial creation of fire	decimal system
plumbing	monogamy
domestic animals	war
tilling the soil—agriculture	law
atomic bomb	education
printing	music
factory system	marriage

Now let us go over the lists to determine how many of these material cultural objects and practices originated in the United States of America. The only one would be the atomic bomb; and that was with the assistance of scientists from other nations, although from nations whose cultures are similar to ours. In the nonmaterial list, none is exclusively and originally "American." While another person might make a different list, certainly it cannot be doubted that each of the items on our list is fundamental. There has been so much diffusion among cultures that practically no culture is without a great deal of indebtedness to the other cultures of the world. If a Russian or a Japanese were to make a similar list he, too, would be forced to the same conclusion that we are—the overwhelming force of diffusion as a culture builder.

This importance of diffusion will become more clear, perhaps, if the student will review pp. 120–122, where it was shown through dozens of illustrations that the great majority of both material and nonmaterial culture contents prevalent in the United States came from other culture areas, some of them from simpler cultures upon which America often tends to look condescendingly.

Basic similarity of invention and diffusion as culture modifiers

The separation of invention and diffusion and the discussion of them as if in opposition to one another may easily lead to the erroneous notion that invention and diffusion are opposites. Actually these processes have much in common as factors in culture building. Both have in common the crucial factor of *acceptance* of the innovation, regardless of the source from which it comes. The final test determining whether or not something new will actually be incorporated into a culture depends upon how well the innovation "fits" with the rest of the culture, particularly with the value system which prevails. If, for example, "efficiency" through the saving of labor and time is a prevailing value, then a labor-saving device, whether invented or diffused, will probably receive a favorable reception. But if the society does not regard labor saving as a desirable objective, the trait, whether invented or diffused, will probably be rejected. The ultimate test is the fitness of the new trait for the prevailing scheme of things. Thus, rural groups have often refused to accept "citified" ways—the new patterns did not "fit" rural values. They seemed, and were, "foreign."

Cultural change is uneven

All of the parts of a culture do not change at the same rate. A persistent characteristic of our culture, for example, is that innovations in material culture seem not to be as strongly resisted as innovations in nonmaterial culture. New ideas in government or morals take longer to be accepted and are more bitterly opposed than innovations in automobile design or kitchen equipment. Apparently people can appraise the value of a material object more readily than they can an idea, particularly if the previous competing idea has had a high value and is deeply ingrained in the prejudice structure.

Is culture inherently static or dynamic?

It is probably already clear that constant change in culture is normal and is, in fact, inherent in the nature of culture itself. It is unfortunate that some earlier writers on culture have somewhat overemphasized the static aspect of culture through undue emphasis upon the importance of the social controls which society imposes on persons. This emphasis upon stability leads often to the erroneous notion that constancy in human affairs is normal and change abnormal.

Human life in society does, however, present something of a paradox. Through the folkways and mores and other social controls, society indoctrinates people and enforces conformity to standards which are not of their making. Yet even while these standards are being imposed, they are already in the process of change. Thus at any given time, in any given society, there is to be observed something of a struggle or conflict between two sets of forces, some making for permanence and stability, and others for change. *But they are all cultural products; one is quite as normal and inevitable as is the other.*

The more "ultimate" effects of
innovation difficult to anticipate

One of the most difficult problems regarding cultural change is the attempt to anticipate or foresee the rate and direction of change in a society. When new artifacts or ideas are introduced, one cannot foresee what all of their ramifications will be. The complications and implications resulting from some one culture trait may forge an endless chain of cause and effect which can entirely revolutionize a society.

The Industrial Revolution in England is a case in point. From the strictly economic point of view, the Industrial Revolution meant merely the shift from the manufacturing of goods in homes or in small groups to manufacturing in large groups. The factory system was made necessary in order to utilize power more efficiently, and later in order to secure lower production costs through the advantages of division of labor. What was originally simply a change in the means of production, however, ushered in a whole new era in all human living. It brought cities of a size never dreamed of before the Industrial Revolution. It brought a standard of living so different that the lowest workman may today enjoy comforts and luxuries unattainable by kings before the Industrial Revolution. The factory system also brought problems. The congestion of cities brought health, traffic, and recreational problems. Crime became more difficult to deal with effectively. Slums developed. Capital and labor, formerly closely allied, have become sharply estranged; and as everyone knows, the nation is periodically inconvenienced by strikes in key industries affecting millions of workmen and creating serious problems for countless millions more. A solution will ultimately be reached, of course, but that solution will become but another link in the endless chain of solution, problem, and solution.

A change in one segment of culture seems almost never to confine its influence to the segment of culture for which it was intended. Discoveries in science bring changes in religion; changes in styles of dress make and break whole industries. The web of interrelationship in culture is so intricate that nothing is isolated or isolatable from anything else.

Change: an inherent theme

While this concludes our present discussion of change in culture and society, the student should not assume that the subject is finished. Change is a recurrent theme in all social science inquiry. It will be discussed, directly or indirectly, in every chapter of this book; and one, especially (Chapter 23), contains a synopsis of a number of the better known and more influential theories regarding change.

SUMMARY

In this chapter we have surveyed the broad sweep of human development from the dawn of civilization, about which we know little, to the dawn of the atomic age, about which we know less. The reasons for our ignorance are, however, not the same in the two cases. We do not know all we would like to know about cultural origins because of the obscurity of antiquity. We are bewildered about the atomic age because we know just enough about the forces of change to be both awe-stricken and somewhat panic-stricken when we attempt to fathom the implications.

No attempt has been made to chronicle the events of human history. That is for the historian to do. Instead attention has been focused in this chapter upon a number of principles involved in the process of social change. These knowledges have been derived inductively from many researches in many different cultures. The principles seem to be:

1. Man's cultural development covers vast periods of time.

2. Throughout most of that time social change has mostly been slow, but the rate of change has been rapidly accelerated in recent years.

3. Many of the basic characteristics of modern society, like democracy, science, and high standards of living, are so new to man's experience that he has difficulty often in knowing what to do with them.

4. Change in culture is inevitable; no culture fails to show evidence of change.

5. The factors making for stability and the factors making for change are both inherent aspects of culture.

6. The rates at which cultures change are very variable. Some societies change very rapidly; others very slowly. Some societies change rapidly for a time, then slowly; others, vice versa.

7. Culture changes by the addition of traits, the loss of traits, or the changed emphasis on existing traits.

8. New cultural elements can arise within the culture (invention) or come from some other culture (diffusion).

9. Invention inevitably involves the use of existing cultural elements in some new combinations. Therefore, the larger the cultural base, other things being equal, the greater the wealth of elements from

which the new inventions can be fashioned. This applies both to culture objects and to ideas.

10. With the possible exception of a few primitive societies, all societies have secured more of their content from diffusion than from their own invention.

11. Most of the inventions represent minor modifications or changes in the details of the culture; the basic patterns of the society are less frequently or radically modified.

12. The eventual effects of inventions are so far-reaching that it is almost impossible to envisage in advance what aspects of a total culture will be changed by some given innovation.

13. The determining factor in the integration of a new artifact or thoughtway into a culture is how the new item fits into the prevailing scheme. No trait is intrinsically of high or low value; it always comes to be evaluated in terms of standards prevailing in the culture, the standards themselves, of course, having been innovations originally.

These, then, are some of the fundamental knowledges about man's cultural development and the processes involved in it. Later chapters (especially in Part IV) will take up in some detail the nature of the society which modern culture change is producing and will consider some of the problems resulting therefrom.

SUGGESTED READINGS

Allen, Francis R., Hart, Hornell, Miller, Delbert C., Ogburn, William F., and Nimkoff, Meyer F., *Technology and Social Change*. New York, Appleton-Century-Crofts, 1957.
An excellent treatment of both the theory and the "content" of modern social change, with special emphasis on the United States. Abundant factual materials.

Cuber and Harroff (See Bibliographic note, p. 40).
Don Martindale, "The Reshaping of Core Institutions," pp. 300–306.

Etzioni, Amitai, and Etzioni, Eva, *Social Change: Sources, Patterns, and Consequences*. New York, Basic Books, 1964.
Considers the processes and events of social change in an inclusive and wholistic way.

King, C. Wendell, *Social Movements in the United States*. New York, Random House, 1956.
Sometimes social change occurs through established institutions in more or less orderly, if not predictable, manner. At other times change occurs through rela-

tively unstructured and seemingly spontaneous social groups; these are customarily called social movements by social scientists.

Mack, Raymond W., *Transforming America: Patterns of Social Change.*
    New York, Random House, 1961.
A general treatment of American society as an emergent. Excellently written with original and important illustrative materials.

Moore, Wilbert E., *Social Change.* Englewood Cliffs, N.J., Prentice-Hall,
    1963.
This view of social change is distinctive in that change is treated not so much as an anomaly as a regular part of the ongoing process of a social system.

Ogburn, W. F., *Social Change.* New York, Huebsch, 1922.
A classic study of the process of social change. Written by the author of the famous "culture lag" theory which, although it is somewhat in disrepute in several of its applications, still contains some measure of basic truth about the differential diffusion of material and nonmaterial culture patterns. Should be read in connection with John Mueller, "Present Status of the Culture Lag Theory," *American Sociological Review*, Vol. 3 (June, 1938), pp. 320–332, and especially J. W. Woodard, "Critical Notes on the Culture Lag Concept," *Social Forces*, Vol. 12 (March, 1934), pp. 388–398.

Philipson, Morris, *Automation.* New York, Random House, 1962.
A series of interpretive essays dealing with the current as well as the projected implications of rapid automation in American society.

Rodnick, David, *An Introduction to Man and His Development.* New
    York, Appleton-Century-Crofts, 1966.
This is an inclusive textbook presentation of the development of man in his many aspects from the beginning of time to the present.

Rogers, Everett M., *Diffusion of Innovations.* New York, Free Press, 1962.
A report on field researches dealing with deliberate innovation. Also deals with theoretical matters.

Shostak, Arthur B., ed., *Sociology in Action: Case Studies in Social Problems and Directed Social Change.* Homewood, Ill., Dorsey Press, Inc.,
    1966.
This is a general anthology dealing with various and sundry efforts and thinkings of sociologists with respect to the direction of deliberate social change—in hospitals, in communities—the reconstruction of disaster areas, desegregation, treatment of alcoholism and delinquency, underdeveloped nations, as well as other foci.

Smelser, Neil J., "Processes of Social Change," in Neil J. Smelser, ed., *Sociology: An Introduction.* New York, Wiley, 1967.

An excellent advanced textbook level treatment of the ideological factors of social change with reference to particular studies. Presents a theory of social change and an excellent summary and critique of historical treatment of the process by sociologists.

STUDY QUESTIONS

1. Why are we unable to state how, when, and where man first began to create culture?
2. Why do we have definite information about some of man's earliest material culture, but only "inferential information" about his nonmaterial culture?
3. Why must we be cautious in the use of "inferential" conclusions from data about culture before the use of writing? Does the use of writing remove the possibility for error? Why?
4. Why is culture not an accumulation of all the culture traits that ever existed?
5. What determines whether culture traits are accepted, rejected, or modified?
6. On what do both material and nonmaterial inventions depend?
7. How do inventions illustrate the proverb that "there is nothing new under the sun"? How do they disprove the adage?
8. Why is it often necessary for an invention to be introduced more than once?
9. What has made possible the increasing rate of inventions?
10. Why is it incorrect to say that a society creates its culture traits?
11. How are invention and diffusion similar? Related?
12. Why do we accept innovations in material culture more readily than we do in nonmaterial culture?
13. How is necessity often the "mother of acceptance" instead of the "mother of invention"? Illustrate.
14. How may the introduction of a new culture trait result in unforeseen changes in a society? Illustrate.
15. How is invention the mother of necessity? Illustrate.

three

BACKGROUND
UNDERSTANDINGS
FROM SOCIAL
PSYCHOLOGY

9
SOME BASIC SOCIAL PSYCHOLOGICAL PROBLEMS

Social psychology is an important but variously conceptualized specialty in present-day behavior science. As the name implies, social psychology is a bridge between psychology and sociology, an interstitial focus of study, which in some respects is presumably like psychology and in other respects presumably like sociology.

There are several ways in which the nature of social psychology can be understood, yet none of them is completely satisfactory when taken alone. To say that social psychology is a bridge between sociology and psychology is to imply that sociology and psychology are distinct. Yet to the student who has studied both psychology and sociology it often becomes apparent that there is considerable overlap with respect to the kinds of material studied, the methods of inquiry, and the suppositions which the practitioners of the two fields typically make. Why, then, should there be a bridge; why should we need an interstitial subject?

If all this seems confusing to the student, it is only because it may also be somewhat confusing to his teacher. Much has been written in an attempt to clearly differentiate psychology, social psychology, and sociology, and a comparable amount of effort has gone into criticizing the differentiation as well as objecting to it. All that one can reliably report at present is that the term *social psychology* and a rather generally established set of ideas and research practices exist in the academic, and to some extent practical, world; that there are substantial numbers of professionals who call themselves social psychologists; that courses in social psychology are widely, if not universally, found in important universities both in psychology and sociology departments; and that a separate professional organization for social psychologists has been in existence for several years, as have professional journals for social psychologists' publications. This evidence taken together would seem to strongly justify the position that this is, indeed, a "field" of present-day behavior science and that its relationship to sociology is sufficiently fundamental that, as in the case of anthropology, its principal ideas and points of view should be examined since they are inextricably intertwined with sociology.

PERSISTENT IDEA CLUSTERS

There is general agreement that the important things about any field of study consist of what it studies and how it studies, that is, its content and methods of inquiry. We shall now give some attention to the emergence of the contemporary social psychological discipline in terms of these two matters.

In the older tradition, 1900 to 1920, people who are today claimed as the precursors of social psychology relied mostly upon case studies, informal observations, and their general intellectual equipment for the necessary information upon which to base generalizations. They made little, if any, use of statistics or other more rigidly controlled observation. In contrast, contemporary social psychologists are much more scientific in the sense that they use laboratory methods, employ advanced statistical procedures, and concentrate upon much more precise data and problems. Moreover, a number of their efforts now have practical applications and, in fact, are often initiated in an effort to solve practical problems, such as studies of morale in military units or factories and dozens of other practical concerns. Specialization and precision have been made possible, of course, in substantial part because pioneers, in this field as in others, had done much of the basic conceptual groundwork on which later students could build. Even the errors of the early students, or more accurately their overgeneralizations and vagueness, provided their followers with the necessary hypotheses and stimuli to facilitate more precise work.

1. On "reality": society and the individual

One of the earliest and continually important conceptualizations with which social psychologists have been, and are still, unavoidably concerned is subsumed in the phrase "society and the individual," sometimes naïvely posed as society *versus* the individual. Such expressions have become a sort of professional shorthand for a larger philosophical idea, namely, which is the more real: (*a*) the live, tangible, acting human being or (*b*) the human collectivity which is customarily called "society." A prima facie case can, of course, be made either way. It has been argued, for example, that the only reality is the individual because all human action, even if it involves nations or armies or other great collectivities, consists basically and fundamentally of the actions of people, who presumably may act in one way or another depending on various conditions and circumstances. Therefore, social scientists ought to study individuals and the forces which bear upon them.

When, however, one begins to focus on the forces which shape individuals—their values, their competencies, their conceptions of reality, their ambitions, and almost everything else about them—one comes to see that such aspects are shaped, channeled, and influenced through participation in the cultures and societies of which these individuals are a part. It would seem appropriate, then, to study larger human collectivities as keys to understanding the individual.

While few social psychologists could today be enticed into what now seems so fruitless a discussion, there are still many laymen and a few philosophers who like to debate whether the individual or society is the more real, the more important, and the more appropriate focus of inquiry.

A half century ago this issue was in substantial measure resolved in a way which has today become a standard thoughtway for behavior scientists. While Cooley [1] is probably not the only sociologist who resolved the issue, his writings have been particularly clear and forceful and his influence great. Cooley said, simply, that the prime reality in question is neither the individual nor society separately, but human life. Human life has an individual *and* a collective aspect, both of which are real, both of which are important, and therefore both of which are appropriate foci of study. The individual and society are the concave side and the convex side, so to speak, of the same arc.

Viewing this arc from the right, the image is manifestly concave; moving around to the left it is manifestly convex; viewed comprehensively it is, of course, an arc with concavity and convexity, both as inherent, inescapable attributes. Thus, whatever one's predilections so far as a particular approach to research is concerned, he has a clear authority to go ahead. He may study an individual or a group of individuals, on the one hand, as tangible aspects of human life, or he may study the larger collectivities such as nations, political parties, ecclesiastical bodies, labor unions, or universities. It is not intended to imply that this is the only philosophical disposition which can be made of an

[1] Charles Horton Cooley, *Human Nature and the Social Order*, rev. ed. (New York, Scribner, 1922), p. 35.

age-old question, but rather that this is a resolution of a fundamental and troublesome question which social psychologists and other behavior scientists have come to accept.

2. On heredity and environment

A second early concern was that of "heredity versus environment." Protagonists of either extreme position are not hard to find among lay contemporaries and, regrettably, also occasionally among professionals, who ought to know better.

Some of the early social psychologists pointed out, first of all, that posing the question in terms of a contest is misleading, although admittedly dramatic. Obviously, for life to continue, even in an unsatisfactory state, the inherited needs of the organism must be nurtured by the environment *in some way* or the organism would perish. The fact of survival, then, is itself tacit acknowledgment of a coincident operation of *both* heredity and environment.

There are important practical implications nonetheless. If it could be determined, for example, that environment (learning) is the more important element, then by concentrating our efforts, we presumably could produce more and better scholars, rehabilitate criminals better, and in many other ways improve the human lot. If we could be convinced that heredity is the more important, then there is much less to be gained by efforts to educate and otherwise manipulate the environment. As we shall see in a subsequent chapter, various kinds of precise research have been carried out in an effort to clarify and establish the interrelationship of hereditary and environmental influences in specific situations. This will be discussed at length in a subsequent chapter. All that is intended to be conveyed here is that one of the big projects of early social psychologists was a preliminary critical look at the heredity-environment issue and a general decision that the two are interrelated. The resolution of *specific* questions requires the discipline of experimental rather than forensic effort.

3. On free will and determinism

One of the old philosophical issues with which social psychologists, along with other students of human behavior, were inordinately concerned was the conflict between explanations of human behavior on the basis of determinism versus a postulated "free will." To state a complicated question very succinctly, the issue comes to something like this: Are human actions *determined* by cultural, biological, and other influences, or is the individual free to *choose* what he will or will not do and become? On a commonsense basis, it is very easy to make a strong case—either way. For example, the free-will advocates say that anyone can assert that he chose to do A rather than B. Yet upon another occasion he may choose B, and someone else may choose A when he chose B, and so on. Introspection convinces most people that they "think about" alternative courses of action, then choose some one and proceed to act.

On the other hand, the advocates of determinism say that all this is deceptively simple, a form of sentimental naïveté. Playing upon every individual at every moment is an innumerable set of influences, pressures, stimuli, and otherwise-phrased forces. It is easy to demonstrate, for example, that because one grows up in a certain society at a certain time in a certain class and is of a certain sex that a great many of his so-called choices are readily predictable to an informed outsider. In other words, choice is in demonstrable ways an illusion, however comforting, which can often with a high degree of accuracy be predicted in advance of the act. Even in matters on which cultures allow alternatives, choices can be accurately predicted in advance, once one knows the "personality structure" of the chooser or the requirements of the situation in which he finds himself. Thus a prima facie plausibility supports either the free-will or the determinist position.

It can probably be anticipated that the position which the social psychologists take is some sort of middle ground. Certain aspects of a person's behavior are determined—unqualified and objectively demonstrable. Certain biological influences, for example, determine certain physical characteristics and behavior. Likewise certain social pressures impose upon an individual requirements so categorical and so well enforced that there are scarcely any exceptions, regardless of a theoretical free choice to behave otherwise. It has been suggested that this kind of determinism is a "soft" determinism. Whether soft or hard, however, the more generic fact should not be obscured, namely that much human action can be reliably anticipated in advance, given the knowledge of the circumstances.

Just as it is easy to maximize determinism, so it is easy to exaggerate in the other direction, often because of insufficient knowledge. So far as existing knowledge is concerned, the most skilled behavior scientists are at present unable to predict, even given a knowledge of the circumstances, how certain persons will in fact behave. Common sense supports the idea of freedom of choice in countless decisions—what to wear on a date, what to order from the menu, for whom to vote, whether to accept a new job, etc. This gives comfort to the free-will advocate, but it may be a false comfort because inability to predict may arise from lack of knowledge of the determining forces rather than constituting any triumph for free will. People who know relatively little about human behavior, for example, are mystified everyday by the choices which adolescents make in the exercise of their presumed free will. Experts, on the other hand, who know something of the forces which typically impinge on this age-group in this society at this time, predict very successfully what adolescents will do, how many will do it, and when. So often, what is a complete mystery to the uninformed is a routine anticipation to someone with the necessary *expertise*.

One more important generalization should be stressed. Looking at the free will-determinism issue over the sweep of a century or so clearly documents the fact that scientific advance demonstrates a narrowing of the operation of free choice. Few informed people, for example, can any longer ignore the fact that many kinds of even serious wrongdoing, which folklore claimed to be a result of someone's "bad choice," are actually the result of forces over which the individual has no control and of which he is not even aware. He does what he must do under the circumstances. He may, nevertheless, retain the illusion of choice; he *thinks* he made the choice, because it is comforting so to think and there is a cultural expectation to that effect. Yet the scientific evidence already is adequate to demonstrate that there was no real choice. Often one does not even identify the theoretical alternatives.

It seems reasonable to expect that science will continue to demonstrate, as it has for some time, that more and more choices are really determined by forces hitherto unknown. One should not assume from this trend, however, that eventually no individual choice can reasonably be expected to exist. It is quite possible that there are relative or absolute limits beyond which determinism may not operate.

The foregoing problem, of course, is probably far, far in the future. It is doubtful whether any but the most dogmatic social determinist of this generation expects to see in his lifetime much more than a perceptible moving ahead of our knowledge regarding determinism. Nevertheless, it would be a mistake to ignore, as some find it comfortable to do, the relentless onward march of our knowledge of the forces which shape human action to such a degree that fewer and fewer mysteries, or even surprises, remain for the person who knows his way about. And finally, for whatever comfort it will bring, it must be acknowledged that our knowledge is at present sufficiently modest that the parlor game of "free will versus determinism" may still continue, even for the relatively informed, as a spirited quasi-intellectual pastime. And, more importantly, persons who are responsible for the behavior of others, such as parents, teachers, and legal officers, are still not equipped with sufficiently definitive knowledge to permit them always to know how a given "choice" by a given individual has been or will be made.

4. On body and mind

The early social psychologists inherited the body-mind dichotomy, or, as most behavior scientists today put it, the "body-mind fallacy." Common sense, reinforced by theology and some philosophy, had long held it obvious that a kind of dualism pervaded the human being. It seemed to require no proof that the human body was a tangible reality with functions which were obvious, sometimes inconvenient, and often troublesome. Yet man seemed to exist on another level, the mental and the spiritual, where he thought and felt, dreamed and feared, felt guilty or proud. This seemed an altogether separate thing, for he could and often did think ill of what his body did, feared what it might do, and sometimes could not control it. Theologians for centuries seemed to the layman to be saying that the body was a rather bad thing on the whole and that the lusts and passions which it fostered had to be kept in stern check by a resolute mind. Thus in the centuries immediately preceding the scientific era, not only was body considered as distinct from mind but there was a rather pervasive assumption that the two were in some kind of necessary conflict—with mind as a rule the hero and body as a rule the villain.

In the light of modern scientific knowledge, the above is, of course, largely nonsense—an excellent illustration not only of the Aristotelian fallacy of postulating opposites but also of a myopic view which overlooked more than it noticed. The first error of the body-mind fallacy lies, of course, in the complete separation of the two. They are in demonstrable ways intimately and inextricably interrelated. Neither exists without the other. The mental and emotional aspect of man intrudes into his physiology, and his physiology profoundly influences his thought processes and emotional states. To some extent the layman recognizes some of the clear connection between the two, as when he says that worry over his job caused an ulcer, or when he observes that his indigestion reduced his efficiency at work or study. The phrase "psychosomatic medicine" has arisen in recent years in an attempt to underscore the fact that psychological and physical processes are inextricably intertwined and that the mental-emotional aspects of a person's being may have profound physical consequences, as well as the reverse. In the second place, to pose body and mind in opposition to one another, as if they were contestants in an athletic event, is a further naïveté. This has probably resulted in substantial measure from the influence of theology, which has for centuries taught the "evils of the flesh" and the "purity of the spirit." Even if we were not the inheritors of this tradition, however, it seems likely that the conflict between body-based desires and mind-based controls would have occurred to many people independently. The whole process of conformity to culture tends to suggest this kind of interpretation. Cultural taboos are chiefly learned intellectually, and many of them consist of inhibitions which are imposed upon the "natural" body processes.

But the matter is not so simple. Desires—even lustful ones, to use an unscientific word—may be intellectually as well as physically based; also, some inhibitions may result from physical causes as well as from psychological ones, notably fatigue or some kind of physiologically-based aversion.

The prevailing contemporary view of the whole body-mind question, then, rejects the extreme separation between the two (dualism) but does not necessarily go the whole way in the other direction either (monism). The clear tendency is to take the middle ground. In certain kinds of research it is quite possible to largely ignore the mental-emotional aspects, as well as vice versa. But he who does so and generalizes too freely is usually somewhat suspect because in the cavalier dismissal of the mental-emotional side of man's nature, there may be and often has been very serious error. Studies have shown, for example, that the I.Q.'s (intelligence quotients) of deprived children have been changed by changing their diets.[2] This came as something of a shock to those who thought that intelligence surely was something "clearly mental." Hundreds of other illustrations could be collected to demonstrate important breakthroughs in knowledge which came about when the customary and convenient separation of body and mind had been discarded. In sum, the above seems to indicate that the fallacy in the

[2] See e.g., Henry E. Garrett, *Great Experiments in Psychology* (New York, Appleton-Century-Crofts, 1957), pp. 239–240. Also treats "physical causes" of I.Q. inconsistency more generally. See, also, W. W. Charters, Jr., and N. L. Gage, eds., *Readings in the Social Psychology of Education* (Boston, Allyn and Bacon, 1963), pp. 12–21.

body-mind distinction was not a categoric one but rather consisted of minimizing or ignoring a connection between two aspects of the human being which present-day behavior scientists of all specialties have come to appreciate as being exceedingly intimate.

5. On "social adjustment"

From the start, social psychologists, like many others before and since, have been concerned with something which has come to be called "social adjustment." Adjustment means simply that a person's behavior, including his desires, is in accord with the prevailing culture. Thus, if a given culture provides that men should be aggressive, a man who desires to be aggressive and behaves aggressively is "adjusted." A man who is shy or who for some reason does not accept the appropriateness is "maladjusted." His personality to this degree does not fit the molds provided in his society. His maladjustment may be relatively minor or it may be gross. And so with the dozens and hundreds of other behavior requirements which an individual faces in whatever society he finds himself.

Part of our practical difficulty, here as elsewhere, derives from the almost universal condition that the discoveries of the expert and the traditional knowledge of the rank and file are geared differently. The rank and file rely, as they probably must, chiefly on tradition and common sense. The experts rely upon objective, scientific knowledge and what appear to be reasonable inferences from such. The resulting scientific knowledge, based upon experimentation or other kinds of rigorous factual testing, claims an authority which the rank and file do not always grant. There is, moreover, a general distrust of the expert, because he seems to talk a different language and he seems to say, when one does understand him, "such outrageous things."

Thus, it is a condition of our present world that there are two separate streams of knowledge concerning the reasons for "maladjustment"—commonsense traditions and scientific information. So far as practical application is concerned, success is held back by both—by science because it does not yet know as much as would be desirable, and by the commonsense traditions because they often impede the use of much of the scientific knowledge which is already available.

There is a great deal more to the question of adjustment and maladjustment. One of the big issues has to do not so much with a strictly scientific question but with a somewhat practical and basically philosophical one. Putting the question bluntly, within what limits is adjustment desirable? It can be demonstrated, for example, that some of the world's greatest works, in the arts as well as the sciences, have come from manifestly maladapted people. One of the greatest composers was a homosexual, as was also one of America's most illustrious poets. Dozens of women of eminence in humanitarian and scientific pursuits have been women unable or unwilling to order their lives in accord with "normal" expectations for women. Numerous scientists, as well as artists, have been recluses; violent hostility has driven people to humanitarian achievements. We could go on objectively in this way for a long, long time.

Yet the whole world cannot be and is not made up of creative giants. For an orderly society, the great mass of people, it would seem, need to behave largely in accord with cultural expectations concerning behavior, or the necessary orderliness which makes society possible would disappear. So runs the logic of the "adjustment above all else" viewpoint.

But the question needs to be posed better. The issue need not be stated in terms of grossly maladjusted people versus robots. Somewhere in between there may be a more moderate and proper sphere for judgment. How much latitude for individuality is safe, beyond which social conformity may be too stifling? There appears to be a general human propensity, more or less present in all cultures but especially acute in some, which places tacit emphasis on the robotized individual. But excessive conformity comes at a bigger price psychologically and socially than many persons realize. Psychologically and personally, conformity comes at the price of acute suffering for many people who find themselves forced into uncomfortable molds by the society, molds which are in sharp contrast to their biological natures or to their psychological requirements. Under these conditions, mental ill health in more or less degree, say many psychologists and psychiatrists, becomes inevitable. In answer to this warning, those defending convention reply with demands for better indoctrination in established values so that individuals will better be able to serve the models which the society currently considers worthy; people's tastes would in this way be better understood by them and more meaningful to them instead of being part of a blind, nerve-wracking drive to conformity.

There is yet another view. Stated tersely it grants that an efficient society requires conformity to certain uniform standards of conduct in order to facilitate orderly interaction. But at the same time it cautions against needless, excessive, or *over*conformity. The reason for being somewhat grudging about too much conformity is that society pays a price for such. The price is a loss of creativity. This, it will be recalled, is the nub of the issue presented by Whyte in *The Organization Man*, to which we referred in the chapter on the mass society. In short, it is not necessary, say the exponents of this view, to be as robotized as people in our society tend to be. Even more importantly, the real loser is the society, which thus loses the benefits which would result from a greater creativity if more individuality were fostered. An added social value which would result from a less strict conception of social adjustment would be a diminished amount and severity of mental illness, since much mental illness is simply nonconformity per se or damage to a person from too great a striving for conformity.

CONTEMPORARY FOCI IN SOCIAL PSYCHOLOGY

Most of the idea clusters which we have just discussed have concerned social psychologists from the beginning and still form a general backdrop for the professional efforts of contemporary social psychologists. But the actual work at the present time does not deal directly with such cosmic considerations as free will, overconformity, the nature of the individual, and heredity and environment as such. Present-day social psychologists work on much more specific questions and hypotheses, collect data of circumscribed and precise sorts, and present findings, as a rule, of rather modest pretensions. These all have implications, to be sure, for the larger issues, but they do not directly test the overall concepts as we have been discussing them.

As we shall see in the following chapters, present-day social psychologists study such varied things as the personalities of identical twins who are reared separately, the effectiveness of altruistic as opposed to selfish appeals in the selling of war bonds, the criteria by which students evaluate their dates, how people make up their minds for whom they shall vote, the extent to which the personalities of children of different social classes are different, and the connections between personality traits and other factors, such as, the relationship between measured intelligence and occupational or social success. In the preceding section, a few studies of an essentially social psychological sort were introduced, for example, the Adorno study of the authoritarian personality in relation to ethnocentrism, national character critiques, and others.

From this inclusive and necessarily highly general account, we turn in the following chapters to more specific problems, concepts, and data. In the treatment of these specific concerns the student will find an admixture of traditional ideas in social psychology with contemporary research and thinking. The technical language of the present-day social psychologist will be introduced and its rationale spelled out. Finally, the unsolved problems and the uneasy generalizations will be acknowledged, too.

SUGGESTED READINGS

Cooley, Charles Horton, *Human Nature and the Social Order*, rev. ed. New York, Scribner, 1922.
This entire book is an examination of the larger question of "how society makes the man and of how man makes society." The early chapter on "society and the individual" is a classic statement of what Cooley called the "organic view" of human life.

Doby, John T., *Introduction to Social Psychology*. New York, Appleton-Century-Crofts, 1966.
A recent textbook in social psychology which is distinctive in several ways, notably in its bridging of social psychology and sociology and in its treatment of broad intellectual themes, like evolution, which contemporary texts tend to ignore.

Hollander, E. P., and Hunt, Raymond G., eds., *Current Perspectives in Social Psychology*. New York, Oxford University Press, 1963.
A systematic analysis of the content and points of view of present-day social psychology.

Sampson, Edward S., ed., *Social Psychology: A Book of Readings*. Englewood Cliffs, N.J., Prentice-Hall, 1964.
A set of readings designed to acquaint the student with the kinds of works and interests which characterize present-day social psychology.

Slater, Philip E., "Social Bases of Personality," in Neil J. Smelser, ed., *Sociology: An Introduction*. New York, Wiley, 1967, Chapter 10.
This is an advanced textbook treatment of a number of issues such as those covered in this chapter. Also constitutes an excellent synthetic discussion of important aspects of socialization.

Smith, Brewster M., "Recent Developments in the Field of Social Psychology." *Annals of the American Academy of Political and Social Science*, Vol. 338 (November, 1961), pp. 137–143.
There is no dearth of books and articles purporting to describe, if not to predict, developments in the field of social psychology. This is a particularly lucid

treatment. The method is to examine the major books published during 1960 and 1961. The author is a psychologist who believes there is a convergence of psychological and sociological conceptions of this field.

STUDY QUESTIONS

1. What evidence do you see in this chapter that behavior scientists find it difficult to observe the neat distinction which they tend to draw between studying "what is" and "what ought to be"?

2. What do you understand is meant by *social psychology?*

3. What are some of the persistent issues with which social psychologists have been concerned? Can you think of any which are not discussed in this chapter?

4. Do you see any reasons in addition to those presented in this chapter as to why so many people still think in terms of society versus the individual?

5. Do you find it easy or difficult to think in terms of determinism? Why do you suppose you think as you do?

6. Explain why the extreme determinist looks forward to the time when there will be no need to postulate a free will.

7. What distinctions do you see between the phrases "body-mind fallacy" and "body-mind unity" (monism)?

8. "Life presents an unending dilemma—one must conform to social requirements but to the extent that he does so beyond a certain point his creativity becomes atrophied." Comment.

9. What is meant by saying that both the society and the individual often pay a "severe price" for excessive conformity?

10. Why is it to be expected that the common sense of ordinary people and the expertise of the behavior scientist will be at odds? Illustrate.

10
SOCIALIZATION AND THE INTERACTION HYPOTHESIS

Not so many years ago you came into the world a polymorphous-perverse little ape with a billion years of biological evolution precipitated, so to speak, in your dimpled organism. You came naked, without shame, without language, food habits, or manual dexterity; ideas, or religious faith; without respect for law and order. . . . You came with no higher desires than to have your capacious belly filled with milk and your somatic and visceral itches scratched by loving hands.

Now you are sophisticated and supercilious [students], weary young intellectuals in a decadent era, murmuring over this, that, and the other in your daily routine, "What a beastly bore!" You are clothed in the choicest fabrics and adorned with the totemic symbols of your respective fraternities. You speak and write the English language—fairly well; and you know better than to eat pie with a knife, at least in public. Some of you can probably play eighteen holes of golf in less than a hundred strokes; some of you can lie beautifully to that effect. Some of you think you know what da Vinci tried to convey by the smile of Mona Lisa. Your desires have multiplied; so have your doubts and fears. You still have somatic and visceral itches, but your scratching technique has, I trust, become much more complicated and effective. Think of yourself as a bawling and puking brat with your nose and bladder in perennial flux, and then look at yourself now. *Mirabile visu!* Isn't Nature wonderful? How did you get this way? That's the first question we shall try to answer.[1]

THREE SEPARABLE FACTORS AFFECT HUMAN DEVELOPMENT

The human being is molded by three separable sets of influences which we may designate at the outset as:

[1] Excerpts from "The Noble Animal," in R. G. Smith, *Fugitive Papers* (New York, Columbia, 1930).

1. His inborn characteristics ("Original Nature");
2. The culture and subcultures in which he lives (Cultural Environment); and
3. The specific noncultural experiences he has (Unique Experience).

Our first task is to examine the nature and content of these three sets of forces.

1. Original nature

a. Some gross distinctions

The term *original nature* is essentially synonymous with heredity. It consists of all those traits and characteristics which a person possesses because he is a specimen of the species *Homo sapiens*. On the surface it would seem easy enough to determine what one owes, so to speak, to biological transmission, yet this scientific problem has been one of the most baffling. Our first step shall consist of separating "heredity" into some of its parts.

Much needless confusion concerning man's original nature has resulted from the failure to distinguish three quite distinct aspects of one's inherited nature. All three are, of course, transmitted to the person through the germ plasm.

1. *Phylogenetic characteristics.* In a very general sense practically all of the individuals of the species are approximately the same. Humans usually have two eyes, their hearts are on the left side, they have the necessary mechanism to enable them to walk erect, they can learn, they require sleep, and so forth.

2. *Ontogenetic variation.* But no two human beings are exactly alike, and sometimes the *extent of individual differences is very great.* Both the genius and the moron are human beings (and might be brothers). Size, weight, and general appearance variations are also obvious examples of this continuous and unpredictable variation in inherited characteristics among human beings.

3. *Dominant "family" traits.* Other inherited individual differences are the result of more predictable heredity and appear to be handed down from parent to offspring in the specific ancestral line. In spite of the fact that studies show rather clearly that intelligence *quotients* are affected by various environmental factors, intelligence per se, that is, innate capacity for learning, usually tends to run in families. This applies to both high intelligence and low intelligence.

Thus, we see that human inheritance presents something of a paradox. Because he is a human being, Joe inherits a collection of traits roughly characteristic of all human beings, but Joe also inherits an almost innumerable array of uniquenesses, some due to the specific parentage he has had and others, as far as we now can determine, to sheer "chance," a term we use to cover occurrences the causal factors of which we do not fully understand and cannot, therefore, predict.

b. The concept *original nature*

At the outset it should be stressed that the term *original nature* or *heredity* is an abstraction. No one can see it or otherwise experience it through his senses. One can see certain *evidences* in humans' behavior, but that which is called "heredity" can be experienced only as an *idea.* It cannot be perceived; it can only be conceived. The idea of original nature is a sort of summary of a number of related facts and interpretations of facts which the scientist has discovered in the course of his experiments and observations. Thus, we observe that at birth the infant cries, he has eyes, he can move his arms and legs, but with apparently no purpose or with little dexterity. Later he gets larger and his dexterity improves. Still later his sexual organs change and he becomes capable of reproduction. Finally, if he lives that long, he usually becomes gray, gets wrinkled, loses physical vigor. Eventually he dies.

We say these acts and characteristics are "due to heredity." But that neither tells us what heredity *is* nor gives us any assurance that our observations are correct. All that one can say with any measure of scientific objectivity is that *heredity* is a general term used to cover those items of human behavior and makeup which we *think* one gets from the fact that he is a specimen of his species and a descendant of his particular ancestral line. All learned behavior and all acquired changes in him are something other than heredity.

One cannot observe heredity directly and is forced to utilize *inferences from observations* of physical structure and of overt behavior. Errors are therefore common and despite the large amount of time which goes into genetic research, *there is much about human heredity in relation to human behavior which the most expert geneticist does not as yet know.*

c. How can the influence of heredity be objectively determined?

At first thought it would seem relatively easy to discover the effects of heredity upon a person's behavior. Several commonsense tests are often employed. (1) One might say that he does not remember *learning* to bite his fingernails and, "therefore, the behavior must have been hereditary." But learning, as we have seen earlier, may be unconscious; or the learning situation from which it came may have been forgotten. Introspection, then, is no satisfactory test. (2) Another spurious test is to compare the behavior of parent and child or brother and sister and, if there are similarities, draw the quick and easy conclusion that the similarities are hereditary. Several errors appear here. First, similarities may as likely be learned from association with the other family members as be due to inheritance. This is especially important when one stops to consider the large amount of time which one spends with his parents and siblings, especially during the early and formative years. In the second place, illusions (false perceptions due to errors in observation or to prejudice or to suggestion) in comparing behavior are common. For example, a father has a bad temper, his child upon one or two occasions shows intense emotional outbursts, and immediately the family members volunteer the sage observation that, "Oh, well, what can you expect? He inherited it from his father." Had there been systematic observation of this child, it would have been clear that the child *rarely* showed instability of emotional control, even under great provocation, and that compared with other children of his age, this child had ample emotional control. The observer's error lay in his previous *expectation* of finding father-child similarity, in short, in an illusion. (3) Chance similarities are often falsely interpreted as causal and even hereditary. Suppose the mother is an alcoholic and at the age of 45 her son also becomes an alcoholic. Often such coincidences are interpreted as evidence that alcoholism is inherited. Actually, there are dozens of reasons why both mother and son might at some time in their lives both be alcoholics and heredity be inoperative.

If one cannot reliably apply the tests of introspection and parent-child comparisons, how then can the influence of heredity be objectively discovered? Actually, what the expert geneticist does is, in more precise form, what the student has been warned against. (1) He examines the person's history for evidences of learning of the observed traits, and (2) he compares individuals in a given ancestral line. The difference, however, between lay and professional examination of such evidence is great. Stripped of technical detail it amounts to *greater* precision in observation by the professional geneticist and requirement of *more, and more reliable, evidence* before a suggested conclusion is accepted as true. And many unsolved problems persist, nevertheless.

2. Cultural environment

The cultures and subcultures in which a person is reared thus might seem on first thought to constitute sets of influences which could easily be studied. Such is not, however, the case. As we have already seen, the culture of a society is not uniform for everyone. Persons of different ages, sexes, social classes, and regions are exposed to radically different patterns of cultural behavior. In fact, it is altogether normal for such cultural specialization to occur. It will, therefore, be necessary in subsequent parts of this and later chapters to break down the totality of culture into more detailed units in order to assay more precisely its many relations to the behavior of the individual.

6. THREE FACTORS AFFECTING HUMAN DEVELOPMENT

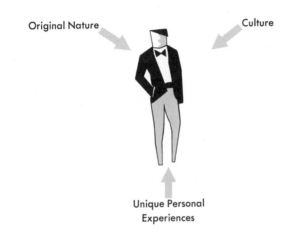

Original Nature

Culture

Unique Personal
Experiences

3. Unique experience

Finally, each individual in the course of living has some experiences which are more or less unique to him. Sometimes one's interpersonal experiences are such that he develops ideas and overt behavior patterns diametrically opposite to those manifested by the majority of persons in his society. The "woman hater," the hermit, the homosexual, the religious fanatic are only a few of many cases in point. It should be noted, however, that all of the above illustrations could also be "normal" behaviors for persons whose cultures contained such norms. But all persons in such categories can by no means be accounted for by their special group-culture connections. Many of our individual likes and dislikes, hopes and fears, are the result of the specific experiences and the unique configurations of experiences which each individual has had.

In the past many writers on sociology and anthropology have ignored or have insufficiently emphasized the noncultural factors in the development of the person. This concept is indispensable if one is to have a more adequate understanding of the forces which shape the human being. At the same time, however, one must be careful not to overemphasize the unique experience factor. Humans are rarely as unique as they think they are.

THE INTERACTION OF ORIGINAL NATURE, CULTURE, AND UNIQUE EXPERIENCE

The three factors are important in interaction, not in mere summation

One must be careful not to think of any of these three factors as being operative independently of the other two. A person's behavior is not the result of original nature *plus* culture *plus* unique experience. Instead it results from the *interplay* of them. Each imposes limitations on the others, and each also facilitates the others. A person, for example, might live in an "excellent environment," as the prevailing values of the culture rate it, and yet not have sufficient intelligence to be able to take advantage of the opportunities which the environment has presented to him. Suppose, again, that there is an individual with an exceedingly high intelligence born into a group which does not have access to schools and in which there is hostility toward formal education. Such a child might conceivably not even learn to read. When an adult he would be illiterate, but he would not be illiterate because of any deficiency in his inherited intelligence; he would be illiterate because his inherited capacities for great learning could not be realized in the environment in which he was reared. Thus, we see that any one factor may limit or even prevent the realization of the possibilities of either or both of the other two.

It is possible to state the interactionist position in the form of three *principles.*

1. *The original nature of a person may prevent his utilizing his culture.*

A society may contain universities, but if a person has insufficient intelligence to learn beyond the elementary school level, the educational opportunities presented by the university have no practical existence to this person. Similarly, a color-blind person cannot participate in the enjoyment of fine color shadings, even though the culture contains them. And so on.

2. *The culture in which a person is participating may limit or prevent the realization of the potentialities of that person's original nature.*

For many centuries women were not permitted to participate in the same kinds of higher education that men were. Throughout these years women of superior intelligence were born and died without any of them being permitted to utilize their intelligence on the higher intellectual planes. The same is found today with respect to some Negroes. In some parts of the United States Negroes are given poorer educational opportunities than whites receive in the same communities. Suppose that there are two children, one white and one Negro, who have identical native intelligence and thus the identical potential capacity for learning. It is obvious that the white child, having greater opportunity to participate in an environment in which his intelligence can be trained, will be able to attain greater educational achievements, not because he is by heredity any brighter but only because he has greater opportunities to utilize the hereditary qualities he natively possesses.

a. Ferals. Of much disputed authenticity but still regarded by some as valid are the studies of ferals. These provide the most extreme demonstration of cultural limitation of original nature. Ferals are human beings who become isolated from all human contacts at a very early age and are reared by animals. Wolves, bears, and apes have been said to "adopt" very young human infants and rear them as they would their own young. Such persons at the age of ten years, although they were normal human beings capable potentially of the same achievements as most readers of this book were at age ten, would actually be unable to read, write, or speak, would probably be unable to walk except on all fours, and would refuse to eat most "civilized" foods. Such ferals, of course, would wear no clothes, and if forced into clothes would tear them off as any wild animal would. Here, then, we have practically a laboratory experiment, without deliberately planning it that way, which gives us a graphic account of what human beings would be like "naturally," that is, if not influenced by any human culture.

b. Isolates. More reliable than inferences concerning ferals are a few more recent and less extreme cases of persons who have been isolated. These individuals have been among humans but in a manner markedly different from that of normal children. One such case, for example, is that of "Isabelle." The record shows that Isabelle at the time she was discovered (six and one half years of age) had been kept in seclusion since birth and in the company of her mother, a deaf-mute. Communication between Isabelle and her mother was, therefore, mainly by gestures. "Her behavior toward strangers, especially men, was almost that of a wild animal, manifesting much fear and hostility. . . . At first it was even hard to tell whether or not she could hear, so unused were her senses. . . . Specialists working with her believed her to be feeble-minded. . . . The general impression was that she was wholly uneducable." [2] Nevertheless, Isabelle was subjected to skilled and intensive instruction. It required one week of ingenious effort to get her to make any vocalization, but within two months she was putting sentences together, and in another nine months could read sentences on a printed page. Seven months later she had a vocabulary of 1500–2000 words. "In short, she covered in two years the stages of learning that ordinarily require six. . . . When the writer saw Isabelle a year and a half after her recovery she gave him the impression of being a very bright, cheerful, energetic little girl." [3] And four years earlier some experts considered Isabelle feeble-minded and uneducable! Why did they make this serious error? Because they failed to recognize, or to allow sufficiently, for the peculiar and subnormal cultural environment in which Isabelle had been nurtured during her first six years.

Similar errors are made almost everyday by many people who are trying to interpret, or to account for, subnormal performance levels of children and adults whose participation in more or less "normal" cultural environment is carelessly assumed. Usually the case is less extreme than that of Isabelle, but the principle is the same: good, or even superior, hereditary equipment is valueless unless the cultural opportunities to develop the hereditary potentialities are present. "How can they know unless they be taught" is indeed a wise adage!

3. *Unique experience may limit or prevent the development of the mutual potentialities of both the culture and the original nature.*

Billy has unusually high intelligence and comes from a family of distinguished men and women. His family is wealthy and therefore able to provide him with the finest educational opportunities that money can buy, plus all the comforts and luxuries which Billy might want. But Billy has developed a hatred of schools, books, and teachers. He is now nineteen. He has spent six years in high school but is still unable to graduate because

---

[2] For further details on the case, and for a detailed comparison of this case with another, see Kingsley Davis, "Final Note on a Case of Extreme Isolation," *American Journal of Sociology*, Vol. 52 (March, 1947), pp. 432–437.

[3] *Ibid.*

he has refused to do any work, has skipped school whenever he could, and for the last two years, has refused even to take an examination.

Here we have an instance of a boy "favored" with an unusual mind and physical health. He also has access to an advanced intellectual level of culture. Both his original nature and his environment contained unusually good opportunities for Billy's personal development. But the potentialities have not been realized, and they probably never will be, because of certain unique experiences which Billy has had. It is not necessary to go into all of the details here, but the facts in Billy's case history show a series of very unfortunate experiences at the hands of a tactless governess who tried in many ingenious ways to force Billy to study at a time when Billy was too young to study the kinds of things she tried to teach him. As a result Billy developed an intense hatred of books, of learning, and, of course, of the governess. Later, when he went to school he carried all of his animosities toward learning with him and readily transferred his antagonism for the governess to an antagonism toward the teacher. No teacher has been able successfully to break down that antagonism. Billy's case is obviously an exceptional one. Most children of superior ability who have opportunities for a superior education do not turn out like Billy. The point is that Billy had also had an unusual set of traumatic experiences with the governess which, fortunately, were unique to him and not typical.

Perhaps enough has already been written to explain what we mean by saying that original nature and culture alone cannot create behavior; they only contain *capacities or potentialities* for the development of behavior, and may or may not actually be translated into acts and thoughts, depending upon the exact kind of personal experiences which the person has had.

POTENTIAL AND REALIZED HEREDITY AND CULTURE

It is useful for the student to distinguish two distinct meanings of heredity and culture which we may term *potential* and *realized*. *Only those items in the environment which are actually experienced by a person can affect him.* Frequently what appears on the surface to be a "good" environment may, for the specific person in it, not be good at all. Billy's environment (p. 174) seemed to be a good one, that is, it had the potentialities from which a rich childhood experience could come. But *for Billy* it was decidedly not good, at least so far as his education was concerned. Billy's governess was a potentially valuable person who might have given Billy a splendid educational start. In fact she had tutored several other children very successfully. But Billy did not actually experience what the governness potentially presented to him. He experienced, instead, almost the antithesis of what one might expect, namely, a hatred for books, learning, and teachers. Another illustration: It is often said that "City dwellers are privileged to live a broad experience since they have daily access to libraries, art galleries, museums, and symphonies." But what proportion of the people of Chicago or New York City avail themselves regularly, if ever, of libraries, art galleries, museums, and symphonic music? Potentially the environment contains these items, but they are not really experienced in the behavior of most people.

The same principle is illustrated on the college or university campus. Potentially each student can secure a rich intellectual and aesthetic development if he devotes all of his time and energy to these opportunities, but as everyone acquainted with the realities of college life in America knows, most students do not actually experience the potentialities of their college. It might be added that their native intellectual acumen is, almost certainly, not the reason for this lack of participation. Rather it is, in part at least, due to the system of values which many students have acquired and which make other things, such as "coke" gatherings, football rallies, and bull sessions, more important than a visit to the art gallery or an evening at a symphony concert.

SOCIALIZATION AS LEARNING

Socialization is the sociologist's inclusive term for the various processes through which the original nature becomes fashioned into the social being. As we have intimated a number of times, people living in different cultures become socialized in different ways, in short, become distinct persons, both in their overt behavior and in their covert ideas, motivations, and thoughtways. A major part of the socialization process consists, of course, of *learning*. It is probably most easy to comprehend this when one considers language. Every person with normal original nature is an "unbiased candidate" for the learning of *any* of the thousands of languages past and present and others to be invented in the future. But before he can speak or understand any of them, he must learn a great many quite complicated skills. In addition to general language, of course, are such specialized communication forms as music, mathematics, and logic. There are also the myriads of kinesthetic skills like typewriting, driving an automobile, or dancing. A moment's reflection readily reveals, then, that the person in society—even a comparatively young one of mediocre performance—has had to learn a great deal.

The layman usually underestimates the complexity of the process of learning. It may come as something of a surprise, unless the student has already studied learning in psychology, to discover that learning is an exceedingly complex process. While there are many kinds of "learning theory" developed by psychologists and social psychologists, no one theory is currently held by a large enough fraction of these specialists to be considered a general agreement. Most of the considerations are, however, quite technical and beyond the scope of an introductory text. Probably the best the student can do at this stage of the game is to think *approximately* about learning in terms of the following concepts:

1. There are *potentials* in the *original nature*, as we have seen in the preceding paragraph.
2. There is an *external environment* consisting of material things, but probably more importantly of other people whose *behavior stimulates* the organism's original nature.
3. The person using his original nature *responds* to the stimuli from the environment. He does *something*, however "crude" or "irrational" it may seem to someone else.
4. These responses result in either *rewards* or *punishments*, pleasure or pain, depending upon how the external environment "treats him."
5. Depending upon the balance of reward and punishment, the person will *continue to respond* in ways which give him *reward* and tend to *refrain*, at least temporarily, from the kinds of responses which recently have brought him *punishment*. Each culture has its own system of rewards and punishments, of course; hence the individual learns the appropriate behaviors as he is rewarded for them.

It must be emphasized that we have written in general terms about learning and have not at this point taken up many of the interesting side lines, such as the complexity of the reward and punishment process, or the apparent contradictions one notes when two individuals are treated apparently the same way, one defining the treatment as reward and the other as punishment. Some of these problems will be treated subsequently, but for the time being we shall be content with the more general theory outlined above.

(Sometimes learning is simply defined as the modification of "behavior" resulting from "experience." Such a definition, however, tells us nothing of the process by which the modification takes place or the reasons for it.)

Through learning, thus, a person can acquire one of two, or more, opposing emotional responses to the same thing. He can learn to love Mama or to hate her; he can acquire a fear of lightning or be amused by it; he can enjoy smoking or loathe it. It was this phenomenon, of course, which we were implying when it was shown in the chapter on "Ethnocentrism" that the people in different societies display antithetical behavior as a result of different cultural experience. Our purpose here is to demonstrate further how learning modifies the behavior of the human being.

Modification of drives

Let us now consider the important question of cultural modification of basic drives, sometimes called "instincts." (The concept of drives is not accepted universally by psychologists, but it seems, nevertheless, useful for clarifying and understanding human behavior.) These organic motivations to fulfill fundamental biological needs such as those for food, sex, and activity are, in considerable measure, the underlying urges which prompt men to act. The modification of these relatively few, powerful urges results in the elaborate repertoire of behavior which each of us demonstrates in his daily life.

Drives, however, should not be confused with overt behavior. This is a common and serious error. The hunger drive may explain why one is hungry and why he seeks food, but is not the explanation for his desire to get a chocolate malted milk or a broiled steak. The specific desires and their related behavior had to be learned by the person. All that the inherited drive provides is the internal stimulation to do *something* about the food need, not any *particular* thing. One learns to go to the refrigerator, or to turn on the oven, or to walk over to the restaurant, but the food drive could be satisfied in an infinite number of other ways.

Fallacy of old "instinct" theory of motivation

Not so long ago many sociologists and psychologists thought that there were universal innate motivations which were common to all humans and even published lists of the presumed universal "instincts." [4] While no two of these lists were alike (itself a suspicious factor in a supposedly scientific endeavor), it was common to see such behavior included as "maternity," "hoarding," and "power." Careful research

[4] See L. L. Bernard, *Instinct: A Study in Social Psychology* (New York, Holt, Rinehart and Winston, 1924) for a classic critique of the older instinctivist psychology. Part of our current trouble is linguistic.

has rather clearly shown the fallacies of these by the demonstration of two decisive facts: (1) These so-called universal instincts are *not* universal at all. There are cultures in which such allegedly instinctive behavior is either unknown or taboo. (2) These "instincts" are found in those cultures where they are consciously or unconsciously taught. In other words, they are mostly *"acquired* attributes."

ORIGINAL NATURE IS PLURIPOTENTIAL (OR MULTIPOTENTIAL)

Perhaps the chief error which is made when persons seek to discover relationships between original nature and actual behavior is the assumption that a given original nature can result in only one kind or type of behavior. In other words, if a man is a capable lawyer, he is assumed to have inherited an intelligence for law. The fact of the matter is, on the other hand, that the man has a high intelligence which might just as well have been used in medicine, business, politics, agriculture, or crime as in the legal profession. This particular man's culture and unique experience resulted in his becoming a capable lawyer. A different culture and unique experience could just as well have resulted in an equally capable personality along some other line which required comparable intelligence and other attributes.

1. *The evidence from cultural variability.* It will be recalled from early chapters dealing with culture variability that very wide differences in human behavior norms can be seen among different peoples of the world. Yet all of these peoples have essentially the same original nature, with the occasional exception of such irrelevant things as skin color, size, and head shape. Thus, apparently man's original nature is sufficiently versatile as to permit him to acquire such divergent behavior norms as monogamy and polygamy, Christianity and Shintoism, democracy and dictatorship, capitalism and communism. While each of the above systems is not exactly the opposite of the other, differences are certainly tremendous.

2. *The evidence from studies of identical twins.* Within a given culture one can also find rather marked behavior differences between persons of similar if not identical heredity. Instances are known in which identical twins, the closest to identical heredity that is possible, show marked differences and contradictions in their behavior.[5]

[5] See, for example, the classic study by H. H. Newman, "How Differences in Environment Affected Separated One-Egg Twins," in T. H. Newcomb and Eugene Hartley, eds., *Readings in Social Psychology* (New York, Holt, Rinehart and Winston, 1947), pp. 1–6.

3. *Intracultural variation.* Every human being has the sex drive, but some people remain celibate while others marry, some are monogamous and others polygamous, some are preoccupied with sex and to others sex is of minor interest. One can discover no actual behavior which the existence of the sex drive requires. It can apparently be "satisfied" by such divergent behaviors as prostitution and the writing of romantic poetry!

A hypothetical problem

It is often an interesting speculation what one would have become if he had not become what he did. Obviously there is no definitive empiric proof that he could have become anything else, but the preponderant *inference* from what we have learned is that he certainly could have become a different person if his culture or his unique experience had been different. An excellent exercise which may be helpful in appreciating the multipotentiality of one's orginal nature is to assume that at birth one changed place with a newborn Japanese or Zulu or Mexican peon infant. In what ways, under such circumstances, would one be different: language, morals, values, interests, dress and personal appearance, skills, education, religion? Certainly if one had not contacted American culture, he could not have the characteristic traits of behavior of American society.

SOCIALIZATION AND MATURATION

As we have seen, *socialization* is a generic term to cover all of the processes and results of learning from other people, either directly in face-to-face interaction or indirectly through reading. It is through socialization that one learns the folkways and mores, the real and the ideal culture patterns of his society, shaped, of course, by the vicissitudes of one's unique experience. *Maturation* refers to those changes in the characteristics and behavior of the person due to biological changes resulting from increasing age, irrespective of one's experience. Children attain puberty and adults usually get gray hair in all cultures. Obviously most of the changes which take place in a human being from birth to death take place because of maturation and/or because of socialization.

A persistent and not yet completely solved problem arises, as we have already seen, when one attempts to discover whether socialization or maturation is the sole or more important factor in some *specific* change. When a child goes through the stage known as puberty, for example, there are certain physical changes which occur and which are undeniably due to maturation. These would occur in any culture. But puberty and adolescence are also characterized by numerous psychological changes and characteristics. Are these psychological changes due to the fact of maturation or to the accompanying changes in the culture of the child which may result from the adult's differing conceptions and treatment of the child after he has attained puberty? The answer to this problem is not completely known, but there is growing emphasis among authorities upon the significance of the changed role of the person as a major causative factor in the psychological disturbances attending adolescence. The point is that many of the differences in the behaviors of the persons in differing age-groups are not so much the result of the difference of their ages per se as of the fact that the social codes require, expect, or suggest different behaviors for persons in the different age-groups.

Socialization defines organic factors [6]

It has already been shown in preceding chapters that society requires certain behaviors and exerts strong pressures toward certain others. The culture of every people, for example, contains certain requirements and prohibitions concerning the human body and its functioning. All modern cultures define certain parts of the human body as taboo for public exhibition. Quite consistently the genital organs are so defined. So strong is this taboo that violations of it are regarded with disgust, and such acts are said to be obscene. Precisely how much exposure is to be permitted, and how close to the genitals the exposure may properly come, is simply a matter of style, the standards for which vary greatly from time to time even within the same society. Urination and defecation are also defined, and more or less elaborate rules for their "correct" execution exist.

Almost nothing involved in the organic makeup of the human being has escaped cultural definition and, of course, for practically every approved practice in some culture, a radically different practice in another culture can be found. Thus, the prevailing attitudes derived from the culture determine for a person how and what he ought to think about every part of his anatomy and every function of his organs. This fact of cultural definition is so thoroughly ingrained in a person's ex-

[6] The original development of this point is by W. I. Thomas and Florian Znaniecki, quoted in "The Definition of the Situation" in T. M. Newcomb and E. L. Hartley, *Readings in Social Psychology* (New York, Holt, Rinehart and Winston, 1947), p. 76.

7. CULTURAL VALUES VERSUS EUGENIC VALUES (In the United States)

Women as Valued **Socially:**		Women as Valued **Eugenically:**
Beauty first		Beauty unimportant
Delicate features		Strong features
No "deep" intellect		High intelligence
Vivaciousness		Seriousness
Slim figure		Sturdy figure
Tiny waist		Ample waist
Small hips		Broad hips
Dainty wrists		Sturdy wrists
and hands		Strong hands
Slender, soft		Solid, sturdy
Tapering limbs		limbs and
and slim ankles		ankles
Tiny feet		Good-sized feet

perience that most persons believe, for example, that "it is natural for all humans to be modest" about exposure of certain organs and "ashamed of" certain acts. So long as the principle is stated this generally, it is not entirely incorrect. The idea frequently overlooked, however, is that cultural variability is so great and that cultural definitions are so varied that modesty norms from one group become meaningless in another. In one culture a woman would be ashamed if her face were seen in public but need have no concern about the exposure of her buttocks. Modesty taboos in some cultures require women to conceal their breasts, while in others they may be exposed with perfect propriety.

If one wishes to understand human behavior, he must recognize that feelings like shame, troubled consciences, or disgust constitute no evidence whatsoever that any given organic act is any more natural or unnatural than another. Man's capacity for variously defining vice and virtue, propriety and impropriety, fastidiousness and boorishness is almost endless. Likewise his propensity for building elaborate cultural mechanism to enforce conformity to some particular standards seems almost boundless. The potentiality of the human organism for antithetical behaviors is almost beyond comprehension. But it must also be clearly understood that in no society is a person really permitted to make up his own mind concerning matters of propriety and impropriety, right and wrong. Instead he comes into a world which is already equipped with the "right" answers to the questions of how he shall behave, right down to the most intimate and personal act. In fact, no one really *knows or can know how he would really feel if his body and body processes were defined through another set of mores.*

SUMMARY

In this chapter we have made some preliminary inquiries into the factors which shape the human being. The human being develops through the *interplay* of three sets of influences which impinge upon him—his inherited organism and all of its functions, the culture which he contacts, and the unique personal experiences he undergoes. It cannot be stressed too emphatically that both the culture and the original nature are significant for human behavior as *reservoirs of potentials* and *not as behavior* per se.

It has been pointed out that the original nature of a person consists of his body structure, reflexes, drives (innate, not as conditioned), intelligence and capacities, temperament, and undirected movement. It has been stressed that these parts of man's original nature are pluripotential or multipotential. Evidence for this principle comes from many sources, chiefly from the facts of cultural variability and from identical twins reared separately. Out of all of the many potentialities for behavior which a given person possesses, socialization eventually molds a single human being with one aggregate of potentialities tangibly realized; the other potentialities never become expressed in any behavior at all.

One persistent problem is that of drawing the line between socialization and maturation. Sometimes it is of practical importance to determine whether a given behavior is due to socialization or to maturation. Although existing techniques for the delineation of maturation and socialization are by no means perfected, they are gradually becoming better.

It must be borne in mind, particularly by the beginning student of behavior science, that the culture in which a person is reared defines virtually every physiological process and physical organ of the body with some of the most deeply ingrained emotional imprints of which man is capable. After these prejudice patterns are entrenched, some persons try to think introspectively about their behavior. They notice that it is easier to behave in one way than in another, that certain alternative ways of behaving, though physically quite possible, are so revolting and disgusting as to be really unthinkable. The tendency is then to jump to the conclusion that the accustomed way of acting or thinking is a necessary part of the original nature of man. Acts or thoughts contrary to the approved ways are presumed to be contrary to original nature. The error lies in omitting consideration of the large amount, and of the intensity, of socialization which accompanies the maturation of the physical organism. It is this socialization which defines which one or ones of all of the physically possible behaviors are to be regarded as approved and habituated and which ones are to be disapproved and discarded. After years of repeated practice of some one mode of behavior, it is easy to overlook the fact that any one of several other alternative practices could in the first place have just as well been established in one's habit structure.

SUGGESTED READINGS

Bernard, L. L., *Instinct: A Study in Social Psychology*. New York, Holt, Rinehart and Winston, 1924.
A classic examination of the instinct hypothesis in the light of the evidence. The student may be interested in considering the implications of the fact that as early as 1924 the instinct idea was in disrepute in the scientific world and yet the idea has wide popular currency today.

Cooley, C. H., *Human Nature and the Social Order*. New York, Scribner, 1922.
This is a classic on human behavior in relation to group participation. While some of its ideas are in disrepute today, the major contributions are unassailable. Especially important seem to be Cooley's treatments of "sympathy," "self," and the nature of society.

Cuber and Harroff (See Bibliographic note, p. 40):
Lawrence Guy Brown, "The Interactional Hypothesis," pp. 108–113; "Human Nature," pp. 127–134; "The Normal and Abnormal," pp. 159–167; Kingsley Davis, "Isolated Children: What they Show," pp. 113–118; Dennis H. Wrong, "The Oversocialized Conception of Man," pp. 121–127.

Eckland, Bruce K., "Genetics and Sociology: A Reconsideration." *American Sociological Review*, Vol. 32 (April, 1967), pp. 173–194.
A reasoned and informed statement of the necessity, which some sociologists tacitly deny, of relating study of genetics with the study of sociology and social psychology, particularly with respect to intelligence, as well as to more general sociological concerns. Technical but important.

Elkin, Frederick, *The Child and Society*. New York, Random House, 1960.
A good attempt to assess the impact of society upon the socialization of the child.

Goodman, Paul, *Growing Up Absurd*. New York, Random House, 1960.
Not so much a sociological study as a vivid, sensitive description of the paradoxes and anomalies in growing up in American society. Highly readable.

Terman, Lewis M., and Oden, Melita H., *The Gifted Group at Mid-life: Thirty-Five Years' Follow-Up of the Superior Child*, Vol. V, *Genetic Studies of Genius*. Stanford, Calif., Stanford University Press; London, Oxford University Press, 1959.
Terman is a distinguished psychologist whose studies of gifted children have become widely known and respected. This work examines his original group in their middle years. Should prove highly interesting and informative reading.

Time Life Books, *The Young Americans*. New York, Time Inc., 1966.
This is not a sociological treatise as such. Rather it is a high quality journalistic account which summarizes a great deal of sociological and other material dealing with the life views and overt behaviors of teenagers and other young Americans.

STUDY QUESTIONS

1. Why is "heredity versus environment" a futile argument? Illustrate.
2. Why does each person inherit a unique original nature? What are the sources of the uniqueness?
3. Why is it difficult to evaluate the influence of culture upon human development?
4. Evaluate: "A person's behavior is the result of original nature *plus* culture *plus* unique experience."
5. How is original nature only a *potential* influence upon the development of behavior? Illustrate.
6. Why do we emphasize the *experienced* part of the environment? Illustrate.
7. Would Mickey Mantle have been an outstanding baseball star in Switzerland? Why?
8. How do the mores of a society determine the naturalness or unnaturalness of normal organic acts? Illustrate.
9. Distinguish ontogenetic and phylogenetic biological traits. Illustrate both.
10. Compare and contrast ferals and isolates.
11. Why is the concept *heredity* an "abstraction"? Illustrate.
12. Why do identical twins reared in the same home develop into different personalities?
13. What types of behavior and potentialities for behavior appear to be the result of original nature? How may these be modified by learning?
14. Why is it difficult to determine the "relative influences" of socialization and maturation upon the behavior of the individual?
15. What is learning? Why is it so important in understanding human behavior?

16. What are the fallacies of the old instinct theory of human motivation? Illustrate.
17. What do we mean by saying that socialization "defines" original nature factors?
18. Why should drives "not be confused with overt behavior"? What connection is there between the two? Illustrate.

11
PERSONALITY
AND VARIABLE
SOCIAL EXPERIENCE

Every man is in certain respects
  a. like all other men
  b. like some other men
  c. like no other man.[1]

PERSONALITY

Preliminary definition

The term *personality* is employed by different behavior scientists in *different ways*. The precise reasons behind the different conceptions and statements involve somewhat advanced considerations, and are, therefore, outside the province of an introductory book. It must suffice to cover only the areas of substantial agreement.

First, it is useful, if not essential, to employ the term *personality* in an inclusive way. Personality includes *all* of the traits and characteristics which make up the person's behavior: his overt habits (such as laziness or golf playing or smoking), his attitudes (like attraction to blonde women or prejudices against Chinese), his mentality, his conception of himself, and any or all other things about him which affect his interaction with other persons. All characteristics, "good" and "bad," physical and mental, overt and covert, are parts of the personality. It should be clear, then, that in the discussion of the original nature, the socialization, and the unique experience of a person we have really been discussing the process of personality formation and development. The term *personality trait* is commonly used to refer to some one aspect of the personality much the same as the term *trait* is used in connection with culture.

As with all concepts, personality is an arbitrarily chosen word, but it has come into common usage among behavior

[1] From Clyde Kluckhohn and Henry A. Murray, *Personality in Nature, Society and Culture* (New York, Knopf, 1948), p. 35.

scientists. Until he gets accustomed to this usage the student may find it necessary to be quite cautious when he encounters the word in his reading of behavior science literature or when he uses the term himself. This use of the word *personality* should not be confused with the term as employed popularly. Speakers or musicians or teachers who are particularly successful and well-liked are sometimes referred to as people "with personality." Having a personality, however, is of no distinction because everyone has a personality. One person differs from another, that is, their personalities are different in many respects, but they all have personalities.

Evaluative adjectives often misleading

Other popular phrases which sometimes cause beginning students confusion are "good personality" and "bad personality." When such terms are used, the speaker or writer ordinarily intends to convey the idea that the person under discussion has certain personality traits which meet with approval or disapproval. Perhaps the subject is friendly, affable, or honest. Since in our culture such characteristics are sought after and admired, it is easy to understand why the evaluation word *good* is employed. The error lies in the lack of qualification of the expression "good personality." The person may have many other traits of his personality which are not good according to customary standards of value. He may be lazy, a drunkard, and a thief, and yet at the same time be generous, affable, and kind. When one has in mind one set of characteristics, he might use the adjective *good;* when he has in mind the other, he might use the adjective *bad* to designate the same person. To avoid this confusion the behavior scientist does not use vague and confusing phrases like good and bad personality. Instead he describes the personality trait as objectively as he can. For example, "John is very intelligent and is usually cheerful" or still better, if he has the necessary facts, "John has an intelligence quotient of 131 and is regarded by most of his associates as a cheerful man." That way it is clear as to exactly what one means and on what evidence the statement is based. The listener may make his own evaluations as to the goodness and badness of the subject in the way the facts are meaningful to him.

The importance of context in evaluation

Another difficulty in the use of *good* and *bad* and other evaluative terms is that goodness and badness are usually valid only in some particular context. Suppose, for example, that a man is a "dreamer." Is that good or bad? It would seem to depend upon what the man did with his dreaming. In certain occupations the ability to dream may be a valuable asset. In others it might constitute a handicap. Few personality traits are inherently good or bad. They acquire their evaluation according to the definitions and requirements prevailing in the culture and/or the judgments of the person who is appraising them.

This is very well illustrated by a character sketch by Willa Cather entitled "The Sculptor's Funeral." The setting is a funeral held in a small town where the body of a promising young sculptor has been brought home for burial. The reader is informed that the young sculptor was regarded as almost a genius by the men in his field. But then one hears another evaluation of the deceased man. This time the farmers who knew him as a boy are speaking. They, too, are evaluating his personality. But they are evaluating it in terms of their culture and their experiences with him. It soon becomes clear that they do not hold this man in very high regard. It seems that he was a queer boy with impractical ideas, and he did thoughtless things. And soon one recognizes that the traits which probably contributed to his fame as a sculptor contributed to his low status in the community of his origin. One might possibly say that he had a bad personality for rural agricultural society but he had a good personality for the profession of sculptor.

It is certainly not to be assumed from this illustration that success in different occupations necessarily requires such diametrically opposite personality traits as the sculptor's funeral account implied. But, as far as it goes, the illustration is valid and the principle true: personality traits are not inherently good or bad. They secure their goodness or badness from the evaluation they receive by people; this evaluation usually embodies the prejudices involved in the folkways and mores of the evaluator's culture.

The next few chapters will take up a number of phases of personality in some detail. The student is not to assume that the areas thus emphasized are necessarily regarded as more important than any others. They are, instead, the areas of personality which the sociologist (and social psychologist) has studied more thoroughly because they fall into his professional province—human social interaction. Other specialists have studied other phases of the personality in such specialized fields of study as physiology and psychology. It is not intended to imply that social norms, for example, as treated in the next chapter, are any more or any less important than the circulatory system as studied in physiology or the nervous system and intelligence as studied by psychologists. It is simply a convenient division of labor to concentrate on the topics which one knows best on the basis of empiric study.

VARIABLE SOCIAL EXPERIENCE

It has already been shown that persons who grow up in the same society do not necessarily behave in the same manner. Most Americans, for example, speak and write the English language sufficiently alike so that ordinary communication is possible among them. But not everyone has learned the English language in the same way or from the same sources, nor are the results exactly the same. Some people are very conscious of their language; they take pride in speaking and writing it with precision and nicety. Others give little thought to language as an art and are quite content with numerous imperfections, often being unaware that they are speaking and writing as poorly as they are. Similarly with other areas of culturally patterned learning. The conditions under which human beings interact seem to involve a considerable range of variation, a sort of "tolerance range" permitted or even provided by the culture.

Meaning of the concept *unique:*
the term is relative

The word *unique* has, like many words, a number of somewhat varied connotations. One of these meanings implies complete singularity, something "new and different" for which there is no counterpart. We do *not* use the term in that way here. By "unique experience" we merely mean that the experience in question is *the experience of that one person*, and we do not intend to imply that no other person has had a similar experience. The word is used as an antonym of "common" or "universal." Like many language usages, the word is employed relatively. There are *all degrees of uniqueness*, varying from insignificant and barely distinguishable variation to diametrical opposites. Uniqueness, moreover, is relative to some standard or norm. Thus, automobile theft is a unique form of behavior as compared to the norms of the whole American society, but is a common behavior form among a group of auto thieves. Many behavior differences among persons are comparable to this illustration. Thus if we are going to study human behavior realistically, we must provide understanding and explanations which will treat both the similarities and the dissimilarities of behavior among persons. The word *unique* may seem too "strong" a word to use when one is intending to convey the sort of meaning which we have just outlined, but this usage seems to be quite reasonable; after all, so long as its meaning is made clear, it can serve as a useful language tool.

The concept *oversocialization*

Probably related to the point which we have just made is a corrective to the usual sociological treatment of socialization expressed by Dennis H. Wrong as late as 1961. Professor Wrong,[2] and others he cites, points out that social psychologists and others tend to overemphasize the importance of overt behavior. Focusing attention only on overt action may seem to prove that a total personality has been molded in accord with culture ideals, whereas feelings and beliefs may not really be in accord with the groups' intentions. In short, there occurs a confusion between mere overt conformity and internalization of the ideas which the overt behavior is presumed to flow from. For example, the child who grows up in a family which is meticulous about religious participations may say his prayers as expected, attend religious meetings, and show that he is indeed conversant with religious concepts. But such acts do not prove, in fact, that he has really internalized the beliefs and concepts which underlie his parents' faith or that he may not have serious doubts and even conflicts in his own mind concerning such behaviors. Another person, however, subjected to the same social and cultural requirements may turn out to be essentially a carbon copy of his socializers' intentions. The difference between the two is the measure of the unique element in experience. More total understanding includes the extent to which an actor's overt behavior is really consistent with his subjective judgments, beliefs, and feelings. Surely, to assume such merely from the observance of overt behavior is to be patently naïve. Indeed, abundant research now available dealing with deviant behavior richly documents the finding that much overt conformity to social requirements is in fact accompanied in many cases by serious doubts and anxieties which frequently erupt into manifest mental illness.

The essential uniqueness of personal experience

It should not be overlooked, then, that uniqueness of experience can as easily be underestimated as overestimated. Perhaps this point will be made more clear if we turn to specific examples. By discussing specific aspects of behavior and various sources of influences on behavior we may bring the factor of social experience into sharper focus.

[2] See Dennis H. Wrong, "The Oversocialized Conception of Man in Modern Sociology," *American Sociological Review*, Vol. 26 (April, 1961), pp. 187–193.

The family: variable models

Some persons speak or write glibly, for example, about what "family life means to the child." But *what kind* of family life? Studies of the actual kinds of relationships existing between husbands, wives, and children show not only a great variety of overt behaviors and attitudes, but reveal also a number of virtual opposites in the realm of family experience. This is true even for families living under what appear to be the same or similar circumstances. Some parents give their children a great deal of freedom even while the children are very young, while other parents dominate almost every act of the child on into adulthood. Some children live in homes where the parents are devoted to one another, where they are considerate of one another's wishes, and where relative harmony exists most of the time. Other children grow up in tension-fraught domestic circles in which for days upon end they can observe nothing but conflict, quarreling, outbursts of ill-temper, and evidences of distrust. With the widespread practice of divorce in the United States numerous children grow up having several different persons in the role of parent, while others have only two parents and sometimes only one. Some parents instruct their children in the ways of good social usage with patience and tact, others by coercion, intimidation, and bribery. Some parents teach their children to be tolerant of different races, nationalities, and social classes, and of persons of varying religious and political viewpoints, while other parents indoctrinate their children, either deliberately or unconsciously, with bitter prejudices, hatreds, and intolerance of many persons and groups with whom they must later live. Some children see in their family circles evidences of high and noble ethical principles of human interaction, of justice, magnanimity, and service, while other children receive object lessons in injustice, dishonesty, and vicious selfishness.

What, then, does "*American* family life mean to *the* child"? Obviously it means different things to different children—and the differences are often radical. Of course, there are some basic similarities, such as the fact that the American family almost everywhere is monogamous, that most mothers give daily attention to the rearing of their children, that most families grow up in single family dwelling units. But these are only the formalities. The really fundamental factors in the formation of character and personality spring from the more detailed and intimate interpersonal relationships and are profoundly affected by the specific conditions under which the child comes of age.

The play group: variable experiences

The child's play group, likewise, provides him with a galaxy of unique experiences which leave their mark upon personality as indelibly as do the experiences in his family group. Children, for example, can be unbelievably cruel to one another. The child who is outcast from the play group because he is a stranger in the community or because he lacks the necessary physical prowess to participate in the traditional games, or is conspicuously dull in his school work, or speaks a foreign tongue frequently becomes the object of painful ridicule and ostracism from the group in which he would like to participate. Case studies of maladjusted adults have shown graphically how the rejection of the child in his play group or school group may lead to serious and permanent animosities and insecurity feelings which may seriously impede or completely prevent normal adult participation in work, recreational, or other groups.

Participations in the play group have also a positive function in the development of virtuous personal traits. Many persons first secure experience in leadership, responsibility, and the necessity for adjusting to other people while they are children and functioning in play groups. But all children do not have the same experiences in the play groups— even though superficially they may *seem* to.

EXPERIENCES ARE DEFINED SUBJECTIVELY BY THE PERSON

It is important to note, however, that it is not simply the experience itself which a person has had that leaves the lasting influence upon him; it is also the way in which the experience is *interpreted* or *defined* by the person himself. It is not uncommon to find cases in which a child or an adult feels rejected by his associates and very sensitive about his social position, when the objective fact of the matter is that he is quite well accepted and is afforded an average or superior prestige. Here is a fundamental principle of social experience. It matters little what the *objective fact* or circumstance may be; it is the *definition or interpretation of the fact* or circumstance *which determines its real effect* upon the person. A few illustrations may help to fix this principle in mind.

Suppose a woman believes that her husband is unfaithful, that whenever he is out of her sight he is pursuing or being pursued by some other woman. Suppose, further, that the facts of the matter are entirely to the contrary, that is, that the husband is and has been completely faithful to his wife. Which is the more significant fact *in determining the behavior of the woman toward her husband and toward other people*—her personal conviction that her husband has been unfaithful or the objective truth that he has not? Obviously since she does not know or will not believe the objective fact, her subjective interpretation alone can form the basis for her judgment and overt behavior. Another illustration. A young man feels that he is "unpopular with girls." The facts are, however, that girls say they like him and are attentive and courteous to him. He says, however, that they are "just putting on an act" because they "feel sorry" for him, that their apparent interest in him is feigned and not sincere. Meanwhile he is embarrassed by what he regards as the absence of personal prestige among women, a loss which he feels very bitterly. This mistaken idea not only causes him much personal unhappiness but forms the basis for certain objectionable traits in his behavior by which some of his associates are becoming increasingly irked. So far as this man's judgment and resulting behaviors are concerned, it is of absolutely no significance that his interpretations do not square with the objective facts. So far as *he* is concerned, it is a fact that he is socially outcast by women; to him there is no other and can be no other "fact." In most other respects the young man is essentially a normal personality—he is a good athlete, successful in his profession, was a good student in school, and is very popular with men.

Thus we see that, so far as the significance to human behavior may be concerned, there are two distinct kinds of "reality": *objective* reality, which can be verified by the observation of almost any number of persons capable of viewing the situation, and *subjective* reality, which consists of what *seems* real to the persons involved. It should be borne in mind that objective reality and subjective reality are not necessarily different for all people all of the time. The point is that they *may* be different, as shown in the above illustrations, and that when they are different it is only the subjective definition which can have significance to the person's behavior. This important fact has led one pioneer student of sociology to write the classic statement, "The imaginations which people have of one another are the solid facts of human life." In our language, the subjective definitions which a person has of himself, of his fellowmen, and of the situations in which he finds himself are the significant influences on his life. What the facts "really are" may coincide with what the person believes they are, or they may not. That is of little consequence to the person, however, who can act and react only on the basis of what he has experienced, not on the basis of something else. If a person is color-blind and cannot distinguish between red and green, then there is no difference between red and green *for him*. The fact that someone else can see the difference is entirely irrelevant to his experience. Likewise, if a man has an "insecurity complex" and believes that no one likes him, it is of no consequence to him that *some other* person knows that people really do like him. To him the fact of being socially disliked is real.

In this and later chapters it will be explained in somewhat greater detail why persons develop characteristic patterns of subjective definitions of situations which differ from the objective facts as seen by the majority of others. Obviously such discrepancy represents a kind of deficiency in social judgment, an ineptness in "sizing up" the world of people for what they really are. But to give it a name, or for that matter to explain how it arises, does not in any way solve the problem. The problem persists and is at the root of many of the misunderstandings between persons and groups whose conflicts constitute so important a part of the web of social life.

WHY ARE PERSONAL SOCIAL EXPERIENCES VARIABLE?

We turn now to a somewhat more systematic treatment of some of the reasons for *discrepancies between the subjective and objective realities*.

A factor in the environment has no consequence to a human being until it is experienced. The process of experiencing one's environment is limited by numerous factors. As you read these words, for example, of how much of your environment are you actually conscious? If you are giving your attention to your reading, and particularly if you are interested in it, there are sounds, smells, and sights in the room of which you are largely unaware and will remain unaware until you cease reading or give less attention to your reading. The same would be true for any activity in which you are engaged. Out of all of the potentials present in any environment, only a part are actually being experienced at a given time by the person "in" that environment.

What conditions may be responsible for the person's failure to participate in all of the potentialities of his environment?

Physical limitations and idiosyncrasies

A tone-deaf person is unable to distinguish the differences in tonal quality which a normal person can. A person of low intelligence cannot assimilate verbal stimuli as fast as a person of higher intelligence. An ill person may be less alert and, therefore, see and hear less than when he is well.

Such factors as these are known to have important practical significances in the ability of children (and adults) to learn. In the classroom situation, where the level of activity must be set on the basis of an average ability, a child may "fall behind" because of such factors as these. Then after he has gotten behind, he may lose status in his group or with the teacher and encounter difficulty at home because of inferior school work. There are numerous instances, for example, in which a child was thought to have been dull when he was merely hard of hearing, or had poor eyesight, or was undernourished. If these conditions were not corrected, however, they could become the genesis of objectionable personality traits which would become a part of his adult personality. Case studies have shown instances in which a man's choice of occupation could be traced to his being chronically ill as a child, thus forcing him to secure his satisfactions from the world of books instead of the more normal world of childhood.

Educational background differentials

Previous education may limit a person's ability to participate in his environment. Suppose a person who has lived his entire life in New York City were to take a walk through the country in company with a farmer who had also been trained as a biologist. Would they see the same things? Obviously not. The city dweller could probably identify a number of the flora and fauna by their popular names. He could probably identify "butterflies," but the scientist could distinguish several dozens of distinct kinds of butterflies. The layman, moreover, would have only the vaguest conceptions of the relationships between the various biological phenomena present. The experience of the two would thus be quite different, not because of any difference in basic intelligence or capacity for observation, but simply due to the differences in their previous training. It is often one's education which gives him the ability to experience the finer distinctions and to understand their meanings. Thus learnings influence learnings *ad infinitum.*

Emotional "blocks"

A person may be "blocked" emotionally in such a way as to limit his experiencing of his environment. From time to time people have very vivid experiences which often leave their mark in the form of intense emotional feelings. These strong feelings are called into operation whenever the person is reminded of the unfortunate episode. Sex education, for example, is often made difficult for some persons because they have previously acquired emotionalized definitions of the wrongness or sinfulness of discussing such a subject. There is a case on record of a college girl who became hysterical during a lecture on the physiology of coitus and rushed from the lecture hall screaming "*My* mother never did anything like that! *My* mother never did anything like that!" Obviously, such a person would not have the same experience in listening to the professor's lecture as another student would whose background of experience had brought her to the lecture with a different emotional orientation to the subject of sex.

Almost everyone has observed instances, either in his own behavior or in the behavior of others, which demonstrate that persons under emotional stress such as anger or grief or love or hilarity give evidence that they do not hear what is being said to them, even though other persons present and not under the emotional stress do. Most of the illustrations of this point which have been presented have been of an extreme sort. But it should be borne in mind that in many other far less dramatic ways, the day-to-day experiences of people are colored by the emotional part of the total experience. Thus, previous emotional experience constitutes a modifying influence accounting in part for the uniqueness of the individual's participation in his immediate environment.

Unequal participation

Another factor affecting the uniqueness of experience is the unequal participation of different persons who are theoretically "of the same culture." Almost everyone participates in only a part of what might be regarded as "his culture." The family in which one is reared opens up for him certain channels of the culture and closes certain others. If the family is a professional family, the children will probably have more contact with the children of other professional families than with children of working class or farm occupations. If the family is Protestant, the child will probably not have an opportunity to participate in the religion of the Catholic church. The child's school and play groups will be largely limited to the children who happen to live in the surrounding neighborhood. The same is true on an adult level. Education, occupation, race, income level, sex, and many other factors limit the extent to which we can participate in groups not appropriate to our categories. Consequently it is normal for each person to have some-what limited understandings of the way of life, and consequently of the problems and points of view, typical of people with other group affiliations.

One of the unfortunate things, many think, about modern specialized urban living is the fact that different groups in the community which are dependent on each other often find it almost impossible to reach a common meeting ground of ideas and actions because they live in such utterly different social worlds, even though living only a stone's throw from one another geographically. Neither employers nor laborers, as a rule, *really* understand the problems and difficulties of the other, because neither is participating, as a rule, in the society of the other. The same is true of different races, different nationality groups, and to some extent different age-groups.

Lack of opportunity to participate

Some persons, moreover, do not have normal opportunity to participate thoroughly in that part of the society to which they supposedly have access.

The writer recalls a girl with whom he went to high school who actually did not participate in the high school as it was; she only went to classes. Her parents rarely permitted her to attend parties, extra-curricular clubs, or athletic games. On those rare instances when she was permitted to go, she was chaperoned by her father who remained closely at her side throughout the event. On the surface one might think that she had had a high school experience but actually she did not. Her high school experience omitted many things which her classmates' education did not. Although she was a very able girl, she developed into "an odd person," say most of her acquaintances. (Excerpt from a term paper)

Similarly, other factors may work to limit a person's participation in the culture to which he seems to have ready access, such as insufficient money, low family prestige, illness, or lack of popularity.

When one considers all of the possible limitations on participation, it is not difficult to understand why personal situations which appear to the outsider to be "identical" are really not so. It helps to explain, for example, why children in the same family, perhaps twins, even though they are of similar or identical heredity and have the "same environment," turn out to be such utterly different people. The point is that the selected and realized part of the total environment may be very different for each, and even that will, in all probability, be defined and interpreted in different ways due to the unique ingredients of the total experience for each individual.

SUMMARY

Personality is here defined as the totality of observed and observable characteristics of a person's behavior. Many of the more subtle traits are covert, of course, and therefore obvious for the most part only to the trained scientific observer, and even then somewhat imperfectly.

It was stressed that it is necessary to avoid vague evaluating terms like *good* and *bad* when speaking of personality because the same personality usually includes traits which would be approved and traits which would be disapproved by the same judge. Evaluative terms are meaningless without references to standards of judgment which are highly variable.

In the latter part of this chapter attention was focused on the ways in which the unique experience of a person affects what he acquires from his environment. It was stressed that the subjective facts which a person secures from his environment, however erroneous, are the real facts so far as he is concerned, and that many times conflicts between persons and groups arise as a result of each one having a different definition of the situation. Correctness is so often only a matter of how one interprets the items under consideration. "The imaginations which people have of one another are the solid facts of human life."

A factor in the environment has no significance to a human being until it is experienced by him, the environment almost always containing many more potentials than any human being ever experiences. Different persons experience different things in the same environment because of individual physical differences in their sense organs, differences in the previous education through which their environment is interpreted, emotional blocks to participation in the environment, the inescapably specialized nature of participation in the larger culture due to one's social class, age, sex, religion, and other group affiliations, and certain superimposed hindrances to participation even in one's immediate group, such as overprotective parents.

SUGGESTED READINGS

Bernard, Jessie, "Teen-Age Culture: An Overview." *Annals of the American Academy of Political and Social Science*, Vol. 338 (November, 1961), pp. 1–12.

A highly interesting treatment of the teenage subculture. The author discusses a number of specifics such as popular songs, the special language of the teenager, class differences, and other aspects of the "leisure class" of youngsters.

Brown, L. G., *Social Pathology*. New York, Appleton-Century-Crofts, 1942.
The most consistent and express use of the unique experience factor in socialization to be found in modern sociological literature. The introductory chapters contain the theoretical formulation of this concept. Some sociologists are of the opinion that Brown may overstate the unique experience factor somewhat, but none would deny that it is a very significant one or that it needs a more prominent place in social-psychological study than it has often gotten from sociologists.

Clark, Kenneth, *Dark Ghetto*. New York, Harper & Row, 1965.
A penetrating discussion of the implications of minority status and inferior racial status so far as socialization is concerned.

Matza, David, *Delinquency and Drift*. New York, Wiley, 1964.
This is a prize-winning study of what could be called the "drift" into delinquency. It shows how the distinctive life experiences of certain young people result in the almost inevitable drift into delinquency behavior.

Schramm, Wilbur, Lyle, Jack, and Parker, Edwin B., *Television in the Lives of Our Children*. Stanford, Calif., Stanford University Press, 1961.
A discriminating study of the differentials in the use and meaning of television by children of different ages, different class background, and different personality structure. Excellent for its stress of the differential effects of the television experience.

Wrong, Dennis H., "The Oversocialized Conception of Man in Modern Sociology." *American Sociological Review*, Vol. 26 (April, 1961), pp. 183–193.
This is a long overdue criticism of conventional sociological naïveté about socialization. It should be required reading for everyone, teacher and student alike, who wishes to be truly sophisticated on the subject of socialization, deviant behavior, conformity, and other standard sociological concepts. This reading is the larger source from which the reading in Cuber and Harroff, *Readings in Sociology*, was taken.

STUDY QUESTIONS

1. What is the difference between "personality" as used by the behavior scientist and the "personality" of popular usage?
2. Why do we say that "everyone has a personality"?

3. What determines the use of "good" and "bad" when applied to personality? Why are these usually unscientific, ambiguous terms? Do they necessarily need to be?

4. How is the concept *unique* experience relative? To what is it relative? What is its connotation as used in this book?

5. Why would "the same experience" not have a similar effect upon any two individuals?

6. How may uniqueness in a person's behavior result from "typical" experiences? How may "ordinary" family life and the "typical" play group be sources of unique experiences?

7. Which is the more important to an individual, subjective reality or objective reality? Why? Illustrate.

8. How does the acceptance of subjective reality instead of objective reality often result in conflict?

9. How does subjective reality color the acceptance and influence of objective reality?

10. Why is any factor in the environment of no consequence to a person unless it is experienced? Illustrate.

11. How is one limited in his experience of factors in "his" environment? Illustrate.

12. Why do we have difficulty understanding the "problems" of others?

13. Do we ever "understand" others' problems completely? Why?

14. Can the "experience" and the "interpretation of the experience" by a person be separated by him? Why?

12
NORMS

BACKGROUND

During recent years, sociologists and social psychologists have found the concept *social norm* to be useful as a term to designate units of learned human action. We have already discussed some aspects of social norms, particularly in our treatment of "folkways and mores." Research and theory on social norms, then, are not to be regarded as new *content* but rather as a more precise way of examining familiar content and as a more precise analytical tool.

Definition: means and goals (ends)

The phrase *social norms* refers simply to *accepted or required behavior for a person in a particular situation*. Thus, folkways and mores are social norms in that they are the expected or required conduct prescribed for people in a given society at a given time.

Social norms may be said to have two parts—*goals* and *means*. An individual, thus, may accept a certain goal but not the approved means for achieving it. This would be illustrated, for example, by the student who wishes to receive a college degree (goal) but who does not accept the prescribed conduct for achieving the goal, such as taking the required courses, attending classes, and securing the necessary grades (means). We shall be concerned with this problem more fully later. Here we wish merely to point out these dual aspects of social norms, and the possibility that the means and ends may not both be accepted by a person at the same time.

How do social scientists discover social norms?

There is probably no perfect or ideal way, but two methods of study are utilized, namely, *direct testimony* (that is, what people *say* about their behavior), and *actual observation* of the behavior in question. The two techniques may not yield the same results. For example, a man may say that he always offers his bus seat to a woman, but actually when someone else observes his conduct, it is noted that he does *not* always, or even often, extend women this courtesy. In the research which we shall shortly discuss, both kinds of data have been utilized; the student will probably make his own evaluations as to the validity of the various procedures.

An important distinction: cultural and social norms

Before examining specific research studies, one more distinction needs to be made, namely, that between norms in the ideal or cultural sense and norms in the actual or social sense. Culturally, norms, as we have seen, are the requirements imposed by the group upon the individual. They refer to the shoulds, the oughts, the obligations, the regulations. These norms may or may not be generally observed in the *actual* conduct of the people to whom they pertain. For example, cheating in the classroom is forbidden by the expressed or tacit rules of the college. The actual behavior of students, however, may vary to considerable degree from this norm. Research has shown that in some classes cheating occurs more often than not. In such cases, the actual norm is opposite to the cultural norm. We see, then, that there are two norms: one is the moral norm, and the other, that which actually happens, called the social norm.

The above problem has given students of human behavior a good deal of trouble. One approach, like the one we have just outlined, is simply to recognize that the two phenomena exist and to study both. A second approach is used by persons who are concerned only with the cultural norms, essentially ignoring the coexistence of contrary behavior. This is the view implied by persons who say that Dr. Kinsey's study of sex, for example, is a waste of time because everybody knows what the approved behavior ought to be, so why make a count of all the delinquents? A third approach is to study only the actual norm, the reason being that, irrespective of what people *ought* to do, the *objective fact* is what people actually *do*. A student with this last approach would say simply, with respect to the Kinsey report, that the American sex mores "are" what Kinsey found them to be, whether the actual behavior constitutes violation or adheres to the ethical ideas. The thoughtful student will recognize that none of these three positions is completely satisfactory. The first position has the disutility of resulting in a kind of double talk which many people find confusing and annoying, as when one says that cheating is taboo as a cultural norm, but cheating in some schools is a majority practice as a social norm. Confusing as it may be, however, this view seems most useful, since the other views "solve" the problem merely by ignoring the contradictory evidence.

With this background, then, we turn to an examination of a few of the better known writings dealing with social norms. The reason for selecting these particular writings is that each contributes something to our understanding of social norms in general. The particular information supplied is mainly for illustrative purposes. To put the matter in another way, we will review a few researches in order to equip us with a set of *concepts* which we can use in thinking, and probably in further research, about any norm or norms in general.

SOME THEORY AND RESEARCH FINDINGS ON SOCIAL NORMS

1. The J-Curve Hypothesis

About thirty years ago, Allport [1] published a research which has come to be widely known for the terse and objective way in which his discoveries were set forth. Allport was concerned with ways in which norms of conduct were followed by people in concrete situations. We have always known that "violations" existed, but what is the proportion of violators and nonviolators and how is the *degree* of violation related to the number of violators? For example, is there a larger number of people who cheat on examinations occasionally than who cheat regularly? Allport first presented findings on motorists' behavior in observing stop signs. The observers watched the actual behavior of motorists and made note of the degree of conformity to the legal norm. They counted the number of persons who completely stopped as they were supposed to, the number who slowed down to something less than a stop, the number who "slightly slowed," and those who completely ignored the sign. When these numbers were plotted on the conventional graph, the J-Curve resulted. It is easy to see why it is called a J-Curve, although it is really a *reverse* J.

The second question that naturally arises is whether the finding that applies to motorists and stop signs is unique to that behavior, or whether other kinds of normative requirements also follow the J-Curve. Accordingly, then, such varied phenomena as length of overtime parking, time-clock records in a factory, observing the sacraments in a church, and religious beliefs were studied.[2] In addition to Allport's own researches, other studies and experiments have been made. They tend to show a general agreement with the J-Curve idea. We would

[1] Floyd H. Allport, "The J-Curve Hypothesis of Conforming Behavior," *Journal of Social Psychology*, Vol. 5 (May, 1934), pp. 141–183.
[2] *Ibid.*

8. THE J-CURVE

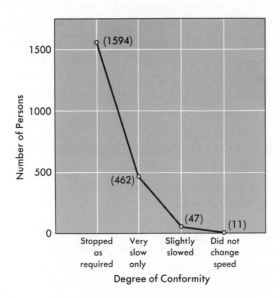

certainly not go so far as to say that the J-Curve is a "universal law" of norm observation, or that all norm-related behavior always follows the J-Curve.[3] Rather it seems warranted to conclude that for many kinds of norm conformity the J-Curve appears to supply the answer to our original questions, namely, what is the distribution of adherence and nonadherence and how does the amount or degree of violations relate to the number of violators?

The J-Curve is useful also in that it demonstrates that there is no simple difference between conformity and nonconformity; instead we see that *degrees* of nonconformity exist and that these differences occur in a pattern.[4]

2. Is nonconformity a general or a specific attribute?

There is a prevailing conception to the effect that people who are nonconformist in some one segment of their lives are necessarily, or likely, to be nonconformist in other segments. Cases selected in order to

[3] The student trained in statistical theory will recognize that the J-shape of the curve results from counting all the cases on one side of the mean of a presumably "normal curve of distribution" as simply "conforming." Since we are not interested in "overconformity," this seems permissible.

[4] Allport found, for example, that the degree of slope of the curve was affected by various conditions, such as the presence of a traffic officer at the intersection, etc. But, nevertheless, a J-Curve results.

prove a point can result in a serious error. Conformity or nonconformity in whatever degree can meaningfully refer only to a specific norm or set of norms. For example, the Amish man who refuses to send his children to public school is a nonconformist so far as his children's education is concerned but is typically a very strict conformist to Christian practices and ideals and practically all other legal expectations. The honor student who is opposed to participation in the Vietnamese war may be, and usually is, quite conformist to other religious, legal, and conventional expectations. Even a large percentage of people who are found guilty of criminal nonconformity are persons whose other aspects of life, such as family life, religion, and recreational habits are essentially conformist. The above is not meant to deny that there are some individuals who may be in a more general sense nonconformist, for example the classic beatnik, but rather to underline the fact that in any large sample of a given kind of nonconformity, the overwhelming proportion of instances will not be so encompassing.

3. The "reference group"

This concept has come into our thinking fairly recently. It has been especially helpful in explaining the nature of nonconformity. Suppose we return to the case of the conscientious objector. A substantial number of conscientious objectors are Quakers. This religious sect has taught for centuries that the pacifistic mode of life is the good life and that all participation in war is morally wrong. Now, when a Quaker refuses military service is he a conformist or a nonconformist? Certainly he is a conformist to the pacifistic norm of the Quaker group ("society and culture"). But in the larger society, which is not pacifistic, he is a violator of the norm requiring military service. Certainly some of the current antiwar dissenters may be conformers to a secular subculture for intellectual reasons. Many kinds of apparent nonconformists fit this pattern. The man who is out of step with the passing procession may simply be keeping step with another drummer. There is no intention here to deny the practical importance to a society of finding more adequate means of dealing with behavior, like the pacifist's, which runs counter to the majority norm. But certainly the student must recognize that there is a vast difference between the Quaker pacifist who refuses military service and another individual who simply refuses to recognize or observe his legal obligations. The latter is a nonconformist in a very different sense.

The student should not minimize the extent to which the reference group concept is useful in studying the normative behavior of people in a society such as ours in which there coexist dozens, if not hundreds, of groups and cultures containing markedly different norms. It is often exceedingly difficult to determine who is the conformist and who is not. Behavior which is nonconformist for a Catholic may be quite conformist for a Protestant, and normative behavior for a coal miner on Saturday night might be radically nonconformist for a minister. To be sure, this complicates the problem of classification in scientific work on human behavior, but we are more concerned with accurate analyses than with the kind of quick, loose categorizing which characterizes many laymen's attempts to "understand" human behavior.

4. Norms of evasion

It will be recalled that earlier we made a distinction between real and ideal cultural patterns (p. 92). The former were defined as what people actually *do* and the latter as what others *expect them* to do, particularly when the behavior is put into words. From the point of view, now, of analyzing norms, a parallel distinction needs to be made. Most people are aware that in many situations a certain behavior requirement exists. To be a conformer one is required to manifest overt conduct in accordance with the requirement. To some norms, however, he is expected also to conform by different, if not actually opposite, behavior and usually does so. What we wish to stress is not merely the coexistence of norms of the real and ideal kinds but rather the fact that the evasion of norms is also patterned and probably could be studied, for example, in terms of such concepts as reference groups and the J-Curve hypothesis.

Putting the problem in another way, it is almost inevitable that this dualism should occur, since, as Williams [5] says, "norms of social conduct never fully define concrete action. A norm is a statement (not necessarily precise) of the course that action should follow, not a description of the action that actually occurs. Social action, on the other hand, is always specific . . . : it is action here and now. . . ." Put by Williams in still another way, "a norm is not a point or a line, but a zone. . . ." Williams goes on to distinguish three characteristic ways in which an individual may react to a social norm.[6]

1. He may accept the norm as morally binding upon him, regardless of whether or not he would be punished for violating. In other words, his conscience is sufficient to insure conformity.

[5] Robin Williams, Jr., *American Society* (New York, Knopf, 1951), pp. 347, 348.
[6] *Ibid.*, p. 353.

2. He may accept the norm but only in a general way as a good thing, but "depending upon conditions" he will allow for a good deal of variation. This is illustrated, for example, when one hears some people excuse men in service from some of the sex standards that they would be expected to follow if they were civilians. One says in effect, "The norm is good but the conditions are such as to excuse violation."

3. He may simply reject the norm categorically. In this case he may attack the norm by trying to get it changed or by defending people who are violators, or he may simply ignore the norm, regarding it as not binding upon him or upon others.

Reflection upon one's own behavior or on the behavior of others will readily supply anyone with numerous illustrations of these three orientations to norms.

A principle which needs to be stressed, however, is that violations of norms, or what we *call* violations of norms, have many of the same social and psychological characteristics as conformity does. Violations are often supported by group "pressures," and the legitimacy of violations is "justified" for the prospective violator. Sometimes, as during the prohibition era or in cases involving graft, it is difficult to determine whether the pressures are stronger toward legal observance or toward violation. Hence, there is a growing tendency for social scientists to use the phrase "*patterns* of norm evasion." [7]

This may at first seem like double talk, but upon further thought will be readily validated by almost anyone's experience. Thus, for example, students who accept the norm of not drinking at a college which forbids students to drink, often at the same time find themselves "under pressure" from other students not only to violate the nondrinking norm but to violate it in specific ways at specific times—almost in a ritual of evasion. It is not uncommon for students to find it difficult to make up their minds whether the group pressure and the rationale rooted in their own consciences more strongly supports the no-drinking norm or some evasion of it.

It has sometimes been said, erroneously we think, that "this just means that there are two norms in the situation." Such analysis does not go far enough because it fails to distinguish a number of important factors, such as that one of the norms has the open and legalized sanction of the community, whereas the other norm is sub rosa, even though widely observed. When a particular individual gets caught, penalties may be expected. There are no such formal penalties imposed upon conformers to the original norm. Hence the admittedly paradoxical phrase "norm of evasion" seems to be a useful way to recognize the

[7] *Ibid.*, Chap. 10, esp. pp. 357 ff.

different nature of the two norms without denying that both are, in a sense, expected behaviors buttressed by certain kinds of "pressures" from other members of the group and justified by common rationales.

It is probably superfluous to belabor a list of evasion norms. In our society most people have encountered them. We will offer only a few illustrations: the norm of classroom honesty and established patterns of cribbing; prohibition and bootlegging; sexual chastity, and a wide variety of norm violations, varying from clandestine "affairs" to prostitution; an income-tax system and systematic patterns of income-tax evasion; ethical standards in all the professions paralleled by well-known and widely practiced ways of "getting around" these ethical commitments. The list could be extended indefinitely.

5. Norm confusion

It is already apparent from what we have said that a person living in a society can normally expect inconsistent demands upon him. Some norm requirements are almost impossible to follow, because they are inconsistent with one another or because the means and ends are not related, in *practice*, the way they are supposed to be in *theory*. For example, a student may attend a university which forbids drinking alcoholic beverages at social gatherings and yet norms of evasion are prevalent. Let us suppose further that such a student is present at the time of a norm violation but does not himself participate in the forbidden behavior. An investigation by the college is undertaken and he is called upon to testify whether there was drinking at, say, his fraternity party. Several means-and-ends norms are immediately confused in this not unusual type-situation. Ordinarily, truthfulness is supposedly a means to such desirable ends as honor among one's associates; but truthfulness *to whom* in this case? If he tells the truth to the investigating committee, he brings dishonor upon his fraternity brothers and very probably also upon himself in the eyes of his fraternity brothers. Actually, he is in a sense being rewarded by lying to the committee and "protecting" his peers. The point is that, regardless of what he does, difficulties ensue and the means-ends relationship between behavior and outcome are confused.

The situation described above is paralleled throughout modern life in our society by countless situations. Many of them are probably far more important in the lives of the people involved than our illustration about the college disciplinary committee. Unavoidably, and with great frequency, the individual encounters problems like those in the above paragraph; and even though there is no actual "investigation," persons very often are required to live with the knowledge that an investigation or exposé *might* take place and that they cannot always trust the means-ends logic which is supposed to order social relations. Thus, the word *normlessness* has come to characterize this confused state of affairs from the point of view of the subjective experience of the person in a norm-confused context.

6. Anomie

Another term which carries a connotation of a somewhat more specific nature is *anomie*. Anomie is difficult to define formally, but roughly the preceding paragraph describes the condition: the various persons in a given category in the society observe different norms, and the relation of means and ends are related differently by different persons.

Anomie, thus, has two dimensions, the one measured by *norm confusion in the society* and the other measured by *confusion within the personality*. Both of these phenomena will be discussed at greater length at later points in the book. Here we are only making the point that in modern society the phenomena of norms, norms of evasion, and anomie are to be regarded as essentially typical conditions and probably permanent ones. Certainly we do not need to stress the fact that such conditions seriously complicate the problem of personal adjustment and the maintenance of order in the society.

7. Internalization of norm conflict

It seems important to stress the apparent fact that inconsistency among norms does not *in itself* automatically bring about personal conflict. For example, there appear to be numerous persons in the United States who see no "conflict" between holding the norm of democracy (equal treatment or opportunity for everyone) and simultaneously holding the norm of segregation for Negroes. Other persons find the two to be in violent conflict and say that their "conscience bothers" them because of the inconsistency between the two norms. But *not all* persons are aware of the large number and serious nature of contradictory norms; even if rationally aware of these contradictions, many are not troubled by indecision or confusion or conscience. In short, there is for some people no emotional dimension to the matter; such persons are said not to have "internalized" the conflict. Thus, only *some* Christians see any inconsistency between the norm of their religion and capital punishment, racial discrimination, or participation in war; other Christians suffer deeply because of these "inconsistencies," and some willingly carry the burden of working to correct them.

SUMMARY

In this chapter we have treated a number of research studies and theoretical efforts which have employed the concept of social norms. We have distinguished, first, between social norms and cultural norms, norms and norms of evasion, and have considered the problem of conformity and nonconformity, especially as it is complicated by the variety of reference groups found in the society. Finally, we have introduced the concept *anomie*, showing how norm conflict gives rise to means-and-ends confusion, to a state approaching normlessness, both for the person and for the society involved. This matter will be treated, also, in other connections later on.

SUGGESTED READINGS

Allport, Floyd H., "The J-Curve Hypothesis of Conforming Behavior," in T. M. Newcomb and E. L. Hartley, eds., *Readings in Social Psychology*. New York, Holt, Rinehart and Winston, 1947, pp. 55–67.
Presents the results of several studies of normative behavior and shows how the J-Curve results.

Haskell, Martin Roy, "Toward a Reference Group Theory of Juvenile Delinquency." *Social Problems*, Vol. 8 (1960–61), pp. 219–230.
Presents a theory which purports to explain delinquent behavior by use of a reference group theory. Presents data based upon a group of boys in a correctional institution and suggests that treatment programs based on the theory may successfully curb delinquency.

Merton, Robert K., "Social Structure and Anomie." *American Sociological Review*, Vol. 3 (October, 1938), pp. 672–683.
A well-known and highly regarded statement of the reason for and type-forms of anomie in American society.

Sherif, Muzafer, and Sherif, Carolyn W., *Reference Groups*. New York, Harper & Row, 1964.
The concept *reference group* is increasingly being used to demonstrate the ways

in which norms form through group exposure, identifications, and pressure. The authors are prominent social psychologists, long known for work on the "psychology of social norms."

Williams, Robin M., Jr., *American Society*, 2nd ed. New York, Knopf, 1960, Chapter 10.
An excellent, sophisticated treatment of causes and types of norm evasion in contemporary American society.

See also the suggested readings following the next chapter.

STUDY QUESTIONS

1. What do you understand the phrase "social norm" to mean? Illustrate.
2. Distinguish "social norm" and "cultural norm." Do you know of any instances in which the two are identical?
3. Show how personal problems may result from the failure of means and ends to be related in practice as they are supposed to be in our ideal culture.
4. What are "reference groups"? How do conflicting reference groups complicate the process of social adjustment for many people?
5. Is conformity a specific or a general trait of personality? What difference does it make?
6. What examples of "patterned" norm evasion have you observed?
7. What is anomie? Why does it occur? What are its consequences?
8. What is meant by the "internalization" of norm conflict? How do you account for the fact that sometimes norm conflict is not internalized?
9. What is the J-Curve hypothesis? Do you consider it the "law" of norm observance? Why or why not?
10. Suggest some research studies which the class could make to test the J-Curve hypothesis.

13
DEVIATION

A great deal of popular comment as well as scientific effort centers around persons who manifest such extremes of behavior that they are conspicuously set apart from the run-of-the-mill or "normal" folk. Genius or talent on the one hand and delinquency or insanity on the other represent opposite variations in personality traits and behavior. Some of the basic understandings concerning such *social variants* constitute the material of this chapter.

DEVIATION

There was a time when behavior scientists used the term *abnormal* to designate the more extreme personalities and types of behavior found among persons in any society. But the word *abnormal* has taken a secondary and more popular meaning implying disapproval and immorality in the minds of many people and is, therefore, not neutral enough to be used as a scientific term, except, perhaps, by the person who is familiar with the difficulties. The term *deviation* is, therefore, coming increasingly into use. Deviation means, simply, that the attribute or action being described varies noticeably or markedly from the ordinary norms characterizing persons in the society. Deviations exist in varying degree as well as kind, and society distinguishes among these in terms of approval and disapproval.

Personality attributes are distributed along a continuum

Deviation of all sorts is a matter of degree. To illustrate: Since the vast majority of persons have an intelligence quotient somewhere between 90 and 110, we speak of both the highly intelligent person (for example, intelligence quotient 140) and the very dull person (for example, intelligence quotient 78) as "deviants" since both vary noticeably from the average. Almost every kind of behavior can be observed and conceived in terms of more or less of some measured attribute, when comparing the person in question to an average. Height, weight, and health are obvious illustrations. Morality, character, or prestige lend themselves quite as readily to such a conceptualization. "There is a little bad in the best of us and a little good in the worst of us" runs the adage. Obviously the difference between the best and worst is not a categorical difference, like black and white, but a difference of degree, like varying shades of gray distributed along a continuum from black to white. Psychological differences like intelligence, inferiority-superiority, and moodiness, or intellectual attributes like objectivity, knowledge attained, or facility with language illustrate the statistical nature of human trait variations. In regard to most attributes human beings range along a series of continuums, each one designed to measure some one attribute of the personality which is under observation. Any given personality will be deviant in some respects.

The extremes of the continuum, of course, contain the persons and acts which attract the greatest attention because they are so conspicuously different from the rank and file. There is a mistaken tendency to think, therefore, of the extremes as being categorically different from all the rest of the group. The error lies in not recognizing that there are differences all along the line and that it is almost impossible to draw the line between adjacent persons along the continuum. The line between the "just passing" and "just barely failing" student in a class is often very hard to draw, just as is the line between the just barely acceptable and just barely rejected man at the army induction station, because the differences are often negligible. But the requirements for satisfactory functioning whether in college or in the army require at least certain minimum competencies, and the line is arbitrarily drawn somewhere between the acceptable and the rejected often on the basis of a "hair's breadth."

Deviation is culturally defined and evaluated

It has recurrently been pointed out that it is the nature of culture and society to define all phenomena which humans can experience. And so the fact of personality deviation comes to be defined in the value system of the culture of each group. The standards or criteria of evaluation are always arbitrary as seen from the outside of the culture but easy to rationalize ethnocentrically.

Deviations may be roughly grouped into those regarded as desirable and those regarded as undesirable. In general the desirable ones enhance the prestige of a person who has them and the undesirable ones lower his prestige. There is, of course, no way outside of the prejudice system of a given culture to determine which behavior items or personality characteristics are to be highly valued and which lowly valued. In the chapter on cultural variability, as well as elsewhere, it has been repeatedly pointed out that extreme differences exist in the definitions of the same acts or of the same traits in different cultures. In some societies, for example, insane people are regarded as sacred.

The beginning student must, therefore, be extremely cautious that he *does not confuse the fact of deviation with the evaluation of deviation.* An admittedly extreme illustration may help to sharpen the distinction. Jesus Christ was certainly a deviant by his own claims, by the kinds of values he embodied in his daily living, and also by the records of the acts he performed. But was his deviancy good or bad, undesirable or desirable, valued high or low? Obviously, it depends entirely upon whom you ask, either among his contemporaries or among yours. Hitler provides another illustration. His deviancy is obvious to almost everyone. If Germany had won the war and succeeded in diffusing its culture into the rest of the Western world, in time he would have gone down in history as one of the greatest of men. Whatever the real traits of George Washington's personality, the personal evaluation of him both by his contemporaries and by posterity was determined by the success of the American Revolution. Had it failed, he probably would have been shot for the crime of treason.

In the ordinary acts of ordinary people the same principle is involved, only less dramatically. In the illustration of the sculptor's funeral discussed in the previous chapter, it was pointed out that the same traits of the same man were valued high and low by the two principal groups in which he participated. By one set of standards he was a failure and by another he was a success. The same would hold true for many of the personal attributes and behaviors of almost anyone.

DEVIATION DEVELOPS THROUGH SOCIALIZATION [1]

Deviant behaviors and characteristics develop through socialization in the same way that conventional behaviors develop. The basic ingredients are one's original nature, his culture, and his unique experience, although, of course, the specific content of each is different from person to person. Case studies of deviant persons as well as seemingly "normal" persons reveal very clearly the large amount of accident, chance, and coincidence which have had a vital influence upon the

[1] This point is very well developed and documented in L. Guy Brown, *Social Pathology* (New York, Appleton-Century-Crofts, 1942).

formation of personality. It is not intended to imply that every person begins life with an original nature equally capable of normality, distinction, or failure. Basic factors like differences in intelligence and physical health, as well as many others, certainly influence the formation of personality as we have already seen. But *there are always alternatives; both the original nature and the environment are multipotential,* and there is no ready device for predicting the outcome precisely.

This principle may be illustrated by the following account.[2]

Old Black Point, Conn., where Willie Colepaugh was born and raised, was an "exclusive" Long Island Sound summer resort, which meant that it had a high gate at its entrance with a sign reading, "PRIVATE BEACH. NO TRESPASSING." Willie lived just outside the gate.

Inside the gate, in their sprawling mansions, lived the summer residents, carefully protected from all people whom their Old Black Point Association considered "not acceptable." The men were stockbrokers who made the three-hour trip from New York every weekend. The women were socialites who gave cocktail parties. The children were scions who were tutored all summer long.

Willie Colepaugh had a different background. His grandparents had worked as servants for Mr. Black, of the New York jewelry firm of Black, Starr and Frost. With his help they bought two summer hotels on the Point, which is 10 miles from New London, and ran them successfully. Willie's father helped around the hotels and later married one of the waitresses. When Willie's grandparents died, the hotels were sold. After that Willie's father sold fish and puttered about as an electrician but never made very much money. Then one year he died of cancer, leaving his wife, his son Willie, and his daughter Louise with a small income from the sale of the hotels. The Colepaughs were very careful with it. Willie's sister worked as a nurse. Willie raked the Old Black Point bathing beach and mowed lawns there. Most of the summer, while the other boys were playing together, Willie worked by himself. In the fall, when there was no work to be done out on the Point, he was free to play. But by then everybody else was gone.

A lot of the time Willie was lonely. So when the first summer boys started to filter back to the Point, Willie would usually look them up. He already knew the reception he would get, but he looked them up anyway. The boys were Willie's age but they seemed older. They had a clean, well-scrubbed look. Willie was sallow and his hair was never cut right. They were educated to speak impeccable English. Willie, who had a nasal twang, said "ain't" and "gonna." They were taught to stick out their chins and say what they thought. Willie had a weak chin and his eyes seemed shifty

2 A. B. C. Whipple, "The Education of Willie," *Life*, Vol. 18 (January 22, 1945), pp. 11–12.

when he talked. A few of the boys were warm and friendly to Willie but found him a dull, unattractive companion. To all the summer boys, who never thought to call him "Bill," Willie was the perfect definition of to-day's term: "meatball."

In the late summer afternoons the summer boys would taper off the day's activities with a game of croquet. It was usually then that Willie would appear, pick up a mallet and make aimless shots about the wickets, waiting to be invited into the game. He rarely was. After a while he went away. At the bathing beach, when Willie flopped down in the sand beside the boys, they decided to swim out to the raft. If he went along they kept swimming until he got the idea.

So Willie went back to his solitary adventures, exploring the islands around the Point and poking into abandoned fishermen's cabins. If he rowed out to Griswold's Island, the boys' favorite picnic spot, and heard noises, he knew he would not be welcome. So he would turn around, row back to the creek, tie up his boat and go home.

After a few summers of the "silent treatment" Willie kept to himself. People who had houses on the waterfront would see him in the early morn-ing or late evening, quietly rowing his boat or picking his way over the rocks, going in no special direction and in no special hurry. Moonlight swimmers would see Willie seated on the "Big Rocks" at the bathing beach, as still as if he were a part of the stone mass. People began to say that Willie was "a little queer," that he "wasn't healthy mentally." But when the time came for the summer boys to go off to Andover and Taft and Hotchkiss, Willie's mother managed to get him into Admiral Farragut Academy in Toms River, N.J.

At the academy Willie buckled down to work. He wanted to get into Annapolis. Although the work came hard for him, he managed to keep his grades just above average. But when his schoolmates greeted him sociably and called him Bill, they found him pretty dull. He kept out of athletics. He was never in on the bull sessions or Coke parties. When he graduated, his yearbook referred to him as the "little obscure gentleman with big castles in the air."

Willie didn't get into Annapolis, but he did get into the Massachusetts Institute of Technology. At M.I.T. he even got a bid to join a fraternity and made a fresh start. But the grind was too tough for him. His marks flopped badly. Twice he was dismissed, went back to Farragut and studied some more. Both times he got back into M.I.T. But his marks stayed low. His social life was even worse. The boys at Phi Delta Theta began to see their mistake and Willie was never actually initiated in the fraternity. He began to drink too much. He became openly surly and violently anti-Semitic. He grumbled at being gypped out of his Annapolis education. Finally, in his loneliness, he went back to the seashore.

Along the waterfront of Boston Harbor, Willie wandered over the wharves and watched the ships come and go. Then one night as an adventure he visited an interned German ship. Soon he was taking candy, gum and cigarets to the crews and listening to them talk about "beautiful Germany" and the Third Reich and Adolf Hitler. Among the homesick German sailors Willie was warmly accepted. Here, suddenly for the first time, he became one of the boys. Willie's education was now complete. When he came back to the fraternity house at M.I.T. he repeated things about "beautiful Germany," and said it was an "outrage" the way the interned sailors were treated. He was expelled from M.I.T. in February of 1941.

The rest of Willie Colepaugh's history was documented by the Federal Bureau of Investigation on New Year's Day. It told how Willie drifted to Philadelphia, was arrested on a draft charge but was allowed to enter the Navy, was discharged from the Navy after four months' service because of his anti-American attitude. After that Willie shipped as a messboy to Lisbon, ducked ashore and volunteered his services to the Nazi government. In the middle of the night 55 days ago Willie came back to the U.S. in a German submarine and landed on a Maine shore very much like his lonely haunts at Old Black Point. Within 33 days he was in federal prison, faced with a military trial as traitor to his country. Back in the town of Niantic, four miles from Old Black Point, the name of Apprentice Seaman William C. Colepaugh has been rubbed from the World War II honor roll. . . .

The thoughtful person will probably note several crucial points in this case history at which the outcome could just as well have been opposite from what it was. Suppose the father had not died, suppose the family had moved away, suppose he had "made the grade" at Massachusetts Institute of Technology? Since he had to learn the attitudes, values, and role of being a Nazi spy, any influence which could have filled his life with a substitute interest, anywhere along the line, could have altered the final outcome radically.

The same principle holds for persons of distinction. In common parlance, they "got the breaks." Our purpose is not to enter into the age-old argument whether the "breaks" make the most of the man or whether the man makes the most of the "breaks." It is sufficient to note that many of the factors affecting a person's distinction constitute factors over which the man has no more control than Willie did over the factors which shaped his destiny. The ordinary success story well illustrates this fact. Whether the boy goes to school or borrows the books from a friend, he still gets access to the books which are not of his making. If the culture did not contain the books, he would never see them.

It seems unfortunate that the folklore of American society has resulted in the cultural entrenchment of numerous myths about success which simply do not square with the facts as they have been observed by students of the process. The chief error seems to lie in the neglect of the socialization factor in the development of the personality which attains the distinction or disapproval. Many people erroneously seem to assume that the behavior in question sprang full-grown from the original nature or from some one item in the total experience of the person. On the contrary, we have found that the human personality is an on-going process and learnings are built upon learnings. Every experience outcome has a potential "other" outcome if circumstances and choices were different anywhere along the line. This does not ignore the factor of inherited differences in the original nature, but even a defective original nature has alternative potential modes of expression in actual behavior depending on the kind of culture and the kind of unique experience such a person has had.

It is well also to note that so-called "good" hereditary factors like high intelligence or physical vigor have frequently become factors in the eventual acquisition of personality deviation of a sort which is disapproved by the norms of the society. Success or failure depends also on what one does with his inherited qualities.

School was always easy for me. By just sitting around and listening to what happened I could always learn enough to pass the examinations pretty well. I never bought a textbook and never studied one single lesson throughout high school. My grades were never high but I never failed a course and my grades averaged more than satisfactory. . . . I also learned quite young that if one is smart he can outwit the ordinary suckers who are really pretty dull. Only dopes work for a living. I've never really done a day's work in my life and I don't intend to. I have always found it possible to work out some kind of a racket and you can always be sure to find some sucker who will do the work for half the gain. I live on the other half. . . . I am now 40 years old and in this scrape which will probably land me in jail. I just overstepped a little—didn't cover up too well. My lawyer tells me I won't get over four years and I may be out in two and a half for good behavior. You can bet that my behavior will be —— —— good. And the boys who sent me up will be working for me yet. (Excerpt from an unpublished autobiography of a criminal suspect)

This man is certainly a deviant in several senses. He is not only a criminal but he possesses basic attitudes not typical of the small city in which he lived. The man had made a small fortune from activities which were clearly illegal, or very close to the border. His case history showed that he had a phenomenally high intelligence, that he was liked by his teachers and fellow students, and that he came from a respected middle-class professional family in a Midwestern city. It was the consensus of the behavior scientists who worked on his case that one of the major factors in the gradual unfolding of his deviant career was his high intelligence, not that the intelligence alone would account for his becoming a criminal, but rather that his high intelligence gave him an opportunity to "get by" easily. The rest of the more normal people about him were readily fooled by his superior wit. Finally, he had developed a mode of life based upon exploitation, and even while being tried for one offense he was already making plans for his next "racket," which he planned to launch when he finished serving the penitentiary sentence for this one. It may be interesting to note that while the man's case was pending, much persuasion and some pressure was brought upon the court by several prominent and respectable people who expressed the view that "this fine man could not possibly have been involved" in such criminal practices as those for which he was being tried. He had been intelligent enough to handle his "public relations" very well.

There is no trait or group of traits in a person's original nature and no social situation which one can be certain will result in any particular outcome for an individual person. Always there are alternatives in the situation; always there is interaction among the factors involved. There is evidence, to be sure, that certain kinds of situations have *greater probability* of producing deviants than others, but there is *no certainty in the individual case.* It cannot be determined in advance precisely how original nature traits, culture, and unique experience will interact to fashion the particular human being.

TYPES OF INADEQUATE DEVIANTS

A useful, overall classification

Broadly speaking, there are three main categories, each with subdivisions, of personal inadequacy: (1) *Physical inadequates.* Such persons cannot discharge the requirements of expected social roles because they are substandard in physical capabilities due to illness, accident, or some combination of these with psychological difficulties. (2) *Intellectual inadequates.* These are persons with insufficient mental ability to discharge the roles which are expected. Classification of mental ability is somewhat arbitrary, the three substandard groups being known as *idiots, imbeciles,* and *morons.* High-grade morons are just barely able to make a living in a few unskilled occupations and in relatively simple cultures. Idiots and imbeciles cannot survive without assistance from other people. Idiots, imbeciles, and morons are usually called *feeble-minded* or *aments*. (3) *Psychological (or psychiatric) inadequates* (sometimes also called *mentally ill,* or *dements*). Persons in this category are usually physically and intellectually normal, but are unable to handle the expected social roles because their mental-emotional functioning is too bizarre. (*a*) The most severe cases of the mentally ill, called *psychotics,* include persons with such mental diseases as schizophrenia, paranoia, catatonia, paresis, and manic depressive psychosis. It is obviously beyond the scope of this book to discuss the nature of each of these behavior disorders. For such information the student is referred to the customary courses in mental hygiene and abnormal psychology. (*b*) Less severe than psychosis is *neurosis,* although the student must not assume that the only difference between psychosis and neurosis is in the degree of the incapacity. Some neurotics are so ill as to require continuous hospitalization, whereas numerous psychotics are at large, some of them occupying positions of responsibility and even sometimes of prominence.

Somewhat distinct from the general run of neurotics are *psychopaths* and/or sociopaths. Briefly, such a person is characterized by "inability to be mindful of routine obligations and insensitive to the rights of others. It is as if they lacked the capacity to appreciate the ethical implications of conduct. . . . In a purely cognitive manner they 'know' that it is 'wrong' to stab a child, to pour acid on a puppy, or to steal money from a blind newspaper vendor. However, they fail to experience the emotional revulsion which crimes of this character arouse in the average man." [3] Less extreme cases of psychopaths are the chronic liars, the sexually promiscuous, and the chronically dishonest. For most positions of trust and responsibility such persons are unfit, even though they may have the intellectual ability and other skills to hold such positions.

The student should bear in mind that the above classification of physical incapacity, intellectual incapacity, and psychological or psychiatric incapacity is *based on symptoms, not on causes.* A mentally ill person may be mentally ill as a result of a physical illness, such as the paretic in the advanced stage of syphilis, while a person who is physically ill may really be a hypochondriac because he is emotionally ill. A person may be feeble-minded, either because he inherited his feeble-mindedness or because of some accident at birth or during childhood.

[3] David B. Klein, *Mental Hygiene* (New York, Holt, Rinehart and Winston, 1944), p. 89.

The close interrelationship between physical and mental disability has received a great deal of attention in recent years through research and writing in the field of *psychosomatic* medicine. While the layman frequently speaks glibly about behavior being "due to" physical *or* mental causes, the expert knows that very often no such clear distinction is accurate, or for that matter even possible.

WHAT MAKES FOR DISAPPROVED DEVIANCY?

The theory of personal responsibility difficult to prove objectively

Many persons fail to measure up to the minimum standards required by the society and are, therefore, more or less conspicuous for their limitations. The criminal, the poor, the mentally defective, the insane, the sick and physically handicapped, the eccentric, and the "unpopular" are all obvious cases in point. In common parlance some of the inadequacies are presumed to be the person's "faults," like crime, while others are presumed not to be the person's fault, like illness. Objective examination of the facts, however, readily reveals that in numerous instances these assumptions completely break down. Some criminals may commit criminal acts as a result of a chain of circumstances over which they have had no real opportunities to exert control. Likewise persons who are ill or physically handicapped may have become so because of their "willful disregard" for health and safety rules, which they understood but "chose" to violate. The better acquainted one becomes with the environmental forces which operate through culture and unique experience the less inclined he is to speak glibly about a person's "responsibility" for either his inadequacies or his distinctions.

It is not meant to deny that humans are not in some measure apparently responsible for their acts but rather that there are many factors which so operate as to turn what are wise choices at one time into unwise choices as events develop. Moreover, in the operation of choice a person can only use the knowledges which have come to him through the culture he has contacted, and these knowledges may quite as easily be incorrect as correct, inadequate as adequate. For example, less than two hundred years ago juries sat in American courts and passed judgments indicating that certain of their neighbors were "bewitched," and some persons were put to death or imprisoned for the crime of witchcraft. Yet these persons, both the witches and the jurors, had no real opportunity to choose to behave on the basis of any knowledge other than the knowledge they had. (It appears probable, incidentally, that the persons charged with "witchery" would today be considered as simply "mentally ill" and would be regarded as fit subjects for hospitalization, not for penitentiaries.)

Causes of disapproved deviancy are numerous and interactive

There are many known causes of disapproved deviant behavior. Some of these are a result of such hereditary factors as low intelligence or congenital illness. In some cases, such as a feeble-minded person, it is relatively easy to detect the obvious reason for his inability to support himself. A somewhat less clear case is that of the criminal, the school dropout, or the business failure. Here usually several factors interact to bring about the observed result, and there is often room for considerable difference of opinion as to which factor or factors are the most important. As is the case with talent there is an *interaction* of factors which affect the eventual outcome; if any one of these factors were significantly different, the final outcome would also be different. Since this is sometimes questioned, an illustrative case may be helpful.

For example, a man is an alcoholic. The case history shows that he began to drink excessively when his business began to fail; his business failed because he gave it little interest and attention after the time his wife deserted him. His wife deserted him because, she said, he spent too much time and money on the business. Meanwhile his father says that the man would have continued to succeed in business if his wife had not demanded an unreasonable proportion of his time and attention and had not been "such a spendthrift." Why, then, is the man an alcoholic? Was it the business failure, or the desertion by his wife, or his father's dislike for the wife, or none of these? Did he spend too much time with his business, or not enough? Obviously, we do not know. Any of these alleged factors *might* be crucial, but it is in turn related to the others in an intricate interaction which is baffling to unscramble. Moreover, there are other men for whom the circumstances might be objectively similar, but they did not become alcoholics.

Causes usually multipotential

A *plausible* "cause" of a socially disapproved outcome might as likely result in an approved outcome. In the above case, for example, the man's devotion to his business could as likely contribute to his success as to his downfall. Hard work, ordinarily regarded by persons in our society as a virtue, seems in his case to have contributed to failure. Obviously, with other conditions being different, notably the wife's attitudes, the outcome so far as the alcoholism is concerned could be radically different. Many, if not most, cases of social inadequacy are similar to the one under discussion here. The subtle interaction of multiple factors makes different outcomes possible, depending on how the factors *interact* with one another.

DEVIATIONS AMONG NEAR NORMAL PEOPLE

Specific traits of adequate persons may be inadequate

One's personality is made up of a large number of traits and behavior patterns. Everyone is deviant in some respects. A man known to the author is deviant in the following ways: He is abnormally short, abnormally good in singing ability, has more than average capacity for lying, is oversexed, is undernourished, and is allergic to camel hair. In all of these respects he is deviant, but is nevertheless a successful, in fact prominent, businessman with an enviable reputation. It is obvious that several of the deviations mentioned above are handicaps to him occupationally, but they do not handicap him *sufficiently* to limit seriously his success. In his personal life, however, some of these deviations are somewhat more important, and probably are also related to his unpopularity on strictly personal grounds. The man's wealth and reputation, however, are such as to protect him from serious social consequences of these inadequacies.

Most persons are a unique combination of deviations from the average, some good and some bad, as judged by the standards of society. The deviations are usually not very extreme and therefore do not detract greatly from overall adequacy. Some persons are adequate to the demands of some situations, but not to others. A man may be an excellent husband and father but inadequate as a businessman. Another man may reverse the two.

Adequacy depends on social requirements

The *same personality traits which contribute to a person's success in one area of his life may also contribute to his inadequacy in another area* where the demands are quite different. This is illustrated, for example, by the cases of men who make conspicuous successes in civilian life but make mediocre successes or fail completely in the army. Or, conversely, there are men who make conspicuous successes in the army and adjust poorly to civilian life. It is almost inevitable that such cases would occur because of the great differences in the duties and privileges of military and civilian life. The standards for judging adequacy are certainly markedly different in many basic ways. Originality, for example, might be more readily appreciated by the boss than by the top sergeant!

Every person, then, has a number of variations in his personality, some of which facilitate and some of which impede successful group adjustment. Since the demands of groups upon the individual differ greatly, traits which are an asset in one situation may be a liability in another. The ultimate test consists of the demands which a situation places upon one.

The increasing standards of minimum competency

It is generally held by students of human behavior that as society becomes more complex and standards of minimum competency rise, the proportion of persons who are inadequate increases. This seems true in spite of our improved methods of education and our better treatment of the persons who have "broken down." This apparent increase in personal inadequacy is probably due to the increases in the kinds and number of demands which society places on a person. *The standards of minimum competence are constantly being raised.* Persons who could "get along" passably well as illiterates in a simple rural society of a generation or two ago would be woefully helpless in the complex urban society of today, where one needs to be reasonably literate merely to move around safely in a community, not to mention being able to sell his services to an employer.

The minimum standards for admission into the various professions and occupations are constantly being raised. The average housewife operates more precise machinery in an average day than a skilled workman would have had access to in the past. Thus, numerous persons break down physically and mentally as well as morally in their attempts to live up to the demands placed upon them. This is not entirely a modern phenomenon, of course. There probably have always been in all cultures and at all times, persons who have not found it possible or who have not wanted to fulfill the requirements set forth for them. Some persons now, as always, find that they are more able than others are to "make the grade." But the proportion who do not make the grade seems now to be greater.

American society is organized to combat some kinds of inadequacy

Since everyone is affected in one way or another by the inadequacy of other persons, and never really knows when he may be inadequate himself due to factors beyond his control, there have arisen many organizations in the United States and elsewhere to cope with the problem. Some are set up to operate on a *preventive* basis and others on a *corrective* or an *ameliorative* basis. Hospitals and public health programs were early recognized as necessary to prevent and treat personal inadequacy due to health factors. The public school system was designed to bring the advantages of both general and vocational training to more persons than were able to afford it under the earlier system of private education. Later, public education was made compulsory because it was found necessary to have a larger proportion of the total population capable of at least the minimum standards of literacy. The great depression of the 1930's brought to public attention the need for setting up national programs for reducing the instances of inadequacy or at least for reducing some of the harmful effects of inadequacy. Thus we have the Social Security system, which provides insurance against unemployment and for old age. Even with this impressive array of organizations and professionally trained personnel, there are many cases which need assistance and do not get it. It appears that inadequate persons are being created even more rapidly than the existing agencies can reconstruct them.

Major social reform and personal inadequacy

There is, of course, another entirely different approach to solving problems of personal inadequacy. If appreciable and apparently increasing numbers of persons are made inadequate by some social condition, it might be possible to eliminate or change the condition in some way. On the surface such an approach seems relatively easy, but it is actually exceedingly difficult to carry into effect. Some conditions have long been known to have important bearing on a number of different kinds of inadequacies. Slums, for example, make for bad health, juvenile delinquency, and higher death rates. But the elimination of slums cannot be done by the stroke of a pen; the problem is much more involved. It is complicated, also, because there are influential persons and groups in the community who, while giving lip service to programs for the elimination of slums, are not willing to make the financial sacrifices necessary to accomplish the objective.

Sometimes, also, the same conditions which create inadequacy also create other conditions or results which are valuable according to the prevailing standards. The big city is a case in point. Certainly the vice, crime, filth, and crowding found in the working-class sections of many American cities must impair the adequacy of many personalities. But large cities also create many benefits which we are apparently unable to secure without also incurring the liabilities. And thus the cities remain.

There is a growing body of opinion which takes the pessimistic, but probably accurate, view that we now have the kind of mass society, both in America and worldwide, which is producing social inadequates at ever increasing rates. There is much factual evidence to support such a view. All factors considered, mental illness seems on the increase. Crime and delinquency, especially of the sociopathic type, seem to show long-run increases. Degenerative physical illnesses, such as heart diseases, are on the increase. Modern machinery places greater strains on the mind, body, and character than many persons can absorb and hence there are appalling accident rates, despite numerous safety measures and improved skills in managing machinery. These conditions may no longer be dismissed as merely the "personal factor" in human life. They are socially created and probably cannot be reduced in severity until there is some kind of basic and fundamental reordering of the social system. What that reordering will be, or should be, and whether it will, or can, be effected in our time are among the tremendous imponderables of our miraculous age.

SUMMARY AND CONCLUSION

Norms of human behavior are a fundamental part of every society. Different persons attain or observe the norms in varying degrees. Thus everyone is to some extent a deviant. Deviancy is of two basic sorts: (1) variation from norms in the direction of superior public approval or distinction, and (2) deviancy in the direction of disapproval or inadequacy to meet minimum social requirements.

Deviation is defined by culture. A given act may have high or low evaluation, depending on the standards of judgment of the culture at the time.

Deviation develops through socialization, through substantially the same processes as does normality or approved conduct. No trait of personality and no situation per se causes deviancy; it is always a matter of the interaction of many factors with the outcome unpredictable in the individual case.

Deviation which is favored is popularly explained by many fallacious ideas. It can be said with assurance that not all kinds of distinction require high intelligence and that high intelligence does not necessarily result in distinction. Personal attributes other than intelligence may contribute to "success."

The same general principles which apply to approved deviancy apply also to disapproved deviancy or inadequacy. It should be emphasized that many popular notions concerning both the causes and types of inadequacy are not tenable in the light of our scientific knowledge. Persons who are generally adequate may be inadequate in certain parts of their personality and vice versa.

It cannot be stressed too greatly that the extent and nature of personal inadequacy is largely determined by the number and kinds of demands which society places on the person. The assumed increase in the amount of personal inadequacy in present society is thus a result not of any "degeneracy" in the human being per se, but rather of an increase in the demands, both physical and mental, which are imposed on the person by the society.

The alarming increase in personal inadequacy in present-day America is being attacked by two kinds of approaches. One approach emphasizes the individual and seeks to guide him by education and other means so as to prevent inadequacies from arising, or seeks to treat inadequacies if they do arise. This is a tremendous task and the need may be greater than our collective ability to meet it. The other approach, through general social reform to remove the causes of inadequacy, is a major controversy in America. It has been only cursorily treated in this chapter.

SUGGESTED READINGS

Becker, Howard S., *Outsiders: Studies in the Sociology of Deviance*. New York, Free Press, 1963.
This is a study of deviation among two groups, marijuana smokers and jazz musicians.

Coser, Lewis A., "The Functions of Deviant Behavior and Normative Flexibility." *American Journal of Sociology*, Vol. 68 (1962), pp. 172–182.

This article is significant in that it takes a positive view of deviance which is largely at odds with the conventional view which tends to see deviance as a "failure of socialization" or a "problem for society." Coser tends to argue that deviance is important in relation to innovation and has important implications for group structure. An important article.

Erikson, Kai T., "Notes on the Sociology of Deviance." *Social Problems*, Vol. 9 (Spring, 1962), pp. 307–314.
An important and highly realistic article designed to correct the tendency for sociologists to "regard deviant behavior as an alien element in society." Deviancy "can often be understood as a normal product of stable institutions, a vital resource. . . ."

————, *Wayward Puritans: A Study in the Sociology of Deviance*. New York, Wiley, 1966.
Conventionally students of deviation frequently make the assumption that it is somehow unique to the present. Undoubtedly there are some uniquenesses, but it is also instructive to consider deviation historically. This is what this book does.

May, Edgar, *The Wasted Americans*. New York, Harper & Row, 1964.
This is a study of one of the anomalies of the affluent society—millions live on relief, willingly or otherwise, during a period of unprecedented abundance and affluence. How does this come about? Why does it go on?

Mizruchi, Ephraim H., and Perrucci, Robert, "Norm Qualities and Deviant Behavior." *American Sociological Review*, Vol. 27 (April, 1962), pp. 391–399.
This is a sophisticated discussion of the relation between the characteristics of norms and deviant behavior with a variety of illustrations. Relates such concepts as *permissiveness* and *anomie* and presents a typology of norms in relation to deviancy.

Pasamanick, Benjamin, M.D., Scarpitti, Frank R., and Dinitz, Simon, *Schizophrenics in the Community*. New York, Appleton-Century-Crofts, 1967.
This is an award-winning book which presents the result of a major experiment in the treatment of one important and apparently growing kind of deviation—mental illness. The implications of this study are far reaching.

Srole, Leo, Langner, Thomas S., Michael, Stanley T., Opler, Marvin K., and Rennie, Thomas A. C., "Mental Health in the Metropolis," in Derek L. Phillips, *Studies in American Society*. New York, Crowell, 1965, pp. 200–258.
A report on the well-known interdisciplinary study of Midtown, a section of Manhattan with 175,000 people. This is probably one of our best indexes of the extent of mental illness, its treatment, and related social facts now available. Also has careful references to other related studies.

Sutherland, Edwin H., *White Collar Crime*. New York, Holt, Rinehart and
Winston, 1961.
This is the classic work on white-collar crime. Later and more detailed studies
have been made, but this pioneer effort by Edwin H. Sutherland will remain the
classic treatment of the subject.

STUDY QUESTIONS

1. Why is *personality deviation* a relative term? Illustrate.
2. How does personality deviation depend upon the culture of a society?
3. How is the development of deviant behavior similar to the development of conventional behavior?
4. Why does man have no control over many of the factors affecting personality development?
5. Why is it impossible to predict with any high degree of certainty what kind of personality will result from a given original nature and a given social situation?
6. Why does the possession of "high" general intelligence not guarantee the achievement of distinction?
7. What part do "special inherited abilities" play in the successful attainment of goals?
8. In what sense is it inaccurate to hold a person "responsible" for his behavior?
9. Why is it difficult to determine the cause, or causes, of any specific pattern of behavior?
10. What problems arise when we attempt to classify personal inadequacy types?
11. Why is "cause" an unsatisfactory basis for the classification of personal inadequacy?
12. Why may the adequate person possess inadequate traits and still be considered a success?
13. What is the relation between the increasing complexity of society and the increasing proportion of persons who are inadequate? What difficulties are there in interpreting this causally?
14. Why and how are we attempting to reduce personal inadequacy in our society? On what basis do some people oppose collective action of this nature?
15. Why would prevention rather than alleviation and reduction of personal inadequacy be more desirable? Why is it difficult to agree upon a program of prevention?
16. Distinguish between aments and the mentally ill. Between psychotics and neurotics. Illustrate each.
17. How does culture affect (1) the creation of mental illness, and (2) the treatment of mental illness. Illustrate.

14
ATTITUDES
AND PUBLIC
OPINION

Research effort on the subject of attitudes has been, and still is, enormous. As early as 1940, for example, both the *American Journal of Sociology* [1] and the *American Sociological Review* [2] published extensive bibliographies on this subject. The former listed 269 references and the latter 200. Many more have appeared since. Despite this tremendous output of scholarly effort, many important questions remain unsolved, and on numerous others there is abundant but contradictory "evidence." In this chapter we shall limit ourselves chiefly to the areas of substantial agreement, leaving the more technical issues to advanced work.

Preceding chapters have already pointed out that human beings are motivated (prompted to act) by their basic organic drives which express themselves in a variety of ways depending upon the manner in which they have been conditioned by culture and by unique experiences. Human motivation is one of the most important and yet difficult aspects of the study of man. Why and how do people develop the likes and dislikes, the attractions and repulsions, the interests and apathies toward other persons, situations, and things?

PROBLEMS OF ATTITUDE STUDY

Definition

An attitude is, first, an orientation or a "tendency to act" in some way toward some person or situation or object or idea. Stated crudely, attitudes amount to likes and dislikes, attractions and repulsions, interests and apathies. They have a basis in original nature as all behavior does, but take specific form through socialization. Once formed they in turn influence further socialization.

[1] H. W. Dunham, Vol. 46, pp. 344–376.
[2] Daniel Day, Vol. 5, pp. 395–411.

Attitudes and overt behavior:
relationships and distinctions

The attitude should always be distinguished from the overt behavior presumably related to it. A teacher, for example, may dislike some student intensely, but because she has a code of professional ethics which frowns upon such discriminations, the teacher "leans over backwards" to be kind, considerate, and helpful to this student. Thus the teacher really tries to conceal her attitude by acting overtly as if her attitude were different from what it really is. In fact she may "act the part" so well as to deceive the student and other people who observe her. But the negative attitude toward the student is still there. It is an ever-present potentiality for overt behavior and may be expressed in the form of overt behavior at any time, perhaps when the teacher is a bit "off guard" or the situation extremely provocative. One of the chief errors made in appraising attitudes is the confusion of attitudes, which are abstract tendencies, with overt behavior, which is a more readily observable and objective fact.

One must be careful not to assume, however, that attitudes and overt behavior are entirely distinct phenomena; they are really intimately related, and it is very doubtful whether they are ever entirely inconsistent. Let us return to the illustration in which the teacher disliked the student. There were really two main attitudes operative in the teacher—her dislike for the student and also her desire to live up to the code of professional ethics which stipulates that she should be fair to all students regardless of personal preferences. Her kind treatment of the student was, thus, an overt response which is quite consistent with her professional attitude. It seems more in line with the facts, then—to interpret this situation as one in which two (if not more) attitude-response patterns were in conflict—her dislike of the student and the desire to behave professionally. The latter attitude was presumably more dominant, and thus she really treated the child with consideration most of the time. Upon the occasions in which she did otherwise, her attitude toward the child predominated over her attitudes of proper professional conduct. Exigencies of living present to all persons at almost all times the same type of conflict which faced the teacher in our illustration. Standards of morality and etiquette confront the expression of our more basic attitudes pertaining to immediate appetitive satisfactions like food and sex. Thus we see that while overt behavior is shaped by attitudes, several attitudes may be operative simultaneously, and some of them may be inconsistent with others. Whatever overt behavior actually occurs, some other potential overt behavior related to the other attitude or attitudes involved must remain unexpressed or inhibited.

Attitudes are learned

There is no way whereby attitudes can arise in a person except through learning. Even those tendencies to act which are associated with the organic drives of food and sex still have to be learned *in the specific form* in which they exist. A man may have an organic need for sex expression, but that does not mean that all women regardless of age, color, appearance, character, or relationship to him would be equally acceptable as sex partners. Quite to the contrary. On the basis of his learned preferences there would be numerous women who would be defined as nonacceptable, even though they would be quite satisfactory to meet the physical requirements of the drive. They would not conform to the man's standards of acceptability as learned through social participation.

Origins may be obscured

Often when laymen try to be introspective and seek out the origin of some attitude, they cannot recall any particular instance or occasion upon which the attitude was learned. Moreover, the attitude seems so fundamentally a part of their behavior that they cannot conceive of their behavior ever having been or being other than it is. Thus, they often refer to the attitude as "natural" or "instinctive" as if it were inherently a part of their original nature. Very few persons, even among those partially trained in behavior science, are sufficiently objective analysts of their own behavior that they can recall when, where, and how they acquired a certain attitude. Seldom, also, can they appreciate fully the degree to which long-standing, emotionally ingrained attitudes can create the illusion of being inherently a part of one.

Attitudes develop gradually

It is a common mistake, also, to assume that some *one* experience or occasion is the sole source from which one acquires a given attitude. While it is possible to acquire an attitude as a result of one, often dramatic, unit of experience, most attitudes are built up gradually over relatively long periods of time and are derived from and through many different kinds of experience. A basic attitude toward the members of another race is a case in point.

Standardization of attitudes through group affiliations

Group affiliations and participations tend to standardize attitudes for the members of the group. We have already pointed out that in the course of growing up in a group with a common culture, a person tends to acquire the attitudes which prevail in that culture. Ethnocentrism (Chapter 7) is perhaps the cardinal illustration of this principle. Through membership in some group whose culture defines a situation in a certain way, a person often has no real opportunity to reach fundamental conclusions which run counter to the prevailing notions of the group. As soon as he shows signs of deviation he becomes the subject of criticism and correction. In short, he is "under pressure" to react in the way in which he is "supposed to." To be sure, his conformity may be more conspicuous in his overt behavior than in his subjective attitudes, but it would be easy to overexaggerate the probability of wide discrepancies between them. A glance at one's own group associates readily reveals the great extent to which similarities in attitude and related overt behavior exist. The things we think "important," what we consider "beautiful," what we define as "wrong," what we consider "practical," what we consider "valuable" are very similar from one person to another in the same group, and in many cases are virtually identical. Among persons participating in other cultures, comparable unanimity of attitude is equally conspicuous. One needs to attain attitudes consistent with those of his associates not only because of pressure to conform but because it usually never occurs to him that there is really any other normal or intelligent way of looking at a given situation.

Attitudes within a group vary, but usually not radically

One should not lose sight of a companion principle, namely, that there may be individual variation, sometimes appreciable, in the formation of individual attitudes within a group. One will readily observe that many of the differences between persons' attitudes are really only relatively minor variations of the general attitude which is predominant. An excellent illustration of this is provided every four years when presidential elections are held in the United States. The campaigns call forth arguments concerning the relative merits of the party platforms and the expressed views of the candidates. But as one analyzes the contents of the party platforms and the stated views of the candidates, he can invariably find many more points of agreement than of disagreement. No major candidate for the presidency in recent years has ever officially expressed attitudes at variance with the fundamental concept of democracy, the customary freedoms, the capitalistic system, or the American Constitution. That is not to deny that one could find some persons at variance with any or all of these values.

As a further illustration of the fact of attitude variation, the following study of the expressed attitudes of five hundred students on the *ideal* number of years which a man *should* serve as President of the United States was made. (1) Seventy percent of the students thought the present system was right without any amendment. (2) The remaining 30 percent split almost evenly as to whether a longer or shorter period would be desirable. (3) Very few persons, about 4 percent, wanted a presidential term shorter than two years or longer than six. (4) Lastly, no one wanted a permanent or an indefinite term of office. Not all issues which one could formulate would, of course, show results of this sort. On questions such as the moral rightness of birth control, the same group tended to divide into opposite camps, some favoring, some opposing. It is noteworthy here, however, that the birth control issue is one of the points of sharp disagreement between Catholic and non-Catholic culture in America. If one then took either group alone and studied attitudinal variations, he would find the same sort of result as in our illustration about the attitudes toward the length of presidential term.

Ambivalence

Thus far it has been implied that a person has only one attitude toward a given thing or person or situation at a given time. Such is not always, of course, the case. It often occurs that the same person's attitudes toward the same subject at the same time are inconsistent with one another. Such a condition is termed *ambivalence*. Most people find that certain occasions arise in which they feel opposite attitudes toward the same persons or things, particularly where strong emotional feelings are involved. Studies reveal that parents are frequently ambivalent toward children, especially unwanted children.

We had not planned to have a child until we had sufficient funds to give the child and ourselves a decent standard of living. But sometimes the best laid plans run amiss and ours certainly did. Junior is now two years old, and to be perfectly frank with you, I don't know whether I love him or hate him—or really I guess I both love and hate him. I love him because he is, like any little child, dependent and lovable. Besides he is mine; he is physically and otherwise a part of my very being. But I hate him, too, because very often when I look at him I realize that even though he couldn't help it, he has been the cause of the greatest tragedy which I shall ever know. As a result of his coming my husband had to give up school and before he gave it up he tried to support the child and me and go to school, too. As a result of this impossible task he so ruined his health that he is destined not to live much longer. What might have been a gloriously happy future for Junior's father and me turns out to be pretty bleak. And regardless of how objective I try to be, at times I find it almost impossible not to think of Junior as the cause of it all. I know he can't help it but that doesn't change the fact that his existence caused it. . . . Of course, I would never tell this to anyone else who could possibly know us, because it would sound so utterly immoral. But it is true, so I have to say it. (Excerpt from an autobiographical paper)

This is by no means an unusual case. Any person with wide counseling experience or who has otherwise had the confidence of many persons will recall numerous instances of ambivalence. Sometimes the person both loves and hates a mate or an occupation or a colleague or his parents. This ambivalence is often so carefully suppressed that it is concealed from the person's associates, and sometimes he does not even realize it very clearly himself.

Personal attitudes may conflict with social expectancies

Frequently ambivalence springs from the conflicts between the attitudes a person actually acquires through his unique experience and the attitudes he is *supposed* to have acquired according to the norms of his culture. Parents, for example, sometimes conduct themselves in such a way that they lose the respect of their children, but the children also have learned that they should "honor" their fathers and mothers. But how can one honor someone whom he does not respect or, more bluntly, how can one honor someone who is not honorable? Most persons resolve the conflict in some measure by behaving overtly in the manner in which they are expected and keeping their disapproving attitudes to themselves. This does not entirely solve the problem, of course, because some people are sensitive to being "hypocrites" and may have mental conflicts resulting from such "insincerities." The chief point to be noted here, however, is the normality and inevitability of ambivalence for many persons in many situations.

STEREOTYPES

One of the most significant ways in which participation in culture standardizes attitudes is through the indoctrination of persons with *stereotypes*. Stereotypes may be regarded as caricatures of persons or situations or things. Newspaper cartoons (*not* comic strips) serve as a convenient illustration. Here, characteristically, we see Uncle Sam with his striped trousers, tall stately poise, and kindly face. We also see the Russian Bear and the British Lion and the anemic, bespectacled college professor in cap and gown clutching a college diploma. The politician, always of more than adequate girth, is smoking an oversized cigar. And, of course, there is the taxpayer, bewildered and exploited. No one, of course, points out that the United States is not a benevolent looking man or that the businessman, the politician, and the college professor are all taxpayers, too, because it is not the purpose to present the whole truth—the graphic fragment is enough.

Some of the conventional stereotypes are complimentary to persons or groups in the category to which the stereotype pertains, others are defamatory, but they are all incorrect. They are incorrect not because it is impossible to find some instances which conform to the stereotype, but because *most of the persons in the class to which the stereotype pertains do not conform to the stereotype.*

If stereotypes are as inaccurate as the above paragraph would imply, why then, do they exist? No one knows exactly why they exist, but it seems to be a reasonable inference, from our knowledge about culture and human behavior, that they are a result of *ethnocentrism combined with the desire for brevity, generality, and simplicity.* There is a certain mental economy in the use of stereotypes. Newspaper editors know that they can usually get across a much more vivid impression to many more people through suggestive stereotyped cartoons than through a brilliant editorial. The stereotype is a kind of mental shorthand through which vivid images are presented to people so simply and so often that the illusion of their accuracy is finally almost completely inculcated.

Stereotypes defined

One of the early students of stereotypes defined them as "preconceptions" of persons, situations, and things "which are dominant over our perceptions" of these things. The key words in this definition are *conception* and *perception*. A *conception* is an idea which has no special time or place reference, and which may be difficult to formulate precisely in objective form. The idea suggested by the word *dog* is a case in point. Everyone knows what dog means, but is it a St. Bernard or a Chihuahua, black or white, long-haired or short-haired, gentle or vicious, male or female? Obviously being a concept, it embraces all of these antitheses. It is thus a generalized abstraction, based upon a great many objective instances, but it often cannot be defined in purely objective terms by the persons who are familiar with the concept. *Perception*, on the other hand, refers to a specific experience. It refers to the physical stimulation which enables one to see, smell, or feel a stimulus, plus the meanings through which he "understands" the experience. Thus one can perceive a man, but only conceive mankind; he can perceive *this* book, but only conceive "books."

Returning to the definition of stereotypes, it will be recalled that according to the definition, the significance of the stereotype to human experience is that through stereotypes *prior conceptions* are predominant over *actual perceptions*. That means that the actual experiences one has with a person or a thing may be overshadowed by the previous conceptions he has had of that same thing. The following case in which a person relates his experience with teachers constitutes an excellent illustration of this point.

Stereotypes in socialization

Before I went to school I was thoroughly enlightened, so it seems, on the subject of teachers. My playmates, my parents, and my friends all passed hints or related anecdotes which led to the conclusion that school would be an unhappy experience, chiefly because the schoolroom would be presided over by a personality called a teacher. Vaguely I got the idea that the teacher was female, but it was also clear that she did not have the feminine attributes of kindness, sympathy, and affection which Mother did. Instead the teacher was a disciplinarian who made people stand in corners and stay after school. Moreover these punishments were not just punishments, but were unfairly meted out by the arbitrary whim of this teacher. . . . I remember upon my return home from my first day at school of telling my mother that I had had a pretty good time of it but had not yet met the teacher. I was noticeably shocked to discover that Miss ———— in whose charge I had been all day was really the teacher. She punished no one, she was friendly and kind and even looked, surprisingly enough, much like Mother. . . . Looking back over my entire school experience I can recall only one case of a teacher who fits the stereotype. Yet whenever the words *school teacher* are mentioned, they call up to me a vivid image of a middle-aged, grouchy, meticulously but outmodishly attired old maid, wearing horn-rimmed spectacles and using very pedantic, but obviously correct, language. (Excerpt from a term paper)

Here we have a splendid illustration of the way stereotypes operate in socialization. Prior to the actual experience with a thing or person or situation, there is usually verbally transmitted information *about* the person, situation, or thing to be experienced. Through this vicarious experience the person learns how the anticipated experience is supposed to be defined, that is, what may presumably be expected. Then, when the experience is actually encountered, one tends to read into it the meanings with which he has previously been indoctrinated. Thus, for example, since people from the Latin countries are supposedly "temperamental," when one observes an Italian or a Frenchman in an outburst of anger, he reacts, "That is just like a Latin—they're very temperamental." Rarely does one pause to try to recollect carefully whether he has really observed a larger proportion of Latin people exhibiting such traits than he has persons from other regions. Nor does he usually stop to think whether the situation he has observed is actually a fair test of the hypothesis at all. As a matter of fact, to most persons there is no hypothesis involved; it is a *fact* that the Scotch are penurious, Italians temperamental, and English stolid. The fact that the evidence may be contrary to most of these stereotypes is not known to most people.

A subsequent chapter on Race will discuss a number of common stereotyped conceptions of Negroes widely held by whites in America on which sufficient research has already been conducted to confirm that the stereotypes are utter fictions. But the stereotypes persist, constituting one of the major handicaps to the treatment of contemporary problems in race relations. The same principle operates with respect to different classes and regions within the United States.

Vicarious and real experience

It has sometimes been said that humans "secure their attitudes from their experiences." This generalization is fairly accurate but only if the vicarious experience which comes to the person through indoctrination with stereotypes is included. Unless the contacts with stereotypes are included as "experience," it would be impossible to account for persons having attitudes so utterly contrary to the real experiences which they have had. How, on the basis of his actual experiences with schoolteachers, could the man whose case was cited above come to the conclusion he did relative to schoolteachers? A woman also reports in her case history that all of her relationships with Jews have shown them to be strictly honest, but that every time she thinks of a business deal with a Jew she expects to be cheated. These are by no means unusual instances. They illustrate the predominance of vicarious early experience over subsequent real experience, especially where stereotypes are involved.

Summary: sociological significance of stereotypes

Stereotypes are very significant sociologically for at least two basic reasons. (1) Stereotypes often represent *institutionalized misinformation, distorted information*, and *caricatured ideas* of places, peoples, and things; and (2) *stereotypes have profound influence on the formation of attitudes pertaining to these areas of experience.*

THE MEASUREMENT OF ATTITUDES

Inadequacy of direct questioning as an index to attitudes

One of the persistent problems facing the behavior scientist is the discovery and measurement of attitudes. On the surface it might seem relatively easy to determine a person's attitude simply by asking him. Experiments, however, have shown (1) that persons are frequently *unwilling to indicate their attitudes, particularly if the attitudes are at variance* with those which they think are *expected* of them in the situation. Thus mothers will not admit having attitudes of dislike for their children, or a sadistic surgeon will not admit that he likes to perform surgery because he likes to see people suffer. It is always easier to talk as if one agrees with the customary conventional notions. (2) Even if they are quite willing to admit the truth, *persons do not always know what their attitudes are.* Most people, in fact, find it difficult to put attitudes into words, even when they feel reasonably sure that they understand what their attitudes are. Limitations of language are serious enough even for the experts who have long and involved schooling and have learned many of the more precise forms of expression. When interrogated regarding his attitudes toward something, the layman often cannot say anything more exact than that he "likes" or "dislikes" it, and perhaps that he likes or dislikes it more or less than something else. But attitudes vary from person to person in intensity, as well as in direction. Also there are many middle-of-the-road positions between categorical likes or dislikes. One may like certain things about the "War on Poverty" and dislike other things. And so on. (3) When a person tries to put his attitude into words the language may seem clear enough to him, but he cannot be certain that it will have the same meaning to the person who reads or hears his statements. Thus, what one *says* about his attitudes may be entirely misleading.

This problem of language is especially pertinent when one is requested to state his attitudes in terms of "Yes" or "No" answers to questions in a questionnaire. There is experimental evidence to show that many persons often do not understand what the questioner is asking or find that they cannot accurately state their own positions through the choices allowed on the questionnaire. The techniques for better questionnaire construction are gradually being refined, but even under the most expert study, questionnaire results are not to be regarded as entirely valid.

Inferential nature of knowledge about attitudes

The root of the problem is that *one really does not study attitudes directly; instead the behavior scientist is forced to infer attitudes from some other behavior* which he considers relevant. It must be realized that answering questionnaires constitutes behavior. The assumptions regarding the connection between the observed behavior and the actual attitude are as likely to be wrong here as in any other kind of behavior. It has been suggested by some scholars that a sharp distinction be drawn between *opinions* and *attitudes,* opinions being merely the verbal statements which are presumed to reflect the attitudes but may not do so in fact, for reasons we have already discussed.

Even when one observes the direct behavior of the subject, he still is in no position to be certain what attitudes the behavior reveals. As we have already seen, several persons may perform the same overt act but be motivated by entirely different attitudes. The persons may be deliberately trying to conceal their real attitudes or may wish to suggest attitudes differing from those which they know they have. The observer, moreover, must be careful not to infer attitudes too freely even from observation of overt behavior.

In spite of all the problems inherent in attitude study, attitudes are of the essence where human behavior is concerned. Although it is readily admitted that it is difficult to prove the connection conclusively, most authorities feel that overt acts result from, that is, follow, the attitudes which people have. Thus, for example, if a man refuses to move into a neighborhood where foreign-speaking people live, it seems reasonable to assume that it is either because he has attitudes which define that situation as undesirable or because he believes that other people in whose estimation he wishes to remain high have negative attitudes toward living in foreign-speaking neighborhoods. Either way the attitude precedes the choice and presumably tends to control it. The idea that attitudes cause behavior, of course, may not stand the test of further research and knowledge. Perhaps we only *think* that attitudes come first and overt acts follow. We may someday learn that some other sequence is the correct one.

THE STUDY OF PUBLIC OPINION

An important category of attitudes pertains to public matters, particularly so in a democracy, where the attitudes, opinions, and judgments of the entire adult population are supposed to be brought to bear upon the decisions of government. It is quite understandable, therefore, that a number of organizations have been established for the purpose of measuring what has come to be called "public opinion" on various issues. Thus, everyone has seen in newspapers and elsewhere from time to time such summaries as the following:

Will vote for Senator Smith	63%
Will vote for Mr. Brown	32%
Undecided	5%

or

Favorable to the Jones Amendment	41%
Against the Jones Amendment	53%
Undecided	6%

or

Think that Russia wants war now	30%
Think that Russia does not want war now	40%
Undecided	30%

Professional opinion as well as lay opinion varies greatly about the efficacy of such opinion summaries. Probably the chief difference between professional and lay opinion is that laymen usually seem concerned simply with the *accuracy* of polls for predicting elections, whereas professional students of public opinion are concerned more with other matters, such as trends in public opinion regarding medical matters, approval or disapproval of the war in Vietnam, or censorship.

WHAT DO PUBLIC OPINION POLLS REALLY MEASURE?

1. As we have already noted, a distinction has often been made between *attitudes* (as we have been using the term) and *opinions*. Opinions constitute efforts to *put attitudes into words*. A moment's reflection will further convince practically anyone that he cannot always or even often put his attitudes into words, because words do not quite convey what he "feels." Moreover, for various reasons, he may not wish to have his attitudes known; when someone inquires about his attitudes, he either replies vaguely or his response deliberately masks what he actually feels. Thus, often poll takers and other questioners do not get attitudes, but rather what are called "verbalisms." Sometimes verbalisms are simply trite, hackneyed phrases which serve the purpose of substituting for more accurate and original reflections of attitudes. To summarize our first point tersely, then, there is reason to doubt whether opinion polls really measure attitudes at all; the reported verbalism may have little if any correspondence to the real feelings—and even less to the real behavior—of the persons questioned.

2. By their very nature, opinion polls present a *static* picture. To be sure, many attitudes are resistant to change, but this is only part of the story. They sometimes also do change, and unless opinion polls are taken at frequent intervals and over long periods, as they rarely are, we are left not knowing whether the attitudes recorded, even though accurate at the time they are collected, have any relevance to public judgment at present.

3. People are suggestible. There is abundant research to show that in statements of opinion persons are strongly influenced by the way the question is asked (tone of voice, facial expression, and the apparent attitude of the questioner). At their best, public opinion interviewers are trained in the art of questioning and in minimizing the factor of suggestibility, but this represents an ideal and it may or may not be realized in practice. Certainly there is evidence to show that the same person, confronted with different verbal forms, will express markedly different attitudes on the same subject. There is reason to believe, then, that there is a subjective factor in the interrogation which may be an important source of error.

4. It is easy to read too much into the results of a poll. There is a tendency to assume, if a person favors, say, a proposed law, that he understands the law and for some reason or other approves of it. Again, there is evidence that such an assumption is not warranted. In a recent experiment conducted by a class in social psychology the following was revealed: 60 percent of the persons interviewed said that they favored

the President's message to the Congress. *But 70 percent of those who said that they favored the message could not tell the interviewers one single item contained in the message!* For all practical purposes, the question might just as well have been "Do you like or dislike the President," or "Do you believe in his program," since a majority of interviewees were apparently reacting to some such idea. As a test of the President's popularity or the reaction to an idea in general such a poll might be quite accurate, but it would be naïve to assume much else in cases of this type. For these and other reasons, then, one may wonder what public opinion polls really measure.

On the positive side, there is much to be said *in favor* of the practice of apprehending public opinion by the polling technique.

1. Polls represent our best, if not our only, statistical measure of popular judgments. However inaccurate they may be in such respects as discussed above, they still seem to be a considerable improvement over the alternative, which would be to guess or infer the content of public preference from even less reliable indices.

2. Where public opinion polls have been used to predict behavior, the more scientific of them have been fairly reliable. The above statement will come as something of a surprise to those readers who have studied the election of 1948, when practically every public opinion poll predicted the election of Governor Dewey over President Truman, whereas President Truman actually won by receiving slightly *less than half* the total votes.[3] How, then, can we say that the polls had a "fair" degree of accuracy? The point is that presidential elections are typically close in the popular vote, few being decided by more than a 5 percent difference and sometimes by an even smaller difference. Therefore, if a poll were 90 percent accurate it could still fail to predict the election successfully. Yet 90 percent accuracy is a high degree of accuracy. It is a serious mistake to judge the efficacy of polls as a whole simply by whether or not they can foretell who will be elected in a given electoral contest.

3. Many of the errors in public opinion polling are due simply to technical details in sampling, question formation, and interviewing. Rapid strides are being made in perfecting these techniques, and there is every reason to believe that the time is not far off when this science may be radically better than it is at present.

[3] Votes cast, in millions:

Truman	24.1
Dewey	21.9
Others	2.8
Total	48.8

Some larger problems

There is, however, a great deal more to public opinion than simply counting the number of people who say "yes" or "no" to some stated question. Taken literally, the "opinion of the public" may cover a great many matters upon which there is substantial, if not unanimous, agreement; and it may include disagreements which, for whatever reason, have never been brought out openly. What can we say, then, about public opinion in this larger and possibly more significant sense?

First, it must be reported that experts in public opinion are in marked disagreement concerning what might be called a "theory" of public opinion, or even, for that matter, what is the meaning of "public opinion." This may seem strange, but it can be profusely documented.

Although there are great gaps in our knowledge about public opinion, we do have a few ideas regarding at least some matters.

1. Public opinion, like private opinion, frequently involves disagreements on particular issues because the *underlying values are in conflict*. Thus, we get a kind of ideological conflict in public opinion between, for example, Christian ideals of the brotherhood of all men and militant nationalism and between humanitarian ideals, on the one hand, and fear of "big government" on the other, should the government try too aggressively to foster humanitarianism. Such conflicts will often arise in practice when a particular issue is raised, such as whether we ought to have more Social Security or less, or the extent and the role of Medicare.

2. While some aspects of public opinion are fairly measurable, such as which of two candidates is preferred for an office, others are exceedingly difficult to measure with existing techniques. Much is left, therefore, to the inferences of observers, and consequently judgments, even among experts, differ widely as to what public opinion is on many matters.

3. We know least, perhaps, about public opinion where there are no immediate issues involved. This is because issues are dramatic, and there is often great practical value in knowing how people stand. Where no issues are drawn, on the other hand, the expense and trouble of a poll are not undertaken. Consequently, so far as poll data are concerned, one gets the impression that disagreement and conflict are pervasive, while, in fact, if a more total inventory of opinion were taken, great areas of virtual unanimity would probably be uncovered.

Such critics consider the present stage of our knowledge about public opinion to be very immature. There is much impatience with the slow groping for important knowledge which characterizes present-day social science. All factors considered, it would seem that a really remarkable advance has been made within the last quarter century in respect to the study of public opinion.

SUMMARY

Attitudes are among the most difficult aspects of socialization to understand, and yet they seem to be among the more important products of socialization which behavior scientists study. The existence and nature of attitudes must always be inferred from verbal and other kinds of behavior, and the problems of drawing accurate inferences are great. Attitudes are learned from experience, but one must be careful to include stereotypes and other kinds of vicarious learning if he is to understand the similarity in the attitude outcomes found among persons within a given group.

Attitudes, like other cultural products, are paradoxical in that they are habituated and hence resist change while changing nevertheless. The changes may be gradual and unconscious, or they may be the result of someone or some group's deliberate planning.

The study of public attitudes and opinions by polling procedures is a relatively new and controversial field. We have discussed the pros and cons of this matter and also some of the broader problems of public opinion study.

SUGGESTED READINGS

Becker, Howard S., and Geer, Blanche, "The Fate of Idealism in Medical School," in Peter I. Rose, ed., *The Study of Society*. New York, Random House, 1967, pp. 165–173. Also *American Sociological Review*, Vol. 23 (February, 1958), pp. 50–56.
A well-known study in adult socialization. Shows how attitudes toward medicine, the role of the doctor, and related matters are changed between entrance and exit from medical school.

Blumer, Herbert, "Attitudes and the Social Act." *Social Problems*, Vol. 3 (October, 1955), pp. 59–65.
Questions, as do we in this book, the current assumption that attitudes direct and control behavior. Suggests a "better" theory of action and suggests ways of studying it. Technical.

Bryan, James H., "Occupational Ideologies and Individual Attitudes of
   Call Girls." *Social Problems*, Vol. 13 (Spring, 1966), pp. 441–450.
While sociologists have often been chided that they give too much attention to
deviant groups, their best work has often been on such subsystems. Here is a
study of modest claims and scope and yet highly informative regarding the
attitude structures of this marginal profession.

Clark, Kenneth, *Black Ghetto*. New York, Harper & Row, 1965.
A moving account of socialization as it affects attitudes in a situation of low
social position and racial segregation.

Coleman, James S., *The Adolescent Society*. New York, Free Press, 1961.
A well-known study of adolescents, their attitudes, their reasons for holding
these attitudes, and other aspects of the subculture of the teenager in American
society.

Doby, John T., *Introduction to Social Psychology*. New York, Appleton-
   Century-Crofts, 1966, pp. 297–317.
A brief, but clear, resumé of "theories of attitude change." A needed accent since
attitudes are so often discussed statically, as if they were inherently changeless.

Fenton, John M., *In Your Opinion*. Boston, Little, Brown, 1960.
A review and analysis of trends over a decade and a half in public opinion on
issues of a political and more general nature. Has a Foreword by George Gallup
on the history of polling and its contribution to U.S. democracy.

Glenn, Norval D., and Alston, Jon P., "Rural Urban Differences in Reported Attitudes and Behavior." *The Southwestern Social Science
   Quarterly* (March, 1967), pp. 381–400.
A perennial concern to both professional social scientists and laymen is the
similarities and differences between rural and urban people. Current stereotypes
accentuate the differences, but research by and large documents their convergence under the impress of the mass society. This study is instructive with
respect to the issue.

Additional readings dealing with public opinion will be found in the suggested readings following the chapter on government.

STUDY QUESTIONS

1. Why does one have inconsistent attitudes?
2. Why must attitudes be learned? Illustrate.
3. Why are some attitudes believed to be "natural" or "instinctive"?
4. What is the connection between attitudes and knowledge?
5. Why do our attitudes *tend* to be consistent with those of our associates?

6. Why do attitudes vary within a group as well as from group to group?
7. Why may a person have inconsistent attitudes toward the same subject?
8. Of what value are stereotypes to the propagandist?
9. How do stereotypes influence the attitudes that we acquire from an experience?
10. How are stereotypes "inaccurate generalizations"?
11. How does vicarious experience as well as real experience determine attitudes?
12. Why is it difficult to measure attitudes? Why must we measure attitudes indirectly?
13. What three major difficulties are involved in the measurement of attitudes?
14. How do attitudes often tend to resist change?
15. How may some attitudes tend to foster social change?
16. How would you define "public opinion"?
17. What are strengths and weaknesses of public-opinion polls as indices of public thinking?

15
THE SELF, SOCIAL ROLES, AND ROLE CONFLICT

SELF ATTITUDES

Definition of "the self"

Among the numerous attitudes which every person has is a group which refers to himself. Very early in his life each person learns that certain attributes of his own personality are important to him through the effect which they have upon other people and, therefore, upon other people's treatment of him. A very young infant soon learns that when he cries, certain consequences follow in the form of changed adult behavior toward him. Perhaps he will be picked up, fed, or talked to. In this simple way a fundamental fact of socialization is brought home to him at a very early age, namely, that *what he does affects how he is treated by others.*

On the adult level, of course, each individual's attitudes about his own personality are exceedingly numerous and much more complicated. They are evidenced in common speech by many recurring phrases with which almost everyone is familiar: "I lost control of myself"; "I hated myself"; "He loves himself"; "She was ashamed of herself"; and so on.

What is the significance of the reflexive word *self* which recurs so frequently and so consistently in the everyday language of people? It seems to be tacit evidence of the existence of a pattern of attitudes which each person has concerning his own personality. *This pattern of reflexive attitudes has come to be called "the self."* Most of this chapter will be devoted to the consideration of how self attitudes and feelings develop, how they become organized, and how they affect and are affected by other behavior.

251

Self and the imagination in process

Perhaps the fundamental understanding necessary to appreciate the nature of the self is to recognize that *each person through his imagination takes a position as if he were outside of his own personality and from this assumed position observes his personality as if he were someone else.* The recurrent phrases "as if" are significant; no one really leaves his own personality in any objective sense. He merely exercises his imagination in such a way that it has the effect upon him of taking a detached position for the purpose of self-observation and appraisal. Actually, of course, the person is really not necessarily any more objective when his self attitudes are operating than when any other attitudes are involved. He does not really "see himself as others see him"; he only thinks he does. His observations of himself may be as erroneous as his observations of anything else. His attempts to evaluate experiences may be confused by stereotypes, faulty observation, and misjudgment. It is, then, a sort of illusion that one has that he is looking at himself the way others would, for in fact he never really knows exactly how others do regard him.

It is essential to note, also, that *attitudes toward himself are frequently not easily verbalized* by the person. One may, in fact, be largely or completely unconscious of how his attitudes toward himself would look to him if he saw them present in someone else, or how they would sound to him if they were actually stated as they exist. Thus, it is not at all uncommon to hear an egotistical person express disapproval of someone else because "he is so egotistical." The egotistical person may not know that he is regarded as egotistical himself. Probably no one has sufficient insight into his own behavior to be conscious of the existence of all of his own attitudes toward himself, and even more certainly, to be objective concerning the accuracy of these attitudes.

Sources of self attitudes [1]

Are the person's attitudes toward himself his own attitudes or a reflection of others' toward him? This way of stating the question sets up a false distinction. A person's attitudes are, of course, uniquely his own, but at the same time they are derived from the attitudes of others toward him as he has observed them. This is not to deny that it is possible for the person to have different attitudes toward himself than those

[1] For an advanced, classic analysis of this and related problems see George H. Mead, *Mind, Self and Society* (Chicago, University of Chicago Press, 1934).

which other people have toward him. The point is that his attitudes result from interaction with other people. In short, self attitudes, like all attitudes, are learned through socialization and are strongly influenced by the culture norms of valuation, as well as by a person's unique experience. There may be uniquenesses in self attitudes just as there may be uniquenesses in the way in which a person writes or speaks, but it is no more correct to ignore the influence of other people on the formation of self attitudes than it is to deny the significance of other people in the formation of one's language patterns. Self attitudes are a social product.

THE "LOOKING GLASS SELF"

The nature of the self may perhaps be more clear if it is described in the manner in which C. H. Cooley [2] conceived of it when he coined the phrase, the *looking glass self*. He explained that there is an ever recurring thinking process going on in each person's mind, and it is characterized by three separable phases.

Step 1. *The imagination of how "I" appear to others*, that is, simply what they see or perceive when they interact with the "I." Strictly speaking, of course, no one can ever know what anyone else experiences when the two interact. All that he can ever know is what he thinks or assumes or has reason to believe they perceive. As a matter of fact "they" may not even see him at all, and yet he may think that they do. Thus the first stage of the looking glass process is *the person's imagination of what other persons perceive about his personality*. If he wears a blue suit he assumes that they see a blue suit. If he is tall, he assumes that they perceive tallness. If he lies to deceive them, he assumes that they believe what he has told them.

Step 2. Once the person believes he knows what others perceive of him, the second phase of the process occurs, namely, *how do they interpret what they see?* Or how do they *evaluate* what they have seen? If the person has a "black eye," he not only assumes that others see the black eye but he is also aware of the ways in which people characteristically interpret a black eye. They may assume, perhaps, that he has gotten the worst of a fight, whereas he actually acquired the black eye in an auto accident. Since having the black eye is not usually a virtue, he probably concludes that others are evaluating him negatively in that respect. Actually, of course, no one may have noticed the black eye,

[2] C. H. Cooley, *Human Nature and the Social Order* (New York, Scribner, 1922), pp. 184 ff.

but since the person knows from past experience that people usually interpret black eyes in certain well-known stereotyped ways, he will probably assume that his black eye has been interpreted characteristically. In other words, the person not only imagines that his behavior is visible to others, he also imagines, as best he can, how that behavior will be evaluated by them. As has repeatedly been pointed out, his estimates of others' evaluation of him may actually be incorrect, but because he knows or thinks he knows what the standards and definitions and criteria of the group are, he feels that he knows how they will be applied to him.

Step 3. On the basis of the above two processes the person derives *feelings about himself,* such as pride, embarrassment, chagrin, depending upon how he thinks the evaluation of himself was made. It should be clear, of course, that *it is the perceived evaluations by others and not the behavior being evaluated which determines the kind of emotion called up.* Let us suppose that a man is among a group of men who are telling risqué stories. He tells one which he considers to be appropriate and the laughter is intense. He probably would judge that his behavior has been evaluated favorably and would be proud of himself. Just at this moment he notices that his mother has overheard the story. It is the same story which the men heard, but he knows that, being a woman and having the kind of standards she does, she will strongly disapprove of his conduct. Instead of being proud, he is now ashamed of the identical act from which he derived pride a moment earlier. Thus, it can be seen that the feelings derived when one's behavior is being judged are not determined so much by the behavior per se as by the way in which one thinks the behavior is defined by other people.

INDIVIDUALITY AND SOCIAL ACCEPTANCE

The false separation of "self" and "others"

Frequently one hears the protest that he should not be "dominated" so completely by what other people think. He should "make up his own mind," "be himself," and "assert his own individuality." Such a view is altogether natural and understandable, particularly after one has experienced pain as a result of others' evaluations. But the advice is sometimes meaningless. So many of the satisfactions of human life result from the approval of oneself by other people that it is impossible to escape very long from the knowledge that *what others think is important,* not only abstractly but also in *many practical ways.* Rewards and punishment are meted out on the basis of others' evaluations. "No man liveth unto himself." This should not be taken to mean that only a robotized individual results. Actually, self formation, like other personality formation, is partly idiosyncratic, but the risks of unacceptance by others are an omnipresent fact of life.

A person learns by trial and error, by joys and pains, and through the operation of the self not only the importance of others' evaluations but also how to secure favorable evaluations. This is essential to him, not merely for the abstract value of "being well thought of" but also for the inescapably practical requirements of successful living. On the basis of other peoples' judgment of one's personality one is given rewards and punishments, promotions and demotions, satisfactions and frustrations in myriads of practical matters from day to day. Small wonder that virtually everyone is interested in "how to make friends and influence people." Most people know how to do it passably well; most would like to do it much better than they do.

Deviant behavior is no exception

It often appears that one knows persons who seem largely to ignore what other people think, who by words and deeds antagonize people at every turn and seem, in fact, to enjoy securing negative evaluations of their conduct from other people. At first thought such persons might seem to constitute an exception to the principle under discussion in this chapter. When they are observed more closely, however, it usually becomes apparent that such persons do not really constitute an exception. Sometimes they have experienced uniqueness in their socialization as a result of which they are spared some of the penalties normally resulting from social disapproval. Not infrequently such persons have enjoyed relatively secure positions in their social worlds. This is well illustrated by the case of a man who was the son of "the wealthiest man in town." He was so secure financially and socially that he was accepted by everyone because no one would dare to offend his father. No one really liked the boy's temper tantrums, his snobbishness, or his boorishness, but no one dared to register disapproval of these behavior patterns because of the fear of incurring the disapproval of the boy's father. When the boy became a man, he did eventually learn through a very bitter experience that he really was held in very low esteem, a fact from which he had been sheltered. He very probably would have learned it normally and gradually if he had been an ordinary child. It would have early been impressed upon him that other persons are usually in a position eventually to make their evaluations felt in some way or another, and that, therefore, one must accede to their judgments. Sometimes, also, the apparent disregard of other people's evaluations can be explained by the poor judgment of the subject, due to low intelligence rather than to unusual socialization. Usually, however, it seems to be the latter.

Social judgment may be faulty and often is

A person's estimation of how his behavior is being evaluated by other people may, as has already been pointed out, be distorted or even completely wrong due to inaccuracies or ineptnesses in his judgment. It should also be noted that another factor contributes to the existence of discrepancies between the evaluation of one's behavior by others and his own estimate of their judgment. Not infrequently persons, because they wish to be tactful or because they are cowed by the real or assumed prestige of another person, may feign approval when they really disapprove certain behavior. Some of the bad manners, for example, of very wealthy or otherwise socially prominent persons may receive tacit approval because no one quite dares openly to voice disapproval of such a high personage. "The King can do no harm." The practical problem, of course, is not so much involved with royalty, but the principle is the same. Indulgent parents have not infrequently treated their children as if the child's defects of character were virtues, and thus have contributed to defective self-appraisal on the part of the child.

INFERIORITY AND SUPERIORITY FEELINGS

Inaccurate self-appraisal commonly recognized

It is a matter of common observation to the layman that some persons realize quite accurately how they "rate" in the evaluations by others. But some people are "egotistical," that is, regard themselves more highly than others generally do. Others feel "inferiorities," that is, regard themselves less highly than other people do. Sometimes, also, superiority feelings are feigned to compensate for more basic inferiority feelings. Thus, the very talkative and assertive person who seems to be overconfident may be behaving in this manner as a camouflage for his fundamental feelings of inferiority. This may be either a conscious or an unconscious adjustment.

Both the person characterized by inferiority feelings and the person characterized by superiority feelings represent a somewhat distorted self-appraisal.

Socialization and distorted self-appraisal: a case

The nature of one's socialization has a great deal to do with the origin or intensification of distorted notions of oneself.

So long as I can remember my parents and my brothers and sisters never permitted me to do very many things on my own initiative. They seemed not to trust my judgment. Someone always accompanied me when I went away from home, as if I were unable to find my way back. Whenever I was sent to the store to buy something, I was always given the exact change as if I would not know what the correct change was. Meanwhile it was not uncommon to be told I lacked "responsibility." For a while I seemed to resent the injustice of the situation. . . . Of course, I did lack initiative; I never got the chance to exercise it. I was like the person who couldn't swim because he never got the chance to try. . . . Eventually, though, I fell in line with the pattern laid out for me. But I do recall feeling upon many occasions that I really did have the ability to do the things which I was always being told I did not have the ability to do. Once in a while by accident a situation would arise in which there was some opportunity to exercise responsibility, initiative, or judgment, but when those situations arose I was so bewildered by my lack of experience in acting on my own that I would hold back a little, preferring to follow rather than to lead. As I see it now, I had learned so well the fallacy that I lacked responsibility that I would not even exercise initiative when I did have the chance. . . . Now as an adult, even though I understand the situation, I still rarely take on any kind of leadership or do any kind of pioneering whatsoever. Time and again I know I have the necessary ability and have seen persons of less ability get along very well. But from force of habit I still hold back. I still think of myself in the way I had learned to think of myself—lacking responsibility, having to be taken by the hand like a child. Even though my friends keep telling me that I can do all sorts of untried things I still cannot get over my lifelong habit of thinking of myself as not equal to the demands of the situation. (Excerpt from an autobiography)

The above is a case which illustrates how a person can develop a lack of confidence in the appropriateness or adequacy of his own behavior as a result of the way in which he believes his behavior has been defined by others. This person has come to think of himself, and particularly of his abilities, as being less good than objectively they are. The reverse can be equally true. The following case is taken from a longer interview with a man who had recently been discharged from a position which had originally been given to him on the basis of his falsified statement that he had had the necessary technical training which the job required.

Question: But why did you try this work, knowing as you must have that it required technical knowledge which you did not have? Was it because you needed a job so desperately?

Reply: No, I quit a job to take this one. Of course, I knew the job required what you call "technical knowledge." That is why I lied about my education. I've never found anything yet I couldn't do. [His record showed that he had been five times discharged for not being able to do his work.] I could have bluffed this thing through if I hadn't gotten a bad break. I've always been smart—not in school, just in general.

Further insight into this case came from the young man's mother, whose interview revealed much more than she apparently intended.

He has always been such a smart boy. When he was eleven years old he fixed my vacuum cleaner. He has always been handy. He always knows what to do. Of course, he makes a lot of mistakes. He spoiled the alarm clock trying to fix it and almost ruined the car when he repaired it, but I've never held these things against him. You know a child always has to be encouraged or you are apt to break their [sic] spirit. I think it is horribly unfair that he has been discharged—they'll be sorry they let so promising a man go.

Thus it appears that his mother's treatment of him and her appraisal of his abilities may have been the reason for his failure to get a balanced view of his abilities and his disabilities. Perhaps he received deserved praise for repairing the vacuum cleaner, but he was never made to understand, apparently, that his failures revealed the limitations of his ability. He did not have to pay for failures—his failures were made to look like successes. Small wonder, then, that at twenty-one he could do "anything" successfully!

GROUP PARTICIPATIONS AND LOW PRESTIGE

There are various adjustments which a person may make to the fact that he believes he has low esteem in certain groups. A simple solution, of course, is that of avoidance of the persons or groups by the standards of which he knows he does not rate. This solution is not always a ready one, however, because he may find that his participation in the group is essential. Compulsory school attendance for the child who does poorly in school is an obvious case in point. He has no choice except to go. One's family may present almost the same problem. Personality difficulties can sometimes be traced to a person's low estimate by those in his family circle.

In my profession, as you know, I enjoy a very high status. My colleagues regard me as a leader and frequently refer their most difficult cases to me. You know, also, that I have received many honors for my work. . . .

But at home it's all different. There I am just another male who compares somewhat unfavorably with the plumber, for the plumber can accomplish something which is tangible and valuable but I can't. Although the source of the difficulty is probably with my wife, my greatest humiliation comes from the way the children, influenced of course by her, think of me. They treat me fairly decently as far as the formal amenities are concerned, but it is always made clear to me in dozens of subtle but unmistakable ways that I am not as useful to anybody in the family as somebody else's husband is to his. This is the reason I have considered a divorce. But, as you know, I can not drive myself to carry it out. There are too many ties and pulls to my family. That will probably result in my enduring the humiliation of rejection. I would rather rate high in the eyes of my two children than in the eyes of all the world. Instead I have the acclaim of the world and the amused condescending tolerance of my family.

There may be good reasons which would account for this husband's low prestige in his family. But that fact is outside the point under discussion. The case illustrates clearly why persons may continue to participate in group situations which continually aggravate the unpleasant feelings of rejection. Sometimes one's occupation presents a comparable problem; he knows he does not have the respect of his colleagues in his occupation, but he cannot leave the group because he is not trained in any other occupation.

GROUP AFFILIATIONS AND SELF FEELINGS

One may also derive self feelings of inferiority or superiority from the position of the group with which he is identified. Groups as well as individuals enjoy high and low prestige in the evaluations of the larger society or community.

I guess I'll never feel well adjusted in any complete sense. Now and then there are times when I feel that people see me as I am and judge me strictly on the basis of how I measure up. But most of the time people never get around to see me as I am. They see, instead, the label and that label is anything but complimentary. They don't see me as a gentleman or as a student or as a football fan or as a physicist. They see instead that I am a Jew. I was born of Jewish parents and that one fact, over which I had no control, stands in the way of my ever being really seen *as a person* by many of the people in my society.

Comparable cases could be found from the autobiographical accounts of Negroes, immigrants, American-born Japanese, and those of many other group affiliations. Group membership, however, works also in the other direction, as the following excerpt from an autobiography illustrates.

I almost feel a little guilty about it, but everywhere I go I am accorded deference and treated with the greatest respect because I was a member of the ——— Division. Actually I had very little to do with the heroic deeds of that outfit. But just because I was *in* it, I find myself not only decorated with hardware, but given all kinds of prestige which any guy likes if he's human.

What, then, can one conclude about the aggregate self, made up of all of the separate prestiges and statuses which a person is accorded by his several groups? Is there such a thing as a "total self" made up of all the selves from all the groups in which one participates? The answer to this question is largely a matter of how one wishes to state it. It should be obvious from the foregoing that the aggregate of one's selves contains a considerable variety of differing prestiges and very probably some downright contradictions from group to group. One could not regard the person, however, as merely an average of these varied selves, because they are not all co-ordinate with one another. Thus high or low status of one group, or of a few groups to which the person attaches greater importance, may fashion his personality with but little important modification by other group evaluations. This can work both ways. The man who was accorded such low status by his family in the preceding illustration came gradually to be a more and more generally insecure man whose inferiority feelings then spread to his professional life. His family evaluation was so important to him that it eventually overshadowed all of the others. For all of these reasons, then, it is difficult to determine in any general sense whether one may accurately speak of a total self, except in a purely academic and abstract sense. One can, with much greater certainty, however, speak of the multiplicity of selves, of the contrast and contradictions among the several selves, and of the way in which certain selves became predominant or subordinate in the total life-pattern of the person.

SOCIAL ROLES

Definition and illustration

Shakespeare wrote that all the world is a stage and men and women merely the actors of the drama of life, speaking their parts and enacting their roles. While this analogy is not wholly accurate, it does contain a near-truth. In each society the standards of the prevailing culture or cultures contain patterns of behavior which are expected or required of persons in the various social positions. Thus, in our society, the man is expected to work and earn a living for his family, expected to do the physically heavier kinds of work in the home, expected to be more stoic than a woman, and expected to show deference in many "little ways" toward women in general and in special ways toward women in various relationships to him. Not all of these requirements, however, are regarded as equally important.

Anyone living in contemporary American society cannot avoid the expectation that he will observe the required behavior norms. Taken together these norms constitute a *pattern of requirements* which Shakespeare probably had in mind when he likened human beings to actors in a play. These societal standards of behavior do show interesting similarities to the parts of a play. The persons carrying them out usually have little if anything to do with the original formulation of the roles they are expected to play. True, one may take liberties with the role, but if he takes too many liberties he runs the risk of making interaction with other people difficult for all concerned, or the risk of being regarded as "queer" or definitely immoral.

We may now define *social role* and the related concept, *status*. Status refers to the position a person holds in the complex of relationships among people, such as mother, teacher, supervisor, or juvenile delinquent. Each status carries with it *a set of culturally defined patterns of behavior expected or required of persons in each status*. It should be borne in mind that the term *behavior* as used in this definition includes, as always, both overt acts and covert behavior such as attitudes, values, and ideas. When persons in different roles think about a given matter, their thinking may and often does differ widely.

The various social roles and statuses, as we have noted earlier, usually fit together. The roles of husband and wife, for example, are *reciprocal*. Each of the obligations imposed upon the man also imposes reciprocal obligations on the woman, and when the two roles function together there results a fairly smooth organization of activities called "family life." When the customary roles are not followed, interaction becomes difficult because others have no way of understanding or evaluating behavior contrary to the role, except to conclude that it is wrong, indiscreet or, at least, eccentric.

Human beings are not mere automatons, however; they fashion the role somewhat, even while they are playing it. Each time, moreover, that the role passes to the next actor it has already become a slightly different role from what it was the preceding time it passed from one person to another. Today's "daughter" soon assumes the status of mother and with it a new role for her.

Ascribed and achieved status and related roles [3]

It is helpful to distinguish between two types of status-role complexes, *ascribed* and *achieved*. Some roles are "ascribed," that is, they are assigned to a person more or less automatically by the culture of a society on the basis of his age, sex, race, or some other category into which he falls. The double standard of sex morality, for example, in which certain behavior is considered right for men but not right for women is a case in point. The person has absolutely no choice where ascription is concerned. The fact that he is male or that he is eighteen or that he is Negro automatically gives him certain role assignments requiring certain behavior of him and tabooing other behavior.

Other statuses are "achieved," that is, the individual has some measure of choice in the matter. Husband and wife serve to illustrate this. Presumably, a person in American society is usually not required to marry, but if he or she chooses to marry, the obligations of the husband or wife role immediately come into operation. With parenthood a new status-role complex is added. Occupational choices also are of this type. Although it is easier to illustrate the strict requirements of occupational roles in such occupations as the ministry or teaching, the same principle holds true for most occupations; aside from the actual discharge of the work duties, other auxiliary and often nonessential behavior requirements are imposed on the person, such as union membership, the kind of clothes he wears, where in the community he may or may not live, and to some extent his language usages.

It is important to note, however, that the difference between ascribed and achieved status is not clear-cut. The assumption of choice in achieved roles is only partially valid because of the many societal

[3] This is essentially the same distinction as Linton's classic treatment of "achieved" and "ascribed" status. See *Study of Man* (New York, Appleton-Century-Crofts, 1936), p. 115.

and other factors which we know limit choice. It is highly questionable, for example, whether we are justified in saying that people who marry really choose to marry or whether they become so conditioned to marriage through living in the society that most cannot choose not to marry. Thus, the ascription aspect seems the predominant factor to be kept in mind.

A person has numerous role participations

Each *person participates, as a rule, in a number of different roles,* perhaps as many different roles *as he has group affiliations.* Thus a more or less typical man in American society plays the following roles in the course of an ordinary week in his life: husband, father, church member, chairman of a committee to buy flowers for a sick lodge brother, foreman at the plant, county golf champion, and usher at the church. Each role requires somewhat different behavior, and each role carries more or less well understood privileges, obligations, and taboos.

Roles change

A given person's statuses and roles change from time to time, of course, and many persons have difficulty in learning or submitting to the requirements of their changing roles. Many of the stock jokes in our and other societies center around the ludicrous things which people do when they are new in their roles. The newlyweds, the newly-rich, parents with their first child, the young man on his first job, the rookie in the army are all funny or tragic depending upon how one looks at each situation, but at least these people are conspicuous because they are having some difficulty in getting accustomed to the requirements of the role.

Roles may be difficult to perform

People do not always find it equally easy to fulfill the requirements of their various roles. If the roles are of the achieved type, it is sometimes possible to escape from the obligations of continued fulfillment of the role. But even this is not always possible in a practical sense. Some persons have found their personalities not well suited to many of the requirements of marriage and parenthood but find other aspects of marriage and parenthood quite to their liking. One can rarely choose only part of a role. He usually has to accept all or none. One may, moreover, sometimes regret the role he has chosen, but often there is no escaping from the choice after it has been made. And in the case of ascribed roles he has no choice at all. A woman may not like the behavior norms expected of her because she is a woman, but she is left no choice.

Roles channel interaction

The significance of roles in determining the way in which people behave toward each other may perhaps be appreciated more fully through an illustration. Suppose that two men are playing as teammates on an amateur baseball team. Here their relationship is one of more or less equality, since the positions they play are almost identical. One of the players is a physician, the other is a lawyer. Suppose that the lawyer gets injured while playing ball and for that reason becomes the physician's patient. Each then has new obligations to the other. The patient is supposed to take orders from the doctor, and the doctor is responsible for the patient's health. Their status positions and resulting behavior are now entirely different because they are in different roles. The sudden way in which events sometimes reverse roles often makes for difficulties in the interaction of persons who formerly had different role relationships. A professor's bright pupil becomes his superior, for example. Both men confess serious discomfort in the situation because the relationship seems awkward, especially at first. The transition from civilian life to army life, and then back again from army life to civilian life requires many extreme role changes in very short periods of time. While there is much joking comment about the day when one's commanding officer might have a job washing the private's car, there is also a very serious aspect to this situation. Many persons are finding and will continue to find it extremely difficult to adjust to new roles thrust upon them by unforeseeable or uncontrollable circumstances.

Roles standardize behavior

Roles standardize behavior in two ways: (1) by *habituating* the person to the requirements of the role as we have already seen, and (2) by *selecting* certain personality types for certain roles. Sometimes it is the selection factor rather than the modification of the person's behavior which is the more important influence making for the similarities one observes among persons in the same role. If it is true, for example, that lawyers are more facile with verbal language, that is, "smoother talkers" than scientists, one should not assume that being lawyers made them smoother talkers. They may have been attracted into the legal profession because they already were smoother talkers. Also, very probably the two factors of selection and modification may work to reinforce each other, and in that way accentuate the similarities among persons in the same or similar roles.

ROLE CONFLICT

During recent years considerable attention has been directed to the personal problems resulting from role conflict. Several aspects of this problem have already been discussed, especially in Chapter 12 in connection with norms and anomie. Our concern here is with conflict among the clusters of norms which make up social "roles." Thus, the discussion pertains to problems already familiar, but in a somewhat different focus of attention.

There appear to be a number of *kinds* of role conflict, and perhaps we should first distinguish among them. The following "types," though overlapping considerably, are at least sufficiently distinct to warrant separate consideration.

1. Some kinds of role conflict

a. Conflict between roles, both (or several) of which are culturally required and constitute, as we say, "social expectations." An example of this would be the conflicting roles of wife (companionship, attractiveness to the male, and so forth) and mother (care of children, housekeeping, rigid daily routines). Time and interest are conflicting, and while some women "manage" to play both roles fairly well most of the time, others fail to do so. Even for those who we would agree were successful as a whole, problems still are common.[4]

b. Conflict due to *confusion in the society with respect to what the given role requirements are.* A classic example here is the present social position of the adolescent. One moment he is expected to carry out the duties and responsibilities of an adult and the next moment he is treated somewhat like a child. Much of the time he does not know in the larger focus whether he is a child or an adult. As one of them once said, "When I want the car on Saturday night, I am just a kid who shouldn't be trusted with the car. But when the car needs repairs I am expected to do as good a job as the old man."

c. Role conflict may take the form which Ruth Benedict calls *dis-*

[4] See, e.g., Mirra Komarovsky, "Cultural Contradictions and Sex Roles," *American Journal of Sociology,* Vol. 52 (November, 1946), pp. 184–189.

continuity.[5] As a person moves from one role to another, he is often provided with few if any training opportunities in which to learn the requirements of the later role. He is thrown sometimes abruptly from one set of behavior requirements to the next. This involves more than simple role conflict. Probably, strictly speaking, the conflict is not with the role at all; it is with the person who is trying to play a new role for which, so to speak, he has had no chance to rehearse. Again, probably overused, the case of the adolescent comes to mind, but there are other examples. The reversals of behavior requirements for the single adult and the married adult, the childless couple and the new parents, or the college man in the army are all cases in point.

2. Effect on personality

What are the consequences to the personality of these various kinds of role conflict? We do not know as much about this process as might be expected. On the surface, and without formal study, probably everyone realizes that incongruities in role requirements pose "problems" for the person. But, obviously, not for everyone and not in equal degree for those who do have problems. Social scientists seem to suggest (but not in our judgment, conclusively *prove*) that (*a*) mental illness,[6] (*b*) crime and delinquency,[7] and (*c*) physical illness all result from role incongruities of the sorts we have discussed. The failure to provide conclusive proof results in part from the difficulties of study. For example, it is easy to show that a given young man became mentally ill in late adolescence just after being inducted into the army. It appears as if the army or the adolescence brought about the illness, but (1) how do we *know* that he would not have become ill if he had not been drafted into the army, and (2) how about the other young men of similar characteristics who did *not* become ill?

3. The factor of internalization: unconscious and conscious conflict

We must again stress the point made on page 210 when we were discussing norm *conflict*. *Role* conflict as seen by an "outsider" may not be felt by the person whose behavior is under consideration. Repeatedly

[5] Ruth Benedict, "Continuities and Discontinuities in Cultural Conditioning," *Psychiatry*, Vol. 1 (May, 1939), pp. 161–167.

[6] See, e.g., Arnold W. Green, "The Middle-Class Male Child and Neurosis," *American Sociological Review*, Vol. 11 (February, 1946), pp. 31–41.

[7] Robert K. Merton, "Social Structure and Anomie," *American Sociological Review*, Vol. 3 (October, 1938), pp. 672–682.

it has been pointed out that many persons whom one would expect to be "caught" in the cross currents of conflicting role requirements (*a*) seem completely unaware of the inconsistencies, or (*b*) if aware, seem to feel no confusion or guilt or other emotion regarding them. They have not internalized the conflict; for them there seems to be no conflict.

There may, however, be adjustmental difficulty, but it is unconscious. Thus, a woman may not be *conscious* of the fact that she wishes to be both a "good wife" in the sense of much time spent with her husband and a "good mother" in the sense that she devotes her time and energies almost continuously and solely to her children. But she may be seriously affected by the conflict on a subconscious basis. All that she may be aware of is that she feels uneasy, is not as happy as she was before or thinks she should be, or feels ambivalent attitudes toward her children or her husband or both. Probably most role conflict for most people most of the time is of this sub- or quasi-conscious sort.

Other somewhat standard illustrations of conscious adjustmental difficulties are found in (1) the drafted man whose roles as a soldier, on the one hand, and as father or husband or lawyer, on the other, may be very taxing; (2) the economist employed by a private concern and working to effect some outcome favorable to the interests of the concern but which is contrary to his role as citizen where the "public interest" may predominate; and (3) the office holder in his role of "party member" and as statesman. Cases are legion. The problem is so prevalent that it may be considered almost normal.

SUMMARY

Each person acquires a set of attitudes concerning himself based upon the evaluations which he has reason to believe other people make of him and of his behavior. Each group contact results in a different set of evaluations and may result in very different self attitudes and feelings. These group evaluations are important factors in feelings of happiness and security.

Each society imposes upon the individual patterns of interaction appropriate to his status which he is required to observe. These we called his social role-status complex. Each person normally plays many different roles intermittently and in succession, and each role may require different behavior of him. This presents difficulties in social adjustment. The problem is often further complicated by the enforced changing of roles, partly as a consequence of the person's choices and partly due to factors entirely beyond his control.

SUGGESTED READINGS

Blumer, Herbert, "Sociological Implications of the Thought of George Herbert Mead." *The American Journal of Sociology*, Vol. 71 (March, 1966), pp. 534–544.
This is a somewhat technical evaluation of the work of one of the two pioneers who have established the concept of *self* as a basic component of personality.

Cooley, C. H., *Human Nature and The Social Order*. New York, Scribner, 1902.
This is the classic work regarding the self. As early as 1902 Cooley explained the nature and social genesis of the self in terms not markedly different from our understandings today.

Goffman, Erving, *The Presentation of Self in Everyday Life*. Edinburgh, University of Edinburgh Social Sciences Research Center, 1956.
An excellent interpretation of the process of "self presentation" in the mass society. Uses the language of the theater. Highly original.

Kemper, Theodore D., "Representative Roles and the Legitimation of Deviance." *Social Problems*, Vol. 13 (Winter, 1966), pp. 288–298.
Deals with role conflict within organized groups. The concepts of *reciprocal deviance* and *parallel deviance* have important implications for understanding how deviant acts may be involved in legitimate role behavior.

Mead, G. H., *Mind, Self, and Society*. Chicago, University of Chicago Press, 1934.
This is a splendid, though somewhat technical, treatment of the self in relation to society. Generally considered to be the outstanding contemporary work on the self.

Mizruchi, Ephraim Harold, "Alienation and Anomie: Theoretical and Empirical Perspectives," in Irving Louis Horowitz, ed., *The New Sociology: Essays in Honor of C. Wright Mills*. New York, Oxford University Press, 1964.
This is a particularly good treatment of a familiar theme in contemporary sociological interpretation, namely whether and how Americans in the mass society are alienated from their historical identifications, particularly with respect to work. A sophisticated and readable paper.

Reckless, Walter C., Dinitz, Simon, and Murray, Ellen, "Self Concept as an Insulator against Delinquency." *American Sociological Review*, Vol. 21 (December, 1956), pp. 744–746.
A careful research on the relations between self attitudes and delinquency.

Reeder, Leo G., Donohue, George A., and Biblarz, Arturo, "Conceptions of Self and Others." *American Journal of Sociology*, Vol. 66 (September, 1960), pp. 153–159.
This is one of the many studies which show the relationship between self conception in the sense in which it is discussed in this chapter and the interaction with other persons.

Seeman, Melvin, "On the Personal Consequences of Alienation from Work." *American Sociological Review*, Vol. 32 (April, 1967), pp. 273–285.
A careful empirical study of the results which flow from alienation in work, a condition exceedingly common in the mass society. Mostly these findings are negative to the popular beliefs that alienation results in intergroup hostility, political apathy, and feelings of powerlessness.

STUDY QUESTIONS

1. Why do people have attitudes concerning their own personalities?
2. Why is it difficult to be wholly objective in observing one's own personality?
3. How are self attitudes "a social product"?
4. How do interpretations of other persons' judgments influence self attitudes? Illustrate.
5. Why are most individuals concerned over the evaluation of their personality by other people?
6. Why do a few individuals *apparently* disregard the evaluation of their personality by other people? Why may this be more apparent than actual? How does evaluation by others vary in different kinds of groups?
7. How are diverse loyalties often the cause of "eccentric" conduct?
8. How may faulty interpretations of the reactions of other people influence behavior?
9. Some people have inferiority feelings while others have superiority feelings. How do both relate to self attitude formation? Illustrate.
10. Why does a person develop different, and often antithetical, patterns of self attitudes in different social situations?
11. Why is it often difficult to adjust to low prestige?
12. How are self feelings of inferiority or superiority related to the position of the group with which one is identified?
13. What is the relation of inferiority and superiority feelings to one another?
14. Why is the person not merely an "average" of his selves?
15. Why is there often conflict between the different roles of the same individual?
16. Why do people sometimes have difficulty in fulfilling the requirements of their roles?
17. How do roles tend to standardize behavior?

four

SOME IMPORTANT AGGREGATIONS, GROUPS, AND SYSTEMS IN MODERN AMERICAN SOCIETY

16
GROUPS
AND SYSTEMS

WHAT IS A GROUP?

Definition

The term *group* has long been a pivotal concept of sociology. Stated tersely, *a group is any number of human beings in reciprocal communication.* It may be well to emphasize certain aspects and implications of this short definition which beginning students, as well as some sociologists themselves, frequently overlook or do not appreciate fully. First, a group refers only to persons *in communication.* Mere physical closeness, if there is no communication, does not make a group. The communication creates the group, not the mere fact of spatial proximity or physical contact. Second, a group may be of any size from two persons to, theoretically and potentially, the entire population of the world. Third, communication need not be face-to-face or by "word of mouth"; it may be indirect through writing or at long range through such instruments as the telegraph. Persons need not "know each other personally" in order to be in communication; they merely need to contact one another via language, oral or written or gestural. Finally, the persons in a group influence each other reciprocally; one-way communication does not form a group. This, of course, does not mean that the various persons in a group influence each other equally.

Groups and social systems

In recent years sociologists have been making increasing use of the concept *social system.* "This model is designed to help one visualize that certain human collectivities (groups) are systems whose parts are interdependent and which, as unities, are in turn interlinked with one another through mutual dependencies. The prerequisites for a social system are two or more people in interaction directed toward attaining a goal and guided by patterns of structured and shared symbols and expectations." [1] A number of understandings of the structure and function of groups can be facilitated by thinking about group interaction in such systemic terms. While the group is a unity, this unity derives from the interconnectedness of the actions of individuals, many of which are quite different from one another. Thus, for example, the various players on a football team behave in quite different ways but as each player performs his particular role, a unity of purpose is achieved. In looser language this is sometimes referred to as "organization." However termed, the basic point is that differentiated individual behavior when linked systemically with other individual behavior provides a structure for interaction. This is true from the largest to the smallest groups. It is relatively easy to understand this point when one is observing the United States Senate or similar formally structured groups, but the point is equally relevant to understanding much less formal group participations such as a date, a family at meal time, or a conference with one's teacher.

Even though group and social system are sometimes used interchangeably, a more careful usage is preferable. Group refers to the actual, observable concrete behaving individuals, while social system is essentially an abstract concept, a model, which focuses upon the roles, their linkages with one another, and the expectations which channel the group interaction. This is a distinction similar to the one made earlier concerning the concepts *society* and *culture*.

"Group" distinguished from other human "collectivities"

The concept of the group may perhaps become more clear when we have distinguished two other kinds of human pluralities—categories and aggregations.

The category. A category is a number of persons who are *thought of together*, whether they are in communication or not. Morons are a category. So also are the males 40 to 44 years of age in the population of the United States, or all the women in the United States who have failed in college. None of these is a group, as we have defined the term, because *these categories of people are not ordinarily in intercommunication.*

The aggregation. An aggregation is a collectivity of persons who are held together in a physical sense by some factor other than inter-

---

[1] Alvin L. Bertrand, *Basic Sociology, An Introduction to Theory and Method* (New York, Appleton-Century-Crofts, 1967), pp. 24–25.

communication. The populations of a country or of the world are cases in point. Aggregations may, of course, be groups also, but all aggregations are not groups because the people involved may not be in interaction.

WHY GROUPING?

Wherever humans are found, they are living in groups. The universality of human grouping has attracted attention, and several false notions have arisen claiming to explain the "reason" for groups. These errors have become so widely diffused that it seems necessary to examine them critically at the outset.

Instinct or learning?

Perhaps the chief fallacy is the widespread explanation of human groupings in terms of an *inherited* "need" or "urge" or "instinct" for group activity. Evidence for this explanation is lacking. It may better be explained without the "instinct" assumption. Group action is universal because each person has become so dependent in so many different ways upon other people that permanent and consistent living outside of groups is virtually unthinkable and impossible. From birth cry to burial, the desires of the human being are ministered to by other humans. While at times interaction with other people may not be wholly pleasant, the overall experience of his life is characterized by association with other people. Having learned, as everyone has, that he needs other people in order to satisfy his wants, there is no alternative. Group living becomes a necessity.

"Common interest" versus functional interdependence

A second popular fallacy pertaining to groups is the "common interest" cliché. Men are said to be found everywhere functioning in groups because they have common interests, and through group participation the common interests are satisfied. Undeniably *some* of men's interests are common, but others are individualized or specialized, while some are openly antagonistic. Observe, for example, the larger number of groups found in the modern community which grow out of men's conflicts with one another. Courts, strike mediation boards, and legislative bodies are only a few of the many groups which come into existence because of conflicts among men. Other groups are made possible only by the fact of divergent, but not necessarily antagonistic, interests.

The marketplace, stores, banks, and schools come into being because different members of the society have different needs which can often be satisfied through interaction among persons whose interests are reciprocal. Thus, the seller and the buyer form a brief group which fulfills the needs of the seller to sell and the buyer to buy. The bank provides a medium through which people who have money to lend for interest may make contact with persons having a desire to borrow money and willing to pay interest for the privilege. Schools arise because there is a category and perhaps also a group of people (teachers) who have talents which they are willing to sell and which the pupils directly or indirectly buy. The teachers' interests are to sell their services and the students' to buy them. Thus it is readily demonstrated that the common generalization to the effect that groups are based on common interest is an oversimplification, or an exaggeration, of one factor which accounts only for the existence of *some* groups. A great many groups are based on divergent interests or antagonistic ones. All of the evidence taken together, however, would seem to indicate that groups are a practical manifestation of our interdependency.

THE PERSON AND HIS GROUPS

Group participations are roles

In preceding chapters it has been pointed out that a major part of each personality consists of patterns of behavior called *roles*. A person's roles are usually numerous in modern society and vary greatly, as a rule, from one another. Through these roles a person's participation in groups is carried on. A personality can be conceived as a collection of group-related roles. While some of each person's behavior may not be obviously related to any distinguishable group, most of his behavior is group-oriented. Segments of John Doe's personality consist of his behavior in the role of Mrs. Doe's husband, first clarinet player in a dance orchestra, member of the bowling team, Chairman of the Board of Trustees of the First Congregational Church, and the son of Mrs. Doe, Senior, to mention only a few. These various group participations are, of course, not equally important to Mr. Doe, nor does he devote an equal amount of time to each of them. It is well to note also that Mr. Doe need not be actually present in a group situation in order to be participating in group-related behavior. Thus when he is practicing on his clarinet he may be quite alone, but this behavior is still related to his functioning in the role of first clarinet player in the orchestra.

It will also be recalled from earlier chapters that group affiliations are important in making John Doe the kind of man he is. It is likewise clear that he chooses his group affiliations, in part at least, on the basis of their congeniality with his personality. Once he begins to participate in a group, his experiences in that group become influences further affecting his personality. One should not lose sight of either of these processes. Both are important to a balanced understanding of the relationship of the person to his group. Persons choose to function in groups in terms of their values and needs; and once persons are participating in a given group, that group in turn influences their values and needs.

Behavior varies with group situations

The visible part of John Doe's personality, that is, his overt behavior, is not the same in all of his groups. His "bowling personality" is very probably not the same as his "husband personality," and both may be quite different from his "church personality." This is an altogether natural outcome of his playing different roles in each of the different instances. Somewhat distinct behavior is expected of him in each situation; and if he wishes to be favorably received by his fellows, or if he wishes to have adequate self-definition, he must behave somewhere near the role norms prevailing in each group.

This fact of variable personality traits under varying group conditions has attracted the attention of moralists for a long time. It has been fashionable to point out the inconsistencies in the behavior of a person from group to group and to decry the fact that the behavior in one group does not "come up to" the standards present in another group. Thus, it is common to hear a devout churchman called a "hypocrite" when he manifests behavior in another group which differs from his behavior in church. It is not our purpose either to condone or to condemn this fact, but rather to explain why it so frequently occurs that people behave very differently from one group to another. The role requirements which the person encounters in each group are, simply, different.

CLASSIFICATION OF GROUPS

Sociologists have devoted a great deal of effort to the difficult problem of classifying groups into types. At first thought this would seem easy to do, but after further reflection it will be found to present numerous difficulties. These difficulties are so great, in fact, that at present we have no overall systematic classification of groups which is entirely acceptable to all sociological scholars. However, considerable understanding of the nature of groups can be derived from a study of some of the attributes or characteristics of groups.

1. A continuum of size

Groups vary along a continuum, one pole of which is the human pair (the smallest possible group), the other of which might conceivably include all of the human inhabitants of the earth as soon as some medium for their intercommunication is devised. In other words, there is no real limit to the size which human groups may eventually reach.

2. A continuum of compulsion

Some group participations are clearly compulsory. The inmate of the penitentiary and the child in school, or for that matter, in his family, represent group participations, over which no choice exists. Participation is thus said to be *nonoptional* in such groups. Other group participations are seemingly matters of choice, although as has been pointed out previously, there always exist numerous *limitations* upon a person's unrestrained or free choice of anything. Still other group participations fall somewhere between choice and outright compulsion. Thus we speak of "pressure" to belong to certain groups. Actually, then, there is a *continuum of compulsion*. At one extreme are the groups over which one has no choice at all, at the other extreme are the groups which he is free to choose or reject, and there are all gradations in between the two extremes.

3. Primary and secondary groups

One important distinction which sociologists have found very useful is that between "primary" and "secondary" groups.

By primary groups I mean those characterized by intimate face-to-face association and co-operation. They are primary in several senses, but chiefly in that they are fundamental in forming the social nature and ideals of the individual. The result of intimate association, psychologically, is a certain fusion of individualities in a common whole, so that one's very self, for many purposes at least, is the common life and purpose of the group. Perhaps the simplest way of describing this wholeness is by saying that it is a "we"; it involves the sort of sympathy and mutual identification for which "we" is the natural expression. One lives in the feeling of the whole and finds the chief aim of his will in that feeling.

It is not to be supposed that the unity of the primary group is one of mere harmony and love. It is always a differentiated and usually a competitive unity, admitting of self-assertion and various appropriative passions; but these passions are socialized by sympathy, and come, or tend to come, under the discipline of a common spirit. The individual will be ambitious, but the chief object of his ambition will be some desired place in the thought of the others, and he will feel allegiance to common standards of service and fair play. So the boy will dispute with his fellows a place on the team, but above such disputes will place the common glory of his class and school.

The most important spheres of this intimate association and co-operation—though by no means the only ones—are the family, the play-group of children, and the neighborhood or community group of elders. These are practically universal, belonging to all times and all stages of development; and are accordingly a chief basis of what is universal in human nature and human ideals.[2]

Nonprimary groups or secondary groups are characterized by a condition of participation in sharp contrast to the primary groups—impermanence, casualness of contact, and fewer ties of deep sentiment among the members. Primary and secondary groups are not to be thought of as two distinct categories, into one of which each and every group could be pigeon-holed. Here again we have a *continuum with poles of primariness and secondariness*, groups differing from one another not categorically, but in the *degree* to which the interacting behavior of the participants is characterized by the attributes of primariness as discussed above.

4. Vertical and horizontal groups

Some groups are made up of members or participants who are alike in their relation to the class system of a society. Thus a union made up of meat cutters or railroad engineers represents a relatively uniform group, the members of which have approximately the same income and approximately the same general prestige rating. Such a group would be considered *horizontal* since, as the word suggests, the persons in the group are about "on the same level" of the society. Of course the use of a geometrical term like *horizontal* to describe a societal phenomenon like class position is not strictly apt. The license for using such a word

2 C. H. Cooley, *Social Organization* (New York, Scribner, 1915), pp. 23–24.

arises from the common language usage implied in such expressions as "higher" and "lower class," people "on the same level," and so forth.

Vertical groups, on the other hand, are groups whose members or participants include persons from a variety of different social classes. The church would be a case in point; well-to-do and poor, people of high status and low, may all be members of the same church. In the vertical-horizontal distinction, as in the preceding ones, there will always occur numerous difficulties in classifying some individual group. The difficulty will disappear if one thinks of the group attributes of horizontalness and verticalness as defined, and then uses these concepts for comparative purposes.

5. Formal and informal groups

Another dimension along which groups can be classified and which facilitates an understanding of their nature concerns the degree of formality-informality which the system incorporates. Formality and informality are not to be regarded as a dichotomous classification but rather as a continuum with formal and informal at the extremes, it being understood, of course, that probably no group has 100 percent formal interaction or 100 percent informal interaction. There are, however, manifest differences among groups with respect to the rigidity of the role behaviors involved, the more rigidly defined roles being characteristic of the more formal group. In a succeeding chapter dealing with bureaucracy one prevalent type of relatively formal organization of contemporary group life will be analyzed in considerable detail.

The importance of nomenclature

The student should become acquainted with this nomenclature regarding groups for at least two reasons. (1) Each of these terms facilitates understanding of the nature of groups because it calls attention to one or more group attributes, like primariness, permanence, verticalness, and so forth. (2) Like all vocabulary, this nomenclature provides one with an economy of effort in communication. Reading and writing about sociological phenomena is made easier and more meaningful when the persons communicating with one another have the common understandings on which the common language is based. The same point has also been made elsewhere in this book. It is repeated here so that the student may be reminded that the technical nomenclature just introduced is not arbitrary or "merely academic," but is functionally justifiable.

Groups have many attributes

Each actual group, whether a husband-wife group, the neighborhood card club, or the Republican party, could be classified somewhere along each of the above continuums. It is not of importance to determine whether the card club is a primary group *or* an optional group *or* a horizontal group. It may be all three. Moreover, it is also a relatively temporary group, and a relatively small group. The card club could, however, be compared with the Republican party in respect to each of these and other attributes. It might then be described as more temporary, smaller, more primary, more horizontal, and possibly more optional. And so for any comparison of two or more groups which one might care to make.

SOME CURRENT TRENDS

Before discussing specific groups it is possible to take an overall view of the general group composition of mass society (Chapter 4) for the purpose of considering some of the outstanding trends in group organization and personal participation in groups.

1. The decline of primary groups

While there are, of course, numerous primary groups still to be found in American society, more and more of the groups in which a person functions are of the secondary type. More important, perhaps, is the decreased amount of time being spent in the remaining primary groups and the corresponding increase in secondary types of participation. Although this trend is more apparent in urban society, it is true in some degree throughout most of the United States.

Various interpretations are placed upon this transition. There are those who decry the trend as one having unfortunate consequences to the personality. Primary groups, it is thought, foster the virtues of loyalty to high ethical standards, devotion to common purposes, and the "we feeling." No one has ever successfully demonstrated, however, that these attributes are *indispensable* to human happiness or efficiency. True, life is *different* when there is less primary group participation, but is it necessarily *inferior?* All that can be objectively determined is that society is changing in that more and more groups are becoming secondary in nature.

Much of the assumed indispensability of primary groups seems to be simply conservative reaction to change. When the kind of human relationship to which one has become accustomed, and from which, therefore, he has derived much pleasure, seems to be declining, it is quite understandable that he would feel a sense of personal loss at the change. But to assert that human life is therefore "deteriorating" seems to be going decidedly beyond the objective facts and into subjective speculation. The evaluation of social change is an entirely legitimate function, but it should not be confused with the objective reporting of the facts. Social change normally brings with it numerous discomforts for persons who have been habituated to, and therefore prefer, the old system. Particularly during a period of transition, some persons are conspicuously aware of their own personal loss and discomforts due to the change. But one must be cautious not to assert that dire consequences for persons *in general* will result, merely because he has observed that he and some people encounter difficulty in their efforts to function in the new way of life. While it is quite possible that the decline of primary groups constitutes a distinct loss of irretrievable human values, at this time social science *lacks the evidence* to assert such as fact.

2. Increasing casualness of group contact: functionaries

In modern life, especially in the larger cities, a person is really not known *as a person* by the other participants in many, if not most, of his groups. Only a fragment, and often a very small fragment, of his personality is known and reacted to by his associates. One neither knows nor needs to know anything more about the man who sells him a suit or drives the bus or serves as his boss or runs the movie projector in his favorite theater, save the one objective fact that this person does his job sufficiently well to meet others' wishes or needs.

Numerous persons in one's group experience, then, associate merely as *functionaries*, not as persons. The word *functionary* is employed because it seems to suggest that the only matter of consequence to the participants in many secondary groups is *how well the functions which the other person is supposed to carry out are actually carried out by him.* Perhaps the bus driver neglects his wife, causes trouble among his in-laws, and has stupid views on politics. In a vague sense, perhaps, one might prefer that the bus driver was a different person, but he would probably not refuse to ride on the bus because of a dislike for these aspects of the driver's personality. It is sufficient that the man drive his bus, arrive on time, and make change correctly; his personal life is usually not known, and even if known, is not regarded as of much consequence to the bus riders. The same applies to the bus riders as viewed by the driver.

Other secondary group contacts, though less casual than the one just discussed, illustrate the same characteristic. Thus teachers are gradually finding it more and more possible to secure employment on the basis of their merits *as teachers*, with less and less attention to the other aspects of their lives not directly related to their functioning as teachers. There was a time, for example, when a divorced woman or a person of radical political views could not possibly secure employment as a teacher, if these facts were known. In pointing out the change, it is not being overlooked that such factors as marital status and political views might be significant to the teacher's functioning as a teacher. The point is that in modern secondary society we are becoming more concerned with her ability as a teacher per se. And so with the other persons with whom one associates. We are usually in no position any longer to secure all, or even many, of the facts of the person's other group participations, and increasingly people take the position that they are irrelevant anyway. It should be borne in mind that it is still not difficult to find exceptions to this trend, especially in rural communities, in other more primary group types of society, or even in some of the more primary group aspects of urban society. The point to be noted is that these instances are becoming less and less prevalent, and thus do not in any way contradict the trend. Moreover, it must be recalled here, as in many other places in this book, that we are describing what is true, not what our personal wishes would like to have true. Thus we are not advocating the increase of mere functionary participation in contemporary groups; we are reporting that it has occurred and that it appears to be increasing.

3. Groups are becoming more specialized

Not only individuals but groups, also, are becoming increasingly devoted to specific purposes and functions and are limiting their activities primarily, if not exclusively, to these purposes. Few persons who live in a metropolitan city of minimum size (100,000) could probably designate by name one-tenth of the organized groups which are to be found in their city. This figure (10 percent) is not entirely an estimate, but was derived from a study in which approximately 700 people were asked to name as many organized groups in their community as they could. These lists were then checked against the list of organized groups having telephones listed in the directory of that city. Only one

person came even near to 10 percent; the majority fell far below 5 percent. Most of them were familiar with the existence of some of the large
groups or of some of the groups in which nearly everyone participated,
such as his family group, school group, or those specialized groups with
which he came in contact. But he was almost entirely unaware of the
great mass of specialized groups permanently organized and functioning in his own community.

4. Transfer of functions away from existing primary groups

Specialized groups have not all grown up because of new or even
basically changed needs of people living under modern urban conditions. Many have arisen as specialized agencies concentrating on functions formerly carried on by primary groups. Thus, the family at one
time supplied many of the needs of its members for which there now
exist such various specialized groups as nursery schools, bakeries, laun-
dries, diaper services, and even organized groups of baby sitters, to
mention but a few. Likewise the functions formerly performed by the
"family doctor" are now divided up among dozens of specialized kinds
of medical groups working in hospitals, laboratories, and special clinics
for almost every organ in the body, each organization having some
specialized sort of function for meeting the health needs of the person.
It is probable, of course, that the opportunity is thus provided for better
health for many people, but the kind of group interaction characterized
by the family doctor and his patients is slowly but surely declining, and
in its place are arising these specialized groups in which a person participates more or less "as a number," participates perhaps a few times in
a lifetime or maybe not at all. The same principle operates in almost
every area of a person's life and is one of the inescapable facts about
modern society.

5. Increasing complexity of overall community structure

With the ever increasing numbers and specializations of groups
comes an almost inevitable complexity of the total group structure of
one's social world. One may properly inquire, in fact, what particular
pattern of groups really constitutes "his" social world. Surely not all
the groups in a city are participated in by anyone, and almost certainly
no one participates in as many as a majority of them. But the groups—

groups within groups, groups serving groups, and groups opposing groups—constitute a veritable maze of human activity. It strains almost anyone's imaginative faculties to conceive of the whole process.

There are those observers who believe that much of the apparent increase in personal inadequacy discussed in Chapter 13 is a rather direct result of the strain placed upon many persons who try to work out their life patterns in this intricate and changing maze. While one cannot be certain that this assumed causal connection is sound, it appears altogether probable that the complexity of modern living, for some people at least, has introduced a strain which they are unable to withstand successfully. This strain seems to take the form of inefficiency, physical impairment, or mental inadequacy as a concomitant of this complexity. It may well be, however, that the observed instances of personal inadequacy which appear to be associated with group complexity are the result not so much of group complexity per se as of a period of early adaptation to a less complex and changing group structure.

6. Institutionalization

Sociologists have coined the term *institutionalization* to describe the process of formalizing interaction in groups. There is a tendency for participation in most groups to become habituated and formalized into increasingly rigid roles. Each person's behavior becomes laid out for him in specified ways, and elaborate rules and regulations exist prescribing the proper procedure for everything from securing a position to building a house. The employer-employee relationship, for example, was on a primary group basis originally. The terms of each man's employment, like wages, hours, the amount and kind of work to be done, were arrived at by direct negotiation, no one being very much concerned if each detail was not worked out precisely. Now the majority of employees in industrial establishments in America never even see their employers. They belong to unions and are represented at wage conferences by officers of the union, whom in all probability they do not know personally either. The employer is likewise represented by some functionary. Eventually an elaborate wage contract is worked out, carrying numerous details stipulating the obligations and privileges, the duties and proper functions of employer and employees, which contract will require the services of a competent attorney to understand completely.

Institutionalization is also illustrated in the organization of any typical American university. When the student presents himself for admission he must be prepared to offer numerous proofs of his qualifications to do college work. No one, it seems, takes his word for anything. He then goes, or his papers are sent, from functionary to functionary. Each term or semester he enrolls for further work he again goes through more or less routinized procedures with deans, department heads, advisers, cashiers, and all of the various assistants which each of these various functionaries has. When he nears graduation, again the formalities come to the fore. Has he the right number of courses, hours, the right "sequences," the prescribed grades, in majors, minors, and electives, and so on and on? To the average student the whole procedure must seem both arbitrary and bewildering, and yet it appears to be necessary. Most of the rules are there for good and sufficient reasons, although sometimes even those who are supposed to know find difficulties in understanding the rules; much less are they able to justify them. The complexity is a result of an attempt to secure efficiency of operation so that students do not get lost in the complex and specialized maze of subgroups in the university. Under the old primary group kind of education, a student could not avoid securing some form of guidance, in case he needed it. He got it continuously and informally in the course of association with the teacher. Now he gets learning from the teacher, guidance from a guidance officer, academic guidance from the academic dean, personal guidance from the personnel dean, and occupational guidance from the occupational information officer. Each person's role is formally set down for him so that he and others may know what is expected, not only of them but of the other people as well. Who occupies a given role does not make much difference so long as the role incumbent, whoever he is, is competent and discharges the functions of the role more or less as prescribed. The roles are often more lasting than the specific incumbents who fill them.

Perhaps the army and navy carry institutionalization of roles to the most extreme form. In military organization everyone almost invariably knows precisely where he belongs in the hierarchy of rank, and knows exactly what his rights and duties are in relation to everyone with whom he could possibly come in contact. The person, then, is a Captain first and Joe Doe second. A glance at another man's insignia is all that is needed in order to know exactly the way he ought to be addressed, as well as many other things relating to the interaction with him. There is a "chain of command" perfected so that under almost any possible condition it can be determined who is in the position of authority and what his rights and limitations are. The difference between military and civilian group structure is, however, not as great as one might at first think. Many civilian groups, such as large-scale industry, may be institutionalized to an extent which is more than a little suggestive of the more extreme forms to be observed in the military. Likewise the group organization of the Catholic church is institutionalized quite thoroughly with a carefully worked out role pattern. There seems to be objective basis for concluding that one of the basic trends in American groups is the extension of formal organization into groups which traditionally have been much more loosely and informally integrated.

7. The rise and dominance of pressure groups

One of the specialized types of groups which is very prominent in modern society is the "pressure group." It exists for the purpose of influencing or controlling the conduct of other persons and other groups. Many groups in modern society, for example, have desires and vested interests which they try to further by influencing governmental decisions in their favor. Labor, industry, agriculture, and the professional groups each have the desire from time to time to secure governmental action or public support for or against some measure or proposal. Some management groups in industry, for example, would like to have labor's right to strike either curtailed or eliminated, while labor, on the other hand, would like to extend its power to secure greater control over the management of industry. Thus each group "puts on the pressure," so to speak, to try to secure enough public support for its point of view so that the elected governmental officials will have no choice but to side with it. The techniques for managing publicity campaigns are involved and costly. Billions of dollars are spent every year in paid advertising, printed hand bills, circulars, booklets, salaries of lobbyists who try to influence government officials in various ways, speakers touring the country, and radio programs. These are only a few of the devices through which pressure groups exert their influence.

A representative type of democracy like the United States lends itself particularly well to the existence of pressure groups. Since public officials are either elected or appointed by those who are elected, they recognize that they can stay in power only so long as the "public" is satisfied, or not too dissatisfied, with their decisions and actions. Thus, pressure groups strive to inflame public opinion on some issues, thus virtually forcing the officials to act in accordance with what is or appears to be "public opinion," or risk defeat at the next election.

Some of the propaganda techniques of pressure groups have periodically been found by courts to be illegal, and a great many more are of dubious legality. Every trick known to the propagandist is utilized to bring about the kind of public opinion he wants. Thus, the citizen is deluged with "information," advice and assertion, claims and counterclaims. Everyone's case is made to seem "convincing," and the conscientious citizen who tries to take an impartial point of view in the interest of the whole society, instead of some special group, finds it almost impossible to get the whole truth or to know what to do after he gets it. He is often in a difficult position to exert any effective influence unless he "joins up" with one side or another. Pressure groups in connection with government will be discussed in a subsequent chapter. This brief treatment has been introduced at this point because pressure groups constitute so prominent a part of the general group structure of modern American society. Pressure groups are, thus, the instrumentalities or the agencies through which the larger groups that they represent strive to win supporters for their points of view.

SUMMARY

Groups are universal aspects of human life. Each person needs group participation because he has grown up in groups and has thus acquired wants, most of which can only be satisfied, directly or indirectly, by other persons.

Some groups are based on common interest among the participating persons, but other groups are based on the divergent interests of their members or even on antagonistic ones.

Each person participates in a variety of groups which differ in importance and predominance in his total behavior. These participations are roles and constitute significant segments of one's personality. Groups likewise consist of segments of the behavior of each of the participants. Behavior can therefore be conceived as readily from the point of view of the group as of the individual. Both are equally "real."

Groups may be classified on the basis of any of their attributes—size, the extent to which the participation is voluntary, the duration of the participation, the extent to which the group is "primary" and "vertical."

Several current trends in the structure of groups were discussed, such as the decline of primary groups, the increasing casualness of group participation, functionary interaction, specialization, complexity of groups, and institutionalization. The nature and significance of pressure groups was also briefly treated, but will be discussed at greater length in the chapter on government.

Most of the rest of the book will be devoted to a somewhat more detailed analysis of each of the principal groups and group patterns making up American society.

SUGGESTED READINGS

Bertrand, Alvin L., *Basic Sociology: An Introduction to Theory and Method*. New York, Appleton-Century-Crofts, 1967.
An elementary textbook written around an explicit social systems frame of reference.

Cooley, C. H., *Social Organization*. New York, Scribner, 1915, Chapters III, IV, and V.
The original statement of the primary group concept by its founder.

Gordon, C. Wayne, and Babchuk, Nicholas, "A Typology of Voluntary Associations." *American Sociological Review*, Vol. 24 (February, 1959), pp. 22–29.
Voluntary associations is a term sociologists use to designate the various organizations of recreational, civic, and religious orientation in which the modern American participates. It is helpful to see familiar organizations viewed in a systematic, typological manner.

Homans, George, *The Human Group*. New York, Harcourt, Brace & World, 1950.
A unique book. Demonstrates how groups can be studied by the use of a very limited set of concepts.

Warriner, Charles K., "Groups are Real: A Reaffirmation." *American Sociological Review*, Vol. 21 (October, 1956), pp. 549–554.
An excellent modern restatement and clarification of some older philosophical questions regarding the "reality" of groups. Discusses nominalism, interactionalism, and realism with clarity and brevity.

Wilson, Logan, "The Sociography of Groups," in G. Gurvitch and W. E. Moore, eds., *Twentieth Century Sociology*. New York, Philosophical Library, 1945, pp. 139–171.
An advanced treatment of human groups. See also Florian Znaniecki, "Social Organization and Institutions," pp. 200–216 in the same source.

STUDY QUESTIONS

1. Why are human groups "necessary"?
2. Why is the "common interest" only a partial explanation for groups?
3. Why does a person in our society have numerous and varied roles?
4. Why would it be difficult to classify all groups into either optional or nonoptional?
5. How could club membership be either primary or secondary group contact? How is this a matter of degree?
6. Are American Legion Posts vertical or horizontal groups? Why?
7. What criteria should we use in determining when the use of technical nomenclature is necessary and desirable?
8. How do sociologists interpret the "decline" of primary groups?
9. Why has there been a growth in casualness of group contacts in our society?
10. How does our present society foster the growth of specialized groups?
11. What is a possible relationship between personal inadequacy and group complexity?
12. Why has there been an increase of institutionalization in our society?
13. How are some civilian group participations similar to military institutionalization?
14. What is the function of pressure groups? Why have they developed in our society? What objectionable features do they have?
15. What is the purpose of classifying groups? What are the dangers? Illustrate.
16. How do the concepts *group* and *social system* relate to each other? Illustrate.

17
BUREAUCRACY: THE PREVAILING MODE OF WORK AND LIFE

Colloquially, the term "bureaucracy" has become an epithet which refers to inefficiency and red tape in the government; but this was not its original meaning, and it is not the way the term will be used in this book.[1]

One of man's most far-reaching social inventions is *bureaucracy*. Max Weber, generally conceded to be the earliest and most systematic student of bureaucracy, traces its origins as far back as ancient Egypt during the period of the New Empire. But for many centuries the bureaucratic method of organizing interpersonal relationships directly affected only relatively small proportions of the people. Today, however, the bureaucratic mode has come to be the prevailing form of human association in nations like our own, where not only government but business organizations, church organizations, charitable enterprises, educational institutions, and, of course, the armed services together provide a web of relationships so pervasive that probably no one could extricate himself from their preponderant influence, even if he should want to. So much, however, of what a person is and what he does, in short of his personality, is a part of bureaucratic organization that it becomes increasingly doubtful whether, except in moments of frustration, most men have any real desire for emancipation from bureaucratic structure, or even much consciousness that there is any alternative way in which they might function. Therefore, a study of the nature of bureaucracy, its influences upon personality both in the work situation and outside, is at once the portrait of modern man and an analytical tool for understanding how he "got this way."

As indicated in the quotation with which this chapter begins, the term *bureaucracy* is to many people an epithet. And

[1] Peter M. Blau, *Bureaucracy in Modern Society* (New York, Random House, 1956), p. 13.

it is quite understandable why persons with aspirations of individuality and self-determination should find themselves, so it seems, harassed by the impediments to action set up by one bureaucracy after another. The social scientific study of bureaucracy is, on the other hand, essentially amoral. Bureaucracy *is* part and parcel of the modern man's social existence. Yet the social scientist, while accepting the scientist's responsibility to be amoral, need not be irresponsible. That is, he may and should be as sensitive to the blunderings, the "inhumanities," and the inefficiencies of bureaucracy as he is to the rather remarkable accomplishments which have been made possible in large, if not decisive, part by bureaucratic organization. In short, then, while we shall take a "natural science" view of bureaucracy, we shall also keep alerted to the diseases of the specimen.

THE NATURE OF BUREAUCRACY

As we mentioned above, Max Weber has systematically set forth the concept of bureaucracy. In so doing he has carefully avoided a simple empirical description of any particular bureaucracy and has confined himself, instead, to a description of the major characteristics of the bureaucratic structure which are common to the wide variety of concrete bureaucratic organizations found in American or any other modern mass society.[2]

The most apparent characteristics of bureaucracy are (1) specialization of tasks for the individual, (2) an intricate and universalistic system of rules, (3) a hierarchy of authority, and (4) impersonality. Now let us examine each of these concepts.

1. Specialization

As early as 1776 Adam Smith, generally regarded as one of the founders of modern economic theory, set forth in his *Wealth of Nations* a classic rationale for the advantage of specialization in carrying out even the most simple task. But even before Adam Smith the common sense of many men had already taught them that if a task is divided up into parts and each part assigned to a different person, the task may

[2] Weber's method is known in the technical nomenclature of social science as the "ideal typical method." The pros and cons of this method of social analysis, its values and shortcomings, constitute one of the more controversial professional issues in contemporary sociological thinking. Examination of this issue is beyond the scope of a beginning course, except for the more astute student. For him, Peter M. Blau, *op. cit.*, pp. 28–43, should constitute provocative and stimulating reading.

be more capably accomplished. Particularly so, if it is done over and over again, because a person can master, obviously, a simpler skill sooner than a more complex one and presumably thereafter makes fewer mistakes than he would if he were performing many tasks intermittently. And so, generally speaking, the larger the bureaucracy the more specialized becomes the duty (or work) of each individual. His duties are carefully set forth in terms of the *office* or *position* which he holds. Thus, in theory at least, everyone's activities mesh with everyone else's to bring about an efficient performance of some total purpose. This purpose may be almost anything—building an automobile, winning a war, training a physician, passing a law, curing the sick—for the list is endless. The behavior of these various specialists must, therefore, be very carefully *prescribed* through an elaborate set of *rules* and *regulations*. This brings us to the second basic characteristic of bureaucracy.

2. A system of rules

Anyone who has had experience with a bureaucratic structure of any size is familiar with such concepts as "the T.O." (table of organization) and "S.O.P." (standard operational procedures). Each bureaucracy has its own system of rules and all, of course, are not equally inflexible or restrictive upon the behavior of the individual. But all have in common a more or less definite set of prescriptions for each person's behavior—(*a*) a set of behavior requirements and (*b*) a set of behavior taboos. Failure of any position holder to observe these duties and taboos is at once a threat to the efficient operation of the bureaucracy and to his security and continuity as a holder of the office. In fact, procedures for handling violations of prescribed behavior are usually included in the rules and regulations, so that even the deviant is handled in an "orderly" way. It is important to note that almost all bureaucratic structures contain violators of rules who seem not to get caught, or if caught, not dealt with as the rules specify. It is also apparent that bureaucracies vary from one to another in the severity of punishment for the violator. Thus, being "called on the carpet" by the Dean may seem so different from a "court martial" that the basic similarity between the two may be overlooked. But both represent given bureaucratic procedures for handling breaches of the pattern of requirement and taboo. Ordinarily, each holder of an "office" or "position" in a bureaucracy is responsible to someone else who is "above him" in the organization. Thus, the rules and regulations provide for a *hierarchy of authority*.

3. Hierarchy of authority

Not only is each individual in a bureaucratic organization under the control of someone above him but he is responsible (except for those in the very lowest echelon) for securing appropriate behavior from those in positions immediately lower than himself. The higher up in the hierarchy of authority a given person functions, the greater is the number of inferiors for whose behavior he must account to his superior. *The authority over inferiors, however, is not absolute*—it is more or less strictly *circumscribed by the rules and regulations.*

Only certain kinds of behavior may be required; other kinds may not. Thus, for example, a supervisor has the right to require that those who work at a given task carry out their work in certain ways, but he does not have the right, in most cases, to determine what they wear or what they eat for lunch. One of the persistent problems in bureaucracy derives from just this distinction—or rather from a failure to observe it carefully. One of the most common complaints of persons who work in bureaucratic situations is that their superiors require of them certain conformities not provided by the rules. This *usurpation* of power may be minor and subtle, or it may be obvious and gross.

Once the concept of hierarchy—superiors and inferiors—is established, it is frequently difficult to secure strict conformity to rules and regulations limiting the extent and kind of authority which the superior may exercise over the inferior. At the same time the existence of elaborate systems of subterfuge frequently make it difficult for the superior to know the true extent to which his inferiors violate the rules, and even if he knows that they do, he may find it more expeditious to overlook the violation than to "make an issue of it." Consequently, while there is in theory a neatly prescribed hierarchy of responsibility and authority, in actual practice authority and responsibility are not so neatly intermeshed as one might assume, if his knowledge were limited to what is contained in the rule book.

4. Impersonality

One of the fundamental principles of bureaucracy is the concept of impersonality. All decisions are supposed to be made according to the rules—sentiment, passion, sympathy are presumably irrelevant to carrying out the purposes of the organization. In fact, even the discretion or judgment of the office holder is sharply limited by the rules. The reason for this may not at first be clear. Judging from the frequency with which complaints about the "inhumanness" and "arbitrariness" of functionaries are voiced by persons who are unhappy with bureaucratic decisions, one would readily draw the inference that "impersonality" was somehow synonymous with "inhumanity." Actually, of course, the bureaucracy becomes efficient to the extent that all cases of a similar nature are handled alike. The phrase "of a similar nature" can and often does become a fiction. For example, suppose that it is decided by the Selective Service system that all men 18 years of age and physically fit must serve in the armed services. Assuming that there are no other qualifying rules, if a man is 18 years of age and if he is physically fit he automatically falls into the category of eligibles for military service, and it is competely unimportant whether there are other circumstances which some "reasonable person" might conclude should warrant an exception being made. Consequently, very frequently "gross injustices," as seen by the person who thinks logically but outside the rules and regulations of the bureaucracy, are perceived; and a person concludes that someone in the bureaucracy who renders a decision is inhuman, senseless, or even stupid.

Moreover, the person in a bureaucratic position may feel that the decision which he has rendered is an unfortunate one—because he has sympathy, is reasonable, or sees the other side—but under the rules of his office there is nothing else that he is free to do. On the other hand, "the rules" may become a convenient excuse for insensitivity or even incompetency in the rendering of vital decisions which have important bearing on the lives and fortunes of people. The incompetent or the insensitive office functionary might be allowed to exercise more discretion than he does, but it is easier to "pass the buck" to "the regulations."

Regardless, however, of such irregularities and incongruities as we have just discussed, the principle of impersonal relationships among the persons in a hierarchical relationship and in the handling of outsiders (clients) whom the bureaucracy is supposed to "serve" must be understood to constitute the essence of efficient bureaucracy, as that form of organization is known to us.

5. Other characteristics

There are, of course, *other aspects of bureaucracy* than those which we have just discussed. A few of these we shall now mention briefly. (*a*) Employment in the upper echelons of a bureaucratic organization is usually referred to as "a career." This means that employment depends upon an individual having certain technical qualifications for the job, such as education, certain kinds of experience, and so on. He is presumably appointed because of these qualifications and not because of friendship with the appointing officer, religious or political affinities, familial relationship to the appointive officer, and so forth. Moreover, "career" implies that the office holder is protected against "arbitrary dismissal." Dismissal must be "for cause" and the causes, again, are specified in the rule book. Thus if an employer has a labor contract with a union, he is not free to dismiss an employee for any reason except the stipulations provided in the contract or by procedures other than those provided in the contract. "Career" also implies systems of promotion and advancement. Advancement is usually achieved by some combination of evidence of merit and seniority, just how much of each varies from career to career and probably, also, despite the rule book, from judge to judge in the specific situation.

There is much complaining, from both members of the bureaucracy and those outside it, concerning its standards of appointment and promotion and the way in which these standards are applied to individual cases. From a strictly objective point of view, it is frequently difficult to determine to what extent the critics are rationalizing prejudices and their own ineptness and how much the career rules in the individual case are archaic or inappropriate.

(b) A sharp distinction is drawn between "official activity" of a person in a bureaucratic role and "the sphere of private life." The theory holds that the holder of office is "entitled" to hold just about any view as a private citizen and to act in any way he pleases within the broad limits of law and informal custom. But in his official capacity all is different. His behavior, in fact his official thoughts themselves, must follow the bureaucratic mold—impersonality, respect for the rules, adherence to the system of inferiority-superiority, and close attention to the limits of his specialization. Some bureaucratic structures, to be sure, are more lenient than others with respect to how sharply this division of private and official capacity must be observed. For example, both a major professor in a large university and a general in the army are high-ranking members of bureaucracies and are expected to observe these distinctions. It is obvious, however, that the general's bureaucratic expectation differs sharply in many respects from the professor's.

Stated in broad terms, then, this is the nature of bureaucracy. As we have said, it is a principle of organization, a mode of relating the behaviors of many people in order to get some task proficiently performed. To this end it presumably makes certain behavioral requirements of the people who function in it. The requirements of bureaucratic organization, like all human inventions, are, however, *imperfectly observed;* and we have noted some of these imperfections, also. We turn now to a somewhat closer look at some of the facts about bureaucracies which have been uncovered by careful research during recent years. Needless to say, one cannot discuss all of the findings. A few must suffice here.

SOME ASPECTS OF CONTEMPORARY BUREAUCRATIC OPERATION

1. Informal organization

Whenever a close look is taken at actual bureaucracies in operation, we find that there exists an informal, primary group-like interaction which operates where it would not be expected to according to the rules and regulations of the bureaucracy. This occurs regardless of how "strict" the bureaucracy may be with respect to the enforcement of its rules and regulations. This informal organization apparently arises spontaneously to fulfill needs which the formal organization cannot supply. These needs are of two kinds, the one personal, the other organizational.

People often find it difficult to be as impersonal as the bureaucratic rules and regulations expect them to be. Hence, there arise friendships and social groupings of various kinds to supply the "human touch"; apparently the bureaucracy, however efficient and strict, cannot stamp these out.

Quite often the informal organization exists, or eventually operates, to circumvent or "get around" the bureaucratic regulations. For example, in one study of an air force base it was discovered that an informal organization existed among key personnel for the purpose of "cutting through the red tape" so as to improve the efficiency of the unit. One ranking officer told the interviewer, "If we did everything G.I. we'd never get a bomber off the ground." This is probably an exaggeration, but in the overstatement lies the essential truth, namely, that it is sometimes more efficient to invent ways of communication than to use the formal ones provided in the ideal culture.

Sometimes, also, the informal organization exists as a "face-saving" device for people who must make decisions and who wish to avoid the embarrassment of making decisions which will be objected to further up the line or which may be reversed by a superior. The techniques here amount to "sounding out" the superior, possibly at a social function which is designed for that purpose but avowedly exists for a different one, or having some trusted friend "put out a feeler," or relying on some other device for "keeping one's ear to the ground."

Quite often these informal organizations are really *subversive*, that is, they thwart the efficient operation of the organization. For example, during World War II in many defense plants a rather intricate system of organized pilfering existed quite openly among employees. In order to operate successfully it was necessary at the minimum to have the cooperation of the worker's immediate superior officer and guards at the plant gates. This apparently was not difficult, since objects as large and heavy as three horsepower electric motors, power saws, and inter-communication systems found their way out of the plant during times when everything, including lunch buckets, was supposed to be checked by the guards at the gate!

The informal organization may exist as a sort of mutual aid system. This is found very often, for example, among the enlisted men in the armed services. In innumerable ways one's lot is made easier by having someone else in the bureaucracy "cover up" or in some other way assist in getting around the rules.

2. Activity programs

Many modern bureaucracies have built in and around their necessary organization a growing network of fringe activities and functions. Large corporations, for example, typically provide recreational facilities, social activities for the wives and children of employees, inter-departmental competitive sports, and even educational and cultural programs. They justify such as efforts to increase employees' sense of belonging as well as to provide channels for off-the-job association of work associates and their families. Critics of this trend have called it a return to feudalism: "one's whole life gets swallowed up by the corporation." Others staunchly defend it as providing a humanizing function to lessen the rigidity and impersonality of bureaucratic functioning. There are probably elements of accurate evaluation in both positions, depending on the motivations in the actual operation of individual structures.

3. Efficiency: myth and fact

According to the classic theory of Weber and others, bureaucracies exist because they are efficient. It can hardly be denied that many of the colossal tasks which organizations are required to perform could hardly be performed otherwise. Yet it would be a serious error to assume, simply, that bureaucracies are efficient. In innumerable and demonstrable ways they are grossly inefficient, when a close look is taken at the more specific tasks which are performed incidental to the gigantic end product. Inefficiencies grow out of at least three aspects of bureaucracy which are so general as to be regarded as inherent—obsolete procedures, incompetent personnel, and simple negligence or dishonesty.

The frequent accusations of red tape in bureaucracies are probably overstated because the complainant sees only his own frustration instead of the larger picture of running the enterprise. It is true, nevertheless, that some bureaucratic organizations are operating under rules which may have been the most efficient possible at the time they were formulated but have become outdated. As evidence that this is increasingly recognized, at least by some bureaucracies, there has arisen a profession of "consulting personnel engineers," variously termed, one of whose main jobs is to assist organizations to modify their rules and procedures periodically in the interests of increasing efficiency. For much the same reason the President or Congress occasionally turns its attention to "reorganizing" the armed services or the Department of Agriculture or the postal service.

One of the conditions which frequently stands in the way of developing the most efficient organization, however, is that of the "outside factors" which are usually given consideration. Thus, for example, for the sake of efficiency a university president might like to eliminate a certain vice-presidency which had been created by his predecessor as a reward for a faithful assistant. But the incumbent is a likeable fellow and has a considerable "following" in the community and on the campus. So perhaps it is wiser not to push the matter, and no doubt an "act of God" will solve it eventually anyway. In government, reorganization for increased efficiency is almost always thwarted, if not completely nullified, by "political considerations." Some years ago, for example, the Hoover Commission for government reorganization, after a prodigious amount of work, set forth a set of monumental suggestions for increasing the efficiency of the government, including the armed forces. Virtually everyone, regardless of political party, who took the trouble to study the recommendations seemed to regard most of them as desirable, yet years after the appearance of the recommendations very little change has been made in governmental structure, because, one must conclude, considerations other than efficiency enter into the decision making.

The balanced view, then, would seem to be that while bureaucracy exists for the purpose of providing an efficient procedure for getting large tasks performed, it is, like all human inventions, an imperfect device; and innumerable inefficiencies creep in and cause waste of one sort or another. Waste of time, money, and personnel are almost everywhere apparent in connection with bureaucracy.

4. Tenure and career: some unsolved problems

One of the dilemmas in bureaucratic structure centers around the concept of *tenure*. "Tenure" means that a person who does his work properly cannot be removed from his office without "demonstrated cause." This is said to be necessary to efficient functioning for several reasons. If persons in positions cannot be fired at the whim of their superiors, they will function more courageously instead of simply courting the favor of the superior. Moreover, persons of superior ability and training are said to be attracted to the organization if they have reasonable assurance that they will be retained and promoted according to seniority and merit. As stated, this rationale for tenure is convincing. Problems, however, arise on other scores. First of all, competency for many bureaucratic tasks is exceedingly hard to measure (for example, just who is and is not a "competent" college teacher), or often competency is fairly easy to measure, but the facts *about* competency and incompetency do not get correctly relayed to the person responsible for hiring and firing, promotion and demotion. This is one of the reasons for the existence of some informal organization—the formation of cliques, the purpose of which is to get to the appropriate superior only such information as will enhance the prestige of clique members and suppress evidence of incompetency which may be well known to persons familiar with the job incumbent. Sometimes rather ingenious and utterly immoral networks of intrigue are formed and perpetuated for long periods in this way.

Moreover, competency is not a constant over the lifetime of the individual. A very promising man at 40 years of age may be placed high in a responsible position for quite objective reasons, but may some time thereafter, either because he is negligent, sick, distracted, or downright dishonest, show materially reduced competency. He may still retain enough power through the informal organization to "cover" his incompetency in various ways and continue more or less indefinitely in his post.

For all of these reasons and many more, the career concept inherent in bureaucracy continues as a mixed blessing to the organization. Some organizations, notably in the business field and civil service, strive to correct these conditions by such devices as periodic merit ratings. But it is exceedingly difficult to outsmart the informal organization and to go against the loyalties of the peer group which tends to protect even those of its members who are admittedly less than adequate in their jobs.

5. Perversions of the bureaucratic philosophy

In theory the bureaucracy in its efforts to be efficient selects and promotes the most efficient people possible and surrounds them with working conditions and rules and regulations which maximize their efficiency. In practice, however, many and devious are the ways of circumventing and even perverting the basic theory. Circumventions such as nepotism (giving preference to relatives and, by extension, to friends), favoritism (giving preference to persons because of past favors granted or future favors to be expected), and other gross practices of this nature shall not be discussed here. These are well known and much publicized and are obvious enough anyway. The kind of perversions of the bureaucratic mode with which we shall be concerned are somewhat more subtle.

One of the most prevalent and most natural deviations results from the normal effort on the part of the career person to "get ahead." In American society, as elsewhere, this is regarded as an altogether legitimate ambition, and most bureaucracies provide ladders of ascent on which the competent and ambitious may climb to positions calling for increasing competency and offering increasing rewards for success. But it is the judgment of persons, ultimately, upon which one's rate and degree of success must rest. The most competent ballistics expert may remain in an obscure, minor position unless and until someone who has the power to advance him (*a*) *recognizes* his competency and (*b*) *acts*. Thus, it readily occurs to the ambitious that if their successes are *apparent* to the *appropriate* people, they will get ahead further and faster. Moreover, in the larger bureaucracy, there is value to being "socially conspicuous" so that when there is an opening one will not be overlooked. "Making contacts" with the right people, ingratiating oneself in one way or another with the right people, may facilitate one's advancement much more than hard work or competency in the strict sense. Putting the matter very bluntly, it is very easy for a person to substitute pleasing his superior, in whatever ways are at his disposal, for doing the best possible job. Many persons particularly adept at this are the first to deny that they operate in this manner. And they may not be altogether dishonest in their denial. It is indeed an easy, almost unconscious, transition from competency (in the strict sense) for the purpose of gaining favor to gaining favor per se, since the end objective is the same anyway.

William Whyte, Jr., in his influential book, *The Organization Man*,[3] underscores another kind of bureaucratic perversion. He points out that the traditional virtues of hard work and excelling others do not fit very well in the bureaucratic mode. The "eager beaver" easily becomes a nuisance, and knowing this he finds it expedient to adopt what Whyte calls the "Social Ethic." Whyte explains that the individual finds himself more or less pressured into a mold of conformity to the prevailing patterns of his colleagues. Since, in the nature of the case, talent is rare and mediocrity abundant, the majority pattern of mediocrity becomes the work mode. (It might be pointed out that the trade union concept prevalent in the building trades as early as the 1920's operated in much the same way. Even though a given man might be able to lay 20 percent more bricks per hour than the union rate, he was not allowed under union rules to do so. The rationale held that although he could work at this rate, most men could not and invidious distinctions among co-workers would be harmful to their mutual interest.)

And so, according to Whyte and others who have observed this closely, a rather easy pace is set and the prime consideration is shifted from getting a job done most brilliantly and effectively to just "getting along well" with colleagues. Whyte reports that this philosophy of "belongingness and togetherness" has become so effectively sold to many leaders of management in business, the armed services, and elsewhere that it is encouraged as an inherently sound basis of operation. Undeniably the "belonging and together" philosophy makes for smoother relations between colleagues and between superiors and inferiors. Annoyances are cut to a minimum and the organization appears to be running smoothly. But the piper must be paid, and the pay comes in the form of loss of talent. If talent is not rewarded—or is actually penalized, as is often the case—a fundamental inefficiency is introduced which no amount of "smooth" personnel management can ever overcome. If Whyte's analysis is correct, and many feel that it is, the basic objective of efficiency in bureaucracy has been perverted to a substitute objective of convenience.

[3] William Whyte, Jr., *The Organization Man* (New York, Simon and Schuster, 1956).

SOME HYPOTHESES AND IMPLICATIONS
REGARDING PERSONALITY

In the preceding section we have discussed some conditions which are *known* on the basis of research and are readily verifiable by anyone who wishes to take the trouble to do so. He may not need, in fact, even to be a technically trained social scientist in order to do his own replication. In the present section, however, our concerns become more technical in the sense that the untrained observer might find it very difficult, if not impossible, to do any very reliable replication. Therefore, we use the term *hypotheses* in the heading which precedes this discussion. This is not to imply that there is no evidence, but rather that the evidence does not have the same degree of ready verifiability as was true in our discussion up to the present.

1. "Bureaucratic personality"

In any social relationship, we may safely theorize, the ideally functioning personality is the personality whose needs, aspirations, and habit patterns correspond identically with the requirements of the roles which the person is expected to fill. If the role, for example, calls for "daring," the kind of person who finds it easy and possibly pleasurable to take chances is, other things being equal, better suited to the role expectations than the person who is quiet, hesitating, looks to other people for decisions, and values security over new experience. Starting from this premise, it is fairly easy to describe the kind of personality which fits most effectively, that is with least tension, into the bureaucratic mode. One study [4] attempted to set forth some of the more salient features of personality which were most expeditious for effective functioning in one kind of bureaucracy. These features were:

1. Previous experience in and preference for functioning in groups which are impersonal, that is, bureaucratic in nature, should increase adaptability.
2. Persons who characteristically follow "institutionally prescribed norms and conduct, irrespective of more personally benefiting behavior" will fit better into a bureaucracy.
3. Persons who "characteristically follow institutionally prescribed norms, irrespective of obligations to others," for example, to parents, siblings, friends, "will function better" in a bureaucracy.

[4] Alfred C. Clarke, Russell R. Dynes, and John F. Cuber, *Social Factors Related to Adaptability of Air Force Pilot Trainees,* U.S.A.F. School of Aviation Medicine, Air University, 1957.

4. Persons who "experience little or no conflict between obligations stemming from bureaucratic rules and regulations" and other life roles, such as religious systems, political views, or moral conceptions, "will show greater adaptability" to effective bureaucratic functioning.
5. Persons who are willing and able "to forego immediate satisfactions in favor of long term goals" will function more effectively in bureaucracies.

Probably anyone who has absorbed the earlier discussion in this chapter would find it relatively easy to understand why each of the above hypotheses should be true. A bureaucracy is characterized by impersonal secondary kinds of relationships. It is rather obvious that if a person has had experience with and has been comfortable in this kind of relationship, he will be more able to function effectively in a bureaucracy than a person without this experience, or a person who does not like this kind of interaction pattern. Persons who play by the rules rather than trying to figure out for themselves what is the appropriate conduct in a given situation will find it easier to do what the bureaucracy requires of them, namely, a faithful, dispassionate, unequivocal carrying out of the prescribed behaviors. If, for example, it is the "policy" of the organization not to employ Jews, then an effective office holder simply does not employ Jews. It is at best a waste of time, and at worst an act of disloyalty, to fret about whether it is desirable or not to have such a policy, and guilt feelings concerning whether one has done right in refusing employment to a Jew would only add to the person's operating inefficiency. The third hypothesis carries this same point a step further. Frequently the bureaucracy may call upon one to perform certain duties which are at variance with one's obligations or ethical precepts which derive from other social relationships such as being a parent or a Catholic or a Mason. The good bureaucrat does his job according to the rules and regulations, whether or not it interferes with such "extraneous considerations." He does not, it is important to note, do so grudgingly. The pilot who is ordered to bomb a village in which his relatives may live, *if he is a good pilot*, simply does what he is ordered, because this is the order. A civilian bureaucracy would call it a "policy." Rarely, of course, are the conflicts as great as the case we have just cited, but the principle is the same.

The fourth hypothesis is quite similar, except that instead of involving conflicts between personal role obligations it involves conflicts between broader ideologies such as religion, moral codes, and the like. The requirement, however, is essentially the same, namely, that the efficient office holder in a bureaucracy, without equivocation, and with a minimum of conflict, carries out policy whether or not that policy conflicts with some moral precept. The logic behind the armed forces' policy of not attempting to integrate conscientious objectors into fighting units is based upon this proposition. The conscientious objectors in all probability would not be efficient fighting men anyway. Ways are provided, therefore, for them to "serve their country" in other ways.

The last hypothesis grows, of course, out of the tenure and career features of bureaucratic positions. The typical career pattern in a bureaucracy is for the incumbent to begin with a relatively low pay and privilege rating and to "work up through the ranks" with increasing increments of both pay and other benefits. In a very real sense, he is thus *paid later* for what he does today—at least it seems so. Some persons find this rather easy to accept, others do not. They want their gratifications and rewards *now* for the disprivileges which they undergo *now*. Such people do not make good adjustment to bureaucracies.

2. Specialization and "trained incompetency"

Probably there would be general agreement that some of the rule requirements for bureaucratic functioning are "good" according to the generally accepted American values. Certainly vocational security, which is maximized in bureaucracy, is a good thing. Tenure, regular salary increments, formalized promotional policies, pensions, and various fringe benefits certainly remove for the individual some of life's most anxiety-producing contingencies. Moreover specialization, while by no means an unmixed blessing, is easy to rationalize. It promotes efficiency, takes some of the anxiety out of carrying out role requirements, permits the person to utilize his specialized training, and so on. For certain kinds of specialization, however, this is in part counterbalanced by the monotony deriving from routinized activities and the sense of being "a cog in the machine" which some people appear not to like.

There have, however, been foreboding shadows cast across the easy assumptions that specialization and impersonality are all that they are rationalized to be. The bureaucratic specialist (as distinct from a pure *skills* specialist, such as a brain surgeon or a die caster) may find that his so-called specialization becomes, as Veblen called it, "trained incapacity." One becomes trained not to have an opinion about things he is not supposed to have opinions about, in short not to be capable of thinking outside of the mold he is supposed to follow according to the rules and regulations. Other critics have coined such phrases as "occupational psychosis" and "professional deformation" to characterize this same condition. Probably most people have observed the hapless plight of one or another person who has a high bureaucratic position involving decision making according to the rule book, but is bewildered when he needs to make a decision affecting his own life for which there are no rules and regulations, no mimeographed handbook defining "our policies" and defining meticulously what is relevant and what is not relevant to the decision!

3. "Overconformity"

So important does it become to the successful person in a bureaucratic position that he conform to the rules and regulations if he does not wish to jeopardize his career that a pronounced tendency to overconformity easily sets in. "An over concern with strict adherence to regulations" induces "timidity and conservatism."[5] The automaton-like individual, whom everyone has seen, may be a caricature, but he is a perfectly natural exaggeration of a tendency which exists in practically any successful bureaucratic functionary—some degree of atrophy of creative expression and personal growth. There are those who feel that this is too great a price in personal value to pay for the obvious benefits of vocational security and paternalistic protection against some of life's contingencies.

SUMMARY, CONCLUSIONS, AND IMPLICATIONS

No matter what may be undesirable to the person or to the society about the bureaucratic mode, bureaucracy is here to stay. Even if it is as inefficient in some respects as its most severe critics claim, even if it has some negative features for the mental hygiene of the individual, no alternative mode for handling the gigantic tasks of big government, massive industry, centralized religion, and mass education has yet been found, or for that matter even envisaged by the fondest dreamer. As indicated earlier, bureaucracy is a human invention—an improvised way of getting big things accomplished—which like all human inventions is something less than perfect for the purpose for which it is intended. Moreover, it is in the nature of inventions, both material and social, to have undesirable consequences in ways quite extraneous to the intended purpose. This is true of practically all institutional arrangements. Probably all that a reasonable evaluator of a society can ask is that the purpose of each bureaucracy be reasonably well achieved and,

[5] For a superb classic discussion of this and other related points, see Robert K. Merton, "Bureaucratic Structure and Personality," *Social Forces*, Vol. 17 (1940), pp. 560–568.

second, if there are inefficiencies and if there are objectionable side effects, that these be eliminated to the greatest degree possible. To a perceptible extent this is being done. Some bureaucratic organizations from time to time have made self-studies for the purpose of improving their procedures. Many personnel policies have been instituted for the purpose of reducing some of the presumably undesirable personality effects. The probability that these changes have been stimulated by selfish rather than by humanitarian objectives does not alter the fact that they may be beneficial to persons attempting to adjust as well as possible to bureaucratic structure.

There is another side to bureaucracy and personality which the critics have not told us much about. First, there are many persons whose personality needs are so well suited to bureaucracy that we can regard it almost as an ideal arrangement for their needs. A number of people have stated that they "can't understand what critics like Whyte and Riesman are talking about." For these people the inadequacies of bureaucracy simply do not exist. Furthermore, the bureaucratic mode, particularly in industry, the military services, and the civil service, has made it possible for persons of rather limited intelligence and skill to make their way in the world reasonably well, and even to make contributions to it. To them intricate specialization is no bugbear, but a godsend. It may also be that the easy pace, impersonality, and resulting low emotional involvement in the job may have some very beneficial mental hygiene effects as compared with self-destructive frantic efforts of the eager beaver, the striver, the rate buster, and the like, spawned in such numbers during the individualistic era out of which we have come. This does not mean that persons in bureaucratic career structures do not have ambition and are not strivers, but rather that some features at least of self-destructive kinds of overexertion which we have known in the past may be somewhat meliorated. If so, this may be good. And finally, as we have said and implied over and over again, there is no alternative to the bureaucratic way for getting gigantic tasks accomplished when we want essentially identical units with interchangeable parts in everything from automobiles to postal service to professional certification. If these uniformities are desired, there is no way to get them other than by some kind of hierarchical organization that will insure some approximation of identical, if minimal, quality standards in everything from canned soup to jet pilots.

At least part of the difficulty with bureaucracy, our attitudes toward it, and our ability to adjust to it is probably a passing thing and much more likely to be felt acutely by our parents than by our children.

For a couple of centuries at least, as Whyte points out so ably, people in our society have been reared in an individualistic tradition of self-reliance and independence. These and other sentiments seem to be violated and thwarted by the bureaucratic mode. It is irrelevant whether they are better or worse than the sentiments of the "social ethic." The point is that they are familiar, emotionally held, and yet thwarted in their free expression. But time changes all and it is not inconceivable that in a generation or so, or even sooner, the bureaucratic way of life and work will seem so completely natural that critics like Whyte may indeed seem to most people to be talking about something that does not exist. Human beings appear to have an almost unlimited capacity, in the long run especially, to rationalize almost any social arrangement as "good," once they have become accustomed to it. If there is any irrefutable lesson from history this is it. And if one wishes to take an even longer look, he can safely prophesy that bureaucracy, too, will have had its day and some other kind of institutional arrangement will take its place; or that the nature of the bureaucratic pattern, already different in many respects from the Weber description, may change at fundamental points, thus making "a new order" by another route.

SUGGESTED READINGS

Blau, Peter M., *Bureaucracy in Modern Society*. New York, Random House, 1956.
A short pocket book of essentially the same scope as the treatment in this chapter. Of particular significance are Chapters 5 and 6, which treat of innovation and democracy in a very simple but penetrating manner.

Eisenstadt, S. N., "Bureaucracy, Bureaucratization and Debureaucratization." *Administrative Science Quarterly*, Vol. 4 (1960), pp. 303–320.
An excellent treatment of two foci in the study of bureaucracy: (1) bureaucracy as a "tool" for efficient operation of social systems and (2) bureaucracy as an "instrument of power" and the continuous expansion thereof.

Etzioni, Amitai, *Complex Organizations: A Sociological Reader*. New York, Holt, Rinehart and Winston, 1961.
This is a highly respected set of readings, from 39 different sources, on various aspects of complex, chiefly bureaucratic, organizations. The articles include some classics from Max Weber as well as some contemporary research-oriented materials.

Evan, William M., and Zelditch, Morris, Jr., "A Laboratory Experiment on Bureaucratic Authority." *American Sociological Review*, Vol. 26 (December, 1961), pp. 888–893.

This is an excellent critical examination of the incongruities between the authority of "office" in bureaucratic organization and simple merit. The article suggests four types of office holders on the basis of the four possible relationships between merit and authority. A significant article.

Gerth, H. H., and Mills, C. Wright, eds., *From Max Weber: Essays in Sociology*. New York, Oxford University Press, 1946, pp. 196–240.
This is generally regarded as a classic treatment of bureaucracy as an "ideal type" social system. The translation is well done.

Merton, Robert K., Gray, Ailsa P., Hockey, Barbara, and Selvin, Hanan, eds., *Reader in Bureaucracy*. New York, Macmillan, 1952.
Probably the best collection of original materials on bureaucracy to be found in one book. Almost any aspect of the subject which one might want to examine can be found here. Extensive bibliography.

Thompson, Victor A., *Modern Organization*. New York, Knopf, 1961.
This is a treatment of bureaucracy written by a nonsociologist. Particularly striking is the treatment of bureaupathology. The author apparently takes the view that complete adjustment to bureaucratic organization is both necessary and inevitable and tends to dismiss as alien considerations a number of problems which typically concern, if not disturb, sociologists.

Whyte, William H., Jr., *The Organization Man*. New York, Simon and Schuster, 1956.
Strictly speaking this is not a sociological treatise, but only so because the author is not a professional sociologist, although he shows unusual familiarity with sociological work. The book has become a best-seller and "organization man" a byword among educated people. The book is critical in the better sense of the word—not carping, irresponsible, objection finding, but an analytical job forcefully carried out.

STUDY QUESTIONS

1. How do you account for the fact that the words *bureaucracy* and *bureaucratic* have come to have such an unfavorable connotation in our society?
2. List some ways in which bureaucracies are efficient and some ways in which they are inefficient. Illustrate wherever possible from your own practical experience.
3. Why is the career pattern in a bureaucracy so much sought after by educated young people?
4. In what ways does the bureaucracy make demands upon its employees outside of work hours and off the job? Why is this so?
5. In what ways can you see present bureaucracies differing from the classic description by Weber summarized in this chapter?

6. Why did the early American settlers have little need for bureaucracy?

7. From your observation do people in or out of bureaucracies work harder?

8. "You have your choice between security and freedom—work in a bureaucracy or outside of it." How do you react to this terse comment?

9. What proportion of people would you say (in the United States) are still working outside of bureaucratic structures? Support your estimate with whatever evidence you can get.

10. List the differences which you have observed from one bureaucracy to another. How do you account for these differences?

11. What informal organization have you noticed in some bureaucratic structure that you have had connection with (military service, college, factory, and the like)? Why do you think this informal organization grows up and what problems does it create for the bureaucracy and for the people in the organization?

12. "Informal organization may facilitate as well as impede the operation of the bureaucratic structure." Explain how both conditions may occur and illustrate wherever possible from your own experience.

13. "Bureaucracy is government from the top down and democracy is government from the bottom up. Coexistence of the two in the same society introduces a dreadful and dangerous paradox." What do you think the author of the above quotation means? Do you agree with him that the coexistence of these two forms is dangerous? If dangerous, dangerous to what and to whom? Do you see any way in which these two seemingly opposite philosophies may coexist in a society like ours?

18
RACE RELATIONS

Race relations in the United States present an excellent example of at least two basic principles of human behavior, both of which have already been discussed and need, therefore, merely to be restated. (1) *Mistaken ideas are as real* to the person who believes them *as accurate ones are.* In other words, the firmness with which one believes something is no criterion whatsoever of its accuracy or validity. History has shown countless examples of men's willingness even to die for some idea which was based on a fundamental untruth. The belief in a "super-race" among Nazi Germans, for example, is only one of many cases in point. Much similar nonsense about race is believed very firmly by millions of Americans. (2) A second fundamental principle which is basic to understanding problems of race is the *inability and/or unwillingness of persons to be equally or comparably scientific about different aspects of the universe.* Thus we find numerous instances in which persons can be scientific and intellectually honest in the realms of chemistry, medicine, or agriculture, but unscientific —if not antiscientific—when thinking about and acting in the realms of race relations or other phases of human behavior. It is important not to overlook the significance of this. Evidence of competence, or even brilliance, of a person in some scientific realm gives no assurance whatsoever that that person will show similar objective thinking ability in another realm. It is common to find persons of distinction in various fields of modern scientific endeavor who show evidence at the same time of the most unscientific ideas concerning race and race relations. A large part of the difficulty in the interaction of the races in the United States is a direct result of the mistaken prescientific ideas about race which have become deeply ingrained in American culture.

It seems instructive, therefore, to discuss at least three separate *aspects* of race and race relations in the United States.

1. The latest *scientific evidence* regarding race as discovered by modern researches in the fields of biology, psychology, sociology, and anthropology.

2. The characteristic *beliefs* held on the same subject. These beliefs are, of course, mostly the survivals from a period before scientific research on man was common. They represent largely prescientific or folk thinking, although sometimes they appear to result from defensive efforts to justify status or to legitimate status change.

3. The *effects of the discrepancies between scientific evidence and popular belief* on the interaction of persons in the various races.

The enlightened student of race relations realizes that the *beliefs about race* and the *facts about race* are often as opposite as the poles. Moreover, it is to be noted that the possessors of the scientific knowledge about race are relatively few in number, because the acquisition of expert knowledge in this field, as in others, is a result of careful specialized study for which many persons lack the ability, the interest, or the time necessary to enable them to master the existing facts. Meanwhile the rank and file rely on the folk "wisdom," the stereotypes, and other nonrational sources of "information" which prevail in the culture.

RESEARCH EVIDENCE PERTAINING TO RACE

1. Race relations viewed historically and cross-culturally

There is a prevailing provincial, if not ethnocentric, view among Americans which makes the tacit assumption that the kinds of attitudes, practices, and problems associated with race in the U.S. are somehow natural or normal whenever different races are in contact. Such is manifestly not true. In fact, patterns of race relations are no exception to the principle discussed earlier, namely that cultures and societies are highly variable in the ways in which they handle and have handled contacts between the races.

An excellent typology of race relations patterns is presented by Brewton Berry in his important and influential book *Race and Ethnic Relations*.[1] In this presentation Professor Berry combines race and ethnic differences, which seems justified in view of the fact that only a relatively few scholars appear capable of using the term *race* in its true biological sense; many habitually confuse religious groups (e.g. Jews) or nationality groups (e.g. Italians) with true race. Here, again, we find a clear illustration of the classic sociological truism that however mistaken ideas may be, they become true in their consequences. Whether Jews are a race or not makes little social difference if in the practical

---

[1] Brewton Berry, *Race and Ethnic Relations*, third edition (Boston, Houghton Mifflin, 1965).

circumstance non-Jews regard Jews as a separate race and treat them as such. There have been instances in which visitors from India were required to observe the same customs required of American Negroes merely because they were darker than the whites. The fact that racially they are not Negroid makes no difference in the way these people are treated, so long as the persons in power are ignorant of the difference.

Professor Berry made a comparison of patterns of race relations through time and across space: a cross-cultural analysis. He was able to identify six more or less distinct patterns which mankind has evolved for structuring the relations of races or groups considered to be races. Throughout time, unlike peoples have upon occasion come into contact through wars, peaceful migrations, trade relations, or even accidentally. Generally humans react to difference in negative terms and since, as a rule, the contacting groups differ in power, one is usually in a better position than the other to impose conditions on the interaction. Sooner or later, however, certain kinds of relationships become institutionalized with the result that it is possible to document the following types.

a. Annihilation

Upon a number of occasions in known history and quite possibly more frequently in pre-history, one race has sought simply to annihilate the other. There are in the Old Testament (third chapter of Deuteronomy and fifteenth chapter of the Second Book of Kings) blood curdling accounts of the complete destruction of cities and peoples. Likewise the Assyrians, Babylonians, and Egyptians have left records indicating that they simply smote their adversaries to the last man, woman, and child. The historian, Toynbee, records how the British completely wiped out the native population of Tasmania within a period of seventy-five years. A more modern attempt at annihilation occurred during the Nazi domination of Europe, during which period 60 percent of the 9.6 million European Jews were in one way or another exterminated. This, of course, was accomplished deliberately with the explanation that the racial inferiority and consequent effects on European culture required such genocide.

b. Expulsion

A second solution to the problem of unlike peoples in contact is the forceful eviction of the less powerful group by the more powerful group. Students of history will recall how Phillip II of Spain had the Moriscos expelled from Spain and how Henry VIII drove the Gypsies from England, or how the Acadians were expelled from Nova Scotia by the British. Examples are abundant. A little publicized historical fact in the United States is that of the expulsion of the Cherokee from Georgia in violation of treaties with these Indians. Over 10,000 Cherokee were placed in stockades and then driven west to the Oklahoma territory under the most brutal and unbelievable circumstances. The federal government officially carried out this expulsion.

c. Assimilation

In other instances unlike peoples solve the problem of their unlikeness by merging their separate cultures, by intermarrying and thus eventually completely losing their separate identities. This is what has happened in substantial measure in the United States so far as the various ethnic groups of the white race, who migrated here from Europe, are concerned. While there have been some "diehards" among various ethnic groups who have insisted upon marriage within their own nationality groups, most second, third, and fourth generation Americans have paid little attention to such extremism. In other parts of the world assimilation of various racial groups has taken place in much the same way.

d. Segregation

Segregation needs little comment for American students, since it has been our most consistent resolution of the race question where Negroes and whites are concerned. At one time or another Negroes have been required to remain separate in residence, church, school, use of public facilities, and even occupation. Some aspects of this segregation, as everyone knows, are now being dissolved by law, but the process is slow and arouses violent objections from many whites.

e. Stratification

At other times and places and to some extent in the United States at present the more powerful race, while not requiring physical segregation of the disadvantaged group, assigns it inferior positions in the distribution of privilege and opportunity. The "inferior" race may be denied equal schooling, entrance into the better jobs even though some members are technically qualified to fill them, and equal rights before the law. In various other ways members of the "inferior" race are "kept in their place." Slavery is, of course, an extreme form of stratification, and this practice has been widespread in history.

f. Pluralism

Pluralistic systems of race relations have been relatively rare although there appears to be a long time trend in this direction. Pluralism means simply that the various race and/or ethnic groups, while retaining their identity, continue to interact with one another with a minimum of conflict. Pluralism is unlike assimilation in that original identities are not lost; they are retained but are not the basis for conflict. The classic case of pluralism is the Jews. For 2000 years they have been scattered over the face of the earth, living in a wide variety of cultures and climates, subject in varying degree to discrimination, nevertheless (with the exception of a brief period in Germany) participating widely in the general society in which they have found themselves. In almost every Western culture and in almost every field of endeavor the names of distinguished Jews are conspicuous. Pluralism with respect to Negro-white relations is, of course, the goal of the various civil rights movements, desegregation programs, "open housing," and nondiscriminatory employment practices which are so much in evidence in the United States at present. When and whether a truly pluralistic situation will obtain is now only a matter of conjecture. There are, however, many areas of the world—Hawaii, for example—where multiple races have co-existed for some time in a remarkably pluralistic set of arrangements.

Thus, we see that almost every kind of relationship system, varying from annihilation and expulsion to assimilation and pluralism, has at some time or other been in existence somewhere in the world. Conflict, thus, is not to be regarded as an inevitable outcome of interracial contact, anymore than segregation and stratification are to be thought "natural." This is not to imply, however, that once established, a pattern of race relations can readily be changed. Certainly no one in the United States today can overlook the strong resistance to modification of historical patterns.

Yet patterns of race relations, like all other kinds of human systems, inevitably do change with time. Little more than a hundred years ago the Negro-white race relation pattern in the United States was one of slave and slave owner, but this pattern did not survive a changed moral conscience and a changing economy. Less than fifty years ago it was virtually impossible for a Negro, however capable, to be employed as a professor in an American university, to be elected to the Senate, or to be appointed to the Supreme Court. Yet all of these and many similar events have occurred within the year—and with increasing frequency.

We move now to a more specific focus on facts and research dealing with race.

2. Extent and number of racial differences minor

Probably the basic popular illusion about race lies in the conception of race itself. On the basis of "commonsense" observation it would appear, for example, that since Negroes are dark (often mistakenly called "black") and whites light (not really white) that a great chasm of difference separates the two. Actually, of course, in the sum total of physical traits of the two races, differences are negligible both in number and importance. All of the races overlap in all of their traits, that is, one can find persons of another race who will possess traits ordinarily characteristic of some given race. For example, some whites can be found with darker skin coloring than some Negroes, and some whites can be found with higher cheek bones than some Mongoloids. What is more important, however, is the fact that careful analyses of the physical makeup of the various races show that they are virtually identical. The blood plasma, for example, of a Negro cannot be distinguished from that of a white of the same blood type. If an internal organ is taken into a laboratory for observation the anatomist has absolutely no way of determining with certainty whether the organ came from a Negro, a Mongolian, or a white.

3. There is no "pure" race

The above items are hardly surprising when one recognizes the fact that *there is no pure race*, that historical and anthropological research has demonstrated that from time immemorial racial interbreeding (though not necessarily intermarriage) has occurred in most parts of the world. Moreover, there are *differences in the physical structure of the subgroups within a given race*. Although the American Negro originally came from Africa, for example, he is no longer, on the average, like the African Negroes, even physically. The differences are accounted for by several facts. First, there has been considerable race mixture in the United States, although very little intermarriage. This began in slave days and has extended to the present time. Some present-day "Negroes" are so light in color that they pass for whites. They probably have more white ancestors than Negro ancestors. Moreover, the American Negro has been isolated from the diverse African Negro stocks from which he descended for a sufficient number of generations that differences are probably appearing because isolation and inbreeding are creating a somewhat different type. Irrespective of the reasons, however, the fact is clear that American Negroes and the various kinds of African Negroes are not the same. Comparable illustrations could be found among other races. The American Indians, for example, are clearly Mongolian, but they are quite distinguishable from the Chinese, Japanese, and other Mongolians.

4. Racial origins explained

Students of race history have now rather well agreed that races probably originated as a result of *mutation, isolation,* and *inbreeding.* The student will recall from his biology that a "mutation" is a somewhat markedly different specimen who appears in a species for no apparent reason and then passes on his somewhat unusual characteristic to his offspring through heredity. In the million years or so during which man has been on the earth there has been ample opportunity for numerous mutations to appear. Then through isolation, due either to geographical factors or to man's self-imposed separateness from others, inbreeding among the offspring of the mutation would tend to perpetuate and magnify the original uniqueness. Differences would also come about through ordinary variation and become intensified by inbreeding. Thus, in time, the original uniqueness of the mutation or the variant could become a commonplace trait of the group. It is possible, moreover, that certain factors in the climate might have had an indirect effect upon the modification of traits, since certain traits have greater survival values in certain climates. Scientists are less sure about this geographical factor than they were at one time, however.

Thus the history of each race is one of isolation and inbreeding on the one hand, and contact and outcrossing on the other. Consequently, there is small wonder that most careful scholars in recent times who have tried to discover one valid criterion for the classification of races have concluded that there is *no satisfactory single criterion for the classification of races,* because there are no pure races and because the races are so basically similar in the first place.

5. Differences in intelligence

One important finding on race pertains to intelligence.[2] The idea has been common in America, for example, that Negroes, as a whole, are inferior in intelligence to whites, as a whole. Superficially, it appears to many that such a conclusion is true because of the high incidence of illiteracy among Negro groups and the small number of Negroes who have attained educational and scientific distinction. A somewhat more careful analysis, however, would reveal that the problem is complicated by several important factors.

[2] The classic and definitive studies of psychologist Otto Klineberg are the cornerstone of our knowledge. See his *Negro Intelligence and Selective Migration* (New York, Columbia University Press, 1935) and *Race Difference* (New York, Harper & Row, 1935).

First, the *American Negro lives in a society dominated by whites and has not been given an equal educational opportunity with whites.* Since, then, Negroes are not given the same opportunities to develop their abilities that whites are, how can we determine whether or not they have comparable inborn capacity for learning, that is, comparable intelligence? There is, basically, only one way to answer this vital question. A group of Negroes and a group of whites must be given the same opportunities for learning and then at intervals both groups can be tested. If differences appear, it may be assumed that those differences are inherited differences and presumably reflect the difference between the two race groups. Even this is not as easy to do as might be at first thought. It is difficult to find, for example, a community which has *really* given Negro children the same opportunity to develop their intelligence as white children have been given. So far as the school alone is concerned there are numerous communities with approximately equal school facilities for Negroes and whites, but it has long been known to educational experts that the preschool and the out-of-school experiences of a child have a great deal to do with the amount and kind of learning which the child acquires in school. The child, for example, who has grown up in a family which speaks precise English has a much better opportunity to learn the language arts in school than does the child in whose home there is illiteracy and a spoken language made up of colloquialisms.

In spite of the difficulty of equalizing the out-of-school experience of children of Negro and white parentage, satisfactory samples of Negroes and whites of comparable social position have been selected for research purposes. Numerous tests of such equalized groups have been made and they have *shown conclusively that there are negligible native intelligence differences between Negroes and whites when both have approximately the same opportunities to learn the kind of material found in the test.* Early studies, incidentally, which did seem to reveal differences in favor of the whites now have been reinterpreted, because the researchers had usually made the error of using samples of Negro and white children whose learning experience had not been truly comparable. In recent years there have been large enough, and sufficiently numerous, valid tests [3] to demonstrate conclusively the absence of important differences in mental ability between Negroes and whites, and also between whites and Mongolians.

[3] See an excellent resumé in Thomas Pettigrew, "Negro American Intelligence," reprinted in Joan I. Roberts, ed. *School Children in the Urban Slum* (New York, Free Press, 1967), pp. 32–57.

Race prejudice not a general condition

It is undeniably true that persons of each race possess character-istic attitudes of distinction from, if not also antagonism toward, mem-bers of other races; in short, that race prejudice exists. Although persons vary in the degree to which race prejudice is manifest, there is no deny-ing that race prejudice is a very widespread phenomenon.

One of the significant things about race prejudice found by per-sons who have studied it is that *it is not directed toward a race in gen-eral, but rather consists of a number of separate evaluations of specific social relationships.* Many persons in the North, for example, do not object to their children attending the same school with Negro children, but do object to having Negroes living in their own neighborhood. Others would accept Negro neighbors, but would object to having their children "date" Negro children. Some persons do not object to working with Negroes or having Negro servants in the home, but would bar Negroes from membership in their lodges or churches. It is significant that race prejudice, in the United States at least, does not so much object to the physical proximity of the other race. There could hardly be a closer physical relationship, for example, than that of hav-ing a colored servant, and yet such relationships are very widely prac-ticed and are, in fact, status-enhancing practices. This has given rise to a useful concept in understanding human relationships. It is not limited to race, but is certainly pertinent to race. It is called *social distance.*

Social distance

Social distance refers to the attitudes of closeness or farness, ac-ceptance or rejection, which persons have toward each other. Social dis-tance can be measured, approximately, through an opinion scale. Such a scale might consist of a series of questions as follows:

1. Would you live in the same city with a Chinese?
2. Would you hire a Chinese as a gardener?
3. Would you hire a Chinese as a cook?
4. Would you permit your children to attend the same university which Chinese attend?
5. Would you work in an organization which employs Chinese at jobs comparable to your own?
6. Would you live in the same apartment house with a Chinese family?
7. Would you permit your son to play on an athletic team with a Chinese?
8. Would you object to your children playing with Chinese children?

9. Would you object to your children dating Chinese children?
10. Would you marry a Chinese?

Here, then, is a series of questions beginning with a relationship permitting great social distance, namely, living in the same city. Succeeding questions are then roughly graduated in degree of reduced social distance, ending with what is probably the most intimate relationship, marriage. It is not to be assumed, for example, that Question 4 implies *necessarily* less social distance than Question 5 does, if both were answered "Yes." The point is that taken *as a whole* this social distance scale moves in the direction of reduced social distance. When scales of this sort are given to large numbers of people the results usually show: (1) considerable individual difference in social distance felt by various persons toward the members of some race; (2) regional-cultural differences such as those between Northern and Southern whites regarding Negroes; and (3) approval or disapproval of races or relationships on the basis of current stereotypes, rather than on the basis of actual personal experience. In one study, for example, numerous persons indicated unwillingness to permit members of a certain race to join the churches to which they belong, and yet admitted further along in the questionnaire that they had never seen or had direct personal experience with persons of the race which they would thus ostracize.

Is race prejudice instinctive?

A common error in thinking about race prejudice is the expressed or implied notion that it is inherited, that one "instinctively prefers his own kind" and recoils from other races. This view is clearly false according to the accumulated evidence which is now available. In the first place, there is no evidence whatsoever that an attitude pattern, like race prejudice, can come to a person through the germ plasm. Patterns of evaluation, like other attitudinal phenomena, are learned through the real and vicarious experience of the person and are strongly influenced by prevailing stereotypes.

Research has revealed such facts as the following, which certainly contradict the idea of innateness of race prejudice.

1. Children—especially very young children—do not show race prejudice. Their likes and dislikes for other children are based upon criteria other than physical appearance. As children get older, of course, and learn more of the adult evaluations, they take on the characteristic race prejudices of their group.

2. Different cultures have radically different patterns of race atti-

tudes. Many American servicemen, for example, who have been stationed in England and France, expressed great surprise that Negro men were accepted socially by the "respectable" white women of these societies. Such behavior would be rare indeed in the United States. Apparently in those cultures, persons had learned radically different patterns for evaluating Negroes. Even within the United States, of course, there are considerable regional differences in the nature and extent of race prejudice. In the South, where race prejudice is regarded as most categorical, it has always been a sign of distinction and high status for white families to employ Negro house servants, even trusting to them such intimate matters as the prepartion of food and care of babies. Surely if there were an innate basis for race prejudice, such intimate physical contact could hardly be tolerated.

Prejudice rooted in history and social status

Race prejudice consists of a pattern of evaluation which is ingrained in the culture. Like all ideological patterns, race prejudice has a history. It can never be understood independently of its cultural history. Thus the differences by which Northerners and Southerners in the United States have traditionally evaluated Negroes cannot be separated from the differential facts of history of these two regions, including such factors as slavery, the Civil War, the Reconstruction period, and the Underground Railway. Race evaluations, moreover, are not the same among all the social classes in a community. To the employer, sometimes, the Negro represents cheaper unorganized labor which may help him in the competitive struggle to produce lower cost goods. But to the white workman who must compete for jobs with the Negro, a very different evaluation of the Negro may be characteristic. He sees the Negro as a potential source of lowered wages. Yet the Negro does not prefer to work for lowered wages any more than the white man does, but he has been forced to accept inferior wages or working conditions because it has become traditional for him to do so. One of the most recurrent issues has been this conflict over equalizing the work opportunities and remuneration for Negroes and whites performing the same tasks.

Cultural entrenchment of prejudice

Race prejudice, then, is accounted for like any other prejudice—tradition, false "facts," inferences from these "facts," and rationalization to support or alter social position, all interrelated into a web of beliefs with which the person is indoctrinated in the course of his socialization. The person has no real opportunity for viewing the matter objectively, because the pressures toward conformity tend to operate so as to keep him in line with the "right way of looking at the situation."

Personal factors in prejudice

Cultural traditions which devalue certain races, however, do not constitute the complete explanation for the existence of prejudice. It will readily be noted by almost any observer that some people are more prejudiced than others who have had comparable cultural participation. One child in a family, for example, may have Negro playmates, whereas his sibling will refuse to play with Negro children. Some men in a white fraternity would welcome Negro members, others would leave the group if a Negro were pledged, and so on.

How, then, can we explain the difference? Two theories are widely held by students of the problem. (1) Some social psychologists explain prejudice difference, like any attitudinal differences, as the result of different life experiences, especially during childhood. They see no reason why everyone should value Chinese any more than why everyone should be sympathetic to the views of the Republican party. Prejudice differences are simply individual differences accounted for like any other attitudinal differences. (2) A second explanation gets us into depth psychology. It holds that prejudice is often an outgrowth of frustration, an aggressive pattern of hostility to compensate for some real or imagined disprivilege. Thus, persons are thought by proponents of this view to vary in the degree, and possibly even in the direction, of their prejudices, depending on the nature and intensity of their feelings of frustration. Although there is some evidence to support this view of the matter, such evidence is by no means conclusive.

Popular belief versus scientific findings

In the foregoing section it has been shown that the various races have all been interbred at various times in man's history. Therefore, no race is pure or for that matter ever wholly distinct from any other. It was shown, moreover, that there are no *significant* inherent intelligence differences between the groups which are commonly designated as "races." Finally, the race prejudice phenomenon has been demonstrated not to be innate, but rather entirely a matter of indoctrination. *Popular belief runs contrary to all three of these demonstrable truths about races and race relations.* The phrase "popular belief" in the above sentence may easily be underestimated. As used here, it refers not merely to the less literate, obscure people in the society but to the whole hierarchy from rich to poor, from moron to genius, with the exception only of the relatively small group familiar with modern research findings on race. Few have ever had any *real opportunity to know the facts* about race. But even when these facts are presented, many refuse to accept them in any practical manner.

CURRENT ISSUES IN RACE RELATIONS IN THE UNITED STATES

Equal rights versus discrimination

Tensions between the races in the United States and elsewhere center around a relatively few basic issues. At the risk of oversimplification these *issues may all be regarded as ramifications of the minority races' desire for the same political, social, and economic rights and duties which whites have.* The political slogan "civil rights" has this generic meaning. One is not to assume, of course, that white society is entirely equalitarian. The point is simply that the basic issue in race relations consists of colored peoples' desire to be treated in the same way as other people of the same ability, the same wealth, the same education, and other comparable traits.

The dominant white group has, of course, already granted the Negro some measure of democracy. In many parts of the country, the Negro may vote and hold office. In many Northern "white" cities, Negro and white children attend the same schools and play on the same athletic teams. In fewer cities, they are permitted to attend the same movies and swim in the same swimming pools.

This democracy is, of course, very irregular and incomplete. It varies, for example, from city to city, and even from neighborhood to neighborhood, in the North. Frequently the democracy is more apparent than real, that is, it appears to be democratic so long as one does not examine the facts too closely. In one city, for example, which has a large Negro population, Negro players are usually found on the high school athletic teams, but in many subtle ways pressure is put upon the coach to keep the number of Negroes down to one or two per team even though, perhaps, there are enough Negroes who excel in the sport that the team might have a majority of Negro players. Thus while Negroes are not categorically rejected, they still do not have equal rights to secure recognition solely on the basis of their merit.

Economic aspects important

The struggle to secure comparable rights for Negroes has an important economic foundation. Negroes constitute competition for whites in whatever jobs the Negroes are permitted to enter. If Negroes can be kept out of a given job, some whites have argued, the whites could not only be more secure in that job but also command better wages. Whether they are right or wrong in this contention is beside the point; the significant fact is that they *think* so and have frequently opposed opening job opportunities for Negroes on the basis of this "reasoning." Employers have often thought it desirable to keep Negroes out of "white jobs" so that Negroes could be employed more cheaply at other jobs. Here, again, the point of view may be sound or unsound economically, but it is widely held and efforts to change meet strong resistance.

"Fair Employment Practices" sharpen the economic issue

There is also a tradition in American social thought which advocates granting equal economic rights to Negroes. This argument is based both on moral grounds and on the "practical" ground of thereby reducing conflict in race relations. The issue has been sharpened in the form of legislation under the name of "Fair Employment Practices." There are recurrent attempts being made to secure legislation requiring employers to hire employees without regard to "race, color, or creed," and with strict regard to competency for the job being filled. Some states and cities had FEP laws in operation prior to the federal civil rights legislation more recently passed.

It is very difficult to evaluate objectively the existing FEP legislation. Cynics often point out that legislation of this sort has often been purposely designed to make evasion easy, thus nullifying its possible effectiveness. Others claim real and important gains for FEP. All that can be reliably reported at this time is that Negro and other minority groups and many persons of the majority group who think in democratic (nondiscriminatory) terms *consider* FEP to be a real gain in the realization of their social ideals. It remains to be seen how well these laws will be enforced and what their effects on race relations will be.

Too much may be expected of FEP

It should not be assumed, however, that present Fair Employment Practices necessarily solve the problem of Negro job and wage discrimination. Many Negroes reside in parts of the country where public opinion would not support such laws even if they were enacted. Furthermore, numerous Negroes work in occupations or establishments which are not covered by Fair Employment Practice laws. Even where Fair Employment Practice laws are effective, it is not always possible to override the prejudice against Negro workmen on the part of fellow-workers and supervisors. These prejudices result in many subtle and largely uncontrollable forms of discrimination. Moreover, the Negro professional person frequently encounters difficulties which legislation can hardly correct. Negro lawyers, for example, have complained of the practical impossibility of exercising their theoretical rights to practice in court because of the widespread prejudice against them on the part of the jury, judge, and legal colleagues. They complain that Negroes patronize white lawyers because by so doing they feel they can get better "breaks" in the courts. Negro physicians, moreover, have reported difficulty in securing specialist consultations, ambulance services, and hospitalization for their patients. They also report that many Negroes select white physicians in order that they may have better access to these specialized services if they should need them.

Legislation as a means of reducing discrimination difficult to evaluate

It remains an unanswered question whether more rapid equalization of privileges for the several races in America will be secured by approaching the matter through legislation. Some advocate legislation because it seems to get results more quickly. It, presumably, forces everyone covered by the law to do what the law requires. These people argue that if the nation waited for the slow change in attitude, decades or centuries might elapse before a more equitable solution could be worked out.

The opponents argue, on the other hand, that laws are effective only insofar as there is public opinion to support them, and that if legislation moves too far ahead of popular thinking, ways of evading the law will become common and enforcement, therefore, almost impossible. They also point out that attempting to bring about social change by force may engender a great deal of ill-will against Negroes by whites who might, if given time, come around to a more democratic conception of race relations. Finally, Fair Employment Practice legislation is said to be undesirable because it tends to build up false hopes among Negroes for a quick and complete settlement of problems through law when there really is no quick and complete solution possible. The result, then, is disillusionment among Negroes and an embittered antagonism among white opponents of Fair Employment Practices.

Both sides of the issue present arguments which are in some measure sound. Under conditions of modern life, however, more and more dependence is being placed upon legislation as a means of handling major social problems, and perhaps this is the reason why the advocates of Fair Employment Practices have already won so many legislative and judicial victories. But the *goals* of such apparently successful programs are still far from being achieved.

Segregation: residential

But jobs and wages are not the entire issue in American race relations. The second large area of conflict concerns segregation, the requirement that Negroes live in areas set aside partly by law and mostly by illegal and unconstitutional tradition as "Negro areas."

The first objection frequently raised is ethical, that Negroes are forced to live in their segregated areas, but whites are not bound by any such requirements. Chiefly, however, the issue centers around the *kind* of living conditions prevalent in the segregated Negro areas. The lowest paid Negroes probably have living conditions somewhat comparable to the lowest paid whites, but as one ascends the scale into the higher income groups, it becomes virtually impossible in most American cities for high status Negroes to find the kind of comfortable housing which they can afford. The goal of "open housing" laws and practices is to correct such injustices. Moreover, it is common to find poorer services and facilities—police protection, fire protection, parks, and playgrounds—in the Negro segregated areas. Another common Negro complaint is that many of the "public" buildings, parks, and cultural centers are virtually closed to Negroes. The same holds true of the better theaters, the better restaurants, and other places of wholesome recreation. (There is great variation, of course, in these conditions among the different areas of the United States.)

There is one aspect of segregation which is frequently overlooked and which has an important practical angle. Very often there is unbelievable crowding in segregated Negro areas of cities as a direct result of segregation. Perhaps when the segregation pattern was started in a city, there was somewhere near ample room for the Negro population *at that time*. Yet, as the Negro population has increased due to large-scale migration to Northern cities, the boundaries of the segregated area have not been comparably expanded. Thus the same area is forced to house two or three times the number of persons for whom it was originally designed. Race riots in large cities are often related to this problem of inadequate room and substandard housing in the segregated area. There has often been a refusal or an inability on the part of the city leaders to provide for additional space to house the growing Negro population. Crowding of any population, Negro or white, is a serious condition and is closely related to many social problems varying from disease to crime.

The view is commonly held that segregation is necessary in order to reduce violence and other undesirable forms of race conflict which might otherwise break out intermittently. We do not have the necessary facts to determine whether this assumption is correct or incorrect. It is probable that the pattern of residential segregation is sufficiently entrenched in the American way of handling race relations that any radical change from this pattern is exceedingly unlikely to be tried for some time to come. It should be clear, however, that the fact of segregation has a great deal to do with the perpetuation of many aspects of the mythology about race and is the source of many of the tensions between the races which have already been discussed. In short, segregation creates problems, whether or not it solves any.

Segregation: educational

The Supreme Court decisions. As this is being written the nation is in the process of adjusting to a group of history-making decisions of the United States Supreme Court proclaiming, in essence, that the segregation of Negroes and whites in public schools is unconstitutional. This means that the South and some places in the North which have traditionally had segregated public schools had created an institutionalized structure which is illegal in the most final sense.

"Compliance." Anyone even superficially acquainted with the "current events" of the last few years is quite aware that compliance with the Supreme Court decisions has been neither universal nor immediate. Inflammatory phrases like "Little Rock," "Save ole Miss," "White Citizens Council," "Ku Klux Klan," "modern carpet baggers," and many more are explosive verbal evidence of the deep emotional

attitudes which many people have toward this issue. From the current magazine, newspaper, and television presentations, of which there has been a plethora during the last five years, one could easily get the impression that everywhere in America, North as well as South, the nation is close to civil war over the integration issue. The fact of the matter is otherwise.

9. CONTRASTS IN INTEGRATION AMONG SOUTHERN AND BORDER STATES

	Percent of Negroes in Schools with Whites
Alabama	.004
Tennessee	2.71
Maryland	48.3
Kentucky	54.4
West Virginia	87.9

Source: Statistical Summary of School Segregation-Desegregation in Southern and Border States, The Southern Educational Reporting Service, Nashville, Tenn., 1963, p. 2.

To be sure, compliance is not uniform in all parts of the country. Although there are exceptions, the general pattern appears to be this: Most areas north of the Mason-Dixon line had already been largely desegregated long before the Supreme Court decisions, so no changes of consequence needed to be made there. The so-called "border states," such as parts of Kentucky, Missouri, and West Virginia presented a mixed picture, even before the Supreme Court decision, and in these states there has been considerable movement in the direction of compliance—not uniformly, of course, but marked. In the "deep South" there has been the least compliance, although it would be a mistake to assume that there has not been some. In this section, many parts of which have a larger Negro population than white, there is still a considerable amount of open defiance and searching for substitute educational arrangements whereby the Supreme Court decision can somehow be circumvented or complied with only technically. It is difficult to see very significant "progress" toward compliance in this area. Many careful observers (as distinct from partisans) are still saying that in parts of this area full compliance will "never" take place.

Mass media. Few persons realize, as we have said above, that considerable compliance has already occurred. This ignorance of the facts needs comment. Why does practically everyone know something, however distorted, about "the Little Rock situation" [4] and know noth-

[4] Wilson Record and Jane Cassels Record, *Little Rock, U.S.A.: Materials for Analysis* (San Francisco, Calif., Chandler, 1960).

ing about the hundreds of school systems which have integrated during the same period? First, compliance with law is normal and open defiance is rare. Hence, defiance and circumvention make big news. This is especially true in respect to racial questions because, oddly enough, both extremist parties to the issue *want* to make news. The extreme reformers want the world to know how unreasonable and even brutal "the white oppressors have been, since they go to such extremes even in defiance of the United States Supreme Court." The conservatives also often want to make the news. They, too, want the world to know that a "philosophy of outsiders" is being forced upon them and that they have been right all along in their contention that integration could not "work." Consequently the problems of transition have been exaggerated, and orderly transition made more difficult in communities where it would have been easier had the atmosphere been less charged with inflammatory clichés diffused from distant crises.

Extremists and moderates. Fundamental social changes of this sort tend to produce, or at least to sharpen, the differences among three more or less distinct personal orientations to the issue. At the risk of some oversimplification, and deliberately ignoring some views which do not fit precisely, one can distinguish these three categories of people: (1) extremist reactionaries, (2) moderates, (3) extremist reformers. The three categories are almost self-defining. The extremist reformers want compliance with the Supreme Court decisions—totally and immediately. The extremist reactionaries desire the reverse—continued segregation, no compromises, open defiance if necessary. The moderates are a mixed group; they are "in between" for several different reasons. The usual moderate position is that compliance must (or should) come about eventually, but since attitudes and conditions are as they are, change must come slowly and "diplomatically." Others are moderates because they are confused, possibly ambivalent, possibly merely indecisive people who do not see the need for clear-cut decisions and decisive action if "drift" can get them by.

The extremists of both varieties make the news—over and over and over again. One itinerant rabble rouser may be jailed a dozen times in a dozen different states for stirring up otherwise more or less complacent people, and get his picture on the front page of a thousand newspapers each time. The responsibility for orderly change, however, invariably rests with the moderates. Moderates usually please neither the reactionary extremists nor the reformist extremists. Moderates, are, on the other hand, wooed and courted by the extremes and at the same time reviled as "wishy-washy," "egg heads," and altogether lacking in principle.

And yet any solution must come from these moderates, since they are the only ones who are in a position to serve as arbiters between the extremists. Usually they also have the responsibility of maintaining some sort of community order during the time the machinations and incriminations of the extremists are being dissipated. In most serious interracial situations moderates have seemed to fare badly so far as community esteem is concerned during the time when the crisis was most dramatic, but as time passes there seems to occur a recognition, however tacit and grudging, that a solution of the problem ultimately rests with this group. Students of social conflict and cooperation can certainly find abundant materials for analysis and theory-testing from this chapter of American history.

Legal forms of segregation. It should be stressed that compliance with the Supreme Court decision in many areas, both North and South, will involve no significant change in existing school arrangements anyway. This is due to a condition which has been called "natural segregation" in the residential areas of the large cities especially. Since school districts are set up on a territorial basis, no problem is posed where all of the students of the district are already Negro or white. Here the officials and the community members, whether cynically or genuinely, can in truth say that there has been complete compliance with the Supreme Court decision because all of the children in the community go to the same school.

"Gerrymandering" is also a convenient way out and probably also is technically legal, although the intent may be to circumvent the issue. The practice of gerrymandering, which started almost a century ago, simply involves manipulation of boundaries of such territorial units as congressional districts or school districts so that persons of a given color are either concentrated in one political unit or divided into two, depending upon whether the purpose is to isolate them into one area, as with segregation, or divide them up, so as to reduce their political power as would be the case in setting up congressional districts. How much gerrymandering has occurred in recent years to avoid school integration is not known. It is, however, commonly alleged and doubtless has to some extent been stimulated as a means of getting around the integration issue. This kind of solution, of course, leaves no one wholly happy except, perhaps, some of the moderates: the reformers feel thwarted in that Negroes still go to Negro schools and whites to white schools.

"Public opinion," propaganda, and the process of change. The dis-

passionate student of social change finds little enlightenment from examining the so-called opinions which opinion poll analysts, newspaper reporters, and even some social scientists have collected in the areas of tension. First of all, many of these opinions, which are stated with such confidence, are based upon premises which, simply, are not true. They represent perennial reincarnations of myths about race which do not now, or never have, squared with the facts about race, yet are widely held. It appears that many persons, and particularly extremists, are capable of frightening distortions of the intellect, which are an affront to the kind of informed intelligence which social science and education have long been trying to effect.

Likewise the appeals to "principles" are usually *selected* principles which can be manipulated to buttress a position taken on quite other grounds. For example, the white supremacy Southerner who maligns the Supreme Court and the proponents of law and order in the government for invading so-called "states' rights" with respect to integration seems hardly to realize that about one hundred years ago another Supreme Court decision, the Dred Scott case, also invaded states' rights by holding that a Negro slave who had escaped to the North was still the property of his owner, even though residing in a state which did not permit Negro slavery. For all the appeal to the higher principles of law, religion, and human dignity, the elementary fact is that for most persons of either extreme position the issue boils down to this: are Negro children in the South to go to school with white children or are they not? All that can be said now is that more and more of them do, but complete compliance with "the law of the land" as interpreted by the Supreme Court will involve a change that will be neither painless, without risk, nor rapid.

Miscegenation

Since post-Civil War days most Southern states and a few Northern ones have had antimiscegenation laws. These laws prohibit the marriage of Negroes and whites and in some instances, by extension, would presumably cover all interracial marriages. At one time thirty states had such laws, but by 1967 only fifteen remained on the statute books.

In a 1967 Supreme Court decision all of these state antimiscegenation laws were declared unconstitutional. It should not be assumed, however, that this will necessarily presage any great rise in Negro-white marriages. The changed legal status is more symbolic than practical. Even in the Northern states where no antimiscegenation laws have existed the number of interracial marriages has been inconsequential.

MINORITY RACES AND PERSONALITY

It will be recalled from previous chapters dealing with personality that considerable evidence exists to show that one's group affiliations, his social roles, and his frustrations fashion the nature of his personality. It would be expected, then, that such patterns as segregation, race prejudice, and discrimination would have some influence upon the kinds of personality traits which the disprivileged members of minority races would characteristically develop. Not all persons, of course, in any minority race, develop the same personality traits any more than all the members of the majority race develop the same personality traits. The point to be noted is simply that the *characteristic kinds* of experience which are recurrently a part of the life-experience of a member of a minority race tend to result in attitudes, values, and ideas which are more or less typical of the minority race person. Some of these recurrent personality patterns will now be discussed.

1. Oppression psychosis

The term *oppression psychosis* aptly phrases one very common minority class reaction. It applies not only to races, but also to other minority groups such as immigrants. Once a class recognizes that it is being discriminated against, it comes gradually to take discrimination more or less for granted. As a member of a minority class, a person expects to be discriminated against and exploited because he has had repeated experience with such discrimination and exploitation. He soon learns that he is not highly regarded by the larger community; and unless he is very cautious, he will be "taken advantage of" in many subtle as well as obvious ways. But he *overlearns the principle*, that is, *he learns to expect discrimination and oppression. Even when it is really not present, he experiences it anyway*. Whites who have tried to be personally friendly with Negroes or who have tried to do generous things for Negro communities have often been met with distrust and suspicion. The Negroes have become so accustomed to being exploited that they have interpreted even good intentions and good deeds as concealed exploitation. The existence of this oppression psychosis has sometimes made it difficult if not impossible for well-meaning whites to assist colored groups or individual members of colored and other minority groups.

2. Exaggerated aggression

Another characteristic personality pattern is the exaggerated militant one, characterized by such phrases as, "They won't shove *me* around," "The best defense is an offense," "I follow the Golden Rule, but I'll do it to them first," "You've got to fight for your rights." Here again, as with the oppression psychosis, it is relatively clear how such patterns *can* develop in a minority class. It is aware of hostile feelings from the outside and has also learned that in order to secure privileges, one must fight for them. Concessions are usually granted grudgingly and sometimes only because of a show of force. Even if no tangible results follow, many persons receive a personal satisfaction from having made a show of force, or even from only having contemplated one. Some superficial observers of Negroes have pointed out that Negroes are "touchy" and that they seem overeager to "make an issue." These traits are illustrative of the kind of reaction here discussed.

3. Subservience

There are also those in the minority group position who are quite willing to accept the inferiority assigned them, and to accept rather literally the biblical admonition not to "kick against the pricks." Thus many Negroes approach whites with undisguised and unfeigned deference, or even in a spirit of genuine humility. It is difficult to determine whether this adjustment to the bi-racial situation results from having been so often and so long "beaten down" or whether some persons are of a mild and unaggressive temperament, irrespective of the racial situation. In any event it is not difficult to find numerous instances of minority class members who appear at least to be quite willing to accept the assigned role without serious objection or outward evidence of resentment. In some minority groups, there have even developed a number of folkways and folklores rationalizing the disprivilege as an advantage in disguise. Among these people often it is a sign of indiscretion, if not immorality, to aspire to those privileges or behaviors or possessions which are characteristically denied to the minority but common among whites. There are Negroes, for example, as well as whites who admonish other Negroes to "keep in their places," not to "get uppety," and in general advise and practice the "Uncle Tom tradition."

OTHER AMERICAN RACE RELATIONS

Thus far, attention has been devoted almost entirely to race relations in the United States and even then mostly to Negro-white relations, almost to the exclusion of Mongolian-white and Mongolian-Negro relations in America and to race relations throughout the vast areas of the world. The emphasis upon Negro-white relations in the United States can be justified by the numerical preponderance of Negroes and by the vast attention this problem has been getting over the last twenty years. Yet the principles involved, such as race prejudice, the false inferences about race which are commonly drawn, and the economic problems resulting are very similar in the Mongolian-white relations (including Indian-white relations). There are, of course, notable differences, too. First, the history of each race is somewhat different. Aside from the American Indians, Mongolians came to the United States more recently than did Negroes, and were brought or attracted here as free men, not as slaves. Orientals have, of course, also been segregated, and the same general form of prejudice and the same general kinds of response to discrimination are patent. There is another historical factor which is notably different in the case of Japanese and American-born Japanese, namely, the additional problems and hatreds brought about by World War II in which Japan was one of the enemy nations. Because of the fears (largely unfounded) that among these Japanese-Americans there might be numerous Japanese secret agents, the Japanese and Japanese-born Americans living on or near the West Coast were forced to leave these areas and take up temporary residence in "relocation" areas under strict supervision. Opinions have differed and still differ widely as to whether such treatment of American citizens by American citizens was either morally right or necessary. Many informed persons believe that the move to force residents into relocation centers was prompted more by hysteria than by established facts pertaining to the conduct of these people.

Relations between the American Indian and whites are familiar to most students of American history in some measure at least. During the earliest period of colonial America, relations with the Indians were on the whole friendly but with a considerable amount of economic exploitation by the whites. Indian "troubles" in colonial America were not as common or as bloody as some of the writers of juvenile history books have made them appear. With the growth of the white population and the movement westward more warfare occurred and on a larger scale.

Much sentimental pity for the Indians and exaggerated accounts of the virtues of the westward-moving whites have left a historical mythology consisting of an admixture of truth and fiction from which it is difficult to extract the true account. Certainly the stereotyped portrayals of the western movie thrillers are grossly inaccurate, but probably very influential in formulating characteristic white attitudes toward Indians. Ultimately, of course, the American Indians were given certain territorial rights to the ownership of large areas of land called "reservations," where they were somewhat supervised but permitted to retain much of their original culture, taking on gradually certain of the material and nonmaterial culture of the white man. This paternalism of the whites, plus the fact that the American Indians neither moved to the cities nor took up agriculture on any appreciable scale, has worked in the direction of reducing potential conflict between whites and Indians on anything approaching the magnitude of Negro-white conflict.

In these differences among Negro-white, Indian-white, and Oriental-white relations in the United States one finds abundant evidence of the basic principle that *it is not so much the fact of race contact but the conditions surrounding the contact which make for tensions and conflict.*

WORLD RACE RELATIONS

When one surveys the relations among the races on a worldwide scale, it becomes increasingly obvious that the manner in which individuals of the various races interact, the kind of cultural traditions through which they interact, are the significant factors making for peace or conflict. The mere fact of a bi- or multiracial situation in itself is of little significance. In general, as we shall see in the next chapter, white men from western European countries have dominated the colored peoples of the rest of the world and have exploited in varying degrees the labor of these people and the resources of the areas in which they live. For a time this exploitation was little protested, but a condition has now arisen in which the colored races are aware of the ways and the extent to which they have been exploited and are threatening in one way or another to force a "new deal." It is difficult to determine at this time to what extent these protests will be effective, or when and in what measure the white minorities who control other races will relinquish their control in time to avoid or ameliorate even more disastrous outbreaks of violence than have thus far occurred.

SUMMARY

The relations among peoples of the various races constitute one of the leading social problems of this generation. This is true not only in the United States but throughout the world. The problem is more complicated than it needs to be because of the widespread existence of false ideas on the subject of race in general and with respect to the specific races involved. Several of the more important fallacies have been discussed, and the scientific evidence against them has been reviewed. Specifically it has been shown that the basic assumption of racial uniqueness is a fallacy, that races are all interbred, that the traits of persons in each race overlap markedly with those of persons of other races, and that a few physical characteristics, like skin color, have become exaggerated out of all proportion to their true significance. It was demonstrated further that race differences in mental ability (intelligence) are minimal. It has also been explained why it required so long a time to discover this fact.

Varying kinds of race relations patterns, viewed cross-culturally, have been briefly reviewed—annihilation, expulsion, assimilation, segregation, stratification, and pluralism. Different societies operating under different conditions of contact and perhaps with different moral perspectives have handled the problem differently. Existing race relations patterns, however, are not eternal. They are subject to change, as are other social and cultural forms.

Race prejudice has been treated most fully in connection with Negro-white relations in the United States. It was shown that race prejudice is not innate, but like most attitudes is learned from experience.

Race tensions in the United States center chiefly around the problem of extending the same measure of democracy to Negro groups which is ordinarily accorded to whites with the same personal, economic, and class attributes. This involves not only economic opportunities for comparable jobs and wages for Negroes but also social democracy now largely denied through enforced segregation of Negroes. Efforts are being made to solve these problems in various ways, and sharp difference of opinion exists as to whether the direct frontal attack through legislation is the best method or not.

Several basic principles of race relations should be apparent from our treatment.

1. There is nothing necessarily inherent in the fact that two or more races which are in contact need necessarily be in conflict, also. Conflict, or the absence of it, results from the manner in which the per-

sons of the races involved interact, the kind of definitions they have of each other, and the kind of traditions which exist.

2. Race relations, like all human relationships, change with the passing of time. Just as slavery had its day and its twilight, so also the particular forms of race relations now present, like segregation, will also probably pass out of existence eventually.

3. Race relations will be influenced for better or for worse by the kinds of policies which the two groups, but especially the dominant group, formulate and carry out. There are wise and unwise methods of handling the problem, but they are not wise or unwise per se. They can be judged only in the light of the values which one tries to attain. Thus if one wants democracy in race relations, for example, then something along the line of Fair Employment Practices and Open Housing is indicated. But if one wishes to perpetuate, or institutionalize, a rigid caste-like subservient colored group, that, too, may be possible, in which case Fair Employment Practices is clearly "undesirable." A problem is posed, however, by those who would advocate this latter objective, namely: Is it possible for a nation to retain democratic ideals in more than mere name if it categorically denies democracy to one out of nine of its population?

SUGGESTED READINGS

Berry, Brewton, *Race and Ethnic Relations*, 3rd ed. Boston, Houghton Mifflin, 1965.
A lucid cross-cultural and historical treatment of race relations in the macro-sociological tradition.

Klineberg, Otto, *Race Differences*. New York, Harper & Row, 1935.
An important original volume by the man who has probably spent more time on refining the techniques for studying race differences realistically than anyone else. This book should be read and pondered well by the person who thinks that there are innate differences in racial mentality.

Mack, Raymond W., *Race, Class, and Power*. New York, American Book, 1963.
A series of research articles which focus around the tensions which characterize the interaction of these strata and substrata of American society.

Myrdal, Gunnar, and others. *An American Dilemma: The Negro Problem and Modern Democracy*. New York, Harper & Row, 1944. 2 vols.
This is generally regarded as the outstanding book on race relations in the

United States. It collects data from many sources and analyzes the interracial problem from many points of view. The author is himself not an American; thus he may be presumed to approach the problem with the prejudices of neither a Southerner nor a Northerner. Should be read by every student of America, whether interested specifically in race or not.

Rose, Peter I., *They and We*. New York, Random House, 1964.
An introductory treatment of the relationships, conflicts, and accommodations among various ethnic groupings in contemporary United States.

Tumin, Melvin M., *Desegregation: Resistance and Readiness*. Princeton, N.J., Princeton University Press, 1958.
It is well known that some persons resist and others cooperate with the laws which have attempted to outlaw segregation. This study reveals the characteristics of those people who do and those who do not challenge and resist the law.

Williams, Robin M., Jr., et al. *Strangers Next Door*. Englewood Cliffs, N.J., Prentice-Hall, 1964.
A study of relationships between various racial and ethnic groups throughout the United States.

STUDY QUESTIONS

1. Why are some people scientific in regard to some things but unscientific in regard to human behavior?
2. Why are there few people with scientific knowledge about race?
3. Why are there no pure races?
4. Why is it difficult to determine if there are differences in mental capacities between Negroes and whites?
5. Demonstrate that race prejudice is not directed toward "a race in general." Show how racial prejudice consists of attitudes toward *specific* social relationships.
6. Why do people often seem "inconsistent" in regard to social distance? Is this *really* inconsistency?
7. Why is race prejudice not inherited? What proof do we have of this?
8. Do "equal" school systems for whites and Negroes guarantee equal educational opportunities? Why or why not?
9. How are stereotypes a factor in race prejudice? Illustrate.
10. What is the basic issue in race relations?
11. How is racial "democracy" often more apparent than real? Illustrate.
12. Why do whites often oppose equal job opportunities for Negroes? How do some employers use this to their advantage?
13. What special difficulties does the Negro professional person encounter?
14. How would a Fair Employment Practices law help to eliminate racial discrimination? How might it increase prejudice?

15. Why is segregation undemocratic? How does it tend to cause racial conflict?
16. How are segregation, race prejudice, and discrimination factors in the development of personality traits? Illustrate.
17. What do you think will be the further effects of the 1954 Supreme Court decision on segregation? Why?
18. What different "patterns" of race relations have existed or now exist?
19. Do you think that there is a "long-run trend" toward social pluralism in the world? Why and why not?

19
POPULATION

While population is a biological reality, it is customarily studied by sociologists because the characteristics and size of populations constitute an important set of conditions with which social systems must deal. This is especially true where great population changes occur within short periods. For example, the American population in the last thirty years has changed from a population which demographers (students of population) called an aging population to a youthful population with currently one half of the people being under 25 years of age.[1] The change has been brought about primarily by the great rise in the post-World War II birth rate, which has since somewhat leveled off. In the 1940's such problems as how to provide for old people and the effects of their possible, undue political influence were seriously considered; today these concerns are superseded by attention to the support and absorption of the teeming teen group into the economy and other social institutions, as well as the possible political effects of so unbalanced a population make-up as we now have. This reversal in little more than a quarter of a century!

Population is important, also, when its distribution changes. The make-up of many American cities has changed radically in the last twenty-five years. First, large numbers of the more affluent members of the community have moved out of the city to newly formed suburbs or even to the open country. Thus the so-called "inner city" is left with a disproportionate population of the poor and is the place where poorer migrants to the city can first secure a financial toe-hold. Quite obviously, under these changed conditions the economic, cultural, and social life of the city must undergo marked changes.

Population is also important both nationally and worldwide because of the consequences of the so-called "population explosion." Customary economic systems and methods of production which were adequate for populations in the past shortly become inadequate when numbers rise sharply. Famine and near-starvation haunt millions upon millions of the world's

[1] "Teen-Age Consumers—Dynamic Force in the United States Economy," *Senior Scholastic*, Vol. 86 (February 25, 1965), p. 5.

residents and pose problems of a political and moral nature even for the more affluent countries. For these and other reasons, then, sociologists continue to be necessarily concerned with understanding the demographic facts of life. We turn our attention, first, to some basic theoretical considerations concerning total populations.

POPULATION AND THE FACTORS WHICH AFFECT IT

World population: the "explosion"

One of the most dramatic changes in the population of the world is occurring at the present time and is known popularly as the *population explosion*. In 1950 the population of the world was slightly less than 2.5 billion; now it numbers 3.25 billion, which means that there has been a 36 percent increase in this short period. This change has not occurred uniformly, a fact which adds to its troublesomeness. Generally speaking, the areas of the world which have increased most rapidly are the areas with the lowest standard of living and the poorest capacity to support large populations due to a combination of poor technology, low educational levels, and sometimes inadequate natural resources. During the years when world population increased by 36 percent, the population of the United States, for example, increased by only 27 percent. When we realize that the population of the United States is only 6 percent of the total population of the world, the importance of this difference becomes more apparent.

Demographers have for some years now been pointing out that at present rates of increase the population is rapidly outstripping the capacity of the earth's surface to produce enough food for even minimal subsistence. Even if the more affluent nations, like the United States and western Europe, were to lower their standards of living radically and distribute the surplus, the core of the problem would scarcely be touched because of the tremendous numbers and the tremendous rates of increase occurring in the underdeveloped countries. A somewhat ironic condition has occurred for the more developed countries. By disseminating medical knowledge to underdeveloped countries, they have kept alive large numbers of the population who would otherwise die. Few if any of these people practice any kind of contraception with the resulting population explosion. While obviously the dissemination of contraceptive knowledge and techniques, such as "the pill," would materially improve the situation, powerful groups in the West, notably but not exclusively the Roman Catholic Church, have opposed the dissemination of contraceptive knowledge and materials to these underdeveloped countries. Hence, the poorest nations are left to bear the staggering consequences of an unbridled population explosion. It should not, of course, be inferred that even if contraceptive materials and information were made available that the world population problem would be totally solved. An *available* technology for limiting births does not necessarily result in its *use*. A considerable reculturation would be necessary in many instances. Nevertheless, there is evidence to indicate that contraceptive technology would be used by many of these people, if made available, and to that extent would slow down the skyrocketing population.

A number of the foregoing generalizations need to be analyzed in somewhat greater detail, and such is the purpose of the following few pages.

Population size dependent on subsistence

At any one time, the absolute size of the population of the world is limited by the ability of the earth at the given time to produce enough food to sustain life. In the United States, where food is normally very abundant and surpluses are the usual problem, one has little conception of the extent to which the stark reality of insufficient food is the major factor determining the number of people who may live. In many parts of Asia, notably China and India, famines occur from time to time as a result of which millions of people die from starvation. Millions more die from time to time from malnourishment and attract no more attention than those in our population who die of heart disease or pneumonia, because these causes of death are widespread and common. There is insufficient land to support the existing population in many parts of the world under the conditions of land use and modes of agriculture used there.

Advanced technology increases
sustenance opportunities

There are several reasons why the population of some nations, such as the United States, is so far removed from starvation. First, the American culture possesses an elaborate technological development which enables the society to utilize many natural resources which the people of simpler cultures cannot use. Moreover, our scientific knowledge enables us to utilize the resources we have in such a way as to yield much greater results. Scientific farming is a case in point. With many crops, an acre of land can produce several times the yield of a hundred years ago. For all practical purposes, a technological culture can almost "create" land, through the drainage of swamps and the irrigation of deserts. Thus, land which would ordinarily be waste land becomes capable of yielding food for human sustenance. The same principle applies in industry as in agriculture. Through man's technical knowledge, he can discover sources of energy like coal and oil, and probably also "the atom," to replace human effort in the production of the necessities of life.

Birth control and living standards

A second factor which enables the American population to remain far above the starvation point is the deliberate limitation of our population through the practice of birth control. Studies show that large numbers of persons practice limitation of the number of children in one way or another and with varying degrees of success. The usual reason for so doing is to enable the parents and the children they have to enjoy what is usually called "a higher standard of living." In other words, our culture contains values which when acted upon result in the voluntary control of population. One is the high valuation placed upon nonessentials in the pattern of living. Strictly speaking, of course, many of the elements of a high standard of living may not be *really* nonessentials. Certainly better balanced diets, better preparation of foods, better medical care, and more education could not be regarded as nonessentials by our standards. But they are nonessentials in the sense that some sort of life *could* be sustained without them, that is, a few more of us might die earlier without these protections, but the vast majority of the peoples of the world "get along" quite well without them.

Most of the items in the American so-called "high standard of living," however, have not the remotest relation to physical health or longevity. Fur coats, big automobiles, expensive amusements, costly but by no means nourishing items of diet, and expensive personal adornment are cases in point. Several Chinese families, for example, could be supported on their standard of living by the money spent by the average middle-class American family on its automobile alone. But this American standard of living, as anyone knows, is very highly valued. It is so highly valued, in fact, that it supersedes another value, also highly held by many, namely that of more frequent parenthood.

It is very difficult to state the situation entirely accurately, how-

10.   Birth Rates, 1961, per 1000 Population

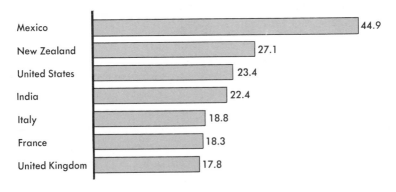

Source: Statistical Office of the United States.

ever, because most people regard the limitation of the number of children as a device for securing a high standard of living for those fewer children whom they do have. In other words, quality rather than quantity of children seems to have become the greater value. To what extent this is all a common rationalization to permit a higher level of living for the parents themselves cannot be determined and perhaps need not be for our purposes. It is sufficient to note that the deliberate reduction in the number of children born keeps the numbers of the total population somewhat reduced and enables those who are living to have a greater share in the available necessities, comforts, and luxuries which the natural resources and the technical knowledge of the culture can produce.

The factors in the "population balance"

No one knows how large a total population the world can eventually support. That number depends upon three factors, none of which can be precisely computed but which can be studied mathematically nevertheless. These factors have already been mentioned but should be analyzed further.

1. *The amount of available land.* Offhand, one might think that the amount of available land could be readily calculated. But man is always making land, practically speaking, by the irrigation of deserts, the drainage of swamps, and even more important, by the discovery of means whereby a given area can produce many times what it formerly did. Man is, thus, really creating land through his agricultural and engineering arts. At this time, there seems to be no discernible limit of the

extent to which man may go in this extension of the resources which can be derived from the earth's surface. At a *given* time, however, the amount of available land sets absolute limits to the number of people who can be kept alive on the earth.

2. *Knowledge concerning the use of land.* The state of the arts of production makes it almost impossible to determine how much sustenance can eventually be derived from existing land or from the land yet to be brought under cultivation or other usage. There seems now no limit to how far man's technical knowledge can *ultimately* go. It cannot be stressed too strongly, however, that *at any given time the state of the arts sets absolute limits to the number of people who can be supported in a given area or in the entire world.*

3. *The "level of living."* The third factor in the balance of population and land is the level (also called "standard") of living. Stated bluntly, the higher the level of living, the lower the population that a given area of the entire world can support. In some parts of the world the standard of living is so low that large populations can exist on small areas of land, but in areas of high living levels, like the United States, the resources can support only a relatively sparse population.

4. *Numbers of people.* As we have implied in the foregoing paragraphs, the number of people which any given land area can or does support is dependent on the other three factors: the amount of land, the state of the arts, and the level of living. Malthus pointed out a long time ago that both theoretically and practically human beings reproduce faster than the advancing state of the arts which must provide the sustenance to support them. Numbers are held down either by starvation on the one hand or voluntary limitation of birth on the other. Voluntary limitation of numbers can be effected either by the practice of birth control or by postponing marriage for women. Migration is sometimes a temporary and local solution to overpopulation, but is of no final aid because it simply transfers the population pressure from the area of emigration to the area of immigration. The total earth must still support the total population as before the migration.

The population factors interact: man's fundamental choice

Thus we see that these factors—the amount of available land, the state of the productive arts both in agriculture and in industry, and the level of living—interact with population in a variety of ways. The interaction may be theoretically explained in the following way. The available land and the state of the arts set up the available sum total of want-satisfying materials. If the population becomes larger, the level of living must be lower because the available goods and services must be divided among more people. If the population becomes smaller, the level of living can be higher. Over a longer period, of course, the existence of aspirations for a higher level of living may, as we have seen, operate in such a way as to reduce the population, and thus the goods and services available to each person become greater. Much of the phenomenal advance of man's ability to produce food and other goods during the last century has been taken up by great increases in the population, but not so great as to prevent higher levels of living for much of Western civilization from also occurring.

The significant fact to be noted is that man has a choice, so to speak, of what he will do with the gain in sustenance which his advancing technological arts provide him. (1) He may increase his numbers, holding his level of living the same; (2) he may increase his level of living, holding his numbers constant; or (3) he may divide the gain somewhat between increased numbers and increased level of living. But increased numbers or increased levels of living can come only from increased sources of sustenance.

The individual case: distribution of goods, not total supply, is often the crucial fact

Thus far we have spoken largely in broad theoretical terms. Actually, the level of living enjoyed by a given person in a society is not so simply determined. According to our reasoning thus far, Henry Ford would have the same level of living as your garbage collector because both are part of the same society. The factor omitted from our discussion, then, is the factor of *individual and class distribution of the total goods and services which the total society produces.*

All of the numerous factors involved in distribution make the subject an involved one and quite beyond the scope of this book. One basic fact, however, can be briefly stated: Each society through the value system of its culture contains a set of standards or criteria on the basis of which the available goods and services are distributed among the social classes and among individuals. Capitalism has one system, communism another. In the United States the system worked out for distributing the profits of the joint efforts of capital, management, and labor has changed somewhat with the coming of labor unions, and more recently with their increased power in determining labor's share of the total product. The prevailing class system of a society, as we shall see in a later chapter, has a great deal to do with how the share of the goods and services which make up a level of living is determined for different persons. History records numerous examples of the coexistence of fabulously high levels of living for one class and pitifully low levels for another, but these conditions are determined by the value system and not by the population problem per se.

Density and population "pressure": a complicated question

Differences in population *density*, the number of persons per square mile, are frequently used as evidence of the overcrowding of some areas. Density figures are frequently misleading, however, unless one knows at least (1) how the population derives its sustenance, (2) how much of the area of the nation consists of tillable soil and how fertile the soil is, (3) whether the climate is favorable or unfavorable to high production, (4) the degree of technological progress, and (5) the extent to which the resident population is being exploited by absentee populations. Thus, for example, India has a population density of 300 persons per square mile, while England has a population of over 800 persons per square mile. Yet living conditions in most of India are difficult, and famines are common. Meanwhile the English level of living is among the highest in the world. England can support the high population density which she does because she has a skilled manufacturing and trading economy, thus enabling the English citizens actually to draw sustenance *indirectly* from the land of the entire world, including India. The population of India, on the other hand, is forced largely to subsist on its own land, much of which is not especially fertile under the kinds of tillage and agricultural knowledge practiced by the Indian farmer. Other examples of the same principle can readily be found. Comparative density figures are valid only when climatic factors, the state of the arts, the natural resources, and the trade relations of the two societies are comparable. Otherwise they are confusing and misleading.

WORLD POPULATION DISTRIBUTION: GEOGRAPHICAL

The population of the world is distributed very unevenly. Over one half of all of the people of the world live in Asia alone; the other half is distributed among the other four continents. At first thought, one might conclude that the Asiatic continent must have either a wealth of food-producing resources or a highly advanced technological culture to enable it to support so large a proportion of the world's people. Actually neither is the case. The chief factor enabling this fabulous population to exist is the low standard of living which prevails for practically all of the population of that continent.

The areas of the world with a high level of living are not the most populous. It is probably objectively true that the United States and Canada now have the highest average level of living to be found in the world, and yet these two nations together contain less than 10 percent of the population of the world. To say that their high level of living is due to any one factor would be to oversimplify what is a complex series of cause-and-effect relationships. Surely the level of living can be higher if the population is kept down by the practice of birth control, but that is not the whole story either. The population of the United States and Canada is favored by a recent history of relative abundance of land in proportion to the number of people on it, and also by a recent period of history during which scientific knowledge and technology have been increasing at a phenomenal rate.

Added to these factors is another one, somewhat less easy to grasp, but certainly important. The nations of the world with the more advanced technology are always in an advantageous trade position with the rest of the world which has a simpler economy. The more advanced society can sell its manufactured goods to the simpler society in exchange for raw materials. This has the effect of expanding the land area from which the people of the complex society may draw. All of these factors are interrelated, but together largely account for the high level of living prevalent in such societies as the United States.

To a considerable extent, the same principles hold for northwestern Europe, but with a few modifications. The Europeans began their technological advance and world trade earlier. They began with a larger relative population and a smaller land area, and probably practiced less birth control. They also began with a traditional kind of distribution which approved great distinctions in income levels for different segments of the society. Finally, modern wars have destroyed and disrupted European economy several times. These factors together largely account for the somewhat lower average level of living in northwestern Europe, although as compared with the Oriental, the European's level of living is relatively high.

WORLD POPULATION DISTRIBUTION: RACIAL

Relative numerical magnitude and location of the major races

The several races are unevenly distributed in the world population. For convenience, we may distinguish three races, although as we have seen, racial classification is difficult: the Caucasoid, or "white" race; the Negroid, or "black" race; and the Mongoloid, or "yellow" race. While exact statistics and wholly useful and agreed upon racial classifications are not available, the student may get some idea of the relative world position of the white race from the following. The combined white populations of North America, South America, Europe, and Australia total less than one billion people. If the dark-skinned people of India are included as "Caucasoid," then a slight majority of the world population would be "white." If the dark Indian people are not classified as "white," then the whites would be exceeded by the near one billion Mongoloids who inhabit chiefly Asia and some of the surrounding islands, including Japan and much of the East Indies. The smallest race group is the Negroid, native chiefly to Africa. There are about 20 million Negroes in the United States who have descended largely from the Negroes who were brought here originally as slaves.

Numbers versus power

It is significant that most of the world is under the economic and political control of the white race. It is sometimes assumed that this prestige and power, out of proportion to its numerical strength, is an outgrowth of the superior intelligence of the white race as a race. This is entirely erroneous. It has now been clearly demonstrated that such great differences in the general intelligence of races do not exist. The dominance of the white race in the world is explained *at this time* by the unique and probably temporary *historical advantage of having invented a set of effective cultural techniques as well as the desire for world control.* The development of Europe and later of America as a manufacturing and trading economy gave the white race the prestige and the power to enforce its position over the other peoples. In order to protect trade relations and guarantee markets and sources of supply, gigantic navies and later armies were built up to hold the advantages gained and to "protect" the higher level of living which a trading and manufacturing economy made possible.

11. THE DIVISION OF WEALTH BETWEEN DEVELOPED AND OTHER AREAS OF THE WORLD

Underdeveloped Countries

Developed Countries

65% of Population and 20% of Income

35% of Population and 80% of Income

Source: Twentieth Century Fund.

How long the ascendancy of the white race will continue is a matter of judgment. No one who is familiar with the facts, however, thinks the white race can hold this position of advantage forever. There are already unmistakable signs, both in the Orient and Africa, that the colored peoples realize the potential power of their numbers and resent their inferior position in the world. There is little doubt that the white race is still far enough ahead in the technical implements of war to continue its dominance in world affairs. The immediate issue in international relations seems, however, not to be racial but rather ideological. The United States and Japan now seem to be aligned against Russia and Communist China, despite recent rifts between them, in the Orient. At this writing it is impossible to determine whether the older identity of philosophy and purpose between Russia and the Communist power in China will continue. Experts differ widely, and the Communist regime in China is too new to be judged by any substantial record of performance. It seems clear, however, that the significant international economic issues at present are not racial, but ideological, with persons of each race on both sides.

It would be a mistake, however, to assume that warfare is the only or even the major way in which the struggle for power between races and nations takes places. In dozens of ways in economic, political, and other relations among nations, the struggle for power is constantly going on. The struggle breaks out in warfare only after an impasse in other means of struggle has been reached. Thus the struggle between the white race and the yellow race for control of the Orient is by no means ended by our victory over Japan or the defeat of the Nationalist forces in China by the Communists there.

Throughout Asia there are very strong feelings against the white man, not only because of the power he has had over these peoples but also because of the *ways* in which he has *used* that power. The existence of these attitudes, of course, does not mean that racial war in the Orient is either inevitable or necessary. It means simply that one must be realistic and face the fact that the white man's position of power in the world, out of proportion to his numbers, is probably only a passing phase in history. Perhaps if the white peoples recognize this fact in time and retire gracefully to a world position comparable to their numerical strength, no serious international racial difficulties need be encountered. On the other hand, it seems likely that the white race will attempt to maintain its power at all costs—even of another war, if necessary. Should this prove to be the case, the outcome is not pleasant to anticipate. Processes like these, of course, may take long periods to work themselves out.

POPULATION MAKEUP AND TRENDS IN THE UNITED STATES

The United States contains 200 million people, 6 percent of the world's population. What is its structure and how is it changing?

1. Changes in the birth rate

Like most countries with the western European type of culture and society, the *long-run* American birth rate had been slowly declining. It cannot be determined whether this decline was due entirely to the practice of birth control or to what extent modern living results in the involuntary infertility of increasing numbers of men and women. Most population research experts, however, seem inclined to attribute much if not most of the decline to the deliberate limitation of families.

After World War II the birth rate in the United States reversed a long-time downward trend and the great "baby boom" occurred. The change was not lasting, however.

12. CHANGE IN AMERICAN BIRTH RATES, 1940–1965

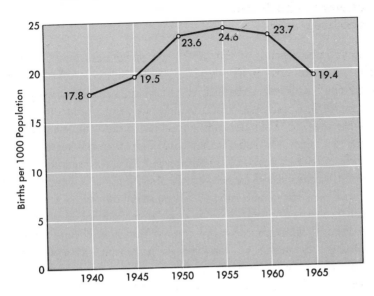

Source: Division of Vital Statistics, U.S. Department of Health, Education and Welfare.

The birth rate for the American population has declined from 24.1 per 1,000 population in 1959 to 23.4 in 1961 to 19.4 in 1965 as reported by the Division of Vital Statistics of the U.S. Department of Health, Education and Welfare.

13. POPULATION OF THE UNITED STATES AND OUTLYING AREAS, 1960 AND 1950

| Area | 1960 | 1950 | Increase 1950 to 1960 | |
			Number	Percent
Total	183,285,009	154,233,234	29,051,775	18.8
United States	179,323,175	151,325,798	27,997,377	18.5
Conterminous United States	178,464,236	150,697,361	27,766,875	18.4
Alaska	226,167	128,643	97,524	75.8
Hawaii	632,772	499,794	132,978	26.6
Commonwealth of Puerto Rico	2,349,544	2,210,703	138,841	6.3
Outlying areas of sovereignty or jurisdiction	237,869	215,188	22,681	10.5
United States population abroad	1,374,421	481,545	892,876	185.4

2. The differential birth rate: a diminishing trend

For many years prior to the 1950's the so-called "middle classes" in America, as elsewhere in Western countries, reproduced themselves at rates greatly lower than the rest of the population. Not only were there more childless and one-child families but even the multiple-child families were smaller. This condition was called the "differential birth rate." It has not been established whether the differential birth rate was due primarily to the practice of birth control, to later marriages in this group, or to "involuntary" infertility. Probably all three factors were involved, and possibly others as well. The extent of this was striking— persons of greater education, and probably innate intelligence, also, were reproducing themselves at appreciably less than the rate required for maintaining themselves; persons of less educational achievement and probably, on the average, lower intelligence were reproducing them- selves at rates much higher than were required to maintain their rela- tive numerical position in the population. Dire predictions were being made to the effect that if this inequality in reproduction were not re- versed, or at least checked, the United States would eventually become "a nation of morons."

The pessimists may have been right, but if current reproduction rates continue, it will take a much longer time for the presumably ad- verse effects to occur. In other words, like the general birth rate, the dif- ferential birth rate has fluctuated during the years since World War II. Demographers are not in full agreement, but there is at least some evidence to indicate that the size of the differential may have been re- duced. But the differential birth rate has not disappeared altogether. Families are still larger, only less markedly so, among the less well- educated, economically less well off classes.

No one knows, moreover, whether the current reduction in the long-trend differential will be permanent or only a temporary phase. Birth rates are a highly inconstant social fact, especially for the classes of the population who, as studies show, have both the necessary knowl- edge and favorable attitudes toward birth control. What might be the effect, for example, of a long depression in which the now quite satis- factory standard of living for college graduates were seriously threat- ened? Would we see, as in the 1930's, a sharp decline in the birth rate? Or, what would the effect be upon family size if a reversal occurred in the current trend toward earlier marriages in these same groups?

14. STATES RANKED BY TOTAL POPULATION, 1960

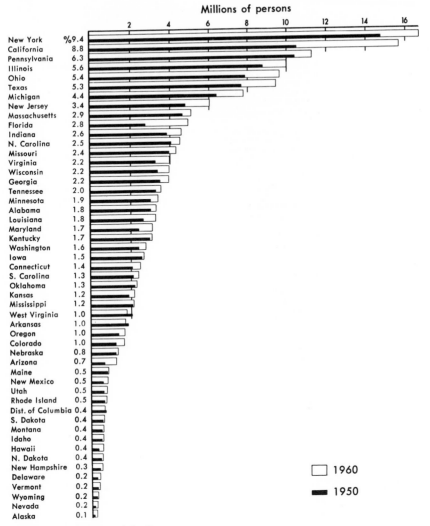

	Millions of persons
New York	%9.4
California	8.8
Pennsylvania	6.3
Illinois	5.6
Ohio	5.4
Texas	5.3
Michigan	4.4
New Jersey	3.4
Massachusetts	2.9
Florida	2.8
Indiana	2.6
N. Carolina	2.5
Missouri	2.4
Virginia	2.2
Wisconsin	2.2
Georgia	2.2
Tennessee	2.0
Minnesota	1.9
Alabama	1.8
Louisiana	1.8
Maryland	1.7
Kentucky	1.7
Washington	1.6
Iowa	1.5
Connecticut	1.4
S. Carolina	1.3
Oklahoma	1.3
Kansas	1.2
Mississippi	1.2
West Virginia	1.0
Arkansas	1.0
Oregon	1.0
Colorado	1.0
Nebraska	0.8
Arizona	0.7
Maine	0.5
New Mexico	0.5
Utah	0.5
Rhode Island	0.5
Dist. of Columbia	0.4
S. Dakota	0.4
Montana	0.4
Idaho	0.4
Hawaii	0.4
N. Dakota	0.4
New Hampshire	0.3
Delaware	0.2
Vermont	0.2
Wyoming	0.2
Nevada	0.2
Alaska	0.1

□ 1960

■ 1950

Source: U.S. Bureau of the Census.

3. Population redistribution in the United States: migration

The population of the United States has been ever changing in its distribution over the territory of the nation. We shall later discuss the radical shift from rural to urban residence. One other aspect of spatial redistribution needs comment here—the differential growth (and de-

15. STATES RANKED BY PERCENT OF CHANGE IN POPULATION, 1960

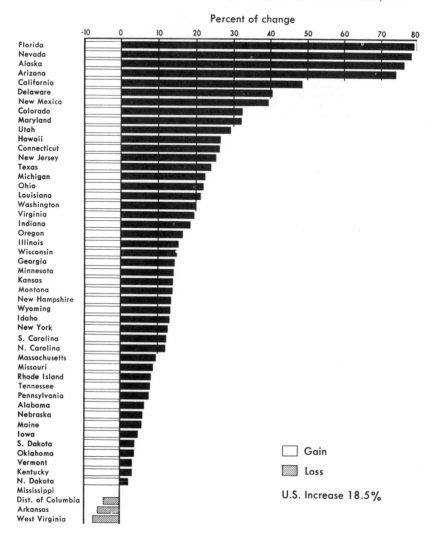

Source: U.S. Bureau of the Census.

cline) among the several regions of the United States. The Far Western
states (especially California) and Florida have shown impressive percentages of growth. While the nation as a whole increased 18.5 percent
in a decade, percentages of growth as high as 80 percent occurred for
some states, whereas other states actually lost population. It should be
noted that states with a stationary population or with small gains, such
as Iowa, Kansas, Nebraska, Pennsylvania, and Maine, actually lost population *proportionately* to the nation as a whole. (See Fig. 13, above.)

16. States Ranked by Percent of Population Urban, 1960

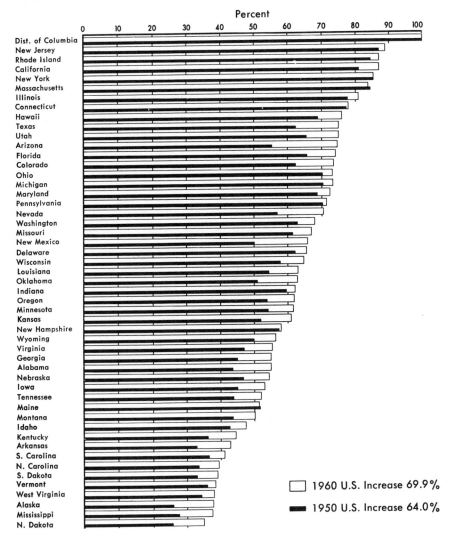

Source: U.S. Bureau of the Census.

4. Negro population: numbers and redistribution

One out of nine persons in the United States is a Negro. This proportion has fluctuated markedly between different periods in American history. At the time this nation came into existence two out of ten Americans were Negroes. The proportion of Negroes then declined until by 1920 only one out of ten Americans was a Negro. This proportion remained constant until the 1950's when the proportion of Negroes began to rise. If present rates of reproduction of Negroes and whites continue, by 1972 one out of eight Americans will be Negro.[2]

The *redistribution* of the Negro population in the United States has been more striking. In 1900 only 10 percent of the nation's Negroes lived in the Northern states. By 1966, due mostly to a rather steady migration, the number of Negroes living in the North and North Central regions had increased 23 percent. During the same period the Negro population living in the Western states increased by 59 percent, while the Negro population in the South showed little change.

SUMMARY

The world population of 3.25 billion is very unequally distributed over the earth. The pressure of population upon the means of subsistence depends upon the state of the productive arts and the level of living, not simply upon the available land. Different parts of the world have different kinds of population problems depending upon how these factors interact to affect them. Theoretically, relief from the population problem can be found through one or another of four possible approaches: control of numbers, expansion of the land area from which sustenance is derived, decline in the level of living, and improvement in the efficiency of the agricultural and manufacturing arts.

In practice, however, each of these theoretically possible solutions presents problems. In the case of limiting numbers, there are the ideological beliefs of certain religions and the educational and technological difficulties involved in implementation of a contraceptive program. The land area of the earth is relatively constant, although through reclamation and the "farming" of the ocean considerable potential exists. Except during certain periods of warfare or political extremism, voluntary declines in the standard of living are vigorously opposed. Nevertheless, under conditions of dire need, living standards may have to go down. Improvement in agricultural and mechanical arts have been very beneficial in the more developed nations, and it is quite possible that new technological frontiers may still be opened.

The *distribution* of a society's want-satisfying goods and services is a somewhat different problem. It depends upon the kind of prevailing ideas concerning who shall have how much of the joint product of the society. There may be, and certainly has been, terrible poverty

[2] Daniel P. Moynihan, "Employment, Income, and the Ordeal of the Negro Family," in Talcott Parsons and Kenneth B. Clark, eds., *The Negro American* (Boston, Houghton Mifflin, 1966), pp. 134–159.

where the overall potentialties of the society could be more than ample if the distribution system were different. The distribution problem, however, should not be confused with the basic population problem.

The various races share in the world population picture very unequally, and this condition introduces some interesting paradoxes, as well as overwhelming world problems. The dominance of the white race should be understood for what it is, a point in history, and not as a demonstration of any inherent superior abilities of white people. Just as there were times in the past when the culture of white people was markedly inferior, so it is entirely possible that again the leadership, prestige, and power may pass to another race. The Orient particularly poses the problem for the future. Resentments against continued white domination are real and deeply held. How long the white race can hold the position of dominance in the world remains problematic.

The population of the United States, consisting of 6 or 7 percent of the world's population, is showing some significant trends. Birth rate trends have been inconstant, reaching an all-time low in the depression years, followed by a sharp rise in the post-World War II years, and now declining again. The differential birth rate continues, although the extent of the differential seems to be becoming less great. The population as a result of the high birth rates of the immediate postwar period has become a younger population. This may hold more important implications for social change than any other demographic fact in recent years.

SUGGESTED READINGS

Petersen, William, *Population*. New York, Macmillan, 1961.
A general book on population with emphasis on the analysis and systematic treatment of populations in their social settings. One of the most recent and authoritative general treatments of the population problem in its broad sociological aspects. Contains figures from the 1960 census.

Shryock, Henry S., Jr., *Population Mobility Within the United States*. Chicago, Community and Family Study Center, University of Chicago, 1964.
One important focus in studies of population concerns its redistribution. This book focuses upon the patterns and magnitudes of population redistribution in the United States.

Simpson, Hoke S., ed., *The Changing American Population*. New York, Institute of Life Insurance Graduate School of Business, Columbia University, 1962.

There are numerous books which have attempted to interpret the demographic facts concerning the American population. None exactly parallels any other, but this one is representative. An abundance of factual materials.

Stockwell, Edward G., "The Relationship Between Population Growth and Economic Development." *American Sociological Review*, Vol. 27 (April, 1962), pp. 250–252.

"One of the major problems confronting mankind today concerns the fact that roughly two thirds of the world's population lives in countries that are characterized by extremely low levels of economic and social well-being. To take a specific illustration, in contrast to an annual per capita income of $1,864 in the United States, recent estimates indicate that about 70 per cent of the countries in the world have annual per capita incomes of less than $400. Furthermore, in most of these countries, death rates have been falling rapidly while fertility has remained at fairly high levels, thus resulting in extensive population increases. It is generally assumed that such persistent population growth in these countries acts to impede the improvement of their current low levels of living, and imposes a real barrier to sustained economic development."

Thomlinson, Ralph, *Population Dynamics*. New York, Random House, 1965.

This is a solid textbook with broad coverage of demographic factors and their sociological implications. Excellent.

STUDY QUESTIONS

1. What are the facts of the "population explosion"?
2. What limits the size of the population of the world at a given time? Why is the phrase "at a given time" important?
3. How do advances in technology permit an increase in population *or* an increase in the available food per person?
4. Why do many American families practice birth control?
5. What are the three major factors that determine the total population the world can support? How is each a factor?
6. What three choices does man have when there is an increase in sustenance?
7. What determines the level of living of a given person?
8. What information besides density of population is necessary to determine if a country has an overcrowded population? Why?
9. Why do the people of the United States and Canada have an average higher level of living than the people of the rest of the world?
10. How does the white race compare in numerical strength with the other races? What implications do you see in this?
11. Why has the white race been able to acquire and maintain political and economic dominance of the world?

12. To what factors are the oscillations in the American birth rate attributed?
13. Why are some people alarmed over our differential birth rate?
14. What have been the demographic changes in the American Negro population during the last twenty years?

20
HUMAN ECOLOGY
AND HUMAN
RELATIONS

ECOLOGY

Biological ecology: symbiosis the key idea

Biologists have discovered that important new light can be thrown on the older knowledge about many species of plants and animals through the study of plant and animal "communities." The several plant and animal species living in a given area depend on one another for their sustenance. This interrelationship between different kinds of organisms living in the same environment is a very complex one. One obvious dependence relationship among organisms is that of parasitism. In other instances, one form of life lives on or near another without in any way injuring it, and may in fact indirectly assist it in its struggle for survival. Some kinds of birds, for example, feed on the excrement of mammals. This in no way harms the mammal and may, in fact, be an indirect benefit as a sanitation factor. Other animals secure their food as scavengers. The possibilities of interdependence are many. *These various kinds of sustenance interrelationships* found in the plant and animal communities have been collectively termed *symbiosis*.

The symbiotic relations of plants and animals constitute a complex "web of life" and "balance of nature," each species being dependent upon other species while still others are dependent upon it. Darwin pointed out, in jest of course, that the number of old maids in a community had an effect upon the abundance of the clover crop. This was his reasoning. The larger the number of old maids, the larger the cat population. The larger the cat population, the greater will be the ravages of the cats on the field mouse population. Since field mice feed on the larvae of bumblebees, the bees would increase in number as a result of the smaller mouse population. With a larger bee population there will be a larger clover yield, because the

clover plant (or some varieties, at least) lacks the power to pollinate itself, its pollination relying on the activity of bumblebees. Thus, he concluded, the greater the population of old maids, the greater the clover
yield! This humorous illustration does show the important fact of intricate and vital interdependence of plant and animal species in any
area. Some of those interrelations are so involved that the findings of
ecologists make some of the most fascinating reading in biological literature. Every species, including man, depends for sustenance upon
other species, and itself provides the basis for the existence of additional
species in an endless chain or "web of life" or symbiotic interrelationship.

Human ecology: intraspecies symbiosis

Sociologists have found the concept *symbiosis* to be applicable also
to the human community. The sociologist, of course, studies *intra*species symbiosis. In other words, the interdependence which the sociologist studies is the interdependence of humans with other humans.

The cardinal concept in studying human symbiosis is *division of
labor*. Human division of labor forms an intricate and complex web of
interdependence between persons, groups, nations, and continents
which becomes more and more intricate and complex as modern society
develops.

Similarities of biological
and human symbiosis

Just as the population of grazing animals in a natural size is limited
by the amount of edible foliage, so the number of persons in any given
occupational specialty is limited by the size of the human population
of the community in question. The number of dentists, filling station
attendants, or lawn-mower sharpeners who can make a living in a given
community is limited. Additional ones simply divide up the available
work among themselves, until such a time as some are forced to drop
out because they cannot secure enough work to make a living. Human
beings can, of course, change occupations or move to another area, and
thus *mobility* or *economic failure* rather than *starvation* tends to be the
result of the oversupply of any of the specialties in the symbiotic pattern.

The abundance of the subsistence which a given individual of the
species can enjoy, whether plant, animal, or human, is determined by

the *abundance of the source of supply and the individual differences in ability to compete.* Thus, if there are too many dentists in a community, all of them will not suffer equally by the oversupply of dentists. Some will continue to secure more work than the others do, and very probably those who secure the least work will be forced to drop out. It is probable, however, that when this or any other occupation is overcrowded, many of the persons in it will find their incomes reduced somewhat, but by no means equally. In many other ways the analogy of the symbiotic interdependence of the plant and animal community and the intraspecies symbiosis of the human community may be made to appear exceedingly similar. But pointing out such similarities should by no means imply that they are identical; the differences are equally important.

Basic differences between human and subhuman symbiosis

The chief difference between human and subhuman symbiotic relationships lies in the fact that for subhuman species the relationships are *purely biological while for human beings the factor of culture intervenes.* Thus the whole symbiotic process becomes materially altered.

For example, in our society we do not permit the persons who are unable to make a living to die; those who are able to make more than a minimum for their subsistence help to carry the others along in some way or other. What may be even more important, humans exert control on many occupations so as to keep the number of persons in those occupations sufficiently low, and thus virtually guarantee not only subsistence but a very liberal supply of it. Furthermore, culture is constantly creating new occupations while related established occupations become obsolete. Sometimes what appears to be overcrowding in an occupation may simply be the result of the occupation becoming obsolete due to social change.

There are other differences between the symbiotic processes in human and subhuman communities, but probably enough has been said to indicate that real and fundamental differences exist. So long as the student recognizes the difference between occupational symbiosis and species symbiosis he will probably find that many of the biological concepts pertaining to symbiosis can be fruitfully employed in studying the human community. A very real error arises, however, when the differences are overlooked. Even human ecologists themselves have sometimes overlooked or minimized the cultural factor.

The spatial pattern of subhuman and human species

As a result of the symbiotic interdependence of species, certain well-known plant and animal *location relationships* can readily be observed. Certain kinds of grass cannot grow under trees because of the shade. Other plants require specific soil types. Animals, too, have their habitats, determined by such factors as climate, sources of food, and the abundance of animals of prey. Because of these spatial regularities it is possible to map many forms of biological life. These spatial patterns, then, arise out of the symbiotic relationships and, therefore, are strikingly similar for the same and related species from community to community in the same general type of geographical and climatic area.

Human communities also have a characteristic spatial patterning. It is based partly on symbiotic relationships, but is by no means solely determined by them. Probably almost everyone has observed the similarity among American cities in the location of the various industries, service establishments, and living arrangements. This is no accident; it is a direct result of the forces of competition among human beings and organizations in various separate but interrelated occupational specialties. So standardized is this spatial pattern that a stranger in a city for the first time has little serious difficulty in finding any of the usual services he might want, even without making special inquiry.

Human ecology defined

Summarizing the foregoing paragraphs, we may now define sociological ecology as *the study of the symbiotic relationships and the resulting spatial patterning of human beings and human institutions in the community*.[1]

While sociology is not the only study of man which treats ecology, sociologists during recent years have built up a considerable body of knowledge on human ecology. This and the following chapter will summarize a number of such understandings.

THE LARGER IMPORTANCE OF HUMAN ECOLOGY

Human ecological theory has in large degree constituted the theoretical underpinning for a great deal of precise and often important practical work in the fields of population, urbanization, and the struc-

---

[1] This is the classic formulation by one of the founders of human ecology. R. D. McKenzie, "Human Ecology," in *Encyclopedia of the Social Sciences* (New York, Macmillan, 1930).

ture of cities and so-called urban regions. It is quite possible that the most important contribution of the ecologist lies, however, not so much in his more precise researches as in his vivid reminder that, despite culture, man is still a member of the "animal kingdom" and that even though he can, through technology, considerably alter many aspects of his dependency upon nature, he has not yet succeeded in eliminating some of the hard facts of biological life. Chief among these hard facts are his sustenance needs, which he meets through a complicated symbiotic dependency both upon other species of animals and plants and by an intricate symbiosis with his fellow humans.

The ecologist's theory and the data which he has assembled also remind all social scientists of the importance of the subsistence, as distinguished from more sentimental, considerations in defining the course of human action. Much of the unfortunate, unsightly, and often unmanageable debris contained in the average American city is understandable in terms of the efforts of some people to maximize their opportunities for the exploitation of their habitats. Moreover, although all people are dependent on one another, the consequences of human action are often remote—these consequences move ahead in expanding zones of influence often vitally affecting persons who had no real interest in or benefit from the original activity. "We are all in it together" in the human community; and if one of us finds it profitable to institute a dump in the direct line of vision of someone else's treasured picture window, the latter learns again the lesson that the human community and everything in it are unavoidably intrusive in so-called "private worlds." Thus there is a "web of life"—other's subsistence efforts, self-interest, and the residues therefrom are normal conditions of human living together.

Some ecologists have used the term *cultural landscape* to call attention to the fact that many human activities involve the creation and maintenance of a physical structure, like freeways and skyscrapers, acres of wrecked cars, as well as parks, playgrounds, and farmsteads. Man himself does not so much live upon the earth as he, in a very real and demonstrable sense, builds a superstructure upon it. And he does this in repetitive ways, so much so that it is relatively difficult to find a really unique urban landscape in which to live and work. Even the processes by which man solves the recurring problems of existence become themselves habituated, because they are strongly compromised by the pre-existing symbiotic and spatial structure which ecological forces have already built.

Symbiosis, the web of life, the balance of nature—these are no aca-

demic phrases; they are words which stand for a stern set of facts of
life which many men like to believe belong only to what is condescendingly called the "lower forms" of life. At best all that man seems able
to do, even with impressive technology, is to meliorate some of the influences and sometimes postpone and deflect the forces; but his inescapable dependency upon the earth and other men for subsistence, he
cannot long overlook.

ECOLOGICAL PROCESSES

So far we have treated ecology largely as a study of the static aspect of symbiotic and spatial patterning. The community is, of course,
a growing thing, and the ecology of growth takes recurrent, standard
forms which the ecologist has studied and to which he has attached
more or less standardized terms.

One basic ecological process is *segregation*. We have already
studied one aspect of segregation in respect to racial segregation. For
different reasons, however, other elements are relegated to more or less
limited locations. Immigrant groups in the larger cities, like other racial
or cultural groups, tend to settle in separate ethnic areas. "Social classes"
also segregate, largely on the basis of income and wealth, with the
ability to pay rent or own real estate as the crucial criterion affecting
location. Types of economic activity are also segregated. Each city has
industrial areas, wholesale business areas, retail shopping areas, and so on.

As the boundaries of segregated areas are broken, there is said
to be an *invasion* of the new area by the formerly segregated activity
or population segment. As the invasion matures and the transition to the
new use or population becomes completed, a *succession* is said to have
taken place.

Other well-known ecological processes are those of *centralization*
and *decentralization*. It is normal for specialized functions, like the
central business district, to become more and more centralized until a
point is reached after which it is no longer efficient to centralize, and
decentralization begins. The retail shopping subcenters which spring
up here and there in larger cities, usually along the main thoroughfares
and at intersections, illustrate decentralization. The same process is at
work in industry. Many industrial and commercial enterprises are now
deliberately breaking up their organization into smaller units and dis-
persing them to different cities. The economies and other advantages
of large-scale enterprise go on only to a point—after that greater economy and advantage result from decentralizing the enterprise.

REGIONS AND URBAN DOMINANCE

The rise of regional organization of American and world society

Prior to the rise of the present American society, this nation was organized along political territorial lines—states, counties, townships, cities, wards—with boundary lines delimiting one from the other. With the rise of large-scale financial and industrial organization, better transportation and communication, and more specialization and interdependence of persons and areas, a new form of territorial organization of people came into existence. The various parts of modern society are now primarily held together not by locality and political ties but by the vital needs of securing raw materials and labor and selling finished products.

Sociologists have attached the term *region* to this modern form of economic organization consisting of major cities and their surrounding and dependent hinterlands. Regions are the real units of modern national, and to some extent even of international, organization. The old political boundaries and localism pale into unimportance as the new cultural unity based on the economics of the large city brings greater and greater homogeneity.

Under the impact of this new large-scale economic organization, political boundaries like those of the several American states have become less and less significant, except as descriptive terms like street names. States and counties still continue to exist, of course, as convenient (and sometimes very inconvenient) administrative units of government for activities such as highway construction, school maintenance, and policing. But so far as the economic organization of the nation is concerned, state lines are more to be regarded as minor nuisances.

Not only individuals specialize; industries specialize, and so even do cities. A given factory or a given city provides certain materials or services for very large areas. Thus New York is virtually the financial center of America, while Chicago is a livestock and meat processing center, and Detroit, the automobile center. Recreation production becomes similarly specialized with movie manufacture in Hollywood, the horse-racing industry in Kentucky, and winter vacationing in Florida and southern California. These specialized centers and areas provide the services for the whole continent and some may even be worldwide in scope. The people in one state may find themselves more vitally concerned with what happens in a remote part of the nation or in some far corner of the world than by the happenings of their local community. A change in women's fashions, for example, may create a depression in an entire city and a boom in another.

Cities are the dominance points of regions

Large cities are, of course, the focal points of the regional organization of the modern world. The converging of all of the railroad, highway, and air lines on Chicago or New York or New Orleans is symbolic of the *dominance* of these cities over their *hinterlands*.

Out over the surrounding area each day are spread fabulous numbers of copies of the big city newspapers, while its radio and television stations broadcast into the homes of persons far removed from the city. The goods people buy are distributed from the great cities to smaller ones and so on down to the tiniest hamlet.

It is not to be assumed that it is only the large cities like Chicago or New York which exert dominance. All cities exert dominance, but over different aspects of life. In fact, it is because it exerts dominance that a given city may live. Agricultural villages have dominance, too. Villages as well as cities secure their dominance because they contain the stores, banks, professional offices, churches, schools, post offices, and all of the service institutions which people use to meet their wants. But the local village does not exert dominance over clothing design, supplying refrigerators, college education, or radio entertainment. For these services the centers of dominance are elsewhere.

One of the relatively new features in American life is this great dominance of urban centers for the organization and control of the society. Although some manufacturing is done in smaller cities, the chief function of small cities is that of distributing goods and services which have been created for the most part in far-away places. The overall direction of modern industry comes from a few very large cities. This relegation of small and especially rural communities to "service station" functions is decried by many people, but seems to have become, nevertheless, already an accomplished fact. The major decisions affecting the pattern of life of the nation, or at least of great areas of it, are made in the large cities and tend, therefore, to reflect urban needs, urban interests, and urban values.

SUMMARY

A branch of sociology called "human ecology" has arisen in recent years for the purpose of emphasizing the study of the symbiotic interrelationships and the resulting spatial pattern of human living. Although many of the concepts employed, like "the web of life," "symbiosis," "spatial pattern," are also employed in the study of plant and animal communities, the student should bear in mind that the factor of culture makes symbiotic relationship among humans fundamentally different from that of plant and animal communities. In the subhuman community the individual must adjust to his environment purely on a physical basis, and the inability to adjust means death. Through the medium of culture, however, humans modify their environment and alter the conditions of survival in various other ways. The important thing to note is that the intraspecies symbiosis resulting from division of labor among humans does make the general ecological approach a fruitful one through which to study certain aspects of collective human life. The ecological approach should be employed with caution.

In the Western mass society, cities are the centers of dominance from which societal influences radiate. There are differing degrees and kinds of dominance, varying from New York City to the crossroads country store, but it is to the large cities that leadership for culture control and culture change has almost completely shifted. The basic ingredients of social life, both material and nonmaterial, are fashioned in the offices, factories, laboratories, and studios of a very few great urban centers. In this regional organization around a few superdominant cities, state and local boundaries mean little. The interdependence and specialization of cities, like the specialization of individuals and of industries, is a fundamental part of modern life. We will discuss some of the characteristics of the contemporary city in the next chapter.

SUGGESTED READINGS

Hawley, Amos H., *Human Ecology*. New York, Ronald, 1950.
One of the two full text-length treatments of the field of human ecology.

McKenzie, R. D., "The Scope of Human Ecology," in E. W. Burgess, *The Urban Community*. Chicago, University of Chicago Press, 1926.
The original statement of the University of Chicago "school" of human ecology by one of the leading ecologists in the United States. May be taken as representative of the first of the two conceptions of ecology discussed in this chapter.

Odum, H. W., *Southern Regions of the United States*. Chapel Hill, University of North Carolina Press, 1936.
A classic. This extensive study of the regions of the South is replete with statistical and other details.

Quinn, James A., *Human Ecology*. Englewood Cliffs, N.J., Prentice-Hall, 1950.
One of the two full text-length treatments of the field of human ecology.

Numerous bibliographic references in the following chapter apply also to this one.

STUDY QUESTIONS

1. What links of the "endless chain" are missing in the old-maid-clover-crop illustration of symbiotic interrelationship?
2. On what factors does the number of profitable shoe repair shops in a community depend?
3. Why do some trades and professions use various devices to limit the number of people entering their field of endeavor? Illustrate.
4. How do human and subhuman ecology differ?
5. How do the economic and cultural explanations of urban development differ? How are they similar?
6. How does our culture tend to be a "money culture"?
7. How is economic relationship the integrating factor in human "webs of life"? Illustrate.
8. How do cities dominate their hinterlands?
9. What is the significance of the increase in urban dominance?

21
URBANIZATION AND THE STRUCTURE OF THE URBAN REGION

In the earlier chapter on the "Mass Society" (Chapter 4) it was pointed out that a rapid urbanization had characterized twentieth-century United States and that the proportion of agricultural and nonagricultural people had reversed itself since the beginnings of the nation. Figure 15 presents the latter generalization dramatically, but actually it *overrepresents* the proportions on farms at the present time for two reasons. (1) The data on which the chart is based is several years old and the shift from country to city continues apace with each passing day. Now (1967) only 6 percent of Americans live on farms, as compared to 9 percent in 1960. (2) All persons who live on farms are *not gainfully employed there*. For growing proportions of urban-employed Americans, farm living has become a certain kind of "having your cake and eating it, too."

MEASURING THE RATE AND EXTENT OF URBANIZATION

As early as 1930 the *majority of Americans*, regardless of occupation, were living *within daily access of metropolitan American cities*. Metropolitan cities were defined by the census in 1930 as cities with a total population of 100,000 or more, including all persons who lived in the contiguous minor political areas with a density of 150 per square mile or more. Thus, cities with populations of 50,000 in the central city plus a sufficiently large suburban development could total 100,000, all of which is considered as "metropolitan" area. There were 96 such metropolitan cities by 1930. The majority of the American people in 1930 lived close enough to these 96 metropolitan cities so that they could conveniently use these cities as their place of work or as shopping and recreation centers, traveling to and from the central city daily.

17. THE SHIFT FROM COUNTRY TO CITY

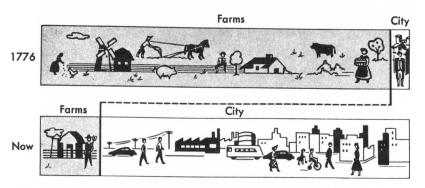

Source: U.S. Bureau of the Census.

"Since 1950 the Census Bureau, urban demographers, and many users of population statistics have found it necessary to gather or apply urban population facts in terms of such more comprehensive units as 'urbanized areas' and 'standard metropolitan areas' (known as SMA). The latter unit, which is now widely used in the United States, deals mainly with the largest and economically most important urban areas. It is defined as containing one or more (but within twenty miles of one another) central cities of 50,000 or over, plus adjacent counties that exhibit arbitrarily defined 'urban' characteristics. . . ."[1] "This expanded unit seems to provide more valid measures of urbanization and, with increasing importance, it allows for more meaningful comparisons of trends. . . ."[2]

In 1960 in the thus-computed "standard metropolitan areas" there lived over 113 million Americans or 63 percent of the American people. Between 1940 and 1960, moreover, almost 80 percent of all population growth occurred in these standard metropolitan areas. All of the rest of the country divided up the remaining 20 percent. At the present there is not available definitive information as to what percentage of Americans live in *daily access* of the standard metropolitan areas, that is, live in or commute to metropolitan cities in connection with their work, but it would seem a reasonable inference from the information we have that over three fourths could be so accounted for, since three out of five actually live in metropolitan areas. Thus, not only urban experience but *metropolitan* urban experience is the daily regimen for more than three out of four Americans.

[1] For details see Alvin Boskoff, *The Sociology of Urban Regions* (New York, Appleton-Century-Crofts), p. 49.
[2] *Ibid.*, pp. 49–50.

18. PERCENT OF CHANGE IN POPULATION, 1950–1960
(In and Outside Central Cities by Size of
Standard Metropolitan Statistical Areas)

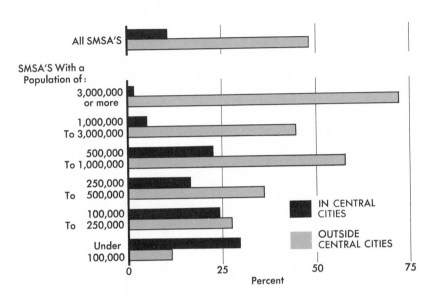

REASONS FOR URBAN GROWTH

The *facts* of urban growth, as we have seen, are reasonably clear. To determine *why* the growth has occurred is not as easy a task as might be thought. Sometimes it is held that people have moved to cities "because they like city life" or because of the attractiveness of the real or imagined higher wages paid in the city. This seems not to be the whole truth, however, because during the early years of great urban growth there had also been occurring an unprecedented recession in American agriculture. Therefore, we do not know whether the migration to the cities was due to the greater attractiveness of the cities or because rural living had become so economically unattractive that many people were left no real choice. Probably the two factors reinforced each other. Assuming that the migrants preferred to move to the city, we still do not know whether they preferred the urban mode of living or were merely willing to endure it for the sake of the somewhat higher wages and standard of living which they would receive, or thought they would receive, in the cities.

It is possible to approach the reasons for the growth of cities from a less personal angle. Cities grew because there was a sufficient demand for labor in the cities to enable people to make a living there. That fact is

19. PERCENT OF POPULATION IN SMSA'S, BY STATES, 1960

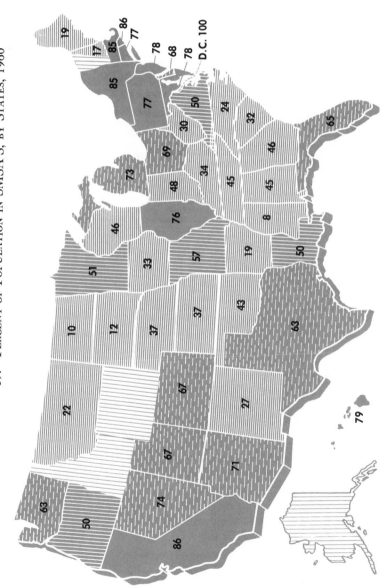

United States
63.0 Percent

0
1-49
50-62
63-74
75 up

19

17
85
86
77

85

77
78
68
78
D.C. 100

50

24

32

65

30

69

73

46

48

34

45

46

51

76

57

45

8

33

19

50

37

43

10

12

37

63

22

67

27

79

67

71

63

74

50

86

20. Percent of Population Urban, by States, 1960

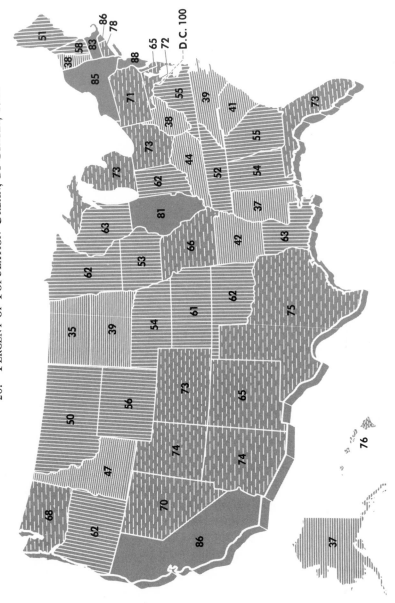

United States
69.9 Percent

Under 50
50-64
65-79
80-100

377

21. Composition of Urban Population, 1960

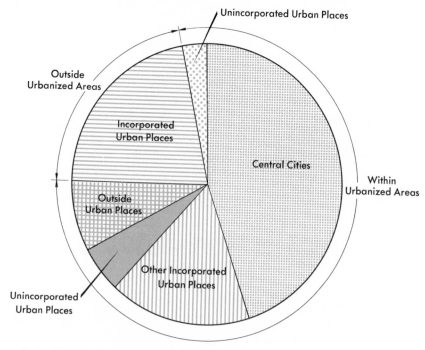

Source: U.S. Bureau of the Census.

fundamental, although one must not assume that everyone who lives in the city actually makes a living there. Numerous persons in the city are supported in whole or in part by philanthropy, even during prosperous times. The point, however, is that the city-dominated economic systems must be economically able to support not only those gainfully employed there but also those unemployed who are directly or indirectly supported by those gainfully employed. Cities have traditionally been able to support their large populations largely because of the presence of the great basic employing units—factories.

It would be a mistake to assume, however, that the production of goods is the sole or even major type of urban employment. Cities are also the centers of the great service institutions: colleges and universities, hospitals, banks, insurance companies, and recreational services of all kinds, to mention a few of the more obvious ones. The affairs of government, moreover, are employing a greater and greater proportion of the population, particularly since the services of government are constantly expanding. These centers of government are, of course, all

22. POPULATION BY TYPE OF RESIDENCE, 1960
(In Metropolitan and Nonmetropolitan Areas)

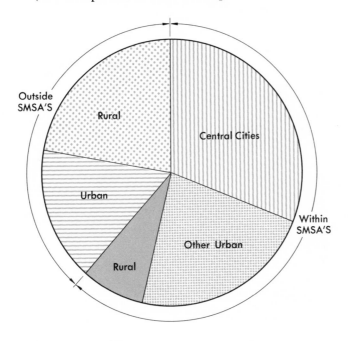

Source: U.S. Bureau of the Census.

located in urban centers. In short, *our society has produced a culture which emphasizes the kind of values and activities which we seem best to carry out when functioning in large, sometimes tremendous, cities.*

THE STRUCTURE OF THE URBAN REGION

1. The concentric circle conception

It has been conventional for thirty years or more for urban sociologists to portray the "structure" of the city in terms of what was called an urban pattern (Figure 21). It was represented schematically by a series of concentric circles, and the encompassed areas were called zones.

Zone I. Approximately in the center of the city is a well-known *central business district* containing retail stores, financial institutions, hotels, eating establishments, theaters, and, on upper floors, the offices of the more important business organizations and professional persons. The central business district is an area of dense population during the working part of the day, yet almost no one lives there, except for the

23. Theoretical Sketch of the Urban Pattern

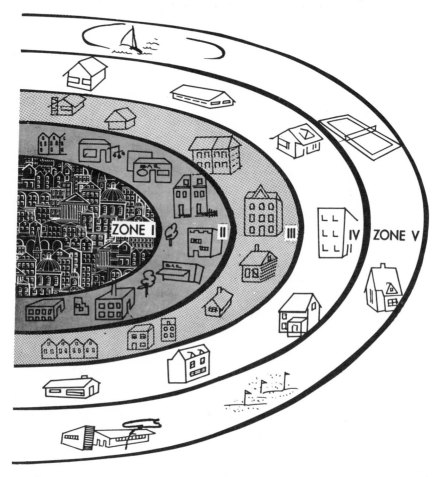

Source: Redrawn from Robert Park, E. W. Burgess, and R. D. McKenzie, *The City* (Chicago, University of Chicago Press, 1925).

transients who occupy the hotels. It is the place where people converge for specific commercial or recreational purposes. Thus the business district is at the center of the city with all transportation lines converging there.

Zone II, called the *zone in transition*, is in the area immediately surrounding the central business district. Conspicuous buildings in this zone are the large, made-over private dwellings, now usually used for offices of persons and businesses which cannot afford the high rental values of the central business district but need a somewhat central location. This is also the area of rooming houses and cheaper hotels. Because it is somewhat centrally located and yet not a costly area in which to live or to maintain a business as compared with the central business district, the zone in transition attracts such establishments as pawnbrokers and second-hand stores, restaurants, and taverns catering to a less discriminating clientele. Very often wholesale business establishments are also located here.

The zone in transition is usually the part of the city in which occurs the greatest concentration of crime and criminals, houses of prostitution, gambling establishments, and similar activities which the ideal culture patterns of the society frown upon, but which enjoy a considerable clientele nevertheless. The resident population of the zone in transition is predominantly male and relatively transient.

This section is called the zone in *transition* because it usually represents an area which, during bygone days when the city was smaller, contained the pretentious homes of the city's most wealthy and prominent people. This was before the day of the automobile, and it was then fashionable for the city's wealthy and elite class to live in the conspicuous houses which now are largely remodeled into office buildings and interspersed with new commercial structures. Thus the area is "in transition" from a residential area of the upper class to the kind of area just described. The transition is relatively complete so far as the function and personnel of the area are concerned, but architectural survivals of the past age are present, although becoming less and less predominant as time goes on.

Also in the zone in transition is the area of the poorer workingmen's homes. This area usually contains the city's "slums," the poorer Negro colonies, and the neighborhoods occupied by immigrants who are not yet assimilated into the American culture. Most of these persons live here not by preference, but because rents are lower and transportation costs to work are likely to be less. The level of living of this area is, of course, low. The area is usually relatively congested. In times of unemployment, this area contains much of the community's relief load because of the narrow margin of financial reserve which the persons who live here can accumulate.

The last decade has witnessed a considerable refurbishing of the zones in transition of many American cities, especially the larger ones. Here has been concentrated most of the urban redevelopment. Old buildings have been razed and relatively modern high-rise apartment houses have replaced them. Networks of expressways and sometimes parks and hospitals now stand in areas which were formerly labeled zones in transition. In short, the kind of transition implied when the model was formed has not been allowed to take place, instead governmental and privately operated planning programs have resulted in a different kind of transition. Federal, state, and city governments continue to work at the staggering task of renovating the inner city to eliminate the substandard housing, overcrowding, and poor public facilities which still abound in some of these areas.

Zone III is also an area of workingmen's homes and usually "shades off" from Zone II gradually. In general the housing is slightly better, although still clearly below average for the whole city. Frequently, in smaller cities especially, Zones II and III virtually run together.

Zone IV. As one goes out further from the center of the city, the housing becomes more modern and less crowded. It becomes apparent that although still a workingman's area, it is definitely better by the accustomed standards for measuring the desirability of housing. Hence it gets its name "area of better workingmen's homes" or "middle-class family area." As compared to Zone III, Zone IV is characterized by more space, fewer children, larger incomes, better housing, and all of the numerous evidences of higher incomes.

Zone V. The gradual increase in the quality of the housing is apparent as one moves even farther out from the center of the city, ending in the fashionable suburbs with the fetching names—the "heights," the "monts," the "brooks," and the "parks." This is the area where there is economic abundance and security. On the whole, it is the area where the city's most prominent and successful business and professional leaders live. Here there is relative cleanliness and modernity. During recent years in a number of cities, better working-class housing has developed in and around some of the formerly exclusive suburban areas. Even mobile home communities can now be found in some cities within reasonable access to some of the more exclusive suburbs. A number of the suburban communities have their own schools, churches, and retail shopping areas. Often they also have their own local government, separately incorporated from that of the central city.

2. The regional conception

More recent developments, however, have necessitated a somewhat different conception of the urban area. As everyone knows, the influence of the city reaches far beyond even the suburban zone. Automobile transportation, particularly when coupled with good freeway systems, makes it possible for people living substantial distances to work and play in the central city with relatively little inconvenience and at modest cost. From the point of view of efficiency, distance has become simply a function of time and cost. Freeway systems have radically reduced both, so that it is no exaggeration to say that much distance has been, for all practical purposes, eliminated.

24. SIMPLIFIED ECOLOGICAL DIAGRAM OF THE URBAN REGION

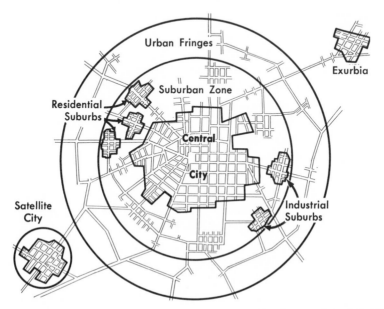

Source: Reproduced from p. 132 in THE SOCIOLOGY OF URBAN REGIONS by Alvin Boskoff. Copyright © 1962 by Meredith Publishing Company. Reproduced by permission of Appleton-Century-Crofts.

Figure 22 is a simplified schematic diagram of the urban region. It is, of course, generalized. Probably no central city has exactly the shape of the one presented here, nor are the various suburbs so distributed. Nonetheless, almost all American cities approximate this kind of structure.

a. Residential Suburbs. As indicated in the chart, modern suburbs are of several kinds, the first major distinction being that of residential as opposed to industrial suburbs. Residential suburbs, moreover, are by no means all the same. Boskoff distinguishes three types.[3] (1) *The traditional upper-class suburb.* This kind of suburb is marked by "a preponderance of long established, high-status families; comparatively little turnover in population"; it tends to have somewhat long standing

[3] Boskoff, *op. cit.*, pp. 134–135. Quotations in the paragraphs describing these three types of residential suburbs, as well as footnotes 4 and 5, all refer to this citation.

and a distinguished history. Some of these suburbs are almost a half century old and are associated in the minds of the city's residents with wealth, privilege, and distinction. (2) *The stable middle-class suburb.* "More recent in origin than the previous type, this suburban form is perhaps the most representative of modern suburbia. It attracts families from the middle income and status range, who seek relatively permanent residence in newly developed segments of the urban fringe. In general, the occupations of this group are concentrated in such professions as medicine, law, teaching, in medium level proprietors, and the more stable executive positions in commercial and industrial organizations." [4] (3) *The "packaged" suburb.* "This is the most obtrusive and controversial type of residential suburb—the recent object of much fiction and impressionistic diagnosis. In contrast to the other types, it is quickly and uniformly carved out of apparent nothingness deep in the urban fringe. Occasionally, it is referred to as the 'mass-produced suburb,' which indicates that most or all dwelling units are faithful replicas of one or two simplified designs and that the area is fully developed 'at birth' rather than a gradual accumulation of physical facilities, housing styles, and population. The packaged suburb reflects an insistent need for respectable but moderate-priced housing, which the stable middle-class suburb cannot satisfy. Most of the residents seem to be highly mobile (geographically and socially), comparatively young, and in the junior executive category of national corporations." [5]

b. Industrial Suburbs. This is a type of suburb about which less has been written than the "dormitory" type of suburb which we have discussed above. In the industrial suburb, people both live and work; obviously the occupation and class make-up of the population is "weighted toward the skilled and semi-skilled categories, and likewise toward lower and lower-middle status groups." The rate of growth in industrial suburbs has been much less than in residential suburbs, probably reflecting the changed occupational structure of the American

[4] Good examples of this type are discussed in John R. Seely *et al.*, *Crestwood Heights: A Study of the Culture of Suburban Life* (New York, Basic Books, 1956); and Alvin H. Scaff, "The Effect of Commuting on Participation in Community Organizations," *American Sociological Review*, Vol. 17 (April, 1952), pp. 215–220.

[5] Studies of this suburban type include: Harold Wattell, "Levittown: A Suburban Community," in William Dobriner, ed., *The Suburban Community* (New York, Putnam, 1958), pp. 287–313; William H. Whyte, Jr., "The Transients," in Llewellyn Miller, ed., *Prize Articles 1954* (New York, Ballantine Books, 1954), pp. 39–112 (these originally appeared in *Fortune Magazine* during 1953); William H. Whyte, Jr., *The Organization Man* (New York, Doubleday, 1956), Part VII. A readable and broad-ranging critique of the packaged suburb is John Keats, *The Crack in the Picture Window* (New York, Ballantine Books, 1956).

people. The proportion of the working force employed in manufacturing has been going down for some time—the dramatic increases in employment have been in service, professional, and clerical occupations.[6]

Characteristics of suburbs

There are several important features of suburbs which warrant special mention if one is to understand the structure of the modern urban region. (1) Residential suburbs have had the highest rate of population increase of an urban or rural community type for the last twenty years. (2) The sex ratio of suburbs is more nearly equal than for any other living area. (3) A higher proportion of both men and women are married in the suburbs as compared to the cities. (4) The average age of suburban populations is younger than that of the central cities. And, as would be expected, there are more children proportional to the number of adults. (5) Suburbs are more preponderantly "white" and, with the exception of the industrial suburbs, more native born.

Functions of the suburbs and resultant problems

The residential suburb has been called "a specialized outpost of the large city." It cannot be a community in the full sense of the word because it is not a place of employment for every resident and does not contain many of the essential services which suburban residents need and which they travel to the city to secure. The shopping center trend somewhat overcomes the incompleteness of the suburb, but there are still businesses which have not relocated in the suburban shopping centers; similarly with institutions of artistic and cultural nature, probably because these cater to so small a proportion of the total population that to decentralize them would destroy their traditional character. There are numerous middle- and even upper-class suburbs which do not contain such essential institutions as hospitals and from which the patrons of theaters and art galleries must travel to the central city for these services. It remains to be seen to what extent the shopping center trend will go in creating a service constellation which is rounded out for suburban dwellers' needs. Even if the shopping center should succeed in this one hundred percent, however, the community would still be fragmentized in the sense that much employment lies elsewhere.

[6] Throughout this chapter we have relied heavily on the formulations of Boskoff, *op. cit.*

From the city's standpoint, the residential suburb is a mixed blessing. Suburban growth adds to the urbanized population . . . But this growth is not immediately expressed in tangible advantages to the city. Until the suburb is absorbed by annexation or is economically linked by the municipal income tax, the central city discovers that suburbia cuts deeply into municipal revenues—principally in personal and real property taxes, sales tax returns, and in business taxes. In addition, Community Chest campaigns inevitably suffer from suburban movements, unless regional agreements encompassing suburban areas are reached.[7]

c. The Urban Fringe. It is more difficult to generalize concerning the urban fringe because it is a more heterogeneous composition of person-types and varies a great deal within itself as to the degree of fragmentation which it represents. Boskoff enumerates several "identifying features" of the usual urban fringe.[8] (1) They are generally located beyond the suburban zone but near major highways. (2) The land use is uncoordinated, an "accumulation of residential, commercial, manufacturing, and special service (private hospitals, cemeteries, etc.) types, with considerable amounts of vacant land." (3) The residential facilities "tend toward lower levels of attractiveness and physical repair." (4) "The employed population tends to be drawn from lower-status categories than are found in the residential suburb." (5) The urban fringe "normally lacks both urban services (e.g. pressurized gas for cooking and heating, adequate water systems, paved streets, etc.) and local social organization, such as its own government, school system, police and fire protection, and churches." It has been called "an institutional desert." (6) The outer rim is intermixed with active agricultural production. (7) Its boundaries are constantly changing.

d. Satellite Cities. The satellite city is a quasi-independent city but has such close dependence on the central city that it is not truly independent. Oftentimes satellite cities are older than the central city of which they have become a quasi-differentiated part. They are usually politically independent of the central city and supply their residents with the full range of community services but mostly of a distinctly inferior quality taken as a whole. Partly this is due to the fact that they are rarely able to afford such urban accomplishments as art museums, symphony orchestras, etc. Sometimes it is admittedly difficult to draw a sharp distinction in an individual case between a larger industrial suburb and a smaller satellite city. The two blur into one another.

[7] Boskoff, *op. cit.,* p. 139.

[8] Boskoff, *op. cit.,* pp. 140–141. All quotations in this paragraph are from this source.

e. Exurbia. The farthest thrust of the urban region is both relatively recent and somewhat rare. Only the very largest cities—New York City, Chicago, and Los Angeles—seem to develop one or more *exurban outposts,* which are located well beyond the fringe in what were originally rural or village communities. The exurban area may or may not be geographically continuous with the more familiar segments of the urban region. But it is nevertheless closely linked with the central city.

Exurbia is generically similar to suburbia, although the exurbanite often refuses to consider himself in the same universe with the suburbanite. Both types represent a basic ambivalence toward the big city; both wish to escape—but not too far (either physically or psychologically) from the cultural magnetism of the metropolis. Exurbia and suburbia differ, however, in their *opportunities* to express this ambivalence and in the *means* used to implement it.

The exurbanite, by virtue of his occupation, has superior opportunities for escape. He (or she) is typically in the "creative" branches of the vast urban communications industry—advertising, commercial art, radio, television, films, magazines, and playwriting. From an ecological standpoint, given the desire to escape, these occupations are significant in that they do *not* require daily attendance at a downtown office or studio. In addition, they yield comparatively large salaries—$20,000 and up, with an average probably around $30,000. Consequently, the exurbanite can easily arrange to live at a considerable distance from the central city, unlike the typical suburbanite.

If exurbia is therefore both residence and workshop, how are specific locations selected? Escape involves physical distance, of course, but also physical *contrast* with the city and some link with previous marks of successful escape. These conditions are satisfied by rural and semirural areas where artists and writers of the recent past lived and worked—e.g., Bucks County, Pennsylvania, and Fairfield County, Connecticut.[9] Exurbia is therefore a specialized, modernized, financially successful version of the artists' colony, located 40–50 miles from the commercial center with which it maintains a sustained symbiotic relationship.[10]

A functioning unity

Despite the differences which we have described and which are in many respects rather dramatic, it must be borne in mind that the modern urban region is a unity. No part exists independently of the others. Some connections, such as those between residential suburbs and the central city are obvious enough. Others, as with the exurbias, might

[9] Boston seems to have acquired an exurban area in Hillsborough and Rockingham Counties of New Hampshire. See *The New York Times,* February 5, 1961.

[10] Boskoff, *op. cit.,* pp. 144–145.

seem less essential. Yet the life of a city is a complex thing and the dependency of the modern city on the "creativity" of its exurbanites can easily, but should not, be underestimated. Dependency in the other direction such as the exurbanite's dependence on the central city is, of course, quite obvious.

Cultural lag in the urban region

It would be difficult to find a more dramatic illustration of cultural lag (that is, uneven rates of change between material and nonmaterial aspects of culture, see p. 421) than one finds typically in the urban region. Most problems of municipal government are essentially of this character. The traditions of local autonomy in police protection, for example, have made it exceedingly difficult to enforce laws and, of course, relatively easy, particularly for the professional criminal, to avoid apprehension. Taxation based on ownership of urban real estate was a fairly adequate way of financing government so long as people lived in the areas where the services were located. But how is the city to finance its central services when most of its more opulent workers live in other political jurisdictions? Several adaptations have been made to such problems as the above, but in each case only after considerable confusion and disorganization and sometimes interminable legal difficulties. Annexation has been one adaptation. This works fairly well for the immediately contiguous residential areas, providing the residents wish to be annexed—and they may refuse for a long time. The city income tax gets at everyone, but this presupposes state constitutions which permit such and/or state legislatures which are sympathetic to the problems of the central city. But even annexation and the city income tax and other expedients are a far cry from a political system which fits the economic and social facts of the urban region.

THE "COMMUNALITY" SUPERSEDES THE COMMUNITY

With new methods of transportation, with changes in types and forms of industry and of industrial organization, and with the domination of a money economy, man has tended to become increasingly detached from the earlier "home community" both physically and psychologically. This current social detachment has significant results for individual personality patterns, for local democratic activity and organization, and for community autonomy.

In the city hundreds of thousands of people are renters. They have little or no stake in the *place* in which they live except that involved in the month-to-month purchase of living space and conveniences. Many of them live in "furnished" rooms and apartments and have few *impedimenta,* except suitcases or trunks. They travel light. They move easily. They have no roots in locality. Even the owners are restless and frequently eye covetously newly-opened subdivisions with newer homes and up-to-the-minute improvements. Witness the recurrent "for sale" signs. Automobiles have widened the territorial range of people and both stimulated and satisfied their urge for adventure. There are sheer pleasures in the swift motion of the automobile and a sense of power in its manipulation. No wonder people spend much of their leisure in their cars, going places and doing things. "Neighboring," especially in the city, has almost become a lost art.

Who lives next door? Why should anyone be concerned unless the nigh-dweller gets too noisy or the children or dogs get into a fight? Today, the local resident is rarely socially dependent upon his neighbors; in fact, he frequently prefers *not* to know them. He chooses friends and associates, not because they happen to live near by, but because they enjoy doing the same things or because their work interests bring them together in a mutual association to protect and advance both their social and economic welfare. A few people may be politically inclined, and they are the ones who serve perennially on precinct and ward committees, especially on the election boards on voting day. Local residents as a whole vote casually or not at all. National elections are lodestones to the voting booths. School board elections tend to be the least interesting and compelling.

The general decline of interest in local affairs does not necessarily mean that people lack social contacts and activities. Within contiguous communities people inevitably gravitate together into congenial groups. If they have common interests they will get together, the only limitation being time and means of transportation. The place need have no special relation to their place of residence, but is determined by its convenience as a meeting place. It is this type of association which may be called "a communality."

The communality is an interest-circle characterized by the social nearness of members whose places of residence may be widely separated. It may be a formal or an informal group, as close-knit as a fraternity, as fluid as a public dance hall crowd. Its members belong, not because they share a place of common residence or are identified with the same community, but simply because they share like interests, ranging from the ephemeral to the relatively permanent. They meet together whenever they find it convenient. . . .

Communalities are as varied as the interests of people. They form a kind of shifting, shimmering overlay above the more stable, earth-bound community. They are territorially detached social groupings, and their activities run the gamut of social, economic, political, and religious concerns. They provide for the socially popular, as well as for the so-called social misfit. Their varied type and makeup permit the crossing of many social boundary lines. As a consequence, they provide opportunities for the expansion of personality in the easy give-and-take of social interaction.[11]

EVALUATION OF URBAN LIFE

Heterogeneity, anonymity, and wide personality range

Urban life is a specialized kind of existence for the human being. From the collective point of view, it may be characterized as *heterogeneous*. Hence a person may develop *highly individualized behavior patterns in the city* which in rural areas would not be tolerated by the mores, not necessarily because the mores are so different but rather because more of the person's behavior is conspicuous in a small and primary group society. With the *anonymity* of the city and the large population from which one may choose his associates, it is possible for the person to indulge his idiosyncrasies and eccentricities as well as find congenial persons like himself if he wants to. The "Greenwich Village" personalities apparently succeed in finding congenial associates among the large and diversified population aggregate of New York City. In a small town the same behavior would result in ridicule if not ostracism, and if the person in question wanted social acceptance he would have no choice but to conform. In the city, on the other hand, through the wider selection of specialized associations, and then by the reinforcement of his unconventional behavior and values through association within the special groups, *wider personality range* may be fostered. Thus, the city population may come to be characterized by greater individual differences as compared to rural areas. Its groups offer a congenial environment for the individualist who wishes to escape from the watchful eye of provincial mores. It does not follow, however, that the city causes the person to become deviant; it may merely make his deviancy more comfortable for him.

It is thought by some students of crime, for example, that the prevalence of crime and criminals in the large city is largely explained in terms of the principle here being discussed. In the large city primary contacts can be largely escaped if one so wishes, and anonymity be made virtually complete. The large population, the mobility, and the anonymity multiply the *opportunities* for behaving in criminal ways,

[11] B. A. McClenahan, "The Communality: The Urban Substitute for the Traditional Community," *Sociology and Social Research*, Vol. 30 (March–April, 1946), pp. 264–271.

and particularly offer better opportunities for escaping detection and apprehension by the law enforcing officials. Thus, a sort of antisocial society comes eventually to be organized. The paradoxical phrase "antisocial society" means that the criminal society is based on values which are contrary to those of the larger society, but the criminal society is, of course, a society in itself.[12]

For the ordinary person, however, who lives and works in the large city, urban living means merely that he must learn a number of specialized techniques required for successful urban living, like learning the folkways of subway travel, being more cautious about being exploited, learning the more formal and superficial way of casual conversation, and other folkways which make no fundamental difference in the important affairs of life anyway. Persons of rural origin usually adjust soon to the new demands of urban life. They tend to retain, of course, certain values and habits from their rural antecedents, but these personality traits seem not to interfere seriously with their successful functioning as urban citizens.

It seems that so far as our present knowledge goes, the chief significance of the city to personality lies in the *greater opportunities* for participation *in the more specialized and individualistic groups if one so desires.* These participations are, however, not universal for urban dwellers, the majority of whom share many of the basic sentiments and values characteristic of the overall culture of American society. Persons reared in the large city learn city ways by the same processes of socialization that rural children learn rural ways, but, as we have seen, their out-of-home participations are characterized by more secondary group contacts. They encounter urban ways and learn urban ways. There is no reliable evidence that the resultant urban and rural personality "types" are then necessarily unique or even clearly differentiated.

The antiurban bias

That urban life is *different* from rural life is obvious enough, but is it, therefore, a *less desirable* mode of life as compared to rural? It has become somewhat fashionable—a sort of intellectual fad—to decry the "terrible conditions" under which people are forced to live in cities. Such provincial judgment and beliefs are understandable enough when they are voiced by rural people whose ethnocentrism would be ex-

[12] See, e.g., W. C. Reckless, *The Crime Problem* (New York, Appleton-Century-Crofts, 1967).

pected to cause them to come to a negative conclusion about a mode of life foreign to them. Somewhat more surprising, however, is the same evaluation coming from some city dwellers themselves. The notion is prevalent both among urban and rural evaluators that urban life is an inferior mode of existence. The indictment is probably familiar to most persons, so we need review it only briefly.

The "indictment" of the city

Cities are said to be noisy, crowded, dirty, and disease laden. Life is monotonous in many specialized occupations; working conditions in numerous factories are not conducive to health and longevity. Even suburbias are said to be inured in a suffocating and insipid "togetherness." Despite a plethora of organizations and activities, children complain of nothing to do and their harassed parents complain of their inability to do anything about it. Activities are so rigidly scheduled as to make the person seem a mere robot. People are said to be "unfriendly, aloof, too reserved, too superficial, and not always trustworthy." Poverty and wasteful luxury abound side by side. The "moral tone" is said to be low, with gambling and prostitution prevalent, and the "sex theme" is much overplayed and commercialized not only in recreational matters but on every hand.

Moreover, urban dwellers are said to be a "self-indulgent and socially parasitic" people because their birth rates are so low. It has been necessary for cities to draw recruits from rural areas in order to maintain even a stationary population. The rural areas rear and educate these migrants at considerable expense; and when it is time for them to make a contribution to their communities, they migrate to the city.

These descriptions may be true enough. Suppose, however, we analyze the indictment further. First, the characteristics of city life can be divided into those which are remediable, that is, can be eliminated or greatly reduced when there is the will to do so, and those which are inherent in the city as a form of living. Among the presumably remediable characteristics are noise, dirt, disease, bad working conditions, excessive speed, and traffic congestion.

Already great strides have been made in many cities toward reduction and elimination of many of these dangers and nuisances. They are no more inherent in the nature of city life than outdoor toilets and folk superstitions are inherent in rural life. Both merely happen to be present at the time, and can be eliminated when there is sufficient knowledge and determination to do so. We do not mean, however, to oversimplify a complex problem when we make this point. Many of the city's difficulties such as traffic fatalities and congestion, smog and smoke nuisances are still very knotty problems. But there is tangible evidence from numerous cities that there are at least partial solutions to these problems within reach, whenever the citizens organize or otherwise cooperate to reduce the severity of such conditions.

Advantages of urban life

In opposition to the indictment of urban life—or rather whatever elements of the indictment still remain—should be placed a series of advantages which can be somewhat objectively evaluated. Urban life permits a great deal of specialization, thus enabling the society better to utilize the diversified talents and interests of its people. Cities, moreover, have taken the lead in providing better water and food inspection, traffic control, specialized medical and hospital facilities, better schools for children, and supervised out-of-school and recreational facilities for children. Cities have largely been the centers for research, education, and scientific development, many of the benefits of which have been extended to rural areas to reduce some of their own more undesirable characteristics.

DEMOCRATIC CONTROL IN URBAN SOCIETY

Much of the prejudice against urban life is due to the lack of knowledge on the part of some civic-minded, responsible citizens as to how they may exert effective collective control to eliminate many of the undesirable conditions of urban living. The city is apparently here to stay, although the biggest cities may become somewhat decentralized. No one seriously claims that urban living does not present problems, but sweeping depreciation of urbanism as a mode of existence seems to be largely wasted effort, unless it contributes to the eventual improvement of at least the improvable aspects of city life.

City dwellers need no longer assume that they must forever accept all of the nuisances and dangers present in the city. Many of these have come down from the recent past and are the result largely of giving free rein to the industrial and commercial interests which largely planned the city on the basis of criteria of financial gain, leaving the economically less favored persons to endure the squalor, while those who planned it now usually live with their families in the more costly and attractive suburbs. The point is not that industrial and commercial leaders deliberately planned the less desirable aspects of city life, but that they were in the past permitted a free hand in laying out the city primarily for the convenience of industry and commerce with practically no concern for the housing and recreational interest of the great mass of citizens of moderate means who have to live in the city because they work there. Nor should the commercial and industrial interests necessarily be blamed for doing what they were permitted to do under the existing laws and customs prevailing at the time when present American cities were being built.

There is growing evidence that enlightened groups of citizens are becoming more aware of their democratic rights to assert themselves on what kind of city they want and then to force the government to bring about the needed changes. Progress in the past has been slow because there were always convenient excuses. A new park would cost too much money. If there were laws requiring industry to reduce the smoke nuisance, industries would move out of the city to other places where the citizens were less exacting in their demands for a clean city. High traffic fatalities resulted from "poor driving," not from narrow streets, insufficient policing, and poor lighting! In time citizens not only have become enlightened concerning their rights under the law and the right to make new law but also have "seen through" much of the propaganda of vested interests who placed their immediate economic welfare over the eventual public good. In several cities great and sweeping improvements have already been planned and the legal barriers have been crossed, with the result that the next decades will probably see appreciable improvements in the livability of many cities. It is unfortunate that persons of the different social classes will probably share unequally in the coming benefits, but in a society organized around pecuniary valuation, greater power goes with greater wealth, and those who do not share too prominently in the distribution of income share comparably in social privileges.

SUMMARY

The modern urban region is at one and the same time one of the newest and most troublesome aspects of human relations. The two aspects are, of course, interrelated. Whenever one aspect of a relationship is changed, other aspects are disturbed, too. And most of the problems of urban living are problems of disequilibrium or disjuncture between the various parts. Admittedly, there is much catching up to do —assuming that that is possible—before urban living will become as harmonious as its critics and dreamers would like.

Yet the facts of urbanization are truly impressive. Metropolitan living is perhaps man's most recent and radical experiment in collective living. In many ways his greatest vulnerability as well as his greatest opportunities are inextricably intertwined in the urban mode.

And fewer and fewer escape the urban mode—or seem to want to. Modern society is, in fact, an urban society.

SUGGESTED READINGS

Boskoff, Alvin, *The Sociology of Urban Regions*. New York, Appleton-Century-Crofts, 1962.
A brief, dependable treatment of urbanization and the American city. This chapter has relied heavily upon Boskoff's data.

Gottman, Jean, *Megalopolis: The Urbanized Northeastern Seaboard of the United States*, Foreword by August Heckscher. New York, The Twentieth Century Fund, 1961.
Megalopolis is an awkward but descriptive word which Gottman uses to stand for the rapidly emerging belts of metropolitan cities which are growing up in Great Britain, Western Germany, the Low Countries, and along the Northeastern seaboard of the United States. This is a stage of urban development a step beyond the SMA as discussed in this chapter.

Mack, Raymond W., and McElrath, Dennis C., "Urban Social Differentiation and the Allocation of Resources." *The Annals of the American Academy of Political and Social Science*, Vol. 358 (1964), pp. 26–32.
Presents some important projections concerning the extent of urbanization in the future and its implications for social class, life style, and other sociological concerns.

Mumford, Lewis, *The City in History: Its Origins, Its Transformations, and Its Prospects*. New York, Harcourt, Brace & World, 1961.
Mumford has been one of the best known critical and persistent writers on the city. In a strict sense he is not a sociologist but rather a general social scientist-philosopher who always has something thoughtful to say.

Wirth, Louis, "Urbanism as a Way of Life." *American Journal of Sociology*, Vol. 44 (July, 1938), pp. 1–24.
A well-known article discussing the significance of urban living to the personality.

STUDY QUESTIONS

1. How do we measure the present extent of urbanization?
2. Compare the 1930 census designation of the metropolitan city with the 1950 standard metropolitan area (SMA).

3. Why were the "large cities" before the Industrial Revolution so small in comparison to modern cities?

4. What changes are taking place in the distribution of American urban population?

5. Why is it difficult to determine the reasons for urban growth? Make what you consider to be the best possible objective statement of the case.

6. What are the reasons for the suburban movement?

7. Compare and contrast the different kinds of residential suburbs.

8. Why are the industrial suburbs not growing rapidly—if at all?

9. If you had a choice, would you prefer to live in a satellite city or a middle class suburb, assuming the same amount of time and cost for commuting to your work? Why?

10. What is there about urban life which makes it so difficult for responsible and informed citizens to solve such persistent problems as traffic and parking management and the adequate financing of services to urban people?

11. What effect do you think the rapidly expanding freeway system will have on the shape of the future urban region?

12. What is meant by the "communality"? Why is it an "adjustment to urbanization"?

13. Is urban life better or worse than rural life? To what extent is the answer to this question an exercise in ethnocentrism?

14. What do we mean by the antiurban bias?

15. Is the exurban dweller primarily urban or rural? Explain.

16. What aspects of urbanism are involved in the "corporation farming" pattern?

22
SOCIAL
STRATIFICATION

DIFFERENTIAL STATUS AND SOCIAL STRATIFICATION

In all human societies from the most primitive to the most modern, persons are accorded *differential status*. Prestige, esteem, honor, and power, which are the manifestations of differential status, tend to be unequally divided among persons in different age-groups, between the sexes, and among those of different occupation, education, and lineage. Most modern societies have formalized some aspects of differential status with the result that groups and persons are placed into categories forming a hierarchy of rank, usually called a "class system" or, somewhat preferably, "social stratification."

The word *stratification* seems appropriate since the different statuses assigned to persons carry with them definitions of "higher" and "lower" value as compared to other categories of persons. In common language we speak of successful persons as "rising" or "coming up," and refer to "higher" and "lower" social position. The valuation implied in these language usages is clear. The people of the society regard certain persons and groups *as if* they were more important or more valuable than other persons and groups. Much formal lip service is paid to the democratic ideal in America which pretends that "everyone is equal to everyone else," but a more realistic examination of actual behavior makes it quite clear that people characteristically think and act in terms of conceptions of higher and lower social position.

Financial status not necessarily a determinant of social position

It is important to emphasize that the possession of wealth and income, which figures so prominently in American social stratification, is not the base of stratification in all societies. Among European royal families, for example, wealth has been a relatively unimportant factor, lineage being much more significant. In other societies education or occupation, irrespective of the income received, is the base on which differential position is determined. Race is sometimes the determining factor. In short, valuation is of the essence, and whatever the society has chosen to value highly may be the basis for affording differential status.

Wealth and income are, of course, not the sole determinants of social position even in the United States, although they are prominent features of the stratification system. Education and occupation also loom large. There are numerous cases of persons of great wealth and income who are not "accepted" by persons of higher status groups because they lack the necessary requisites of education and the "right occupation." Professional people, for example, are not among the most highly paid groups in the United States, but usually are quite acceptable in higher class society because they have other high-status, prestige-providing attributes. In most local communities, family background and length of residence are also factors affecting the person's class position.

FORMS OF SOCIAL STRATIFICATION

Taking a broad view of all societies, past and present, it is possible to distinguish certain recurrent forms or types of social stratification. Although the stratification systems of specific societies vary from one another in important details, they can be best comprehended by examining two sharply contrasting, or "polar," types: "caste" and "open class."

Caste

The most rigid form of social stratification is the *caste*. Membership in a caste is determined by birth. One inherits a caste position from which, with few exceptions, he cannot rise or cannot fall. In some instances membership may be acquired in a caste through marriage or adoption, but such instances are clearly exceptional. Caste is, therefore, a permanent basis of stratification for the person. It cannot be overemphasized that placement in a caste system is not determined by one's personal qualities, whether good or bad, or by the talents or wishes of the person. Lineage is the chief criterion.

No modern Western nation is characterized by a caste system, although there are certain caste-like attributes to be found in several. The position of Negroes in the United States, for example, has certain attributes of caste. Until recently Negroes and whites were forbidden by law to intermarry in fifteen American states, and some jobs are still closed by law or custom to Negroes. Segregation in some degree is practically universal. In spite of these facts, however, the position of the Negro in the United States is probably not truly one of caste. Segregation is not complete. Many occupations are shared by Negroes and whites, and the two races are not set apart by different dress or insignia of rank or the possession of exclusive caste goods. Furthermore, *within* the Negro group there is also social stratification based upon the same general kind of valuation that one finds in the dominant white society.

Caste stratification consists of rigid hereditary placement of the person irrespective of personal attributes or desires. Caste is often characterized by endogamy, occupational prohibitions and requirements, segregation, distinguishing caste attire and possessions, or some combination of these.

"Open-class" system

Open classes are distinguished largely in terms of the degree of ease and the frequency with which persons change position. An open-class system may be defined as a class system which does not place categorical limitations on the person with respect to his class position. This means that admission to another class is determined chiefly, if not solely, by whether he possesses the necessary skills pertinent to the role of the class to which he aspires, whether higher or lower in the hierarchy. So long, for example, as persons are barred from occupations because of color, creed, family background, or similar considerations, an open-class system cannot be said to exist. The open-class system may also be conceived as a "democratic" system, that is, a person's status is accorded strictly on the basis of his own personal fitness for the various roles which a given class position requires.

A continuum of stratification systems

The various forms of social stratification found in actual societies may be thought of as *positions along a continuum*. Caste and open class represent the extremes. Probably no perfect caste system or open-class system has ever existed, although some societies have come quite close to each. Thinking in terms of this continuum will tend to emphasize the fact that actual societies distribute themselves along a continuum, varying from one another *in the degree to which the individual secures his position by virtue of his own abilities and attributes, and the corresponding ease with which he may change his position if he has the requisite personality to meet the requirements of another stratum.* Stated in another way, societies vary along the continuum on the basis of the degree to which they impose categorical limitations on a person's social status and/or assign permanent position to persons on the basis of inheritance.

Thinking in terms of a continuum will also assist the student to comprehend the important fact that systems of social stratification, like all sociocultural phenomena, are *constantly changing*. A given society may move constantly and consistently in the direction of caste-like tendencies or open-class tendencies, or it may move for a time in one direction and then reverse itself. These sudden reversals have often taken the form of revolutions, like the Russian Revolution or the French Revolution, as a result of which the whole stratification system has been radically altered in a very short space of time. Like all social change, modifications of stratification may occur either through slow evolutionary development or through sudden revolution.

WHAT IS THE STRUCTURE OF AMERICAN SOCIAL STRATIFICATION?

While the facts of differential status, privilege, and power are obvious enough even to the untrained observer, it becomes exceedingly difficult to determine the precise system or pattern of stratification which characterizes American society. Different professionals, presumably of equal competency, see the system differently—sometimes radically so. An important sophistication should result from examining a number of their conceptions.

The three-classes theory

Traditionally we have loosely referred to upper, lower, and middle "classes," but how can one determine objectively that there are three "classes" rather than four, five, or seventeen? Furthermore, assuming for the moment that there are really three classes, to which of the three, for example, does the public school teacher belong? Measured by income she might conceivably be in the lowest of the three classes, and yet she sometimes enjoys the privilege of participating socially in many ways with members of the upper class. Furthermore, is the "class system" of an Iowa county seat town comparable in any realistic sense with the class system of an Atlantic seacoast metropolitan city? From these and other questions which could readily be formulated, it becomes apparent that it is no easy task to determine the class structure of the United States.

Two-class theory

The Lynds, in their famous *Middletown* [1] books, which are classic and penetrating analyses of a middle-size American city and more or less typical of much of Midwestern America, have made extensive use of a rough two-class conception of stratification which they term simply "the working class and the business class." The terms hardly need definition. "Business class" is used loosely to include persons engaged in commerce and the management of industry and persons in the roles ordinarily called the professions. While professional persons are not concerned strictly with business, some of them, like lawyers, veterinarians, and many physicians, are essentially highly trained persons who sell services rather than goods. Hence, they come very close to the business class because of the size of their income and their general social acceptance by business-class people. When issues are drawn between business and working-class interests, professional persons have, in the past at least, almost invariably "lined up" with the business-class point of view. One should not assume that all business-class persons necessarily receive higher incomes than working-class persons, for such is not the case. *On the average*, however, business-class persons do receive superior incomes, but their community position does not depend entirely upon how much money they receive.

Five- and six-class theories

Other students of American classes, for example, Warner in the famous Yankee City Series,[2] conceptualize the class hierarchy in terms of six classes. Critics of these studies, both professional and lay, have often made the point that even these somewhat elaborate formulations do not present a satisfactory explanation of the nature of the class structure of the more or less typical American community. The chief difficulty in accurately describing the class system lies in the fact that

[1] Robert Lynd and Helen Lynd, *Middletown* (New York, Harcourt, Brace & World, 1929) and especially *Middletown in Transition* (New York, Harcourt, Brace & World, 1937).

[2] See, e.g., W. L. Warner and Paul Lunt, *The Social Life of a Modern Community* (New Haven, Yale University Press, 1941).

25. An Outline of the "American Class Structure"

Ideal Typical Class	Percent	Central Value	Other Prominent Values	Miscellaneous
Upper Class Two categories: (a) "self made" man (b) inherited "position"	1%	"Gracious Living"	Not especially concerned with making money. "Family" important; "reverence" for the past.	Most will be in the *Social Register* and *Who's Who*. "He is usually much less overbearing than is the middle-class man."
Upper Middle Class Two categories: (a) "old middle class" (independents in business and professions) (b) "new middle class" (salaried men, the bureaucratic official)	9%	"Career"	Education—almost all are college graduates. "Outgoing" personality; fluent talker. Capacity to sacrifice for future success. Careful attention to "public behavior and reputation."	Class "contains many newcomers." Much spatial as well as occupational mobility. A deliberate "lack of tradition."

THIS IS THE LINE "BETWEEN THE BIG PEOPLE AND THE LITTLE PEOPLE"— "THE BASIC SPLIT IN OUR STRATIFICATION ORDER."

Ideal Typical Class	Percent	Central Value	Other Prominent Values	Miscellaneous
Lower-Middle Class "Semi"-professional "Petty"-professional "Petty"-agriculture Foremen "Many skilled craftsmen"	40%	"Respectability"	High School education and/or "some additional special training." Aspire to college for their children. "Most regular churchgoers of our society." Strong moral attitudes. Home ownership "a symbol of stability" and respectability.	"Often not sure where they belong." "Most will never get very far, and after they have outlived the romantic dreams of youth, they know it." "Solid citizens"

Working Class Typically a "semi-skilled factory operative."	"Get by"	40%	A complete separation of "life" and "work." Live "comfortably"—a faith that added gadgets are per se achievement Not much participation in community life.	"Not much point in working hard to get somewhere because there is no place to go." Work life is essentially routine.
Lower Class	"Apathy"	10%	Fatalistic Hedonistic "Live beyond the pale of respectability" Irregular employment Unstable family life	Live in substandard houses. No sense of future being "better." Recipients, in one way or another, of much charity.

Source: Compiled from many sources, but chiefly from a summarization by Joseph Kahl, *The American Class Structure* (New York, Holt, Rinehart and Winston, 1957), esp. Chap. 7. "Class" names, percentages, and "central values" are Kahl's distillation from abundant sources.

there are classes within classes; and unless one is quite familiar with the value patterns of the groups in question, he can easily err in his judgment as to where in the status hierarchy a given person or family really "belongs." Class differences are most easily appreciated when the observer is comparing persons of wide class discrepancy, and are not so clear when the rank difference is slight.

The continuum theory

In rather sharp contrast to all of the foregoing conceptions of the American stratification system is a point of view which we may call the *continuum theory*. This theory holds, simply, that there are no sharp —or for that matter objectively discernible—lines of demarcation which set off one so-called "class" from another, but rather that prestige and power differences are numerous and distribute themselves by almost imperceptible gradations along a continuum from top to bottom. The continuum theory is buttressed by a considerable number of field researches which have been done both in large and small communities and in a number of different regions in the United States.[3]

It should be stressed that there is no disagreement between adherents to the continuum theory and the categorical theories with respect to the *facts* of differential status or to the *effects* of these differentials upon individuals and the society. The only point at issue concerns whether or not there are agreed upon lines of demarcation which break up the continuum into a distinct number of strata.

Classes as ideal types

Despite apparent disagreement among various research workers and theoretical writers about social class, there are nevertheless certain agreements which should not be ignored. Moreover, some of the apparent differences are the result of how one looks at the evidence. Joseph A. Kahl in his excellent book, *The American Class Structure*,[4] sets forth an "ideal type" classification which is consistent with the bulk of our data and yet avoids the overstatement and oversimplifica-

[3] See, e.g., Gerhard E. Lenski, "American Social Classes: Statistical Strata or Social Classes?" *American Journal of Sociology*, Vol. 58 (September, 1952), pp. 139–145; Stanley Hetzler, "An Investigation of the Distinctiveness of Social Classes," *American Sociological Review*, Vol. 18 (October, 1953), pp. 493–497; Thomas E. Lasswell, "A Study of Social Stratification Using an Area Sample of Raters," *American Sociological Review*, Vol. 19 (June, 1954). For a fuller treatment of this matter see John F. Cuber and William F. Kenkel, *Social Stratifications in the United States* (New York, Appleton-Century-Crofts, 1954).

[4] Joseph A. Kahl, *The American Class Structure* (New York, Holt, Rinehart and Winston, 1957).

tion which often tend to mar otherwise good research. Kahl begins sensibly: "Let us avoid that argument altogether [the question of precise divisions between the levels] and admit that we will discuss five classes as a matter of arbitrary decision, based on the criteria of convenience in synthesizing the results of various investigators with a minimum of distortion to each." [5]

What, first, are "ideal types"? "They are not precise descriptions of reality, but scientific constructs which indicate that there are patterned relationships among . . . variables; they hang together in a meaningful way." [6] There is really little that is wholly new about the ideal type method of analysis, other than the name and some of the types themselves. Everyone has used ideal types, is familiar with some of them, and also probably familiar with the difficulties in their use. Here are a few popular ideal type constructs in common use in everyday language—"career girl," "swinger," "hippie," "brain," "loner." Almost any normal American knows what these mean and knows some people who more or less accurately "fit" the meaning. He also knows, or should, that there are people who partially fit the type and yet do not fit as perfectly as others do. Moreover, even for the person who fits quite well there are some aspects of his personality which are not accurately subsumed by the type which he admittedly fits. Despite the difficulties, however, the construct is useful for the person who knows how to employ it, though clearly an impediment to clear thinking for the too literally-minded person who cannot quite see that the useful abstraction and the concrete reality are not the same thing. It should perhaps be noted that we have used a number of ideal type abstractions in this book, among them bureaucracy, stratification, group, caste, primary group, and many more.

Now, what are Kahl's conclusions as to the ideal type classes in American society? What percent of the families of each community fall into each? And what are some of the main characteristics of each of the classes? *The answers to these questions will be found in the tabular summary on pages 402 and 403.*

The problem of interpretation

Kahl warns, again in his summary, against a too literal and too formalistic interpretation of these materials. "These ideal-type classes are helpful abstractions, but cannot be used without practical judgment; they will help us order our thinking about the complexities of

[5] *Ibid.*, p. 186.
[6] *Ibid.*

26. Occupational Prestige Ratings, United States, 1963

Rank	Occupation	Norc Score	Rank	Occupation	Norc Score
1	U.S. Supreme Court Justice	94		chestra	78
2	Physician	93	35	Author of novels	78
3	Nuclear physicist	92	36	Economist	78
4	Scientist	92	37	Official of an international labor union	77
5	Government scientist	91	38	Railroad engineer	76
6	State governor	91	39	Electrician	76
7	Cabinet member in the federal government	90	40	County agricultural agent	76
8	College professor	90	41	Owner-operator of a printing shop	75
9	U.S. representative in Congress	90	42	Trained machinist	75
10	Chemist	89	43	Farm owner and operator	74
11	Lawyer	89	44	Undertaker	74
12	Diplomat in the U.S. foreign service	89	45	Welfare worker for a city government	74
13	Dentist	88	46	Newspaper columnist	73
14	Architect	88	47	Policeman	72
15	County judge	88	48	Reporter on a daily newspaper	71
16	Psychologist	87	49	Radio announcer	70
17	Minister	87	50	Bookkeeper	70
18	Member of the board of directors of a large corporation	87	51	Tenant farmer—one who owns livestock and machinery and manages the farm	69
19	Mayor of a large city	87	52	Insurance agent	69
20	Priest	86	53	Carpenter	68
21	Head of a department in a state government	86	54	Manager of a small store in a city	67
22	Civil engineer	86	55	A local official of a labor union	67
23	Airline pilot	86	56	Mail carrier	66
24	Banker	85	57	Railroad conductor	66
25	Biologist	85	58	Traveling salesman for a wholesale concern	66
26	Sociologist	83	59	Plumber	65
27	Instructor in public schools	82	60	Automobile repairman	64
28	Captain in the regular army	82	61	Playground director	63
29	Accountant for a large business	81	62	Barber	63
30	Public school teacher	81	63	Machine operator in a factory	63
31	Owner of a factory that employs about 100 people	80	64	Owner-operator of a lunch stand	63
32	Building contractor	80	65	Corporal in the regular army	62
33	Artist who paints pictures that are exhibited in galleries	78			
34	Musician in a symphony or-				

Rank	Occupation	Norc Score	Rank	Occupation	Norc Score
66	Garage mechanic	62	79	Coal miner	50
67	Truck driver	59	80	Restaurant waiter	49
68	Fisherman who owns his own boat	58	81	Taxi driver	49
69	Clerk in a store	56	82	Farm hand	48
70	Milk route man	56	83	Janitor	48
71	Streetcar motorman	56	84	Bartender	48
72	Lumberjack	55	85	Clothes presser in a laundry	45
73	Restaurant cook	55	86	Soda fountain clerk	44
74	Singer in a nightclub	54	87	Sharecropper—one who owns no livestock or equipment and does not manage farm	42
75	Filling station attendant	51	88	Garbage collector	39
76	Dockworker	50	89	Street sweeper	36
77	Railroad section hand	50	90	Shoe shiner	34
78	Night watchman	50			

Source: Reprinted from Robert W. Hodge, Paul M. Siegal, and Peter H. Rossi, "Occupational Prestige in the United States, 1925–1963," *The American Journal of Sociology*, Vol. 70 (November, 1964), pp. 290–292, by permission of the University of Chicago Press. Copyrighted 1964 by The University of Chicago. Based on over 3000 random interviews by the National Opinion Research Center.

social realities, although they may encourage us to assume falsely that a community can be neatly divided with each family tagged and placed in its niche." [7] This comes very close to saying, as we have implied above, that there is a sort of paradox in the American class structure. While, on the one hand, these ideal-types are clearly discernible, yet, on the other hand, there is a very significant number of individuals and families who cannot be categorized accurately in this structure. If one focuses his attention upon the clear cases he concludes that there are discrete classes. If he focuses on the many unclear, mixed, exceptional cases, he concludes that there is a continuum. It would seem that Kahl's procedure and the sophistication with which he presents his conclusions imply clearly that there is merit and danger in both the discrete classes and the continuum theories, when either is accepted without regard for the other evidence.

The exceptions

Lastly, some comment is needed concerning those rather numerous instances, no one knows exactly how many, of individuals and families who do not fit into the overall structure. Why? (1) In many instances the case does not fit because the person or family is *highly and suddenly*

[7] *Ibid.*

mobile. They have some characteristics of the class they are trying to move into and other characteristics of the classes from which they have come. The *nouveau riche*, or *nouveau* poor, or the college professor who spent his boyhood in a city slum, or the Eastern businessman who grew up on an Iowa farm may be hard to classify, especially during their younger years, because they have something of the old and something of the new and one is not sure where to put them. Often they do not know where to put themselves, although usually they are more oriented to their hopes than to their origins. (2) Even though most marriages are homogamous (apparent tendency of likes to marry likes), a considerable number are heterogeneous with respect to class background. During the early years of adult life a family does not know where to place itself, nor does the community know where to place it. If one observes the career orientation and education of the husband, a family may look like "upper-middle," but if one focuses on the style of life and the recreational patterns of the wife, the family would have to be classed with her "working-class" origins. In time, assimilation will probably take place and classification may become easier. (3) Just as persons upwardly mobile are hard to classify, so are persons in *families that are slipping*. They may cling to old values but "feel squeezed because they no longer can buy the prestige they believe they are entitled to." (4) Then, there are the people who are *simply different*. Actually, there are two varieties here, those who really *are* different— individuals whose tastes or life patterns do not square with people of similar occupation or income—and a second group who make a self-conscious point of being different, because somewhere they have acquired a conception of the appropriateness of being "not like other people." Many times it is difficult to distinguish the two, and for our purposes that may not be necessary. Whether they are genuinely individualist or merely phony, there are enough persons and families of this sort to make classification difficult. Finally, (5) there is a class almost outside of the class structure which is quite numerous, oftentimes economically affluent, and cannot quite be ignored—the professional criminal groups and their associates in morally marginal occupations like gambling. These persons and families frequently have external characteristics—homes, automobiles, clothes, and recreational patterns —which strongly resemble the upper-middle class. Some of their values do, also. Yet a clear and generally recognized line of demarcation shuts them off from the mainstream of American society.

One further qualification, lest the ideal class picture that we have used here be taken too literally. There are marked variations from region to region in the United States and from community to community within a region. A mining town in Kentucky is not like Lexington and probably no community in Kentucky is like any community in Connecticut, except in the barest outline.

With these qualifications in mind, then, the student of American social stratification may, with sound empirical evidence behind him, think in some such terms as we have outlined.

SOCIAL MOBILITY AND THE AMERICAN STRATIFICATION SYSTEM

One of the fundamental American values, especially prevalent in that range along the continuum which we call "the middle classes," is the importance of what is called "getting ahead," by which is usually meant getting into an occupation and securing an income higher in the American value system than that of one's father. For males this is accomplished through such varied devices as getting an education, "working up" in an open bureaucratic system such as the army or some large corporation, and, of course, by "working hard." For women, getting ahead is usually accomplished by marrying a man who is getting ahead, although among unmarried career women the rationale is similar to men's.

There is sharp controversy among sociologists, as well as other observers of the American scene, concerning two aspects of social mobility: (1) *How many* persons actually succeed in getting further up the social ladder than their parents? (2) Is the number who do *increasing* or *decreasing?* One might think this an easy set of facts to acquire, but actually the problem, though much investigated, is still without a definitive answer. There is, of course, no dearth of persons unhampered by the requirement of objective fact who are willing to speak dogmatically on one side or the other of this controversy.

Varied interpretations

Joseph Kahl, whose work we have relied upon considerably in this chapter, applies an old sociological principle rather adroitly in his attempts to explain why persons in different positions in the hierarchy typically believe diametrically opposite things about the American stratification system. First of all, the statistics we have yield differing, almost opposite, conclusions. For example, "Sixty-nine percent of the business elite is recruited from other levels." This suggests considerable openness. But it is also true that the business elite is "recruited from its own level 7.7 times oftener than from other levels. This suggests a closing process at work." But we must look further. Would it not be expected that persons from the business elite, quite apart from any favoritism which they might later receive, would start out in life with a "favorable handicap" in the competitive struggle? They are familiar with the motivations, aspirations, and style of life of this group. They have access to the right kind of education and to various kinds of social contacts which a person from the lower echelons has to learn and sometimes even struggle to acquire.

It is understandable, too, why typically persons in different class positions *feel* differently about the openness of the system. "We should expect that at the upper levels there should be a feeling of openness, for so many have climbed. At the bottom . . . a sense of a closed system, for so many have remained. And the men at the unskilled level should be confused, for there has been much movement in both directions." [8]

SUMMARY

Differential status is a universal aspect of all societies past and present, primitive and modern. In most societies, differential status becomes formally organized or institutionalized into systems of social stratification such as caste and open-class arrangements. The essential difference among these forms of stratification is the extent to which the individual person is permitted to achieve his class status on the basis of his personal merit, irrespective of categorical placement or categorical limitations on placement.

Placement in the American stratification system is the result of a number of factors, some obviously economic like wealth and income, others indirectly economic like possessions and education, while still others may or may not be related to economic matters, such as family background or the possession of a special talent. It is difficult to determine the relative importance of these factors. Although the primacy of pecuniary valuation is clear, it is not the sole factor.

It is exceedingly difficult to outline the structure of the American stratification system. Some students appear to have found two, three, four, five, and six distinct classes! Others, aware of the lack of agreement, prefer to consider the American system as a continuum, rather than as a set of discrete classes.

Regardless of the above issue, the fact and significance of position to the person's well-being can hardly be exaggerated. From cradle to

[8] Kahl, *op. cit.*, p. 263.

grave, position in the stratification hierarchy is one of the most important facts circumscribing the formation of personality and the freedom
of action of the person.

SUGGESTED READINGS

Baltzell, E. Digby, *The Protestant Establishment*. New York, Random
    House, 1964.
A well-known and influential book relating the class system in America, particularly the WASP (White-Anglo-Saxon-Protestant) segment, to the so-called
melting pot. A forthright statement in vigorous language.

Crockett, Harry J., Jr., "The Achievement Motive and Differential Occu-
    pational Mobility in the United States." *American Sociological Review*,
    Vol. 27 (April, 1962), pp. 191–204.
This is one of the better studies, of which there is a plethora, which attempts to
relate the achievement motive (ambition) to mobility. One of the important
consequences of studying this research is that it heightens one's appreciation of
the complexity of the popular assumption that high ambition and social mobility
simply "go together."

Dobriner, William, *Class in Suburbia*. Englewood Cliffs, N.J., Prentice-
    Hall, 1963.
This study shows that suburbia, often treated as if it is a unified class system,
really represents a variety of different class identifications and characteristics.
An excellent antidote to the easy generalizations about *the* suburbanite.

Hodges, Harold M., Jr., *Social Stratification: Class in America*. Cambridge,
    Mass., Schenkman Publishing Co., 1964.
An up-to-date study of elements of stratification with special reference to data
on the American scene.

Lasswell, Thomas E., "Orientations Toward Social Class." *American Jour-
    nal of Sociology*, Vol. 65 (May, 1960), pp. 585–587.
This is an important refinement concerning attitudes ("orientations") toward
social classes. Distinguishes between mass and pluralistic stereotypes. This may
help to explain some of the inconsistencies found in the research on class attitudes.

Lenski, Gerhard, *Power and Privilege*. New York, McGraw-Hill, 1966.
A provocative and creative study of stratification which differs from most others in that the dimension of power is given pivotal treatment: "Who gets what
and why?"

Veblen, Thorstein, *The Theory of the Leisure Class.* New York, Heubsch, 1919.
This is a classic. It advances the theory that class position is affected, if not determined, by "conspicuous consumption" and the obvious use of leisure. Vigorously written.

STUDY QUESTIONS

1. What is meant by *social stratification?* Why is this concept a figure of speech?
2. Distinguish between differential status and a class system. Illustrate.
3. Discuss the *pros* and *cons* of the question whether persons in superior positions deserve their privileges.
4. Is there anything inconsistent about a stratification system and democratic ideals? How is it necessary to qualify one's answer to this question?
5. Why is it difficult to discover how many "classes" there are in America?
6. What aspects of caste are found in the position of the American Negro?
7. Why is it difficult to determine whether the American stratification system is moving toward caste or toward more "open" class?
8. What is the "continuum theory"? What evidence supports it? What evidence contradicts it?
9. What utility do you see in the phrase "class struggle" as applied to American society? What disutility?
10. How does stratification affect socialization?
11. Why is it difficult to determine whether social mobility is increasing or decreasing in the United States?

five

MAJOR SOCIAL INSTITUTIONS AND SYSTEMS

23
THE STUDY OF SOCIAL INSTITUTIONS AND SYSTEMS IN PROCESS

The behavior of people in a society has been conceptualized by social scientists in two main ways—we may call these, figuratively, the *atomistic* and the *molar*, or in the more technical nomenclature of contemporary sociology, *micro-analysis* and *macro-analysis*. On the one hand, behavior can be seen and studied largely as the actions of specific persons, their ideas, and their overt acts. This way of looking at the matter was taken in the chapters on social psychology. There we reviewed the research and thinking of social scientists in terms of such concepts as the socialization of the person, personality, norms, attitudes, self, personal deviation, and especially social roles. If we pursued our studies of the individual far enough and deeply enough we could *presumably* come to know everything knowable about human behavior. In contrast to this atomistic approach, there is another which we have termed the *molar*. Instead of focusing directly on the behavior of individuals, the scholar might focus on the collective aspects of human behavior. For this there is an old and strong tradition in sociology, probably older than the atomistic approach. In other words, the student of human behavior can focus on such large units of behavior as are suggested by the collective nouns *government* or *the family*, largely ignoring the specific people involved.

A key concept in this approach is *institution*. What do sociologists mean by the term and why is it useful as an analytical tool?

THE NATURE OF SOCIAL INSTITUTIONS

Little of the technical nomenclature of social science has given scholars as much difficulty as has the concept *institution*.

The difficulty has stemmed largely from the fact that the word had a vague but somewhat established core of meaning in the layman's language before the social scientists began to use it. That core of meaning, variously stated, was to the effect that certain basic values and the activities which embody them are important and relatively permanent aspects of each society. Thus the family, government, and other major segments of the society are usually referred to as "institutions." But a great many other phenomena, for example, capitalism, liberty, and some particular university or mental hospital, are also called "institutions." Hence the confusion.

The first essential to bear in mind is that the *term* institution *is an abstraction*, such as the abstraction involved in such generic nouns as government, man, life, or behavior. One cannot *perceive* any of these things. He can see *a* man, can observe *a* government, can observe *a* life or some *one* behavior. He cannot possibly see all men past and present. Therefore, we say, that one must *conceive of* an abstraction, like "man," though he may *perceive* some specific instances which approximate the abstraction conceived. So it is with an institution, such as the family, education, or religion. The words stand for ideas which are derived not from any one government or one religion, but from many governments and many religions, past and present, embracing both their similarities and their differences.

What are the *characteristics* or attributes of institutions? Angell's particularly perceptive and lucid treatment follows: [1]

Institutions are *systems of social relationships* to which people feel loyal because these systems are judged to *embody the ultimate values that these people have in common.* . . . Their acceptance need not be rational or conscious; it is often traditional or emotional. This is obviously true of such long established institutions as the family.

Societal institutions . . . are institutions expressive of so broadly shared an orientation that they *become the focuses around which the life of a society revolves.* There may be a few in the population who are indifferent or even hostile; but they are regarded as queer, and they are powerless to prevent the reception of the institutions by the next generation.

Institutions are *accepted not merely by all who actually participate in them but by all who share the common orientation.* For example, a bachelor can accept the institution of the family and believe it conducive to the realization of the highest values he cherishes. . . . Though the individual is within the structure he does not feel it as constraining. A father plays his

[1] R. C. Angell, *The Integration of American Society* (New York, McGraw-Hill, 1941), pp. 25–27 (italics ours).

role in the family loyalty, not from fear of legal sanctions if he does not, but from a *sense of the importance of* the family in the scheme of things that he values. . . .

Institutions and organized groups [2]

It is important to note a *distinction between the institution, which is an abstract nucleus of values* centering around some segment of human life, *and the specific organization and groups through which institutions are actually expressed*. For example, it is probably true that no two existing families in the United States are exactly alike in the manner in which they are organized, the purposes which they fulfill, or the activities which they carry out. In fact, striking contrasts exist. Moreover, a number of families are broken up due to divorce. Yet the institution of a permanent monogamous family is part and parcel of the culture of this society, and any deviations or variations from monogamy or permanence, even though they are numerous, are usually viewed as unfortunate occurrences and often regarded as morally wrong. (In a very real sense a divorced family illustrates the institutional principle of permanent monogamy quite as well as does a conventionally unified family. The divorced family had to secure legal permission to be dissolved and had to show cause before it would be possible under law for the courts to grant the couple the right to an exception to the institutional rule of abiding monogamy.)

In many other ways the *close relation of institutions* and associations or groups could be illustrated. The essential point is that *groups tend to embody institutions when viewed as a whole, but specific groups may embody institutions very imperfectly*. Therefore, one cannot infer the institutions in a society merely from the observation of one or a few groups, because he may find in the groups he chooses important variations or downright exceptions to the institutional pattern. One can *infer* institutions only from a broad and extensive, as well as deep and intensive, study of a great many existing groups, associations, or organizations of a society.

INSTITUTIONAL CHANGE

One of the persistent characteristics of man in society is his recurring inconsistency in wanting to have his cake and eat it, too. Nowhere is this more manifest than in the ways in which he acts overtly, and also

[2] This classic distinction is the work of Robert MacIver. See, e.g., his *Society: A Textbook of Sociology* (New York, Holt, Rinehart and Winston, 1937).

thinks and feels, about his institutions. Men constantly change their institutions; at the same time they pretend to cherish institutions and the traditions and sentiments which lie behind them and to hold them inviolate against the insidious pressures making for change.

The process of institutional change is almost always controversial and sometimes fiercely so. At the present time, for example, it is not at all uncommon to hear the term *communist* applied by many persons to other persons who simply wish to change some aspect of some institution. The use of the epithet and its companion terms *un-American* and *subversive* gives evidence of the fact that many find it difficult, if not impossible, to think calmly about the process of institutional change, preferring apparently to derive security from the ethnocentric logic that he who wishes something changed should be *ipso facto* suspect of malicious destruction of the sacred traditions. Strangely enough, the same persons who so violently oppose change in some one institutional pattern are themselves often advocates of change in some other one. A decade or two ago, for example, many were convinced that labor unions were "un-American" because they involved the introduction of a quasi-monopoly in the labor market; the same persons could see nothing "un-American" or subversive in a creation of large mergers in business which had as their purpose exactly the same type of outcome as labor unions did, and which were equally "foreign to our tradition." Or, to take another illustration, it is not at all uncommon for persons who employ married women to assert vehemently that "woman's place is in the home."

So general is this *ambivalence toward institutional* change that it should probably be regarded as a normal condition in the process of social living. All are dependent upon the securities provided by our institutions and so it seems altogether natural to view with alarm evidence which suggests that we may be bereft of some security through change in an institution. At the same time, men are to some extent rational beings, and frequently in their attempts to solve problems they discover that older institutional forms stand in the way of achieving desirable objectives, and that, if something were changed, goals could be better attained. This is perhaps the reason why the same individual may be simultaneously pushing for change in one institution and complaining about change in another, or be agitating for change in one aspect of an institution and opposing change in another aspect. Thus, the typical person is not opposed or favorable to change per se, but reacts to change selectively, depending upon how he assesses its effects upon his aspirations and values.

SOME OTHER SOCIOLOGICAL THEORIES
OF INSTITUTIONAL CHANGE

1. Sumner [3]

Sixty years ago, when social science was very young indeed, Sumner, who was then studying folkways, mores, and institutions, suggested three reasons why persons were unable to prevent change in institutions, no matter how great the effort in attempting to do so.

a. Failure of 100 percent transmission of culture. Anyone who has attempted to teach an abstract concept like "justice" or "loyalty" or "respect for women" or "property rights" to a child will readily recall innumerable instances, some of them often humorous, indicating how difficult it is to transmit an ideology from one person to the next. Communication is not perfect enough, teachers are not sufficiently skilled and perhaps not diligent enough, and moreover, the neophytes have wills of their own. Complaints of the elderly that youth are "going to the dogs" are as hoary as is the race, and the recurrent frustration of the parent is that he has failed to transmit to his youth the verities which he feels are fundamental.

b. Change in external conditions. Institutions are not things apart from the world of technological devices and geographical factors. Before the miracles wrought by science were commonplace, for example, it was much easier for more people to believe in a *personal* Deity, who watched over each and every person individually with the tenderness and wisdom of a loving parent. But now that we know what causes thunderstorms as well as most illnesses, and have created through the hydrogen bomb the capacity to devastate the earth and its people, the naïve faith of some of our forebears is much harder for many to accept. The point is not whether they are "right" or "wrong" in their difficulty, but simply that in one social setting a given ideology is much easier to accept than in another.

c. The strain for consistency. It will be recalled that in a discussion of culture it was pointed out that the various parts of a culture are often disharmonious, and sometimes great inconsistencies coexist. The same holds for our institutions, since they are essentially cultural. For a long time, for example, we have had a tradition in the family that the parents, being older, are therefore wiser than the children. Yet, in many ways, because of superior educational opportunities, children may actually be wiser than their parents in many matters. Thus we have the con-

[3] W. G. Sumner, *Folkways* (Boston, Ginn, 1907).

tradiction between fact and theory which presents a strong impetus for change in the parent-child relation. Somehow, in the long run, said Sumner, inconsistencies in the various cultural forms will be resolved; and, however they are resolved, some element must thereby have been changed.

2. Cooley [4]

Another early contribution to our theory of institutional change came from another sociological pioneer, C. H. Cooley. Cooley saw the process of institutional modification as a recurring cycle, consisting of four stages, each one inevitably bringing about the next. If we start at the stage of *efficiency* we find that the institutional forms (values, roles, attitudes) are well suited to carrying out human needs. Tersely, *the forms carry out the functions* satisfactorily. This happy condition does not go on for long, however, because, as we have already seen in the paragraphs above, conditions external to the particular institution in question may virtually force modification. This gives rise to the stage which Cooley calls *formalism,* that is, the forms to which behavior is supposed to conform do not carry out the function very well. This makes the institution somewhat inefficient because what people are re-quired to do is inappropriate for fulfilling their needs. Following for-malism, says Cooley, the institution becomes *disorganized.* While formalism could be characterized as "mechanism supreme" over func-tion, disorganization is "mechanism going to pieces." In a very strict and literal sense there is no longer an institution, for the standardization of behavior inherent in the institution gives way to a sort of anarchy in which no one knows what to expect as all pursue their needs individual-istically.

Many believe, for example, that the family institution today is in such a stage of disorganization. *The* role of women is impossible to de-fine in American society. Instead there are *many* roles for women—the "career" role, the "homemaker" role, the "glamour girl" role, to men-tion only three—and the inconsistencies among them are sometimes dramatic. During the confusion of the state of disorganization there is experimentation, says Cooley, with a variety of new ideas and behav-ioral forms, some of which work well in filling human needs and some of which do not. Eventually it becomes clear to many that some values and overt behavior patterns are better than others, these become wide-spread, and we are back to the original stage of institutional efficiency.

[4] C. H. Cooley, *Social Organization* (New York, Scribner, 1925), Chapter 30.

The cycle repeats itself, however; eventually, tendencies to formalism again creep in and the cycle begins anew.

Many modern sociologists feel that Cooley's theory is too general to be of great utility, because, to be sure, no one knows when "efficiency" will give rise to "formalism" or formalism to "disorganization." Nor can it very objectively be determined precisely when an institution is in one stage and when in another. Nevertheless, other sociologists feel that Cooley's generalized theoretical statement of the matter is useful—especially pedagogically—to explain some aspects at least of the recurring process of institutional modification.

3. Ogburn [5]

Somewhat later than Cooley and Sumner, another sociologist, Ogburn, set forth what has become a widely known theory of institutional change, called in the sociologists' argot the *theory of cultural lag*. Briefly Ogburn's theory is this: Society consists of two interdependent systems, similar to what we have earlier called *material culture and nonmaterial culture* (pp. 79 to 80) or more preferably, technology and a value system. A value system is most widely and firmly held when it is in harmony with the material facts in the technological system. For example, if an economic system needs capital for expansion, then the value of thrift makes for efficiency, because if people save money it can be invested and this facilitates the expanding economy. But if the economy is overexpanded, that is, if we have all the factories and other material resources which we can use, then the practice of thrift becomes negative; and the more persons save the more they contribute to the disruption of the economy. The gist of Ogburn's thesis, then, is that culture in general, including institutions, is continuously in the process of keeping values caught up with the more rapidly changing technological elements to which they unavoidably have reference.

Ogburn's theory has been severely criticized by a number of sociologists, the main lines of criticism being that technological change is not always in *advance* of value change, that values may change independently of, as well as in response to, changes in technology. Despite these criticisms, some sociologists feel that Ogburn, like Cooley and Sumner, has contributed something useful toward the understanding of institutional change, if nothing more than to have pointed out that the various parts of an institution change unevenly, with unequal resistance, and that the dislocations caused by uneven change create serious problems.

[5] William F. Ogburn, *Social Change* (New York, Heubsch, 1922).

We have reviewed these classical sociological theories of institutional change, then, not because any of them is a complete or wholly satisfactory explanation of what appears to be a complicated, evasive, and subtle process. Rather we have considered them because each of these represents a well-known and influential theoretical explanation with which the student of society ought to be somewhat conversant. The perfect explantion has not yet been formulated.

SOME MODERN ANALYTICAL CONCEPTS FOR STUDYING INSTITUTIONS

More modern sociologists than those whose theories we have just examined have approached the question of institutions and change from a less general focus. They have formulated concepts designed to illuminate one aspect or another of the nature of institutions and of the process of change. Several of these concepts deal with the *function* of institutions, that is, with what institutions "do."

1. Function and dysfunction

Although it is by no means always easy to discover what an institution does in a society, it may be necessary to make the attempt. Apprehending the functions of an institution is deceptively easy. In a very general sense, function is obvious—the function of the school is to teach, the function of the government is to govern. But, *how?* And what is "the function" of the family? Of religion? Our quest is not an easy one.

But let us suppose that we can reach agreement that an institution has certain stated functions. A list for the family might, for example, include the function of producing and rearing children, the function of regulating sex relations among adults, and the function of providing a system for the creation, maintenance, and passing on of property rights. There are probably other functions, but let us use these three for pedagogical purposes. Having agreed, then, that the family exists for these purposes, we then turn to a more detailed analysis of the behavior patterns which typically are subsumed within it. Upon doing so, we note that some of the typical forms of family behavior contribute clearly to the *facilitation of these functions*. These have been termed, appropriately, the "functional aspects" of the family. Specifically, we could list the division of labor between man and woman and the joint ownership of property as functional elements.

But all aspects of the modern American family do not facilitate the carrying out of basic functions. Some actually *impede the realization of the functions.* For example, some married women are employed outside the home; sometimes this employment is financially unnecessary and may have a baleful influence upon the children. Yet the trend toward the employment of married women with children is growing. Moreover, many of the recreational and leisure-time activities of the modern family detract materially from the well-being of the children, both in the financial deprivations which result and in the separation of the children from parental influence. Such patterns as these, which interfere with carrying out the basic functions, are called *dysfunctional.* Every institution has its dysfunctional elements, and speaking very generally, the efficiency or inefficiency of the institution is in direct proportion to the severity of the impact of the dysfunctional elements upon the functional elements.

Putting the matter in the way in which we just have has, of course, been something of an oversimplification. If one were to make a thorough functional-dysfunctional analysis of an institution, he would encounter at least the following very difficult problems. First of all, it is not always apparent what the fundamental purposes of an institution are. That is, different persons will not agree as to what the functions of an institution are or ought to be. As we shall see in some detail in a subsequent chapter on educational institutions, different persons and groups in a society disagree very sharply as to what functions are or are not appropriate to education. Obviously, if we cannot agree on purpose, it would be impossible to determine what is functional and what is dysfunctional, since practices cannot be functional or dysfunctional per se; they can be functional or dysfunctional only in terms of the agreed purpose.

Furthermore, the several functions of an institution may be in themselves inconsistent with one another. This can be illustrated in institutions of higher education, which are frequently charged with two objectives, often without recognition that they are inconsistent—to "teach students to think" and to teach students only the approved moral, political, and economic values. It is relatively easy to achieve either of these purposes, so long as one is not required also to do the other. Now, suppose we are trying to decide whether a course in "Anarchistic Philosophy" is functional or dysfunctional in a college. If we are trying to teach students to think, the answer would certainly be "yes"; but if we are trying to teach students only the approved values of American society, then the answer would be "no." Again, let us return to the illustration of the outside employment of married women with children. From the point of view simply of carrying out the child-rearing function, outside employment is probably dysfunctional. But on the other hand, from the point of view of increasing the family's standard of living, such employment might be both rational and functional.

Despite the above objections, however, the concepts of function and dysfunction in institutions seem useful. Surely we need to recognize that everything which exists is not necessarily equally good for the carrying out of given human purposes; some norms of behavior facilitate certain objectives and others impede. Even though we cannot reach complete agreement, even within ourselves, as to precisely what is functional and what is dysfunctional, the attempt to determine this should yield useful insights into the nature of institutions and the persons within them.

2. Manifest and latent functions

Another pair of concepts which some have found useful are *manifest* function and *latent* function. If we look at an institution closely, we will observe that it performs two kinds of functions that are essentially different. The first of these has been termed the *manifest* function, that is, literally, the obvious, apparent, largely agreed-upon function. The latent functions of an institution are usually less obvious and may, in fact, be disapproved by the values of some groups in the society —or even within the institution in question. Merton [6] aptly illustrates the distinction with reference to the political machine. The political machine is generally regarded as unequivocally bad, and a strong case can be made to discredit it through the use of democratic criteria: patronage follows from loyalty to the party rather than from competency for the office held; votes are garnered by techniques which have little, if anything, to do with the merits of the issue or the qualifications of the candidate; and bribery and other kinds of "honest graft" are too common to need documenting, especially in the large city political rackets. Despite these facts and periodic attacks upon the machine system, the political machine, varying in detail from one city to another, seems here to stay. Obviously, then, the machine must *do something*—must perform some function. Among the functions which Merton mentions are these: "the precinct captain is forever a friend in need . . . food baskets and

---

[6] Robert Merton, *Social Theory and Social Structure* (New York, Macmillan, 1949), pp. 70–81.

jobs—setting to rights minor scrapes with the law . . . looking after the bereaved—the whole range of crises when a feller needs a friend." Merton emphasizes that the precinct captain's function to the rank and file is not wholly *what* he can do, but also the *way* in which he can do it—no red tape, no records, no loss of self-respect, all of which go with the formal legal means of getting assistance. But the political machine also serves another group, says Merton—business, both legitimate and illegitimate. Many times a business, large or small, wishes to "get something done" which may be illegal; or it merely wishes to expedite something which is legal, but wants to avoid the "red tape" and time loss that result from following correct channels. There are other functions as well, but perhaps enough has been said to indicate what Merton means. His point is that within institutions—in this case, government, or more specifically party organization—will be found subgroups and activities which may seem to work at cross purposes with the functions of the institution. But they perform functions, and sometimes quite useful functions, which are latent in the realities of the social system in which they operate.

Obviously the manifest and latent concepts are related to the functional and dysfunctional elements, although they are by no means the same. The latent function may or may not be dysfunctional in the original sense in which we used the terms.

The concept of sociopathy

Related to the foregoing is the concept *sociopathy*.[7] We are familiar with the concept of biopathy (malfunction of the organism) and psychopathy (malfunction of the person). Sociopathy refers to the malfunction of the society, or some part thereof. An institution may be said to be sociopathic, according to Bain, when it fails to satisfy needs effectively; when it interferes with the satisfaction of human needs by other institutions; when its ideology contains internal inconsistencies; when it fails to adjust to technological and ideological changes in its own and related institutions; and when it wastes human and other resources.

Obviously, there will not be clear agreement among all observers that a given condition, such as the waste of student talent in educational institutions by employing outmoded instructional techniques, is sociopathic. Nevertheless, the concept has utility in focusing, like the con-

[7] Read Bain, "The Concept of Sociopathy," *Sociology and Social Research*, Vol. 38 (September–October, 1953), pp. 3-6.

cept dysfunction, upon the fact that all aspects of institutions are not of the same order of utility to man. Perhaps that is why there develop from time to time strong demands by some persons at least for the modification of some aspect or another of various institutions.

DIFFICULTIES IN THE STUDY OF INSTITUTIONS

In a superficial but important sense, everyone is his own expert on the institutions of his society. Practically every person stands willing, even if not very able, to discuss with conviction any institution which one may mention. Few persons will admit much doubt that they know what is right or wrong with the government or with the family, what religion does, and what the schools ought to do!

On the contrary, sociologists and other social scientists who devote their professional lives to the analysis of institutions find their task difficult and elusive. So subtle are many of the aspects of institutions that they escape even the studied scrutiny of the trained sociological eye. And even when the professional student of an institution has objectively discovered some truth, and that truth has been verified by other scholars, it is not at all uncommon to have the findings summarily rejected by some much less able individuals who are accustomed only to analyze the grosser dimensions and are content only with conventional explanations.

1. Multiple causation

At several points in this book we have referred to the principle of multiple causation. Broadly speaking, one of the main differences between the layman and the social scientist lies in the latter's awareness of the multiplicity of factors that bring about a given condition. The layman, on the other hand, usually tends to seize upon some one or two factors to explain a situation, when actually a dozen or more are manifestly operative. This is especially true in connection with institutional change. Practically any man on the street "knows" without a moment's reflection why there is a high divorce rate, while experts who have spent a lifetime studying this fact would be very reluctant to offer even a definitive *list* of the reasons.

2. Problems of measurement

Ideally, in order to describe or to indicate the degree or direction of change, it is necessary to measure the phenomenon in question. In many aspects of sociology, measurement has become highly refined, but for the most part studies of institutions still remain in the pre-measurement stage. There are several reasons for this. First, many of the *questions* which both laymen and professionals ask about institutions are *not in such a form that the relevant phenomena can be measured.* For example, a current issue centers around whether public schools are doing a better or a worse "job of educating our youth" than did the schools, say, of twenty years ago. This might at first seem to be an easy question to answer, but upon further examination it becomes practically a conundrum. To be sure, we can measure how well high school graduates of today spell, write, or read. But the high school graduates of twenty years ago are now adults and no one knows with certainty how they spelled and wrote and read when they were graduated. Furthermore, education is more than merely the langauge arts. How can we measure the effectiveness of education on such vital intangibles as character, citizenship, and personality? Would liberals and reactionaries agree, moreover, as to what good "citizenship traits" are? It has probably already become apparent that what at first appeared to be a simple question about the functioning of one part of one institution has become virtually unanswerable in scientific, objective terms. This does not mean, of course, that we are devoid of *all* knowledge, or that there is no utility in discussing the question with whatever factual material we have; but we must say that the ideal of scientific definitiveness appears yet far, far away.

3. Statistical interpretation

The alert student will readily recognize that abundant statistical materials are available on a great many aspects of institutions. The census reports the American family size to two decimal places. The Bureau of Labor Statistics publishes cost-of-living indexes every month for the nation as a whole and also for principal cities. The FBI publishes crime rates of several sorts. Economists can tell us how much the average family makes per week and how many pounds of ham are consumed per capita per year. And so we might go on and on indefinitely. Are not these statistical data useful for something? Do they not describe certain dimensions of American institutions?

The answer to the above question, to be accurate, must be "yes" *and* "no." Part of the problem, at least, resides in the fact that very few persons are trained well enough in statistical matters to know how to *interpret* most of the statistical data which they may be able to *read.* Sometimes, despite abundant statistical materials, a commonsense answer to "how many" cannot be given. For example, there are at least five different methods for measuring the divorce rate, all of which are reliable and useful for certain purposes. The conclusions which could safely be drawn from these data are that anywhere from one in three or four to about one in twenty-five marriages end in divorce! What, then, is "*the* American divorce rate" in which everyone seems interested?

Another difficulty with statistical data is that sometimes it is *designed deliberately to mislead*. Many private sources, and also some public ones, compile statistics on some aspect or another of American institutions; regrettably their purpose is not strictly to achieve accuracy. Add, then, to the difficulties of interpretation, the mischievous distortion of the facts; and there is small wonder why so many despair of trying to get at the truth of larger social questions by the statistical route. The expert in some measure can, but the layman had best be very cautious.

4. Semantic confusion

Of necessity, in the analysis of institutions, as in other matters, we use language. Language is supposed to facilitate communication by rendering it more precise and objective. But here again we encounter a dubious legacy. Most college students have already recognized that the same word means different things to different people; also any discussion can be turned into a debacle by calling someone a "liberal," since the word has almost as many meanings as there are participants. Similarly what is "progressive" education, or for that matter what is "education," what is "democratic" government, what is "free enterprise," *ad infinitum?*

Sometimes it is naïvely thought that only the uneducated share this confusion, that once one has "cultivated his mind" he will be able to rise above the frantic semantics of the usual popular discussion. Unfortunately, this faith is not always vindicated. Addressing himself to university students and teachers, the eminent Max Weber, a German sociologist, once distinguished two kinds of words. He said that words might be used either as "plowshares to loosen the soil of contemplative thought" or as "swords" with which to do battle "against the enemy." [8] Probably no one is free, even the educated, from a confusion of the two. Unfortunately, even in professional discussion and in serious, high-level professional writing, there is evidence, particularly when discussing institutional issues, that the high level of objectivity so rigorously

---

[8] Quoted in Logan Wilson and W. L. Kolb, *Sociological Analysis* (New York, Harcourt, Brace & World, 1949), p. 11.

taught to graduate students is not always manifest among their teachers.

These difficulties notwithstanding, social scientists of various kinds, along with laymen, continue to think about institutions in ways which best suit their various purposes. Generally speaking, academic men have fewer axes to grind, by training and circumstance have fewer vested interests, and at least at times approximate the ideals of objectivity.

In this spirit of trying to be objective, the following five chapters will each be devoted to a somewhat detailed discussion of some of the more salient aspects of each of the five major institutions, those which sociologists seem generally to agree are the pivotal ones in American society—family, government, education, the economy, and religion.

SUGGESTED READINGS

Bain, Read, "The Concept of Sociopathy." *Sociology and Social Research,* Vol. 38 (September–October, 1953), pp. 3–6.
A short, well-written statement suggesting the use of the concept *sociopathy* to interpret certain institutional conditions.

Hertzler, J. O., *American Social Institutions: A Sociological Analysis.* Boston, Allyn and Bacon, 1961.
Hertzler has been an authority on American social institutions for at least thirty years. This treatment of American institutions, on a high level of generalization, will be found useful for an overview of the American institutional structure.

Inkeles, Alex, and Geiger, Kent, *Soviet Society: A Book of Readings.* Boston, Houghton Mifflin, 1961.
A carefully selected and critically presented set of readings on Soviet society drawn from a variety of sources. It covers a variety of topics from ideology and economic life to "everyday living." As an authoritative treatment this is hard to duplicate.

Lipset, Seymour Martin, *The First New Nation.* New York, Basic Books, 1963.
An excellent book which not only identifies contemporary American values but does so through a consideration of their historical development.

MacIver, R. M., *Society: A Textbook of Sociology.* New York, Holt, Rinehart and Winston, 1937.
A classic statement of the theory of institutions and associations.

Merton, Robert, *Social Theory and Social Structure.* New York, Macmillan, 1949.

An advanced treatment of a number of Merton's original contributions to institutional theory. For the more advanced student.

Williams, Robin, Jr., *American Society*. New York, Knopf, 1960.
An excellent treatment of American institutions from the structural-functional point of view. See esp. Chapters 6, 7, 8, 9.

STUDY QUESTIONS

1. What is meant by an "institution"? Why does the abstractness of institutions present difficulties for the student?
2. Distinguish between institutions and associations.
3. What examples of ambivalence toward institutional change have you observed among persons you know?
4. Why are so many people ambivalent toward institutional change?
5. Explain the theories of Sumner, Cooley, and Ogburn regarding change in institutions.
6. Why is the cyclical theory of institutions (Cooley) very difficult to apply to concrete cases?
7. What criticisms do you see of the culture lag hypothesis with respect to institutions? Despite these criticisms, what utility does the theory have?
8. Select some organized association with which you are familiar and discuss some of its functional and dysfunctional elements.
9. What are some of the manifest and latent functions in your college or university? Do you think the faculty would agree with your choice of latent functions? Would the public?
10. What similarities do you see between the concept of sociopathy and the concept of dysfunctionality? Illustrate.
11. Illustrate multiple causation in relation to the change in some institution with which you are familiar.
12. Why is it difficult to secure the necessary information frequently required in order to answer questions of institutional change and also of efficiency?
13. Explain how we may have abundant statistical information about an institution and still be unable to understand many aspects of it.
14. What is meant by "semantic confusion" in relation to institutional analysis? Why does this condition exist?

24
MARRIAGE
AND THE FAMILY

In previous chapters we have discussed several significant aspects of the family institution and have advanced a number of basic principles pertaining to it. The family is a universal social grouping found in broad outline in every society. Family makeup, however, is highly variable, including such divergent forms as polygyny, polyandry, and group marriage, as well as the monogamous form with which Americans are familiar. The requirements of the roles of husband, single adult, married adult, parent, and child are likewise radically variable. What is characteristically male behavior in one society may be typically female behavior in the other. Authority for governing the family may be vested solely or largely in the husband, solely or largely in the wife, or may be a combination of these two.

The family, like all social forms, changes. The rate and direction of change has varied considerably at various times and among various societies, but the fact of change has never been successfully resisted by any people which social scientists have been able to study. Considerable effort is often put into contriving ways and means of preventing family change through law, church dogma, and informal public pressures. At best these devices serve only to reduce the speed of change (if they even achieve that), but they cannot prevent change.

Not only do the norms of family life vary but so also do specific families vary from the norms characteristic of the larger society of which they are a part. Thus, in any society one can find individual cases of marked variation from the general family pattern. Numerous married women in our society, for example, are employed outside the home. Some couples are deliberately childless, and in some families greater authority is held by the wife. Moreover, it is common knowledge that there is widespread variation in the standards of sex conduct to which different people adhere.

With this background in mind, we now turn to a somewhat more specific treatment of the contemporary American family.

431

27. Trend of U.S. Marriage and Divorce Rates, 1887–1965

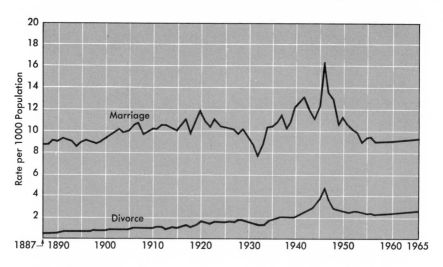

Source: Public Health Service, U.S. Department of Health, Education and Welfare.

STRUCTURAL AND FUNCTIONAL CHARACTERISTICS OF THE MAJORITY AMERICAN FAMILY

Viewed in bold outline, and disregarding the special cases such as the Amish, the entertainment subculture, the beatniks, the racketeer, and the mountain whites, the "American" family structure at the mid-twentieth century can be subsumed in a number of general dimensions. It should be clear to the student by now that the following statements must be of a high order of generality, that is, all of them do not apply to every specific family and even when they do apply, they do not all apply equally. These characteristics taken together, however, describe the *typical* or majority American family structure. A number of these characteristics are also found elsewhere in the world, but together they describe an overall pattern probably found most typically in the United States and Canada.

1. A small or "nuclear" family

The American family is typically small in two senses. Perhaps most important, it is usually comprised only of a married pair and their sub-adult children. This is in sharp contrast with many parts of Asia, and to a less striking degree elsewhere in the world, where the "great family" or "extended family" is found, consisting of a number of re-

lated pairs, their children, and a miscellany of older and variously related adults. In the great family structure a household may include
fifty or more persons. The nearest suggestion of the great family that
we find in America is the awareness of kinship ties with relatives, but
these kin do not usually share a common domicile nor own property
jointly nor have much responsibility for each other's well-being. In
relatively recent years the number of American homes in which periph-
eral family members, such as grandparents or aunts and uncles, are
part of the family circle has materially declined. So general is the small
family that in some communities it is difficult to buy a new house with
more than two, or at most three, bedrooms.

In a second sense the American family is a small family, namely
with respect to the number of children born to each married pair. "By
their practices and stated ideals, it seems that Americans do not want
families of six or more children and also strongly reject a no-child or
one-child family. The emerging value . . . is toward a moderate size
family of two to four children." [1]

2. Equalitarian ideals

The American family is in the process of emerging from a patriarchal tradition in which superior power and prestige were vested in
the male, and especially in the older male. Children, moreover, were to
be "seen and not heard," and while typically treated with sentimental
affection, few persons thought it necessary or desirable to take the
wishes of children, or especially their judgments, at all seriously.

The process of emergence from this patriarchal tradition is not yet
complete—if it ever becomes so. Generally speaking, women have received more *theoretical* legal, political, and economic equality with men
than they have *actual* social equality. Put in another way, the attitudes
of men and to some extent of women, also, are not as equalitarian as one
might think from listening to inspirational speeches and editorials about
the complete emancipation of women. At present many more men than
women go to college, and a much higher percentage of men than of
unmarried women are gainfully employed.

Even casual observation reveals the fact that the man who has a
truly equalitarian concept of women in such diverse roles as important
political office-holder, automobile driver, or business executive is indeed rare. This does not mean that impressive evidence could not be

[1] William F. Kenkel, *The Family in Perspective* (New York, Appleton-Century-
Crofts, 1966), pp. 225–226.

marshaled to show that the equalitarian ideal is *growing* in acceptance, but rather that it has not yet become a *fait accompli.*

Why, then, do we say that one of the structural characteristics of the American family is an equalitarian ideal? There are two justifications for such a position. First, compared to our antecedents and to most of our contemporary cultures, the American family system is more equalitarian than it is patriarchal. In the second place, as an ideal cultural norm, equalitarianism is held as an almost sacred principle. Despite the contradictions to be found in real behavior, few Americans would question the *principle* that women are and ought to be the equals of men in all social matters. The evidences of a smarting conscience and a defensiveness about overt behavior or attitudes inconsistent with that ideal constitute a tacit admission of the omnipresence of the equalitarian ideal which should not be overlooked.

The situation with respect to children, while less frequently discussed, is quite similar. Particularly in the more educated classes, but to a considerable extent elsewhere, also, there is a growing recognition of the morality as well as the practicality of allowing children and very young adults an increasingly large measure of freedom of judgment and action. Again, as with women, survivals from the older tradition are evident and the change has come about very unequally from family to family; but comparisons with other cultures and with our own recent past certainly give evidence of the emergence of this kind of equalitarianism, too, in America.

3. Happiness orientation

This caption may strike some readers as a little strange. Do not people always prefer happiness? Possibly so. But the American family is deemed to be the chief *source* of what is here called "happiness," and the chief reason for entering into, or escaping out of, a particular marriage is almost universally regarded in terms of whether the change will make the persons more "happy." The fact that many of these individual judgments may be erroneous is beside the point. We are simply stressing the fact that happiness is regarded as a particularly desirable thing, and marriage and family life are supposed to contribute largely to it. To be sure, persons in certain religious traditions, and to some extent everyone, hold certain values of duty in relation to marriage; but by and large duty values are subordinate to happiness values as the *raison d'être* of marriage and family life in America today.

4. Apparent instability

Partly as a result of the foregoing characteristics, the American marriage and family system appears to many to be an unstable one. Alarmists are found on every editorial staff and in many pulpits, and at least one can be found in every bull session. The theme is well worn—there is a high and rising divorce rate, sexual irregularity is common, parents cannot control their children as they should, so large a part of the population is transient with no community and friendship "roots" anywhere, and so on. The facts as stated are essentially correct. There is an uncomfortably high proportion of marriages which end in divorce, desertion, and informal separation, or endure in spite of interminable incompatability and unhappiness in the family circle. Moreover, all of these have a baleful influence upon children and also, of course, upon the adults, both those directly and those indirectly involved. There is no denying the fact that in most communities a substantial number of parents, if not a majority, seem either unwilling or unable to control the behavior of their adolescent children sufficiently to avert a substantial amount of officially recorded juvenile delinquency, and even more goes undetected.

But are these signs of instability or simply of a new order of things? The conventional view of divorce, for example, is one of couples willfully pursuing their own desires, irrespective of moral obligations. But many Americans think that there is another interpretation of the evidence. The overwhelming percentage of divorced persons marry again, and usually quite soon. While all of the evidence is not yet available, there is certainly enough to indicate that the success rate of second marriages is, in contrast to the folklore, high. Apparently divorced persons, like single persons, have no lack of faith in marriage as a way of life, despite the fact that American society makes rather comfortable provision for the unmarried, both economically and socially. The American population is becoming increasingly a married population. This fact seems not generally known, despite the ample documentation of it in the United States census for a number of decades now.

The foregoing is not to be taken as categorical that the American family, taken as a whole, should be regarded as either stable or unstable. Rather it is intended as a caution against a too quick acceptance of partial facts and questionable logic often marshaled to buttress a traditionally comfortable conclusion. Certainly, however, there is an *apparent* instability, and what may be even more important, there is a widespread *belief* among professional and lay people that the American family system is dangerously unstable. This belief, even if erroneous, is a significant fact in shaping the expectations and judgment of people regarding their own and others' families.

5. An apparent defunctionalization

The European and early American family of the nineteenth century performed a larger number of functions for its members than the present family does. In addition to rearing somewhat larger average families than are reared today, the home was to a considerable extent a small manufacturing unit for making clothing, for canning and other food processing, and often for the growing of food. Moreover, much of the recreational activity of the people was centered in the home and in neighborhood primary groups. The early family also performed numerous welfare functions such as care of the aged, the sick, and destitute relatives.

It is evident that in each of the respects mentioned above, the American family's functions have declined or been transferred to other groups. A host of service institutions from bakeries and delicatessens to beauty salons and diaper services have grown up to do work formerly done by the family members for themselves and each other. Public schools take children at an earlier age, and nursery schools, in the cities especially, are available for the care of preschool-age children. Government and private charity are more and more taking the family's place in caring for the aged, the destitute, the handicapped, and the sick. Health needs are increasingly cared for in hospitals and clinics. Schools not only take children at an earlier age but occupy the children's time through extracurricular activities for longer hours. And so on.

There are those who decry this trend, pointing out that so many of the traditional family functions have been transferred to other institutions that the family is left with "nothing to do." Such a view of the matter seems hardly accurate as a general interpretation, although perhaps in certain instances it might be applicable. It is quite possible that the family may have taken on functions which are less conspicuous than those it has lost, but possibly more important. For example, the standards of child rearing have certainly risen during the last fifty years. This applies not only to the physical requirements of feeding, clothing, and health provision but also to psychological services to the child of which increasing numbers of parents are becoming conscious.

Perhaps the time formerly spent in baking bread and making children's clothes may now be spent in studying children's nutritional needs and in supervising and planning the child's recreation. Moreover, there is some evidence to indicate that husband-wife companionship may be greater when less time must be devoted to the economic aspects of the family. There is no assurance, of course, that such will be the case always, but the point is that to many couples companionship with one another and recreational activities in common are important values, and values which can be attained only if there is available time for such activity. No one can scientifically determine, of course, the answers to such imponderable questions as whether the "old-fashioned family" was, on the whole, "better" or, on the whole, "not so good" as the present family. All that can be said is that the present family's functions and activities are *different* and that the difference is such as to provide the *possibility* for what are commonly regarded as improvements in the quality of child rearing and husband-wife companionship.

6. Morality: real versus ideal patterns of conduct

Morality, too, is somewhat different. Opinions differ widely concerning the extent of moral change and the desirability of it. The sociologist usually does not become as excited about changes in morality as some persons do because of his familiarity with the facts of moral variability in past times and in other cultures. Objectively it can be shown through sample studies that in various ways moral standards have changed during the past generation or two. The change has been most apparent with respect to women. The facts are sufficiently well known that they need not be rehearsed here. Suffice it to say that there is less disapproval of women's smoking, drinking alcoholic beverages, and having premarital sex experience. There is also less disapproval of birth control and divorce, and an increasing toleration of some kinds of extramarital freedom on the part of married persons.

These changes have come very unequally in different regions, different social classes, and different religious groups. The change is more apparent in the "real" behavior of persons than in the "ideal" culture patterns. There is wide discrepancy between the *actual sexual behavior* of people and the current *laws and verbal pronouncements* pertaining to sex. When asked, persons will often assert that certain conduct is wrong categorically, but will admit to such acts themselves and to the approval of such acts among their friends. The inconsistency, if it be inconsistent, is rationalized by the "logic" that it is good for other people, or for children, or for appearances, to give lip service to higher standards of morality than are actually observed in one's own personal conduct. Whether such a view is correct or incorrect, desirable or undesirable, is probably not for the social scientist to pass judgment upon; in the interest of accuracy it is necessary, however, to report such facts as these, since they are significant factors in human behavior. (The student should be cautious in the use of the cases with which he is familiar as a basis for reaching conclusions regarding moral conduct. His sample may be atypical without his realizing it.)

7. An institutionalized diversity

This heading is, taken literally, a paradox: "institutionalization" connotes formalization and standardization and thus stands in apparent contradiction to "diversity." But in a less strictly literal sense the phrase is apt. Families vary radically in everything from their standard of living to their sex morality, and there is no dearth of persons who insist on the propriety, if not the morality, of this wide diversity. "A man's home is his castle" is no empty sentiment. Rather it is a long-established principle, particularly appealing in individualistic America, that individuals and families have the privilege, if not even the moral obligation, to do quite as they wish, so long as they do not interfere with the same right of others. To be sure, there are the contrary influences of standardization, like "keeping up with the Joneses" and the hypersensitivity to the latest fad and fashion and to what has been called "the strong voice of Mrs. Grundy over the back fence." Yet the fundamental principle subsumed in the vernacular "it's none of anybody else's business" is firmly established in American family culture. It is not at all uncommon to hear vigorous defenses of various modes of family living by persons who themselves have a strong preference for other modes but insist on the principle that each family has the right to its own idiosyncrasies, if not the obligation to "be themselves."

These, then, are some of the more salient features of the American family structure at this time. The student will recognize that the above paragraphs contain a considerable variety of types of evidence and exercise considerable judgment concerning what the evidence means. Some of the evidence is based upon specific studies, which are by no means infallible, but at least approximate the goals of scientific objectivity. Other evidence consists of essentially informal observations. Finally, some of the logic involved in the interpretations may be idiosyncratic to the particular observer. All of these diverse materials constitute the "evidence" for the conclusion drawn, and while none is infallible, taken together they constitute a reasonable facsimile of what sociologists have concluded about the functional-structural characteristics of the contemporary American family.

SOCIETAL REGULATION OF THE FAMILY

Despite a popular pleasing fantasy to the contrary, the family is by no means a social system independent of the larger society. The latter will not allow it to be, and never has. In many diverse ways other segments of the society seek to shape the structure of the family, and to some extent succeed in doing so. We shall consider in the following paragraphs three aspects of societal influence on the family: (1) legal regulation, (2) guidance of family behavior, (3) indirect and sometimes even unintentional general effects.

1. Legal control

In the past, and usually in primitive societies, societal controls upon the family were largely *informal*. "The strong voice of Mrs. Grundy over the back fence" was usually enough to keep most people approximately in line with the behavior required of them by the social codes. Informal public opinion is effective enough as a guide so long as society is largely primary group oriented. But with the rise of large cities, secularized thinking, a great deal of movement from place to place, and the increasing impersonality of behavior, informal controls have become largely superseded by *legal controls*. In many more ways than most persons realize the modern American family is regulated by law.

a. Each of the fifty states has its own set of laws pertaining to marriage, divorce, and the family. Great variations occur from state to state. One student of family law has pointed out, for example, that the same person, without so much as moving from the driver's seat of his automobile, could by traveling fifty miles pass through three states under the laws of which he would be variously a single man, a married man, and a bigamist! [2] Numerous other similar legal entanglements are easily found. Many persons are of the opinion that this variation from state to state is undesirable, and attempts have been made to secure federal legislation and/or constitutional amendment in order to unify state laws. It now appears doubtful that any such reforms will occur soon.

[2] If a man had two common-law wives, he would be a bigamist in a state which recognizes common-law marriages; in a neighboring state only the first common-law marriage would be recognized whereupon he would be merely a married man, while a third state recognizes no common-law marriage, so he would be a single man.

b. Some uniformities do, however, exist. State laws usually prohibit marriage to certain categories of persons such as the feeble-minded, the insane, and the epileptic. All states set minimum age limits at which persons may legally marry. These age limits, however, vary several years among states. No couple may legally marry without securing *permission* from the state in the form of a "marriage license," and the license is increasingly often granted only after other conditions, such as a blood test, have been met.

c. Once a couple is married, their relationships to each other and to any children which may be born to them are regulated by the law. The husband is required to support his wife and children, and failure to do so may result in fine, imprisonment, or both. Adultery or "fornication" or "illegal cohabitation" are serious crimes. The state laws stipulate which of the parents or whether both are the legal guardians, and set forth the kind and extent of legal responsibility which parents have for the conduct of their children. State laws usually require children of certain ages to attend school and sometimes require parents of children who have communicable diseases to be quarantined for stipulated periods. Several states have sweeping laws providing severe penalties for adults, including parents, who in any way "contribute to the delinquency of minors." Moreover, the laws set various requirements pertaining to the inheritance rights of adults and children either under terms of a will or in the absence of a will.

d. Each state regulates divorce as well as marriage. In the various states as many as ten to eighteen different grounds for divorce are provided in the statutes. The right to a divorce, contrary to much popular belief, is a prerogative of the state, not of the individual. "Giving" a spouse a divorce is often spoken of glibly, as if it were in the power of a mate to give his spouse a divorce in the same sense as he could give his spouse money or property. Divorces can be given only by courts, and even then the courts are limited by the laws of the states within which they have jurisdiction.

e. The enforcement of all of these laws is, of course, highly variable. Persons falsify their age and get married contrary to the law. Public officials are sometimes negligent, and persons to whom marriage is theoretically denied are often permitted to marry anyway. Some of the laws pertaining to marriage and particularly to sex conduct are openly violated, and prosecution is practically negligible. Perjury and collusion, especially in divorce cases, are almost the rule rather than the exception. Taken as a whole, the laws of marriage and of divorce represent one of the most confused areas of legal practice found in the

United States. Perhaps the chief factor in this confusion is the discrepancy between the requirements of the law and the wishes and desires of the people who theoretically, but not actually, make the law.

In spite of the above condition it should not be overlooked that the "rights" of persons in regard to marriage, parenthood, childhood, inheritance, and divorce are only such rights as the laws stipulate. While it is true, as we have seen, that the laws and the values of the people may be at a variance, this condition should not obscure the basic fact that marriage is a legal status made possible by the law, and the rights and duties related to it are protected by the law. In the long run, perhaps, the law tends to approximate the values of "the people"; but values are so variable, traditional ideal mores loom so large in many persons' thinking, and legislative inertia is so great that contradictions such as we have noted seem "normal."

2. Family guidance services

It is common knowledge that many persons meet with great unhappiness in family life. Not only are divorces numerous but many couples who do not seek divorces are exceedingly unhappy in their marital state. Not only adults but children as well are frequently severely frustrated by the family situation in which they find themselves. While conclusive evidence does not exist to prove the assumption, it is commonly held by persons familiar with the facts that personal unhappiness in connection with family living is on the increase. Certainly a consciousness of unhappiness is widely felt.[3]

It seems probable, moreover, that there is more domestic maladjustment than there needs to be, that many of the tensions grow either out of ignorance of the mates or out of ill-advised matings in the first place. Accordingly, there has arisen a movement to educate people more fully about various areas of marriage, varying from sex behavior to budgeting. Books have been written and courses in college and even in high schools have been introduced for the purpose of acquainting as many people as possible with as much knowledge as is available concerning marriage. This is a new movement. Prior to World War I it was practically impossible for a person, even if he wanted, to get any reliable guidance of a scientific nature regarding marriage. All that was available was the folk wisdom, the homespun philosophy, and the platitudinous advice of friends and relatives and of a few intuitive poets

[3] John F. Cuber and Peggy B. Harroff, *The Significant Americans: A Study of Sexual Behavior Among the Affluent* (New York, Appleton-Century, 1965).

and moral leaders. Gradually it has occurred to more and more people that the scientific method could be applied to the discovery of the basic principles and facts involved in marriage.

While there is much yet to be learned, considerable progress has already been made along at least three lines: (a) prediction of success and failure in marriage; (b) courses in preparation for marriage; and (c) counseling techniques applied in individual cases by experts in human behavior for the purpose of treating difficulties that have arisen and disposing of them or adjusting to them before too serious results have occurred. We shall now discuss each of these three forms of education and guidance.

a. Marriage prediction

There are two important pioneer studies which formed the initial factual basis for the prediction of success or failure in marriage: the Burgess and Cottrell [4] study conducted by two sociologists and the Terman [5] study conducted by a psychologist. These studies, though somewhat different in method and results, are much the same. Both provide a factual basis for determining in advance the probabilities that a given person will have high, low, or average marital adjustment. The originators of these predictive instruments have been careful not to claim too much for them, but the experience of numerous persons who have used them extensively for actual predictions has indicated that they are quite reliable and accurate.

The technique is not difficult. On the basis of a number of questions about a person's background, a score is obtained. Then this score is compared with the results of the original study summarized in a table. Thus, the person contemplating marriage may be informed that persons whose marital prediction scores are like his have shown a certain percentage of very successful marriages, a certain percentage of less successful marriages, and so on through five categories of success and failure.

The test cannot predict with certainty that a given marriage will succeed or fail any more than the findings of a physical examination would necessarily guarantee how long a person will live. Like the physical examination, the marriage prediction results can show a person approximately what the *probabilities* are, on the basis of numerous other cases that have been examined.

[4] E. W. Burgess and Leonard Cottrell, *Prediction of Success and Failure in Marriage* (Englewood Cliffs, N.J., Prentice-Hall, 1939).

[5] Lewis M. Terman, *Psychological Factors in Marital Happiness* (New York, McGraw-Hill, 1938).

Up to the present, of course, marriage predictions have been made for only a negligible proportion of the total marrying population. Sometimes even when the results are available the persons involved may not use them; some couples may marry even though the prediction indicates that the marriage is not advisable. There seems some reason to believe, however, that in the future greater use will be made of marriage prediction as a basis for determining who is suitable to marriage and who is not, and also perhaps at what time marriage is indicated for a given pair.

Some persons mistakenly assume that the chief value of marriage prediction lies in the prevention of divorce. Of far greater significance, however, would seem to be the insight which marriage prediction can give a couple concerning the degree of adjustment which they may expect, where they will fall on a continuum marked by high happiness on the one extreme and just barely avoiding divorce on the other. As the availability of marriage prediction becomes more popularized and more trusted, and as the prediction techniques are improved, probably greater use of these promising devices may be made.

b. Marriage courses

About half of the colleges and universities in the United States now have one or more courses designed to inform students on the subject of marriage, or at least on some aspects of it. These courses vary a great deal in content, popularity, and probable effectiveness. Many are of limited value, if not useless, because of the strict censorship concerning the discussion of sex and other important aspects of the problem. Others are weakened materially because they are oriented too obviously around a desire to indoctrinate the students with certain "moral" precepts rather than to inform them honestly on such subjects as sex, birth control, and divorce. Some courses are not effective because they are taught by persons whose intentions are good but whose scientific knowledge is not up to date in the several fields of knowledge which such courses should include. In spite of these criticisms, numerous scientifically valid courses are to be found, and it is usually reported that such courses are popular with students. Gradually better textbooks are being written and better trained teachers for such courses are becoming available.

There are, however, numerous *unsolved problems in marriage education*. First, there is no evidence to prove that such courses really result in better matings and happier marriages. There is evidence from other areas of education that the successful completion of courses is no indication whatsoever that the knowledge contained in the courses will be successfully applied by the students who have taken the courses. In other words, the possession of accurate knowledge about sex or budget-making gives no assurance that the person who has the knowledge will be able to *use it successfully* in his own life. Studies now in progress may supply reliable answers to the question of effectiveness of marriage education. All that we possess now is the faith and the hope that marriage education may in practice help persons to achieve more success and happiness in marriage.

In the second place, there is no complete agreement as to who should be responsible for guiding marriage education. It is often held that the person's home and family should be the source of this instruction in regard to marriage and family, but it is obvious that numerous families are unwilling or unable to offer much reliable guidance, even though they are themselves successful. Others, moreover, have failed themselves and hence often do not have the confidence of their children. Some think that the church should assume the responsibility for marriage education. But a large proportion of the population is not actively interested in organized religion, and a large proportion of the churches are neither interested nor competent in this area. This leaves the task to the school which, in spite of its shortcomings, may be the only agency which could possibly be effective in marriage education.

At the present time marriage education is largely limited to the college level. This eliminates the vast majority of the marrying pairs categorically, because they do not attend college. And even among those who do, only a small proportion take marriage preparation courses.

It is possible that the most effective marriage education for the masses of people is presented by the movies, television, and popular fiction. Almost every movie and every work of fiction has a man-woman theme. Thus, over a period of years the average person sees enacted before him a few hundred family sequences which are almost certain to influence him in some way in the formation of the values and conduct of his personal life. There is a prevailing notion that this movie and fiction influence is an undesirable one, but evidence is lacking which would enable us to determine even what the influences of movies and fiction are, much less to evaluate the worth of such influences.

c. Marriage counseling

Another significant development which shows some promise in assisting persons to adjust more successfully in their family roles is the rise of marriage, or domestic relations, counseling. Counseling is done by a variety of persons who are by no means equally well trained for this technical work. Marriage counseling of a sort has been done in the past by the clergyman and by the family physician. Both of these functionaries have enjoyed a great deal of respect and have generally been regarded as proper persons in whom to confide concerning matters of relative intimacy.

For their time the clergyman and the family doctor probably represented the best kind of sympathetic listener and advice-giver that was available. But neither of these functionaries is a marriage counselor in the professional sense of the word, because neither has been trained very extensively in the *sciences of human behavior*. More recently there has developed a professional field of marriage counseling staffed by psychologists, social workers, psychiatrists, and sociologists. Some physicians, ministers, and lawyers also are becoming competent in this practice.

It is not our purpose here to discuss the professional training necessary or the techniques used by marriage counselors. It must suffice to point out that such a professional service exists but is mostly limited to the larger cities, and that this service is being used increasingly by persons who are unable to solve their marriage problems themselves. Since this field is a new one and not subject to much legal control, there also exist numerous charlatans and quacks who pose as competent counselors, extorting sizable fees from persons in trouble who do not know how to choose an ethical and competent counselor when they need one. The quack counselor, like the quack doctor, does the profession and his clients a great deal of harm. Legal control of the quack counselor is even more difficult than that of the quack doctor because counselors are not yet licensed, and thus the state has little control over them. Perhaps before many years have passed, minimum standards of competence for counselors will be agreed upon so that counselors can be licensed and only properly trained persons permitted to practice.

As in the case of marriage education, it is difficult to determine objectively how effective counselors really are. One never can determine what the conditions would be if the counselor had not been consulted. There is some reasonably objective evidence, however, which seems to indicate that many of the persons who use the service of counselors feel that they have been helped by counselors, and sometimes markedly so.

3. Indirect societal influences

Perhaps the most profound influence on the family, emanating from other institutions and societal conditions, is unintended. Practically every occurrence has implications for the family. Some of the obvious instances are wars which separate, sometimes permanently, husbands and wives as well as parents and children, disrupt educations and occupational careers, and often work havoc with property and standards of living. We can only guess, for example, what the effects upon a generation of children may be when so many of them have had the limited and abnormal relationships with fathers characteristic of war periods.

Less dramatic social changes also have their influences upon the family institution. We can take the space to mention only a few, but these illustrations may help to demonstrate a general point and facilitate further thinking on the part of the student. Earlier in this book it was pointed out that the Industrial Revolution and other technological developments have transformed the nation from a land of farmers and small town dwellers into a nation of city dwellers and nonagricultural workers. The whole impact of this change upon family behavior is not yet fully known, but some of the broader influences are apparent, such as the change from the family as a producing and consuming unit to that of a consuming unit only, the separation of the place of employment from the home itself, the isolation of all family members except the breadwinner from the process of production, the growing and changed reliance upon money as the source of practically every desirable thing, and all of the attending problems of urban living which we have discussed earlier.

Even more specifically, each technological change has its impact upon the family. Whatever their beneficial effects, household appliances have revolutionized the role of women, and not all of the consequences can be considered good. The automobile sounded the death knell to chaperonage and hastened virtual, if not actual, maturity by several years.

But all of the social influences upon the family have not been technologically caused. Education, particularly of women, has established new concepts of life and of living. Changes in religious emphases and philosophies have presumably also had their influence. Governmental programs, like social security for older people and college educations for veterans, represent significant changes from anything previously known to family experience. And so we might go on and on, but perhaps enough has been said to indicate that the family is not, and apparently cannot be, a thing apart from the larger society. It is influenced by what goes on outside, sometimes dramatically and sometimes by slow, insidious increments, often termed "pressures," to change. Resistances, rooted in older family traditions, may sometimes weaken the impact; but rarely, if ever, can the outside forces be successfully and permanently resisted.

THE PERSON AND THE CHANGING FAMILY PATTERN

Mental hygiene problems

We have already seen that in numerous ways the traditional American family is being modified. These changes have been described largely in objective language, in terms of such factual statements as the decline of male authority, the increasing outside employment of married women, the changing moral code, the decline in the size of the family, and the increase in divorce. Describing these conditions in such objective language *tends to minimize the seriousness of the problems encountered by the person who tries to adjust his ideas and conduct relating to family life during a period of change.*

It is easy to describe, for example, the increase in the out-of-home employment of married women and to point out the objective fact that there is nothing inherently or necessarily permanent about the traditional role of women in the home. But to the man whose ideals and values of family life were learned from participation in the older family type, it may be exceedingly difficult to *accept* this change even though he can *understand* it in a purely rational way. To him, "family" means a wife in the home and not a second "breadwinner." To him "family" means a single family dwelling, a white picket fence, and children around, not a high-rise apartment with maid service, a nursery school, and most of the meals in a restaurant. *Rationally*, of course, he can understand that his wife has as much "right" to a career as he does, and usually he does not wish to deprive her of the things she wants. But he still cannot escape from the fact that the values he holds and the conceptions of family life which are meaningful to him are not products of rational judgments and considerations of justice, but are the unconscious, nonrational images and sentiments which are the results of his socialization. He cannot escape from these, often, even though he might like to. To many thousands of men in the United States the outside employment of their wives constitutes a fundamental and persistent frustration of their basic wishes. Many persons do not have sufficient insight to recognize this condition as frustration because it may be largely unconscious, but its effect upon happiness and feelings of security is often very evident to the professional analyst of human behavior.

It is not only the man who finds personal problems resulting from this change in the family pattern. On the surface it would seem that the woman has had the advantage of securing her "freedom." But frequently there are complications for her, too. First, she is likely to possess some of the same traditional family habits and values of home-making and to accept them as a woman's proper activity. But she cannot do these things and work outside the home, too, without encountering difficulties. The difficulties may take the form of overwork due to attempting two jobs at once. In some cases husbands have been known to expect too much domestic activity on the part of an employed wife, not because they consciously wish to be unreasonable but because unconsciously they think in terms of woman's traditional role in the home. Sometimes health problems for the woman result from the attempt at doing double duty. Not infrequently working wives, because they do not *really* accept that role, develop hostilities toward their husbands because the men are unable "to take care of" them.

In these and many other ways, social change may bring additional personal problems to those persons upon whose lives the social change impinges.

While the illustration of employment of married women has been used here, it is not to be assumed that this is the only or even major problem brought about by social change in the family. Changes in morality have often created tortuous problems for both husbands and wives. Persons of radically different moral codes, without realizing it, may fall in love or even marry. Under such conditions tensions are almost inescapable. Under the emotional stress of being in love or of devotion to the mate, persons have often behaved in ways which have resulted in serious "guilt complexes."

Likewise, the transfer of functions from the family has ostensibly freed women from much household drudgery, but only to leave many of them confused and bewildered because they have too much time on their hands and do not know how to use it to advantage. Illustrations could be multiplied almost indefinitely; together they reinforce the important generalization that change in the family pattern creates problems for many persons. Husbands and wives frequently have had different value-backgrounds which seemed unimportant before or at the time of marriage. After marriage they have discovered that their basic conceptions of what family life ought to be were different. These values are often not only markedly different, but sometimes basically incompatible. This factor is an important one in numerous cases of divorce or domestic discord and has caused intense personal unhappiness.

Evaluation of change

It is not to be assumed from the foregoing discussion that change in the family pattern is to be disapproved merely because it has brought unhappiness to some people. In the first place, whether one disapproves or not, change will inevitably occur. No useful purpose is therefore achieved by decrying it. Moreover, many of the changes which bring personal unhappiness and disorganization to individuals during the period of transition may bring important benefits to many generations thereafter. For instance the decline of male dominance may have been a frustrating experience to many males, but this change made possible the emergence of a freer personality for women. This transition could be justified not only on moral grounds but also in that it probably resulted in objective benefits in the long run for men, also.

There has been an unfortunate tendency in the recent past for some students of human behavior to oppose change and especially rapid change on the grounds that it disorganized and frustrated the persons whose values had been fashioned by the older regime. It is true enough that social change is confusing, but since it is also inevitable, and since it can be demonstrated that many of the benefits of modern living were made possible only by the effects of change, it seems both useless and ill-considered to oppose change per se. It would seem better to seek to understand the change and to adjust as rationally as possible to it, or to steer it in certain beneficial directions.

It does not follow, either, merely *because change is inevitable, that all specific changes are necessarily inevitable or that all changes are to be equally approved.* It appears that we have arrived at a stage in social development, in America at least, in which it is possible somewhat rationally to decide what kind of a social system we want, and then use our influence to get it. Merely because past attempts to control social change have frequently been unsuccessful is no assurance that they will always be doomed to failure. Democracy failed many times before it succeeded, but it did eventually succeed. The same logic can be applied to the family. Although it is undeniably true that most persons cannot think objectively about the family in such fundamental respects as evaluating monogamy itself, it is also true that recent generations have seen societal approval of basic modifications in the family system such as the increased use of divorce, of birth control, and of a somewhat more scientific rearing of children. It is not being asserted here that these changes are desirable or undesirable in themselves, but rather that they illustrate how the family can be modified even during relatively short periods. It is a debatable question, of course, whether these changes were the result of deliberate planning or the unconscious result of impersonal forces making for change, which merely happened to work out in these ways. Certainly, however, if a given couple decide to limit the number or time of birth of their children, they must have a desire so to do. Or if a woman wishes to have a career as well as marriage, one must presume that she wants a career. When sufficient numbers of people do these things, the family pattern has been changed. It seems reasonable to conclude that the change represents deliberate choice on the part of at least some of the people of the society in which the change has occurred. In formulating this interpretation we have not overlooked the fact that underlying a person's desire to change from the traditional way of behaving, there are other influences over which he perhaps has no control. Yet when a significant number of persons desire to have a somewhat different kind of life than has traditionally existed and choose to implement their desires by action to bring about what they want, it would seem justifiable to regard these changes as rational and deliberate.

SUMMARY

We began this chapter by discussing a number of typical structural and functional characteristics of the majority American family, namely: that it is a small family, both in the sense that each pair lives separately from its kin and also in that the number of offspring per married pair is relatively small as societies go; that equalitarian ideals with respect to women and children are growing in acceptance; that a happiness orientation pervades its ideology; that there is at least an apparent instability and an apparent defunctionalization; that morality manifests wide real-ideal discrepancies; and that wide diversity from social norms is encouraged.

The larger society influences the family, both deliberately and unintentionally, through regulatory laws, through guidance services such as education and marriage counseling, and possibly most importantly through the unintentional consequences of other social changes great and small.

Change in the family pattern comes usually at a considerable price in mental-emotional strain to many people. It is unfortunate but probably inevitable that a rapidly changing society exacts this toll through the process of first indoctrinating individuals with the importance of certain values and then, through rapid change, making it virtually impossible for the individual to live by the ideals which he has been so fervently taught. Although it cannot be proved statistically, it seems not unlikely that the high incidence of mental ill-health in our society may well be an outgrowth of the trauma which many people experience in their efforts to find happiness and fulfillment in their most intimate institutional setting, marriage.

SUGGESTED READINGS

Bernard, Jessie, *Remarriage: A Study of Marriage.* New York, The Dryden Press, 1956.
One of the more careful studies of what happens to personality when remarriage occurs.

Cuber, John F., and Harroff, Peggy B., *The Significant Americans: A Study of Sexual Behavior Among the Affluent.* New York, Appleton-Century, 1965.
A study of man-woman relationships among the American upper middle class in all principal occupations. The study is based on 437 extensive interviews. Presents some new typologies concerning marriage as well as other aspects of the man-woman world. Replete with quotations from the interviews.

Getzels, Jacob W., and Jackson, Philip W., "Family Environment and Cognitive Style: A Study of the Sources of Highly Intelligent and of Highly Creative Adolescents." *American Sociological Review,* Vol. 26 (June, 1961), pp. 351–359.
"Two groups of adolescents were studied: (a) those exceptionally high in intelligence (IQ) but not concomitantly high in creativity, and (b) those exceptionally high in creativity but not concomitantly high in intelligence (IQ). The groups were found to differ not only in intellective and social behavior, but to have their source in differing family environments." (From the abstract to the article.)

Goode, William J., *World Revolution and Family Patterns.* New York, Free Press, 1963.
This is an excellent analysis of the way in which family systems are modified under the influences of rapid and dramatic change in other systems to which the family perforce must also relate.

Hunt, Morton, *The World of the Formerly Married.* New York, McGraw-Hill, 1966.
A highly readable study of a growing subculture, the divorced. Studies life

styles, reassimilation into marriage, success and failure of remarriage. Exceedingly reasonable and replete with quotations from the research interviews.

Kenkel, William F., *The Family in Perspective*. New York, Appleton-Century-Crofts, 1966.

This is an excellent general book on the study of the family organized around the four principal frames of reference within which different researchers have worked. This is a sophistication of which no other textbook on the family takes such explicit note.

Komarovsky, Mirra, *Blue-Collar Marriage*. New York, Random House, 1964.

While sociologists' data are somewhat deficient in high quality discussions of marriage at the blue-collar level, this study is a notable exception. Replete with case materials. Should be highly interesting, as well as informative of marriage at this level of American society.

Nimkoff, M. F., ed., *Comparative Family Systems*. Boston, Houghton Mifflin, 1965.

A well-known sociologist of the family presents in this book an interesting and readable account of family systems in different parts of the world.

Reiss, Ira L., *Premarital Sexual Standards in America: A Sociological Investigation of the Relative Social and Cultural Integration of American Sexual Standards*. New York, Macmillan, 1960.

There have been many census-like descriptions of sexual behavior of both subcultures and, as in the case of Kinsey, of samplings of the entire population. But standards are something else. Reiss' reexamination, for example, of the Kinsey data in the light of attitudes involved in the overt acts is an important addition to the literature.

Rodman, Hyman, *Marriage, Family, and Society: A Reader*. New York, Random House, 1965.

An uncommonly good reader on the family. The selection of articles and the interlaced comments by the author show genuine sophistication. It is books like this which demonstrate, rather than merely assert, that the sociological analysis of marriage is truly professional.

Winch, Robert F., *Mate Selection: A Study of Complementary Needs*. New York, Harper & Row, 1958.

This study is based on the author's well-known theory of complementary needs as the basis for love and marriage. This theory stands somewhat in opposition to the more familiar theory that homogamy in personality traits is the more plausible theory accounting for mate selection.

STUDY QUESTIONS

1. What typical structural characteristics of the family do you think were omitted in this treatment?
2. Why do you think so many people are so sure that the family is disintegrating? Why are sociologists, for the most part, less sure?
3. Why do individual families vary from the norms of their own society?
4. Why do happenings in other areas of society affect the family?
5. What are the indications that impermanence is becoming a family characteristic?
6. How do the functions of the present American family differ from those of the early nineteenth-century family?
7. Illustrate several ways in which the real family patterns differ from the ideal patterns.
8. In what ways may changing family patterns be sources of frustrations? In what ways may changes remove or reduce frustration?
9. What type of marriage guidance was available prior to 1920?
10. Of what value are the techniques of predicting success or failure in marriage?
11. Why are marriage courses offered in schools? What are the limitations of these courses?
12. What are the limitations of marriage counseling?

25
ECONOMIC
SYSTEMS

Since one of the well-established social sciences, economics, is devoted to the study of economic activity, it needs to be demonstrated that the efforts of sociologists can add something to what economists have already discovered. In other words, the burden of proof that there is such a thing as *sociology* of economic activity and institutions rests with the sociologist. What can he add and why?

When the sociologist makes a study of economic institutions he has the advantage of a *different perspective;* he is trained to see different things, and even the same things in different ways. By and large the sociologist's observations of economic matters tend to go beyond those of the economist. The sociologist is more interested in the *wider social effects* of economic matters and also with the *less apparent aspects.* For example, what are the effects of job specialization upon personality, upon recreational activity, and upon family life? Or, again, how are economic attitudes created and changed? What makes men work, especially after the basic necessities of life are achieved? What is the role of ideology in the economic-social system? These are a few of the kinds of questions which sociologists have been concerned about in their studies of the economic aspects of modern society.

REVIEW OF PREVIOUS RELEVANT MATERIALS

It will be recalled that in the chapter on cultural variability we pointed out that economic activities, like all other kinds of social action, vary markedly from one society to another. People prize different things, have very different attitudes toward wealth, and have radically different concepts of what constitutes property. Not only is there variation from place to place but there is an endless process of change continuously reshaping economic institutions. Some of the changes have been little short of dramatic. A little over a hundred years ago white men owned property rights in Negroes in the

United States and were free by both law and informal custom to buy and sell Negro men, women, and children like livestock. During the 1920's the manufacturing, sale, and transportation of alcoholic beverages was illegal (unconstitutional), and any persons engaged in such business were, by definition, criminals. Less than fifty years ago an employer had the legal right in many places in America to hire strike breakers as a means of forcing his employees to come to his terms, and he also had the legal right to fire employees for belonging to labor unions. These few illustrations should help the student to recognize that economic matters have the same variability in time and place that characterizes other aspects of society.

The economic system is an aspect of culture and has the same dual relationship to personality that all culture does, namely, it *creates wants* and other habits (secondary drives) through socialization of the person. Moreover, in varying degree, it *satisfies these wants*, the whole process being so subtle that most people are probably not aware that they are so largely fulfilling destinies not of their own making. Unfortunately, also, all wants are not satisfied, hence the ever-present phenomenon of *frustration* and the various adjustments men make to frustration.

Thus, what we call "the economic system" really inheres in the attitudes and habits of people. The meshing of these attitudes and habits, through the various interdependent social roles which people continually play, creates a more or less orderly and predictive social structure which, when viewed collectively, we call the "economic system" or "economic institutions."

SOCIAL STRUCTURE OF THE AMERICAN ECONOMY

Competitive tendencies versus monopolistic tendencies

Many of the things (goods, prestige, services) which people seek are relatively scarce, at least scarce enough so that everyone, as a rule, cannot have as much of them as he wants. Hence, human effort of various sorts, varying from hard work to criminal activities, goes into the process of "making a living" and "getting ahead." This often rivalrous activity typically takes a form in the United States which we call *competition*, that is, each person or group of persons banded together tries to outstrip others in securing scarce "utility" (goods, services, or prestige). By the prevailing American norms, this competitive effort is construed as productive of the greatest good to the greatest number. Thus, we speak of a "competitive economy" in the sense that the rivalries of individuals is the accepted basis for securing scarce things.

But as any student of history knows, the *actual* economy is not and has not ever been entirely a competitive economy. There are also *monopolistic* tendencies. Some individuals and groups have learned that there are advantages in *avoiding* or *circumventing competition*. The so-called "trusts" of a half-century ago were simply devices whereby supposedly competing firms arranged to avoid actual competition through such devices as interlocking directorates, "gentlemen's agreements," and the like. Other more modern avoidance of competition is found in the so-called *merger* in which one organization, whether a local grocery store or a coast to coast railroad, simply buys out its competitors or a large enough percentage of them, hopefully to be in a better position to control price and other aspects of the enterprise.

All monopolistic tendencies, however, are by no means those of industrial and commercial organization. Labor unions constitute another kind of monopolistic tendency, operative chiefly through the exercise of the strike or threat of strike and collective bargaining with employers, so that individual workers do not really compete with one another any more than do the separate industries operating under "gentlemen's agreements." Farmers' cooperative organizations are of a similar character. Rather than competing with one another, individual producers band together in order to market their products or purchase their supplies more advantageously as large units.

It is not our purpose here to make a complete listing of all of the various techniques which are used by industry, labor, agriculture, and the professions to circumvent the operation of competition as the determiner of income and price. We are simply concerned with making the point that it is a mistake to view the existing economic system in the United States as *either* a wholly competitive one *or* a wholly monopolistic one. There are elements of both, and a strong case can be made for the pre-eminence of either by those who choose to ignore the evidence on the other side, as is so common in popular economic-political discussion. Opinions differ radically as to whether the *major* factor determining distribution of goods in American society is the competitive tendencies or the monopolistic tendencies. It is not our purpose to attempt to arbitrate this complicated and explosive issue either. Our purpose is simply to make clear that both of these opposing tendencies are present and are inextricably intertwined in the structure of the American economy.

Massive organization

The American economic organization consists of the interaction of large, sometimes gigantic, organizations which make decisions vitally affecting the destinies of millions of people, both within and outside their own constituencies. It is not uncommon to hear laboring people complain that they have no real *personal* voice in the negotiation of the labor contract under the terms of which they must work. While it is true that they often have the opportunity to vote on the acceptance or rejection of a contract, they are obligated to abide by it, even though they have voted against it as members of a sizable minority. Similarly, individual stockholders of such gigantic corporations as United States Steel, Standard Oil (N.J.), or American Telephone and Telegraph may highly disapprove of some of the decisions and policies of the corporations of which they own a part. They are as powerless as are the workers who disapprove of some of the tactics or policies of their

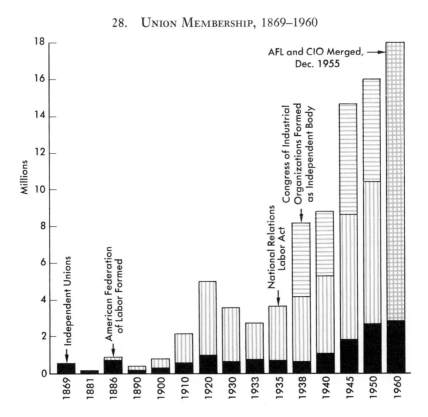

28. UNION MEMBERSHIP, 1869–1960

Source: Bureau of Labor Statistics.

union. Of course, both have *theoretical rights:* the worker can withdraw from the union and the stockholder can sell his stock. But what is he to do then? Whether they like it or not, most Americans in their economic affairs are obliged to accept their lot as relatively small and individually powerless cells in a gigantic structure which wields tremendous and often decisive final power in economic matters. We do not intend to imply that there is any evidence of overwhelming dissatisfaction with this state of affairs, but simply that even if there were, there would be no escaping this fact or the consequences which follow from it.

29. CORPORATE PROFITS, 1960

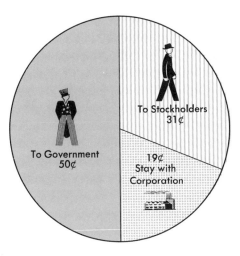

Source: U.S. Department of Commerce.

The economic order as an arena of conflict

Typically, the economic institutions of our society are in conflict with one another and within themselves. The conflicts between management and labor, between competing firms, and between government and specific economic organizations are well known. Practically any daily newspaper chosen at random will carry a number of news stories about these conflicts. Sometimes they are "settled" through the courts, and not infrequently they eventually reach the Supreme Court. But in a real sense they are never settled, because ours is a dynamic economy; and while adjustments of conflicts are made from time to

time, these adjustments are usually only temporary breathing spells
before the next crisis.

Government: the ultimate economic arbiter

Increasingly as time goes on the *federal government* has come to
be the *final decision-maker* in a growing number of economic matters.
This is due to the basic fact that the government is the *ultimate holder
of power*. If any one of the great power organizations—labor, business,
the professions, or agriculture—can influence or control the decisions of
government, it can in fact control the economic aspects of the society—
at least until the next election. Consequently, each economic organization is, perforce, also a political organization because it needs to be a
political organization in order best to carry out some of its economic
functions in the best interests of the persons it represents. Thus, organized labor wants to elect members of Congress favorable to the
labor viewpoint and wants also to see jurists with the same ideologies
appointed. Business interests, not always or necessarily opposed to those
of labor, but often so, also have their political preferences, and so does
organized agriculture, and the American Medical Association, and so
on and on.

As long as we have political democracy in America, we can expect
a recurring "battle for men's minds" as each of these interest groups
tries to "sell" the voters on the idea that their own political-economic
interests are also the voters' best political-economic interests. The
propaganda techniques are devious and also expensive in these days of
radio and television. In one important sense it is naïve to speak of the
government as the "controller" of economic organization, because one
of the functions of economic organizations is to try to control the government. Probably the greatest problem of practical politics for a
political party is to make its decisions in such a manner as to satisfy the
greatest number of persons in the various conflicting groups and thus
secure or retain the allegiance of the majority of the voters. This is
perhaps why political parties try to be all things to all people, for such
is necessary to their survival.

ECONOMIC INSTITUTIONS AND THE PERSON

Frequently one hears the expression that something is a "purely
economic" matter. Upon closer scrutiny it will usually be found that
there is no "purely" economic phenomenon, because economic matters
also have noneconomic implications and consequences. Let us take, for

example, the intricate division of labor which now characterizes all industrial employment and, for that matter, practically all employment in our society. Presumably, this high degree of specialization has come about because it is efficient. There are those who question this, but we are not inclined to challenge the common assumption. But what are the *consequences* of an intricate division of labor?

Practically no one who works in industry literally makes anything any more. To be sure he performs a task, and possibly a very intricate and technical one; but what does he have to see or to show at the end of a day's or a week's labor which would be the equivalent for the craftsman of an earlier day who alone made a pair of shoes or built a house or polished a diamond? Has something gone out of the life of the worker who cannot identify his own product? Suppose a man works on the assembly line at the Ford Motor Company. Is there any psychological satisfaction as he sits on his porch and watches the Fords go by? Does he proudly say to himself, "I may have tightened the bolts on the two muffler brackets underneath that convertible"? On the other hand, perhaps what Veblen called the "instinct of workmanship" is not a necessary concomitant of good personal adjustment. Perhaps good wages and short hours and a Ford of his own to drive and a place to picnic with his family and a television set on which to watch his favorite ball team may be all that a man needs from an economic system in order to feel that he lives fully and well. These are among the abiding enigmas of the modern worker—whether white collar or gray collar—in an economic system, so many aspects of which are too new for most persons to have a set of traditions to guide them.

The impress of the economy upon persons is important even for those who are not "in" the economy in the sense of employment. Youth is a dramatic case in point. Due to compulsory school attendance laws and strong pressures to continue education into the twenties, a large segment of American people experience the economy mainly as *consumers*. The extent of participation in the current affluence is dependent, of course, on the economic affluence of the parents and the relatively minor additions which may come from part-time employment. Yet all analyses of the American market for goods continually stress the growing importance of the youthful consumer, whose tastes have come to dominate not merely styles of clothing, records, and musical instruments, but even automobile design. Meanwhile, the more thoughtful youth experience a serious and growing anxiety as they approach the point at which, whether after high school, college, or professional school, they must take their places somewhere in the impersonal, highly bureaucratized, and complex system. Due to the thoroughness of their training, they are aware of the importance of their ability to make a living and the effect which their new role in the economy will have upon everything in their personal lives from the

30. OUR JOBS CHANGE

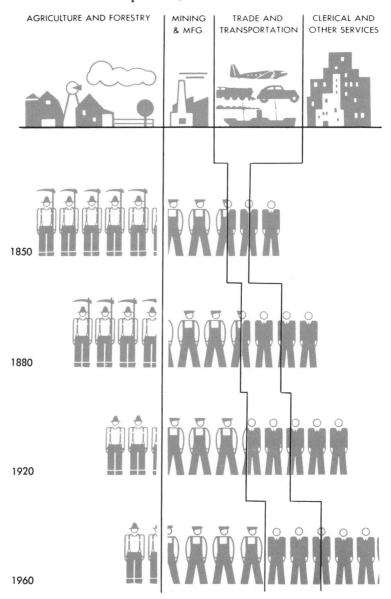

Each symbol represents 10 percent of all gainful workers

Source: National Industrial Conference Board.

places they live and the goods they can afford to the qualities of life and living which they can provide for their families. Nor can they help being aware of the widespread dissatisfactions of those who are somewhat older, those who have already experienced the hard realities of making their way in the system. By and large, the strictly financial returns of economic participation are, as compared with the recent past, relatively promising. But for many the more subtle psychological dimensions leave much to be desired. Alienation from work, serious tensions of an interpersonal nature with work associates, inability to control work assignments, or even an uneasiness of being ever at the mercy of bureaucratic superiors has yielded a general cultural legacy which many of the young quite naturally approach with apprehension. Much of the interest in the Peace Corps, Vista, and other idealistic programs of service is said to stem from a reaction against what youth defines as a too materialistic, too psychologically dissatisfying economy.

Personal security—psychic and economic

Surely it can be objectively demonstrated that the modern American economy has weakened, for most people, the link between *personal responsibility* and *economic well-being*. A person may have security or insecurity, and either may occur *independently of his skill or integrity*. Technological changes periodically render certain occupations practically obsolete. Changes in consumer habits, and even whims, may bring poverty or bankruptcy to the managers and workmen who supply some consumer good or service. Business cycles of prosperity and depression bring waves of poverty and plenty which to the average man are overwhelming and unpredictable, and before which forces he is largely powerless. It is easy enough for the poets to write inspiring lines about men who are "masters of their fate" and "captains of their souls," but in such "clutches of circumstance" as depressions, wars, and changing technology, few individual persons can shape their destinies in fact!

One of the most baffling public problems is that of discovering ways and *means of protecting persons from the more severe ravages of insecurity*. Two aspects of the problem stand out as distinct: (1) protecting the person from some of the obvious *physical effects* of insecurity by providing him with such varied assistance as old-age pensions, sickness and accident insurance, unemployment insurance, Medicare, liberalized credit in times of crises, and direct relief when needed; and (2) protecting the person from the *psychological ravages* of insecurity and anxiety feelings. The latter is the harder to achieve since, as we have seen in the early chapters dealing with social phychology, human beings are not altogether rational in their definitions of self and in their analyses of situations. Many case studies of persons show that insecurity feelings and anxieties are prominent and consistent aspects of the personality, and they do not respond readily to rational treatment. It appears doubtful, moreover, that dealing with individuals will be sufficient to cope with the seriousness and the extensiveness of the problem, because its roots lie deep in the social organization of American and other Western societies. Rapid and unpredictable change, particularly when one's experience and status depend so much on jobs, wages, and prices as they do, creates mental and emotional hazards of momentous proportions for great masses of people.

ECONOMIC IDEOLOGIES

Underlying any economic organization is some "ideology" or rationale which gives meaning and credibility to the system and helps to hold the allegiance of the people involved. Such terms as *capitalism, communism,* and *socialism* are terms which stand for groups of related values which constitute the rationales for some economic system or another. It is more difficult than it might at first appear to give accurate definitions of these various rationales. The politician or public agitator from either the "right" or the "left" who wants simply to embroil passions or win unthinking allegiance does not usually trouble himself to define his terms, with the result that most people have fallen heir to a dubious legacy of name calling and sloppy semantics in this important area. During recent years the terms *communistic* and *communist* have been used in so many ways—sometimes by the same person—that it becomes virtually impossible to find any core of meaning beyond the fact that when the term is applied to someone or something, we may safely assume that the user of the term is displeased. It is, therefore, more than ordinarily difficult to put into careful scholarly language those cores of meaning which the various economic ideologies have come to have. But we shall try.

Modern economic systems can be classified in several ways. Because each system has many attributes, there are many possible classifications. Thus, economic systems can be classified on the basis of the amount of government control, on the basis of the importance attached to economic activity, on the basis of complexity, or on almost any other basis. An exhaustive treatment of each of these classifications would involve a series of books. Within the brief scope of this book it will be possible to focus major attention on only one of these differences, namely, *the relation between economic activity and government control*. There are five major economic systems in this classification: capitalism, regulated capitalism, socialism, fascism, and communism.

1. Capitalism

Capitalism is an economic philosophy which grew up in Europe in the eighteenth century. It spread to America and flourished during the nineteenth century and the beginning of the twentieth century.

One might assume, as many do, that capitalism means simply the private ownership of property. But all economic systems have some private ownership of property. One of the important distinctions between them is the *amount and kind* of private property which the system permits, and the *degree of absoluteness* of private control over the property held. We turn now to an examination of these questions.

a. Ownership versus control of property. Ownership of property rights is always conditional. Phrases like "unlimited freedom of ownership," "completely owned private property," are misleading and inaccurate, because no society permits anyone the unconditional use of any property right. Some of the common limitations require the payment of taxes and the requirement not to use the property in such ways as would interfere unduly with other people's rights or privileges. Thus, a person who owns an automobile is permitted to use it only so long as he pays the taxes required and uses it in accordance with the provisions of the law. The same principles hold true in the ownership of a home, or a herd of swine, or a radio. Building codes require the observance of many regulations before one is permitted to construct a house on his own lot, and one can be prohibited from playing his radio if it interferes unduly with his neighbor's sleep. Examples could be multiplied to an impressive total, but the legal principle is probably clear, namely, that there are no absolute property rights in ownership, and that for the public good or the protection of other people, even those property rights which have been traditional are becoming increasingly abridged by law.

Capitalism has been a system which permits very great, although not unlimited, freedom to the owner of capital. Early in the history of the United States, for example, if a man had money enough he could build a noisy, unsightly, and unhygienic factory in the heart of the residential area of a city. If he owned the land, he could do with it as he wished. Gradually there has been established, although not without great struggle, the legal principle that the *interest of others in the use of private property is a legitimate and constitutional one.* But what are "legitimate interests" of other people in the use of one's private property? Does the ownership of a factory carry with it the right to dump refuse into the river, endangering the health and property of those who live downstream? There was a time when American courts upheld the legality of such action. Does the ownership of a railroad give the right to pollute the city with smoke in the vicinity of railroad yards and terminals, or does the collective interest justify forcing the railroads to use electric locomotives within the city limits? Some laws to that effect are now in operation. Does the ownership of an industrial establishment carry with it the right to refuse to employ workmen who are affiliated with a union? According to existing law, the management of large industry has no such right, but in the past such rights did exist. Thus, it can readily be seen that the amount and kind of control and the values underlying the control are, like all societal phenomena, highly relative.

b. Public properties. Capitalistic societies for over a hundred years have recognized that certain property rights should not be premitted to be privately owned. Roadways, rivers, harbors, and the postal system are cases in point. There were times in American history when certain improved roadways, called "turnpikes," were privately owned, and the persons who used them were required to pay rental in the form of "tolls." This arrangement was not permitted indefinitely. A comparable condition still occurs occasionally in the case of toll bridges and a few toll roads in the United States, but these are either state owned or almost completely controlled by the government. There is usually provision for the ultimate restoration of these facilities to complete public ownership. The logic underlying the prevention of private ownership of these properties is simply that they are limited in number and constitute "natural monopolies." It is usually thought that the private ownership of natural monopolies would not be consistent with the public interest; it would give too much power to the owners of these properties.

c. Public utilities. The extension of this logic to such public utilities as electric light and power, telephone, gas, and water is at present a controversial one. It is sometimes held that these systems should be operated at cost or else that the profits should go into the government treasury. Public utilities are now governmentally regulated in many respects, but the profits from most of these industries accrue to the owners of stock. A few cities own some of their public utilities in the form of electric light systems, street railways, and water supply systems. So-called public utilities in the United States present a currently confused picture between private ownership, public ownership, and private ownership with public control.

2. Regulated capitalism

In the discussion of capitalism it has been noted that more and more regulation is being exerted over the use of private property on the theory that the public interest requires it. These controls have now become so numerous and so extensive that many observers believe that private or pure capitalism can no longer be said to be in existence. By the gradual process of increasing control, capitalism is said to have become transformed into quasi-capitalism or regulated capitalism. This new system still has some of the attributes of the old capitalism, but also has many new features as we have seen. This is true not only in the United States but also in most of Europe as well. Regardless of the terminological argument, the facts are clear, namely, that some aspects of the laissez-faire capitalism characteristic of the nineteenth century have passed from the American scene.

3. Socialism

Although there are many different varieties and definitions of socialism, there is one common core of meaning which the term has. *Socialism* is an economic system which permits private ownership, but the *major* industries are regarded as public utilities. In other words, under socialism income may accrue to the absentee owner whose capital is invested in an industry, but the industry as a whole is supervised by the government in the public interest, not in the private interest of the owner alone. Production is said to be primarily "for use" and not primarily for profit. Inherent in the socialistic idea is a need for a relatively large number of controls upon industry, agriculture, commerce, and the professions.

The Labour government in England for a time after World War II was perhaps the clearest case of a modern, large nation which was socialistic. Some observers judge that England is presently still "relatively socialistic." It is difficult to determine at precisely what point controlled capitalism becomes socialistic, just as it is difficult to determine at what point capitalism becomes controlled capitalism.

4. Fascism

A mixed form of controlled capitalism and socialism known as *fascism* arose in prewar Europe, especially in Spain, Italy, and Germany. Under fascism the economic system usually comes under rigid governmental regulation. On the surface, this might seem to be like socialism. The distinction, however, lies in the *purpose* of the control, that is, control in whose interests? Whereas under socialism the control is designed to be in the interests of the whole society as nearly as possible, under fascism a relatively small group of wealthy persons, governmental and army functionaries are favored, almost to the exclusion of everyone else. Lip service may be paid to objectives which sound socialistic, but the evidence is clear that the interests of this small class, not the interests of the rank and file, are regarded as paramount. The fascist systems of Germany and Italy were, of course, virtually destroyed when their leaders were defeated in war. Not so in Spain. Moreover, observers report that fascist ideas are again growing up in Germany and Italy. At present, however, fascism is not a prominent system, although its potentialities are omnipresent.

5. Communism

Communism represents the complete or "logical extreme" of both government ownership and government control. It differs from socialism in that very little or no private ownership is theoretically permitted. "The wealth belongs to the people." Incomes may, however, be unequal.

Communism as an economic *philosophy*, however, should not be confused with the economic *system* found in present-day Russia and popularly called "communistic." Russia represents a specific form of economic system which is a unique combination of socialism, fascism, and communism, just as the United States represents an admixture of capitalism, socialism, and regulated capitalism.

The modern world has had less experience (if any) with pure communism than with any of the foregoing economic forms. It is believed by some that there is a worldwide trend in the direction of a more communistic-like society. This reasoning is based upon a number of facts but represents a mode of analysis which goes considerably beyond the facts. To assume that the trend toward increasing government ownership and control of producers' goods will become as complete as that of communism represents either a hope or a fear, depending on one's values, but not a fact.

SUMMARY

In this chapter we have discussed some of the findings and theories of sociologists regarding economic institutions, especially of American society. We have pointed out that both competitive practices and monopolistic practices coexist in the structure of the American economy, that a few massive organizations make the essential decisions shaping the economy, that the economic order is typically an area of intense conflict, and that government is of necessity the ultimate economic arbiter when other agencies cannot settle their own differences.

The subject of economic ideologies, fraught as it is with confusion, suspicion, and distortion of fact, was discussed briefly. We differentiated five types of economic rationale—capitalism, regulated capitalism, socialism, fascism, and communism—pointing out some of the salient characteristics of each.

SUGGESTED READINGS

Berle, A. A., and Means, G. W., *The Modern Corporation and Private Property*. New York, Macmillan, 1933.
This is a classic study of the realisms involved in modern business organization in the United States. Contains both theoretical and empiric materials.

Brodersen, Arvid, *The Soviet Worker*. New York, Random House, 1966.
A study of the relationship between labor as an interest group and government in the Soviet Union. Will prove instructive for comparing the relationship of government and labor in the Soviet Union and in the United States.

Hamilton, David, "The Ceremonial Aspect of Corporate Organization." *American Journal of Economics and Sociology*, Vol. 16 (October, 1956), pp. 11–23.
An "off-beat" and highly provocative discussion of the nonfunctional (perhaps even dysfunctional) aspects of current ritualism regarding corporate organization.

Jones, Peter d'A., *The Consumer Society*. Baltimore, Penquin Books, 1965.
This is a historical-economic study of developments in capitalism through various stages resulting in the emergence of what can now be called the "consumer society."

Moore, Wilbert E., *The Conduct of the Corporation*. New York, Random House, 1963.
The role of the corporation in the larger American society has been the object of considerable apprehension and debate. This book attempts to assess this role in contemporary society in the light of current practices.

Nosow, Sigmund, and Form, William H., eds., *Man, Work, and Society*. New York, Basic Books, 1962.
A collection of materials which will help the student to appreciate the kinds of interests and points of view which the sociologist brings to the study of occupations, with particular reference to American society.

Seligman, Ben B., "The American Corporation: Ideology and Reality." *Dissent*, Vol. 11 (Summer, 1964), pp. 316–327.
An excellent article comparing and contrasting the actual conduct of the American corporation with the way it is supposed to be conducted according to the simplitudes of general public assumption. An excellent study of real vs. ideal in an important American system.

Shostak, Arthur, and Gomberg, William, eds., *Blue Collar World*. Englewood Cliffs, N.J., Prentice-Hall, 1964.
This is a collection of studies of the American worker which taken together tend to provide a realistic image of his contemporary and future position in the American system.

STUDY QUESTIONS

1. Why does the sociologist "dabble" in economic matters, instead of leaving the field to economists?
2. What is incomplete in saying that an economic system "fulfills human needs"?
3. What "monopolistic tendencies" can you mention in addition to those cited in this chapter?
4. "It is easier to see competitive action in our economy than monopolistic action." What did the author of this statement probably mean? Explain.
5. Is there anything undemocratic about massive economic organization? Why or why not?
6. In what ways do we have capitalism in the United States today?
7. Why is it incorrect to say simply that we now operate under a system of "free enterprise"?
8. How has the relationship between the ownership and control of property changed?
9. Why do we have public ownership of certain types of property?
10. To what extent do we have socialism in the United States?
11. How do capitalism, controlled capitalism, socialism, fascism, and communism differ? How are they similar?
12. Why is it difficult to determine the "public interest"? Why do some groups claim that government regulation "stifles initiative"? How may some stifling of initiative possibly benefit the "public interest"?
13. Why do groups often attempt to make their own selfish interests appear to be the "public" interests?
14. What changes in our economic system have contributed to the growth of personal insecurity?
15. Why are we a nation of increasingly insecure and dependent people and also the "richest nation on earth"?

26
GOVERNMENT

Much which has previously been discussed in this book has important bearing on government, and it may be well to begin with a review and an application of already acquired insights.

Government is a social system and as such it shares the characteristics of the genre. The system operates with a cultural blueprint which is intended to spell out the operation of the system. This is usually codified in constitutions, bills of rights, magna chartas, and other "enabling documents." The system, however, operates through people, actors who play specialized and interlocking roles. These roles are numerous and intricately interlaced among elected officials, appointed officials, in some nations hereditary officials, and various and sundry categories of persons in such varying role categories as students in a state university, convicts in a penetentiary, soldiers on guard duty, employees on a highway construction crew. All of these roles and diffuse activities are held together typically by bureaucratic organization with all of the advantages and ills which we have already examined. The activities of government exist to carry out certain functions, but as in all bureaucracies, dysfunctional elements become entrenched and frequently governments are unable to carry out their functions efficiently, such as the perennial difficulty of maintaining law and order during periods of general unrest.

The governmental system operates not only in a network of interactions of the people involved in it and served by it, it has important influences upon other social systems on a collective level. Thus, governments usually regulate marriage and business and exert important, though not always definitive, regulatory powers over educational institutions and the churches in nations which have an "established church."

Governmental systems, however, are also *affected by* other systems and structures. First, and notably, governmental systems must function within limits sometimes set by other governmental institutions around the world. Once Russia initiated the space age with the first Sputnik, there seemed no alternative for the United States but to expend a prodigious amount of income and activity on what has since come to be called "the space race." The awakened consciousness and growing aggression of Negroes with respect to their life circumstances have refocused the attentions of legislators and court systems and very probably have had many other influences which we do not yet fully apprehend. New technology, like television, not ony completely alters the patterns of political campaigns but makes for a visibility of governmental action which is new in human history. Pictures of actual war scenes can be seen in almost every household twenty-four or forty-eight hours after they happen. When public officials make statements, the public hears every hesitation, sees every grimace, in short, can react to a far more total experience than merely reading a statement in a newspaper. While we do not fully understand as yet what these and other influences on government may portend, it becomes dramatically obvious that they shape the structures and functions of government systems, even though they may originate completely outside of the province of the governmental system.

Thus, government is quite as much a sociological institution and social system as is a family or a school; and the principles of socialization, role enactment, normality and deviation, and all the rest apply.

Government is unique among the social systems of modern society, however, in that it is the *ultimate source of power*. Although other institutions have power of various sorts, their power is always limited and if necessary is contravened by the overruling power of government. Thus, we might speak of the government as the "superinstitution" or "supersystem" because of this power to override or overrule any and all of the other groups in the society.

The foregoing does not mean that some of the other systems (especially in a *democratic* society) do not also exert power on government. Surely it is apparent from our discussion of economic institutions in the preceding chapter that in many ways such massive power-wielding blocs as labor unions and giant corporations significantly affect the conduct of government. In less obvious ways, religious and educational institutions also place limits upon the arbitrary actions of government. The careful observer will note that governmental agencies as a rule are very reluctant to challenge outright either the churches or the great economic power blocs. Nevertheless, despite the qualifications mentioned in this paragraph, government must be recognized as the ultimate power-wielding agency of modern society, even though that power is often exercised with caution and may be countervailed by other power centers.

SOME SYSTEM CHARACTERISTICS OF AMERICAN GOVERNMENT

1. Government is multifunctional

When we attempt to spell out in concrete forms the various functions which are subsumed in the phrase *to govern*, the number and variety of functions found is indeed impressive. At the present time the federal government includes the following in its kaleidoscope of functions: it compiles and publishes statistics of hundreds of sorts from the cost of living to the estimated number of wild ducks; through the Bureau of Standards it tests thousands of products from insecticides to airplanes; it maintains an army, navy, and air force; it fixes the prices (via parity supports) of a number of farm products; it supervises the Indian reservations; it owns and operates the postal system; it maintains millions of acres of national parks and forests; it regulates railroad rates, improves harbors, builds highways and airports; it maintains what is probably the world's most complete library; it supervises the taking of strike votes; it carries on directly and by subsidy thousands of research projects each year in every recognized branch of science; it manages the largest old-age insurance business in the world. And this is only a beginning! State governments make and enforce traffic laws, regulate marriage and divorce, run institutions of higher education, maintain agricultural experiment stations, regulate telephone and other public utility rates, license liquor dispensers, operate mental institutions, and regulate insurance companies. Local governments enforce public health laws, run elementary schools, regulate traffic, control the building and remodeling of houses, grant permits to bury the dead, own and operate art galleries, hospitals, and public recreational facilities. Some cities own and operate street railways; and practically all own and operate water purification plants and sewage disposal systems and provide such miscellaneous services as garbage collection, fire fighting, and street paving. And, again, we have only begun!

Sociologists MacIver and Page [1] have suggested a classification of governmental functions which may be helpful in evaluating our growing governmental colossus.

1. "Functions *peculiar* to the State"—maintenance of order, the attainment of justice, and protection of a system of property rights.
2. "Functions for which the state is *well adapted*"—conservation of natural

[1] Robert M. MacIver and Charles Page, *Society: An Introductory Analysis* (New York, Holt, Rinehart and Winston, 1949), pp. 458–463.

resources, control of monopoly, and the maintenance of public services such as parks, museums, schools, and playgrounds.

3. "Functions for which the state is *ill adapted*"—these will "vary with the conditions," but in general are functions which do not serve the needs of the *entire* community, such as religion, literary and artistic production or evaluation.

4. "Functions which the state is *incapable* of performing"—"controlling people's opinions," regulating morality (not the same, of course, as requiring "lawfulness").

It will probably be apparent that there is room for considerable difference of opinion concerning what specific functions would belong in categories two and three, since there is a thin line, indeed, between them. Surely we know that in practice the government of the United States has frequently become involved in functions which serve primarily special groups, and sometimes relatively small ones at that.

Ambivalence toward expanding governmental functions. One of the common clichés heard constantly in American society, especially during political campaigns, is that "the government is getting too big" or "the government is interfering too much in the affairs of other institutions." Usually, when one requests more specific information, the complainant is at a loss to explain precisely *what* functions of government he would abandon. But, even if he would enumerate some, his influence would be nullified by the next complainant who is a strong supporter of the functions which the first one would eliminate. It appears that, regardless of the party in power, the number and scope of federal governmental functions continue to grow. There are several reasons for this growth, but two seem to predominate: (1) the continuing pressure of some group to secure governmental service or support, or the desire to enlist the power of government to achieve control over someone else; and (2) the political advantage of adding functions so that additional patronage can be controlled, patronage being a powerful device in the practical politics of securing and maintaining political support. Partisanship is, of course, a powerful factor affecting judgments in such matters as these, and most persons find it difficult to be charitable about the motives of persons in their political outgroups.

2. Ideological unclarities

The ideological basis of American government has by no means the unanimity of popular acceptance which the Fourth of July orator so confidently asserts. To be sure, there is a *near unanimity in the words we use* but *not in the concepts* for which they stand. Probably two cores of controversy, both centering around the word *democracy*, largely subsume the issues.

Is American government a democracy? Most persons will say that it is, but a highly vocal minority can increasingly be found who insist that it is "not a democracy, but rather a republic." Generally speaking, persons who stand for more limited activity in public welfare and less regulation by the government and who hold strongly to "states' rights" adhere to the republic concept. This makes a strong rationale for a more limited pattern of functions and a freer reign for powerful interest groups who oppose present regulations of themselves, but not necessarily of others.

Even if American government is a democracy, *what does democracy mean?* Compressing a wide variety of concepts of democracy, two quite distinct patterns of opinions and action stand out: (*a*) democracy means *equal treatment* of everyone by the government, and (*b*) democracy means a governmental obligation to create *equality of opportunity*. The difference between these two is radical. If everyone is treated equally, inequality is inevitably fostered. If, for example, the physically handicapped person is treated the same as the normal person, inequality becomes augmented with the passing of time. If the poor are taxed equally with the rich, the poor can only get poorer and the rich richer. If everyone is charged the same fee for an education, then more education can be afforded only by the more wealthy, and again inequality becomes cumulative. This may be precisely what the equal treatment proponents want, although they rarely say so.

The opposing concept of democracy holds that it is the business of the government so to control the society that persons of unequal actual opportunity will have equal opportunity as a result of governmental action. For example, this is the rationale behind much of the social-welfare activity of governments, both federal and local. In application it means that if a boy is blind or his parents poor, he should not be required to pay the same tuition rates as a normal child whose parents have average ability to pay for his education. It means in practice that if a politically powerful group is in conflict with a less empowered group, it is the obligation of the government to intercede in favor of the weaker so as to equalize the conflict. The implications of this difference in the concept of democracy is fundamental. Many times disagreements pertaining to whether this or that program is in "the public interest" really amount to which of these two widely held concepts of democracy one favors. Not many persons seem able to articulate the difference succinctly, but it is usually clear from the larger context of what they say which of these ideologies is preferred.

A given person is not always consistent in his adherence to one or the other of these concepts. A man may, for example, hold to the equal treatment concept of democracy when he opposes a progressive income tax, but hold an equality of opportunity viewpoint, too, when he advocates larger scholarship stipends for monetarily poorer students.

These conflicting themes constitute an important backdrop against which the contemporary governmental issues of the day are debated. It is not uncommon to hear one group called by another "un-American" and its ideology "foreign," when actually both viewpoints are indigenous to America. The fact that governmental ideologies are not often rendered explicit may be a factor in the seemingly endless maelstrom of claim and counterclaim in the practical conduct of political decision in the United States.

3. Real versus ideal practices

At several points throughout this book we have emphasized the nature and importance of the distinction between real and ideal patterns. The study of government presents another striking example. Suppose, for example, someone wholly unfamiliar with American government were to read the American Constitution and all of its amendments for the purpose of understanding how Americans are governed. While he would no doubt learn something about the form of American government, he would receive a very unrealistic, not to say downright inaccurate, impression concerning the actual working of the American federal government.

First, there is no mention of political parties or lobbies or pressure groups, yet these are of the very essence of the American mode of government. Also he would read in the Constitution that every four years the American people go to the polls to select a group of officials called "electors," who later meet to deliberate upon and to choose some man to serve as President for the next four years. Nothing is said of political parties holding nominating conventions, candidates representing each party traveling over the land trying to convince voters, party workmen who exchange support of the party for promise of appointment to office if the party wins. Nothing is said in the Constitution which will lead its readers to understand that usually before midnight of election day it is common knowledge who is elected President, even though the electors do not meet for some weeks thereafter.

It is imperative that the student understand that the *formal legal structure of government is only a part of the actual organization and working of government. Customs and traditions are built up over the years which supplement and sometimes contravene the formal legal Constitution.* Thus, while the amendments to the Constitution of the United States permit Negroes to vote and enjoy the same civil and economic rights as whites, it is common knowledge that in large areas of the nation voting rights are denied. Almost everywhere Negroes are somewhat disprivileged with respect to the civil liberties which they enjoy. These are only a few ways in which informal patterns of government supersede the formal ones. We shall now compare the theory and the practice of the American governmental system in several respects.

Representation: myth versus fact

Theoretically the people in each territorial unit, county, city, ward, or state, periodically elect persons who sit in legislative bodies to pass the laws by which the people are governed. In *theory* these *representatives are the official spokesmen for all the people who live in the territorial unit from which the legislator is elected.* Evidence is overwhelming that this theory of representation contains much myth.

1. As we have seen in previous discussions, *the people of each territorial unit are divided into interest groups* such as farmers, workmen, businessmen, prohibitionists, Protestants, parents, pacifists, and so on. It would be *impossible,* even should the legislator wish to do so, *to represent all* of these divergent and opposing interest groups. As it works in practice, most legislators tend to sense and to *serve certain group interests* rather than others. The groups which tend to be served are not necessarily the groups which contain the largest number of potential votes, but rather are the groups which seem to possess sufficient *power* to dethrone the politician through indirect means of influencing voters. Thus, powerful business interests, strong labor unions, owners of newspapers and radio stations, leaders of well-organized religious groups "have to be catered to," because even though they represent minorities, they possess sufficient power to threaten the security of the legislator at subsequent elections.

2. Under the American system *large minorities and sometimes majorities are actually not represented.* If a clear issue is drawn in the election, the side that wins even by a bare margin tends to regard its victory as a "mandate from the people" to put into effect the policies which it espoused in the campaign. Possibly election constitutes a mandate from *some* of the people, but certainly not from all of the people.

While there are, of course, exceptions, the tendency is all too prevalent for law-makers to serve those interest groups which they personally represent and toward which they have loyalties, and those groups which they believe have enough power in the community to facilitate reelection in the future. The recurrent scandals which have been revealed through the years in both of the major political parties in the United States present rather telling testimony of the behind-the-scenes dealings which are made by candidates for public office. Campaign funds, editorial support, and votes are all too frequently bought—not bought in the sense that a contract for sale is drawn up—but "bought" in the sense that a tacit gentlemen's agreement is made to the effect that if a party or a candidate is supported, he will, if elected, serve the wishes and objectives of those who assisted his election or who contributed funds, time, or influence to his support.

Wherever the ideal of truly democratic government is current and the people are well informed relative to the realities of political operation, there is concern regarding the real extent to which current American government is really representative of the wishes and interests of the majority of people. No easy or quick solution seems imminent, but agitation will probably continue so long as current unrepresentative practices continue.

Propaganda: special interest groups

It has been pointed out repeatedly that special interest groups continually try to strengthen their position by securing as many converts to their point of view as possible. Thus, for example, during the period in American history when it was considered to the advantage of industry to secure high tariffs, much energy was devoted by business groups to convincing workmen and farmers that their interests also would be served by a high tariff policy. Organized labor in more recent years has tried to "sell" as many people as possible on the philosophy that high wages benefit not only the workmen who receive the high wages but others as well, because the expenditure of the high wages will constitute a stimulus to prosperity. It is outside the province of this book to evaluate the soundness or fallacy of any of these economic arguments. Our concern is rather with the examination of the ways and means through which special interest groups try to win adherents among persons not directly a part of the interest group but useful to their interest as political power allies in the struggle to manipulate government.

Almost every large organized group in America sponsors under one name or another a *public relations* department. It is the duty of this public relations department to sponsor the cause of the interest group through supplying information to newspapers, bringing "pressure" on legislatures, providing speakers, and in any way possible gaining favor for the program and policies of that particular interest group. These public relations officers often organize and sponsor what are called "pressure groups," whose name well describes their purpose, namely, to exert influence either directly upon legislators or indirectly through voters for the purpose of winning favor for their cause.

Financial power a vital factor in the success of pressure groups

Frequently the possessors of the largest funds ultimately succeed in winning the most adherents. This is not necessarily due to an unethical use of money, such as bribery, but rather due to the fact that the *group which possesses the funds can purchase the services of skilled persons to represent the cause and can purchase organized means of reaching the public, such as newspaper space, time on radio and television, and can support skilled personnel called lobbyists to convince legislators or coerce legislators into giving ear to the wishes of the group represented.* It then becomes the duty of the hirelings of the pressure group to present the case of the group to "the public" so that the public will really believe that the group is serving the public's interest rather than the interest of the propaganda group. It is, of course, possible that the interest of some group and that of the public *might* be wholly compatible, but in numerous and obvious instances the propaganda can easily be demonstrated not to be in the public interest at all.

Propaganda techniques designed to rationalize "causes"

Although there are many devices used by propaganda experts, propaganda resolves itself into a process of rationalizing some group's desires or intentions or programs to make them appear to be in the "best interest" of someone else. Moreover, it is to the propagandist's advantage usually to conceal his real motive. Thus it would be difficult, if not impossible, to go before the American people with a frank and outright request by farmers for higher prices so that they, the farmers, could enjoy a higher standard of living. Such an appeal might win support from some altruistic people, but would largely be ignored. Instead the propagandist would make it appear that great public danger would lurk in the failure to provide farmers with higher prices. He would not necessarily *falsify* the facts, but would *select* the facts which would serve the purpose and make the cause of higher farm prices appear to be necessary to the national defense, the public welfare, or the struggle against communism.

31. LOBBYING IS BIG BUSINESS

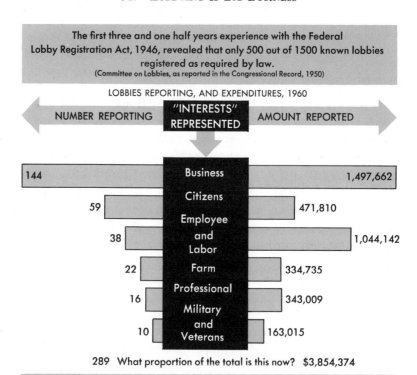

The first three and one half years experience with the Federal Lobby Registration Act, 1946, revealed that only 500 out of 1500 known lobbies registered as required by law.
(Committee on Lobbies, as reported in the Congressional Record, 1950)

LOBBIES REPORTING, AND EXPENDITURES, 1960

NUMBER REPORTING	"INTERESTS" REPRESENTED	AMOUNT REPORTED
144	Business	1,497,662
59	Citizens	471,810
38	Employee and Labor	1,044,142
22	Farm	334,735
16	Professional	343,009
10	Military and Veterans	163,015

289 What proportion of the total is this now? $3,854,374

The "vagueness" and nonenforcement of the current law is such that the number reporting and the expenditures reported give only the most approximate underestimates of the real scope of lobbying in the Federal Government.
(Congressional Quarterly, 1961)

Not only does a propagandist strive to rationalize the real objective which he serves, he usually finds it advantageous to use *catch phrases to which the public is already conditioned*, and then in some way to *attach the catch phrase to the cause favored or the cause opposed*. Thus it is usually safe in America to make an opposed program appear to be "communistic" without troubling oneself to define communism, or really to determine whether the matter in question has any connection with communism or not. The propagandist has learned that most people are unwilling or unable to think effectively on the more involved public issues and that they tend to rely on sweeping and loosely-used concepts. These concepts usually have a more precise meaning, but in order to understand that meaning more knowledge is required than most people have.

Propaganda, then, seems to be an inherent part of the realistic operation of American government, not necessarily because the government itself conducts or authorizes the propaganda, but because the decisions of the men who constitute the government and the decisions of the voters are so largely influenced by the public relations and pressure tactics of special interest groups. These groups strive to gain support for their program by making them appear to be laden with virtue and the public interest, and by making those of their opponents seem fraught with grievous dangers and contrary to the American way of life, the sanctity of the American home, if not also the will of God!

Patronage

Americans tend to think of office holders as persons who secure their position by election. While the more prominent public officials such as the President, senators, and members of the House of Representatives are elected by the people, vastly more persons who administer the affairs of government are appointed. This is not only true of minor officials, but applies to such important office holders as the President's Cabinet, the United States Supreme Court, ambassadors to foreign nations, and representatives to the United Nations. The tradition has become established in American government that the appointees of the numerous offices, from Secretary of State to the postmaster at the crossroads general store, receive their appointments in part as a reward for political service to some elected officer who either makes the appointment or arranges for the appointment. The phrase "the spoils system" may perhaps overdramatize the matter, but it is essentially correct: to the winner of the election belongs the "spoils" of appointing to numerous offices those persons who helped him get elected. While the Civil Service system has placed certain limitations upon the cruder operation of the spoils system, it has by no means eliminated it. Most of the really important policy-making, administrative, and judicial positions are outside the scope of Civil Service control.

The *elected official* who is responsible for the appointments to office is, of course, *not entirely free* to pass out political offices on the basis of his personal wishes. Appointive officers are in the public eye almost as much as elected ones, and the elected official who chooses too many unpopular appointive subordinates may find his popularity jeopardized by his misjudgment or favoritism. At least, then, one may say that the appointive official must present a minimum degree of competence for the position as well as claiming the favor of his appointer. Probably public officials vary greatly in the extent to which their decisions concerning appointees are dominated by the desire to render the best possible public service as opposed to the desire to pay their political debts.

In many other ways the actual organization of government shows striking deviations from the publicly proclaimed and formally stated ideals or constitutional principles. We have limited this discussion to some of the realities involved in representation, propaganda, and patronage. It is not to be assumed that these are the only features—or even the most manifest ones—in the real-ideal cleavages within governmental institutions.

SOME RESEARCH FINDINGS CONCERNING VOTING BEHAVIOR

In a society which allows universal suffrage, the act of voting and the process of deciding how one will vote constitute one of the most important and objective indices to government. How do people make up their minds for whom they shall vote? More specifically, how important are the various kinds of propaganda which emanate from the contending sides during the campaign? A definitive answer to this question is not possible, but a few relevant factors have been fairly well established by research.

First, there is evidence that people do not expose themselves equally to both sides of the propaganda. They give attention selectively, that is, if they are Republican they are much more likely to listen to the Republican speeches, read Republican campaign literature, and associate in friendship and interest groups with other Republicans. This has the effect, of course, of insulating the voter to some extent from what the other side may have to say.

Second, there is evidence to indicate that "economic interest" is not as strong a determinant of party identification as some earlier studies seemed to imply.[2] Apparently party identification is multifactoral and other factors, such as the religion of the candidate, personal popularity, and noneconomic issues such as nationalism or morality,

---

[2] E.g., the findings of Richard Centers, *The Psychology of Social Classes* (Princeton, N.J., Princeton University Press, 1949); and A. W. Jones, *Life, Liberty and Property* (Philadelphia, Lippincott, 1941).

combine with strictly economic interests in such a way that there is no clear correlation between a man's economic interests and the way he votes.

A factor which might contribute to this lack of correlation between economic interest and party allegiance is that it requires a fair degree of sophistication on the part of the voter to determine where his best economic interests really lie. One of the time-honored rules of practical politics is to hold to broad generalities on economic issues when writing platforms and making speeches. Rarely do candidates state their full past voting records on controversial economic questions; and even if they did, it is doubtful that a high enough percentage of the voters understand the intricacies of the legislative process well enough to know how to interpret a man's voting record.

Third, political apathy, as evidenced by nonvoting, is an important factor. The widespread failure to exercise the voting franchise casts doubt on the assumption that there actually is the great desire to participate in government which some political theorists have asserted. Even in presidential elections, with all their fanfare and publicity, only 55 to 65 percent of the voters vote, while in local elections it is not uncommon for only 20 percent of the eligible voters to vote. Political apathy is distributed unevenly in the population—more men than women vote, more older than young people vote, more persons in higher social position vote, and well-educated persons vote more than the less well educated.

Voting for the same party, irrespective of the issues, the candidates, or the nature of the times, seems to be the preponderant pattern. About 70 to 80 percent of the voters regularly vote for the same party, and at least one study showed that 77 percent of the voters voted for the same party that their parents and grandparents did.

If party voting is repetitive, why is it that the parties in power change periodically? Several factors contribute to this condition. Most elections, even the so-called "landslides," are really very close. If as few as 5 percent of the voters voted otherwise, most political outcomes would have been reversed. It is the small group of independent, open-to-change voters who hold the margin of victory in most elections.

SUMMARY

Government is the superinstitution of modern society. Modern government is multifunctional, despite the widespread ambivalence toward the continuing growth of governmental functions. On the operational level, governments work through bureaucracies. The familiar dualism between real and ideal patterns which pervades the entire society, as we have seen, applies conspicuously in government, notably with respect to representation, patronage, and pressure groups. There is considerable ideological unclarity underlying American government, particularly with respect to whether or not our government is a democracy and, if so, what kind.

Studies of voting behavior show that voting is primarily traditional, which fact is buttressed by the selective manner in which people expose themselves to political information. Economic self-interest appears not to be as strong a determinant of party affiliation as has sometimes been claimed. Meanwhile, political apathy remains a conspicuous part of the practical political scene.

SUGGESTED READINGS

Alford, Robert R., *Party and Society*. New York, Rand McNally, 1963.
An excellent sophisticated discussion of "the politics of diversity" in the United States, illustrated with data on class and regional voting since the 1930's.

Baily, Stephen Kemp, *Congress Makes a Law*. New York, Random House, 1964.
A richly documented account of the process through which a proposal becomes a federal law. In our terms, a case study in the contrast between the real and the ideal processes of law enactment.

Burdick, Eugene, and Brodbeck, Arthur J., *American Voting Behavior*. New York, Macmillan, 1959.
This is an interesting book for two reasons—first, because it provides a reappraisal of a number of highly respected studies of voting behavior in the mass society; second, because it brings together 22 different authorities with various interpretations on this important subject.

Greer, Scott A., *Governing the Metropolis*. New York, Wiley, 1962.
The processes of practical politics illustrate many sociological principles, particularly with respect to the governing of the metropolis, the system par excellence, of the mass society. This is descriptive and interpretive.

Gusfield, Joseph R., "Mass Society and Extremist Politics." *American Sociological Review*, Vol. 27 (February, 1962), pp. 19–30.
This is an excellent discussion of a number of explanations for the extremist political ideas and organizations which appear to be inherent in the mass society. The article discusses conditions in the mass society which provide support for democratic political norms and suggests that isolation from mass culture, and not mass culture itself, accentuates extremist views.

Key, V. O., Jr., *Public Opinion and American Democracy*. New York, Knopf, 1961.

A readable and inclusive work by one of the long-time students of public opinion and American government.

Kornhauser, William, *The Politics of Mass Society*. New York, Macmillan, 1959.

Kornhauser has been a long-time student of voting and other aspects of political behavior in the mass society. There is a persistent view that the mass society is vulnerable to totalitarian, and particularly fascist, tendencies. Kornhauser examines the concepts of mass society and pluralism very critically, at least so far as the political implications are concerned.

Lipset, Seymour Martin, *Political Man*. Garden City, N.Y., Doubleday, 1963.

A collection of papers on sociological causes and consequences of American politics.

Lipset, Seymour Martin, and Rukkhan, S., eds., *Party Systems and Voter Alignments*. New York, Free Press, 1967.

An up-to-date, mature study of the commitments of various classes of voters to the several parties. This is an excellent compilation, as well as including some interpretive analyses by the editors.

Monsen, R. Joseph, Jr., and Cannon, Mark W., *The Makers of Public Policy*. New York, McGraw-Hill, 1965.

A continuing interest among sophisticated social scientists has to do with decision-making in the mass society. Who are the decision-makers, how are they related, how are decisions made, how do these decisions relate to public opinion? This book is instructive with respect to these questions.

Woods, Robert C., *Suburbia: Its People and Their Politics*. Boston, Houghton Mifflin, 1963.

A close look at the political views and practices of suburban populations. Increasingly it is this segment of society which seems likely importantly to influence political decision now and in the future.

STUDY QUESTIONS

1. What limit do you see to the extent to which governments may increase their functions?
2. What do you think of Page and MacIver's classification of government functions?
3. What latent functions do you see in government? And how clear an agreement would you expect to find on the subject among informed people?

4. Why do you think the ideological unclarities in American government developed?
5. Where do you stand on the meaning of democracy? Why?
6. Are you familiar with any other real-ideal contradictions in American government than those discussed in this chapter?
7. Are the real-ideal contradictions in American government diminishing or increasing? Why do you think so?
8. How do you account for the large amount of political apathy characteristic of American people?
9. "The balance of power in most elections is held by 3 or 4 percent of the independent voters." Why is this true?
10. Why do not more people follow their economic self-interest when choosing political allegiances?
11. What limitations do you see upon the "absolute power of government"? Would you prefer to see these limitations diminished or increased and why?

27
EDUCATION

Probably because education is so important to the perpetuation of all social systems, education receives a large share of attention, and also criticism. In the mass society, education is for the most part accomplished through special institutions designed for this purpose. To the extent that distinct social systems for education are set up there is the strong probability that they will not socialize exactly in the way in which other systems intend.

Practically everyone has been exposed in informal conversation, if not through formal study, to a plethora of complaints to the effect that educational institutions in American society fail to accomplish various stated and implied purposes. There is the complaint that educational institutions do not prepare young people adequately to assume the kind of jobs which they want and need. There is also the objection that "character," "responsible citizenship," "discipline," and other presumably necessary adult competencies are not well or effectively taught. Schools are accused of being "too academic" to serve the needs of the working-class child and not academic enough to serve the needs of the professionally-oriented youngster. Few seem to realize that a mass educational system, particularly if it is compulsory, can hardly be expected to achieve pluralistic goals, particularly when it is typically operated with an inadequate budget and sometimes with substandard personnel. In a society which has transferred so much of its socialization to a separate institution, and which represents such a kaleidoscope of subcultures, it is small wonder that no one seems satisfied.

Several of the harder realities of education as a social system in American society fail to be appreciated, not only by the thoughtless critics but even by the more sober analysts. First of all, education must be understood as being carried out by one of the nation's largest bureaucracies, and therefore the whole process falls heir to the limitations of bureaucratic enterprise. Like other institutions, educational institutions possess latent functions, some of which are dysfunctional to the achievement of the manifest functions. For example, incorporation of a tenure system, while it provides protection for the capable, creative teacher, at the same time also provides a cloister, a protected refuge, for the borderline incompetent. While the elaborate paraphernalia of student counseling and guidance present a potential for helping some students to escape the limitations of their own class position, there is at the same time set up a pattern of power and influence of teachers over students which may run contrary to parental wishes and sometimes to the students' own best interest. All of this not because of base motives on the part of anyone, but simply because the apparatus of large-scale organization under the harassment of limited budgets and the inadequacy of certain personnel is simply not up to the task which it has been assigned.

Among the abiding dilemmas of education in the mass society are these: Despite increasing sophistication on the part of teachers and administrators, an alarming proportion of students "drop-out" before completing their educational goals. With the minimum requirements for employment constantly being raised, the high school dropout borders on unemployability or only marginal employability for the rest of his life. Particularly for the male, this poses problems to other people, since his wife and children will also be dependent upon his earning power for their own levels of living. Moreover, since the dropout is rarely employable at his age, he becomes an active candidate for other kinds of deviation, notably delinquency, crime, and probably mental illness. While the high school dropout has received a great deal of attention, the college dropout poses a more complicated question. The problem is not so much his survival in the economy as the waste of talent which the problem poses. In one study reported in the press at the time of this writing, a University of California research revealed that on the basis of a presumably reliable test for creativity, a sample of three colleges studied revealed a higher proportion of creative students in the dropout category than were graduated by these colleges. If the system is unable to retain more than half of its most creative clientele, then manifestly there is something wrong.

What may be wrong may also be, under the circumstances, unavoidable; and this poses a further dilemma. Education is an increasingly expensive enterprise. Not only is the paraphernalia of education increasingly costly—laboratories, libraries, classrooms, teachers' salaries —but the proportion of the population requiring such services is on the increase. Earlier we pointed out that one-half of the population is currently under 25 years of age. It is expected that a clear majority of this group will enter and presumably expect to complete college, and a growing proportion will extend education into graduate school and professional school. How can a society afford, whether through public expenditure or private, to support, at ever-increasing costs, so large a proportion of its people through these long, unproductive years? Idealists from time to time point out that if we diverted, say, half of our liquor budget, or 20 percent of our space budget, to educational purposes, the problem might be solved. But how is such a suggestion to be implemented? Who, incidentally, is the "we"?

On another level, educational systems are experiencing the consequences of their own bureaucratization. One of these processes is the emergence of teachers from employee status to professional status. In substance this means that as bureaucratic role players, teachers are increasingly beginning to assert the prerogatives of other professionals, namely, to take on to themselves more and more of the responsibility for carrying on the educational enterprise. They are more aggressive about curriculum content, tenure, participation in administration, and salaries. Teachers' strikes, a rarity even a decade ago, are today a common occurrence, particularly in the larger cities. The issues are not merely higher pay; they fan out into a wide spectrum of objectives which come down to an insistence that their professional status be recognized in the conduct of the educational enterprise.

Juxtaposed against teacher professionalism is a long-established tradition in American society centering around such clichés as "local control of education" and parents' "right" to a major voice in education. Perhaps at one time these were functional, but at the present time, with the exception of some middle-class parents, most parents are manifestly incompetent to serve as the overseers of education. Subject matter is too advanced and techniques simply too complicated for most parents to comprehend, much less to direct intelligently. Nonetheless, legally and sentimentally the tendency is to try to operate with the old cultural blueprint; and the fact that this blueprint bears little resemblance to the realities of the present day requires more sophistication than most can muster.

These, then, are only a few of the underlying facts, trends, and enigmas which interact with other hard realities to make the formal socializing institution as much a battleground for system conflict as an effective socializer for system functioning. It is intended that the rest of this chapter will spell out some of the culture traditions which are involved in the educational blueprint, some of the institutional anachronisms which of necessity follow, as well as some of the attempts at rational control of the educational system.

THE FUNCTIONS OF INSTITUTIONAL EDUCATION

1. The universal function of education

Education is a universal process found in all human societies. Everywhere and at all times man has thought it necessary to bring up his young by indoctrinating them with the culture of his society. Part of that indoctrination he does deliberately by formal teachings, either through the family or through organized education or religion. Some societies, however, do very little formal educating of their young. For example, the Manus people of New Guinea do not have schools, books, teachers, or even an alphabet. Yet the Manus child learns the Manus language, the religion, the morals, and the etiquette required in order to function successfully in the Manus society. Much of this learning is, of course, informal and unconscious. The child learns by imitation and by the suggestion and examples of his associates. In short, the Manus child, like the American child or the child of any other society, learns the skills, the ideas, and the values which he needs to know in order to be able to function in his society. This we may term "the universal function of education." Stated briefly, it consists of the *conditioning of the plastic and growing human being so that he will be able to function in a society made up of a similarly conditioned people.* This every society needs to do for a substantial number, though not necessarily all, of its members in order to remain intact. If the society fails to achieve this objective, its nature changes, or it may go out of existence as a society entirely. In a sense, the ultimate requirement for the continuity of any society is the ability successfully to perpetuate itself by indoctrinating its offspring with the folkways and mores which enable it to exist. This preservation of its cultural heritage is indispensable to the continuity of any society.

As we have previously noted, of course, no society reproduces itself identically in successive generations. This is simply another way of saying that the indoctrination of the young has always been incomplete, or that once indoctrinated, the people do not remain that way. This fact of social change, however, should not obscure the fundamental fact that even in the most revolutionary society there is much that is old in the postrevolutionary social order. Living with other people would be incomprehensible unless there were a fundamental basis of understanding, a common heritage of language, and some agreement upon values. Without these common denominators a society would simply fall apart, or perhaps to put it more accurately, there would be no society at all. Not only, then, is the indoctrination of the young with the prevailing culture a universal educational process, it is also an indispensable one for the existence of the society.

2. The variable functions of education

After the universal, indispensable societal need is met, there remain considerable alternatives as to the form, content, and purposes which a society may incorporate in its educational efforts. Education may be formal or informal; it may be dominated by the family, by the government, by organized religion, by a semi-independent agency such as the school in America, or by some combination of these. Education may be extended to both sexes or limited to one. The sexes may be segregated during some or all of their formal education, or they may be educated together. The culture of the society may condone or encourage almost universal education, or may limit education to certain social classes. Education may be concerned with training people for vocations, or it may be limited to liberal or spiritual or aesthetic matters. It may be the purpose of education to mold people along a single basic pattern as closely as possible, or it may be considered desirable to encourage individuality and individual differences in greater or lesser degree. The educational system may exist for the purpose of indoctrinating or for encouraging "free thinking" along certain lines. In short, there is almost no end to the differences which can be found in the educational systems and philosophies now existing or that have existed in the known past.

3. Purposive and implicit education

The prevailing American view is to think of education as synonymous with the school. This leads to numerous faulty interpretations and unreasonable hopes. It is doubtful if one should assume that the school is even the chief educational agency in modern society. The teaching-learning process, whether so intended or not, is a continual process of socialization of the person literally from the cradle to the grave. Only a small part of the total education time of even the most learned person is spent in school, and learning occurs continuously through a wide variety of media outside of school—from movies, radio, television, the church, political speeches, newspapers, magazines, books, informal association with other persons, and from myriads of other sources.

As an institution, on the other hand, education is the function of the societally-sponsored school system from the nursery school to the postgraduate college. While such agencies as the movies, the play group, or the poolroom undoubtedly have influence upon the formation and modification of the personality, they do not exist primarily for that purpose. Their "educational functions" are incidental to other functions. *In the broadest sense, education is synonymous with the socialization of the person; in its stricter sense, education as an institution consists of the programs of the formal educational organization of the society* and the effects of these programs on the persons influenced by these organizations.

32.   SOURCES OF PUBLIC SCHOOL SUPPORT, 1960

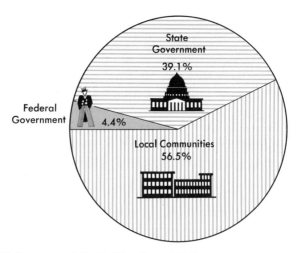

Source: U.S. Department of Health, Education and Welfare.

4. Education interacts with the total society and may foster change

The educational system is, as we have seen, a creature of the society; but it is sometimes so operated that instead of serving the intended purposes of the society, it may also modify the society. There are those who think that the contemporary American educational system is doing precisely that. It was originally established and supported by a capitalistic and somewhat democratic society. It was given freedom under the law to formulate in some measure its own policies and objectives, but that freedom is by no means complete. Segments of the American educational system then became "liberal," that is, chose to examine and to criticize many aspects of the government and society which created and supported the educational system. These segments succeeded in creating critical, usually called "liberal," attitudes on the part of the system's products, the pupils, some of whom became politically liberal and used their knowledge for the purpose of changing the larger society.

This liberalism, then, became the point of attack by those persons and groups who are, or were, hostile to change in the traditional *modus operandi*. School and teachers are often attacked, not to say castigated, for informing pupils regarding some of the failures of the society and encouraging them to study some of the proposals for reform.

It is entirely possible that part of the pressure for change may be traced to the encouragement of "critical thinking" by some teachers and that this may be a stimulus to social change. However, forces other than the educational system will be found to have shared in the process. But certainly the school system, especially the university system, appears to have exerted an appreciable influence toward liberal social thinking in America. It is desirable, therefore, that the educational system of America be examined for the purpose of determining (1) what values and philosophies are promulgated in the educational system, (2) what influences other institutions exert upon the system of education, and (3) what main lines of evaluation of these values, philosophies, and proposals are current in the present American culture.

IDEOLOGICAL ROOTS OF THE EDUCATIONAL SYSTEM OF THE UNITED STATES

1. "Liberal" education

The phrase "liberal education" is used in somewhat different ways by different persons, but it has one core of meaning in common acceptance. Liberal education stands *in contrast to indoctrination*. It is the philosophy that a person should be made familiar not only with the values and ideas and precepts of his own culture but also with other cultures, both past and contemporary. It holds, for example, that even though a man is Protestant, he should be familiar with the history of Catholicism and the ideas of the great Catholic thinkers. Thus a liberally educated person will probably have read Hitler's *Mein Kampf*.

But why spend time reading a book written by the one-time leader of an enemy nation? Hitler is dead, and probably also is much of Germany's Nazism. A liberally educated man, however, would want to be familiar with the content of *Mein Kampf*, not because he wishes necessarily to accept any of its preachments, but simply because it has been an influential book in fashioning, or at least in representing, one of the great movements in modern Europe. The same logic would hold for studying the *Communist Manifesto* and the works of St. Thomas Aquinas.

The liberal would study science, also, not necessarily because he wishes to become a scientist or otherwise put his scientific knowledge to "practical" use, but rather because science is a significant part of modern culture and the scientific mode of thinking is an important one. Liberal education, of course, does not neglect the study of one's own culture, but tries to get the student to *see his own culture within the perspective of the larger stream of ideas, men, and events which antedate and surround it.*

Liberal education, however, has its *opponents*. It has been attacked because of the "moral relativism" which the liberally educated tend to develop. Moral relativism means the recognition that there are *many* different moral-ethical-religious-political systems, each of which has its own logic and justification, none representing a corner on the whole or sole "truth." It is easy for the liberally educated person to become a moral relativist. Having familiarized himself with other ideas and philosophies, with others' attempts to rationalize different thought systems than his own, he may tend to lose some of his cruder ethnocentrism. During the early period of World War II, the complaint was commonly heard that America's educated young men, because they could "see" both sides more clearly than the ignorant, would not have sufficient enthusiasm to fight for their own nation's side since they could see virtue and fault in both sides. The implication of these critics was to the effect, then, that ignorance of other cultures would be an asset because one could feel more secure in the all-sufficiency and perfection of his own!

Another criticism of liberal education is that it is "impractical," by which is usually meant that it does not necessarily fit one for a special job, with the possible exception of such liberal professions as journalism, ministry, politics, and perhaps teaching. This criticism really is beside the point, of course, because liberal education was never claimed by its proponents to be vocational education. No one claimed that knowledge about American history or the Magna Charta would per se make a better filling-station attendant or a more effective salesman. The projected values of liberal education are those of better citizenship, broad understanding of the universe, and a perspective on change. Liberal education values emancipation over ethnocentrism, objectivity over bigotry.

2. Vocational education

Another root of American formal education, and to a considerable extent a reaction to liberal education, has been the rise of an emphasis on special training for specific jobs. Emphasis on vocational education extends from the professional schools of the great universities down to the junior high school. Most metropolitan cities have one or more high schools, often called "vocational high schools," which specialize in training children for such job fields as stenography, agriculture, printing, carpentry, and machine shop work.

The theory underlying this movement is obvious enough. (*a*) The trained person does better work, receives better pay and more rapid advancement, as a rule, than the less well trained. (*b*) There has, however, been a second factor in the rise of vocational high schools. Many boys and girls, either because they lacked ability or because they lacked interest, were found not to be well adjusted in the conventional academic high school. Since compulsory school attendance laws and laws prohibiting the employment of children existed in most states, these persons who were not well adjusted to the conventional high school had to be placed somewhere. The vocational high school seemed to be a logical place. (*c*) There were also those people who favored the vocational high school on the ground that many people could not afford the time or the money for the "luxury" of a liberal education. They could make time count for more in dollars and cents by using their school time to train them for some job. This philosophy has a strong appeal in a society in which pecuniary values are as prominent as they are in the United States.

The *critics of vocational education* have taken the position, first, that much time is wasted in vocational education. Not very many children know what occupation they wish to follow when they are in junior or senior high school. Even if they did know, it would be possible to learn the necessary skills in a much shorter time and with much better results if training were received directly as apprentices in the training departments of large corporations, or in specialized trade schools for adults. Critics have also contended that often the standards of work in vocational schools have been low and technically obsolescent. Moreover, the availability of vocational schools and courses has tended to encourage vocational school work for students capable of attaining more advanced educational objectives.

CONTEMPORARY ISSUES

The unending stream of recent criticism and revaluation, of varying quality and intent, which has been leveled against American educational institutions may be summarized under about seven captions, several of which have already been mentioned briefly in the preceding paragraphs. *It will not be our purpose here to suggest how our educational problems may be solved nor which of the critics is right about the various issues and their resolution.* Our purpose is simply to present a *systematic analysis of the revaluation process taking place,* giving some historical perspective and occasionally indicating, where it is known, what degree of fact underlies the alleged inadequacy. Solutions will be discussed from time to time to illustrate various points, but these illustrations are not to be taken as recommendations or endorsements of any one plan over another. It is to be expected that students, like everyone else, will have certain preconceptions and will favor certain changes and certain solutions over others. Presumably, also, students having the opportunity to be better informed in some matters may formulate opinions which have better bases in empirical reality and may have more sophisticated rationales for their preferences.

1. Content

One of the most persistent charges leveled against American educational institutions is that at all levels, but especially in the high schools, something called "content" is neglected. By content is usually meant a somewhat formal and academic mastery of certain traditional subject matter areas, for example, history, mathematics, American government, or English usage. There seems little doubt that the average student is today required to know considerably less about these than formerly. If the number of days a student goes to school remains roughly the same as it was a generation ago, and, as is the case, he now receives academic credit for such subjects as auto driving, home economics, tractor repair, physical education, typewriting, and "life adjustment and social relations," then he is of necessity going to spend less time on, and presumably therefore will learn less about, the traditional and so-called basic subjects. It should be pointed out, however, that no one knows, empirically that is, that this is the case, because it is impossible to com-

pare what an average high school student now knows about such subjects with what, say, his parents knew when they graduated from high
school. Besides, and perhaps more importantly, it is of greater significance what one has learned five or ten or twenty years after high school
than what he knows at examination time in high school. There is considerable research to show that very little of formal learning is long
retained after school years, unless the student uses it in college or in an
occupation, or cultivates certain academic interests as an avocation.
This may or may not be an argument against teaching him these things
in the first place, however.

It is interesting to the observer of the conflict to note that formal
education in science and mathematics is regarded by many critics as
superior content in education. The preoccupation with these subject
matter areas, to the neglect of others like English, literature, world
history, or government, is probably due to the accent on science drama-
tized by the accomplishments and ambitions of the space age. With the
Russian nation as our only effective challenger for world leadership,
the Russians' competency has become a matter of frenzied concern.
Hence the clamor for more scientific and mathematical content at the
expense of all else.

In spite of differences in emphasis and focus, however, the most
pervasive criticism of American education today is that by accenting
vocational education, well-adjusted and well-rounded personalities, and
education as a thoroughly pleasant activity, we have reached the point
where we do not educate enough.

2. "Discipline"

Practically everybody, it seems, is concerned about the "lack of
discipline" in educational institutions as manifest by their products.
Again, this means different things to different people, but the core idea
seems to be that there has come about a changed attitude toward work
and responsibility in general. It is alleged that schools have ceased in
considerable measure to require "enough" and *difficult enough* work,
especially from the superior students. (Probably the inferior ones work
as hard as ever to keep their heads "above water.") This has the twin
effects, it is claimed, of students actually learning less than they would
if they "really had to work" and not really ever learning that one has
to put forth considerable effort, perhaps under unpleasant circumstances, in order to achieve competence. A refinement of this idea holds
that in large measure the only real test of their own competence which

many students experience is either on the athletic field or in their successes and failures in social relationships. The net effect, it is claimed further, is to ill-prepare the student for his maximum vocational achievement or for various kinds of social responsibilities which often involve much unpleasant and hard work. Whether these allegations are true or false is very difficult to ascertain objectively. We are here concerned only with the fact that they are current, widespread, and may have bearing on the kinds of changes which may be forthcoming in American education.

3. "Fads and frills"

Many critics, it seems, are "agin' fads and frills." It is not always easy, however, to determine precisely what constitutes a fad or a frill. Apparently what most critics deplore is the substitution of many of the newer educational activities for the traditional content courses. Overemphasis on extracurricular activities is under considerable reappraisal. By "overemphasis" is meant that while the extracurricular activity may in itself be wholly desirable, it becomes undesirable when it interferes with or takes precedence over other activities equally or more desirable.

Educational institutions have in part been caught by their own adaptive practices and their own successes. For example, one can make a very good case for auto driving as a high school subject. What could one possibly teach a high school student which would be more vitally related to his own safety and the safety of others than how to handle an automobile correctly? Moreover, the activity is dramatic and has high immediate interest value. Small wonder, then, if students become much more interested in things like auto driving, putting on high school dances, and various vocational courses. The fads and frills do seem to "take over."

4. Athletic "overemphasis"

Considerably fewer but apparently a growing number of critics are concerned about athletic overemphasis. The criticism is directed at public performances of school teams, rather than intramural physical exercise. What these critics lack in numbers they may make up in the logic of their case. Many communities which are hard pressed for funds to operate their educational institutions would impress a foreign traveler as "school plants" consisting of magnificent gymnasiums and athletic fields surrounded by secondrate classrooms with substandard equipment. It is typical for football coaches to receive salaries higher than any of the teachers of academic subjects. Typically, the equipment of the athletic teams is more modern than the equipment in the laboratories or the books in the libraries. Communities become excited over such issues as whether or not changing a coach will increase the probability of having a championship team. All of this activity and all of this expenditure so that a couple of dozen young men of superior physique, who need physical education less than anyone else, may put on a dozen or so hour-long exhibitions per year before their fellow students and townspeople! So runs the critique.

Then, also, there are nuisance factors, such as the added efforts required to keep some outstanding athletes academically eligible for athletic participation even under very minimal scholastic requirements. On the college level, there are the dubious ethics involved in holding to technical compliance with the ethics of noncommercial athletics and yet, in the scramble for top talent, coming up with a winning team. It is held by many that this whole preoccupation with athletics gives the student, and especially the athlete, a very effective—but necessary?—lesson in duplicity and cynicism.

One solution to this problem has been suggested: That each community should set up two more or less parallel institutions: (*a*) a school in the strict, traditional sense, devoid of any athletic functions whatever except, of course, intramural physical activities in which all students participate; and (*b*) in addition, something which might be called a "youth agency" for all the young people in the community whether or not they go to school. This youth agency would have charge of all athletic and social activities and would have its own budget, personnel, and, probably, buildings. No one would need to be concerned about the academic eligibility of athletes, any more than the school is now concerned about the athletic eligibility of all of the students. This, it is argued, would be thoroughly democratic, would allow the school to specialize in education, and would have the added value of enabling the community to better see what it is paying for each function, relative to what it is getting.

5. Anti-intellectualism

By anti-intellectualism is meant that the total impact of public school education, and to some extent college, too, has come to have the effect of depreciating intellectual pursuits in favor of other kinds of values. The popular term "egghead" which came into existence about

1950, while not related directly to education at that time, was a manifestation of a widely held contempt for the man of learning and for intellectual pursuits generally. Anti-intellectualism is in the nature of the case a subtle, *if true*, aspect of education. Certainly no one openly advocates that students not be intellectual, not learn, or not seek intellectual development. Instead, to the extent that this criticism of education is true, it results from intellectual pursuits getting crowded out in the pursuit of other values, such as facilitating the life adjustment and vocational skills of the student, assisting him to develop his physical potentials, supplying him with sex education, providing him with "meaningful life experiences," and so on. Most of these and other objectives have come into education during recent decades, and their exponents have done an effective job of demonstrating their merits. No one, it seems, has been successful in selling either all the students or the entire community, or, for that matter, even many in the teaching profession itself, on the merits of learning *à la* the liberal arts tradition which we have discussed earlier. Studies of the attitudes of college students have indicated that these anti-intellectual attitudes even survive through the college years, that insofar as college students work hard in their academic pursuits, most of them do so for nonintellectual reasons, that is, for such objectives as getting into a profession or occupation, or more immediately, getting into a fraternity or sorority and remaining in one, or remaining eligible for some extracurricular interest which requires certain scholastic levels. The popular courses on most college campuses are usually not the courses in which the students are held to high intellectual achievement. The numbers of students to whom truly intellectual pursuits hold a high priority are few, and such students are often not highly regarded in the status structure of the campus community.

Some critics have even charged that anti-intellectualism has become prevalent among the teachers themselves, particularly in the public schools. A disproportionate part of a teacher's training period is said to go into methods of teaching, "understanding" of children, and the practical management of the school plant, leaving little time and often less interest in the development of the teacher as an educated person in the sense that he is conversant with significant ideas, literate in the fuller sense, and intellectually curious. Obviously these criticisms, if true, apply very unequally to the teaching profession. The disturbing thing to many people is that they should apply to *any* teachers whatsoever. Critics have been more articulate in their statement of this criticism than in their presentation of any practicable means for correcting it.

6. "Class bias" in the school system

During recent years American education has become increasingly criticized for its antidemocratic, or at least nondemocratic, practices. It is argued that instead of providing an instrumentality through which all American youth, regardless of race or economic status, can avail itself of educational opportunity, the American educational system has become a class-biased agency. The benefits of education are not available to all American youth on an equal footing. At least four separate indictments are made, all supported by statistical evidence.

1. Many persons of high intellectual ability are denied admission to college and graduate school because they cannot afford to pay the costs of higher education. Statistics show clearly that many thousands of talented men and women *in the lower economic groups* do not go to college and graduate school. During the past, as now, some have been aided by scholarships, loans, and other forms of aid, but the amount of such aid and the number of persons aided is far below the need. In various ways financial aids have improved in recent years, however, and if this trend is continued, the loss of talent may be lessened.

2. Our educational system discriminates against Negroes on all levels of education. Per pupil costs of Negro-segregated schools in parts of the South are appreciably lower than for whites in the same communities, and sometimes the discrepancies are appalling. The same is true on the college level.

3. Less easy to prove statistically is the charge that lower-class children do not receive equal treatment in many schools, either as a result of administrative policy or because of the class bias of teachers who are recruited mainly from the so-called middle class and consequently manifest the ideas and prejudices characteristic of middle-class culture. They simply do not understand life realities of the lower-class child, even if they try.

4. Negroes, Jews, and lower-class people are said to be discriminated against very generally, and sometimes quite openly, by the professional schools, which either categorically deny admission to such groups or admit them in small numbers, even though there are numerous persons in these groups who adequately meet the scholarship and character standards ostensibly set for admission to these schools. This is a difficult charge to prove conclusively, but enough fragmentary evidence is presented here and there to make the charge plausible at least.

Why, now, should a society be concerned about matters such as these? Suppose there is class bias in the educational system—does not such bias exist throughout the society and give rise to no comparable clamor for reform elsewhere? (*a*) What these critics have in mind is that the educational system is an important resource of the total society and that the benefit of it should be democratically shared, since we claim to be a democratic people. (*b*) Even more important, perhaps, is a practical consideration. Failure of a society to educate its potential leadership results in a net loss of trained talent to the entire society. If there are, as one set of statistics seems to show, over half a million American youth of college age who have the mentality to do *B* level college work or better and who are not now in college because their admission is denied for one reason or another, then the entire society, not merely those individuals, is the loser. The potential physicians, teachers, and scientists who are not trained constitute an irreparable loss of talent. Hence both ethical and practical considerations cooperate to demonstrate that class bias in regard to education constitutes a significant unsolved problem in American education.

7. Is American education free or is it subservient to other systems?

It is commonly held that the United States has a "free" educational system. The word *free* is intended to connote that schools, although they are largely supported by the government, are free from political and religious domination. There is growing doubt, however, that the American system of public education is as free as it is alleged to be.

The issue in the public schools

The formal organization of public schools would imply that education there is not dominated by government or religion. Local schools are under the control usually of boards of education elected by the real-estate property owners in some states and by all citizens in others. These school boards appoint the chief executive officer of the system, who in the large cities is usually called a "superintendent" or "commissioner." Presumably he runs the educational system as he thinks best, and presumably he is appointed because he is a capable professional man whose training and experience qualify him for the office. Both of these assumptions are, in many cases, not borne out by the facts. Many school administrators are not really permitted to operate the school systems in the manner in which they deem wise, nor are they chosen always strictly on the basis of their professional competence. In one way or another, there is recurrent meddling and dictating to school administrators by the various and sundry pressure groups of the community. During recent years there have been startling revelations, for example, concerning the choice of textbooks. Books have been discarded, not on the basis of their merit, but rather because they have been too accurate in revealing certain truths about American history or some aspect or other of the economic system. Presumably, someone does not want the truth taught in our free public schools!

There are, of course, *great variations from community to community* with respect to the degree of freedom permitted. Paradoxical as it may seem, one of the chief and recurrent problems of public school administration in America is the *struggle to maintain the freedom in fact which is granted in name*. There seems little doubt that there are still powerful groups of persons in the United States who conceive of the function of education as being largely that of the indoctrination of children with some one set of ethnocentric values to the exclusion of all others. Not infrequently school boards have made it an express policy to appoint only such administrators as will be "safe," meaning conservative about innovation in either the methods or the contents of teaching, and have required that the same policy be enforced in the selection and promotion of the teaching personnel. Some observers believe that this condition is growing worse, and some that it is growing better, but the facts, of course, are difficult to secure.

The issue on the college level

Colleges and universities face the same basic problem, although they are not as subject to direct local community censorship as are the more elementary schools. The tradition has somehow been established that higher education may pursue the truth much more independently than public schools in those instances in which truth lies along lines contrary to the values of the power groups of the community. But the difference between colleges and elementary schools is only in degree. Basically, colleges and universities must depend for their support on (1) public funds which are controlled by state legislatures, (2) public funds controlled by city boards of education, or (3) voluntary endowments and gifts of philanthropic persons or institutions. Thus the *universities are really only as free as the holders of these "purse strings" permit them to be*. College and university administrators and professors alike hold tenure always subject to the wishes of those who pay their salaries. This fact is made obvious periodically when some state legislature, philanthropist, or pressure group conducts an investigation, stages a "red hunt," or demands the dismissal of some officer or teacher. But the latent power is there all the time, and the consciousness among teachers that it exists probably constitutes an important limitation on the kinds of research undertaken, the publication of research findings, and the kinds of materials presented in the classrooms. There are undoubtedly persons in educational roles who disregard, overlook, or deliberately challenge the pressure groups which scrutinize public education; but it seems probable that such persons are clearly in the minority. It could hardly be otherwise.

The role of the scholar is a cultural anachronism

It is probably inevitable that there would exist some discrepancy between the values held by certain groups in the community and those held by the scientist and scholar. The scientist and scholar is a seeker after the truth, a discoverer of the new, a critic, an analyst of those things which the average man takes for granted. His worth is usually judged by professional standards in which originality, creativeness, and discovery are very prominent. The scholar is a pioneer, ever pushing out on the periphery of human ignorance. But each new discovery runs the risk of antagonizing persons and groups who have vested interests in the previous untruth, or who conceive their function as that of perpetuating the old, not because they wish to be "backward" but because they may believe sincerely that their old values are the right ones. Thus, when certain branches of organized religion rose up to quell the teaching of the theory of evolution in the universities, they did so either because they refused to accept the scientists' findings or because they believed that widespread knowledge of evolution would destroy the authority of the Bible and of the church. Similarly, when some conservative people opposed the study of Russia in American colleges and universities, they did so because they believed that such knowledge about another economic culture would weaken the loyalty and faith of American youth in their own economic system. Regardless of the motives, the *fact* of pressure groups and their constant influence upon American higher education should not be overlooked.

Probably one of the distinct attributes of American culture has been the existence of the semi-autonomous educational system, which in spite of its control is still the freest mass educational system with which man has had experience in his whole history. There are those who believe that out of this fact grows much of the distinctiveness of American culture. When one considers the fundamental problems of ethnocentrism, the significant fact seems not to be that education and the scholar are inhibited, but rather that they are as free as they are.

33. KEY RECOMMENDATIONS OF PRESIDENT'S COMMISSION ON HIGHER EDUCATINN

① Guarantee of a good high school education to every qualified youth

② Federal scholarships up to $800 a year, to go to 20% of all college students

③ Federal fellowships to $1500 a year for 30,000 graduate students

④ Elimination of tuition fees for first 2 years of publicly-controlled colleges; cut in other tuition fees to 1938-39 level

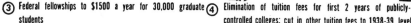

⑤ Discontinuance by all colleges of discriminatory practices—withholding of federal funds from violators

⑥ Establishment of more free, public, community colleges

⑦ Continued growth of privately controlled and supported institutions

⑧ A more comprehensive program of adult education

SUMMARY

Education may be considered synonymous with socialization. Wherever there is learning, whenever there is modification of behavior, there the teacher-learner process is operating. From cradle to grave, education is occurring. Every group with which one is in contact is an educational influence, although, of course, there are great differences between groups as educational agencies. Aside from the school system, and quite as important as the school system, are the family, the play group, radio and television, the movies, the church, newspapers, magazines, and books.

Education, as a formal system, consists of the organized deliberate program of teaching. The universal function of formal education is one of indoctrination of the infant and growing person into the culture of his society. This may be done in a startling variety of ways and for very different purposes, and therefore there are many variable functions of education.

The educational system of the United States is currently characterized by numerous clashes among different schools of thought concerning the advisability and the relative importance of such emphases as liberal education, vocational education, and others. The main arguments for and against each of these have been summarized.

According to our idealized culture patterns, American education is and ought to be free, that is, not influenced by other institutions such as church, state, or economic groups. While American education is probably the freest educational system in the world, there are many ways in which various pressure groups exert effective control over both public and private education in the United States. In many respects colleges and universities are freer from some of the cruder aspects of this control, but they are by no means immune to it. (Note the chart "Key Recommendations of the President's Commission on Higher Education" on page 505. None of these recommendations, made by the commission in 1947, has been withdrawn since that time; rather, all of them are still active issues, showing that, even during a period of strong public concern, modifications are brought about very slowly.)

Conflict between education and other aspects of the society is probably inevitable because of the difference in the roles of the scholar and most of the rest of society. The scholar is an innovator, a searcher for truth, while many of the other agencies of society, for one reason or another, are the perpetuators of old traditions. It is quite understandable that the custodians of the old would find themselves in conflict with the diffusion of new discoveries and would seek to control, if not prevent, the diffusion of such knowledge as is either misunderstood or contrary to the pre-existing values. Authoritarian societies have solved the problem by sharply limiting or entirely prohibiting the activities of scholars, at least so far as the diffusion of their findings is concerned. One of the significant earmarks of democracy is its attempt at least to maintain a semi-autonomous community of scholars and learners, called a "free educational system." If democracy is not to be reduced and eventually lost, many scholars of education warn, constant effort must be directed at the groups and forces which are ever seeking to subordinate education to other societal interests.

SUGGESTED READINGS

Bereday, George Z. F., Brickman, William W., and Read, Gerald, with the assistance of Schlesinger, Ina, eds., *The Changing Soviet School.* The Comparative Education Society Field Study in the U.S.S.R. Boston, Houghton Mifflin, 1960.
Since the spectacular scientific successes of the Russians, much attention has been given by some Americans to the Russian educational system. This is a very good "inside view" of Soviet education based upon the direct observations of 70 members of the Comparative Education Society who spent a month in the Soviet Union during 1958.

Chandler, B. J., Stiles, Lindley J., and Kitsuse, John I., eds., *Education in Urban Society.* New York, Dodd, Mead, 1963.
One of many books which combine the views of various people concerning the educational enterprise. This book focuses on the impact of urbanization on the school system.

Conant, James B., *The American High School Today: A First Report to Interested Citizens.* New York, McGraw-Hill, 1959.
This has been an influential book by a former president of Harvard University who, after retirement, devoted himself to developing a balanced, fact-laden critique of the American high school. While almost ten years old, this book still stands as a solid documentary on this pivotal institution.

Corwin, Ronald G., *A Sociology of Education.* New York, Appleton-Century-Crofts, 1965.
A wide variety of books have been labeled "the sociology of education." This one is distinctive in that it deals with sociological realities in the public school system rather than with a miscellany of information and viewpoints. The foci of attention are upon the emerging patterns of class, status, and power in the public schools and the implications of class and power differentials upon the condition of the social system devoted to education. A fresh approach.

Jewett, Robert E., "Why the Able Public School Teacher Is Dissatisfied."
    Educational Research Bulletin, Vol. 36 (October, 1957), pp. 223–234.
Report on an excellent study of why the better teachers leave teaching—*not*
salary.

Mills, C. Wright, "Mass Society and Liberal Education," in Irving Louis
    Horowitz, ed., *Power, Politics and People: The Collected Essays of
    C. Wright Mills.* New York, Oxford University Press, 1963, Chapter 9.
C. Wright Mills, macro-sociologist as well as social critic, presents a vigorous
assessment of the effect of the realities of the mass society upon the traditional
concepts of liberal education.

Mizruchi, Ephraim Harold, "Educational Values and the American Dream,"
    in Ephraim H. Mizruchi, *The Substance of Sociology.* New York,
    Appleton-Century-Crofts, 1967, pp. 101–109.
An excellent article interlacing American success values, the realities of the
stratification system, and American education.

Sanford, Nevitt, ed., *The American College: A Psychological and Social
    Interpretation of Higher Learning.* New York, Wiley, 1962.
"A set of articles on student society and culture, student performance, and the
effects of college education."

Riesman, David, *Constraint and Variety in American Education.* Lincoln,
    University of Nebraska Press, 1956.
A very readable and provocative account of a number of aspects of American
higher education. Draws a number of important distinctions among professors
and institutions which ought to be better understood than they often are.

Roberts, Joan I., ed., *School Children in the Urban Slum.* New York, Free
    Press, 1967.
A collection of a wide variety of materials dealing with the characteristics of
children in the urban slum, their tussle with education and education with them,
all done in a thoroughly scholarly and professional manner. A must book for
people with professional interests in education.

Ryans, David G., *Characteristics of Teachers: Their Description, Compari-
    son, and Appraisal. A Research Study.* Washington, D.C., American
    Council on Education, 1960.
This is a report on a ten-year research costing $200,000 undertaken in an at-
tempt to determine whether it would be possible to identify and predict success
in teaching. In one sense the study failed, that is, there is no neat way to identify
a good teacher, but in another sense it is useful in that it demonstrates that good
teaching cannot be "guaranteed" by easy techniques of personnel selection.
Teaching is apparently still a very subtle interactional process—a social process
which eludes even very competent researching.

STUDY QUESTIONS

1. Distinguish between education and the school system. Why is this distinction important in American society?
2. Why is it difficult to determine the educational significance of radio and movies?
3. What reason is there to believe that the influence of movies is not as great as is commonly assumed?
4. What is the "universal function" of education, and why is it universal?
5. What are the "variable functions" of education, and why may they be variable?
6. Explain: "Education is a function of the *total* society."
7. Define and evaluate "liberal" education. To what extent is your evaluation biased by your social class position and aspirations?
8. Is American education free? What qualifications does one need to make in his answer to this question?
9. What do you consider to be the chief problems facing American education today?
10. "Education is the acquisition of culture." Criticize.
11. Are literacy statistics a fair index to the educational level of a nation or of a region? Why?

28
RELIGION

WHAT IS RELIGION?

To define religion in formal terms is difficult, both for the person doing the defining and for the person trying to understand the definition. Part of the difficulty arises from the wide variety of accepted conceptions of "religion," and part from the ethnocentrism regarding religion which dominates many people. It is difficult, for example, for a contemporary American Christian to understand that such behaviors as erotic dancing, body mutilation, or prostitution can be religious rites in some societies. As we have seen in the chapter on cultural variability, *practically every phenomenon in the universe is or has been regarded as supernatural by the logic of one or more cultures, and practically every act of which the human being is capable has somewhere and sometime had a sacred significance.* It is necessary, therefore, to formulate a conception of religion which will include its universal aspects and its variable ones as well.

Although there are numerous ways of objectively defining religion, we may state it this way: religion is a culturally entrenched pattern of behavior made up of (1) sacred beliefs, (2) emotional feelings accompanying the beliefs, and (3) overt conduct presumably implementing the beliefs and feelings.

These three aspects are closely interrelated, but may be separated from one another for the purpose of analysis.

1. Beliefs

Fundamental to all religions are beliefs concerning the nature of the universe and man in relation to it. In the thought-ways of each culture, it is usually possible to make a rough division between two spheres or orders of knowledge. One type of knowledge consists of phenomena which the people regard as natural, earthly, mundane, and satisfactorily understood on a matter-of-fact basis. There is an additional group of phenomena which are regarded as sacred, understandable, and explained by modes of logic not usually objectively verifiable. Thus the universe tends to be divided into what we may call the *natural* and the *sacred*. Any particular item, of course, may fall into the natural or the sacred category on the basis of how the culture of the group in question happens to define it. Thus, for example, thunder and lightning may be regarded as a mere meteorological phenomenon brought about by natural causes, or thunder and lightning may be regarded as an arbitrary phenomenon reflecting the will of some nonnatural force or power or person. Epidemics and catastrophes have also been defined in both of these ways. So with practically every item of the universe.

Science and religion. This explains in some measure the perennial quarrel between science and religion. As science makes each new stride in the understanding of some phase of the universe, its matter-of-fact or "natural" explanation may come into conflict with the sacred (and usually supernatural) explanation held by religious dogma. Organized religion frequently strives in one way or another to rationalize its prescientific conceptions, because only by so doing can it retain its prestige and its reputation for being correct.

It should be noted, of course, that all scientific discoveries do not run counter to religious belief, but only such scientific explanations as challenge the pre-existing religious conception. Thus, for example, the theory of evolution challenged the Christian notion that man was a special creation, brought forth in the Garden of Eden precisely as he exists today. But the findings of biochemical research concerning vitamins or the endocrine glands encounter no violent religious opposition because there have been no religious teachings about them which the research findings have called into question.

It is not only in highly scientific cultures such as our own that religious beliefs and scientific knowledge are in conflict. Incidents have been revealed by anthropological researches which show that even among primitive peoples there have occurred discoveries of natural causes of phenomena which came to the attention of the people, and thus challenged the current religious beliefs.

Those religious beliefs having to do with proper conduct, such as the Golden Rule are, of course, not readily susceptible of any scientific examination because they are not based upon any assumptions of cause and effect. If one should be charitable, then being charitable is a virtue by its own definition, and science can neither validate nor invalidate the desirability of charitable acts per se. On the other hand, if one were admonished to be charitable in order that he live longer, then it could be scientifically determined whether the persons who performed more charitable acts or greater charitable acts did actually live longer.

Extrascientific nature of many religious beliefs. It is probably already clear from the foregoing that religious beliefs are usually neither scientific nor unscientific, but rather tend to be *extrascientific.* They constitute explanations concerning phenomena about which science has not secured or cannot secure empiric data. They are values which are accepted because they seem right or important. It is, of course, possible for religious belief to be scientific, if the sacred is in line with scientific truth, or unscientific, if it asserts explanations or causes which science in the same culture has already discovered to be false. But much current religious belief in contemporary America is extrascientific rather than demonstrably scientific, unscientific, or antiscientific.

Most religious beliefs secure their validity by authority or logic or tradition and not by scientific proof. Thus in the Christian conception, God inspired the writing of the Bible. God being the Supreme Authority, the Bible must represent the ultimate in authority. "Thus saith the Lord" then becomes an order which takes precedence over kings or emperors. Other religions, likewise, have their authorities who claim their right to reveal ultimate truth either categorically, like the assertion that Jesus is the Son of God, or by the supposed self-evident logic of the truths which they proclaim.

2. Emotional feelings

Sacred beliefs usually have strong emotional concomitants of awe, fear, reverence, love, humility, hate, in fact of every emotion of which man is capable. This results in part from the manner in which religious beliefs are taught, and also because of the great importance which is attached to the beliefs and the values which they represent. Again, one should be very cautious about his ethnocentrism. The emotional feeling-tone characteristic of Christian religion is by no means universal. Worship, for example, as Americans know it and the sentiments and emotions of "love" as Christians are taught these sentiments are variable instances in the great panorama of religious experience. It is, in fact, very difficult to determine what the religious "feelings" of another religion really are. It is quite probable that they are so different that our concepts such as love, fear, or hate, familiar enough in American culture, do not even have a counterpart in many other religions. We really do not know how the Bushman or the Hottentot or the Toda "feels" about his religious concepts. We know merely that they do feel intensely, because their behavior, like ours, shows evidence of strong emotions.

3. Propitiation

In the logic of each religion there is a set of behaviors which constitute proper religious conduct. These acts are called *propitiation*. In the Christian tradition, for example, observance of the Christian moral code, prayer, tithes and offerings for the support of organized religion, deeds of charity, church attendance, and formal ceremonies like baptism, confession, and communion illustrate these devices. If one inquires as to why these things are done, he is told that they "are pleasing to God" or that they have some connection or other with the disposition of one's soul after death. In short, there are cause-and-effect relationships in religion between what one does and how the universe will treat him.

Propitiatory devices include practically every act of which the human being is capable. Antitheses of every religious act can be found in the propitiatory practices of some other culture. Thus by the logic of one religion, fasting is acceptable in the eyes of the supernatural, while feasting is so regarded in the next. Kindness and gentleness are virtues in one religious system, while brutality is approved in the next. Public assemblage is the form of religious participation in one society, while the mores of another require that all religious activity be done in solitary confinement. One people sacrifices in the name of religion, and another is acquisitive in the name of religion. Dancing is a religious rite in one society and is regarded as the work of Satan in the next. Sexual behavior, of course, comes in for its share of propitiatory definition. One set of religious mores defines sexual behavior as something disapproved by the deities, with the possible exception of procreation, while in other societies sex orgies and religious prostitution become the means of appeasing the gods. Truly man's capacity for contriving varied religious ways seems almost boundless.

Taboo. Taboo represents propitiatory devices of a negative sort, that is, the person should abstain from certain acts which are presumably inimical to the desires of the gods. Thus, the abstinence from certain foods on certain days or the refusal to indulge in certain pleasing behaviors are regarded as virtues, and presumably result in keeping one in the good graces of the gods.

Duty. (Some analysts use the general term "magic" to designate positive propitiatory acts.) Propitiation also works affirmatively. Sometimes the gods are said to be pleased by positive acts. Sacrifices, good deeds, and religious observances illustrate this form of propitiation.

Belief, emotion, and propitiation are interrelated

Having thus separated religious belief, "feelings," and propitiation, for purposes of discussion, it might have been suggested that these three aspects of religion are more separate and separable than they really are. Actually, of course, all three are bound together into a more or less logical whole. None is meaningful apart from the other two. One has deep emotional feelings because he has certain religious beliefs, and having those beliefs he observes whatever taboos seem appropriate and participates in the pertinent magic as a means of implementing his emotions and beliefs about religious matters. It is quite possible, of course, that one's sacred beliefs may not require intense feelings or formal propitiatory behavior, but taking the religions of man as a whole, the pattern outlined is overwhelmingly present.

THE FUNCTIONS OF RELIGION

Probably the functions of religion can best be discussed in two somewhat separate categories—functions to the individual and functions to the society. While the two are obviously intertwined to some extent, they are easier to comprehend when looked at separately.

To the individual, the functions of religion of the prevailing kinds found in the United States seem to center largely around the facilitation of security feelings. Life here, as in every society, is fraught with insecurity, varying in seriousness from the uncertain and final fact of death to the endless number of more minor frustrations, such as the vagaries of a lover or the vicissitudes of economic life. Whether one be powerful or weak, he is still unable to understand, much less control, the forces of the external universe. Religion provides him with such understandings, and in some measure even with control. This brings a sense of peace and sometimes even of power; it provides certainty, or at least an explanation, of the unknown; it provides answers to the conundrums of life, whether the answers take the form of strict taboos or of general principles. Religious conversion and religious experience are, for those persons who have experienced them, real, and sometimes abiding, life fulfillments of a profound nature. In a sense we might term this a mental hygiene function of religion to the person.

For the society, probably the chief function of religion is its strong reinforcement of the moral order, since religions derive their authority from sources which are above and beyond the will or reason of mortal men. Earlier we made a point that the distinctive function of government was that it represented the ultimate of power in a society; similarly, the unique function of religion is that it provides for its society of believers a source of *ultimate moral authority* beyond all question.

Other functions of religion can be isolated, but they are clearly subordinate to the foregoing. For example, most of the prominent religions in the United States provide for periodic public assembly both for public worship and for a variety of other social and recreational facilities. For many persons these group participations constitute an important and meaningful life activity, providing such varied fulfillments as "a sense of belonging," a reinforcement of faith, an opportunity to publicly demonstrate convictions, and the satisfaction of doing something overt to represent gratitude for religious blessings.

34.   CHURCH MEMBERSHIP UP (In Percent of Population)

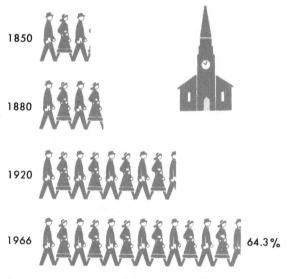

1850

1880

1920

1966   64.3%

Each symbol represents 5 percent of population

Source: *Yearbook of American Churches* and *World Almanac.*

When we examine these varied functions of religion we observe that, as is the case with other institutions, there is *room for* disagreement concerning which functions are vital and which are not, which elements are functional and which dysfunctional, which latent functions can or should be perpetuated. Moreover, there are in the United States an appreciable number of persons to whom organized religion is of little or no importance—and even a small group who overtly oppose religious institutions altogether. Apparently for them the personal functions of religion are either met by some other activity or they continue to live with the functions unperformed.

We shall turn now to an examination of some of the structural characteristics of organized religion in the United States through which these and other functions are currently being performed.

SOME STRUCTURAL CHARACTERISTICS OF AMERICAN RELIGIOUS SYSTEMS

1. Diversity

Religious institutions in America present a panoramic picture. First, there is the well-known trichotomy of Catholic, Protestant, and Jewish, to which we should add the companion fact that the nonmembers of this trichotomy at this time account for approximately a third of the total population. Protestantism, as is well known, is divided into over two hundred different denominations, some of the larger of them quite similar to one another in a number of respects. Yet radically different doctrines, beliefs, and practices are clearly manifest throughout the list.

Within the various denominations, moreover, there are the familiar cleavages between fundamentalists and modernists, liberals and conservatives, and the segregation of Negro and white. Judaism has its three-way split among the Orthodox, the Conservative, and the Reformed. Catholicism to the outsider often gives the appearance of strict uniformity, because it is the most hierarchically governed religious group, but Catholics themselves are the authority for pointing out that there are appreciable differences also within the Catholic Church from region to region and between one ethnic background and another.

In American society, if a man identifies himself as "a religious man," one cannot with certainty conclude which among the many hundreds of patterns of belief and practice he will manifest.

2. An operating unity

It would be an error to leave the impression, however, that religious institutions in America are as fragmentized as the above facts alone would indicate. Despite rather radical doctrinal differences among Catholics, Protestants, and Jews, for example, there exist in many communities operating unifications of these varied bodies. Clergymen of all three religious faiths may belong to a single clergymen's organization.

On a national level, through the National Conference of Christians and Jews, all three main religious groups sponsor a number of projects jointly and work for better feeling among their membership. Within Protestantism there is a great deal of movement of members from denomination to denomination. Despite doctrinal differences there is a practical operating unity sufficiently great that it is often difficult to know, unless one looks at the sign outside, which of a number of churches he is worshipping in.

It is very difficult to account for or to interpret this paradox of diversity and uniformity. When focusing upon one set of facts, like interfaith prejudice, or upon some local community with a Catholic-Protestant fight on its hands, it would appear that diversity, if not warring conflict, is the chief characteristic. On the other hand, there are equally dramatic evidences that, especially within Protestantism, but even to some extent among the three large faiths, there is a willingness and an ability to minimize differences and work together. Objectively, all that we can report is that both facts are manifest and that from time to time one or the other becomes accented.

3. Ecumenicism

Ecumenicism refers in broadest terms to a movement within Christendom toward greater unity. Its most sweeping official form is, of course, within the structure of the Catholic Church, which has sponsored an Ecumenical Congress devoted almost as much to the reconciliation of conflicts within its own various traditions as to growing coexistence with non-Catholic Christian groups. Within Protestantism, the movement is officially marked by an increasing number of mergers of Protestant denominations on a national scale. Involved in ecumenicism, perhaps more by accident than by intent, is also, particularly so far as the Catholics are concerned, a growing insistence on a voice accorded to laymen in the operation of the system. Viewed in terms of practical accomplishments, the ecumenical movement has not been particularly impressive; but viewed against the backdrop of centuries of separation and rigidification of belief and practice, even the few breaks with custom may be highly significant.

Ecumenicism as a formal change in system operation may perhaps be less important than ecumenicism as a state of mind on the part of diverse groups of Christians. This, too, is difficult to assess partly because of the recency of the movement and partly, also, because the consequences of changed attitudes are sometimes difficult to detect.

Certainly it is clear that a vast amount of discussion of the desirability of ecumenicism constitutes an important dialogue among church members and nonchurch members alike and that the general tenor of this discussion is to the effect that, practical difficulties notwithstanding, it is desirable that differences in Christendom be played down in the interest of emerging with a more monolithic Christian institution. This break with traditional ethnocentrism on religious matters, even if only verbal, is an important change.

4. Separation of church and state

Under the American Constitution the government may create no official or state religion, and the right of every individual to religious freedom is asserted as fundamental. These two principles, called "the separation of church and state" and "religious freedom," have, however, presented continuing problems of interpretation, raising issues which frequently reach the Supreme Court for final adjudication. A number of issues are still up in the air, despite Supreme Court decisions —or at least partly so. If a religion, for example, holds pacifism as one of its sacred tenets, has the government the right to force military service upon a person in violation of his religion? To what extent and in what forms may the public schools carry on religious instruction without violating the Constitution and the religious freedom of persons of no religious faith or of a faith which is not satisfied with the kind of religious education the schools present? If some religious groups also provide general education for their members (parochial schools), to what extent are they entitled to public monies to assist in their educational program? If a religious group is numerous enough in a community or a state to hold a majority of the votes, does it thereby acquire the right to enact laws which are binding upon everybody, if these laws contain behavior proscriptions which nonmembers of the church do not hold? These are only a few of the unending problems which are constantly reappearing, ever in new forms. It is apparently much easier to proclaim a separation of church and state and a right to religious freedom than it is to carry these principles out in practice.

5. Real-ideal cleavages

A number of times we have alluded to the fact that the ideal beliefs and behavior patterns espoused by institutions are paralleled by a coexisting set of real patterns which are often at variance. Both are cultural in the sense that they are shared by many persons, learned through association with others, and reinforced by systems of reward and punishment. It is common knowledge—and the subject of an uncommon amount of gossip—that persons in organized religion, and sometimes the organizations themselves, are caught up in the same ideal-real contradictions that characterize secular institutions. Many persons find it relatively easy to excuse or even condone the ideal-real contradictions in secular institutions, but find it more difficult to do so in the sacred. One study, for example, based upon a sample of Protestant *church members* in Detroit, revealed that a substantial proportion of church participants either were not familiar with the religious teachings of their respective denominations or did not agree with these teachings even though they were familiar with them. A sample of *clergymen* showed substantially the same condition, except that the clergymen were somewhat more likely to *know* where their churches stood on doctrinal matters, but a majority of them did not agree with some of the doctrinal stands taken by their own denominations. Certainly no study is required to document the fact that the behavioral requirements which churches prescribe to their followers are summarily violated, or simply ignored, by substantial numbers of persons who nevertheless consider themselves members in good standing. Moreover, the persons in control of the churches know that their recommended behavioral norms are being ignored, but retain the erring ones as members in good standing. Thus there coexist two codes, one readily verbalized and exacting in its requirements, and the other, which one is less willing to talk about, standing in many respects in striking contrast.

In making the above observations there is no intention to imply any necessary wrongdoing or even inconsistency on the part of persons or institutions to whom the remarks apply. Our concern here is description, not judgment. Our purpose is simply to point out that one of the structural characteristics of organized religion in the United States is this real-ideal dualism. The moralist may call it moral "duplicity," but the sociologist simply moral "dualism."

6. Expanding functions

Organized religion, it appears, has taken one important cue from government. Its recent history is marked by the continuing addition of function after function, until now the larger urban churches, particularly, carry on so many activities for their members that one finds it difficult to extricate the essential or pivotal functions of religion from a study of the activities of religious institutions. In addition to public worship services of the traditional sort, the time-honored ministrations to the sick and bereaved, and the giving of religious instruction, urban churches of all three of the major faiths typically sponsor such activities as the following: competitive athletic leagues in the major sports, summer camps, premarital education for young people, Boy Scout and Girl Scout troops, public affairs forums, magazines on political reform and social justice, public lectures on such secular topics as sex, atomic weapons, and extrasensory perception, along with the somewhat more traditional assortment of picnics and parties. It is not difficult to demonstrate the relevance of each of these activities to carrying out the broad principles of Judaic-Christian ethical religious tradition. Wholesome recreation may be as important to the development of Christian character as the memorization of the Beatitudes. One consequence of this expanding program of activities in an effort better to attain the allegiance of members (or to serve them better) is that it gives organized religion a highly variable, and debatable, functional program. There are those who view this proliferation of activities by religious institutions as a source of weakness, and those who view it as a source of strength. Both are in part probably correct. We are, however, reporting only the fact, namely, that American churches are typically carrying on an ever-expanding variety of activities.

7. Stratification: within and between religious institutions

Religious institutions in America are stratified in at least two ways. First, the various religious organizations draw unequally from different social levels. For example, whereas 46 percent of the Episcopalian Church is made up of professionals, owners, manufacturers, or officials, only 13 percent can be so claimed by the Baptist Church. Or to put it another way, while 14 percent of the Roman Catholics and 11 percent of the Baptists are college trained, 53 percent of Episcopalians and 36 percent of the Presbyterians are in this category.[1]

On the local community level, almost all studies of stratification have reported that the various Protestant churches, even in small cities and villages, are arranged hierarchically. A disproportionate percentage, sometimes overwhelming, of the highest status persons will be found in one church, while at the other extreme, another church will serve

[1] Bernard Lazerwitz, "A Comparison of Major U.S. Religious Groups," *Journal of the American Statistical Association*, Vol. 56 (September, 1961), pp. 568–579.

predominantly the lowest status groups. Finally, there is the fact, unpleasant to many devout churchmen, that organized religion, more than any other institution in society, segregates Negroes and whites, even in communities which have long since abolished segregation in the public schools, theaters, and restaurants.

These facts of stratification serve to illustrate that even an institution which derives its sanction from suprahuman sources, and which more than any other institution proclaims the principle of the brotherhood of man, still apparently in its practical functioning compromises with the imperatives imposed by outside institutions and traditions with radically different rationales.

SUMMARY

Although religion may be variously defined, it seems helpful to conceive of it in terms of belief, emotional concomitants of belief, and propitiatory devices. Thus defined, religion exists in every culture, although the specific beliefs and propitiatory practices vary radically from society to society.

The functions of religion in the United States are difficult to verbalize, but, briefly, fulfill both individual and societal purposes. To the individual, religion brings deep emotional security in a changing, sometimes strange, and often frightening social world; to the society, religion presents an authoritative rationale for a moral order.

American religious institutions are characterized by the seeming paradox of wide diversity and an operating unity; by a theoretical, but perennially disturbing, separation of church and state; by dramatic real-ideal behavioral cleavages; and by an ever-expanding galaxy of organization activities. There is clear evidence of stratification (despite equalitarian pronouncement) both within and among churches in the community.

SUGGESTED READINGS

Glock, Charles Y., and Stark, Rodney, "Is There an American Protestantism?" *Transaction*, Vol. 3 (November–December, 1965), pp. 8–13, 48–49.

This is a report on a very significant statistical analysis of the attitudes and beliefs of Americans. It tends to show that differences *within* various denominations are wide, or in other words, that important differences in American

Protestantism are no longer those *between* denominations but rather different views which cut across denominational lines. An important study.

Herberg, Will, *Protestant, Catholic, Jew*. Garden City, N.Y., Doubleday, 1955.
This has been an influential book which assays the tradition of religious trichotomy in American society and considers the implications of this triumvirate for American culture.

Knudten, Richard D., ed., *The Sociology of Religion: An Anthology*. New York, Appleton-Century-Crofts, 1967.
A carefully edited, selected, and interpreted collection of key materials dealing with religious organization in contemporary America. Several classics will be found here. The juxtapositions dramatically illustrate the conditions of existence of American religion, especially Protestantism.

Lenski, Gerhard, *The Religious Factor*. Garden City, N.Y., Doubleday, 1961.
A comprehensive research conducted in Detroit which attempts to relate religious identification and other social facts such as conditions of family life and various social attitudes. Statistical.

Mayer, Albert J., and Sharp, Harry, "Religious Preference and Worldly Success." *American Sociological Review*, Vol. 27 (April, 1962), pp. 218–227.
This is an interesting examination of the relationship between religious preference and worldly success based on a sample of persons taken from metropolitan Detroit from whom data was secured by interview. In a general way it sustains some of the assumptions involved in Weber's thesis concerning the Protestant Ethic, although with important qualifications. Also documents the high achievement patterns of Jews.

Simmel, Georg, *Sociology of Religion*, translated from the German by Curt Rosenthal. New York, Philosophical Press, 1960.
In recent years the sociology of religion has taken form as an important sociological specialty. For the student interested in this, a treatment of the subject over a half century ago by a European sociologist should prove enlightening.

Williams, Robin M., Jr., *American Society*. New York, Knopf, 1960, Chapter 9.
As in other chapters of this excellent book, Williams' treatment of religious institutions is complete and penetrating.

Yinger, J. Milton, *Religion, Society and the Individual*. New York, Macmillan, 1957.
A comprehensive textbook on the "Sociology of Religion." Emphasis throughout is on the interrelation of religion and the total social setting. Scholarly.

STUDY QUESTIONS

1. What are the functions of religion to the person? To the society?

2. What are the institutional characteristics of religion in America? In what ways do you think the institutional characteristics facilitate the realization of basic functions and in what ways do they impede the realization of these functions? Explain.

3. How do you explain the coexistence of democratic ideals of brotherhood in religion and the fact of segregation and other stratification in religious institutions?

4. Why is it difficult to formulate a universal definition of religion?

5. Why are most people intensely ethnocentric in their ideas and attitudes about religion?

6. How does culture determine which phenomena are natural and which supernatural?

7. What determines a society's specific religious forms?

8. Why is there often conflict between science and religion? Why is this not always true? Illustrate.

9. What is the basic difference between science and religion?

10. How may the sudden loss of an absolute belief in a Supreme Being create mental ill-health?

11. Why may religion be regarded as rational? What is the criterion of rationality?

12. Why are propitiatory devices not the same in all societies? Why are they not the same in all religions in the same society?

13. What is ecumenicism? What is your estimate of its influence? In your time? Later?

six

SOCIAL ORGANIZATION, SOCIAL POWER, SOCIAL PROCESSES, AND SOCIAL EVALUATION

29
ORGANIZATION AND DISORGANIZATION IN SOCIAL SYSTEMS

It is a matter of common observation that the persons and groups making up a social system are "somehow held together." The purpose of this chapter is to present a more adequate conception of some of the reasons for this social *cohesion* and of some of the factors working for and against it among the institutions comprising present-day American society.

The various institution-systems of society like family, government, and religion are *not isolated from one another*. Instead they influence each other in many significant ways. For example, depressions and prosperity are aspects of the economic system of society, but numerous researches have shown that the recurring waves of prosperity and depression have profound influence upon marriage rates, divorce rates, and birth rates, which are certainly aspects of the family. More recently we have seen that there is a close relationship between government and economic activity, and science-education and religious beliefs. In almost innumerable other ways, *reciprocal influence* can readily be shown.

THE BASES OF SOCIAL SYSTEM ORGANIZATION

It is probably unnecessary to elaborate the basic societal fact of interdependence. Previous chapters have contained numerous data pertaining to this condition. Perhaps the cardinal process throughout human evolution from primeval man to modern man has been the extension of interdependence. With each elaboration of the division of labor, the helplessness of the individual human being and the small group becomes more manifest. Man is inherently helpless and dependent upon others in the infant stage, but modern man has magnified this dependence upon others to include the entire life span. This fact of interdependence has both symbiotic and nonsymbiotic phases.

1. Symbiotic interdependence

In the chapter dealing with human ecology, it was stressed that the intricate system of division of labor which characterizes modern life necessitates a somewhat elaborate social organization simply for the purpose of coordinating the efforts and activities of the specializing persons and groups. It has been suggested that a person could receive a graphic appreciation of the extent of his symbiotic dependence by tracing the items appearing on his breakfast table back to their origins. Such an effort would show vividly how dozens, if not hundreds, of specialized functionaries have contributed energies and talents to the production, transportation, and fabrication of the simplest tableware and the most fundamental items of diet. At almost innumerable points the activities of each functionary or group must be coordinated with others, or the entire web of interdependence breaks down. Thus, one aspect of the organization of society, the symbiotic one, can be appreciated.

Railroads, airplane lines, telephone and telegraph systems are the *mechanical media* through which much social organization is carried out. If modern man is to draw his sustenance from widespread geographical areas, he must transport raw materials and fabricated items from their production points to their consumption points, and also maintain a system of communication through which he can regulate the whole structure of symbiotic relationships. Much of the rivalry among modern nations stems from their competition for access to the desirable sources of raw materials and the protection or construction of the mechanical media for trade, such as that of the British Empire which has aptly come to be called its "lifeline."

2. Nonsymbiotic bases of interdependence: values and ideologies

Sustenance considerations are by no means the only forces which hold societies together. Cultural factors such as common religion, national loyalties, and common language are value-patterns which form another type of sociological tie.

Sharing common symbols and values has for centuries united people, sometimes even running against the logical ties based on symbiotic need. The Jews, for example, have maintained a sense of unity despite the fact that some are rich and some are poor, some are highly intellectual and others not much touched by the intellectual life, some are devoutly religious, others only marginally so. But because of a sense of common origins a certain kind of unity prevails. Other examples are found among such religious unities as Catholics or Baptists or Mennonites. Apart from religion are other ideological unifying factors, suggested by such meaningful labels as "left wingers," "conservatives," "liberals." What all of these diverse groups have in common is a commitment to a set of beliefs about what is important and how one should react to this importance.

The interdependence of symbiotic and value ties

It is futile to argue whether the symbiotic ties *or* the cultural ties are more "important" or more "fundamental" in the maintenance of social integration. Both are important and both are fundamental. Raising such an issue as this seems almost like a modern version of the trite and meaningless question of whether man's "physical or mental" nature is the more important. The issue is meaningless because human life, whether for an individual or for a society, is an inextricable unity of both the biological and the ideological aspects. Each person is born into a society with one or more cultures. In the course of his socialization he acquires numerous needs, some of them appetitive, like his food wants, his standard of living, or his sex wishes. These learnings which formulate much of his behavior result from his organic biological needs and from the specific forms which these needs are given by the folkways which he learns. Usually he is unaware that there are really any alternative ways of meeting the problem of human existence. If he grew up in American society, "food" means three meals a day consisting of certain folkways like desserts and *hors d'œuvres*, white bread with butter, sitting at the table, and so on. Likewise sex needs are oriented to married heterosexuality, influenced by the prevailing standards of beauty and prestige, and more or less related to monogamy. Thus, almost inescapably he learns that these objectives are attainable only from and through the behaviors of other people. In short, he learns his roles and statuses which are links in the chains of mutual interdependence with other people. Except in an abstract academic sense, the value-unity of the people of a society is largely inseparable from their symbiotic unity. Thus, the average American's emphasis on pecuniary values has a symbiotic aspect since it is related to his sustenance needs, but it also has a sentimental aspect since many phases of it have no discernible connection with symbiotic needs at all. Long-wheel-base automobiles, fur coats, and other aspects of "conspicuous consumption" can be adequately understood in terms of their status value.

3. Instrumental social arrangements

Subsistence requirements and the common values hold people together. These ends are achieved through the operation of various types of systems. Bureaucracy and primary group organizations are contrasting cases in point. These diverse behavior-systems may be regarded as *instruments* (means) for achieving subsistence and other *values* (ends). One of the persistent theoretical questions which has intrigued (and harassed!) some sociologists for a long time now is whether a separation of means and ends is really defensible, that is, whether people do not react toward what some theoreticians call means and ends in essentially the same manner. When a man says, for example, that "we ought to support the church" is he not treating an organization designed to achieve certain ends as if the organization were an end itself? Or similarly in the case of "respect for the law." Surely law is an instrumentality for the achievement of other values such as justice, orderly adjudication of disputes, continuity in social relations, and so on. Whether, then, what we have here called instrumental agencies of a society are to be regarded as of a different order than the end-goals of sustenance and common value orientations or not, the point should not be obscured that: The man-made institutional arrangements, quite apart from their purposes, are unifying or organizing factors; they are commonly regarded by peoples as values; and they have the effect of regulating behavior. This regulatory function results in furthering predictability in human affairs—the final proof of system organization.

SOCIAL DISORGANIZATION

Traditionally sociologists and other writers and thinkers about social conditions have observed a recurring societal condition which they call *social disorganization*. Modern research and thinking, however, has raised serious questions concerning this concept. In fact, the criticisms have become so basic and their implications so profound, that it now appears at least doubtful that the concept *social disorganization* can be retained as a valid one to the person who desires to think realistically about human behavior and society.

A classic view of the matter

One of the classic statements of the disorganization concept was made by Cooley in 1909.[1]

[1] C. H. Cooley, *Social Organization* (New York, Scribner, 1909), pp. 347–351.

In this state of things general order and discipline are lacking. Though there may be praiseworthy persons and activities, society as a whole wants unity and rationality, like a picture which is good in details but does not make a pleasing composition. Individuals and special groups appear to be working too much at cross purposes; there is a "reciprocal struggle of discordant powers" but the "harmony of the universe" does not emerge. As good actors do not always make a good troupe nor brave soldiers a good army, so a nation or a historical epoch—say Italy in the Renaissance—may be prolific in distinguished persons and scattered achievements but somewhat futile and chaotic as a system.

A well-ordered community is like a ship in which each officer and seaman has confidence in his fellows and in the captain and is well accustomed to do his duty with no more than ordinary grumbling. All hangs together, and is subject to reason in the form of long-tried rules of navigation and discipline. Virtue is a system and men do heroic acts as parts of the day's work. . . .

Cooley, and others since his time, thought that there was some kind of necessary connection between general social disorganization and individual personal disorganization.[2]

Old institutions are passing away and better ones, we hope, are preparing to take their place, but in the meantime there is a lack of that higher discipline which prints the good of the whole upon the heart of the member. In a traditional order one is accustomed from childhood to regard usage, the authority of elders, and the dominant institutions as the rule of life. "So it must be" is one's unconscious conviction, and like the seaman, he does wise and heroic things without knowing it. But in our own time there is for many persons, if not most, no authoritative canon of life, and for better or worse we are ruled by native impulse and by that private reason which may be so weak when detached from a rational whole. The higher morality, if it is to be attained at all, must be specially thought out; and of the few who can do this a large part exhaust their energy in thinking and do not practise with any heartiness the truths they perceive.

We find, then, that people have to make up their own minds upon their duties as wives, husbands, mothers, and daughters; upon commercial obligation and citizenship; upon the universe and the nature and authority of God. Inevitably many of us make a poor business of it. It is too much. It is as if each one should sit down to invent a language for himself; these things should be thought out gradually, cooperatively, each adding little and accepting much. That great traditions should rapidly go to pieces may be a necessary phase of evolution and a disguised blessing, but the present effect is largely distraction and demoralization.

[2] *Ibid.*, pp. 351–352.

The student will probably already have noted that social disorganization is not caused, or even attended, merely by the fact of physical conflict. That is purely incidental. Disorganization is manifest by the fact that persons are behaving in ways not consistent with the approved manner in which they were supposed to behave while playing their respective roles.

The essence of disorganization is that the *customary and approved ways of behavior no longer prevail.* This tends to cause or reflect confusion. Thus, for example, persons who are expected to be subordinate may not abide by their role; and numerous other kinds of unexpected or "abnormal" behavior are in evidence.

"Disorganization" of the family

Thus, some students of the family have suggested that the modern American family is disorganized because many persons secure divorces, some couples deliberately do not have any children, some women have careers outside their homes instead of devoting their time and energies to homemaking and child rearing, and various kinds of new moralities can be observed in the actual lives of many married men and women. Since the traditional roles of husband and wife presume permanent monogamous marriage, reproduction, and women in the role of homemakers and child bearers, these new patterns of behavior which are appearing on a large scale constitute a sort of evidence that many people are not playing the roles which have been traditional. Thus, the modern American family is said by some observers to be "disorganized."

"Disorganization" of economic institutions

Disorganization is also alleged in the economic sphere. Until relatively recently, as we have seen, our capitalistic culture has been organized around the concepts of private property in capital goods and free enterprise. The owner or manager of the factory or mine had the right to hire and fire labor as he chose. He had the right to make any kind of product he wanted and market it in any way he chose, with only a few limitations imposed upon him in the case of extremely harmful goods or extremely untruthful advertising or labeling. He had the right to set both the wages and conditions of employment with no interference either from government or from organized labor. If the worker did not like the conditions of employment in the old order, he could, of course, quit.

Gradually, as we have seen, each of the above mentioned role-prerogatives of the owners and managers of capital goods, and also of

labor, has been modified by changes in law or custom. In large industries, especially, the employer no longer has the exclusive right to fire
or hire a specific man without cause. Certainly it is now not legal to
discharge a man because he belongs to a labor union as was once the
case. Strikes are common and sometimes prolonged. Moreover, the
seller of *some kinds* of merchandise is no longer permitted to charge
any price which he can get, and certain minimum quality standards are
set by law. It is common to hear numerous and vigorous complaints
that the new practices and policies are "ruining" business, and there is
much yearning for the "good old days."

There is no denying that there is an element of truth in the complaints of many persons who allege that they are confused or even
wronged by the new patterns of economic activity. Although it is difficult to get precise facts, it appears that many persons are refusing to
obey some of the new laws; and some are finding legal, as well as illegal,
ways of circumventing the operation of the laws. In short, there is uncertainty, because the roles have changed and because significant numbers of persons are unwilling or unable to follow the new roles. Some
are hoping that by large-scale violations, the new role requirements may
be altered or repealed completely. Other persons, on the other hand,
are quite satisfied with the "new order." They approve of greater rights
for labor and continuation of excess profits taxes, and even favor some
increased governmental control of manufacturing and distribution to
"protect" consumers. They regard such marked modifications of laissez-
faire as wholly proper.

"Disorganization" in education

Educational institutions manifestly are thought to be in a state of
disorganization. At the ideological level, as we have seen in a preceding
chapter, there is conflict over what education basically is and what it
exists for, raising the perennial unsolved question of vocationalism
versus liberal education. Moreover, while we profess to value education
highly, we tend to be penurious with respect to teachers' salaries. The
result is that persons with talent for education are attracted away by
industry and other professions because we pay public school teachers
less than we do long-distance truck drivers. Again, while we profess to
value education highly, most communities still surround the teacher
with various kinds of restrictions on what he may teach, as if to deny
that education is really desired except insofar as it incorporates the
prejudices of the comparatively uneducated. Manifestly, it appears as
if Americans sometimes are unable to make up their minds as to how

we wish to resolve the implications of preachment and the realities of practice. Quite possibly the growing rash of teachers' strikes is partly a consequence of such contradictions as these.

"Disorganization" in contemporary American religion

Contemporary religion presents a comparable panorama of change and confusion. Church doctrines, as we saw in the chapter on religion, clash with one another on fundamental issues. Some churches are following programs and teachings which are largely new, and there is much confusion concerning the wisdom of these new philosophies and policies. Criticisms of the church are heard from both the inside and the outside of this age-old institution. Confusion, experimentation, large-scale and open violation of time-honored taboos, all give evidence that the traditional role pattern has broken down and that no generally accepted new ones seem yet formulated; disorganization is said to exist.

"Disorganization" in government

Government, too, shows symptoms of disorganization when seen against the backdrop of established traditions. Presumably a democratic government should mirror "the judgments of the people"; it should carry out their mandates, yet the flow of influence appears to be in the reverse direction. Government officials seem quite as much the creators of public opinion as the creatures of it. The governmental bureaucracy, contrary to democratic idealism, tends to operate as a separate culture, continuously rendering decisions in important matters for which there is no medium for review. While grassroots opinion is given great lip service in political campaigns, no one seems much to know or care what its perceptions and judgments may be on such vital matters even as war and peace. The Supreme Court is designated as the final arbiter as to what is constitutional and what is not, and yet persons of all levels of literacy summarily reject the authority of the Court whenever the judgments run contrary to ethnocentric judgments, as demonstrated by reactions to the Court's decisions on civil rights and the separation of church and state.

DIFFICULTIES WITH THE TRADITIONAL CONCEPT OF DISORGANIZATION

It will probably appear to the person who has just read the foregoing paragraphs that the term *disorganization* is indeed an apt one to describe such conditions as were there discussed. It usually seems quite clear that formerly there was organization and now the organization has "somehow broken down." Why not call this condition, then, disorganization? Perhaps the reason for sociologists' *growing* (but by no means universal) reluctance to do so may best be shown by a more careful consideration of the symptoms and of the criteria which supposedly indicate disorganization.

From our discussion of the allegedly disorganized aspects of American society, it will probably be clear that the criteria employed for judging disorganization consist of such conditions as the "breakdown of social controls over the behavior of the individual," changes in the social roles, experimentation with new roles, and confusion among the persons behaving. On the surface it might appear, moreover, that such conditions as these are obvious enough and can easily be seen or even measured. Why do they, then, not denote social disorganization?

How can role-disintegration be distinguished from mere role-change?

The crux of the problem lies in the *inability to distinguish between the so-called breakdown of a traditional role and the appearance of a new role*. It is certainly an obvious conclusion from the many facts and interpretations contained in this book that man is the kind of being who can live and be happy under a wide variety of social conditions. Since, for example, many millions of modern men are living under communism and under modified capitalism, one cannot but conclude that both of these systems are workable, even though quite different from one another, and both quite different from laissez-faire capitalism.

It will also be recalled that attention has been repeatedly drawn to the *fact of ceaseless social change*. Since, then, change is always occurring and new roles or role requirements are constantly appearing while others are disappearing, how can we be sure that the conditions which we called disorganization are not merely the emerging new organization for the coming societal mode? *They only seem to be disorganization because we are familiar with the roles which have come out of the past, but we are unfamiliar with the roles which are shaping up for the society of tomorrow.* For example, when the Negro slaves of the South were made free men, the roles of the Negroes as well as of their former owners were abolished—or radically altered, whichever way one prefers to state it. In either event, the customary folkways and thoughtways were destroyed or at least rendered inoperative in the new scheme. There were experimentation and confusion, but the experiment and confusion were really the process of trial and error in the development of new roles for Negroes and whites such as are now quite familiar. Suppose that there had been a group of sociologists describing the Negro-white situation in the South at that time. They would very probably have concluded that conditions were disorganized, because they were new and strange, and would probably have been more or less nostalgic for the good old days when everything was "under control," when everyone knew what to expect in the behavior of everyone else.

The current civil rights movement is a more contemporary case in point. In this age of demonstrations, it is difficult to know whether those who are agitating for change are simply disruptive forces bent upon making a shambles of existing law and order or whether they are the harbingers of a new and more democratic social system in which Negroes and whites may coexist on the basis of their individual merits rather than on the accidents of pigmentation. Quite predictably, there would be a sharp difference of opinion on the question between those who favor and those who oppose the effort. Probably no contemporary can pass any reliable judgment on the issue, for contemporaries are necessarily handicapped because they can operate with only one of two necessary conditions for objective appraisal: they have the perspective of hindsight but not the privilege of foresight.

It should not be concluded, however, that there is no utility in the concept of *disorganization*. The concept is useful certainly to describe conditions such as riots, earthquakes, and similar disruptions of accustomed social organization. These conditions may truly present *disorganization* because of their *relatively short duration* and the strong probability that after the period of confusion, order *will return on approximately the same pattern as existed prior to the interruption*.

SUMMARY

Societies are held together by symbiotic interdependence and by common value orientation. Neither of these can be asserted as primary or more fundamental. The human being becomes habituated both to the symbiotic aspect and to the value aspect in the course of his socialization. Thus, society, through socialization, creates the person's social needs and wants. It also provides him with rationalizations, which are more or less consistent with the existing social structure. Social integration lies both in the behavior patterns of the persons of the society and in the formal organization of the society through the rules, laws, and other written paraphernalia of organization.

From the illustrations and interpretations contained in the foregoing paragraphs it should be clear that much of what has been traditionally called "disorganization" is objectively indistinguishable from normal social change. The confusion and experimentation which allegedly are symptomatic of disorganization are quite as clearly indicative of adjustment to the demands and requirements of new roles.

Much erroneous thinking, moreover, has been introduced into the literature on social change as a result of the use of the word *disorganization*. Disorganization carries an implication of disapproval and abnormality and suggests that it is an unfortunate and temporary condition, whereas social change is a quite normal condition and quite as likely to bring about better as worse social conditions. In fact, both desirable and undesirable social change are characterized by new social roles, and in their early stages are difficult for many persons to master, resulting in confusion and diverse evaluation. Such is, however, the normal pattern of change in human affairs. Therefore, social disorganization is becoming less useful as an objective concept in the vocabulary of the sociologist.

Value disunity and conflict within a society have been frequently interpreted as evidence of a lack of societal integration and construed to forebode ill. Such a thesis is difficult either to defend or to attack *conclusively*. The difficulty may lie in the fact that symbiotic unity alone is difficult to appraise as a unifying force. Perhaps, also, the kinds of common value unity which seem to be passing from American society were only an aspect of a transitory period of history and have been erroneously construed as an indispensable aspect of society per se. Such considerations as these, notwithstanding their importance, are in the domain of the not-yet-agreed-upon areas of sociological theory.

SUGGESTED READINGS

Elliott, Mabel A., and Merrill, Francis E., *Social Disorganization*, 4th ed. New York, Harper & Row, 1961.
This has long been a standard textbook-level treatment of social disorganization. This fourth edition contains the authors' point of view and will give the critical student an excellent idea of the utility and disutility of approaching social problems from this point of view.

Greer, Scott A., *Social Organization*. New York, Doubleday, 1955.
A brief general booklet on various aspects of social organization.

Lynd, R. S., and Lynd, H. M., *Middletown in Transition*. (See footnote, p. 401.)

Chapter XII, "The Middletown Spirit," is an effective handling of a very difficult phase of the social organization of Middletown. The authors attempt to verbalize the values which Middletown holds. Should be read thoughtfully as an index to the Middletown, and also American, mind. The concluding chapter, "Middletown Faces Both Ways," is also useful for the same purpose.

Williams, Robin M., *American Society*, 2nd ed. New York, Knopf, 1960, Chapters 13 and 14.
A good treatment of the problem of social integration.

STUDY QUESTIONS

1. Distinguish between symbiotic and nonsymbiotic kinds of interdependence. Illustrate.
2. Why is it preferable to think in terms of "symbiotic" and "nonsymbiotic" interdependence rather than in terms of "symbiotic" and "cultural"?
3. What are "instrumental social arrangements"? Illustrate.
4. How much value disunity can a society tolerate without disintegration? Why is this question difficult to answer?
5. What has "social disorganization" traditionally meant?
6. Why is it difficult to be objective in describing and interpreting social disorganization? Illustrate.
7. How is social change related to what has been called social disorganization?
8. Evaluate: "A strike is an example of social disorganization."
9. Why can disorganization frequently be approached through a study of roles?
10. What do a person's vested interests have to do with his evaluation of social change? Illustrate.
11. Why are the severe mental hygiene problems of persons experiencing social change not an adequate criterion for judging the desirability of the change?
12. Why is it often impossible to distinguish change and disorganization in society?
13. What criterion does this chapter suggest as valid for distinguishing disorganization from change per se?
14. State the case for considering present economic conditions in the United States as "disorganized."
15. Criticize your reply to Question 14.
16. Why can we not determine objectively whether the American family is disorganized or not? Illustrate.
17. What would be lost if the social scientist dropped the phrase "social disorganization" from his vocabulary? Might the concept live on anyway? Why?

30
SOCIAL POWER
AND POWER
STRUCTURES

American sociologists have long neglected systematic and critical analysis of the factor of power in human affairs. It has been alleged, probably not without some basis in fact, that part of this neglect grew out of timidity. Sociologists are quite aware that in a self-consciously "democratic" and "free" society people cherish the belief that their affairs are controlled "by the people," that their leadership is subject to popular mandate, and are quite uncomfortable with any facts and interpretations which even hint that they do not enter importantly in decision-making and in the conduct of public affairs. Once one inquires closely, however, into the realities of power holding and use, he typically discovers facts and reaches inferences which contradict the naïve and simplistic popular faith. If he openly discusses his findings, he is likely to offend two groups—the naïve who feel an affront to their cherished illusions, and perhaps even more importantly, those who hold or exercise important power and prefer that that fact remain unnoticed.

Nonetheless, while sociologists as a group have neglected the study of power, a minority have focused on it; and a small but classic heritage of respected contributions has been accumulated. Max Weber, a German sociologist who has had a profound influence upon American sociologists, identified power as one of the three main dimensions of social class.[1] American sociologists, however, sometimes only tacitly, have related power to stratification in two ways: (1) differentials in power constitute one of the roots of differential status and privilege on the one hand, and (2) once given a stratification system, differential power becomes a crucial factor in its solidification and perpetuation.

[1] See H. H. Gerth and C. W. Mills, *From Max Weber: Essays in Sociology* (New York, Oxford University Press, 1946), pp. 180–195; and A. M. Henderson and T. Parsons, *Max Weber: The Theory of Social and Economic Organization* (New York, Oxford University Press, 1947), pp. 424–429.

One of the early descriptions of some of the subtleties in differential power appeared in the second of the two classic volumes on *Middletown* [2] written by the Lynds about thirty years ago. Middletown, it is now known, is Muncie, Indiana, a Midwest city probably unique in no important way except that it was twice within a ten-year period, before and during the great depression, subjected to a systematic and brilliant analysis by two leading social scientists. In the second volume the Lynds' attention was drawn to an aspect of the power dimension beyond the earlier difference between what they called "the working class and the business class" and their differential abilities to control their own and the community's affairs. The Lynds examined a particular family, called the X Family, from the point of view of its influence (power) upon a wide variety of facets of the collective life of Middletown. They skillfully avoided a muckraking approach and overstatements about "excessive domination" and imputation of motives on the part of these obviously powerful individuals. They were content to stick to the facts, tacitly acknowledging that whether or not there was intention to exert undue influence over community affairs, such an outcome was virtually inevitable in view of the wealth of the family, its prestige in the community, and the many positions of strategic importance which members of the family held. Reading this richly factual account leaves one clear insight into the potentials for differential power which are wrapped up in the traditions, sentiments, and local culture of the typical American city. Many other studies of local power systems are now available, some of which add important qualifications and additional dimensions to our understanding.[3]

In recent years an influential study, widely read and criticized both pro and con, is that of C. Wright Mills, *The Power Elite*.[4] Unlike the Lynds and others, Mills turned his attention away from specific communities and looked at power from the point of view of the entire society. He identified a group whom he called "the Power Elite," a relatively small group of influential people in industry, government, and the military who because of the positions they hold—rarely elective—wield enormous power over the lives and fortunes of the people of the

[2] Robert Lynd and Helen Lynd, *Middletown in Transition* (New York, Harcourt, Brace & World, 1937).

[3] See, for example, Floyd Hunter, *Community Power Structure* (Chapel Hill, University of North Carolina Press, 1953); Ritchie P. Lowry, *Who's Running This Town?* (New York, Harper and Row, 1965); W. Lloyd Warner and associates, *Democracy in Jonesville* (New York, Harper and Row, 1949); W. Lloyd Warner, J. O. Low, Paul S. Lunt, and Leo Srole, *Yankee City*, edited and abridged in the Yale University Press edition, 1963.

[4] C. Wright Mills, *The Power Elite* (New York, Oxford University Press, 1956).

nation, and for that matter of the world. Those in the "higher circles" of American decision-making, Mills pointed out, are rarely known except by a few of the most sophisticated people; their decisions are not, except in the most general sense, subject to democratic control, and yet they enjoy a sort of celebrity status and have built a *sub rosa* social system of their own. They operate with a value system oftentimes quite at odds with those presumably upheld by the larger society. Some critics feel that Mills somewhat overstated the case, or at least that the factual information appearing in the book did not completely sustain some of the generalizations that followed. Others feel that his portrayal of a largely hidden and politically irresponsible small and enormously powerful group was sufficiently documented to constitute an important characteristic of present mass society.

We turn now to the examination of some additional efforts of professional social scientists and to some important distinctions in the study of power.

SOME DISTINCTIONS

Anyone who gives attention to the matter quickly discovers that the word *power* is widely used by professionals and laymen, alike, and that usages vary enormously in both connotation and denotation. Since this conceptual unclarity exists, attention should first be given to some kind of tightening up of these diffuse meanings. The political scientist Robert A. Dahl [5] begins his analysis with what he calls "a common sense definition of influence." "A influences B to the extent that A gets B to do something that B would not otherwise do." The measure of influence, then, is the amount and direction of change in B's behavior from what it would have been had the influence not been successfully exerted. This, however, says much more easily than it can be operationalized: How can one ever be certain what someone *would have done*, if he has not in fact done it. Commonsense tests must be relied upon. If someone says he would have done something had it not been for some influence which restrained him, then we have a prima facie case for effective influence. Yet this allegation might be in error, either deliberately to mislead or because the person was not sufficiently aware of his own intentions. Other inferences are also possible, as when someone has been acting in a certain manner for some time, influence is brought to bear, and the behavior then changes. Again, one cannot be certain that the behavior might not have changed anyway or might not

[5] Robert A. Dahl, *Modern Political Analysis* (Englewood Cliffs, N.J., Prentice-Hall, 1963).

have changed for other reasons than the influence being assessed. Unless one is to abdicate all responsibility for power analysis, however, some judgment must be reached, admittedly sometimes from tenuous evidence, along some such lines as the foregoing. And this is perhaps one reason why there is so much disputation on the subject of influence (and power).

In discussing the more general concept *influence* it seems plausible to equate *influence* and *power*, except that accepted usages tend to imply certain distinctions. One of these is that only the more coercive forms of influence represent power. Thus, for example, if someone is persuaded by another's logic, he has manifestly been influenced but in no clear way coerced to act in accordance with the new persuasion. There is, to be sure, a fine line here, as when persuasion, as is often the case, includes subtle intimidations. A case in point would be the traditional clergyman's persuasion that if an individual performs certain acts, he will suffer eternal damnation in hell. His parishioner is, of course, free not to accept the clergyman's logic; but if he is already committed to a belief in hell and its connection with his present behavior, then he is as much intimidated as persuaded to abstain. Perhaps the most difficult aspect of the entire analysis applies to the subtle forms of power in which the power wielder, through control of the channels of communication, persuades the person to define his own best interests as those which the power wielder intends. This is, of course, the nub of the propaganda problem. Facts and interpretations are so presented that one comes to believe and act, not under apparent duress, but under the illusion that these are "his own" desires. Thus, the "battle for men's minds" is perhaps the most general, pervasive, and unending power struggle in the modern world.

A fundamental distinction in the use of the concept *power* must be made between *legitimate* and *nonlegitimate* power (or control). Legitimate power, sometimes called "authority," is control over a person or a group which derives from the position which the society accords to the power holder. The police officer is a case in point. He has the authority to direct one's movement within certain limits, to interrogate, and even to take a person into custody. This authority, however, is not arbitrary or unlimited. It is carried out by him as the delegated arm of the society. Similarly, with the power of various office holders in corporations or military organizations or ecclesiastical hierarchies. The formal role requirements simply specify that in order to operate the social system, various role incumbents shall exercise prerogatives which must be recognized by the others. The authority, then, functions as the personification of the regulation which is necessary to maintain order in the system and to facilitate the achievement of the goals of the system.

It is, however, typically difficult to find persons in authority who meticulously limit their control within the limitations of their specified legitimate authority. Everyone knows of instances, for example, of police officers who usurp power in excess of their legal role. Several Presidents of the United States have been accused of usurping power from other branches of government or of taking power directly through the use of executive orders, which are not prescribed in the Constitution or in current legislation. In countless lesser ways, persons encounter in their day-to-day activities instances in which teachers, foremen, social workers, or committee chairmen exert control over the behavior of other people beyond the limits of the legitimate authority. Despite an inordinate amount of complaint about such *usurpation*, it continues and ever reappears in a wide variety of standard forms. We turn now to an examination of some of the devices whereby, whether intended or not, individuals and groups exert power contrary to, or at least exceeding, the legitimate power which is assigned them.

Perhaps the most crude device is *intimidation*. In this well-known practice, power is achieved by threat. The threat may take the form of exposure of information or, more subtly, the form of an offer to withhold legitimate control in return for something. In its crudest form, of course, intimidation is recognized as blackmail and is legally punishable. But usually, because of its secretive character and the difficulties involved in exposure, an inordinate amount of intimidation actually occurs in this or any other society. Gross forms of intimidation may go on with surprising openness in a society for decades, as, for example, the intimidation of Southern Negroes by white sheriffs, voting officials, and even teachers. Sometimes charitable enterprises are financially supported by people who have no particular interest in them, but who make contributions under threat of public embarrassment to business or professional reputations if support is not forthcoming. There are many forms of genteel intimidation which have become so much a part of accepted behavior that they are taken for granted.

Manipulation is an even more subtle form of power. Here the intent is to secure an individual's conformity by the indirect route of causing him to identify the interests and intentions of the power wielder as his own. The many and devious forms of propaganda, censorship of part of the total truth, and the enormously effective techniques of sophisticated advertising all have this purpose in common. What makes it difficult to disassociate the mere dissemination of information from true manipulation is that few people are sufficiently sophisticated to distinguish between information and propaganda, guidance and exploitation. It is, moreover, sometimes difficult to identify the motivations of the manipulator. If it were always easy to recognize the intention, as in the case of the candidate running for office or the advertiser "pushing" his product, there would be little concern. But when the business advertiser subtly pushes political philosophy or the secular teacher proselytizes for his own religious values, one's capacity for discrimination may indeed be taxed.

Whether a separate device or merely a special form of manipulation, *suggestion* is also a source of power. Because persons vary greatly in prestige and because many find it comforting to be in accord with the ideas and practices of prestigeful people, the prestigeful person possesses a kind of power whether he wishes it or not. Studies of innovation of such seemingly dissimilar practices as scientific farming and hair styles have established the fact that prestigeful persons are often directly responsible for the changed behavior of others not merely in those areas where status is acknowledged but in other areas quite remote. This may, of course, result in benefits to the follower but can also be to his detriment. Again, unless one has some reliable way to impute motives, he cannot tell whether the follower is exploited or aggrandized by this kind of control over his behavior. Certainly many illustrations will occur to anyone which selectively could document both possibilities.

Other distinctions can, of course, be made; but at least the foregoing will give an idea of some of the complexities involved in the recognition that persons differ greatly in the amounts and kinds of control which they exert over others' affairs. Part of this control is directly exerted over individuals, but possibly the most important forms involve the differential access of persons to the decision-making processes in a society. This is important on all levels, from the selection of a football coach for the local high school to whether or not the nation will go to war. And in the formulation of such decisions, all of the foregoing forms and perversions of power are frequently involved.

ASSESSING POWER

Dahl [6] points out that there are several ways to observe power relations. Although he is writing about political systems, the methods are equally applicable to other social systems. First, one can assume, with some prima facie justification, that a person's power simply emerges from his position in a bureaucracy; thus the rules and regulations per-

[6] *Ibid.*

taining to his position spell out each person's power. The weakness here, of course, is that the basic assumption is "shaky." People vary enormously in their use (and abuse) of official power and, of course, much power can emanate from an individual who holds no official position whatever. Second, says Dahl, one can rely on judges—people close to and in a position to observe the power process. This is relatively "simple, quick, and economical" and is often used by historians. The disadvantage is "that it puts us at the mercy of the judges." They may be fallible or deliberately misleading. A third method is to study the way in which decisions are actually made and carried out. Who initiates proposals, who favors and who opposes, whose judgment wins out, over what areas does who or what group win out more often, and so on. There are difficulties here, too, however. The student of the process must be rather close to the actual happenings, but even then it is easy to miss the subtle moves—active participation and vocal activity can easily obscure the more subtle and effective ways of "getting things done."

Further insight can be gained, Dahl intimates, by looking at "common errors" which analysts of power, lay and professional alike, tend to make.

1. It is often assumed that those who *participate* in a decision necessarily *influence* it. This is, of course, the error which people make when they assume that a person who holds nominal office necessarily makes the decisions which emanate from that office. "Powers behind the throne" are a time-honored institution. Sometimes the official is simply expressing the consequences of someone else's decision, as when a Dean readmits a dismissed student whose father is a potential donor of a much needed telescope for the campus observatory!

2. The word *powerful* is often overextended. A person typically holds power in certain realms but not necessarily in others. This can readily be appreciated if one thinks concretely about instances in human relations with which he is personally familiar. A fraternity member may have great power in securing favors from the college administration but lack the power to get himself elected president. Parallels occur throughout all social systems. This is not to deny, however, that one of the differences among individuals and groups is the fact that some are able to assume effective power in more areas than are others.

3. Distinctions must always be made among varying *degrees* of power, even in a given realm. For example, defeated candidates are not thereafter wholly powerless; they simply have less and different legitimate power than those who won the election.

4. Even though it should be obvious, clear evidence of past and present power will not necessarily foretell future power. Again, as in all social forms, there is a clear tendency toward continuity, but this is always counterbalanced by inevitable and relentless forces making for change.

To this list of Dahl's we would add the following:

5. The assumption that a power holder is necessarily in this position by his own intent can be erroneous. Numerous instances can be assembled to demonstrate that some people have power thrust upon them by the circumstances of their familial connections, possessions, or the offices to which they are elected or appointed. Of course, in an abstract and unrealistic sense, one can always refuse to exercise such power, but in the hard realities of social life, this is an unrealistic notion. Doubtless, of course, consciousness of power excesses are much more likely to arise from the actions of people who actively seek power, yet this should not becloud the fact that power holding is not always or necessarily by intent of the holder.

6. Power may be sought for reasons which are altruistic as well as self-seeking, conscious as well as unconscious. One may, of course, be naïve in accepting cynical assertions of altruistic intent by self-seeking power wielders or be unaware of the fact that self-seeking may be rationalized by the power seeker himself because he is not conscious of his own motives for self-aggrandizement. Psychological analyses of once powerful figures such as Adolph Hitler and Napoleon are numerous, and every school child has been exposed to at least vulgar versions of these interpretations. To point out that sometimes the interpretations have been in error should not blind one to the realization that power seekers do not always know what their real motivations may be. This is no less true for altruistic than for selfish exercise of power, if for no other reason because the same purposes may be self-aggrandizing for the power holder and manifestly beneficial for the people over whom the power has been successfully exerted (for example, "benevolent dictatorship"). This is a knotty problem and many historical and other disputations about it are rampant. However, the realistic analyst of power ought at least to recognize that diverse motivations and varying degrees of consciousness are operative.

Up to now our discussion has focused on the acts and motivations of the power wielder. It should be remembered that, as in other social situations, the principles of interaction and the concepts of role and status apply. The person upon whom influence is exerted is an active part of the social system and his behavior, too, incorporates a wide variety of motivations, responses, and counter-behaviors which affect the quality of the interaction and the goals achieved. Any number of possible responses are obvious—one may quietly yield to pressure from power groups, or may try to avoid confrontation, or may make a counter-move exerting his own power. In each one of these responses, and countless others, the quality of the interaction is importantly affected. The student need only recall the various responses and counter-responses in the civil rights movement in this country today in order to cite numerous examples.

POWER STRUCTURE

The concept *power structure* is increasingly coming into use. It is probably the sociologists' unique contribution to the understanding of power. Our discussion so far has been essentially psychological, that is, we have explained how power operates, legitimately and otherwise, in the direct control of one person's behavior by another. But usually power does not operate so directly or personally; it operates indirectly but effectively through the established social systems.

Everyone is to some extent familiar with the systems of legitimate power which operate in the major institutions—for example, government, churches, educational institutions, athletic leagues. Procedures are established for changing regulations, handling participants who do not play their roles as required, recruitment of persons for roles, handling of grievances within the organization, and so on. Usually these relationships among persons in authority are set forth in a constitution, by-laws, a charter, or some other enabling document.

But as knowledgeable persons have long since learned, there typically coexists parallel to this established structure of power an informal, loosely organized group of individuals who exert important power directly upon the formal structure. So general are these *sub rosa* power structures in American society that some have taken on an almost institutional character themselves. In New York politics, for example, Tammany Hall has long been a powerful political organization, even though its key personalities have often not held any elective or appointive political office. And in almost every community, once one understands its inner workings, there are counterparts to Tammany Hall.

The informal power structure typically has a number of identifying characteristics: (1) The group is relatively small. (2) The persons in the power structure are usually not elected or appointed, but instead hold their positions of power for a variety of other reasons, chiefly because they can exercise some effective controls over the decision-making processes of the established system. Thus, a union boss, or a man of exceptional wealth, or a newspaper publisher, or a military hero, each for a different reason not only may feel that his counsel ought to be important, say in the local university, but may be in a position to bring his power to bear in devious ways, even though he functions quite outside of any official position in the university. For example, since the university must be concerned with its public image, the editorial policy of the newspaper can have a great deal to do with the public's image (and therefore support) of the university and of its administration or staff. Thus, it may be to the mutual advantage of the two to get along amicably, that is, for the newspaper to "go easy" on criticism of the university in return for some other concession which the university can grant, such as an appointment policy which favors "safe," i.e. conservative, professors or a heavy emphasis on intercollegiate sports.

From time to time there come to public attention some truly scandalous instances of various "unholy alliances" which have demonstrably not been in the interest of the public or of the established organization. No one knows how many unmentioned or unreported instances of this sort exist, but it is generally reported by persons who study power that power arrangements of this sort are quite typical.

It should be recognized that informal power structures may exist for altruistic or at least publicly beneficial purposes. It will be recalled from our discussion of bureaucracy that frequently informal organizations arise to get around red tape or to circumvent incompetent role incumbents or for other reasons to serve the best interests of the organization when the established channels fail to do so. This is also true on the community level where a chamber session of some self-appointed group may be the community's only hope for important improvement.

"WHO'S RUNNING THIS TOWN?"

As pointed out earlier in this chapter, community studies have been an important part of professional attempts to study power. Sociologists have gone far beyond the early influential works mentioned and have identified typologies, developed more careful methodologies, and formulated important distinctions to make analysis more precise. One such study which adds important qualifications and additional dimensions to our understanding is that of Ritchie P. Lowry, *Who's Running This Town?* [7] This recent study of community power structure illus-

[7] Lowry, *op. cit.*

trates a number of theoretical problems and research procedures and
may be helpful to secure some appreciation for the present status of
research on community power. *Who's Running This Town?* is a study
conducted within the last ten years in a city of 30,000 in California,
which the author calls Micro City. As the title indicates, the basic purpose was to answer the question, "Who is running this town?" The
search for answers led to a number of discoveries and refinements of
existing theories and typologies which make this an important work.

Three theories of power structure

Before launching into the actual investigation, it was necessary to
take a theoretical position with respect to the nature of power in a
community. Three such basic positions are extant in the literature and
have to some extent been discussed in the preceding pages. One widely
held view is the *Elitest Theory*. This is illustrated by Mills' *The Power
Elite* and holds in effect that definitive power is held by a relatively
small group of individuals who exercise control upon the established
institutions. Membership in this small coalition emerges from the
coalescence of power for each individual as he pools his influence with
others to effect definitive control over the nation or the community.
The characteristics of the community-centered elitest group are usually long-time membership in the community, wealth, membership in
many community organizations, political interest—with or without past
or present office holding—more than average education but not highly
educated or of professional status, and, of course, the desire to control.
Usually elitest groups have connections with a variety of the institutions of the community, for example, one may be a newspaper publisher, another a banker, another prominent in religious circles, and so
on. This elitest clique, it is alleged, really runs the social system,
whether community or nation, while the people who *appear* to do so,
that is, hold office, are really only "power legitimizers" carrying out
the mandate of the "powers behind the throne."

Lowry rejects Elitest Theory as a sufficient explanation of community power, not because it does not have considerable factual basis
but because *in itself* it does not account for other sources and patterns
of power exercise.

Second, there are the *Mass* theories of community power. This is
not so much *a* theory as a nucleus of more or less implicit theories, with
a common core of "negative orientation." Scholars who see community
power in this light tend to concentrate upon "alienation, apathy, and
other forms of disassociative behavior, because they are natural conse-

quences or at least attributes of the mass society." [8] Through abdication of leadership by the masses, their potential power goes by default to some small clique interested in assuming that power. This is similar to the Elitest Theory but differs importantly in that the masses are presumed to be powerless because of the nature of the society and not so much because elitest groups usurp definitive power.

Lowry rejects Mass theories as sufficient explanation of community power because, while he grants that such characteristics as alienation and apathy may be quite normal in the mass society, they do not preclude a democratic power system. Alienation and apathy may encourage such "open power" groups as political parties to vie with each other for the "uncommitted" voters. In other ways, also, Lowry seems to feel that the Mass theories overstate their case.

Pluralistic theories, as the name implies, hold that contemporary community power, and national power as well, is fragmentized among a considerable number of what have come to be called "veto groups," each of which hold, as John Galbraith phrased it a number of years ago, "countervailing power" over each other and over the society. For example, labor unions through such practices as strikes, collective bargaining, and lobbying can exert sufficient strength over employers' groups and the public to secure gains in income which others would be unwilling to grant were it not for the power held by the labor group. Similarly, management has sources of power which limit the theoretically vast power involved in the right to strike. If for no other reason, persons in this social class are better able than are laborers to survive financially during periods of work stoppage. Likewise, political parties or factions within them hold power through their support by voters and contributors who presumably are committed to the positions which such groups take. Certain newspapers and magazines, through their freedom to discuss or to withhold items of information, as well as in their editorializing practices, have manifest power, too. Yet all of these seemingly great powers are confronted by that of other groups, also powerful, who take opposing stands. The farm bloc is countervailed to some extent by labor unions and by management groups. Liberals who feel that welfare state policies should be expanded are countervailed by conservative groups who hold to a restricted concept of government action. And so on.

Lowry concludes, as do we, that none of these three prevailing theoretical emphases is wholly adequate: "The ultimate dilemma of community power studies is, of course, the fact that all of these theo-

[8] *Ibid.*, p. xx.

retical approaches may be relevant as explanations of particular segments of community context." [9] And, we would add, none completely
explains the structure of power in most situations. Lowry feels that
there is need to incorporate viewpoints from all three approaches and
designates his own study as such a "hybrid." Community leadership in
American society, he says, is typically pluralistic and grows out of the
"continuing conflict between community myth and reality." Communities typically hold ideologies and myths about themselves which
they perpetuate in various ways through their newspapers, sermons,
and informal public comment. Yet these myths are recurrently confronted by contrary hard realities which cannot be ignored indefinitely.
New perspectives come from newcomers to the community and even
from the community's own citizens who are more educated, traveled,
and otherwise exposed to larger purviews. While this incessant conflict
between myth and reality gives rise to alienation, apathy, and disorganization, it also is a stimulus to the rise of forms of leadership based on
consensus and compromise. Most of Lowry's book discusses the details
of this process.

Cosmopolitans, locals, and mediators

For a number of years sociologists studying leadership in community institutions have been using Merton's distinction between *Cosmopolitans* and *Locals*. "In general ideological orientation the local
leader is parochial and provincial. His attentions are directed mainly
to the problems and issues of the small community as an isolated and
insulated grouping within the context of larger society. [For example,
he is jealous of local prerogatives, fearful of state or federal interference
with schools.] The Cosmopolitan leader, on the other hand, is ecumenical and sophisticated. His significant reference groups and affiliations transcend the local community." . . .[10] He is usually well educated
and his reference groups tend to be professional groups who are national and even international in their perspectives. The Cosmopolitan,
whether or not he in fact does so, is free to move from community to
community because his occupational qualifications are technical, standardized, and widely recognized. He does not depend merely upon
local community reputation. Locals tend to hold elective office; Cosmopolitans, if they hold office, hold appointive offices which require
special professional status. To illustrate, possibly oversimply, the school

[9] *Ibid.*, p. xxii.
[10] *Ibid.*, p. 121.

board members are likely to be Locals; the superintendent, Cosmopolitan. The local hospital board members, Locals; the superintendent and professional staff, Cosmopolitans.

Lowry makes an important addition to Merton's dichotomy, which he accepts as illuminating but too "simplistic." He does not deny that both Locals and Cosmopolitans exist in considerable numbers in any community, but he discovered in Micro City that there is also a third and crucially important group, whom he calls the *Mediators*. "The mediating leader is so termed because of the fact that he maintains overlapping memberships and informal relationships with both Local and Cosmopolitan groups. He acts as a kind of buffer and channel of communication between Locals and Cosmopolitans." [11]

Lowry distinguishes between two types of Mediator, the Conservative-Mediator and the Utopian-Mediator, and outlines a profile of each. The Conservative-Mediator tends to be a businessman of a semiprofessional nature, such as pharmacist or insurance broker. He received most of his formal education outside the community. If he was not born in Micro City, he came from a similar one. He usually has terminated his education with a bachelor's degree. He maintains a great many memberships, not only in local organizations but in state and national ones as well. The Utopian-Mediator "may be a college professor, minister, attorney, housewife, or businessman." He has lived in the community around ten years. He differs from the Cosmopolitan professional in that he defines his professional duties as primarily toward the *local* community. His education is more extensive than the Conservative-Mediator, typically including a graduate or professional degree.

Thus, there emerges a picture of the leadership structure of Micro City. At the two extremes are the provincial Locals and the sophisticated Cosmopolitans. They have so little in common in viewpoint, history, and worldview that they find it difficult even to communicate with one another. Between them, organizationally as well as intellectually, are the Mediators, the Conservative-Mediators a little closer to the Locals, the Utopian-Mediators a little closer to the Cosmopolitans. This sets up the pattern for the "dynamics of leadership" and power in Micro City. The Locals and the Cosmopolitans largely talk past each other, each to their own group, but they both talk to the Mediators and listen to them because they need what the Mediators can do in the community. The Locals constitute most of the elitest tendencies which Micro City has, and there is as elsewhere, of course, an ill-defined category of apathetic

[11] *Ibid.*, p. 144.

and alienated people who couldn't care less about such public issues as urban development, supervised summer playgrounds, or where the expressway will be located. But some *are* concerned for any of a variety of reasons and so they get involved in the dialogue which results in whatever decision takes place. The talents of the educated are more and more needed because the exhortations of the Locals based upon tradition and sentiment are no longer enough to solve the pressing problems of community living. The Mediators, since they have interest in common with both the Cosmopolitans and Locals, keep the dialogue going and indirectly keep the several viewpoints operative in the pluralistic process of decision-making.

Returning to the question with which the study began, "Who's running this town?" Lowry concludes that *no one* "really runs" the town. The system is not only pluralistic, that is, different types of leaders play important roles, but the *structure*, not persons per se, holds the ultimate source of power. Doubtless some individuals are personally more powerful than others, but the main point seems to be that individuals come and go and yet the social structure of power goes on, much as the faculty of a high school or college may come and go but the system of roles which has been established tends to be stable, even though a few changes can be identified from time to time. Insofar as changes take place in Micro City, and presumably elsewhere, too, they take place through the influences of the most fluid group in the power structure, the Mediators, but even they cannot function without their dependence upon the special kinds of power which the Locals and the Cosmopolitans each possess.

Some implications from Micro City

What can one learn from the intensive analysis of Micro City which will help him to understand the power structure of macro America? While no single community study can provide definitive answers for the macro society, some implications can nonetheless be deduced.

1. The sources and forms of power are demonstrably pluralistic, although it is well to remember the ever-present tendency for elitest groups to form and usually to have considerable influence for indefinite periods. They tend, however, to be challenged by countervailing groups, although the time required for effective challenging of elitest power may sometimes be considerable.

2. Much seems to depend on how much the society or community, like the residents of Micro City, looks to its myths and ideologies and

how much to the sterner realities of present circumstances. The two are perpetually at odds with each other, and there seems to be no dearth of persons willing to take one side or the other in the struggle.

3. The provincial concepts of the Locals and the rootlessness of the Cosmopolitans, each has its ideological vulnerabilities and strengths, so when actual decisions have to be made, such as whether or not to go to war, whether or not to make an issue of civil rights, the final action is usually in the form of some kind of compromise carried off by a coalition of Mediators who can communicate with the extremes in fashioning a solution which the countervailing power groups can all live with, at least for the time being.

4. But issues are rarely finally settled. They emerge again and again in new forms, and the Mediators are faced anew with the challenging tasks of further decisions.

5. Putting the matter this way, however, may come dangerously close to a naïve, simplistic, and utopian concept of democracy. Actually, the Mediators have their work cut out for them because groups, as well as individuals, do not as a rule give up power easily, nor can they evaluate alternative actions objectively, much less charitably. Usurpation, intimidation, exploitation, as well as downright falsification are all involved in the hard realities of the power struggle.

6. The legitimate power structures seem constantly at guerilla war with the vigilante, *sub rosa* structures; and these, too, take on ever new forms and coalitions.

7. Traditional phrases like "democratic decision-making," "authoritarianism," "dictatorship" do not fit the realities of the current condition, partly because they oversimplify a much more complex process and partly because they make assumptions about the nature and use of power which are simplistic, too. Here, as elsewhere, man's ingenuity, as well as his naïveté, in culture building is in clear evidence.

SUMMARY

Sociologists and other social scientists, although somewhat tardily, have begun to take important steps in the analysis of social power and power structures. A basic distinction in the exercise of power is that between legitimate and nonlegitimate power, the former being an essential component of all social systems, the latter constituting a much less systematic and visible set of motives and techniques such as control by manipulation and intimidation. Much of the effectiveness of non-legitimate power comes as the indirect consequence of control of the channels of communication and sources of potential power through certain institutions such as banking and employment.

Power structures, the social systems through which power is exerted, are likewise legitimate and nonlegitimate. The former are open; power holders are known and the limits of their authority are spelled out in law and custom. The nonlegitimate power structures, on the other hand, are relatively small, less visible, and ordinarily not subject to democratic control, except upon occasion and then indirectly. This is even true when the activities are clearly illegal or otherwise contrary to the principles of the legitimate power structure.

We have examined in some detail Lowry's analysis of community power in Micro City; reviewed his evaluations of Elitest, Mass, and Pluralistic power models; and surveyed his analysis of the roles of Locals, Cosmopolitans, and Mediators. The careful analyst of community, or national, power structures seems to us forced by the evidence to recognize that there is clear merit to several of these theoretical models and that no simplistic explanation yet exists which would completely explain the operation of power and power structures in American society.

SUGGESTED READINGS

Dahl, Robert A., *Modern Political Analysis.* Englewood Cliffs, N.J., Prentice-Hall, 1963.
This is essentially a political science book, but it is of a strongly sociological orientation; the insights and typologies are exceedingly provocative.

————, *Who Governs?* New Haven, Yale University Press, 1961.
A study of the relationship between power and democratic process in American society.

Keller, Suzanne, *Beyond the Ruling Class.* New York, Random House, 1963.
A study of elitest groups functioning in American society.

Lenski, Gerhard, *Power and Privilege.* New York, McGraw-Hill, 1966.
With power as the pivotal concept, this book questions, "Who gets what and why?" A provocative and readable discussion.

Lowry, Ritchie P., *Who's Running This Town?* New York, Harper & Row, 1965.
This book was used prominently in the preparation of this chapter, but there

are many other important insights and data which deserve to be studied by anyone interested in community power.

Mills, C. Wright, *The Power Elite*. New York, Oxford University Press, 1960.

This is an influential and controversial book which advances the theory that there exists at the pivotal decision-making points of American society a relatively small group of nonlegitimate elites who virtually control collective decisions.

Monsen, R. Joseph, Jr., and Cannon, Mark W., *The Makers of Public Policy*. New York, McGraw-Hill, 1965.

Spells out the dimensions of power as they relate to decision-making in the mass society.

Presthus, Robert, *Men at the Top: A Study in Community Power*. New York, Oxford University Press, 1964.

A representative study of the decision-making echelon in the American community.

STUDY QUESTIONS

1. Why have sociologists been so slow in taking up the study of power? Can you think of any reasons additional to those in the text?
2. Why is power difficult to define and even more difficult to measure?
3. Can you think of any more effective ways to measure power than those outlined in this chapter?
4. Distinguish legitimate and nonlegitimate power.
5. What examples of legitimate and nonlegitimate power have you come across in the various social systems you have participated in?
6. Explain why so many social thinkers identify nonlegitimate power as the enemy of democracy.
7. What examples of usurpation, intimidation, and manipulation have you observed?
8. Distinguish between power and power structures.
9. What are the general characteristics of informal power structures?
10. What are the main findings of Lowry's *Who's Running This Town?*
11. What similarities and differences do you think obtain between Micro City and your home base?
12. Distinguish "Elitest," "Mass," and "Pluralistic" concepts of power. Illustrate each.
13. What are meant by "Cosmopolitans," "Locals," and "Mediators"? What are the characteristics of each?
14. Explain how the functions of Cosmopolitans, Locals, and Mediators interact to bring about community, as well as national, decision.

31
SOCIAL INTERACTION: THE PROCESSUAL TRADITION

As everyone knows, or should know, virtually everything in the social milieu is in the process of change. Sociologists have frequently been taunted by other observers of the social scene for being too inclined to stress the structural, orderly, cultural, repetitive, and predictive aspects of society and human relations to the neglect of the more dynamic or processual phases. These critics are more than a little right but by no means completely so. Just as it is easy to exaggerate the rigidity of human relationships, so it is easy to exaggerate the fluidity, and it is therefore doubtful whether anyone hits the balance exactly right.

In any event, what has come to be called in professional jargon "the processual approach" is an old one, in American sociology at least. One of the classic textbooks, Park and Burgess' *Introduction to the Science of Sociology*,[1] placed considerable emphasis upon the social processes in human interaction and identified four basic "forms" of interaction. The purpose of this chapter is to interpret this important tradition and to clarify the forms of social interaction which are as manifest now as they were when Park and Burgess wrote, almost fifty years ago.

The interaction of groups and of individuals tends to follow a relatively *few basic types or forms*. Their existence apparently has been obvious enough to have attracted the interest of the layman, because his language patterns contain standard words and precepts which reveal a more or less accurate conception of some of these basic forms of interaction. *Competition* and *cooperation* are perhaps the best known. These concepts are well enough understood by almost everyone, so that formal definition seems to be largely unnecessary.

[1] R. E. Park and E. W. Burgess, *Introduction to the Science of Sociology* (Chicago, University of Chicago Press, 1921).

We shall turn now to a somewhat more detailed treatment of competition and cooperation as important basic forms of social interaction. Probably in all societies both cooperation and competition have existed side by side in the daily behavior of the people, but the folklore relating to them shows serious misunderstandings.

COMPETITION

Competition: a subcultural life necessity

The basic factor underlying competition is that there is a limited quantity of many items of value which groups or persons strive to secure. If the item of value exists in such abundance that there is enough for everyone's needs, then no competition takes place, regardless of how precious the items might be. Thus, under normal conditions people do not compete for air and water, even though these two materials are essential for the continuation of life. But under occasional artificial conditions of scarcity of air and water, competition for these commodities can be and has been extremely acute.

The basic life drives of the human being are usually expressed either through, or as the result of, competitive endeavor. Food and sex needs are cases in point. For any given person these needs are fulfilled only because he, or someone else acting for him, was able to secure them in the face of varying desire by others.

Competition: a cultural value in some societies

Many of the objectives for which human beings compete do not derive their values from the sustenance needs of the human organism, but rather from the nonrational value patterns of the culture. Men and women compete for such goals as golf championships and political offices, not because these things have any discernible connection with the quality or quantity of their physical existence, but because these quite artificial distinctions reflect superior status upon their possessors.

Status competition for intangibles is often acute

It may already be apparent that some of the most intense competitions in which people engage have as their objective the attainment of intangible items of value. This is true not only in modern societies such as ours but among primitive peoples and among culture-types quite different from ours. At the risk of oversimplification, it may be said that the intangible objects for which people compete are rationalized as worth the severe competitive effort because the successful attainment of the objective reflects superior status on the person who is successful in the competition. This is always contingent, of course, upon the fact that the particular rivalry in question, and also the goal, are approved by the value system of the society in which the person desires to secure the higher prestige rating.

Forms of competition

There are several *subtypes of competition* which ought to be distinguished from one another.

Absolute and relative competition. In some forms of rivalrous interaction, the competition is defined in such a way that only one person can normally claim to have become the successful partisan or the victor. Championships are for the most part of this sort. There is only one winner of the Kentucky Derby or of the world championship baseball pennant. There is only one President of the United States at a time. All other competitors must have been eliminated before anyone can claim success.

Other competitions are simply *matters of degree.* People compete for money, prestige, and fame. But no one expects to attain all of the money or all of the prestige or all of the fame. He often realizes before he begins the competition that he probably can never aspire to even the top 50 percent, but he competes anyway, striving to secure as much as possible of whatever items of value he desires to acquire.

Personal and impersonal competition. Competition may also be classified as *personal* and *impersonal.* In personalized competition the competitors strive with one another, each consciously trying to defeat his rivals at the polls, on the golf course, in court, or at love. Each competing person is aware of the existence of his competitors and recognizes that in some way or another the competitors' claims must be eliminated before he can attain his objective.

On the other hand, some competitions are largely de-personalized. In the present competition between labor and management over wages, for example, there is no necessary personal focus for the rivalry. While it is true that each side bargains through specially designated representatives, everyone knows that these representatives are *only functionaries or spokesmen* and that they could be replaced by other functionaries or spokesmen without in any way altering the outcome. The rivalry of various industrial concerns which produce competitive products may constitute an even better illustration of impersonal competition. Each is courting public favor through advertising, attempting to build a superior product, or providing better service for its customers. But the customers and the managers of the enterprise never meet and do not know each other, nor do the competing workers and managers usually regard themselves as competitors in the personal sense.

Competition is seldom "pure"

Competition is usually *accompanied by some joint or cooperative effort*. When two athletic teams or two industries compete, it can easily be overlooked that a great deal of cooperation among the persons within the group is necessary in order to achieve a more effective organization as a competing unit. Moreover, in many forms of competition there is evidence of cooperation even among the rivals. They cooperate in abiding by the rules of the "game" as recognized by the culture, and in many other ways, also. It is true, of course, that in these instances mentioned, the cooperative effort is subordinate to the competitive purpose; but it seems important to note that the competition in order to be effective seems often to require considerable cooperative effort both within and between the competing units.

The importance of culture in patterning competitive effort

There is a prevailing tendency to overlook the large role played by culture in group or individual competition. Many persons tend to think and talk about competition as if they believed that the competitive process was inherent in the original nature of the person without any significant molding through cultural experience. While we are not here denying that rivalry may be rooted in original nature, it is necessary to emphasize the basic cultural learning superimposed upon and built into the person as a result of living in a specific culture at a specific time; this cultural experience in turn steers the competitive bent in certain directions.

1. A continuum of the importance of competition

We may roughly classify cultures along a continuum on the basis of the importance which each culture attaches to competitive interaction. Some cultures are highly competitive and attach great prestige to the person who is successful at competitive effort. Other cultures devalue competition and sharply reduce the number and importance of personal prestiges which result from it. Ours is a highly competitive culture, and there is a pronounced ethnocentric tendency to assume that the values and behaviors approved in our culture are somehow inherent in the scheme of things. Actually, of course, such is not the case.

2. Culture defines the forms of competition

In addition to the overall emphasis upon competition, culture defines this form of interaction in numerous basic ways.

a. The values of the culture determine the basic *items which are regarded as desirable.* Wealth, for example, may or may not be defined as a worthy personal attainment. The same with education or with physical attractiveness or with romantic love.

b. Culture, moreover, defines the *propriety or impropriety of attempting to attain given values by competitive effort.* The religious and ethical systems of many peoples, for example, disapprove of rivalrous means of attaining certain values. Covetousness along specified lines is very frequently frowned upon. In our society, on the other hand, it is considered altogether proper that the several men who desire a given woman as their wife should compete with one another for the purpose of "winning" her. There are other cultures, however, in which this method of securing a mate would be considered inappropriate, if not indecent.

c. The *culture* of a people *defines who may and who may not compete for a given item of value.* This is most pronounced, as we have seen, in caste and caste-like societies, where it is regarded as inappropriate and therefore virtually impossible for a person of one caste to compete with a person of another caste for the same item of value. Abundant illustrations of this principle can be found in the United States pertaining to white and colored persons. Many jobs, areas of residence, and educational opportunities from which Negroes are categorically excluded illustrate the way in which the culture defines who may or who may not compete for the attainment of a given value.

d. Finally, *culture formulates and enforces more or less recognized rules for competitive effort.* Competition is almost never unrestrained. The epithet *cheat* has wide currency in the thoughtways of almost every people. The cheat is not necessarily the person who has violated some carefully worded law or rule or regulation. He is more often the person who does not follow the informal customs which are supposed to regulate the rivalry and keep the competition "clean." The cleanliness of competition, of course, is entirely a matter of definition. Whether the rivals for the affections of a given girl who fight it out in the alley are playing the game "clean" or "dirty" depends upon the unwritten rules of the game of courtship among the group in question. In one community such behavior would be regarded as altogether fair, but in another group it would be defined as contrary to the standards of "decency" which ought to obtain among courting rivals. At one time in the United States a man who was insulted by another man could defend his honor successfully only by challenging the other to a duel. The society of that time condoned such behavior, but today's society would not. In at least these four ways, then, the prevailing culture of a people institutionalizes the competitive process. Like all forms of culture these approval-disapproval patterns are highly variable in time and space.

3. Competition as a real and as an ideal pattern in economic life

The culture of American business extols the virtue of competition. Competition is said to be the "life of trade" and the basis of the "American way." If a person were naïve, he might reach the conclusion that our economic life implements competition wherever possible. The more sophisticated observer of the economic sphere, however, will note that practice departs very radically, and at many points, from these idealizations of competition; that there are many efforts to *avoid* competition.

The student will recall from his study of American history that one of the most recurrent problems which America has faced has been that of large-scale cooperation between supposedly competing businesses, usually called "monopolies" or "trusts." Device after device has been invented by the management of industry for concealing the extent and kind of cooperative effort among supposedly competing business enterprises. Time and again when competitive bids have been opened for the construction of a public building, road, or bridge, identical bids have been made by all the competitors. Obviously such unanimous agreement is not the result of chance. There have also been "gentlemen's agreements," conclusively proved in court, whereby competing concerns have agreed on certain prices and have agreed not to change prices without consulting each other. Other "gentlemen's agreements" have concerned wage rates and agreements not to compete in certain areas. These and other techniques of avoiding competition have now become public knowledge.

Labor, more recently, has begun to follow the pattern set by industry. Individual workmen do not really compete with one another in large union-dominated industries. In fact, the workman who does too much work is penalized by his fellow union members, and promotions and discharges are forced by union contract to follow seniority and not individual differences based upon competitive effort in doing a job.

Thus, the economic sphere in America presents an interesting paradox, or at least inconsistency, between the ideal and real practice of competition. Competition is said to be the basis of economic life, and yet at almost every opportunity to establish monopoly, competition has been willingly reduced or eliminated entirely. The realistic observer of the whole process is left with no choice but to conclude that in practice free competition apparently does not work as well as it is alleged to work, else it would not be crushed so frequently.

COOPERATION

In some ways, but not in all, cooperation may be regarded as the antithesis of competition. The interaction is oriented toward *joint achievement of a goal*. It will be recalled that in the above discussion of competition, it was pointed out that competition and cooperation may coexist in a situation, such as in the behavior of the members on an athletic team, or a political party, or a business, who cooperate with one another for the purpose of competing more effectively.

Cooperation also a basic life necessity

It is perhaps not surprising that in a society as dominated by the competitive ideology as is the American, there would be so little recognition of the obvious fact that cooperation is a necessary activity. If mother and infant did not cooperate, the infant would die of starvation; if lovers did not cooperate, the resulting frustration would create emotional havoc indeed; if the members of armies, athletic teams, college faculties, police departments, fraternities, industries, and communities did not cooperate in many vital and continuous matters, life as we know it could not exist. Because our society extols the virtues of competitive effort, our attention tends to focus upon it; and we fail to note the extent to which cooperative forms of interaction are prominent aspects of our practical life collectively and our lives individually. A few moments of careful reflection should serve to demonstrate, however, that cooperation is an *indispensable* requisite of human life in this and all other societies. To this end we shall examine cooperation as a form of social interaction.

Cooperation and self-interest

It is often held that cooperative activity is difficult to achieve because "individuals are basically selfish," and their alleged selfishness makes it difficult, if not impossible, to subordinate their individual wills to the collective enterprise. The chief factor overlooked in such a conception of the matter is that there is no *necessary discrepancy between selfishness and cooperation.* A person may be seeking to further his self-interests by competitive activity, by cooperative activity, or by both. Competition and cooperation are merely two somewhat distinct means of attaining *either* self-interests or self-subordination as objectives. Either objective can sometimes be served by either means or more often by some combination of the two. Probably the reason for the close linking of self-interest and competition is a result of the coexistence of these two values in American culture. In short, it is an ethnocentric view of the matter.

Forms of cooperation

It has already been shown that there are several kinds of competition. Cooperation, likewise, is of several forms.

1. The most obvious form of cooperation consists of behavior which results from loyalty or at least adherence to the same objective. In that sense, the citizens of a community cooperate for the purpose of building a school or lynching someone. In that same sense, we may say that the diverse groups making up the United States cooperate for the purpose of winning a war.

2. Cooperation may also be of a form frequently called "*antagonistic cooperation.*" This paradoxical expression seems to be a rather apt one. Frequently persons cooperate for no reason other than for the purpose of organizing their basically opposing desires or interests. When employer and employee agree to a conference for the purpose of arriving at a wage settlement, they are, in a sense, cooperating, but they

are cooperating as a means of attaining a set of objectives fundamentally at variance with one another. The employee wants high wages and the employer low wages. Each side realizes that it is vitally dependent upon the other and that there is no alternative but to work out some sort of an arrangement cooperatively.

3. Other cooperation is the result of unavoidable *mutual dependence* of two or more persons and groups. The interest may not be the same nor yet clearly antagonistic. The overall organization of society through the *division of labor is a largely unconscious form of cooperation due to mutually necessary economic interdependence.*

4. We have already seen that it is often necessary that the members of a group cooperate in order that they may compete more successfully with some other group.

5. Finally, cooperation may result from the *superior power of a group with which one must cooperate* because there is no real alternative. In this sense many individuals and groups in Germany and in Japan cooperated with the Allied armies of occupation after the war. Obviously people in such circumstances would prefer not to be held under the absolute authority of a conquering power, but since they have been vanquished in war, they cannot escape this domination. Hence, they elect to cooperate in order that they may secure better treatment than they would if they resisted. In a similar manner children must cooperate with teachers in some degree at least, and also citizens with traffic policemen.

The role of culture in patterning cooperative effort

Culture is the determining factor in defining the propriety or impropriety of cooperative effort, very much the same as we observed in the case of competition. The particular culture *defines certain goals as most appropriately attainable through cooperation.* Thus, members of a family are supposed to cooperate with one another in the attainment of joint values, and members of an organization such as a church or labor union or board of directors are supposed to be characterized by behavior patterns reflecting cooperation. There is no inherent reason, in most cases, why the opposite form of interaction might not be quite as workable. Yet because one has been indoctrinated with one view rather than another, the way in which his thinking has been fashioned usually seems to him to be more natural or more logical.

Just as some societies tend to emphasize competition as the preferred overall form of interaction, so *other societies place cooperation in a preferred value position.* It is to be noted, of course, that no society is entirely and consistently competitive nor is any society entirely and consistently cooperative. In each society there will be found elements of both forms of interaction, but the relative predominance of one or the other in the total pattern of behavior constitutes whatever justification there may be for such phrases as "competitive society" or "cooperative society."

Obviously, therefore, we can find no objective basis for categorically approving or disapproving of cooperation as a form of interaction. Such evaluation depends largely, if not solely, on the values which the evaluating person holds. As a rule, to most persons in contemporary American society, competition seems to be the more virtuous basic orientation to human interaction. As we have repeatedly pointed out, this superior valuation is altogether natural since our society is one in which, in theory at least, competition is the more approved method of behavior. Obviously, competition will seem more normal and natural than cooperation for exactly the same reason as English will seem more normal and natural than Chinese and that Christianity will seem a more normal and natural religion than Shintoism.

This is understandable enough in view of the close relation between culture and individual behavior. It may not be so obvious, however, that because of the American preoccupation with competition, much actual cooperation which occurs passes unnoticed or is inadequately appraised. Thus, the person gets a distorted or even downright misleading idea of the nature of his own society and of the processes at work in it. His perceptions of his own behavior and that of other people may thus become more fictitious than real, and his *practical* decisions and actions which he bases on these perceptions become correspondingly falsely based.

CONFLICT

Some of the rivalrous interaction among the persons and groups in a society takes place within the more or less culturally approved channels which we have called competition. But there are other rivalries which are less controlled, less within the recognized and accepted "rules." In the absence of agreed-upon standards for carrying out the rivalry, crude hostility and more intense forms of struggle become common. Rivalry of this sort is less easy to define than is competition, but tends to be called *conflict* by students of social interaction.

Historical development of the concept of *conflict*

The first sociologists to attempt a formal differentiation of competition and conflict, Park and Burgess, made the distinction in terms of impersonality and continuity.

"Both competition and conflict are forms of struggle. Competition, however, is continuous and impersonal, conflict is intermittent and personal." [2] This early formulation has not proved entirely satisfactory to modern sociologists, or for that matter even to laymen. Certainly present-day usage of the word *competition* includes rivalries which are conscious and personal (competition for a job, a championship, a woman, or selling a car) and such competition may be continuous, even for extended periods.

Gillin and Gillin have sought a distinction by tracing the etymology of the two words. "It is clear . . . that . . . both terms involve the idea of rivalry or striving against someone who wants the same thing, but that the striving of competition is much less violent than that of those in conflict. Even with all the nuances of the two words there yet remains something of the distinction between *seek* and *strike*." Accordingly they define conflict as "the social process in which individuals and groups seek their ends by directly challenging the antagonist by violence or the threat of violence." [3] Here, then, the distinction is drawn in terms of "violence or the threat of violence." The *Dictionary of Sociology* [4] defines conflict in more general terms as "a process-situation in which two or more human beings or groups seek actively to thwart each other's purposes, to prevent each other's interests, even to the extent of injury or destroying the other. . . . Conflict may exist in varying degrees. . . . It may be organized or unorganized, transitory or enduring, physical, intellectual, or spiritual." Without offering this as an iron-clad definition, because current sociological usage is still varied, we can consider it as, loosely, our working definition of *social conflict*.

Competition and conflict frequently difficult to distinguish

There are numerous cases in which rivalrous behavior has some aspects of competition and some aspects of conflict according to the

[2] *Ibid.*, p. 574.

[3] John L. Gillin and John P. Gillin, *Cultural Sociology* (New York, Macmillan, 1949), pp. 589, 625, respectively.

[4] Edited by H. P. Fairchild (New York, Philosophical Library, 1944), pp. 58–59.

definitions which we have suggested. Capital-labor rivalries, interracial rivalries, and business-government rivalries are frequently of this sort.

Suppose we illustrate with business-government rivalry. We have pointed out several times that one of the basic social trends in America is the increasing control of business by governments presumably in the "public interest." Some, but not necessarily all, of this control has been opposed by business interests. Propaganda campaigns have been launched, both by business groups and those groups which have favored more government control, such as some consumer groups and some labor groups. In these propaganda campaigns there has been much misrepresentation of facts, if not downright falsification. Moreover, very clever techniques have been used, often through conventional advertising channels, which appear to have been designed to be deceptive. Instances of bribery and intimidation of public officials are by no means infrequent.

Do these constitute competition or conflict? They have some aspects of competition in that there are *some* rules, some standards of decency, which can still be observed. Whether this is due to the presence of ethical standards on the part of these groups or due to fear of court action and other kinds of public censorship cannot, of course, be determined. It is clear, however, that there is some observance of rules by both sides. On the other hand, there are aspects of conflict in the situation. It seems difficult, indeed, to rationalize the deliberate deception by propaganda as other than "cheating" for the purpose of winning adherents in a debate. Similarly, some of the actions of pressure groups in influencing legislators constitute more nearly the tactics of the racketeer than those of responsible citizenship. And yet it is entirely possible that these ethically reprehensible practices may have become so widely practical and accepted that they already constitute competitive practices, rather than conflict techniques.

The same difficulty is presented by other large-scale rivalries in American life. The conflict between liberal and traditional religion and between some of the large religious bodies shows the same combination of competitive and conflict rivalry. Certainly some aspects of the rivalrous interaction between the races in the United States fall into this same borderline zone between competition and conflict. Even though we must candidly admit that in these and other specific instances rivalrous interactions have aspects of both types, other rivalries are much more clearly conflict. Revolution, riots, lynching, wars, and the street fight are obvious cases of conflict.

A second look at conflict

There is a pronounced tendency among both professional sociologists and laymen to regard conflict as an undesirable, pathological, destructive force. Evidence for the foregoing statement is abundant and has been documented in a stimulating book.[5] But there is another side, a positive side, to conflict which also needs to be appreciated in order to balance one's view. We need to "correct a balance of analysis which has been tilted in the other direction." [6]

While conflict is undeniably a destructive force in social relationships, such as those between and among the various races, religions, and political partisans of our time, it is the fact of conflict which also *unifies* groups, even if only for the purpose of better carrying on what they believe to be desirable and constructive reform or maintaining worthy traditions, whatever the case may be. There is also a "safety valve" function of conflict. "Our opposition makes us feel that we are not completely victims of the circumstance." [7]

The foregoing is not to be taken as an assertion that all conflict is socially constructive or as a denial that some conflict is not seriously destructive to a society. It is well, however, to remember that many of what we now regard as fortuitous products from history have been won by conflict—our independence as a nation, the separate identity of many religious organizations, the emancipation of slaves, and in less dramatic ways, the establishment of such prized institutional arrangements as the public school system, the emancipation of women, the organization of labor, the rights of freedom of speech, press, and religious belief, and many more.

The nub of the matter seems to be this: Conflict is an inherent, natural part of the ongoing socialization process, both for the individual personality and for the group. Like most natural processes it has both positive (beneficial) and negative (destructive) effects, although it is not always easy or possible to reach agreement as to which is which. Differing value positions from which a given conflict may be interpreted will often result in varied judgments as to whether the conflict was, on balance, good or bad. But surely no one can deny that without conflict, without a mechanism to resist undesirable forces, life as we know it would be impossible. Much of the history of civilization may

[5] Lewis A. Coser, *The Functions of Social Conflict* (New York, Macmillan, 1956).
[6] *Ibid.*, p. 8.
[7] George Simmel, *Conflict* (New York, Macmillan, 1955), p. 19.

be interpreted as a slow, and sometimes heart-rending and forceful, process of regulating conflict so that its natural exercise may result in a minimum of negative effects—trial by legal process instead of by mob action, the Articles of War, the ethics of a "fair" fight being cases in point. But conflict is always at the core—only the forms it takes are "humanized" and some of the cruder effects meliorated. This brings us to the related social process—accommodation.

ACCOMMODATION

Competition and conflict do not go on forever. Frequently they become so intense or so wasteful or so time-consuming that they are terminated. In their place are substituted other kinds of relationships, nonrivalrous in nature, between persons and groups. One of these is accommodation. *Accommodation refers to a permanent or temporary termination of rivalrous interaction which, while not necessarily settling the issue involved in the rivalry, permits the rivalrous parties to function together without open hostility at least in some respects.*

Forms of accommodation

It is neither possible nor necessary to present an exhaustive list of the specific forms of accommodation which one finds in a society. Since these forms are *social expedients for reducing or resolving rivalries,* inventions occur from time to time so that even a complete list at one time might be outmoded before it is published. We shall limit ourselves, therefore, to brief comment on a few of the recognized and long-established forms of accommodation.

1. The *truce* is found in almost every society in some form or other. It consists merely of the cessation of rivalry for a definite or indefinite period with the issues in no sense settled.

2. The *compromise*. Each party agrees to certain concessions, but still retains the right and the power to engage in furtive rivalry. This is also an old and well-established practice found in such dissimilar social situations as legislatures and families.

3. Temporary *subordination-superordination* arrangements are also widespread. Under this form of accommodation, one or the other of the rivalrous parties secures a partial advantage or "upper hand." This is recognized by both sides, and there is devised, often more or less tacitly, some sort of working arrangement which gives the subordinate person or group something less than victory but something more

than defeat. This is somewhat similar to compromise, of course, the difference being in the fact that under compromise there is an assumption of approximate equality in the strength of the rivaling parties, whereas under subordination-superordination arrangements it is unmistakably clear that one group is dominant over the other, but not completely so.

The armistice with Japan illustrates subordination-superordination arrangements rather clearly. In return for permitting the Allies to land peacefully in Japan, the Japanese were promised better treatment than they would have received had the Allies landed forcibly. It had been recognized by both sides that Japan was virtually defeated, the only questions remaining were two: how conclusively was Japan already defeated, and how soon would this be formally recognized? Thus, the Japanese pacifically subordinated themselves in return for some concessions. The basic conflict between Japan and the Occidental nations was not immediately settled in any final sense; it was only accommodated for the time being under these arrangements.

4. *Arbitration* provides for the termination of a rivalry on the basis of a decision reached, and possibly also enforced, by some third party. Courts constitute a conspicuous example of arbitration, but in the everyday affairs of ordinary people there are innumerable occasions in which third parties intervene in rivalries, and terminate them at least temporarily.

5. *Toleration* represents a form of accommodation of which there is abundant evidence. Frequently there is no formal truce, no agreed upon arrangements for terminating the rivalry, no arbitrator, but by informal procedures each party to the rivalry agrees to "put up with" the existence of the other rather than to assume the effort, inconvenience, or expense of further rivalry. Sometimes there is an ethical principle involved, such as we find in the democratic ideal, in which it is generally granted that persons of dissimilar views and behaviors also have the "moral right" to exist and "be free." So long as all sides to the rivalry recognize and accept this principle, some conflicts can be controlled if not, in time, eliminated entirely. These various forms of accommodation may be lasting or very temporary.

The significance of culture
in social interactions

It may appear obvious to the student, but it is a fact not to be overlooked, that cultural standards play a significant role in working out the pattern of accommodations. The forms of accommodations are themselves, of course, culture; they are men's inventions for systematically handling the problem of rivalrous interaction when rivalry is no longer desired.

Culture, moreover, defines which rivalries are or are not accommodable. To attempt to accommodate certain rivalries is regarded as inappropriate, and a person or group which consents to terminate such rivalries may lose "honor" or "face" or prestige by so doing.

The same principle is often involved in more personal interaction. Suppose a husband discovers that another man is showing inappropriate attentions to his wife. Being a peace-loving and democratic gentleman, he decides to do nothing about the situation. He decides to practice the philosophy of "live and let live." In such a situation most persons would condemn the husband almost as much as the wife, since rivalries of this sort are regarded as "dishonorable." The issue must be sharply drawn and settled promptly if the husband is to "save face" and maintain his status in the eyes of many conventional people.

The society also establishes and enforces organized means of accommodation for the purpose of settling certain types of personal and group rivalries which are regarded as undesirable, dangerous, or unnecessary. The court system, as we have seen, has this as one of its purposes. In more recent times the court system has been supplemented by other kinds of deliberative bodies such as strike mediation boards and various other federal and state boards and commissions.

Less formally enforced societal pressures impinge upon the conflicts of ordinary people in the ordinary daily affairs of life. Thus, if two gentlemen disagree upon some basic matter and a rivalry develops, it is often considered "good form" not to gossip about it, to refrain from making an overt issue of it, and most assuredly not to enter into fistic combat concerning it. One may find himself in a rivalrous relationship with his neighbors because of the inconveniences involved in the perennial fights between the neighbor's dog and his own. Obviously, both have loyalties and both may have deeply injured pride, but the standards of etiquette are such that probably neither of the two men involved would want to make "too much" of an issue of these incidents. Each tolerates the intolerable situation because there is nothing else to do about it—if one wishes to remain a "gentleman."

The thoughtways of the culture also provide numerous rationalizations to support the ego of the person who has accommodated a rivalry. He would not "stoop" to such behavior as that of his opponent. It is "better to be a gentleman than to win" the issue. One must "see first things first" and "not jeopardize larger values to attain more minor ones." One should "live and let live." One has to "give and take." And so on and on.

ASSIMILATION

Some competitions and conflicts tend, in time, to disappear because one side becomes overwhelmingly stronger than the other, and there is no longer any basis for effective rivalry. Or the persons and groups which make up one faction may decline in numbers, move away, or change their minds. The rivalries between native populations and immigrant groups frequently show a cycle of conflict resulting in the eventual disappearance of the basis for conflict, because in time, the differences which were the basis for conflict have disappeared. A third generation Pole or Swede or Slovak is no longer a Pole or Swede or Slovak; he is an "American." He talks, acts, and thinks along the same lines as the American of many more generations. Most people are no longer conscious of the matter of origins, and even the tell-tale names come to be almost wholly ignored.

It should be emphasized that not all group distinctions disappear so soon or so completely. Some may even be accentuated with the passing of time. Thus, a third-generation German or Russian tends to be readily accepted in American society as an American—provided he is not also a Jew. In the latter case his Jewish group affiliation tends to persist, but for no really inherent reason. Groups merely fix on certain facts of difference, and this fixation tends to perpetuate certain differences while others shortly disappear. The *long-run* tendencies, of course, are for group differences within a society to be reduced through the diffusion of one group's traits into the other's, until eventually the differences have largely disappeared. Some religious differences seem to be among the most difficult to assimilate; the categories Protestant, Catholic, and Jew are among our most persistent group antagonisms.

Assimilation may be defined, then, as the *gradual process whereby cultural differences (and rivalries) tend to disappear.* Obviously some differences and rivalries disappear more slowly than others, and some may even be accentuated with the passing of time.

Forms of assimilation

It is possible to distinguish different kinds of assimilation. (1) A person who has been socialized in one culture may later come in contact with another culture. Through interaction with people in the second culture, he gradually, but seldom wholly, becomes assimilated into it. If the cultures are not too dissimilar and the prejudice patterns not too sharp, this may be accomplished in a relatively short period. But otherwise an entire lifetime may pass with the personality still "marginal," that is, having traits and characteristics from both of the cultures, sometimes in marked conflict with one another.

(2) Two cultures may merge into a third culture which has aspects of both, but is still somewhat distinct. At one time in the United States rural and urban societies were rather radically different in a number of respects. Such factors as isolation, the nature of the farming industry, and rural institutions contributed to a personality type rather conspicuously different from that of the more cosmopolitan and secular urbanite. These differencies have now largely disappeared in many parts of the United States. Farm homes contain the same paraphernalia as city homes. Farm and urban people participate in the same recreational patterns, and many close friendships cut across the old somewhat sharp rural-urban lines. While the differences have not been entirely eliminated, they have certainly been remarkably reduced.

(3) Assimilation may occur, also, in small groups—even in the pair group consisting of mates. Dissimilar patterns of overt behavior and ideas often tend in time to disappear. As the persons interact, each becomes acquainted with the other's behavior and consciously or unconsciously often tends to conform more closely to the other. (This does not preclude, of course, the appearance of new differences which may appear simultaneously in the new interaction.)

The "marginal man"

The assimilation of a person into a culture other than the one in which he was originally socialized requires considerable time and may, in fact, never be completed within an individual's lifetime. For a considerable period the person's behavior is usually an admixture of the two cultures to which he has been exposed. He is thus said to be a *marginal man*. This condition of marginality has received the attention of sociologists and social psychologists for some time. The marginal man, because he has been partially socialized by each of two cultures, does not fit very well into either culture. The extent and seriousness of his idiosyncrasies depend in part, of course, upon the particular kind of cultures involved. If the ideologies and overt behavior patterns of the two are greatly dissimilar or in direct conflict with one another, his problems of adjustment would tend to be more severe. If, on the other hand, the cultures in question differ only in superficial details, the fact of marginality may present no serious problems of adjustment.

The marginal man experiences *two kinds of difficulties*. One group of problems is *subjective*. He frequently finds it difficult to reconcile the opposing ideas and contradictory ways of the two cultures. One student of the process writes at length about how the marginal man is "poised in psychological uncertainty" between two cultures, not knowing which one is to be followed at the points where the two conflict.

His condition is further complicated by the *objective problems of social rejection*. Neither group feels that this marginal person quite "belongs" to it. The result is that the marginal man loses his security in the original group from which he has grown away, while not yet securing acceptance and security in the new group whose culture he has, perhaps, not yet fully mastered, understood, or accepted.

Large numbers of marginal men are found among (1) the second-generation immigrant groups, (2) American-born and American-reared Japanese, and (3) Jews who do not observe the traditions of the traditional Jewish religion. (4) To a lesser extent the person of rural origins who moves to the city as an adult, or the native urban dweller who takes up residence in a rural community, represents a mild form of marginality. (5) Similarly the person of humble family background who marries into a wealthy social group, or for some other reason makes a radical change in his position in the social hierarchy, also illustrates marginality. Thus, we see that there are all degrees of marginality found in a society such as ours in which there are numerous, somewhat distinct, cultural streams.

SOCIAL INTERACTION CONCEPTS ARE ABSTRACT

It is well for the student to bear in mind that terms like *competition, cooperation, assimilation,* and *accommodation* are, after all, highly abstract language usages. As ideas or concepts they have utility for the analysis of the interaction of human beings and groups. But the generality of these terms as formally defined here and elsewhere tends to minimize the actual variations found in the interactions which one observes in specific situations. For example, "competition" for grades in a college course, "competition" in a football game, and "competition" in winning a court case may all seem to be "the same" in an abstract sense, but the actual behavior involved in each individual instance may be greatly dissimilar. It should be recalled that under each of these interaction types we have discussed a number of subtypes. Even these are somewhat generalized concepts, but they are much more realistic and specific than the four major types which have been treated. It is well for the student who has not yet become accustomed to thinking about human behavior in such abstract terms to strive to keep the general type and specific subtype as distinct as possible in his thinking. At best, the study of social interaction requires a high level of abstract thinking. It is nevertheless an important aspect of the study of human behavior.

Difficulties of study notwithstanding, the processes of human interaction are ever with us; and the solution of our individual and collective problems requires, often, that we understand them in order to act with maximum intelligence.

SUMMARY

An objective evaluation of competition and cooperation is very difficult for most persons because of cultural bias. The prevailing folkways and thoughtways of one's own culture create a barrier of prejudice which is exceedingly difficult to cross over, even for purposes of theoretical analysis. The characteristic American reverence for competition usually makes it very difficult for Americans to understand that many of the objectives which we attain through competitive effort are attained in other societies through cooperative effort. This applies as much to material matters as to psychological satisfactions such as prestige or status.

The prevailing culture of a society defines such fundamental considerations as whether competition or cooperation is the superior virtue, what objectives of life may be properly regarded as attainable by competition and what ones by cooperation, who may or may not compete or cooperate, what the rules and regulations for the various competitions are to be, as well as many other basic considerations.

It cannot be stressed too emphatically that, regardless of cultural preferences one way or another, in each society there are elements of both competition and cooperation in the makeup of the total pattern in interaction. No society is entirely cooperative or entirely competitive. Differences are matters of degree.

Differences in the needs, wishes, and values of the persons and groups which make up a society frequently give rise to a form of rivalrous interaction which is less well controlled by the society than is competition. This relatively unrestrained rivalry is called conflict. Numerous rivalries in society have characteristics of both competition and conflict and are, therefore, somewhat difficult to classify categorically. This should not becloud the fact that here are still two quite distinct rivalrous interaction patterns: the one which is worked out more or less clearly within rules, and the other which is expressed somewhat outside such regulation. At the present time in American society it would be difficult to classify the rivalries between capital and labor, business and government, white and colored peoples, or traditional and liberal religion as either competitions or conflicts, because they all have attributes of both.

Some rivalries eventually become accommodated, that is, rivalrous interaction ceases for the time being, either because some person or group has secured the "upper hand" but has not won a clear-cut victory or because the rivals conclude that the rivalry is too destructive, unnecessary, or for some other reason should be terminated. This gives rise to a number of forms of accommodation such as truces, compromises, temporary subordination-superordination arrangements, arbitration, or toleration, as well as numerous other forms which we have not discussed here. The prevailing cultural ideologies exert a great influence upon the extent and kind of accommodation which the persons and groups in a society will utilize. Cultural values also largely determine which rivalries are accommodable without losing face or honor. Sometimes the society sets up and enforces adherence to such accommodation agencies as courts, arbitration boards, and the like. Also the thoughtways and language clichés of the society assist the accommodating groups to rationalize the cessation of a rivalry.

Some differences among persons and groups tend to disappear in time and are said to have become assimilated. Other rivalries persist over long periods. During the period before which assimilation becomes complete, the person being assimilated may go through a period of marginality during which time he belongs wholly to neither culture, either by his own acceptance or by the acceptance of him in the groups concerned. Thus, the marginal man has both subjective and objective difficulties. Marginality may last for the major part of a lifetime, and in some cases minority groups may go through several generations of marginality before assimilation becomes final.

SUGGESTED READINGS

Coser, Lewis, *The Functions of Social Conflict*. New York, Macmillan, 1956.
A study based upon, but by no means limited to, George Simmel's classic treatment of conflict. Contains many fresh interpretations.

Glazer, Nathan, and Moynihan, Daniel Patrick, *Beyond the Melting Pot*. Cambridge, MIT Press, 1963.
A study of some of the less assimilated ethnic groups in New York. Tends to

show that assimilation is by no means an inevitable process but rather depends on circumstances.

Gordon, Milton M., *Assimilation in American Life*. New York, Oxford University Press, 1964.
A book which takes a realistic look at the so-called "melting pot" in America at the present time by assessing the roles of religion, class, and nationality in this erratic process.

Kropotkin, P. A., *Mutual Aid, A Factor of Evolution*. New York, Knopf, 1922.
This small book was written as an antidote to the overemphasis upon competition as a factor in life, which has been current since the appearance of Darwin's *Origin of Species*. It is Kropotkin's thesis that mutual aid is a significant form of behavior not only on the human level but also in many subhuman forms of life. A significant book.

Park R. E., and Burgess, E. W., *Introduction to the Science of Sociology*. Chicago, University of Chicago Press, 1921.
The classical formulation of the sociological processes which have formed the structure for this chapter will be found in this book.

Rose, Arnold M., ed., *Minority Problems*. New York, Harper & Row, 1965.
In this collection of articles dealing with intergroup relations will be found abundant illustrations of the sociological processes elaborated in this chapter.

Stagner, Ross, "Conflict in the Executive Suite." *Transaction*, Vol. 3 (January–February, 1966), pp. 39–42.
A study of the way in which conflict is handled in high-level corporate disputes.

Stonequist, E. H., *The Marginal Man*. New York, Scribner, 1937.
A well-known volume dealing with the historical and social-psychological aspects of the persons with multicultural participations.

STUDY QUESTIONS

1. How does our society foster competition?
2. Why do people compete for intangible "items" of value?
3. Why are some competitions "only a matter of degree"?
4. How can advertising be an indication of personal or impersonal competition?
5. Why does cooperation often accompany competition?
6. How does the type and degree of competition within a society depend upon its culture?
7. How is competition related to cultural values?

8. Why do men of different races usually not compete for the affections of the same girl?

9. What determines whether a given kind of competitive interaction is "clean" or "dirty"?

10. Why is the theory of competition in present American economic life more of an ideal than a real pattern?

11. How is competition "a waste of human effort"? Is this true often or rarely?

12. How may competition result in impaired physical and mental health?

13. Is cooperation the antithesis of competition? Can this be an "illusion" due to our ethnocentrism?

14. Why is it possible sometimes to achieve the same goal by competition, cooperation, or a combination of the two?

15. Why are some goals attained by cooperation while others are attained by competition?

16. How does a society determine the relative values of competition and cooperation?

17. How may conflict grow out of competition? Vice versa?

18. Why is violence "not the essence of conflict"? Illustrate.

19. Why is it often difficult to distinguish between competition and conflict? Illustrate.

20. Why may accommodation be regarded as a form of cooperation?

21. Describe five common forms of accommodation. How does the problem situation involved determine the form of accommodation? Will this vary from society to society? What, then, do you conclude from this?

22. How do assimilation and accommodation differ?

23. How is the "marginal man" a result of incomplete assimilation? Explain.

24. Why does the marginal man have both subjective and objective problems? Illustrate.

32
SOCIAL PROBLEMS AND SOCIAL EVALUATION

Certain societal conditions such as crime, poverty, juvenile delinquency, prostitution, the high auto accident rate, and unemployment are usually regarded as undesirable and are usually termed loosely as "societal problems" or "social problems." From superficial observation it seems obvious to many that these conditions are problems of "society" because the solution of them is beyond the control of any one person or group. Either prevention or amelioration of these conditions seems to require some sort of *collective* societal action. But as one delves further into these social problem phenomena, he encounters numerous fundamental, theoretical, as well as practical, difficulties which seem rarely, if ever, to have occurred to many observers and commentators. These issues concern us in this chapter.

WHAT MAKES A SOCIAL PROBLEM?

Harmfulness not always an objective criterion

Suppose we begin with the elementary supposition apparently made by most people, namely, that a social problem is an undesirable social condition. What makes it undesirable? Is it undesirable because it is thought to be harmful? What are the *criteria* of harmfulness? Immediately one finds himself in the realm of values. Under a democratic value system, for example, the caste-like position of the segregated and underprivileged American Negro is often regarded as harmful, or at least undesirable, because it runs contrary to the democratic ideal of "equality regardless of color, race, or creed." In a caste society, on the other hand, segregation and discrimination constitute quite normal and equitable aspects of society, not problems at all.

"Harmful" to whom?

Moreover, it is important to note that a given societal condition *may be demonstrably harmful to one class or group, but have no direct or discernible harmful effect on another class* of people. A current case in point concerns various "pockets of poverty" in the midst of a general economic affluence in American society. Parts of Appalachia and the deep South dramatize the situation. According to a U.P.I. (July, 1967) report of a congressional committee hearing, a group of Harvard University physicians under the auspices of The Field Foundation, Inc. of New York found that two- and three-year-old children in parts of Mississippi and Alabama were living under conditions of such physical deprivation that they were "beyond medical help," were suffering from malnutrition and starvation rendering them "not one whit better than in the northern parts of Kenya." Nine out of ten of these children, the study reported, had never in their lives seen a doctor. "By the time they are two or three they have suffered irreparable damage to their bodies and minds. They need food and vitamins and every kind of rehabilitation—particularly blood transfusions." For probably nine out of ten Americans this careful scientific observation borders on the incredible. The same economic system which provides fraternity housing and convertibles for college students also encompasses the circumstances just described. Is there, then, anything "harmful" about the system of distribution which results in such juxtapositions as the above?

Harmful conditions may be rationalized as desirable

Evidence of the harmfulness of a social condition seems not to result in an awareness that a social problem condition exists. Sometimes *harmful conditions are rationalized as inevitable or as indirectly beneficial.* "The poor you shall always have with you" has frequently been quoted in a context suggesting that society should not concern itself unduly with the poor, because poverty is presumably inevitable anyway. In the past perhaps more than at present, theologians have frequently rationalized painful or harmful conditions as punishment meted out by a just and angry Deity for people's willful infractions of Divine decree. Human suffering has, moreover, often been rationalized as indirectly "good for the people, because it builds character, fortitude, and appreciation of spiritual values."

From these illustrations it becomes apparent that a clear-cut definition of social problems in terms of harmfulness is exceedingly difficult. It seems necessary, then, to consider some other formulations of social problems theory. Such an effort not only will serve better to define the varying conceptions of social problems but should add appreciably to one's understanding of the social problems themselves.

Challenge is the first step in problem definition

As we have already noted, history provides instances of deplorable social conditions which have been accepted by persons living under them, either because they were thought to be inevitable aspects of human life or because they were rationalized as desirable. Slavery, poverty, death from preventable causes, famine, racial discrimination, caste exploitation of the underprivileged, and war have for most of man's history constituted quite acceptable forms and products of human living. *In our generation, however, each of these conditions is under attack.* They are no longer accepted either as inevitable or defensible by many people. Much attention is centered around the prevention and treatment of these and other similar conditions. In short, the conditions mentioned above are "problems" in *this era of* man's history, because *man has now acquired values and ideas which are contrary to such conditions and which result in his calling these traditional conditions into question.*

The ideology of rational control of society

Perhaps the chief relevant value which modern man espouses is the *ideology of rational control of society*. Man has traditionally tended to accept the inevitability of his social world as he found it, but modern man, in Western civilization at least, has rebelled against such complete acquiescence to the tyranny of custom. He possesses what has been called "the planning ideology," the notion that he has the *right* and the *power* to alter such parts of his social world as he wishes changed. The use of such expressions as "modern man" is not, of course, wholly accurate. *Some* modern men in Western civilization possess the planning ideology, and there are enough of such to make a concerted and consistent impact of effort in the direction of rational modification of many parts of the social structure. Thus, in America we have groups working to remove racial discrimination and prejudice. In most of the modern nations there are groups working in the direction of eliminating war. And so with other conditions which are called the *problem areas* of modern social life. In fact, it is the efforts of these groups and the counter-efforts of their opponents which make certain aspects of modern life problem areas. Probably no condition, however intolerable one might think it is, is a self-evident social problem; the *problem* inheres in the *fact of challenge*, not in the deplorable condition per se.

Amelioration or attack on causes

There is room, also, for sharp value disagreement concerning whether an undesirable condition should or can be *eliminated completely* or whether its harmful effects should or can *only be ameliorated* somewhat. Thus while many persons and groups oppose slum clearance projects to provide reasonably modern housing for low-income groups, these same persons may favor assisting individual slum dwellers who have personal problems which arise from poor housing. Thus, some persons will approve and even contribute to free clinics for the treatment of the health needs of slum dwelling people, but will oppose the abolition of the slums which produce the bad health through crowding, lack of sanitation facilities, bad ventilation, and the other unfortunate concomitants of life in the slum areas.

The emphasis upon amelioration rather than upon basic solution of causative conditions has been justified on the ground that amelioration is immediate, whereas fundamental solutions usually require considerable time to be worked out. This logic is no doubt valid, as stated, but the history of purposive social change, in America at least, shows that ameliorative programs, instead of being used only as temporary expedients, *may* often become permanent programs instead. Thus, the sources of undesirable social conditions may remain unmodified long after it is possible to control or eliminate them.

A social "problem" is created by the conflict of group values

We are now ready to formulate our concept of a "social problem." *A social problem arises whenever some group or groups in a society try to change an existing condition.* As we have seen in foregoing paragraphs, it is not the condition per se which makes the problem, because of the great capacity of human beings to rationalize a wide variety of circumstances as satisfactory or even beneficial. The problem arises when some group large enough to make its influence felt in some way makes a case against the condition and offers some solution or change with regard to it.

Normally, when an existing social condition is challenged, some groups arise to defend the condition which has been attacked. When the first white men attacked the system of Negro slavery, there were others who arose to justify it. When some women protested the right of men to keep them disfranchised, there were those who rose to defend the status quo. Thus, *there occurs a clash of values regarding the challenged condition.* The ensuing conflict creates the problem condition for the society.

The student often has difficulty understanding this concept of social problems. Perhaps a current example will help to make the point more clear. At present, one of the nation's sharpest political and social issues pertains to the so-called civil rights legislation, designed to remove some of the discrimination against Negroes which has existed in this nation since the Reconstruction period. No one would contend that the plight of the Negro is worse now than in 1840 or in 1910. Probably, objectively, it is better now. There is a problem now, and much less so in 1840 and in 1910, because now there are large groups and more powerful groups which are openly challenging the discrimination system and proposing that it be changed. The problem exists now because these various groups are espousing different proposals. The problem will close only when each side yields to compromise from among the various proposals and the agitation ceases. When agitation ceases, the so-called "intolerable condition" may or may not be objectively any better for the Negroes. But the *society* would no longer have a problem if no one made an issue of the discrimination matter.

A second illustration is presented by the so-called mental illness problem in the United States today. Many authorities on human behavior are currently concerned with what they call a "mental hygiene problem" in the United States. It is evidenced by such conditions as the high Selective Service rejections of young men with various kinds of mental-emotional personality deviations and the large number of army discharges for the same reasons. The National Institute of Mental Health reports a rising number of admissions to state and county mental hospitals, as well as a rapidly rising cost per patient. And this does not even include statistics for the many privately treated individuals, not to mention those in need of treatment and unwilling or unable to obtain it. It is impossible and probably unnecessary to review all of the evidence here, but the fact of an appalling amount of human unhappiness and inefficiency due to mental-emotional disturbances is obvious. It is obvious, that is, to the person acquainted with the facts. It appears not to be obvious to the rank and file of American people. It appears doubtful whether one may yet say that this condition is "a problem" in the minds of the rank and file in the same sense that crime, the auto accident rate, or the cancer death rate is a problem to them. On the basis of the evidence we now have, the actual danger of harmful effects to the average person may be greater from the mental hygiene problem than from the auto accident problem, the cancer problem, or the crime problem. So long as present apathy remains, it is doubtful whether practical, effective treatment of this mental hygiene condition can be expected. In the realistic sense, then, there is a condition which a few informed people know to be deplorable, but it is no "problem" to the majority.

Three levels of value-conflict in regard to a social problem

Value-conflict usually centers around three separate phases of a social problem.

1. Sometimes the clash of values relates, as we have seen, to the issue *whether or not a problem really exists.* It is highly doubtful whether there is any general awareness on the part of the average, or even the better informed, American of the seriousness of poverty pockets in American society. The prevailing opinion seems to be that our nation is enjoying a period of unusual affluence and that there is no "real problem" of poverty on any appreciable scale. The government's so called "War on Poverty" has been subjected to an inordinate amount of ridicule in the press and elsewhere, partly because there is doubt in some circles that a poverty problem "really" exists. In the ensuing dialogue, some sort of decision will ultimately be reached as to whether or not there is a poverty problem. Most social problems go through this stage of definition or formulation before any consideration of what ought to be done about the condition can be considered.

2. Once a consensus (not necessarily a majority view) has been formed that an undesirable condition exists, the value clash shifts to a consideration of *whether or not the problem condition is susceptible to treatment by the society.* Not infrequently persons and groups take the position that "of course" some given social condition is harmful, but that nothing can be done about it effectively because the problem is "too big" or "inheres in human nature" or would "be made worse" by efforts to attack it directly.

Sometimes the proponents of this view are, of course, sincerely of the opinion stated, but there is also evidence that the difficulties of successful attack on some social problems have been exaggerated by certain persons and groups in order to discourage or delay efforts to improve the conditions. Owners of real estate in slum areas, for example, have

been known to exaggerate the difficulties of constructing better housing because at least some of them have considered it to their financial
interest to keep the slums. In other words, if the argument could be
shifted from discussion of the seriousness of the problem to the mag-
nification of the difficulties of solving the problem, the same end would
be attained, namely, inaction. Thus the opponent of reform would remain, in the eyes of some people at least, a person who is not insensitive
to the plight of the slum dweller. Such insincerity is not uncommon.

3. But even among those who sincerely wish the problem attacked
and solved, sharp *disagreement concerning alternative means of attaining this objective is possible,* in fact, probable. Frequently, this involves
values, too. Many persons will admit, for example, that the large-scale
consumption of alcoholic beverages, particularly by the "heavy
drinker," is an undesirable condition. It can easily be demonstrated, for
example, that health problems, child support problems, auto accidents,
work inefficiency, and similar results affecting other people follow excessive drinking. There would, moreover, be little disagreement that
these conditions are harmful. But what should be done? Is a return of
prohibition warranted? Some think so. Should there be restrictions on
the hours during which alcoholic beverages are sold in public places?
Some people think that the only real solution is one of "education."
Whatever social problem one chooses to consider, disagreements concerning ways and means are numerous, and much discussion is usually
required before there develops a sufficient consensus so that some one
course of action can be launched.

WHAT OUGHT TO BE THE ROLE OF THE
SOCIOLOGIST IN TREATING SOCIAL PROBLEMS?

The theory that the sociologist is a social physician

The sociologist is often popularly regarded as a treatment authority, as a sort of "social doctor." Proponents of this view make a
good case by analogy. They argue, for example, that one takes the
advice of the physician, not the garbage collector, when questions of
health are at stake. When one wants legal advice he secures the counsel
of an attorney, not a baseball player. He has his automobile checked
and repaired, if necessary, by a specialist in auto mechanics, not by a
pharmacist. Why not, then, be consistent, and utilize the social scientist
similarly? Why not give him the responsibility for determining what

social conditions are healthful and beneficial, which ones are to be regarded as pathological, and, therefore, require special attention?

Critique of the theory

On the surface the "social doctor" theory appears sound. But the analogy, like many analogies, is more apt than sound when carried to its logical end. Suppose we examine the authority of the physician in health matters. While he is generally regarded as an authority on health matters, *his authoritative position does not result directly from his competence. It exists rather from his acceptance as an authority*. The people of no society appear as yet to be willing to entrust to any group of social science experts the sole or even major responsibility for determining *in the social realm* what is good and bad, and what is to be done about it. It is possible that the time *may* come when the expert social scientist may be permitted to exercise his competence in this way, but at present that time seems remote. The prevailing position taken by people with respect to social problems is that *they* know what they want, their major difficulty being that of convincing others to accept their point of view and finding capable leadership to implement that point of view. Only to a limited extent is the social scientist's counsel sought and even when it is, his advice rarely goes beyond some very circumscribed project.

Sociologists' influence is indirect

The foregoing is not to be construed as meaning that social science experts are entirely ineffectual in the practical treatment of social problems. There are probably practical effects which result from their research and judgment, but these effects are largely *indirect*. Most social scientists are affiliated with the teaching staffs of American colleges and universities. In the exercise of their normal duties they teach classes dealing with social problems varying from the care of the physically handicapped to the control of public utilities. They also write articles and books and are in considerable demand as lecturers and consultants to various practical action projects. Thus, the students in their classes and others outside formulate attitudes and values under the guidance of the professional students of society. Meanwhile the findings and judgments of social scientists also get into the general stream of public discussion through their writings and speeches. It is impossible to determine precisely how effective these indirect influences are, but it appears probable that they have at least some influence upon both public consciousness of social problems and popular consideration of possible solutions. But the influence cannot be calculated precisely.

Social scientists are often too objective for direct partisanship

Probably the most serious weakness of the social problems expert is also his greatest strength. Most careful scholars studying social problems follow the dictates of *scientific inquiry*, namely, objectivity, caution in reaching conclusions, and the critical retesting of facts before final conclusions are reached. However important these attributes may be from the scientific point of view, they constitute what seem to be *impediments in the practical situation*. The findings of social scientists are not usually partisan enough to capture any group's enthusiasm; they are usually not dogmatic enough to give quick conclusions and simple recipes for action, nor are they usually dramatic enough to capture the popular mind. Thus the charlatans, or the pseudo-scientists, or the opportunistic politicians with their simple clichés and dramatic oversimplifications of the facts usually have an initial advantage in winning popular support or popular antagonism to some program or proposal which serves the interest of some special group. The initial advantage, however, in the long run especially, cannot always be retained. The expert in his usually cautious, undramatic, and objective manner does convince some people, and the various competing and extremist quacks sometimes neutralize each other, thus providing the opportunity for the findings and recommendations of the expert to receive consideration and sometimes, even, to become the basis for action.

Scientists' and partisans' views are eventually fused

It may already be apparent from the foregoing discussion that there is much truth both in the notion that social problems ought to be defined and solved by the society and in the notion that they ought to be defined and solved by the expert. Neither view appears in the actual situation to be wholly correct or wholly incorrect. Fundamentally, of course, there can be no social problem until there is an awareness that a certain condition is undesirable. Nor is there likely to be a problem for long if there is complete agreement on the values involved. The essence of the problem condition is conflict or clash of different groups with different values, out of which conflict solutions or attempted solutions or inactivity may result.

But one of the interest groups whose values appear in the total situation is the group of social science experts who possess a certain power and influence by virtue of their positions as teachers, writers, speakers, and consultants. Although they cannot dominate the discussion or the conclusion, they can influence it, and sometimes significantly.

How can we use the social science expert?

The immediate issue which seems to face democratic societies like America is not whether we are to turn over the analysis and treatment of the social problems to the social problems experts, but rather whether the findings and the judgments of the social problems experts are to be given a more or a less prominent place in the whole discussion of social problems. The experts will have some influence so long as American education remains at least partially free, but in the immediate future the amount and kind of audience which will be given to the expert is problematical. Some would have the expert politely, or impolitely, ignored, leaving the evaluation and solution of social problems largely to the partisans representing this or that special interest group, each with his special axe to grind. Other persons, however, are becoming increasingly conscious of the existence of a "general interest" or "the public good" or the "general welfare" and seem increasingly to be insisting that public councils should include the best informed and most objective, as well as the least informed and most partisan, persons.

SOME BASIC UNDERSTANDINGS CONCERNING SOCIAL PROBLEMS

While it is not the purpose of this chapter to enter into a discussion of specific social problems such as crime or unemployment or racial tensions, it is still possible to present certain discoveries and observations concerning social problems in general. Some of these understandings have already been explained in this and other chapters and need, therefore, only to be briefly reviewed.

1. The principle of multiple causation

Since this point has been previously made, we shall limit ourselves to a brief illustration. The mental hygiene condition mentioned earlier springs from many known causes and probably from some which are not yet known. The nature of family life, certain school procedures, employment practices, and uncorrected physical defects are only a few of the many known causes. Likewise, the auto accident rate, which currently results in around 50,000 deaths in the United States per year, results from many causes: high speed, poor driving habits, poor roadways, mechanical defects in automobiles, intoxication, confused traffic laws, inadequate policing, to mention but a few. In formulating practical reforms it is sometimes necessary to concentrate largely on *certain* causes and disregard others in order to get started on *some* course of action. The danger lies, however, in the unconscious overlooking of the principle of *multifactor causation* and proceeding as if the matter were entirely in hand, when in reality only one small part actually is.

2. Causes of social problems may be unknown or uncontrollable

It should not be inferred from the foregoing that all of what are popularly called "causes" of social problems are either known or, at the existing state of our knowledge, controllable. Careful students of social problems tend not to think in terms of "causes" the way popular writers and laymen so often do. *Cause* is a slippery concept when used in regard to social phenomena, and even the most careful students of social problems have made serious errors in cause-and-effect thinking. The difficulties arise from several facts. First, what are called "causes" are themselves effects of other causes, and thus one must go far back of a given condition to understand its *chain of cause and effect*. Control, moreover, is not easy even if causes be known, because the *given cause usually has numerous effects*, some desirable and others undesirable.

3. Solutions to social problems have multiple and often unfavorable effects

Rarely can solutions to social problems be restricted so that they affect only the condition for which they were designed. Instead they ramify in many subtle and sometimes exasperating ways. When America tried the prohibition experiment just after World War I, few persons, even the opponents of prohibition, realized that this "noble experiment" would give rise to the large and powerful pattern of organized criminal practice which it did. Nor could many have envisaged the extent to which this organized system of law violation would infiltrate into the ranks of law enforcement officers, thus bringing about one of the most scandalous and degenerate periods of law enforcement in American history.

This principle of multiple effects of social action has sometimes been misused by the opponents of some social reform. It has become a common opposition technique to exaggerate the detrimental by-products of the proposal for change. There exists, of course, always the inescapable problem of balancing benefits against detriments in appraising any social condition or proposal for change. Fundamentally, this again involves values. In fact, judgments of benefits themselves are values and are subject to the same wide variations among persons and groups which we have so often discussed in previous chapters. This inescapable problem of evaluation even further complicates the practical treatment of problems.

4. Solutions may run counter to other cherished values

It should not be overlooked that so-called solutions to social problems also constitute or bring about conditions other than those which they are supposed to remedy. For example, it has been suggested that the auto accident rate could be materially reduced by requiring each automobile to be equipped with a governor which would prevent the car from being driven faster than forty-five miles per hour. Assuming for the moment that this would materially reduce casualties from auto accidents, it is clear, also, that such a policy would make basic alterations and inconveniences in the personal habits of many people. The time consumed, on long trips especially, would be appreciably increased. For high-salaried persons whose time is valuable, this would constitute a material economic loss. Moreover, the automobile industry for many years has been concentrating on the production of more speedy automobiles. If a maximum speed of forty-five miles per hour were put into effect, the "progress" of many years of research and engineering would be wasted and competing industries in the automobile field would be obliged to find new bases for competition. Moreover, speed has an intangible psychological value to some people. Living as we do in a rapidly moving cultural configuration, time saving has become a value in itself. Many persons would feel greatly deprived if forced to travel at reduced auto speeds. It is not intended in raising these questions either to favor or to oppose the speed limitation proposal, but rather to point out that there are always by-products to solutions to undesirable conditions. This fact serves often as a deterrent to the introduction of some specific solution, and, of course, multiplies the possibilities for value disagreement among the advocates of the several alternatives designed to solve or ameliorate the social problem.

5. Social problems are closely interrelated with social change

It has sometimes been alleged simply that "social problems grow out of social change." While this is undoubtedly somewhat true, it is an oversimplification of a much more complex relationship. While problems do grow out of social change, they also create social change. This is most readily illustrated when one considers that modern society often "does something" about its social problems. These *solutions constitute social change.* When Congress passes a law for the purpose of correcting some undesirable social condition, the provisions of that law eventually become part of the organization and structure of the society and change the society from what it was before the law was passed. Social change also may terminate or reduce social problems while at the same time creating new ones.

6. Social problems affect a society differentially

The so-called "harmful" effects of a social problem do not always, or even often, affect all of the people in a society in the same way. A case in point concerns agriculture and the price disparity suffered by American agricultural people following the end of World War I at least. While this condition was obviously harmful to farmers as an income group and was probably injust on ethical grounds, it served as a temporary benefit to the urban buyers of agricultural produce who enjoyed the privilege of somewhat lower prices than would have obtained if farm prices had been on a parity with nonfarm prices.

The wage rates of both Negroes and women are somewhat below the wage rates for white men doing the same quality and quantity of work. Moreover, the problem of unemployment is a far more stark reality to working-class members than to business-class members of the society.

7. Social problems are usually interrelated with one another

Social problems do not exist in the air-tight compartments in which they are frequently discussed, especially by laymen. Many times a given condition can quite as logically be regarded as an aspect of one social problem as of another. For example, the high divorce rate is a result of many conditions, among them the emancipation of women from many traditional home duties, careers and outside employment for married women, and the decline of the patriarchal authority. Each of these conditions also has other problem aspects as we have already seen in the chapter on the family. Moreover, divorce creates still other problems, such as that of providing a somewhat near normal family life for the children of divorced parents.

8. Social problems may arise from or be increased by generally desirable social change

Most persons would grant that the emergence of women as persons with comparable freedom to men has constituted a desirable social change. Women are now free to acquire an education, provide for their own livelihood, follow careers of their own choosing, and participate in many recreational practices formerly tabooed to them. But the emancipation of women has also created problems, such as the inequities between men's and women's wage rates and tensions between husbands and wives resulting from differing conceptions of the nature, extent, and implications of women's emancipation. Many women are attempting both marriage and a career, and not a few are failing in the double duty of careerist and parent. The children of *some* employed women are receiving substandard family life and subsequently their first introduction to juvenile delinquency. Mechanical inventions such as the automobile have also brought mixed blessings. While the auto has made it easier for the family to spend a pleasant weekend in the country, it has also made it possible for criminals better to elude the law enforcement officers because of the quick and anonymous character of auto transportation.

9. Individual persons often cannot by their own efforts escape the influence of some social problems

The effects of certain social problems are among the chief risks or hazards of modern societal living. However wealthy or virtuous the separate human being may be, he is still practically powerless to protect himself or his children from all of the impacts of the many social problems such as auto accidents, epidemics of disease, and the changing social roles of women or children, to mention only a few. Whether he realizes it or not, and regardless of whether he approves of it, the fact remains that the modern human is so interdependent that it is practically impossible for him to insulate himself, so to speak, from social influences or to protect himself from many of the collective hazards. This is one of the most convincing arguments for collective control of social problems. *No* man lives solely unto himself.

ARE WE HYPERCONSCIOUS OF SOCIAL PROBLEMS?

It has been suggested that contemporary America is "hypersensitive" concerning its social problems. Many of the conditions which are currently being decried, and for which solutions are being sought, are said to be problems which have always existed. "After all, some men have always been unemployed, some families always broken, some people always poor, some children always born out of wedlock, someone always violating laws, and someone always being in some way disprivileged, exploited, or discriminated against." "All that is new and different," say the complacent ones, "is the form which these personal misfortunes take and the big play which they are given by the sentimentalists."

It is altogether possible that *part* of the difference between past and present may lie in the changed consciousness of social trouble areas. At present many persons are less willing than their ancestors were to accept human suffering or inefficiency or discrimination as inevitable. Gradually man has learned that he need not accept the inevitability of any particular social system or any part of it. Particularly in a democratic society, there is a growing consciousness of power on the part of many disprivileged persons and groups, who propose to use this latent power in an effort to remove or at least to ameliorate those conditions which seem not conducive to their welfare. Thus, perhaps there may be some truth in the hyperconsciousness thesis.

But the modern world is to a considerable extent a new world. The web of interdependence has become almost a maze. As we have seen in the section on personal inadequacy, many persons get lost in the maze. The modern world is also new in its impersonality. Some of the prototypes of modern social problems did exist in the past, but their effects were somewhat ameliorated by the mutual aid practices of the primary group society of that time. With the decline of primary groups, one is forced to utilize secondary groups with their impersonal power tactics in his struggle for existence. "Less than a living wage" means something very different to the man in modern society, where the relations between employer and employee are impersonal and where almost every item of life has a pecuniary value.

Moreover, there exists clear statistical evidence that the actual number of persons affected by at least some modern social problems has appreciably increased. Crime is more prevalent, divorce is more frequent, more children face juvenile court judges, more persons are permanently unemployable because they lack the physical or mental abilities required in order to meet modern societal demands of minimum adequacy.

The above is not intended to convey the impression that modern life is necessarily inferior because it is different. It is only meant to document the fact that the accelerated rate of social change, the existence of great personal insecurities, and the rise of new values have made the modern world the kind of a world in which the existence of many and serious social problems are normal and critical aspects of human life. To minimize either the normalcy or the criticalness of these social problems is to be naïve and unrealistic about the kind of world in which we are living.

SUMMARY

We began this chapter with the formulation of a working definition of the concept *social problem*. A social problem is a social condition over which there is a disagreement concerning desirability. Different groups are usually differentially affected by, and related to, a given social condition; and hence a clash of value judgment regarding the condition gives evidence of the existence of the social problem through popular discussion.

Badness, seriousness, and harmfulness of social conditions are matters of definition and judgment; and hence there is often a clash of values on the question of whether a given condition is a problem condition at all, and, if so, which among several alternatives is the proper course of action with respect to it. Democratic values and the planning ideology seem to have affected strongly the thinking about social problems in America and other nations of similar culture.

In the process of making the members of a society aware of the existence and seriousness of a social burden, the social scientist may play an indirect part. Being a scientist, he does not usually enter vigorously into the realm of advocacy, but rather tends to play his role in terms of research and the diffusion of his findings through teaching, speaking, writing, and more recently, consultant work. Some persons, including some social scientists themselves, think this to be a mistake, and the immediate future may show a somewhat different role characteristically played by those in the field of social science.

Social problems have been the object of much sociological and other social scientific research. From these researches we have learned that:

1. Social problems consist of those social conditions which the current values so define, and are often not inherently problems at all.
2. Social problems usually have many causes, in so far as causes can be determined.
3. Solutions or adjustments to social problems also have many ramified effects, often being unpredictable at the time the solution is introduced.
4. Social problems are closely interrelated with social change, some of them resulting from social change, others bringing about social change, and some social change resulting from the elimination or reduction of social problems.
5. Social problems affect the various groups and classes of a society differently, some problems being in reality class problems which are made into general problems by the efforts to secure solutions to them.
6. Social problems are usually interrelated with one another, aggravating the severity of one another, and sometimes apparently "causing" one another.
7. Social problems may arise from social controls (laws) which are evaluated as good, on the whole, but have undesirable concomitants or by-products.
8. Individual persons by their own efforts cannot often protect themselves from the influence of social problems, all persons being more or less "in it together" in many cases.

It has been suggested that perhaps modern man is hypersensitive regarding his collective social conditions, that social problems may be made to appear more numerous and more severe than they "really are," and that modern social problems have had counterparts in past societies when less attention was given them. Probably modern man is somewhat more conscious of trouble areas in modern society now that he has the democratic ideal and the knowledge of the power to control social life. He probably is less willing to accept all existing sets of conditions as his unalterable destiny. In addition, considerable objective evidence exists to support the idea that many social problems are increasing in respect to the number of persons affected, and probably also in the severity of the effects. It seems not to follow from this, however, that modern life is per se less good than the past; it is instead only a different kind of world, a world in which change is rapid, great personal insecurities are common, and new values about collective living make for a more dynamic approach to the conditions of life. It is quite as tenable that these characteristics may make the modern world a better one rather than a "worse" one. Many believe that a society which espouses democracy, as we do, should not long tolerate many of the conditions which we have here discussed, because the existence of these social problems constitutes a practical denial of equality of opportunity.

SUGGESTED READINGS

Dynes, Russell R., Clarke, Alfred C., Dinitz, Simon, and Ishino, Iwao, *Social Problems: Dissensus and Deviation in an Industrial Society*. New York, Oxford University Press, 1964.
This is a theoretically sophisticated treatment of the problem and valuation aspects of contemporary society. The authors advance and consistently use an original conceptual approach. Highly recommended.

Deutscher, Irwin, "The Social Causes of Social Problems: From Suicide to Delinquency." *Publications of the Youth Development Center*. Syracuse, Syracuse University, 1962.
A clear and forthright statement, well illustrated and historically documented, of the relationship between social-structural conditions and certain consequences which are now conventionally called social problems.

Fuller, Richard, "The Problem of Teaching Social Problems." *American Journal of Sociology*, Vol. 44 (November, 1938), pp. 415–435.
Develops the thesis that social problems are defined by the culture through the clash of value judgments of the various persons and groups participating in the culture. Evaluation of the Fuller thesis by several other representative sociologists follows the main article.

Harrington, Michael, *The Other America: Poverty in the United States*. Baltimore, Penquin, 1963.
This has been an exceedingly influential book, being among other things informally credited with convincing President Kennedy that the poverty problem in America deserved top priority. Well-written and authoritative.

Horton, Paul B., and Leslie, Gerald R., *The Sociology of Social Problems*. New York, Appleton-Century-Crofts, 1960.
A standard text on social problems which attempts to analyze a set of social problems from three different theoretical viewpoints.

Meissner, Hanna H., ed., *Poverty in the Affluent Society*. New York, Harper & Row, 1966.
One of several books published in recent years calling attention to the fact that despite a general affluence there is stark, dramatic poverty in many segments of the American population—rural and urban, Negro and white.

"Symposium on Social Problems in the Soviet Union." *Social Problems,*
    Vol. 7 (Spring, 1960), entire issue.
This issue of *Social Problems* is devoted entirely to the social problems of the
Soviet Union. It is exceedingly informative to note the many parallels as well as
differences in such matters as mental illness, public welfare, crime, religion, and
sex in present-day Soviet Union. Excellent antidote to the ethnocentrism sponsored perhaps inadvertently by too much reliance on the horror tales of casual
visitors and professional tub-thumpers.

STUDY QUESTIONS

1. Why can we not define social problems simply as the undesirable conditions in a society? Illustrate.
2. To what extent are social problems really social *class* problems?
3. Illustrate the importance of rationalization in social problem discussions.
4. How are social problems defined in this chapter?
5. Explain what is meant by "the ideology of rational control of society."
6. Why is a "consensus" not the same as a "majority agreement"?
7. Why is it almost impossible to evaluate proposed solutions to social
   problems objectively?
8. What principles should one bear in mind when discussing the causes of
   social problems? Illustrate.
9. What is the role of the social problems expert in the "treatment" of social problems? What are his strengths and his weaknesses?
10. Explain: "Social problems are both cause and effect of social change."
11. Are we hyperconscious of social problems? Discuss pro and con.
12. Why is a genuinely democratic person, other things being equal, more
    likely to be conscious of social problems?
13. What do you consider to be the leading social problems in present
    American society? Justify your choice.

INDEX